EFFECTIVE

A powerful way for students to learn how to apply and use core concepts covered in the text chapters.
More and more professors who teach strategy courses are finding that simulations are every bit as effective as case analysis in providing students with a means of applying what they have read about in the text chapters.

Students are assigned a senior executive role.
Students' strategy-making and decision making skills are put to the test. In this learn-by-doing exercise, students gain hands-on experience in crafting a competitive strategy and in making decisions relating to product quality, production, workforce compensation and training, pricing and marketing, and financing of company operations.

Assurance of Learning.
Wonder how well your students perform globally, or perform against accreditation standards? A Learning Assurance Report is automatically produced and displays how well each student performed relative to all other students worldwide.

See what the buzz is all about

Visit the Web site **www.mhhe.com/thompsonsims** to register for a demonstration and to read what your colleagues are saying about BSG and GLO-BUS.

Business Strategy Game (BSG)

www.bsg-online.com

McGraw-Hill Irwin
Strategy Simulations

GLO-BUS

www.glo-bus.com

Gregory G. Dess
University of Texas
at Dallas

G. T. Lumpkin
Texas Tech University

Alan B. Eisner
Pace University

Strategic Management

Creating Competitive Advantages

fourth edition

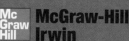

McGraw-Hill Irwin

Boston   Burr Ridge, IL   Dubuque, IA   New York   San Francisco   St. Louis
Bangkok   Bogotá   Caracas   Kuala Lumpur   Lisbon   London   Madrid   Mexico City
Milan   Montreal   New Delhi   Santiago   Seoul   Singapore   Sydney   Taipei   Toronto

STRATEGIC MANAGEMENT: CREATING COMPETITIVE ADVANTAGE

Published by McGraw-Hill/Irwin, a business unit of The McGraw-Hill Companies, Inc., 1221 Avenue of the Americas, New York, NY, 10020. Copyright © 2008, 2007, 2005, 2003 by The McGraw-Hill Companies, Inc. All rights reserved. No part of this publication may be reproduced or distributed in any form or by any means, or stored in a database or retrieval system, without the prior written consent of The McGraw-Hill Companies, Inc., including, but not limited to, in any network or other electronic storage or transmission, or broadcast for distance learning.

Some ancillaries, including electronic and print components, may not be available to customers outside the United States.

This book is printed on acid-free paper.

1 2 3 4 5 6 7 8 9 QPD/QPD 0 9 8 7

ISBN-13: 978-0-07-338121-3
ISBN-10: 0-07-338121-7

Senior sponsoring editor: *Doug Hughes*
Developmental editor: *Laura Griffin*
Marketing manager: *Anke Braun Weekes*
Senior project manager: *Harvey Yep*
Production supervisor: *Debra Sylvester*
Design coordinator: *Jillian Lindner*
Lead media project manager: *Susan Lombardi*
Cover design: *Pam Verros*
Interior design: *Pam Verros*
Photo researcher: *Jeremy Cheshareck*
Typeface: *10/12 Times Roman*
Compositor: *Aptara, Inc.*
Printer: *Quebecor World Dubuque Inc.*

Library of Congress Cataloging-in-Publication Data

Dess, Gregory G.
    Strategic management : creating competitive advantages / Gregory G. Dess,
G.T. Lumpkin, Alan B. Eisner. — 4th ed.
        p. cm.
    Includes index.
    ISBN-13: 978-0-07-338121-3 (alk. paper)
    ISBN-10: 0-07-338121-7 (alk. paper)
    1. Strategic planning. I. Lumpkin, G. T. II. Eisner, Alan B. III. Title.
HD30.28.D4743 2008
658.4′012—dc22   2007034062

Dedication

To my family, Margie and Taylor;
my parents, Bill and Mary Dess;
and Walter and Eleanor Descovich
—Greg

To my lovely wife, Vicki, and my colleagues
at Texas Tech University
—Tom

To my family, Helaine,
Rachel, and Jacob
—Alan

About the Authors

Gregory G. Dess is the Andrew R. Cecil Endowed Chair in Management at the University of Texas at Dallas. His primary research interests are in strategic management, organization–environment relationships, and knowledge management. He has published numerous articles on these subjects in both academic and practitioner-oriented journals. In August 2000, he was inducted into the Academy of Management Journal's Hall of Fame as one of its charter members. Professor Dess has conducted executive programs in the United States, Europe, Africa, Hong Kong, and Australia. During 1994 he was a Fulbright Scholar in Oporto, Portugal. He received his PhD in Business Administration from the University of Washington (Seattle).

G. T. (Tom) Lumpkin is the Kent Hance Regents Endowed Chair and Professor of Entrepreneurship at Texas Tech in Lubbock, Texas. He received his PhD in management from the University of Texas at Arlington and MBA from the University of Southern California. His research interests include entrepreneurial orientation, opportunity recognition, strategy-making processes, and innovative forms of organizing work. He has published numerous research articles and book chapters. He is a member of Editorial Review Boards of *Entrepreneurship Theory & Practice* and the *Journal of Business Venturing.* Professor Lumpkin also conducts executive programs in strategic and entrepreneurial applications of e-commerce and digital business technologies.

Alan B. Eisner is Professor of Management and Graduate Management Program Chair at the Lubin School of Business, Pace University. He received his PhD in management from the Stern School of Business, New York University. His primary research interests are in strategic management, technology management, organizational learning, and managerial decision making. He has published research articles and cases in journals such as *Advances in Strategic Management, International Journal of Electronic Commerce, International Journal of Technology Management, American Business Review, Journal of Behavioral and Applied Management,* and *Journal of the International Academy for Case Studies.* He is the Associate Editor of the Case Association's peer reviewed journal, *The CASE Journal.*

Preface

We welcome you to the Fourth Edition of *Strategic Management: Creating Competitive Advantages!* The author team and our colleagues at McGraw-Hill/Irwin are very gratified with the positive market response that our three previous editions have received. And we are most appreciative of the constructive and extensive feedback that many strategy professionals, who have taken the time to carefully review and critique our work, have provided. We are always striving to improve our product and many of their ideas have been incorporated into the book. We're pleased to acknowledge these many contributors later in the Preface.

In a few words we'd like to revisit the fundamental question: Why did we write the book in the first place? After all, there are already some good strategy textbooks available. The author team felt that there was a need for a book that students would find both relevant and readable, but at the same time challenging. In essence, our tagline could be: "Strong enough for the professor, but made for the student." Perhaps, one of our reviewers, Professor Stephen Vitucci (Tarleton State University–Central Texas), said it best: "I want it to be rigorous but something they can read and understand. The Dess, Lumpkin, and Eisner text I am currently using is exactly what I like and, more importantly, what my students need and like."

To earn such praise, we have endeavored to use an engaging writing style free of unnecessary jargon, to cover all the traditional bases, and to integrate some central themes throughout the book that are vital to understanding strategic management in today's global economy. Among these themes are globalization, technology, ethics, and entrepreneurship. We bring concepts to life with short examples from business practice to illustrate virtually every strategy concept in the book, and we have provided over 90 Strategy Spotlights—more detailed examples—to drive home key points.

We have also included three separate chapters that other strategy texts usually do not have. These chapters focus on timely topics about which all business students should have a solid understanding: the role of intellectual assets and knowledge in value creation (Chapter 4), entrepreneurial strategy and competitive dynamics (Chapter 8), and the value of fostering entrepreneurship in established organizations (Chapter 12). We also provide an excellent set of cases to help students analyze, integrate, and apply strategic management concepts.

When we developed *Strategic Management: Creating Competitive Advantages*, we did not, of course, forget the instructors. You certainly have a very challenging (but rewarding) job. And we want to do our best to help you. We provide a variety of supplementary materials that should help you in class preparation and delivery. In our chapter notes, for example, we did not simply summarize the material. Rather, we always kept in mind (consistent with the strategy concept) value added. To that end, we always asked ourselves: What can we do to add value to the process of teaching and learning? Thus, we provide numerous questions to guide discussion and at least 12 boxed examples to supplement material that is already in the chapter. And, we might add, the author team completed the entire test bank themselves. We have worked hard to provide instructors with a complete package that should make your classes relevant, rigorous, and rewarding for both you and your students. We felt so strongly about this that we developed almost all of these materials ourselves; that is, we didn't "farm them out" to others, as many textbook writers often do. We really believe that this enables us to ensure a high level of quality and consistency in all of our materials.

We'd now like to address some of the major substantive changes in the Fourth Edition. New features we have added we feel "add value" for both instructors and students. And what remains the same—are key features that have been consistent throughout all of our editions.

What's New: Highlights of the Fourth Edition

We have endeavored to add new material to the chapters that reflect both the feedback that we have received from reviewers and the challenges faced by today's managers. While we have added chapter material, we have been careful to avoid "chapter creep." That is, we've worked hard to tighten our writing style and cut redundant examples to illustrate concepts. Thus, our chapters have remained about the same length—and in some cases, have been shortened.

Here are some of our major changes for the Fourth Edition:

- **Ten of the 13 opening Learning from Mistakes "minicases" that lead off the chapters are totally new.** And others have been carefully updated. Unique to this text, these vignettes are all examples of what can go wrong, and they serve as an excellent vehicle for clarifying and reinforcing strategy concepts. After all, what can be learned if we simply admire perfection? **In addition, about half of our 90 Strategy Spotlights are new and many others have been updated.**
- **Four to six "Reflecting on Career Implications" for each chapter.** This feature will help instructors drive home to students the immediate relevance/value of strategy concepts. It focuses on how an understanding of key concepts helps business students early in their careers. This should dramatically enhance the relevance of course material.
- Approximately a dozen key terms for each chapter are defined in the margins of the pages. This was in response to reviewer feedback and should improve students' understanding of core strategy concepts.
- Content (Strategy Spotlights and Exhibits) has been broken out into art or tables to aid learning and improve the visual appeal of our chapters. Further, we strive to avoid long paragraphs, instead focusing on shorter paragraphs with many indented examples. All of these efforts are directed at improving readability and impact.
- The addition of two detailed experiential exercises in the Instructor's Manual that were co-authored by one of the textbook's authors. Atkinson Company deals with managers facing a retrenchment situation in which they have to determine a "rank order of layoff." Plastico is about a management team that must make a quick decision on how to address a serious quality problem that has arisen. But all of the key players have conflicting roles and expectations! These exercises have been used in many contexts, including executive education. They both have a strong game component that makes it enjoyable for students. But, more importantly, Atkinson and Plastico are excellent mechanisms to drive home key course concepts.

Our major content changes for each chapter include:

- **Chapter 1 introduces the concept of "ambidextrous behaviors."** Such behaviors enable managers to help their firms take advantages of existing opportunities as well as explore new opportunities. Among the four ambidextrous behaviors that we discuss is taking initiative and being alert to opportunities beyond the confines of one's own job. This topic has immediate relevance for business graduates.
- **Chapter 3 addresses some of the potential downsides of the balanced scorecard.** Too often, books only focus on the advantages and benefits of concepts that are popular in the business world. Here, as with other concepts in the book (for example, five forces analysis and emotional intelligence), we take a more even-handed approach. This provides a more realistic, critical mind-set for students.
- **Chapter 4 has many useful additions. We provide a detailed discussion of social networks and their implications for knowledge management and career success.** We'd all probably agree that this is a real hot topic in strategic

management (and related fields), and it is supported by a substantial amount of research. We discuss the relative advantages of being part of multiple unconnected networks in a network (i.e., bridging structural holes) and being central to a single network. For example, being a key part of multiple networks (which may represent several departments in a firm) helps individuals gain a greater variety of information sources and contacts which enables them to add more value to their organization and enhance their career success. **We addresss how many firms are developing effective strategies to attract, develop, and retain Generation Y employees.** This is a contemporary issue that all types of organizations face. And of course, it is very relevant to today's students. **And the closing section discusses the importance of firms protecting their intellectual property.** To this end, firms often rely on patents, trademarks, copyrights, and noncompete clauses. However, managers must ensure that their firms develop dynamic capabilities to ensure that they are able to reconfigure knowledge and activities to attain sustainable advantages in the marketplace.

- **Chapter 5 expands our discussion of the industry life cycle.** We discuss how firms can avoid the maturity phase and establish a growth trajectory through "reverse" or "breakaway" positioning. At times, the industry life cycle (the S-curve) is taken as a given. However, our presentation provides insights into how the concept can be addressed more creatively.

- **Chapter 7 introduces the concept of "regionalization" to supplement our discussion of the globalization of the world's economy.** Most multinationals compete in only one or two regions (i.e., North America, Europe, Asia). Why? There are substantial differences (such as language, culture, political/legal institutions) across regions that pose significant challenges for managers. We address the strategic implications, which should spur students' interests in international issues.

- **Chapter 8 (Entrepreneurial Strategy and Competitive Dynamics)** has been completely reconfigured. Part of the chapter (competitive dynamics) is entirely new and addresses the cycle of actions and responses that are initiated when a new player enters a competitive marketplace. This is a "hot issue" in strategy and has important implications for competitive advantage—the core topic of our book. We address competitive dynamics for such rivals as XM and Sirius (satellite radio) and AMD and Intel (chip-makers). The first part of the chapter draws on material that was previously part of Chapter 13 on creating new ventures.

- **In our first three editions, Chapter 8 focused on digital and Internet strategies.** Based on reviewer feedback and the salience of the Internet in the business world and society in general, we have distributed the material that was formerly in Chapter 8 throughout the book: **Chapter 2** addresses how the Internet affects the five forces, **Chapter 3** (appendix) discusses how the Internet adds value, and **Chapter 5** discusses the impact the Internet has on competitive advantage.

- **Chapter 9 addresses one of today's major governance issues—the "backdating" of stock options.** This topic raises critical ethical concerns. By March 2007, about 140 U.S. companies were under investigation by the SEC; 75 firms planned to restate earnings because of backdating, and 66 executives have lost their jobs. Clearly, this issue should raise both emotions and discussion among business students!

- **In Chapter 12, we draw on McGrath and Keil's work on the value captor's processes.** We address how employment practices such as finding the optimal mix of experienced players with new talented and diverse employees can spur experimentation in new venture teams. Given Generation Y's urge to work in progressive and innovative organizations, this topic will be highly relevant.

What Remains the Same: Key Features from Earlier Editions

We've discussed some of the most important changes that we have made to improve *Strategic Management* and keep it fresh and up-to-date. Now, let's briefly address some of the exciting features that remain from the earlier editions.

- *Traditional organizing framework with three other chapters on timely topics.* Crisply written chapters cover all of the strategy bases and address contemporary topics. First, the chapters are divided logically into the traditional sequence: strategy analysis, strategy formulation, and strategy implementation. Second, we include three chapters on such timely topics as intellectual capital/knowledge management, entrepreneurial strategy and competitive dynamics; and, fostering corporate entrepreneurship, and new ventures.

- *"Learning from Mistakes" chapter-opening cases.* To enhance student interest, we begin each chapter with a case that depicts an organization that has suffered a dramatic performance drop, or outright failure, by failing to adhere to sound strategic management concepts and principles. We believe that this feature serves to underpin the value of the concepts in the course and that it is a preferred teaching approach to merely providing examples of outstanding companies that always seem to get it right! After all, isn't it better (and more challenging) to diagnose problems than admire perfection? As Dartmouth's Sydney Finkelstein, author of *Why Smart Executives Fail,* notes: "We live in a world where success is revered, and failure is quickly pushed to the side. However, some of the greatest opportunities to learn—both for individuals and organizations—come from studying what goes wrong."[1] We'll see how, for example, Ford Motor Company's strategic misfires doomed the best-selling car in the United States—the Taurus; how Coors' inability to recognize and act on health trends left its low-carb product, Aspen Edge, in Anheuser-Busch's dust; and, how major flaws in corporate governance has enabled executives like KB Homes' CEO, Bruce Karatz, to enrich themselves—via the backdating of stock options—at shareholder expense.

- *Consistent chapter format and features to reinforce learning.* We have included several features in each chapter to add value and create an enhanced learning experience. First, each chapter begins with an overview and a set of bullets pointing to key learning objectives. Second, as previously noted, the opening case describes a situation in which a company's performance eroded because of a lack of proper application of strategy concepts. Third, at the end of each chapter there are five different types of questions/exercises that should help students assess their understanding and application of material:

    1. Implications of chapter material for career success.
    2. Summary review questions.
    3. Experiential exercises.
    4. Application questions and exercises.
    5. Ethics questions

Given the emergence of Internet and e-commerce, each chapter contains at least one exercise that involves the use of the Internet.

- *Clear articulation and illustration of key concepts.* Key strategy concepts are introduced in a clear and concise manner and are followed by timely and interesting examples from business practice. Such concepts include value-chain analysis, the resource-based view of the firm, Porter's five forces model, competitive advantage,

[1]Personal communication, June 20, 2005.

boundaryless organizational designs, digital strategies, corporate governance, ethics, and entrepreneurship.

- *Extensive use of sidebars.* We include over 90 sidebars (or about six per chapter) called "Strategy Spotlights." The Strategy Spotlights not only illustrate key points but also increase the readability and excitement of new strategy concepts.
- *Integrative themes.* The text provides a solid grounding in ethics, globalization, and technology. These topics are central themes throughout the book and form the basis for many of the Strategy Spotlights.
- *Implications of concepts for small businesses.* Many of the key concepts are applied to start-up firms and smaller businesses, which is particularly important since many students have professional plans to work in such firms.
- *Not just a textbook but an entire package. Strategic Management* features the best chapter teaching notes available today. Rather than merely summarizing the key points in each chapter, we focus on value-added material to enhance the teaching (and learning) experience. Each chapter includes dozens of questions to spur discussion, teaching tips, in-class group exercises, and about a dozen detailed examples from business practice to provide further illustrations of key concepts.

Student Support Materials

- **Online Learning Center (OLC)** The following resources are available to students via the publisher's OLC at www.mhhe.com/dess4e:
  - Chapter quizzes students can take to gauge their understanding of material covered in each chapter.
  - A selection of PowerPoint slides for each chapter.
  - Links to strategy simulations the Business Strategy Game & GLO-BUS. Both provide a powerful and constructive way of connecting students to the subject matter of the course with a competition among classmates on campus and around the world.

And purchasing access to our premium learning resources right on the OLC Web site provides student with the following value-added resources:

  - Pre- and Post-tests. Students can access the online pretest prior to reading the chapter, answer the questions, study the chapter, and then take the posttest to see what they have learned.
  - A handful of content (for instance, quizzes, Pre- and Post-tests, narrated slides, and videos) is also available for iPod download to help students prepare for exams on the go.

Instructor Support Materials

- **Instructor's Manual** Prepared by the textbook authors, the accompanying IM contains summary/objectives, lecture/discussion outlines, discussion questions, extra examples not included in the text, teaching tips, reflecting on career implications, experiential exercises, and more.
- **Test Bank** Prepared by the authors, the test bank contains more than 1,000 true/false, multiple-choice, and essay questions. It has now been tagged with learning objectives as well as Bloom's Taxonomy and AACSB criteria. **Assurance of Learning Ready** Many educational institutions today are focused on the notion of assurance of learning, an important element of some accreditation standards. Dess 4e is designed specifically to support your assurance of learning initiatives with a simple, yet powerful,

solution. Each test bank question for Dess 4e maps to a specific chapter learning outcome/objective listed in the text. You can use our test bank software, EZ Test to easily query for learning outcomes/objectives that directly relate to the learning objectives for your course. You can then use the reporting features of EZ Test to aggregate student results in similar fashion, making the collection and presentation of assurance of learning data simple and easy. **AACSB Statement** McGraw-Hill Companies is a proud corporate member of AACSB International. Recognizing the importance and value of AACSB accreditation, the authors of Dess 4e have sought to recognize the curricula guidelines detailed in AACSB standards for business accreditation by connecting selected questions in Dess 4e the general knowledge and skill guidelines found in the AACSB standards. It is important to note that the statements contained in Dess 4e are provided only as a guide for the users of this text. The statements contained in Dess 4e are provided only as a guide for the users of this text. The AACSB leaves content coverage and assessment clearly within the realm and control of individual schools, the mission of the school, and the faculty. The AACSB does also charge schools with the obligation of doing assessment against their own content and learning goals. While Dess 4e and its teaching package make no claim of any specific AACSB qualification or evaluation, we have, within Dess 4e labeled selected questions according to the six general knowledge and skills areas. The labels or tags within Dess 4e are as indicated. There are of course, many more within the test bank, the text, and the teaching package which might be used as a 'standard' for your course. However, the labeled questions are suggested for your consideration. **EZ Test,** a computerized version of the test bank, can also be found on the Instructor's Resource CD-ROM. This flexible and easy-to-use electronic testing program allows instructors to create multiple versions of tests from book-specific items with a wide range of question types, including adding their own. And any test can be exported for use with course management systems. And now **McGraw-Hill EZ Test Online** is accessible to busy instructors virtually anywhere—in their office, at home or while traveling—and eliminates the need for software installation. It gives instructors access to hundreds of textbook question banks and millions of questions when creating tests. Instructors can view question banks associated with their textbook or easily create their own questions. Multiple versions of tests can be saved for future delivery as a paper test or online. When created and delivered with EZ Test Online, individual tests are immediately scored, saving instructors valuable time and providing prompt test feedback to students. To register please visit http://www.eztestonline.com/.

- **PowerPoint Presentation** for the text consists of more than 400 slides incorporating an outline for the chapters tied to learning objectives. Also included are multiple choice and discussion Classroom Performance System (CPS) questions as well as additional examples outside of the text. And (Case Study PowerPoint slides . . .) Case Study PowerPoint slides are available to facilitate case study coverage.
- **Instructor's Resource CD-ROM** All instructor supplements are available in this one-stop multimedia resource, which includes the Instructor's Manual, Test Bank, PowerPoint Presentations, and Case Study Teaching Notes.
- **Online Learning Center (OLC)** The instructor section of www.mhhe.com/dess4e also includes the Instructor's Manual, PowerPoint Presentations, Interactive Case Grid, and Case Study Teaching Notes as well as additional resources.
- **Enhanced Cartridge for Blackboard and WebCT*** The Enhanced Cartridge is the perfect tool for instructors teaching a hybrid course or a course completely online requiring substantial online content. Resources such as Pre- and Post-tests, iPod content,

---

*Please ask your McGraw-Hill representative about the availability of our Enhanced Cartridge materials for other course management platforms.

interactive skills exercises, and self-assessments help students to learn and apply concepts and allow you to monitor their progress.

- **The Business Strategy Game and GLO-BUS Online Simulations** Both allow teams of students to manage companies in a head-to-head contest for global market leadership. These simulations give students the immediate opportunity to experiment with various strategy options and to gain proficiency in applying the concepts and tools they have been reading about in the chapters. To find out more or to register, please visit www.mmhe.com/thompsonsions.

Additional Resources

- **McGraw-Hill/Primis Custom Publishing** You can customize this text. McGraw-Hill/Primis Online's digital database offers you the flexibility to customize your course including material from the largest online collection of textbooks, readings, and cases. Primis leads the way in customized eBooks with hundreds of titles available at prices that save your students over 20 percent off bookstore prices. For more information, please visit www.primisonline.com/dess or call 800-228-0634.
- **Group and Video Resource Manual** is an instructor's guide to an active classroom. This electronic manual for instructors includes a menu of items you can use as teaching tools in class. Included are detailed teaching notes and PowerPoints for self-assessments, test your knowledge exercises, and the Manager's Hot Seat DVD as well as new group exercises, complete with any handouts or worksheets you'll need to accompany them.
- **Manager's Hot Seat** This interactive, video-based software puts students in the manager's hot seat where they have to apply their knowledge to make decisions on the spot on hot issues such as ethics, diversity, working in teams, and the virtual workplace. This resource is available for student purchase with the Dess text. Resources to support these videos are located in the Group and Video Resource Manual.
- **Dess in eBook** format. Real texts—Real Savings! Are you interested in giving your students the option to access the textbook contents digitally, with interactive, dynamic features and save your students some money? If so, our eBooks are for you. They are identical to our printed textbooks and cost about half as much. Your students will be able to search, highlight, bookmark, annotate, and print the eBook! McGraw-Hill Higher Education's eBooks can be viewed online on any computer with an Internet connection or downloaded to an individual's computer. For more information, please visit http://ebooks.primisonline.com/ or contact your McGraw-Hill representative.
- *BusinessWeek* subscription. Students can subscribe to *BusinessWeek* for a special rate in addition to the price of the text. Students will receive a passcode card shrink-wrapped with their new text. The card directs students to a Web site where they enter the code and then gain access to *BusinessWeek*'s registration page to enter their address information and set up their print and online subscription. Please ask your McGraw-Hill/Irwin representative for more information.
- **Standard & Poor's Educational Version of Market Insight.** McGraw-Hill/Irwin is proud to partner with Standard & Poor's Market Insight ©. This rich online resource provides six years of financial data, key ratio summary reports, and S&P's exclusive "Industry Surveys" that offer an in-depth look at industry trends, projections, and competitive analysis for 500 top U.S. companies in the renowned COMPUSTAT® database. The password-protected Web site is the perfect way to bring real data into today's classroom for use in case analysis, industry analysis, and research for team and individual projects. Learn more at www.mhhe.com/edumarketinsight.

Acknowledgments

Strategic Management represents far more than just the joint efforts of the three co-authors. Rather, it is the product of the collaborative input of many people. Some of these individuals are academic colleagues, others are the outstanding team of professionals at McGraw-Hill/Irwin, and still others are those who are closest to us—our families. It is time to express our sincere gratitude.

First, we'd like to acknowledge the thorough, constructive reviews that we received from our superb team of reviewers and symposia participants. Their input was very helpful in both pointing out errors in the manuscript and suggesting areas that needed further development as additional topics. We sincerely believe that the incorporation of their ideas was critical to improving the final product. These professionals and their affiliations are:

Reviewers for the 4th Edition

George S. Cole, *Shippensburg University*

Keith Credo, *Auburn University*

Tracy Ethridge, *Tri-County Technical College*

Naomi A. Gardberg, *Baruch College, CUNY*

Stephen V. Horner, *Arkansas State University*

Jay J. Janney, *University of Dayton*

Helaine J. Korn, *Baruch College, CUNY*

Zhiang (John) Lin, *University of Texas at Dallas*

Kevin Lowe, *University of North Carolina–Greensboro*

Rickey Madden, Ph.D., *Presbyterian College*

John R. Massaua, *University of Southern Maine*

Fatma Mohamed, *Morehead State University*

Floyd Ormsbee, *Clarkson University*

Ralph W. Parrish, Ph.D., *University of Central Oklahoma*

Annette L. Ranft, *Florida State University*

William W. Sannwald, *San Diego State University*

Mark Shanley, *University of Illinois at Chicago*

Alan Theriault, *University of California–Riverside*

Karen Torres, *Angelo State University*

Craig A. Turner, Ph.D., *East Tennessee State University*

S. Stephen Vitucci, *Tarleton State University–Central Texas*

N. Wasilewski, *Pepperdine University*

Marta Szabo White, *Georgia State University*

John E. Wroblewski, *State University of New York–Fredonia*

Second, the authors would like to thank several faculty colleagues who were particularly helpful in the review, critique, and development of the book and supplementary materials. While Greg was at the University of Kentucky, faculty in the strategic management area were extremely generous with their time. They provided many excellent ideas and contributions for the book's first edition. Accordingly, he would like to thank Wally Ferrier, Gordon Holbein, Dan Lockhart, and Bruce Skaggs. His colleagues at the University of Texas at Dallas also have been helpful and supportive. These individuals include Mike Peng, Joe Picken, Kumar Nair, John Lin, Seung-Hyun Lee, Tev Dalgic, and Jane Salk. His administrative assistant, Mary Vice, has been extremely helpful. Former MBA student Naga Damaraju, along with two doctoral students, Ted Khoury and Erin Pleggenkuhle-Miles, have provided many useful inputs and ideas. He also appreciates the support of his dean and associate dean, Hasan Pirkul and Varghese Jacob, respectively. Tom would like to thank Gerry Hills, Abagail McWilliams, Darold Barnum, Mike Miller, Rod Shrader, James Gillespie, Lou Coco, and other colleagues at the University of Illinois at Chicago, for their continued support. Tom also thanks Keith Brigham, Rod Magee, Todd Moss, Tyge Payne, Jeremy Short, Bill Wan, Abby Wang, and Andy Yu at Texas Tech University, as well as Tammy Branham, Claudia Cogliser, Bill Gardner, Liana Guajardo, Ron Mitchell, Morag Nairn, and Ritch Sorenson for their support. Special thanks also to Jeff Stambaugh for his vital contribution to new materials prepared for the Fourth Edition. Tom also extends a special thanks to Benyamin Lichtenstein for his support and encouragement. Both Greg and Tom wish to thank a special colleague, Abdul Rasheed at the University of Texas at Arlington, who certainly has been a valued source of friendship and ideas for us for many years. He provided many valuable contributions to the Fourth Edition. Alan thanks his colleagues at Pace University and the Case Association for their support in developing these fine case selections. Special thanks go to Jamal Shamsie at Michigan State University for his support in developing the case selections for this edition. And we appreciate Doug Sanford, at Towson State University, for his expertise with one of our new pedagogical features—the key terms in each chapter.

Third, we would like to thank the team at McGraw-Hill/Irwin for their outstanding support throughout the process. This begins with John Biernat, formerly Publisher, who signed us to our original contract. John was always available to provide support and valued input during the entire process. In editorial, Doug Hughes and Laura Griffin kept things on track, responded quickly to our never-ending needs and requests, and offered insights and encouragement. Once the manuscript was completed and revised, project manager Harvey Yep expertly guided us through the production process. Susan Lombardi did an outstanding job in helping us with the supplementary materials. Design Coordinator Jillian Lindner and freelance designer Pam Verros provided excellent design and art work. And finally, we thank Krista Bettino, Anke Braun Weekes, and Mike Gedatus for their energetic, competent, and thorough marketing efforts.

Finally, we would like to thank our families. For Greg this includes his parents, William and Mary Dess, who have always been there for him. His wife Margie and daughter, Taylor, have been a constant source of love and companionship. Greg would also like to recognize two very special people—Walter and Eleanor Descovich, his uncle and aunt, who live in Massapequa, Long Island. They have been a constant source of love and encouragement to him through the years and have raised four wonderful children. They might not write about such ideas as leadership and trust, but they sure practice it! Tom thanks his wife Vicki for her constant love and companionship. Tom also thanks Lee Hetherington and Thelma Lumpkin for their inspiration, as well as his mom Katy, and his sister Kitty, for a lifetime of support. Alan thanks his family—his wife Helaine and his children Rachel and Jacob—for their love and support. He also thanks his parents, Gail Eisner and the late Marvin Eisner, for their support and encouragement.

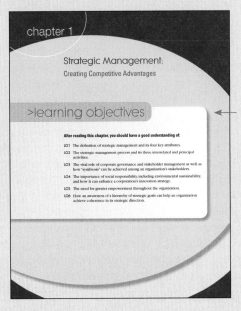

Learning Objectives

Learning Objectives now numbered LO1, LO2, LO3, etc. with corresponding icons in the margins to indicate where learning objectives are covered in the text.

Learning from Mistakes

Learning from Mistakes are examples of where things went wrong. Failures are not only interesting but also sometimes easier to learn from. And students realize strategy is not just about "right or wrong" answers, but requires critical thinking.

Learning from Mistakes

Robert Atkins, a cardiologist, was the founder of the original low-carbohydrate, high-protein diet.[1] He wrote several books that popularized his Atkins diet, including his best seller, *Dr. Atkins New Diet Revolution*, that sold over 10 million copies worldwide. As we will see below, in the beer industry, one firm—Anheuser-Busch—took quick action and benefited from this popular diet trend. Others, including Coors Brewing, were slow to react and paid the price.

In September 2002, Anheuser Busch became one of the pioneers in the low-carb category by launching Michelob Ultra. The brand rapidly became the leader, capturing 5.7 percent of the light beer market by March 2004. The company had jumped on the wave early and rode it during the upsurge of the low-carb trend, which peaked during that year. Clearly, this was an attractive market segment: Beer experts had estimated that about half of the $60 to $70 billion U.S. beer market is from light beer sales as Americans continue to seek out beers that won't add to their waistline.

Coors, in contrast, didn't enter the low-carb market until March 2004—after Michelob Ultra had begun to erode Coors Light's market share. The Coors low-carb brand, Aspen Edge, was too little, too late. By the time Aspen Edge was launched, it faced very stiff competition. In addition to a powerful leader in the segment, Michelob Ultra (which, of course, benefited from Anheuser Busch's deep pockets and marketing prowess), there were already over a dozen other low-carb rivals. These included Rolling Rock, which had introduced Rock Green Light, and Miller Brewing, which had begun to promote the fact that its staple, Miller Lite, had only 3.2 carbs. Further, there were several imported beers, including Martens Low Carbohydrate, brewed by Brouwerij Martens in Belgium.

Even though Coors invested $30 million in Aspen Edge's launch, its sales peaked at just 0.4 percent of the beer market in July 2004. Then its market share began to slide and it was discontinued in April 2006.

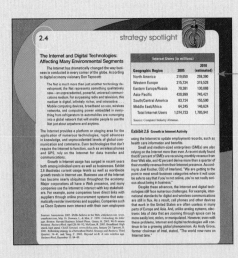

Strategy Spotlight

These boxes weave themes of ethics, globalization, and technology into every chapter of the text, providing students with a thorough grounding necessary for understanding strategic management.

Key Terms

Key Terms defined in the margins have been added to improve students' understanding of core strategy concepts.

strategic management the analyses, decisions, and actions an organization undertakes in order to create and sustain competitive advantages.

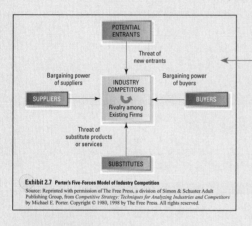

Exhibit 2.7 Porter's Five-Forces Model of Industry Competition

Source: Reprinted with permission of The Free Press, a division of Simon & Schuster Adult Publishing Group, from *Competitive Strategy: Techniques for Analyzing Industries and Competitors* by Michael E. Porter. Copyright © 1980, 1998 by The Free Press. All rights reserved.

Exhibits

Both new and improved exhibits in every chapter provide visual presentations of the most complex concepts covered to support student comprehension.

Reflecting on Career Implications

This new section before the summary of every chapter consists of examples on how understanding of key concepts helps business students early in their careers.

Reflecting on Career Implications . . .

- *The Value Chain:* Carefully analyze where you can add value in your firm's value chain. How might your firm's support activities (e.g., information technology, human resource practices) help you accomplish your assigned tasks more effectively?
- *The Value Chain:* Consider important relationships among activities both within your firm as well as between your firm and its suppliers, customers, and alliance partners.
- *Resource Based View of the Firm:* Are your skills and talents rare, valuable, difficult to imitate, and have few substitutes? If so, you are in a better position to add value for your firm—and earn rewards and incentives. How can your skills and talents be enhanced to help satisfy these criteria to a greater extent? More training? Change positions within the firm? Consider career options at other organizations?
- *Balanced Scorecard:* In your decision making, strive to "balance" the four perspectives: customer, internal business, innovation and learning, and financial. Do not focus too much on short-term profits. Do your personal career goals provide opportunities to develop your skills in all four directions?

support materials

Online Learning Center (OLC)

Online Learning Center (OLC):
www.mhhe.com/dess4e is a Web site that follows the text chapter-by-chapter. OLC content is ancillary and supplementary germane to the textbook. As students read the book, they can go online to take self-grading quizzes, review material, or work through interactive exercises. It includes chapter quizzes, student PowerPoint slides, and links to strategy simulations The *Business Strategy Game* and GLO-BUS. Additional value-added resources are available by purchasing premium content via the OLC. These include Pre- and Post-Tests, narrated slides, and videos—all of which are available for iPod download.

The instructor section also includes the Instructor's Manual, PowerPoint Presentations, Case Study Teaching Notes, Interactive Case Grid, Video Guide, and Case Web Links as well as all student resources.

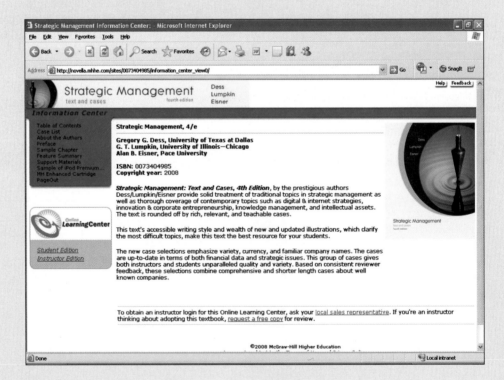

Enhanced Cartridge

The Enhanced Cartridge walks students through each chapter with Pre- and Post-tests, iPod content, interactive skills exercises, and self-assessment helping them learn and apply concepts while also allowing instructors to monitor their progress along the way by feeding directly into the gradebook.

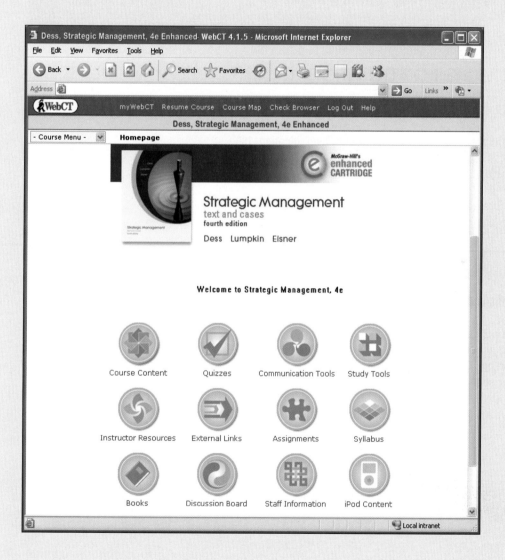

Brief Contents

Contents

part 3 Strategic
    Implementation 301

Strategic Analysis

Chapter 1
Introduction and Analyzing Goals and Objectives

Chapter 2
Analyzing the External Environment

Chapter 3
Analyzing the Internal Environment

Chapter 4
Assessing Intellectual Capital

Strategic Formulation

Chapter 5
Formulating Business-Level Strategies

Chapter 6
Formulating Corporate-Level Strategies

Chapter 7
Formulating International Strategies

Chapter 8
Entrepreneurial Strategy and Competitive Dynamics

Strategic Implementation

Chapter 9
Strategic Control and Corporate Governance

Chapter 10
Creating Effective Organizational Designs

Chapter 11
Strategic Leadership Excellence, Ethics and Change

Chapter 12
Fostering Corporate Entrepreneurship

Case Analysis

Chapter 13
Case Analysis

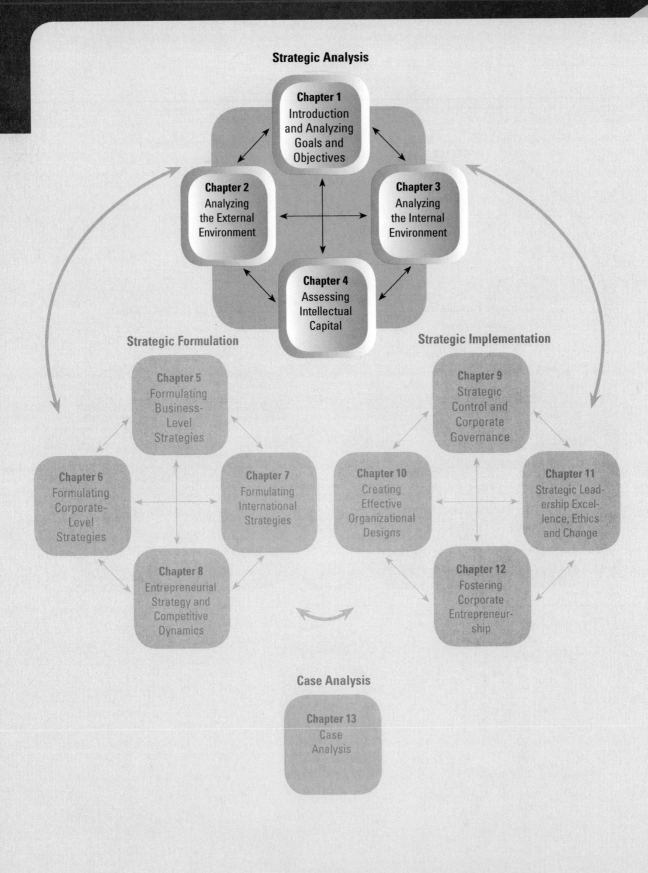

Strategic Analysis

Chapter 1
Introduction and Analyzing Goals and Objectives

Chapter 2
Analyzing the External Environment

Chapter 3
Analyzing the Internal Environment

Chapter 4
Assessing Intellectual Capital

Strategic Formulation

Chapter 5
Formulating Business-Level Strategies

Chapter 6
Formulating Corporate-Level Strategies

Chapter 7
Formulating International Strategies

Chapter 8
Entrepreneurial Strategy and Competitive Dynamics

Strategic Implementation

Chapter 9
Strategic Control and Corporate Governance

Chapter 10
Creating Effective Organizational Designs

Chapter 11
Strategic Leadership Excellence, Ethics and Change

Chapter 12
Fostering Corporate Entrepreneurship

Case Analysis

Chapter 13
Case Analysis

Strategic Analysis

Strategic Management:
Creating Competitive Advantages

>learning objectives

After reading this chapter, you should have a good understanding of:

LO1 The definition of strategic management and its four key attributes.

LO2 The strategic management process and its three interrelated and principal activities.

LO3 The vital role of corporate governance and stakeholder management as well as how "symbiosis" can be achieved among an organization's stakeholders.

LO4 The importance of social responsibility, including environmental sustainability, and how it can enhance a corporation's innovation strategy.

LO5 The need for greater empowerment throughout the organization.

LO6 How an awareness of a hierarchy of strategic goals can help an organization achieve coherence in its strategic direction.

$\mathcal{W}$e define strategic management as *consisting of the analyses, decisions, and actions an organization undertakes in order to create and sustain competitive advantages.* At the heart of strategic management is the question: How and why do some firms outperform others? Thus, the challenge to managers is to decide on strategies that provide advantages that can be sustained over time. There are four key attributes of strategic management. It is directed at overall organizational goals, includes multiple stakeholders, incorporates short-term as well as long-term perspectives, and recognizes trade-offs between effectiveness and efficiency. We discuss the above definition and the four key attributes in the first section.

The second section addresses the strategic management process. The three major processes are strategy analysis, strategy formulation, and strategy implementation. These three components parallel the analyses, decisions, and actions in the above definition. We discuss how each of the 13 chapters addresses these three processes and provide examples from each chapter.

The third section discusses two important and interrelated concepts: corporate governance and stakeholder management. Corporate governance addresses the issue of who "governs" the corporation and determines its direction. It consists of three primary participants: stockholders (owners), management (led by the chief executive officer), and the board of directors (elected to monitor management). Stakeholder management recognizes that the interests of various stakeholders, such as owners, customers, and employees, can often conflict and create challenging decision-making dilemmas for managers. However, we discuss how some firms have been able to achieve "symbiosis" among stakeholders wherein their interests are considered interdependent and can be achieved simultaneously. We also discuss the important role of social responsibility, including the need for corporations to incorporate environmental sustainability in their strategic actions.

The fourth section addresses factors in the business environment that have increased the level of unpredictable change for today's leaders. Such factors have also created the need for a greater strategic management perspective and reinforced the role of empowerment throughout the organization.

The final section focuses on the need for organizations to ensure consistency in their vision, mission, and strategic objectives which, collectively, form a hierarchy of goals. While visions may lack specificity, they must evoke powerful and compelling mental images. Strategic objectives are much more specific and are essential for driving toward overall goals.

Learning from Mistakes

One of the things that makes the study of strategic management so interesting is that struggling firms can become stars, while high flyers can become earthbound very rapidly. For example, consider Ford Motor Company. As this pioneer of the auto industry begins its second century of existence, it is struggling for answers to a variety of problems.[1]

> Ford Motor Company's losses for the year 2006 alone were a staggering $12.7 billion! And even by the company's own projections, they do not see a return to profitability until at least 2009. Along with continuing losses, the company is also experiencing shrinking market share and a stock price that has not risen above single-digit levels in many years. According to analysts at Morgan Stanley, Renault-Nissan may overtake Ford as the world's number three automaker as early as 2007. As the company struggles to avoid drowning in a sea of red ink, one cannot but help wonder how this pioneer of the auto industry went into a downward financial spiral after years of comfortable profits and innovative products. While a number *[continued]*

of errors may have contributed to this decline, nothing illustrates their poor strategy and mismanagement more compellingly than the decision to discontinue the production of the popular Taurus sedan.

Introduced in 1985, the Taurus won acclaim as a symbol of American automotive renaissance. It was admired for its sleek aerodynamic design which was revolutionary for its time. Often referred to as a "jellybean" or a "flying potato" for its futuristic styling, the car was an instant hit, selling 263,000 units in its first year of production. The designers at Ford had spotted an interesting trend among North American car buyers: They were moving away from big, cushy American cars to better handling European models. They catered to this trend by offering a car with stiffer suspension, more interior room, firmer seats, better ergonomics, and more trunk space. They also added a number of "surprise and delight" features such as a cargo net to hold grocery bags in the trunk, and rear seat head rests and heat ducts. In 1989, the Taurus SHO (Super High Output) model was introduced.

After a very successful six-year run, the car was revamped for the 1992 model year, maintaining the overall oval shape, but adding new body panels, slimmer headlights and smoothed-out body sides. The result was a less controversial, more refined design, which catapulted Taurus to the position of the highest-selling passenger car in the United States with sales of nearly half a million units that year. From 1992 to 1996, Taurus was America's best-selling car, instilling a sense of pride in American manufacturers that they could indeed compete with their Japanese rivals and win. It also reversed Ford's financial losses of the early 1980s, contributing immensely to its profitability.

The signs of the decline of Taurus began in the late 1990s. In 1997, Toyota Camry edged out Taurus for the number one spot in the passenger car segment. By 2006, the Camry was outselling the Taurus two to one and Taurus sales had slid below 200,000 annual units. By October 2006, after 21 years and sales of 7.5 million cars (not counting its sibling Mercury Sable), Ford announced the decision to discontinue production of the Taurus.

The obvious question in the minds of millions of loyal customers was: How did the proudest brand of the last two decades come to such an inglorious end? "It didn't keep pace. That's the whole story in four words," claims Joel Pitcoff, Taurus' marketing manager of the mid 1990s. For nearly a decade, Ford treated the Taurus strictly as a cash cow, leaving the car virtually unchanged and with little advertising support. Instead, the company's focus was on high-margin products such as big-size trucks and sport utility vehicles. Meanwhile, competitors had copied and refined many of the attractive features of the Taurus. While the increasingly sophisticated American customers who had plenty of choice in the overcrowded passenger sedan market walked away from the product, Ford focused mainly on the volume intensive but less demanding fleet sales to rental car companies. When the sudden spike in oil prices in mid-2005 sent customers scurrying for more fuel efficient vehicles, Ford was caught flat-footed with virtually no desirable product to offer. "They put no money into the product for the last several years," said Jack Telnack, the original Taurus' chief designer, who retired in 1998. "They just let it wither on the vine. It's criminal. The car had a great reputation, a good name. I don't understand what they were waiting for."

While all of Ford's financial woes cannot be attributed to the demise of the Taurus, it is symptomatic of the many ills that have brought this once proud company to the brink of losing the industry leader position it had enjoyed for decades. Some of the causes of their problems are external in nature, such as the high retiree health benefit costs, the saturation of American markets by numerous producers from Japan and Korea, and the sudden doubling of oil prices. But, in the final analysis, most of Ford's wounds are self-inflicted. Their excessive reliance on trucks and SUVs for profits showed that they had forgotten all the lessons they learned from the oil price increases of the early 1980s. Ford spent $5 billion in the late 1990s in their ill-conceived effort to introduce a "world car." Introduced as the Ford Contour *[continued]* and its sibling the Mercury Mystique, the cars were an instant flop. To starve a successful brand that had captured the imagination of the public and contributed to the resurgence of the company was perhaps the biggest mistake of all.

Responding to the public uproar in the aftermath of the discontinuation of the Taurus brand, the company announced in early 2007 that it would reintroduce the brand by renaming the Ford Five Hundred the Taurus. Only time will tell how customers will respond to this reincarnated Taurus.

Today's leaders, such as those at Ford, face a large number of complex challenges in the global marketplace. In considering how much credit (or blame) they deserve, two perspectives of leadership come immediately to mind: the "romantic" and "external control" perspectives.[2] First, let's look at the **romantic view of leadership.** Here, the implicit assumption is that the leader is the key force in determining an organization's success—or lack thereof.[3] This view dominates the popular press in business magazines such as *Fortune, Business-Week,* and *Forbes,* wherein the CEO is either lauded for his or her firm's success or chided for the organization's demise. Consider, for example, the credit that has been bestowed on leaders such as Jack Welch, Andrew Grove, and Herb Kelleher for the tremendous accomplishments of their firms, General Electric, Intel, and Southwest Airlines, respectively.

More recently, Carlos Ghosn has been lionized in the business press for turning around Nissan's fortunes in the worldwide automobile industry. He transformed huge losses into a $7 billion profit, eliminated $23 billion of debt, and made Nissan the world's most profitable volume producer.[4] And, in the world of sports, managers and coaches, such as Bill Belichick of the New England Patriots in the National Football League, get a lot of credit for their team's outstanding success on the field.

On the other hand, when things don't go well, much of the failure of an organization can also, rightfully, be attributed to the leader. For example, when Carly Fiorina was fired as CEO of Hewlett Packard, the firm enjoyed an immediate increase in its stock price of 7 percent—hardly a strong endorsement of her leadership! The failure of Ford's top management to halt their continuing losses and market erosion finally led the company's board to hire an industry outsider—Boeing's Alan Mulally.

However, this reflects only part of the picture. Consider another perspective called **external view of leadership.** Here, rather than making the implicit assumption that the leader is the most important factor in determining organizational outcomes, the focus is on external factors that may positively or negatively affect a firm's success. We don't have to look far to support this perspective. For example, Ford Motor Company's decline can be attributed partly to a number of external factors. The rising healthcare costs in the United States and the company's pension obligations make it practically impossible to make a profit. Further, the sudden increase in the cost of gasoline after years of steady or declining prices caused a sudden reversal of consumer preferences from high margin SUVs to more efficient vehicles. These developments had serious negative effects not just on Ford, but also on General Motors and Daimler Chrysler.

The point, of course, is that, while neither the romantic nor the external control perspective is entirely correct, we must acknowledge both in the study of strategic management. Our premise is that leaders can make a difference, but they must be constantly aware of the opportunities and threats that they face in the external environment and have a thorough understanding of their firm's resources and capabilities.

Clearly, the fortunes of the U.S. automobile manufacturers have declined in recent years. However, the Japanese automakers, led by Toyota and Honda, have been steadily gaining market share in the United States and have established a strong position in the rest of the world. According to some estimates, Toyota may become the world's biggest automotive company as early as 2009, unseating General Motors from the number

romantic view of leadership
situations in which the leader is the key force determining the organization's success—or lack thereof.

external view of leadership
situations in which external forces— where the leader has limited influence— determine the organization's success.

● An aerial view of the extensive damage caused by Hurricane Katrina taken the day after the hurricane hit (August 30, 2005).

one spot that it has occupied for more than 70 years. What explains the ascendancy of the Japanese companies? Consider four factors:

- They are miles ahead of their U.S. counterparts when it comes to fuel efficiency. Toyota's hybrid car, the Prius, already sells more than 170,000 units in the United States per year while the U.S. companies have no competing product. Gasoline prices are significantly higher in other countries compared to the United States. Therefore, the Japanese automakers' smaller and more fuel efficient vehicles have greater global appeal.
- Despite recent improvements by U.S. auto companies, the Japanese manufacturers still lead in quality and reliability. This is based not only on customer perceptions but also on surveys by J. D. Power & Company, although the gap has narrowed in recent years.
- They have avoided the excessive product proliferation that reduces the effectiveness of the U.S. manufacturers.
- Their recently built manufacturing plants in the United States have lower healthcare and pension costs because of their younger workforce and few retirees.

Before moving on, we'd like to provide a rather dramatic example of the external control perspective at work. On August 29, 2005, Hurricane Katrina had a devastating impact with the loss of many lives and much property damage. Strategy Spotlight 1.1 shares some insights on how this natural disaster placed tremendous constraints on the influence that leaders had on their firms' performance in a variety of industries.

What Is Strategic Management?

Given the many challenges and opportunities in the global marketplace, today's managers must do more than set long-term strategies and hope for the best.[5] They must go beyond what some have called "incremental management," whereby they view their job as making a series of small, minor changes to improve the efficiency of their firm's operations.[6] That is fine if your firm is competing in a very stable, simple, and unchanging industry. But there aren't many of those left. As we shall discuss in this chapter and throughout the book, the pace of change is accelerating, and the pressure on managers to make both major and minor changes in a firm's strategic direction is increasing.

Rather than seeing their role as merely custodians of the status quo, today's leaders must be proactive, anticipate change, and continually refine and, when necessary, make dramatic changes to their strategies. The strategic management of the organization must become both a process and a way of thinking throughout the organization.

Defining Strategic Management

strategic management the analyses, decisions, and actions an organization undertakes in order to create and sustain competitive advantages.

>LO1
The definition of strategic management and its four key attributes.

Strategic management consists of the analyses, decisions, and actions an organization undertakes in order to create and sustain competitive advantages. This definition captures two main elements that go to the heart of the field of strategic management.

First, the strategic management of an organization entails three ongoing processes: *analyses, decisions,* and *actions.* That is, strategic management is concerned with the *analysis* of strategic goals (vision, mission, and strategic objectives) along with the analysis of

The Impact of Hurricane Katrina on Some Industries

August 29, 2005, Hurricane Katrina resulted in the loss of several thousands lives and hundreds of billions of dollars in lost property. Below, we discuss some of the industries that have been particularly hard hit and a few that will benefit.

- Immediately after the hurricane, lumber prices surged. Katrina devastated sawmills and plywood plants on the Gulf Coast and wiped out "vast inventories of wood products," according to one industry newsletter. Up to 1 million board feet of lumber on the docks of New Orleans was destroyed.

- Coffee futures soared. About 27 percent of all U.S. green coffee stocks, some 1.6 million 60 kilogram bags, were stored in New Orleans.

- The nation's breadbasket is also reeling. Katrina knocked out ports where grain-filled barges go upstream to be reloaded, pushing demand and prices up. One company, Colusa Elevator Company in Illinois (which has five grain elevators), has seen the price of corn soar from 42 cents per bushel to 71 cents.

- The tourist and convention business has been hard hit. The tourist business employs 84,300 people in New Orleans. Airlines have been forced to cancel flights, and hotels have halted bookings. Officials at the Omni Hotels in Irving, Texas (which owns two New Orleans hotels) canceled all reservations during the month following Katrina. And the convention business has suffered. The American Association of Retired Persons (AARP) which was scheduled to hold its annual meeting in late September in New Orleans was canceled. Registration had hit 25,000.

- Clearly, some industries will benefit once the rebuilding begins. "From a bank's perspective . . . it's good economically in the same paradoxical way that war is good economically for a lot of people," according to bank research analyst Eric Reinford of SNL Financial in Charlottesville, Virginia. "Natural disasters historically have been a boon for banks because they'll be lending and speeding up the processing of loans." Other big industry winners are construction companies and materials makers. The stocks of these companies soared immediately after Katrina hit.

Sources: Woellert, L., Palmeri, C., & Reed, S. 2005. Katrina's wake. *Business-Week*, September 12: 32–40; and, Lavelle, M. 2005. The (big) ripple effect. *U.S. News & World Report*, September 12: 33–35.

the internal and external environment of the organization. Next, leaders must make strategic decisions. These *decisions,* broadly speaking, address two basic questions: What industries should we compete in? How should we compete in those industries? These questions also often involve an organization's domestic as well as its international operations. And last are the *actions* that must be taken. Decisions are of little use, of course, unless they are acted on. Firms must take the necessary actions to implement their strategies. This requires leaders to allocate the necessary resources and to design the organization to bring the intended strategies to reality. As we will see in the next section, this is an ongoing, evolving process that requires a great deal of interaction among these three processes.

Second, the essence of strategic management is the study of why some firms outperform others.[7] Thus, managers need to determine how a firm is to compete so that it can obtain advantages that are sustainable over a lengthy period of time. That means focusing on two fundamental questions. First: *How should we compete in order to create competitive advantages in the marketplace?* For example, managers need to determine if the firm should position itself as the low-cost producer, develop products and services that are unique and will enable the firm to charge premium prices, or some combination of both.

Second, managers must ask how to make such advantages sustainable, instead of highly temporary, in the marketplace. That is: *How can we create competitive advantages in the marketplace that are not only unique and valuable but also difficult for competitors to copy or substitute?*[8,9]

Ideas that work are almost always copied by rivals immediately. In the 1980s, American Airlines tried to establish a competitive advantage by introducing the frequent flyer program. Within weeks, all the airlines did the same thing. Overnight, frequent flyer programs became a necessary tool for competitive parity instead of a competitive advantage. The challenge, therefore, is to create competitive advantages that are sustainable.

Michael Porter argues that sustainable competitive advantage cannot be achieved through operational effectiveness alone.[10] Most of the popular management innovations of the last two decades—total quality, just-in-time, benchmarking, business process reengineering, outsourcing—all are about operational effectiveness. **Operational effectiveness** means performing similar activities better than rivals. Each of these is important, but none lead to sustainable competitive advantage for the simple reason that everyone is doing them. Strategy is all about being different from everyone else. Sustainable competitive advantage is possible only through performing different activities from rivals or performing similar activities in different ways. Companies such as Wal-Mart, Southwest Airlines, and IKEA have developed unique, internally consistent, and difficult-to-imitate activity systems that have provided them with sustained competitive advantages. A company with a good strategy must make clear choices about what it wants to accomplish. Trying to do everything that your rivals do eventually leads to mutually destructive price competition, not long-term advantage.

> **operational effectiveness**
> performing similar activities better than rivals.

who are our rivals?

The Four Key Attributes of Strategic Management

Before discussing the strategic management process in more detail, let's briefly talk about four attributes of strategic management.[11] In doing so, it will become clear how this course differs from other courses that you have had in functional areas, such as accounting, marketing, operations, and finance. Exhibit 1.1 provides a definition and the four attributes of strategic management.

First, strategic management is *directed toward overall organizational goals and objectives.* That is, effort must be directed at what is best for the total organization, not just a single functional area. Some authors have referred to this perspective as "organizational versus individual rationality."[12] That is, what might look "rational" or most appropriate for one functional area, such as operations, may not be in the best interest of the overall firm. For example, operations may decide to schedule long production runs of similar products in order to lower unit costs. However, the standardized output may be counter to what the marketing department needs in order to appeal to a sophisticated and demanding target market. Similarly, research and development may "overengineer" the product in order to develop a far superior offering, but the design may make the product so expensive that market demand is minimal. Therefore, in this course you will look at cases and strategic issues from the perspective of the organization

think of Paris Cruise example

Exhibit 1.1
Strategic Management Concepts

Definition: Strategic management consists of the analyses, decisions, and actions an organization undertakes in order to create and sustain competitive advantages.

Key Attributes of Strategic Management

- Directs the organization toward overall goals and objectives.
- Includes multiple stakeholders in decision making.
- Needs to incorporate short-term and long-term perspectives.
- Recognizes trade-offs between efficiency and effectiveness.

rather than that of the functional area(s) in which you have had the most training and experience.

Second, strategic management *includes multiple stakeholders in decision making*. Managers must incorporate the demands of many stakeholders when making decisions.[13] **Stakeholders** are those individuals, groups, and organizations who have a "stake" in the success of the organization, including owners (shareholders in a publicly held corporation), employees, customers, suppliers, the community at large, and so on. We'll discuss this in more detail later in this chapter. Managers will not be successful if they continually focus on a single stakeholder. For example, if the overwhelming emphasis is on generating profits for the owners, employees may become alienated, customer service may suffer, and the suppliers may become resentful of continual demands for pricing concessions. As we will see, however, many organizations have been able to satisfy multiple stakeholder needs simultaneously. For example, financial performance may actually be greater because employees who are satisfied with their jobs make a greater effort to enhance customer satisfaction, thus leading to higher profits.

Third, strategic management *requires incorporating both short-term and long-term perspectives*. Peter Senge, a leading strategic management author at the Massachusetts Institute of Technology, has referred to this need as a "creative tension."[14] That is, managers must maintain both a vision for the future of the organization as well as a focus on its present operating needs. However, financial markets can exert significant pressures on executives to meet short-term performance targets. Studies have shown that corporate leaders often take a short-term approach to the detriment of creating long-term shareholder value. Consider the following:

> According to recent studies, only 59 percent of financial executives say they would pursue a positive net present value project if it meant missing the quarter's consensus earnings per-share estimate. Worse, 78 percent say they would sacrifice value—often a great deal of value—to smooth earnings. Similarly, managers are more likely to cut R&D to reverse an earning slide if a significant amount of the company's equity is owned by institutions with high portfolio turnover. Many companies have the same philosophy about long-term investments such as infrastructure and employee training.[15]

Fourth, strategic management *involves the recognition of trade-offs between effectiveness and efficiency*. Closely related to the third point above, this recognition means being aware of the need for organizations to strive to act effectively and efficiently. Some authors have referred to this as the difference between "doing the right thing" **(effectiveness)** and "doing things right" **(efficiency)**.[16] While managers must allocate and use resources wisely, they must still direct their efforts toward the attainment of overall organizational objectives. Managers who are totally focused on meeting short-term budgets and targets may fail to attain the broader goals of the organization. Consider the following amusing story told by Norman Augustine, former CEO of defense giant, Martin Marietta (now Lockheed Martin):

> I am reminded of an article I once read in a British newspaper which described a problem with the local bus service between the towns of Bagnall and Greenfields. It seemed that, to the great annoyance of customers, drivers had been passing long queues of would-be passengers with a smile and a wave of the hand. This practice was, however, clarified by a bus company official who explained, "It is impossible for the drivers to keep their timetables if they must stop for passengers."[17]

Clearly, the drivers who were trying to stay on schedule had ignored the overall mission. As Augustine noted, "Impeccable logic but something seems to be missing!"

Successful managers must make many trade-offs. It is central to the practice of strategic management. At times, managers must focus on the short term and efficiency; at other times the emphasis is on the long term and expanding a firm's product-market scope in order to

stakeholders
individuals, groups, and organizations who have a stake in the success of the organization, including owners (shareholders in a publicly held corporation), employees, customers, suppliers, and the community at large.

effectiveness
tailoring actions to the needs of an organization rather than wasting effort, or "doing the right thing."

efficiency
performing actions at a low cost relative to a benchmark, or "doing things right."

Four Ambidextrous Behaviors: Combining Alignment and Adaptability

Julian Birkinshaw and Christina Gibson studied a wide variety of employees, ranging from senior executives to front-line workers. Their research was a collaboration of the University of Southern California, Booz Allen Hamilton, Inc., and the World Economic Forum. There were a total of 4,195 respondents from 41 business units in 10 multinational companies.

The research identified four ambidextrous behaviors in individuals:

They take the initiative and are alert to opportunities beyond the confines of their own jobs. For example, a regional sales manager for a large computer company, in discussions with one large client, became aware of the need for a new software module that no company currently offered. Rather than try to sell the client something else or just pass the lead on to the business development team, he took it upon himself to work up a business case for the new module. Once he received the go-ahead, he began working full time on the development of the product.

They are cooperative and seek out opportunities to combine their efforts with others. A large beverage company's marketing manager for Italy was primarily involved in supporting a newly acquired subsidiary. She was frustrated with the lack of contact she had with her peers in the other countries. Rather than wait for someone at headquarters to act, she began discussions with peers in other countries that led to the creation of a European marketing forum. This group met quarterly to discuss issues, share best practices, and collaborate on the marketing plans.

They are brokers, always looking to build internal linkages. On a routine visit to the head office in St. Louis, a Canadian plant manager for a large consumer products company heard discussions about plans for a $10 million investment for a new tape manufacturing plant. He inquired further into these plans, and on his return to Canada, he called a regional manager in Manitoba, who he knew was looking for ways of building his business. With some generous support from the Manitoba government, the regional manager bid for, and ultimately won, the $10 million investment.

They are multitaskers who are comfortable wearing more than one hat. For example, the operations manager in France for a major coffee and tea distributor was initially charged with making the plant run as efficiently as possible. However, he took it upon himself to identify new value-added services for his clients. He developed a dual role for himself, managing operations four days a week and on the fifth day developing a promising electronic module that automatically reported impending problems inside a coffee vending machine. He arranged corporate funding, found a subcontractor to develop the software, and then piloted the module in his own operations. The module worked so well that operations managers in several other countries subsequently adopted it.

In summary, such ambidextrous behaviors encourage action that involves adaptation to new opportunities but is clearly aligned with the overall strategy of the business. Such behaviors are the essence of ambidexterity, and they illustrate how a dual capacity for alignment and adaptability can be woven into the fabric of an organization on the individual level.

anticipate opportunities in the competitive environment. For example, consider Kevin Sharer's perspective. He is CEO of Amgen, the giant $12 billion biotechnology firm:

> A CEO must always be switching between what I call different altitudes—tasks of different levels of abstraction and specificity. At the highest altitude you're asking the big questions: What are the company's mission and strategy? Do people understand and believe in these aims? Are decisions consistent with them? At the lowest altitude, you're looking at on-the-ground operations: Did we make that sale? What was the yield on that last lot in the factory? How many days of inventory do we have for a particular drug? And then there's everything in between: How many chemists do we need to hire this quarter? What should we pay for a small biotech company that has a promising new drug? Is our production capacity adequate to roll out a product in a new market?[18]

ambidexterity the challenge managers face of both aligning resources to take advantage of existing product markets as well as proactively exploring new opportunities.

Some authors have developed the concept of **"ambidexterity"** which refers to a manager's challenge to both align resources to take advantage of existing product markets as well as proactively explore new opportunities. Strategy Spotlight 1.2 discusses ambidextrous behaviors that are required for success in today's challenging marketplace.

The Strategic Management Process

>LO2
The strategic management process and its three interrelated and principal activities.

We've identified three ongoing processes—analyses, decisions, and actions—that are central to strategic management. In practice, these three processes—often referred to as strategy analysis, strategy formulation, and strategy implementation—are highly interdependent. Further, these three processes do not take place one after the other in a sequential fashion in most companies.

Intended versus Realized Strategies

Henry Mintzberg, a very influential management scholar at McGill University, argues that conceptualizing the strategic management process as one in which analysis is followed by optimal decisions and their subsequent meticulous implementation neither describes the strategic management process accurately nor prescribes ideal practice.[19] In his view, the business environment is far from predictable, thus limiting our ability for analysis. Further, decisions in an organization are seldom based on optimal rationality alone, given the political processes that occur in all organizations.

Taking into consideration the limitations discussed above, Mintzberg proposed an alternative model of strategy development. As depicted in Exhibit 1.2, decisions following from analysis, in this model, constitute the ***intended* strategy** of the firm. For a variety of reasons, the intended strategy rarely survives in its original form. Unforeseen environmental developments, unanticipated resource constraints, or changes in managerial preferences may result in at least some parts of the intended strategy remaining *unrealized*. On the other hand, good managers will want to take advantage of a new opportunity presented by the environment, even if it was not part of the original set of intentions. For example, consider the wind energy industry.[20] In September 2004 the United States Congress renewed the wind tax credit. Legislation in 19 states now requires that electricity providers offer a certain percentage of "green" (i.e., renewable) energy. Such legislation, combined with falling clean energy costs and rising prices for coal, oil, and gas, have created a surge in demand for competitors such as GE Wind Energy, which makes large turbines and fan blades. Not surprisingly, such businesses have increased hiring and research and development, as well as revenue and profit forecasts. The final ***realized* strategy** of any firm is thus a combination of *deliberate* and *emergent* strategies.

In the next three subsections, we will address each of the three key strategic management processes: strategy analysis, strategy formulation, and strategy implementation.

Exhibit 1.3 depicts the strategic management process and indicates how it ties into the chapters in the book. Consistent with our discussion above, we use two-way arrows to convey the interactive nature of the processes.

intended strategy
strategy in which organizational decisions are determined only by analysis.

realized strategy
strategy in which organizational decisions are determined by both analysis and unforeseen environmental developments, unanticipated resource constraints, and/or changes in managerial preferences.

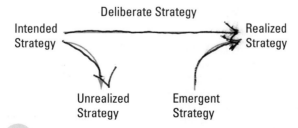

Exhibit 1.2 Realized Strategy and Intended Strategy: Usually Not the Same

Source: From Mintzberg, H. & Waters, J. A., "Of Strategies: Deliberate and Emergent," *Strategic Management Journal,* Vol. 6, 1985, pp. 257–272. Copyright © John Wiley & Sons Limited. Reproduced with permission.

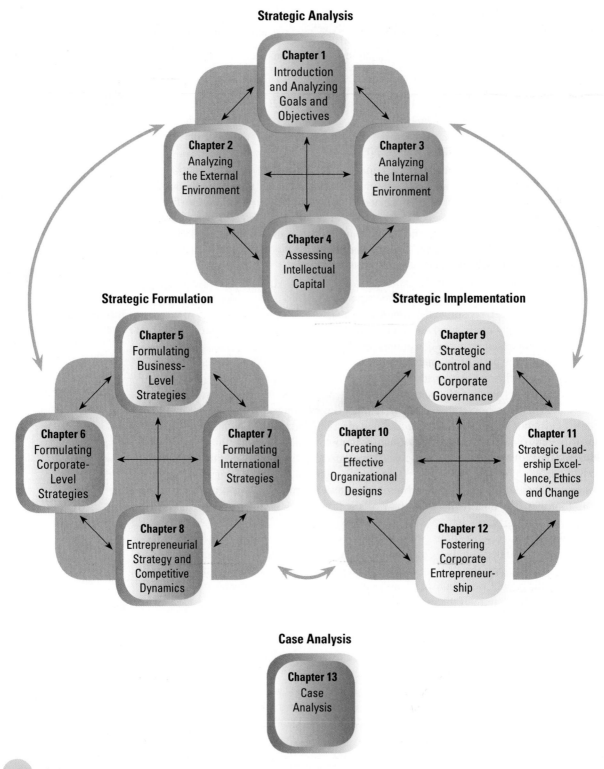

Strategic Analysis

Chapter 1
Introduction and Analyzing Goals and Objectives

Chapter 2
Analyzing the External Environment

Chapter 3
Analyzing the Internal Environment

Chapter 4
Assessing Intellectual Capital

Strategic Formulation

Chapter 5
Formulating Business-Level Strategies

Chapter 6
Formulating Corporate-Level Strategies

Chapter 7
Formulating International Strategies

Chapter 8
Entrepreneurial Strategy and Competitive Dynamics

Strategic Implementation

Chapter 9
Strategic Control and Corporate Governance

Chapter 10
Creating Effective Organizational Designs

Chapter 11
Strategic Leadership Excellence, Ethics and Change

Chapter 12
Fostering Corporate Entrepreneurship

Case Analysis

Chapter 13
Case Analysis

Exhibit 1.3 The Strategic Management Process

Strategy Analysis

Strategy analysis may be looked upon as the starting point of the strategic management process. It consists of the "advance work" that must be done in order to effectively formulate and implement strategies. Many strategies fail because managers may want to formulate and implement strategies without a careful analysis of the overarching goals of the organization and without a thorough analysis of its external and internal environment.

Analyzing Organizational Goals and Objectives (Chapter 1)   Later in this chapter, we will address how organizations must have clearly articulated goals and objectives in order to channel the efforts of individuals throughout the organization toward common ends. Goals and objectives also provide a means of allocating resources effectively. A firm's vision, mission, and strategic objectives form a hierarchy of goals that range from broad statements of intent and bases for competitive advantage to specific, measurable strategic objectives.

As indicated in Exhibit 1.3, this hierarchy of goals is not developed in isolation. Rather, it is developed in concert with a rigorous understanding of the opportunities and threats in the external environment (Chapter 2) as well as a thorough understanding of the firm's strengths and weaknesses (Chapters 3 and 4).

Analyzing the External Environment of the Firm (Chapter 2)   Managers must monitor and scan the environment as well as analyze competitors. Such information is critical in determining the opportunity and threats in the external environment. Two frameworks of the external environment are provided. First, the general environment consists of several elements, such as demographic, technological, and economic segments, from which key trends and events can have a dramatic impact on the firm. Second, the industry environment consists of competitors and other organizations that may threaten the success of a firm's products and services.

Assessing the Internal Environment of the Firm (Chapter 3)   Useful frameworks are provided to identify both strengths and weaknesses that can, in part, determine how well a firm will succeed in an industry. Analyzing the strengths and relationships among the activities that constitute a firm's value chain (e.g., operations, marketing and sales, and human resource management) can be a means of uncovering potential sources of competitive advantage for the firm.

Assessing a Firm's Intellectual Assets (Chapter 4)   The knowledge worker and a firm's other intellectual assets (e.g., patents, trademarks) are becoming increasingly important as the drivers of competitive advantages and wealth creation. In addition to human capital, we assess how well the organization creates networks and relationships among its employees as well as its customers, suppliers, and alliance partners. Further, technology can enhance collaboration among employees as well as provide a means of accumulating and storing knowledge.

Strategy Formulation

A firm's strategy formulation is developed at several levels. First, business-level strategy addresses the issue of how to compete in a given business to attain competitive advantage. Second, corporate-level strategy focuses on two issues: (a) what businesses to compete in and (b) how businesses can be managed to achieve synergy; that is, they create more value by working together than if they operate as stand-alone businesses. Third, a firm must determine the best method to develop international strategies as it ventures beyond its national boundaries. Fourth, managers must formulate effective entrepreneurial initiatives to succeed in highly competitive and dynamic environments.

Formulating Business-Level Strategy (Chapter 5)   The question of how firms compete and outperform their rivals and how they achieve and sustain competitive advantages goes to the heart of strategic management. Successful firms strive to develop bases for competitive advantage, which can be achieved through cost leadership and/or differentiation as well as by focusing on a narrow or industrywide market segment. We'll also discuss why some advantages can be more sustainable (or durable) over time and how a firm's business-level strategy changes with the industry life cycle—that is, the stages of introduction, growth, maturity, and decline.

Formulating Corporate-Level Strategy (Chapter 6)   Corporate-level strategy addresses a firm's portfolio (or group) of businesses, asking (1) What business (or businesses) should we compete in? and (2) How can we manage this portfolio of businesses to create synergies among the businesses? We explore the relative advantages and disadvantages of firms pursuing strategies of related or unrelated diversification. We also discuss the various means that firms can employ to diversify—internal development, mergers and acquisitions, and joint ventures and strategic alliances—as well as their relative advantages and disadvantages.

Formulating International Strategy (Chapter 7)   When firms enter foreign markets, they face both opportunities and pitfalls. Managers must decide not only on the most appropriate entry strategy but also how they will go about attaining competitive advantages in international markets. Many successful international firms have been able to attain both lower costs and higher levels of differentiated products and services via a "transnational strategy."

Entrepreneurial Strategy and Competitive Dynamics (Chapter 8)   Entrepreneurial activity aimed at new value creation is a major engine for economic growth. For entrepreneurial initiatives to succeed viable opportunities must be recognized and effective strategies must be formulated. Actions by new, entrepreneurial entrants threaten existing players and evoke competitive responses designed to maintain a strong competitive position. Such competitively dynamic environments provide both opportunities and significant challenges for entrepreneurial firms.

Strategy Implementation

Clearly, sound strategies are of no value if they are not properly implemented. Strategy implementation involves ensuring proper strategic controls and organizational designs, which includes establishing effective means to coordinate and integrate activities within the firm as well as with its suppliers, customers, and alliance partners. Leadership plays a central role, including ensuring that the organization is committed to excellence and ethical behavior. It also promotes learning and continuous improvement and acts entrepreneurially in creating and taking advantage of new opportunities.

Strategic Control and Corporate Governance (Chapter 9)   Firms must exercise two types of strategic control. First, informational control requires that organizations continually monitor and scan the environment and respond to threats and opportunities. Second, behavioral control involves the proper balance of rewards and incentives as well as cultures and boundaries (or constraints). Further, successful firms (those that are incorporated) practice effective corporate governance. They must create mechanisms to ensure that the actions of the managers are consistent with the interests of the owners (shareholders) of the firm. These include an effective board of directors, actively engaged shareholders, and proper managerial reward and incentive systems. Various external mechanisms such as the market for corporate control, auditors, banks, analysts, and the financial press often help to ensure good governance.

Creating Effective Organizational Designs (Chapter 10)   To succeed, firms must have organizational structures and designs that are consistent with their strategy. For example, firms that diversify into related product-market areas typically decentralize decision making by implementing divisional structures. In today's rapidly changing competitive environments, firms must ensure that their organizational boundaries—those internal to the firm and external—are more flexible and permeable. Often, organizations develop strategic alliances to capitalize on the capabilities of other organizations.

Creating a Learning Organization and an Ethical Organization (Chapter 11)
Effective leaders set a direction, design the organization, and develop an organization that is committed to excellence and ethical behavior. In addition, given rapid and unpredictable change, leaders must create a "learning organization." This ensures that the entire organization can benefit from individual and collective talents.

Fostering Corporate Entrepreneurship (Chapter 12)   With rapid and unpredictable change in the global marketplace, firms must continually improve and grow as well as find new ways to renew their organizations. Corporate entrepreneurship and innovation provide firms with new opportunities, and strategies should be formulated that enhance a firm's innovative capacity. Within corporations, proactiveness and autonomous entrepreneurial behavior by product champions and other organizational members are needed to turn new ideas into corporate ventures.

We've discussed the strategic management process. In addition, Chapter 13, "Analyzing Strategic Management Cases," provides guidelines and suggestions on how to evaluate cases in this course. Thus, the concepts and techniques discussed in these 12 chapters can be applied to real-world organizations.

Let's now address two concepts—corporate governance and stakeholder management—that are critical to the strategic management process.

The Role of Corporate Governance and Stakeholder Management

>LO3
The vital role of corporate governance and stakeholder management as well as how "symbiosis" can be achieved among an organization's stakeholders.

Most business enterprises that employ more than a few dozen people are organized as corporations. As you recall from your finance classes, the overall purpose of a corporation is to maximize the long-term return to the owners (shareholders). Thus, we may ask: Who is really responsible for fulfilling this purpose? Robert Monks and Neil Minow, in addressing this issue, provide a useful definition of **corporate governance** as "the relationship among various participants in determining the direction and performance of corporations. The primary participants are (1) the shareholders, (2) the management (led by the chief executive officer), and (3) the board of directors."[21] This relationship is illustrated in Exhibit 1.4.

corporate governance the relationship among various participants in determining the direction and performance of corporations. The primary participants are (1) the shareholders, (2) the management (led by the chief executive officer), and (3) the board of directors.

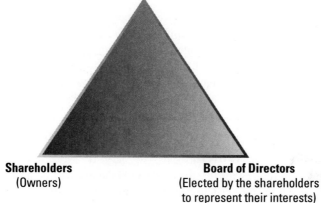

Management
(Headed by the chief executive officer)

Shareholders
(Owners)

Board of Directors
(Elected by the shareholders to represent their interests)

Exhibit 1.4 The Key Elements of Corporate Governance

The board of directors (BOD) are the elected representatives of the shareholders. They are charged with ensuring that the interests and motives of management are aligned with those of the owners (i.e., shareholders). In many cases, the BOD is diligent in fulfilling its purpose. For example, Intel Corporation, the giant $35 billion maker of microprocessor chips, is widely recognized as an excellent example of sound governance practices. Its BOD has established guidelines to ensure that its members are independent (i.e., not members of the executive management team and do not have close personal ties to top executives) so that they can provide proper oversight, it has explicit guidelines on the selection of director candidates (to avoid "cronyism"), and it provides detailed procedures for formal evaluations of both directors and the firm's top officers.[22] Such guidelines serve to ensure that management is acting in the best interests of shareholders.[23]

Recently, there has been much criticism as well as cynicism by both citizens and the business press about the poor job that management and the BODs of large corporations are doing. We only have to look at the recent scandals at firms such as Arthur Andersen, WorldCom, Enron, Tyco, and ImClone Systems.[24] Such malfeasance has led to an erosion of the public's trust in the governance of corporations. For example, a recent Gallup poll found that 90 percent of Americans felt that people leading corporations could not be trusted to look after the interests of their employees, and only 18 percent thought that corporations looked after their shareholders. Forty-three percent, in fact, believed that senior executives were in it only for themselves. In Britain, that figure, according to another poll, was an astonishing 95 percent.[25] Perhaps worst of all, in another study, 60 percent of directors (the very people who decide how much executives should earn) felt that executives were "dramatically overpaid"![26]

To drive home the point, consider the humorous perspective of Russell T. Lewis, CEO of the New York Times Company, in a recent speech:[27]

> Not long ago, CEOs were regarded as captains of industry—among the country's best and brightest talents—at least that's what I've been telling my parents, and they seem to have bought the line. Today, however, CEOs and their CFOs are highly reviled defendants in felony criminal proceedings. And their companies are the subjects of billion-dollar shareholder lawsuits. Things have gotten so bad that any day now I expect *Fortune* magazine to come out with its list of "Most Wanted CEOs." No doubt this will soon be followed by a spin-off of a popular TV program. I can see the promo now: "Tonight at 8 PM—Help us catch America's Most Wanted CEOs . . . they could be hiding in our hometown."
>
> But, folks, the final indignity for this particular CEO concerns my own parents: my loving 87-year-old mother—a former public school teacher and my unfailingly supportive 94-year-old father. They no longer brag about me to the clerks at the Lake Worth, Florida, Publix supermarket. Yes, folks, it has gotten that bad.

Clearly, there is a strong need for improved corporate governance, and we will address this topic in Chapter 9. We focus on three important mechanisms to ensure effective corporate governance: an effective and engaged board of directors, shareholder activism, and proper managerial rewards and incentives.[28] In addition to these internal controls, a key role is played by various external control mechanisms.[29] These include the auditors, banks, analysts, an active financial press, and the threat of hostile takeovers.

Zero Sum or Symbiosis? Two Alternate Perspectives of Stakeholder Management

Generating long-term returns for the shareholders is the primary goal of a publicly held corporation. As noted by former Chrysler vice chairman Robert Lutz, "We are here to serve the shareholder and create shareholder value. I insist that the only person who owns the company is the person who paid good money for it."[30]

Stakeholder Group	Nature of Claim
Stockholders	Dividends, capital appreciation
Employees	Wages, benefits, safe working environment, job security
Suppliers	Payment on time, assurance of continued relationship
Creditors	Payment of interest, repayment of principal
Customers	Value, warranties
Government	Taxes, compliance with regulations
Communities	Good citizenship behavior such as charities, employment, not polluting the environment

Despite the primacy of generating shareholder value, managers who focus solely on the interests of the owners of the business will often make poor decisions that lead to negative, unanticipated outcomes. For example, decisions such as mass layoffs to increase profits, ignoring issues related to conservation of the natural environment to save money, and exerting excessive pressure on suppliers to lower prices can certainly harm the firm in the long run. Such actions would likely lead to negative outcomes such as alienated employees, increased governmental oversight and fines, and disloyal suppliers.

Clearly, in addition to *shareholders,* there are other *stakeholders* (e.g. suppliers, customers) who must be explicitly taken into account in the strategic management process.[31] A stakeholder can be defined as an individual or group, inside or outside the company, that has a stake in and can influence an organization's performance. Each stakeholder group makes various claims on the company. Exhibit 1.5 provides a list of major stakeholder groups and the nature of their claims on the company.

There are two opposing ways of looking at the role of stakeholder management in the strategic management process.[32] The first one can be termed "zero sum." In this view, the role of management is to look upon the various stakeholders as competing for the organization's resources. In essence, the gain of one individual or group is the loss of another individual or group. For example, employees want higher wages (which drive down profits), suppliers want higher prices for their inputs and slower, more flexible delivery times (which drive up costs), customers want fast deliveries and higher quality (which drive up costs), the community at large wants charitable contributions (which take money from company goals), and so on. This zero-sum thinking is rooted, in part, in the traditional conflict between workers and management, leading to the formation of unions and sometimes ending in adversarial union–management negotiations and long, bitter strikes.

Although there will always be some conflicting demands, there is value in exploring how the organization can achieve mutual benefit through *stakeholder symbiosis,* which recognizes that stakeholders are dependent upon each other for their success and well-being.[33] That is, managers acknowledge the interdependence among employees, suppliers, customers, shareholders, and the community at large. Consider Outback Steakhouse:[34]

> Outback Steakhouse asked their employees to identify on a six-point scale how strongly they agreed or disagreed that Outback's principles and beliefs (P&Bs) were practiced in their particular restaurants. The turnover rate of the hourly employees in the group most strongly agreeing that the P&Bs were their stores' guiding ethos was half what it was in the group most strongly disagreeing. Five times as many customers in the strongly agreeing group indicated that they were likely to return. Further, at the strongly agreeing group's restaurants, revenues were 8.9 percent higher, cash flow was 27 percent higher, and pretax profit was 48 percent higher. Not surprisingly, it is now mandatory that Outback managers conduct this survey.

Social Responsibility and Environmental Sustainability: Moving beyond the Immediate Stakeholders

Organizations cannot ignore the interests and demands of stakeholders such as citizens and society in general that are beyond its immediate constituencies—customers, owners, suppliers, and employees. That is, they must consider the needs of the broader community at large and act in a socially responsible manner.[35]

social responsibility
the expectation that businesses or individuals will strive to improve the overall welfare of society.

Social responsibility is the expectation that businesses or individuals will strive to improve the overall welfare of society.[36] From the perspective of a business, this means that managers must take active steps to make society better by virtue of the business being in existence.[37] Similar to norms and values, actions that constitute socially responsible behavior tend to change over time. In the 1970s affirmative action was a high priority and during the 1990s and up to the present time, the public has been concerned about environmental quality. Many firms have responded to this by engaging in recycling and reducing waste. And in the wake of terrorist attacks on New York City and the Pentagon, as well as the continuing threat from terrorists worldwide, a new kind of priority has arisen: the need to be vigilant concerning public safety.

>LO4

The importance of social responsibility, including environmental sustainability, and how it can enhance a corporation's innovation strategy.

Today, demands for greater corporate responsibility have accelerated.[38] These include corporate critics, social investors, activists, and, increasingly, customers who claim to assess corporate responsibility when making purchasing decisions. Such demands go well beyond product and service quality.[39] They include a focus on issues such as labor standards, environmental sustainability, financial and accounting reporting, procurement, and environmental practices. At times, a firm's reputation can be tarnished by exceedingly poor judgment on the part of one of its managers.

> In 2006, Judith Regan, a publisher at HarperCollins, was set to publish a book by O. J. Simpson called *If I Did It,* detailing how he would have committed the 1995 murder of his ex-wife Nicole Brown Simpson and her friend, Ron Goldman. The book was characterized by Regan as O. J.'s "confession," and it earned the world's outrage as an "evil sweeps stunt" that will likely be remembered as a low point in American culture. Regan's boss, News Corporation Chairman Rupert Murdoch cancelled the book and the TV special that was also planned. But this was not before pre-orders for *If I Did It* cracked the Top 20 on Amazon.com. Not surprisingly, Judith Regan was fired.[40]

A key stakeholder group that appears to be particularly susceptible to corporate social responsibility (CSR) initiatives is its customers.[41] Surveys indicate a strong positive relationship between CSR behaviors and consumers' reactions to a firm's products and services. For example:

- Corporate Citizenship's poll conducted by Cone Communications found that "84 percent of Americans say they would be likely to switch brands to one associated with a good cause, if price and quality are similar."[42]
- Hill & Knowlton/Harris's Interactive poll reveals that "79 percent of Americans take corporate citizenship into account when deciding whether to buy a particular company's product and 37 percent consider corporate citizenship an important factor when making purchasing decisions."[43]

Such findings are consistent with a large body of research that confirms the positive influence of CSR on consumers' company evaluations and product purchase intentions across a broad range of product categories.

Cause-related marketing is another example of the growing link between corporate social responsibility and financial objectives. Such marketing generally features promotions in which a portion of the purchase price of a product or service is donated to a social cause: It essentially links marketing and corporate philanthropy. Strategy Spotlight 1.3 discusses how American Express became one of the pioneers of this emerging trend and significantly benefited.

American Express: Using Cause-Related Marketing Effectively

American Express (AmEx) has benefited from favorable public relations, and financially, from its cause-related marketing initiatives. Back in 1983, in connection with the restoration of the Statue of Liberty project, it promised that it would contribute to this initiative a portion of the amount that consumers charged on their American Express cards. The resulting campaign made marketing history. It eventually donated $1.7 million to the cause. But AmEx card use increased 28 percent and new card applications increased 17 percent. Cause-related marketing has grown significantly from $125 million in 1990 to $991 million in 2004, and the figure is expected to continue to increase.

According to a recent Cone Corporate Citizenship Study, cause-related marketing can both reinforce consumer relationships as well as strengthen employee morale. For example, 84 percent of respondents said they would like to switch brands to one associated with a good cause, and 92 percent of Americans said that they have a more positive image of companies and products that support good causes. Similarly, 57 percent of employees wish that their company would do more to support a social issue, and 75 percent of Americans would consider a company's commitment to social issues when deciding where to work.

Sources: Vogel, D. J. 2005. Is there a market for virtue? The business case for corporate social responsibility. *California Management Review,* 47(4): 19–36; 2002 Cone Corporate Citizenship Study, Cone, Inc.

The Triple Bottom Line: Incorporating Financial as well as Environmental and Social Costs   Many companies are now measuring what has been called a **"triple bottom line,"** which involves assessing financial, social, and environmental performance. Shell, NEC, and Procter & Gamble, among other corporations, have recognized that failing to account for the environmental and social costs of doing business poses risks to the company and its community.[44]

The environmental revolution has been almost four decades in the making.[45] It has changed forever how companies do business. In the 1960s and 1970s, companies were in a state of denial regarding their firms' impact on the natural environment. However, a series of visible ecological problems created a groundswell for strict governmental regulation. In the United States, Lake Erie was "dead," and in Japan, people were dying of mercury poisoning. Clearly, the effects of global warming are being felt throughout the world. Some other examples include the following:

● Solar cells can be organized into arrays, such as this one, to provide electric power for industrial, commercial, and residential customers. Solar power is a more sustainable, environmentally friendly option than nuclear power plants or coal- and oil-fired power plants.

- Ice roads are melting, so Canadian diamond miners must airlift equipment at great cost instead of trucking it in.
- More severe storms and rising seas mean oil companies must build stronger rigs, and cities must build higher seawalls.
- The loss of permafrost and protective sea ice may force villages like Alaska's Shismaref to relocate.
- Yukon River salmon and fisheries are threatened by a surge of parasites associated with a jump in water temperature.

- Later winters have let beetles spread in British Columbia killing 22 million acres of pine forests, an area the size of Maine.
- In Mali, Africa, crops are threatened. The rainy season is now too short for rice, and the dry season is too hot for potatoes.[46]

Stuart Hart, writing in the *Harvard Business Review,* addresses the magnitude of problems and challenges associated with the natural environment:

> The challenge is to develop a *sustainable global economy:* an economy that the planet is capable of supporting indefinitely. Although we may be approaching ecological recovery in the developed world, the planet as a whole remains on an unsustainable course. Increasingly, the scourges of the late twentieth century—depleted farmland, fisheries, and forests; choking urban pollution; poverty; infectious disease; and migration—are spilling over geopolitical borders. The simple fact is this: in meeting our needs, we are destroying the ability of future generations to meet theirs . . . corporations are the only organizations with the resources, the technology, the global reach, and, ultimately, the motivation to achieve sustainability.[47]

Environmental sustainability is now a value embraced by the most competitive and successful multinational companies.[48] The McKinsey Corporation's survey of more than 400 senior executives of companies around the world found that 92 percent agreed with former Sony President Akio Morita's contention that the environmental challenge will be one of the central issues in the 21st century.[49] Virtually all executives acknowledged their firm's responsibility to control pollution, and 83 percent agreed that corporations have an environmental responsibility for their products even after they are sold.

For many successful firms, environmental values are now becoming a central part of their cultures and management processes. And, as noted earlier, environmental impacts are being audited and accounted for as the "third bottom line." According to one 2004 corporate report, "If we aren't good corporate citizens as reflected in a Triple Bottom Line that takes into account social and environmental responsibilities along with financial ones—eventually our stock price, our profits, and our entire business could suffer."[50] And, according to a KPMG study of 350 firms: "More big multinational firms are seeing the benefits of improving their environmental performance. . . . Firms are saving money and boosting share performance by taking a close look at how their operations impact the environment . . . Companies see that they can make money as well." Strategy Spotlight 1.4 discusses how Adobe Systems benefits financially from its environmental initiatives.

The Strategic Management Perspective: An Imperative throughout the Organization

Strategic management requires managers to take an integrative view of the organization and assess how all of the functional areas and activities fit together to help an organization achieve its goals and objectives. This cannot be accomplished if only the top managers in the organization take an integrative, strategic perspective of issues facing the firm and everyone else "fends for themselves" in their independent, isolated functional areas. Marketing and sales will generally favor broad, tailor-made product lines, production will demand standardized products that are relatively easy to make in order to lower manufacturing costs, research and development will design products to demonstrate technical elegance, and so on. Instead, people throughout the organization must strive toward overall goals.

The need for such a perspective is accelerating in today's increasingly complex, interconnected, ever-changing, global economy. As noted by Peter Senge of MIT, the days when

How Adobe Systems Benefits from "Being Green"

In June 2006, Adobe Systems, the $2 billion software maker, became the first firm to receive a platinum award from the nonprofit U.S. Green Building Council. Platinum certification of Adobe's buildings was based on ratings in six categories: sustainability; water efficiency; energy efficiency and atmospheric quality; use of materials and resources; indoor environmental quality; and innovations in upgrades, operations, and maintenance.

Thus, Adobe's San Jose headquarters is the greenest corporate site on record in the United States. What is more impressive is that Adobe earned the honor by retrofitting

Sources: Nachtigal, J. 2006. It's easy and cheap being green. *BusinessWeek*, October 16: 53; Warner, J. 2006. Adobe headquarters awarded highest honors from U.S. green building council. *Adobe Press Release*, December 6; and, Juran, K. 2006. Adobe wins top California Flex Your Power! Award for energy efficiency. *Adobe Press Release*, July 3.

its two existing office towers (approximately 1 million square feet). Most of the 151 buildings that have received the council's gold ratings (a "step" down from platinum) are new structures.

By installing everything from motion detectors to waterless urinals, the firm has reduced its electricity use by 35 percent and its gas consumption by 41 percent since 2001. In addition, it conserves 295,000 gallons of water each month. And, during this time, the company's headcount has shot up 80 percent!

Adobe is proving that building "green" isn't just good citizenship—it is profitable. Adobe has invested approximately $650,000 for energy and environmental retrofits since 2001. The retrofits on the two office towers have resulted in approximately $720,000 in savings to date, for a total return on investment of approximately 115 percent. Randy Knox III, Adobe's director of real estate, facilities, and security, comments, "This isn't some pie-in-the-sky kind of thing the enviros are pushing. It really works."

Henry Ford, Alfred Sloan, and Tom Watson (top executives at Ford, General Motors, and IBM, respectively) "learned for the organization are gone." He goes on to say:

> In an increasingly dynamic, interdependent, and unpredictable world, it is simply no longer possible for anyone to "figure it all out at the top." The old model, "the top thinks and the local acts," must now give way to integrating thinking and acting at all levels. While the challenge is great, so is the potential payoff. "The person who figures out how to harness the collective genius of the people in his or her organization," according to former Citibank CEO Walter Wriston, "is going to blow the competition away."[51]

Managers need to anticipate and respond to dramatic and unpredictable changes in the competitive environment. With the emergence of the knowledge economy, human capital (as opposed to financial and physical assets) has become the key to securing advantages in the marketplace that persist over time.

To develop and mobilize people and other assets, leaders are needed throughout the organization.[52] No longer can organizations be effective if the top "does the thinking" and the rest of the organization "does the work." Everyone must be involved in the strategic management process. There is a critical need for three types of leaders:

- Local line leaders who have significant profit-and-loss responsibility.
- Executive leaders who champion and guide ideas, create a learning infrastructure, and establish a domain for taking action.
- Internal networkers who, although they have little positional power and formal authority, generate their power through the conviction and clarity of their ideas.[53]

Sally Helgesen, author of *The Web of Inclusion: A New Architecture for Building Great Organizations,* also expressed the need for leaders throughout the organization. She asserted that many organizations "fall prey to the heroes-and-drones syndrome, exalting the value of those in powerful positions while implicitly demeaning the contributions of those who fail to achieve top rank."[54] Culture and processes in which leaders emerge at all levels, both up and down as well as across the organization, typify today's high-performing firms.[55]

Top-level executives are key in setting the tone for the empowerment of employees. Consider Richard Branson, founder of the Virgin Group, whose core businesses include retail operations, hotels, communications, and an airline. He is well known for creating a culture and an informal structure where anybody in the organization can be involved in generating and acting upon new business ideas. In an interview, he stated,

> [S]peed is something that we are better at than most companies. We don't have formal board meetings, committees, etc. If someone has an idea, they can pick up the phone and talk to me. I can vote "done, let's do it." Or, better still, they can just go ahead and do it. They know that they are not going to get a mouthful from me if they make a mistake. Rules and regulations are not our forte. Analyzing things to death is not our kind of thing. We very rarely sit back and analyze what we do.[56]

To inculcate a strategic management perspective throughout the organization, many large traditional organizations must often make a major effort to effect transformational change. This involves extensive communication, incentives, training, and development to strengthen a strategic perspective throughout the organization. For example, under the direction of Nancy Snyder, a corporate vice president, Whirlpool, the world's largest producer of household appliances, brought about a significant shift in the firm's reputation as an innovator.[57] This five-year initiative included both financial investments in capital spending as well as a series of changes in management processes, including training innovation mentors, making innovation a significant portion of leadership development programs, enrolling all salaried employees in online courses in business innovation, and providing employees with an innovation portal that allows them access to multiple innovation tools and data. We discuss Whirlpool's initiatives in more detail in Chapter 11.

We'd like to close with our favorite example of how inexperience can be a virtue. It further reinforces the benefits of having broad involvement throughout the organization in the strategic management process (see Strategy Spotlight 1.5)

Ensuring Coherence in Strategic Direction

Employees and managers throughout the organization must strive toward common goals and objectives. By specifying desired results, it becomes much easier to move forward. Otherwise, when no one knows what the firm is striving to accomplish, they have no idea of what to work toward. As the old nautical expression puts it, "No wind favors the ship that has no charted course."

Organizations express priorities best through stated goals and objectives that form a **hierarchy of goals,** which includes its vision, mission, and strategic objectives. What visions may lack in specificity, they make up for in their ability to evoke powerful and compelling mental images. On the other hand, strategic objectives tend to be more specific and provide a more direct means of determining if the organization is moving toward broader, overall goals.[58] Visions, as one would expect, also have longer time horizons than either mission statements or strategic objectives. Exhibit 1.6 depicts the hierarchy of goals and its relationship to two attributes: general versus specific and time horizon.

Organizational Vision

A **vision** is a goal that is "massively inspiring, overarching, and long term."[59] It represents a destination that is driven by and evokes passion. A vision may or may not succeed; it depends on whether everything else happens according to a firm's strategy. As Mark Hurd, Hewlett-Packard's CEO, humorously pointed out, "Without execution, vision is just another word for hallucination."[60]

Strategy and the Value of Inexperience

Peter Gruber, chairman of Mandalay Entertainment, explained how his firm benefited from the creative insights of an inexperienced intern.

Sometimes life is all about solving problems. In the movie business, at least, there seems to be one around every corner. One of the most effective lessons I've learned about tackling problems is to start by asking not "How to?" but rather "What if?" I learned that lesson from a young woman who was interning on a film I was producing. She actually saved the movie from being shelved by the studio.

The movie, *Gorillas in the Mist,* had turned into a logistical nightmare. We wanted to film at an altitude of 11,000 feet, in the middle of the jungle, in Rwanda—then on the verge of a revolution—and to use more than 200 animals. Warner Brothers, the studio financing the movie, worried that we would exceed our budget. But our biggest problem was that the screenplay required the gorillas to do what we wrote—in other words, to "act." If they couldn't or wouldn't, we'd have to fall back on a formula that the studio had seen fail before: using dwarfs in gorilla suits on a soundstage.

Source: Gruber, P. 1998. My greatest lesson. *Fast Company* 15: 88, 90.

We called an emergency meeting to solve these problems. In the middle of it, a young intern asked, "What if you let the gorillas write the story?" Everyone laughed and wondered what she was doing in the meeting with experienced filmmakers. Hours later, someone casually asked her what she had meant. She said, "What if you sent a really good cinematographer into the jungle with a ton of film to shoot the gorillas. Then you could write a story around what the gorillas did on film." It was a brilliant idea. And we did exactly what she suggested: We sent Alan Root, an Academy Award–nominated cinematographer, into the jungle for three weeks. He came back with phenomenal footage that practically wrote the story for us. We shot the film for $20 million—half of the original budget!

This woman's inexperience enabled her to see opportunities where we saw only boundaries. This experience taught me three things. First, ask high-quality questions, like "What if?" Second, find people who add new perspectives and create new conversations. As experienced filmmakers, we believed that our way was the only way—and that the intern lacked the experience to have an opinion. Third, pay attention to those with new voices. If you want unlimited options for solving a problem, engage the what if before you lock onto the how to. You'll be surprised by what you discover.

Leaders must develop and implement a vision. In a survey of 1,500 senior leaders, 870 of them CEOs from 20 different countries, respondents were asked what they believed were a leader's key traits. Ninety-eight percent responded that "a strong sense of vision" was the most important. Similarly, when asked about the critical knowledge skills, the leaders cited "strategy formulation to achieve a vision" as the most important skill. In other words, managers need to have not only a vision but also a plan to implement it. Regretfully, 90 percent reported a lack of confidence in their own skills and ability to conceive a vision. For example, T. J. Rogers, CEO of Cypress Semiconductor, an electronic chipmaker that

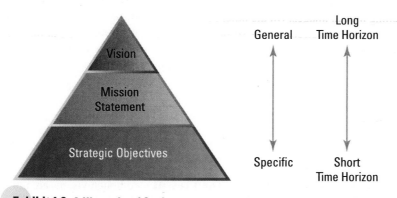

Exhibit 1.6   **A Hierarchy of Goals**

faced some difficulties in 1992, lamented that his own shortsightedness caused the danger, "I did not have the 50,000-foot view, and got caught."[61]

One of the most famous examples of a vision is Disneyland's: "To be the happiest place on earth." Other examples are:

- "Restoring patients to full life." (Medtronic)
- "We want to satisfy all of our customers' financial needs and help them succeed financially." (Wells Fargo)
- "Our vision is to be the world's best quick service restaurant." (McDonald's)

Although such visions cannot be accurately measured by a specific indicator of how well they are being achieved, they do provide a fundamental statement of an organization's values, aspirations, and goals. Such visions go well beyond narrow financial objectives, of course, and strive to capture both the minds and hearts of employees.

The vision statement may also contain a slogan, diagram, or picture—whatever grabs attention.[62] The aim is to capture the essence of the more formal parts of the vision in a few words that are easily remembered, yet that evoke the spirit of the entire vision statement. In its 20-year battle with Xerox, Canon's slogan, or battle cry, was "Beat Xerox." Motorola's slogan is "Total Customer Satisfaction." Outboard Marine Corporation's slogan is "To Take the World Boating." And Chevron strives "To Become Better than the Best."

Clearly, vision statements are not a cure-all. Sometimes they backfire and erode a company's credibility. Visions fail for many reasons, including those discussed in the following paragraphs.[63]

The Walk Doesn't Match the Talk   An idealistic vision can arouse employee enthusiasm. However, that same enthusiasm can be quickly dashed if employees find that senior management's behavior is not consistent with the vision. Often, vision is a sloganeering campaign of new buzzwords and empty platitudes like "devotion to the customer," "teamwork," or "total quality" that aren't consistently backed by management's action.

Irrelevance   Visions created in a vacuum—unrelated to environmental threats or opportunities or an organization's resources and capabilities—often ignore the needs of those who are expected to buy into them. Employees reject visions that are not anchored in reality.

Not the Holy Grail   Managers often search continually for the one elusive solution that will solve their firm's problems—that is, the next "holy grail" of management. They may have tried other management fads only to find that they fell short of their expectations. However, they remain convinced that one exists. Visions support sound management, but they require everyone to walk the talk and be accountable for their behavior. A vision simply cannot be viewed as a magic cure for an organization's illness.

Too Much Focus Leads to Missed Opportunities   Clearly, one of the benefits of a sound vision statement is that it can focus efforts and excite people. However, the downside is that in directing people and resources toward a grandiose vision, losses can be devastating. Consider, Samsung's ambitious venture into automobile manufacturing:

> In 1992, Kun-Hee Lee, chairman of South Korea's Samsung Group, created a bold strategy to become one of the 10 largest car makers by 2010. Seduced by the clarity of the vision, Samsung bypassed staged entry through a joint venture or initial supply contract. Instead, Samsung borrowed heavily to build a state-of-the-art research and design facility and erect a greenfield factory, complete with cutting-edge robotics. Samsung Auto suffered operating losses and crushing interest charges from the beginning. And within a few years the business was divested for a fraction of the initial investment.[64]

An Ideal Future Irreconciled with the Present   Although visions are not designed to mirror reality, they must be anchored somehow in it. People have difficulty identifying with a vision that paints a rosy picture of the future but does not account for the often hostile environment in which the firm competes or that ignores some of the firm's weaknesses.

Mission Statements

A company's **mission statement** differs from its vision in that it encompasses both the purpose of the company as well as the basis of competition and competitive advantage.

Exhibit 1.7 contains the vision statement and mission statement of WellPoint Health Network, a giant $57 billion managed health care organization. Note that while the vision statement is broad based, the mission statement is more specific and focused on the means by which the firm will compete. This includes providing branded products that will be tailor-made to customers in order to create long-term customer relationships.

Effective mission statements incorporate the concept of stakeholder management, suggesting that organizations must respond to multiple constituencies if they are to survive and prosper. Customers, employees, suppliers, and owners are the primary stakeholders, but others may also play an important role. Mission statements also have the greatest impact when they reflect an organization's enduring, overarching strategic priorities and competitive positioning. Mission statements also can vary in length and specificity. The two mission statements below illustrate these issues.

- To produce superior financial returns for our shareholders as we serve our customers with the highest quality transportation, logistics, and e-commerce. (Federal Express)
- To be the very best in the business. Our game plan is status go . . . we are constantly looking ahead, building on our strengths, and reaching for new goals. In our quest of these goals, we look at the three stars of the Brinker logo and are reminded of the basic values that are the strength of this company . . . People, Quality and Profitability. Everything we do at Brinker must support these core values. We also look at the eight golden flames depicted in our logo, and are reminded of the fire that ignites our mission and makes up the heart and soul of this incredible company. These flames are: Customers, Food, Team, Concepts, Culture, Partners, Community, and Shareholders. As keeper of these flames, we will continue to build on our strengths and work together to be the best in the business. (Brinker International, whose restaurant chains include Chili's and On the Border)[65]

Few mission statements identify profit or any other financial indicator as the sole purpose of the firm. Indeed, many do not even mention profit or shareholder return.[66] Employees of organizations or departments are usually the mission's most important audience. For them, the mission should help to build a common understanding of purpose and commitment to nurture.

> **mission statement** a set of organizational goals that include both the purpose of the organization, its scope of operations, and the basis of its competitive advantage.

Exhibit 1.7
Comparing WellPoint Health Network's Vision and Mission

Vision
WellPoint *will redefine our industry:* Through a new generation of consumer-friendly products that puts individuals back in control of their future.

Mission
The WellPoint companies provide health *security* by offering a *choice* of quality branded health and related financial services *designed* to meet the *changing* expectations of individuals, families, and their sponsors throughout a *lifelong* relationship.

Source: WellPoint Health Network company records.

NextJet's Change of Mission

The dot-com crash was only the first blow to NextJet, Inc., a Dallas-based business launched in 1999 to ship packages overnight. The bigger blow came with the September 11 terrorist attacks, when passenger airlines were forced to add security and reduce flights. One of NextJet's strengths was its nationwide network of local courier services that got packages to and from airports, all coordinated through their proprietary software that could determine the optimal routing. However, the company's business model fell apart when it could not rely on the airlines to get packages between cities quickly enough to make the added cost for same-day delivery worthwhile.

Rather than give up, NextJet reinvented the business around the idea that its most important asset was the software itself. The company's new mission received almost immediate validation when its software was deployed successfully at United Parcel Service (UPS).

Sources: Goldstein, A. 2002. NextJet is hoping that its software can deliver. *Dallas Morning News,* December 4: 1–3; Nelson, M. G. 2001. NextJet network adds wireless. *Information Week,* April 30: 34; Anonymous. 2004. Who's who in e-logistics. www.americanshipper.com, September; and Hudspeth, B., & Jones, J. 2004. Service parts and logistics: Should you in-source or outsource? *3pl line,* www.inboundlogistics.com, October.

NextJet's software provides Atlanta-based UPS with tools for setting online rates and tracking packages. While a lot of same-day business did evaporate when corporations tightened the reins on spending, some things can't wait overnight to be shipped. For example, makers of hospital equipment may need to ship critical parts within a few hours. NextJet's software can help shippers make important decisions in less than a second, finding the fastest and most economical route among air, truck, and courier operations. In addition to UPS, its customers include FedEx, Greyhound, and Menlo Worldwide.

NextJet serves a very large industry segment—Service Parts & Logistics (SPL). The annual expenditures for spare parts in the United States are estimated to be $500 billion. And managers have increased their focus on the importance of effective logistics operations, given its potential impact on a firm's income. After all, whether or not a production line is running can often depend on the quick and effective installation of relatively inexpensive spare parts.

NextJet currently has 50 employees and four offices in the United States, and it seems to be on the right track with its new mission. Although executives at the privately held company will not disclose financial results, they say they are about to complete their third consecutive profitable quarter.

Profit maximization not only fails to motivate people but also does not differentiate between organizations. Every corporation wants to maximize profits over the long term. A good mission statement, by addressing each principal theme, must communicate why an organization is special and different. Two studies that linked corporate values and mission statements with financial performance found that the most successful firms mentioned values other than profits. The less successful firms focused almost entirely on profitability.[67] In essence, profit is the metaphorical equivalent of oxygen, food, and water that the body requires. They are not the point of life, but without them, there is no life.

Although vision statements tend to be quite enduring and seldom change, a firm's mission can and should change when competitive conditions dramatically change or the firm is faced with new threats or opportunities. Strategy Spotlight 1.6 provides an example of a firm, NextJet, that changed its mission in order to realize new opportunities.

strategic objectives
A set of organizational goals that are used to operationalize the mission statement and that are specific and cover a well-defined time frame.

Strategic Objectives

Thus far, we have discussed both visions and missions. Statements of vision tend to be quite broad and can be described as a goal that represents an inspiring, overarching, and emotionally driven destination. Mission statements tend to be more specific and address questions concerning the organization's reason for being and the basis of its competitive advantage. Strategic objectives are used to operationalize the mission statement.[68] That is,

Exhibit 1.8
Strategic Objectives

Strategic Objectives (Financial)

- Increase sales growth 6 percent to 8 percent and accelerate core net earnings growth from 13 percent to 15 percent per share in each of the next 5 years. (Procter & Gamble)
- Generate Internet-related revenue of $1.5 billion. (AutoNation)
- Increase the contribution of Banking Group earnings from investments, brokerage, and insurance from 16 percent to 25 percent. (Wells Fargo)
- Cut corporate overhead costs by $30 million per year. (Fortune Brands)

Strategic Objectives (Nonfinancial)

- We want a majority of our customers, when surveyed, to say they consider Wells Fargo the best financial institution in the community. (Wells Fargo)
- We want to operate 6,000 stores by 2010—up from 3,000 in the year 2000. (Walgreen's)
- We want to be the top-ranked supplier to our customers. (PPG)
- Reduce greenhouse gases by 10 percent (from a 1990 base) by 2010. (BP Amoco)

Sources: Company documents and annual reports.

they help to provide guidance on how the organization can fulfill or move toward the "higher goals" in the goal hierarchy—the mission and vision. Thus, they are more specific and cover a more well-defined time frame.

Setting objectives demands a yardstick to measure the fulfillment of the objectives.[69] If an objective lacks specificity or measurability, it is not very useful, simply because there is no way of determining whether it is helping the organization move toward its mission and vision.

Exhibit 1.8 lists several firms' strategic objectives, divided into financial and nonfinancial categories. While most of these strategic objectives are directed toward generating greater profits and returns for the owners of the business, others are directed at customers or society at large.

For objectives to be meaningful, they need to satisfy several criteria. They must be:

- *Measurable.* There must be at least one indicator (or yardstick) that measures progress against fulfilling the objective.
- *Specific.* This provides a clear message as to what needs to be accomplished.
- *Appropriate.* It must be consistent with the vision and mission of the organization.
- *Realistic.* It must be an achievable target given the organization's capabilities and opportunities in the environment. In essence, it must be challenging but doable.
- *Timely.* There needs to be a time frame for accomplishing the objective. After all, as the economist John Maynard Keynes once said, "In the long run, we are all dead!"

When objectives satisfy the above criteria, there are many benefits for the organization. First, they help to channel employees throughout the organization toward common goals. This helps the organization concentrate and conserve valuable resources and work collectively in a more timely manner.

Second, challenging objectives can help to motivate and inspire employees throughout the organization to higher levels of commitment and effort. A great deal of research has supported the notion that individuals work harder when they are striving toward specific goals instead of being asked simply to "do their best."

Third, as we noted earlier in the chapter, there is always the potential for different parts of an organization to pursue their own goals rather than overall company goals. Although well intentioned, these may work at cross-purposes to the organization as a whole. Meaningful objectives thus help to resolve conflicts when they arise.

Finally, proper objectives provide a yardstick for rewards and incentives. Not only will they lead to higher levels of employee motivation but they will also help to ensure a greater sense of equity or fairness when rewards are allocated.

In summary, an organization must take care to ensure consistency throughout in how it implements strategic objectives. Otherwise, employees and organizational units will be acting at cross purposes, resources will be wasted, and people will become unmotivated. Consider how Textron, a $10 billion conglomerate, ensures that its corporate goals are effectively implemented:

> At Textron, each business unit identifies "improvement priorities" that it must act upon to realize the performance outlined in the firm's overall strategic plan. Each improvement priority is translated into action items with clearly defined accountabilities, timetables, and key performance indicators (KPIs) that enable executives to tell how a unit is delivering on a priority. Improvement priorities and action items cascade to every level at the firm—from the management committee (consisting of Textron's top five executives) down to the lowest levels in each of the company's 10 business units. Says Lewis Campbell, Textron's CEO, "Everyone needs to know: 'If I have only one hour to work, here's what I'm going to focus on.' Our goal deployment process makes each individual's accountabilities and priorities clear."[70]

As indicated in this example, organizations have lower-level objectives that are more specific than the strategic objectives that we have focused on in this section. These are often referred to as short-term objectives—essential components of a firm's "action plan" that are critical in implementing the firm's chosen strategy. We discuss these issues in detail in Chapter 9.

Reflecting on Career Implications . . .

- **Attributes of Strategic Management:** How do your activities and actions contribute to the goals of your organization? Observe the decisions you make on the job. What are the short-term and long-term implications of your decisions and actions? Have you recently made a decision that might yield short-term profits but might negatively impact the long-term goals of the organization (e.g., cutting maintenance expenses to meet a quarterly profit target)?
- **Intended versus Emergent Strategies:** Don't be too inflexible in your career strategies; strive to take advantage of new opportunities as they arise. Many promising career opportunities may "emerge" that were not part of your intended career strategy or your specific job assignment. Take initiative by pursuing opportunities to get additional training (e.g., learn a software or a statistical package), volunteering for a short-term overseas assignment, etc.
- **Ambidexterity:** Avoid defining your role in the organization too narrowly; look for opportunities to leverage your talents and your organization's resources to create value for your organization. This often involves collaborating with people in other departments or with your organization's customers and suppliers.
- **Strategic Coherence:** Focus your efforts on the "big picture" in your organization. In doing this, you should always strive to assure that your efforts are directed toward your organization's vision, mission, and strategic objectives.

Summary

We began this introductory chapter by defining strategic management and articulating some of its key attributes. Strategic management is defined as "consisting of the analyses, decisions, and actions an organization undertakes to create and sustain competitive advantages." The issue of how and why some firms outperform others in the marketplace is central to the study of strategic management. Strategic management has four key attributes: It is directed at overall organizational goals, includes multiple stakeholders, incorporates both short-term and long-term perspectives, and incorporates trade-offs between efficiency and effectiveness.

The second section discussed the strategic management process. Here, we paralleled the above definition of strategic management and focused on three core activities in the strategic management process—strategy analysis, strategy formulation, and strategy implementation. We noted how each of these activities is highly interrelated to and interdependent on the others. We also discussed how each of the 12 chapters in this text fits into the three core activities.

Next, we introduced two important concepts— corporate governance and stakeholder management— which must be taken into account throughout the strategic management process. Governance mechanisms can be broadly divided into two groups: internal and external. Internal governance mechanisms include shareholders (owners), management (led by the chief executive officer), and the board of directors. External control is exercised by auditors, banks, analysts, and an active business press as well as the threat of takeovers. We identified five key stakeholders in all organizations: owners, customers, suppliers, employees, and society at large. Successful firms go beyond an overriding focus on satisfying solely the interests of owners. Rather, they recognize the inherent conflicts that arise among the demands of the various stakeholders as well as the need to endeavor to attain "symbiosis"—that is, interdependence and mutual benefit—among the various stakeholder groups. Managers must also recognize the need to act in a socially responsible manner which, if done effectively, can enhance a firm's innovativeness. They also should recognize and incorporate issues related to environmental sustainability in their strategic actions.

In the fourth section, we discussed factors that have accelerated the rate of unpredictable change that managers face today. Such factors, and the combination of them, have increased the need for managers and employees throughout the organization to have a strategic management perspective and to become more empowered.

The final section addressed the need for consistency among a firm's vision, mission, and strategic objectives. Collectively, they form an organization's hierarchy of goals. Visions should evoke powerful and compelling mental images. However, they are not very specific. Strategic objectives, on the other hand, are much more specific and are vital to ensuring that the organization is striving toward fulfilling its vision and mission.

Summary Review Questions

1. How is "strategic management" defined in the text, and what are its four key attributes?

2. Briefly discuss the three key activities in the strategic management process. Why is it important for managers to recognize the interdependent nature of these activities?

3. Explain the concept of "stakeholder management." Why shouldn't managers be solely interested in stockholder management, that is, maximizing the returns for owners of the firm—its shareholders?

4. What is "corporate governance"? What are its three key elements and how can it be improved?

5. How can "symbiosis" (interdependence, mutual benefit) be achieved among a firm's stakeholders?

6. Why do firms need to have a greater strategic management perspective and empowerment in the strategic management process throughout the organization?

7. What is meant by a "hierarchy of goals"? What are the main components of it, and why must consistency be achieved among them?

Key Terms

romantic view of leadership, 7
external view of leadership, 7
strategic management, 8
operational effectiveness, 10
stakeholders, 11
effectiveness, 11
efficiency, 11
ambidexterity, 12
intended strategy, 13
realized strategy, 13
corporate governance, 17
social responsibility, 20
triple bottom line, 22
hierarchy of goals, 24
vision, 24
mission statement, 27
strategic objectives, 28

Experiential Exercise

Using the Internet or library sources, select four organizations—two in the private sector and two in the public sector. Find their mission statements. Complete the following exhibit by identifying the stakeholders that are mentioned. Evaluate the differences between firms in the private sector and those in the public sector.

Name			
Mission Statement			
Stakeholders (✓ = mentioned)			
1. Customers			
2. Suppliers			
3. Managers/employees			
4. Community-at-large			
5. Owners			
6. Others?			
7. Others?			

Application Questions Exercises

1. Go to the Internet and look up one of these company sites: www.walmart.com, www.ge.com, or www.fordmotor.com. What are some of the key events that would represent the "romantic" perspective of leadership? What are some of the key events that depict the "external control" perspective of leadership?

2. Select a company that competes in an industry in which you are interested. What are some of the recent demands that stakeholders have placed on this company? Can you find examples of how the company is trying to develop "symbiosis" (interdependence and mutual benefit) among its stakeholders? (Use the Internet and library resources.)

3. Provide examples of companies that are actively trying to increase the amount of empowerment in the strategic management process throughout the organization. Do these companies seem to be having positive outcomes? Why? Why not?

4. Look up the vision statements and/or mission statements for a few companies. Do you feel that they are constructive and useful as a means of motivating employees and providing a strong strategic direction? Why? Why not? (*Note:* Annual reports, along with the Internet, may be good sources of information.)

Ethics Questions

1. A company focuses solely on short-term profits to provide the greatest return to the owners of the business (i.e., the shareholders in a publicly held firm). What ethical issues could this raise?

2. A firm has spent some time—with input from managers at all levels—in developing a vision statement and a mission statement. Over time, however, the behavior of some executives is contrary to these statements. Could this raise some ethical issues?

References

1. This section draws from the following articles: Maynard, M. 2006. Gone but not forgotten. *New York Times,* October 28: C1; McCracken, J. 2007. Big three face new obstacles in restructuring. *Wall Street Journal,* January 26: A1 & A8; Edmondson, G. 2007. Putting Ford in the rearview mirror. *Business Week,* February 12: 44; and, McClellan, B. 2006. The Ford Taurus is dead, but what an amazing run. *Ward's Dealer Business,* December 1, np.

2. For a discussion of the "romantic" versus "external control" perspective, refer to Meindl, J. R. 1987. The romance of leadership and the evaluation of organizational

performance. *Academy of Management Journal* 30: 92–109; and Pfeffer, J., & Salancik, G. R. 1978. *The external control of organizations: A resource dependence perspective.* New York: Harper & Row.

3. A recent perspective on the "romantic view" of leadership is provided by Mintzberg, H. 2004. Leadership and management development: An afterword. *Academy of Management Executive,* 18(3): 140–142.

4. Anonymous. 2005. Face value: The 10 billion dollar man. *The Economist.* February 26: 66. Interestingly, this article speculated that Mr. Ghosn could add approximately $10 billion to the market value of Ford or General Motors if he were to sign on as Chief Executive Officer. Such a perspective is clearly consistent with the "romantic view" of leadership. For an insightful perspective on the challenges faced by Mr. Ghosn as he assumes the roles of CEO for both Nissan and Renault (which owns 44 percent of Nissan), refer to: Edmondson, G. 2005. What Ghosn will do with Renault. *BusinessWeek,* April 25: 54.

5. For an interesting perspective on the need for strategists to maintain a global mind-set, refer to Begley, T. M., & Boyd, D. P. 2003. The need for a global mind-set. *MIT Sloan Management Review* 44(2): 25–32.

6. Porter, M. E. 1996. What is strategy? *Harvard Business Review* 74(6): 61–78.

7. See, for example, Barney, J. B., & Arikan, A. M. 2001. The resource-based view: Origins and implications. In Hitt, M. A., Freeman, R. E., & Harrison, J. S. (Eds.), *Handbook of strategic management:* 124–189. Malden, MA: Blackwell.

8. Barney, J. 1991. Firm resources and sustained competitive advantage. *Journal of Management,* 17(1): 99–120.

9. Much of Gary Hamel's work advocates the importance of not focusing on incremental change. For example, refer to Hamel, G., & Prahalad, C. K. 1994. *Competing for the future.* Boston: Harvard Business School Press; see also Christensen, C. M. 2001. The past and future of competitive advantage. *Sloan Management Review,* 42(3): 105–109.

10. Porter, M. E. 1996. What is strategy? *Harvard Business Review,* 74(6): 61–78; and Hammonds, K. H. 2001. Michael Porter's big ideas. *Fast Company,* March: 55–56.

11. This section draws upon Dess, G. G., & Miller, A. 1993. *Strategic management.* New York: McGraw-Hill.

12. See, for example, Hrebiniak, L. G., & Joyce, W. F. 1986. The strategic importance of managing myopia. *Sloan Management Review,* 28(1): 5–14.

13. For an insightful discussion on how to manage diverse stakeholder groups, refer to Rondinelli, D. A., & London, T. 2003. How corporations and environmental groups cooperate: Assessing cross-sector alliances and collaborations. *Academy of Management Executive,* 17(1): 61–76.

14. Senge, P. 1996. Leading learning organizations: The bold, the powerful, and the invisible. In Hesselbein, F., Goldsmith, M., & Beckhard, R. (Eds.), *The leader of the future:* 41–58. San Francisco: Jossey-Bass.

15. Samuelson, J. 2006. A critical mass for the long term. *Harvard Business Review,* 84(2): 62, 64; and, Anonymous. 2007. Power play. *The Economist,* January 20: 10–12.

16. Loeb, M. 1994. Where leaders come from. *Fortune,* September 19: 241 (quoting Warren Bennis).

17. Address by Norman R. Augustine at the Crummer Business School, Rollins College, Winter Park, FL, October 20, 1989.

18. Hemp, P. 2004. An Interview with CEO Kevin Sharer. *Harvard Business Review,* 82(7/8): 66–74.

19. Mintzberg, H. 1985. Of strategies: Deliberate and emergent. *Strategic Management Journal,* 6: 257–272.

20. Carey, J. 2005. Tax credits put wind in the sails of renewables. *BusinessWeek.* January 10: 94.

21. Monks, R., & Minow, N. 2001. *Corporate governance* (2nd ed.). Malden, MA: Blackwell.

22. Intel Corp. 2007. *Intel corporation board of directors guidelines on significant corporate governance issues.* www.intel.com

23. Jones, T. J., Felps, W. & Bigley, G. A. 2007. Ethical theory and stakeholder-related decisions: The role of stakeholder culture. *Academy of Management Review,* 32(1): 137–155.

24. For example, see The best (& worst) managers of the year, 2003. *BusinessWeek,* January 13: 58–92; and Lavelle, M. 2003. Rogues of the year. *Time,* January 6: 33–45.

25. Handy, C. 2002. What's a business for? *Harvard Business Review,* 80(12): 49–55.

26. Anonymous, 2007. In the money. *Economist,* January 20: 3–6.

27. From Lewis, Russel T., "The CEO's Lot is Not a Happy One . . ." *Academy of Management Executive: The Thinking Manager's Source,* 16(4): 38–39, Copyright © 2002 by Academy of Management. Reproduced by permission of Academy of Management via Copyright Clearance Center.

28. For an interesting perspective on the changing role of boards of directors, refer to Lawler, E., & Finegold, D. 2005. Rethinking governance. *MIT Sloan Management Review,* 46(2): 67–70.

29. Benz, M. & Frey, B. S. 2007. Corporate governance: What can we learn from public governance? *Academy of Management Review,* 32(1): 92–104.

30. Stakeholder symbiosis. 1998. *Fortune,* March 30: S2.

31. For a definitive, recent discussion of the stakeholder concept, refer to Freeman, R. E., & McVae, J. 2001. A stakeholder approach to strategic management. In Hitt, M. A., Freeman, R. E., & Harrison, J. S. (Eds.). *Handbook of strategic management:* 189–207. Malden, MA: Blackwell.

32. For an insightful discussion on the role of business in society, refer to Handy, op. cit.

33. Stakeholder symbiosis. op. cit., p. S3.

34. Sullivan, C. T. 2005. A stake in the business. *Harvard Business Review,* 83(9): 57–67.

35. An excellent theoretical discussion on stakeholder activity is Rowley, T. J., & Moldoveanu, M. 2003. When will stakeholder groups act? An interest- and identity-based model of stakeholder group mobilization. *Academy of Management Review,* 28(2): 204–219.

36. Thomas, J. G. 2000. Macroenvironmetal forces. In Helms, M. M. (Ed.), *Encyclopedia of management.* (4th ed.): 516–520. Farmington Hills, MI: Gale Group.

37. For a strong advocacy position on the need for corporate values and social responsibility, read Hollender, J. 2004. What matters most: Corporate values and social responsibility. *California Management Review,* 46(4): 111–119.

38. Waddock, S. & Bodwell, C. 2004. Managing responsibility: What can be learned from the quality movement. *California Management Review,* 47(1): 25–37.

39. For a discussion of the role of alliances and collaboration on corporate social responsibility initiatives, refer to Pearce, J. A. II., & Doh, J. P. 2005. The high impact of collaborative social initiatives. *MIT Sloan Management Review,* 46(3): 30–40.

40. Anonymous, 2006. If I did it. *BusinessWeek.* December 18: 108.

41. Bhattacharya, C. B., & Sen, S. 2004, Doing better at doing good: When, why, and how consumers respond to corporate social initiatives. *California Management Review,* 47(1): 9–24.

42. Cone Corporate Citizenship Study, 2002, www.coneinc.com.

43. Refer to www.bsr.org.

44. An insightful discussion of the risks and opportunities associated with global warming, refer to: Lash, J. & Wellington, F. 2007. Competitive advantage on a warming planet. *Harvard Business Review,* 85(3): 94–102.

45. This section draws on Hart, S. L. 1997. Beyond greening: Strategies for a sustainable world. *Harvard Business Review,* 75(1): 66–76, and Berry, M. A. & Rondinelli, D. A. 1998. Proactive corporate environmental management: A new industrial revolution. *Academy of Management Executive,* 12(2): 38–50.

46. Carey, J. 2006. Business on a warmer planet. *BusinessWeek,* July 17: 26–29.

47. Hart, op. cit., p. 67.

48. For a creative perspective on environmental sustainability and competitive advantage as well as ethical implications, read Ehrenfeld, J. R. 2005. The roots of sustainability. *MIT Sloan Management Review,* 46(2): 23–25.

49. McKinsey & Company. 1991. *The corporate response to the environmental challenge.* Summary Report, Amsterdam: McKinsey & Company.

50. Vogel, D. J. 2005. Is there a market for virtue? The business case for corporate social responsibility. *California Management Review,* 47(4): 19–36.

51. Senge, P. M. 1990. The leader's new work: Building learning organizations. *Sloan Management Review,* 32(1): 7–23.

52. For an interesting perspective on the role of middle managers in the strategic management process, refer to Huy, Q. H. 2001. In praise of middle managers. *Harvard Business Review,* 79(8): 72–81.

53. Senge, 1996, op. cit., pp. 41–58.

54. Helgesen, S. 1996. Leading from the grass roots. In Hesselbein, F., Goldsmith, M., & Beckhard, R. (Eds.), *The leader of the future:* 19–24. San Francisco: Jossey-Bass.

55. Wetlaufer, S. 1999. Organizing for empowerment: An interview with AES's Roger Sant and Dennis Blake. *Harvard Business Review,* 77(1): 110–126.

56. Kets de Vries, M. F. R. 1998. Charisma in action: The transformational abilities of Virgin's Richard Branson and ABB's Percy Barnevik. *Organizational Dynamics,* 26(3): 7–21.

57. Hamel, G. 2006. The why, what, and how of management innovation. *Harvard Business Review,* 84(2): 72–84.

58. Our discussion draws on a variety of sources. These include Lipton, M. 1996. Demystifying the development of an organizational vision. *Sloan Management Review,* 37(4): 83–92; Bart, C. K. 2000. Lasting inspiration. *CA Magazine,* May: 49–50; and Quigley, J. V. 1994. Vision: How leaders develop it, share it, and sustain it. *Business Horizons,* September–October: 37–40.

59. Lipton, op. cit.

60. Hardy, Q. 2007. The uncarly. *Forbes,* March 12: 82–90.

61. Quigley, op. cit.

62. Ibid.

63. Lipton, op. cit. Additional pitfalls are addressed in this article.

64. Sull, D. N. 2005. Strategy as active waiting. *Harvard Business Review,* 83(9): 120–130.

65. Company records.

66. Lipton, op. cit.

67. Sexton, D. A., & Van Aukun, P. M. 1985. A longitudinal study of small business strategic planning. *Journal of Small Business Management,* January: 8–15, cited in Lipton, op. cit.

68. For an insightful perspective on the use of strategic objectives, refer to Chatterjee, S. 2005. Core objectives: Clarity in designing strategy. *California Management Review,* 47(2): 33–49.

69. Ibid.

70. Mankins, M. M. & Steele, R. 2005. Turning great strategy into great performance. *Harvard Business Review,* 83(5): 66–73.

chapter 2

Analyzing the External Environment of the Firm

>learning objectives

After reading this chapter, you should have a good understanding of:

LO1 The importance of developing forecasts of the business environment.

LO2 Why environmental scanning, environmental monitoring, and collecting competitive intelligence are critical inputs to forecasting.

LO3 Why scenario planning is a useful technique for firms competing in industries characterized by unpredictability and change.

LO4 The impact of the general environment on a firm's strategies and performance.

LO5 How forces in the competitive environment can affect profitability, and how a firm can improve its competitive position by increasing its power vis-à-vis these forces.

LO6 How the Internet and digitally based capabilities are affecting the five competitive forces and industry profitability.

LO7 The concept of strategic groups and their strategy and performance implications.

S trategies are not and should not be developed in a vacuum. They must be responsive to the external business environment. Otherwise, your firm could become, in effect, the most efficient producer of buggy whips, leisure suits, or slide rules. To avoid such strategic mistakes, firms must become knowledgeable about the business environment. One tool for analyzing trends is forecasting. In the development of forecasts, environmental scanning and environmental monitoring are important in detecting key trends and events. Managers also must aggressively collect and disseminate competitor intelligence. The information gleaned from these three activities is invaluable in developing forecasts and scenarios to minimize present and future threats as well as to exploit opportunities. We address these issues in the first part of this chapter. We also introduce a basic tool of strategy analysis—the concept of SWOT analysis (strengths, weaknesses, opportunities, and threats).

In the second part of the chapter, we present two frameworks for analyzing the external environment—the general environment and the competitive environment. The general environment consists of six segments—demographic, sociocultural, political/legal, technological, economic, and global. Trends and events in these segments can have a dramatic impact on your firm.

The competitive environment is closer to home. It consists of five industry-related factors that can dramatically affect the average level of industry profitability. An awareness of these factors is critical in making decisions such as which industries to enter and how to improve your firm's current position within an industry. This is helpful in neutralizing competitive threats and increasing power over customers and suppliers. We also address how industry and competitive practices are being affected by the capabilities provided by Internet technologies. In the final part of this section, we place firms within an industry into strategic groups based on similarities in resources and strategies. As we will see, the concept of strategic groups has important implications for the intensity of rivalry and how the effects of a given environmental trend or event differ across groups.

Learning from Mistakes

Robert Atkins, a cardiologist, was the founder of the original low-carbohydrate, high-protein diet.[1] He wrote several books that popularized his Atkins diet, including his best seller, *Dr. Atkins New Diet Revolution,* that sold over 10 million copies worldwide. As we will see below, in the beer industry, one firm—Anheuser-Busch—took quick action and benefited from this popular diet trend. Others, including Coors Brewing, were slow to react and paid the price.

In September 2002, Anheuser Busch became one of the pioneers in the low-carb category by launching Michelob Ultra. The brand rapidly became the leader, capturing 5.7 percent of the light beer market by March 2004. The company had jumped on the wave early and rode it during the upsurge of the low-carb trend, which peaked during that year. Clearly, this was an attractive market segment: Beer experts had estimated that about half of the $60 to $70 billion U.S. beer market is from light beer sales as Americans continue to seek out beers that won't add to their waistline.

Coors, in contrast, didn't enter the low-carb market until March 2004—after Michelob Ultra had begun to erode Coors Light's market share. The Coors low-carb brand, Aspen Edge, was too little, too late. By the time Aspen Edge was launched, it faced very stiff competition. In addition to a powerful leader in the segment, Michelob Ultra (which, of course, benefited from Anheuser Busch's deep pockets and marketing prowess), there were already over a dozen other low-carb rivals. These included Rolling Rock, which had introduced Rock Green Light, and Miller Brewing, which had begun to promote the fact that its staple, Miller Lite, had only 3.2 carbs. Further, there were several imported beers, including Martens Low Carbohydrate, brewed by Brouwerij Martens in Belgium.

Even though Coors invested $30 million in Aspen Edge's launch, its sales peaked at just 0.4 percent of the beer market in July 2004. Then its market share began to slide and it was discontinued in April 2006.

Successful managers must recognize opportunities and threats in their firm's external environment. They must be aware of what's going on outside their company. If they focus exclusively on the efficiency of internal operations, the firm may degenerate into the world's most efficient producer of buggy whips or carbon paper. But if they miscalculate the market, opportunities will be lost—hardly an enviable position for their firm.

In *Competing for the Future,* Gary Hamel and C. K. Prahalad suggest that "every manager carries around in his or her head a set of biases, assumptions, and presuppositions about the structure of the relevant 'industry,' about how one makes money in the industry, about who the competition is and isn't, about who the customers are and aren't, and so on."[2] Environmental analysis requires you to continually question such assumptions. Peter Drucker labeled these interrelated sets of assumptions the "theory of the business."[3] Most would agree that Coors would have benefited from a more rigorous environmental analysis— in particular the growing popularity of low-carb products. By the time Coors took action, the low-carb boom had already peaked.

A firm's strategy may be good at one point in time, but it may go astray when management's frame of reference gets out of touch with the realities of the actual business situation. This results when management's assumptions, premises, or beliefs are incorrect or when internal inconsistencies among them render the overall "theory of the business" invalid. As Warren Buffett, investor extraordinaire, colorfully notes, "Beware of past performance 'proofs.' If history books were the key to riches, the Forbes 400 would consist of librarians." And Arthur Martinez, former chairman of Sears, Roebuck & Co., states, "Today's peacock is tomorrow's feather duster."

In the business world, many peacocks have become feather dusters or at least had their plumage dulled. Consider the high-tech company Novell, which went head-to-head with Microsoft. Novell bought market-share loser WordPerfect to compete with Microsoft Word. The result? A $1.3 billion loss when Novell sold WordPerfect to Corel. And today we may wonder who will be the next Wang, Delta Airlines, or *Encyclopaedia Britannica.*

Creating the Environmentally Aware Organization

>LO1

The importance of developing forecasts of the business environment.

So how do managers become environmentally aware?[4] We will now address three important processes—scanning, monitoring, and gathering competitive intelligence—used to develop forecasts. Exhibit 2.1 illustrates relationships among these important activities. We also discuss the importance of scenario planning in anticipating major future changes in the external environment and the role of SWOT analysis.[5]

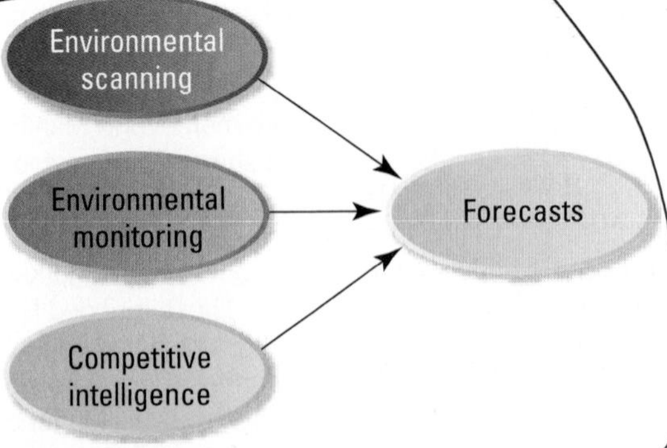

Exhibit 2.1 **Inputs to Forecasting**

The Role of Scanning, Monitoring, Competitive Intelligence, and Forecasting

>LO2
Why environmental scanning, environmental monitoring, and collecting competitive intelligence are critical inputs to forecasting.

Environmental Scanning   **Environmental scanning** involves surveillance of a firm's external environment to predict environmental changes and detect changes already underway.[6] Successful environmental scanning <u>alerts the organization to critical trends</u> and <u>events before the changes have developed a discernible pattern and before competitors recognize them.</u>[7] Otherwise, the firm may be forced into a reactive mode.[8]

Sir John Browne, former chief executive officer of petroleum company BP Amoco, described the kind of environmental changes his company was experiencing.

> The next element of the change we've experienced is the growth in demand, and the changing nature of that demand. The world uses eight million more barrels of oil and 30 billion more cubic feet of natural gas every day than it did in the spring of 1990. The growth of natural gas in particular has been and continues to be spectacular, and I believe that change can legitimately be seen as part of a wider, longer-term shift to lighter, cleaner, less carbon-intensive fuels.[9]

environmental scanning surveillance of a firm's external environment to predict environmental changes and detect changes already under way.

Consider how difficult it would be for BP Amoco to develop strategies and allocate resources if it did not scan the external environment for such emerging changes in demand.

At times, your company may benefit from studies conducted by outside experts in a particular industry. A. T. Kearney, a large international consulting company, identified several key issues in the automobile industry, including.[10]

- *Globalization.* This is not a new trend but it has intensified, with enormous opportunities opening up in Asia, central and eastern Europe, and Latin America.
- *Time to Market.* Despite recent improvements, there's still a gap between product development cycles in the United States and Europe compared to Japan. This gap may be widening as Japanese companies continue to make improvements.
- *Shifting Roles and Responsibilities.* Design responsibility, purchasing, and even project management and systems engineering are shifting from original equipment manufacturers to integrators/suppliers.

Consider how disadvantaged you would be as an executive in the global automobile industry if you were unaware of such trends.

Environmental Monitoring   **Environmental monitoring** tracks the evolution of environmental trends, sequences of events, or streams of activities. They may be trends that the firm came across by accident or ones that were brought to its attention from outside the organization. Consider the automobile industry. While environmental scanning may make you aware of the trends, they require close monitoring, which involves closer ongoing scrutiny. For example, you should closely monitor sales in Asia, central and eastern Europe, and Latin America. You should observe how fast Japanese companies and other competitors bring products to market compared with your firm. You should also study trends with your own suppliers/integrators in purchasing, project management, and systems engineering. Monitoring enables firms to evaluate how dramatically environmental trends are changing the competitive landscape.

environmental monitoring a firm's analysis of the external environment that tracks the evolution of environmental trends, sequences of events, or streams of activities.

One of the authors of this text has conducted on-site interviews with executives from several industries to identify indicators that firms monitor as inputs to their strategy process. Examples of such indicators included:

- *A Motel 6 executive.* The number of rooms in the budget segment of the industry in the United States and the difference between the average daily room rate and the consumer price index (CPI).
- *A Pier 1 Imports executive.* Net disposable income (NDI), consumer confidence index, and housing starts.

- *A Johnson & Johnson medical products executive.* Percentage of gross domestic product (GDP) spent on health care, number of active hospital beds, and the size and power of purchasing agents (indicates the concentration of buyers).

Such indices are critical for managers in determining a firm's strategic direction and resource allocation.

Competitive Intelligence   **Competitive intelligence** (CI) helps firms define and understand their industry and identify rivals' strengths and weaknesses.[11] This includes the intelligence gathering associated with collecting data on competitors and interpreting such data. Done properly, competitive intelligence helps a company avoid surprises by anticipating competitors' moves and decreasing response time.[12]

Examples of competitive analysis are evident in daily newspapers and periodicals such as *The Wall Street Journal, BusinessWeek,* and *Fortune.* For example, banks continually track home loan, auto loan, and certificate of deposit (CD) interest rates charged by peers in a given geographic region. Major airlines change hundreds of fares daily in response to competitors' tactics. Car manufacturers are keenly aware of announced cuts or increases in rivals' production volume, sales, and sales incentives (e.g., rebates and low interest rates on financing). They use this information to plan their own marketing, pricing, and production strategies. Exhibit 2.2 provides some insights on what CI is (and what it isn't).

The Internet has dramatically accelerated the speed at which firms can find competitive intelligence. Leonard Fuld, founder of the Cambridge, Massachusetts, training and consulting firm Fuld & Co., specializes in competitive intelligence.[13] His firm often profiles top company and business group managers and considers these issues: What is their background? What is

competitive intelligence a firm's activities of collecting and interpreting data on competitors, defining and understanding the industry, and identifying competitors' strengths and weaknesses.

Exhibit 2.2

What Competitive Intelligence Is and Is Not!

Competitive Intelligence *Is* . . .	Competitive Intelligence *Is Not* . . .
1. **Information** that has been analyzed to the point where you can make a decision.	1. **Spying.** Spying implies illegal or unethical activities. It is a rare activity, since most corporations do not want to find themselves in court or to upset shareholders.
2. **A tool** to alert management to early recognition of both threats and opportunities.	2. **A crystal ball.** CI gives corporations good approximations of short- and long-term reality. It does not predict the future.
3. **A means to deliver reasonable assessments.** CI offers approximations of the market and competition. It is not a peek at a rival's financial books. Reasonable assessments are what modern entrepreneurs need and want on a regular basis.	3. **Database search.** Databases offer just that—data. They do not massage or analyze the data in any way. They certainly don't replace human beings who make decisions by examining the data and applying their common sense, experience, and intuition.
4. **A way of life, a process.** If a company uses CI the way it should be used, it becomes everyone's job, not just the strategic planning or marketing staff's. It is a process by which critical information is available to those who need it.	4. **A job for one smart person.** A CEO may appoint one person as the CI ringmaster, but one person cannot do it all. At best, the ringmaster can keep management informed and ensure that others become trained to apply this tool within their business units.

Sources: Imperato, G. 1998. Competitive intelligence—Get smart! *Fast Company,* April: 26–29; and Fuld, F. M. What competitive intelligence is and is not! www.fuld.com/whatCI.html.

strategy spotlight

2.1

Ethical Guidelines on Competitive Intelligence: United Technologies

United Technologies (UT) is a $28 billion global conglomerate composed of world-leading businesses with rich histories of technological pioneering, such as Otis Elevator, Carrier Air Conditioning, and Sikorsky (helicopters). It was founded in 1853 and has an impressive history of technological accomplishments. UT built the first working helicopter, developed the first commercially available hydrogen cells, and designed complete life support systems for space shuttles. UT believes strongly in a robust code of ethics. In the last decade, they have clearly articulated their principles governing business conduct. These include an antitrust guide, an ethics guide when contracting with the U.S. government and foreign governments, a policy on accepting gifts from suppliers, and guidelines for proper usage of e-mail. One such document is the Code of Ethics Guide on Competitive Intelligence. This encourages managers and workers to ask themselves these five questions whenever they have ethical concerns.

Sources: Nelson, B. 2003. The thinker. *Forbes,* March 3: 62–64; and The Fuld war room—Survival kit 010. Code of Ethics (printed 2/26/01).

1. Have I done anything that coerced somebody to share this information? Have I, for example, threatened a supplier by indicating that future business opportunities will be influenced by the receipt of information with respect to a competitor?

2. Am I in a place where I should not be? If, for example, I am a field representative with privileges to move around in a customer's facility, have I gone outside the areas permitted? Have I misled anybody in order to gain access?

3. Is the contemplated technique for gathering information evasive, such as sifting through trash or setting up an electronic "snooping" device directed at a competitor's facility from across the street?

4. Have I misled somebody in a way that the person believed sharing information with me was required or would be protected by a confidentiality agreement? Have I, for example, called and misrepresented myself as a government official who was seeking some information for some official purpose?

5. Have I done something to evade or circumvent a system intended to secure or protect information?

their style? Are they marketers? Are they cost cutters? Fuld has found that the more articles he collects and the more biographies he downloads, the better he can develop profiles.

One of Fuld & Co.'s clients needed to know if a rival was going to start competing more aggressively on costs. Fuld's analysts tracked down articles from the Internet and a local newspaper profile of the rival firm's CEO. The profile said the CEO had taken a bus to a nearby town to visit one of the firm's plants. Fuld claimed, "Those few words were a small but important sign to me that this company was going to be incredibly cost-conscious." Another client retained Fuld to determine the size, strength, and technical capabilities of a privately held company. Initially, it was difficult to get detailed information. Then one analyst used Deja News (www.dejanews.com), now part of Google, to tap into some online discussion groups. The analyst's research determined that the company had posted 14 job openings on one Usenet group. That posting was a road map to the competitor's development strategy.

At times, a firm's aggressive efforts to gather competitive intelligence may lead to unethical or illegal behaviors.[14] Strategy Spotlight 2.1 provides an example of a company, United Technologies, that has set clear guidelines to help prevent unethical behavior.

A word of caution: Executives must be careful to avoid spending so much time and effort tracking the actions of traditional competitors that they ignore new competitors. Further, broad environmental changes and events may have a dramatic impact on a firm's viability. Peter Drucker, often considered the father of modern management, wrote:

> Increasingly, a winning strategy will require information about events and conditions outside the institution: noncustomers, technologies other than those currently used by the company and its present competitors, markets not currently served, and so on.[15]

● The sales of printed encyclopedias were decimated by CD-ROMs.

Consider the fall of the once-mighty *Encyclopaedia Britannica*.[16] Its demise was not caused by a traditional competitor in the encyclopedia industry. It was caused by new technology. CD-ROMs came out of nowhere and devastated the printed encyclopedia industry. Why? A full set of the *Encyclopaedia Britannica* sells for about $2,000, but an encyclopedia on CD-ROM, such as Microsoft *Encarta,* sells for about $50. To make matters worse, many people receive *Encarta* free with their personal computers.

Environmental Forecasting   Environmental scanning, monitoring, and competitive intelligence are important inputs for analyzing the external environment. However, they are of little use unless they provide raw material that is reliable enough to help managers make accurate forecasts. **Environmental forecasting** involves the development of plausible projections about the direction, scope, speed, and intensity of environmental change.[17] Its purpose is to predict change. It asks: How long will it take a new technology to reach the marketplace? Will the present social concern about an issue result in new legislation? Are current lifestyle trends likely to continue?

Some forecasting issues are much more specific to a particular firm and the industry in which it competes. Consider how important it is for Motel 6 to predict future indicators, such as the number of rooms, in the budget segment of the industry. If its predictions are low, it will build too many units, creating a surplus of room capacity that would drive down room rates. Similarly, if Pier 1 Imports is overly optimistic in its forecast of future net disposable income and U.S. housing starts, it will order too much inventory and later be forced to discount merchandise drastically.

A danger of forecasting is that managers may view uncertainty as black and white and ignore important gray areas. Either they assume that the world is certain and open to precise predictions, or they assume it is uncertain and completely unpredictable.[18] The problem is that underestimating uncertainty can lead to strategies that neither defend against threats nor take advantage of opportunities. In 1977 one of the colossal underestimations in business history occurred when Kenneth H. Olsen, then president of Digital Equipment Corp., announced, "There is no reason for individuals to have a computer in their home." The explosion in the personal computer market was not easy to detect in 1977, but it was clearly within the range of possibilities that industry experts were discussing at the time. And, historically, there have been underestimates of the growth potential of new telecommunication services. The electric telegraph was derided by Ralph Waldo Emerson, and the telephone had its skeptics. More recently, an "infamous" McKinsey study in the early 1980s predicted that there would be fewer than 1 million cellular users in the United States by the year 2000. Actually, there were nearly 100 million.[19] As humorously noted by Jane Bryant Quinn, a business writer: "The rule on staying alive as a forecaster is to give 'em a number or give 'em a date, but never give 'em both at once."[20]

At the other extreme, if managers assume the world is unpredictable, they may abandon the analytical rigor of their traditional planning process and base strategic decisions on gut instinct. Such a "just do it" approach may cause executives to place misinformed bets on emerging products or markets that result in record write-offs. Entrepreneurs and venture capitalists who took the plunge and invested in questionable Internet ventures in the late 1990s provide many examples.

A more in-depth approach to forecasting involves scenario analysis. **Scenario analysis** draws on a range of disciplines and interests, among them economics, psychology, sociology, and demographics. It usually begins with a discussion of participants' thoughts on ways in

environmental forecasting the development of plausible projections about the direction, scope, speed, and intensity of environmental change.

>LO3
Why scenario planning is a useful technique for firms competing in industries characterized by unpredictability and change.

scenario analysis an in-depth approach to environmental forecasting that involves experts' detailed assessments of societal trends, economics, politics, technology, or other dimensions of the external environment.

Scenario Planning at Shell Oil Company

Preparing to cope with uncertainty is one of the biggest strategic challenges faced by most businesses. There are few tools for coping with strategic uncertainty, especially over medium- to long-term horizons. One technique that has proved its usefulness is scenario planning.

Scenario planning is different from other tools for strategic planning such as trend analysis or high and low forecasts. The origins of scenario planning lie with the military, which used it to cope effectively with multiple challenges and limited resources.

In the 1960s and 1970s, Shell combined analytical tools with information to create scenarios of possible outcomes. The result of the 1973 oil embargo was a sharp increase in crude oil prices, short supplies of gasoline for consumers, and a depressed world economy. However, Shell's strategic planning, including the use of scenarios, had strongly suggested that a more unstable environment was coming, with a shift of power from oil companies to oil producers. As a result of the precautionary actions it took, Shell was in a better position than most oil companies when the 1973 embargo occurred. Shell also uses scenario planning to plan major new oil field investments because elements of risk can be identified and explored over a considerable period of time.

Sources: Martin, R. 2002. The oracles of oil. *Business 2.0,* January: 35–39; www.touchstonerenard.co.uk/Expertise/Strategy/Scenario_Planning/scenario_planning.htm; and Epstein, J. 1998. Scenario planning: An introduction. *The Futurist,* September: 50–52.

The Shell process of scenario planning involves the following stages:

1. Interviews with people both inside and outside the business, using an open-ended questioning technique to encourage full and frank answers.
2. Analysis of interviews by issue in order to build a "natural agenda" for further processing.
3. Synthesis of each agenda to draw out underlying areas of uncertainty/dispute and possible interrelationships among issues.
4. A small number of workshops to explore key issues to improve understanding and identify gaps for further research. These generate a wide range of strategy options.
5. A workshop to identify and build a small number of scenarios that may occur in the next 10 to 15 years or even later.
6. A testing of strategy options against the scenarios in order to assess robustness (i.e., whether or not a given strategy is effective under more than one scenario).

Other practitioners of scenario planning include Levi Strauss, which uses scenario planning to consider potential impacts of everything from cotton deregulation to the total disappearance of cotton from this planet. Also, a German insurance company anticipated the fall of the Berlin wall and made plans to expand in central Europe. And in 1990 when Nelson Mandela was released from a South African prison, he met with a panel that helped him create scenarios to chart out the country's future. Scenario planning helps by considering not just trends or forecasts but also how they could be upset by events and the outcomes that may result.

which societal trends, economics, politics, and technology may affect the issue under discussion.[21] For example, consider Lego. The popular Danish toy manufacturer has a strong position in the construction toys market. But what would happen if this broadly defined market should change dramatically? After all, Lego is competing not only with producers of similar products but also on a much broader canvas for a share of children's playtime. In this market, Lego has a host of competitors, many of them computer based; still others have not yet been invented. Lego may end up with an increasing share of a narrow, shrinking market (much like IBM in the declining days of the mainframe computer). To avoid such a fate, managers must consider their future in a wider context than their narrow, traditional markets. They need to lay down guidelines for at least 10 years in the future to anticipate rapid change. Strategy Spotlight 2.2 provides an example of scenario planning at Shell Oil Company.

SWOT Analysis

To understand the business environment of a particular firm, you need to analyze both the general environment and the firm's industry and competitive environment. Generally, firms compete with other firms in the same industry. An industry is composed of a set of firms that produce similar products or services, sell to similar customers, and use similar methods of production. Gathering industry information and understanding competitive dynamics among the different companies in your industry is key to successful strategic management.

One of the most basic techniques for analyzing firm and industry conditions is **SWOT analysis.** SWOT stands for strengths, weaknesses, opportunities, and threats. SWOT analysis provides a framework for analyzing these four elements of a company's internal and external environment. It provides "raw material"—a basic listing of conditions both inside and surrounding your company.

The Strengths and Weaknesses portion of SWOT refers to the internal conditions of the firm—where your firm excels (strengths) and where it may be lacking relative to competitors (weaknesses). Opportunities and Threats are environmental conditions external to the firm. These could be factors either in the general environment or in the competitive environment. In the general environment, one might experience developments that are beneficial for most companies such as improving economic conditions, that cause lower borrowing costs or trends that benefit some companies and harm others. An example is the heightened concern with fitness, which is a threat to some companies (e.g., tobacco) and an opportunity to others (e.g., health clubs). Opportunities and threats are also present in the competitive environment among firms competing for the same customers.

The general idea of SWOT analysis is that a firm's strategy must:

- build on its strengths,
- try to remedy the weaknesses or work around them,
- take advantage of the opportunities presented by the environment, and,
- protect the firm from the threats.

Despite its apparent simplicity, the SWOT approach has been immensely popular for a number of reasons. First, it forces managers to consider both internal and external factors simultaneously. Second, its emphasis on identifying opportunities and threats makes firms act proactively rather than reactively. Third, it raises awareness about the role of strategy in creating a match between the environmental conditions and the firm's internal strengths and weaknesses. Finally, its conceptual simplicity is achieved without sacrificing analytical rigor.

We discuss the analysis of the external environment in the following sections of this chapter. We will also address some of the limitations of SWOT analysis in Chapter 3.

SWOT analysis a framework for analyzing a company's internal and external environment and that stands for strengths, weaknesses, opportunities, and threats.

The General Environment

The **general environment** is composed of factors that can have dramatic effects on firm strategy.[22] Typically, a firm has little ability to predict trends and events in the general environment and even less ability to control them. When listening to CNBC, for example, you can hear many experts espouse totally different perspectives on what action the Federal Reserve Board may take on short-term interest rates—an action that can have huge effects on the valuation of entire economic sectors. Also, it's difficult to predict future political events such as the ongoing Middle East peace negotiations and tensions on the Korean peninsula. In addition, who would have guessed the Internet's impact on national and global economies in the past decade or two? Such dramatic innovations in information technology (e.g., the Internet) have helped keep inflation in check by lowering the cost of doing business in the United States at the beginning of the 21st century.

general environment factors external to an industry, and usually beyond a firm's control, that affect a firm's strategy.

>LO4

The impact of the general environment on a firm's strategies and performance.

We divide the general environment into six segments: demographic, sociocultural, political/legal, technological, economic, and global. First, we discuss each segment and provide a summary of the segment and examples of how events and trends can impact industries. Second, we address relationships among the general environment segments. Third, we consider how trends and events can vary across industries. Exhibit 2.3 provides examples of key trends and events in each of the six segments of the general environment.

The Demographic Segment

Demographics are the most easily understood and quantifiable elements of the general environment. They are at the root of many changes in society. Demographics include elements such as the aging population,[23] rising or declining affluence, changes in ethnic composition, geographic distribution of the population, and disparities in income level.

The impact of a demographic trend, like all segments of the general environment, varies across industries. The aging of the U.S. population has had a positive effect on the health care industry but a negative impact on the industry that produces diapers and baby food. Rising levels of affluence in many developed countries bode well for brokerage services as well as for upscale pets and supplies. However, these same trends may have an adverse effect on fast food restaurants because people can afford to dine at higher-priced restaurants. Fast-food restaurants depend on minimum-wage employees to operate efficiently, but the competition for labor intensifies as more attractive employment opportunities become prevalent, thus threatening the employment base for restaurants. Let's look at the details of one of these trends.

The aging population in the United States and other developed countries has important implications. The U.S. Bureau of Statistics states that only 14 percent of American workers were 55 and older in 2002.[24] However, by 2012 that figure will increase to 20 percent, or one in five, of all U.S. workers. At the same time, the United States is expected to experience a significant drop in the percentage of younger workers aged 25 to 44, making it increasingly important for employers to find ways to recruit and retain older workers. Similarly, the National Association of Manufacturing estimates that as baby boomers continue retiring and the economy grows, the United States will have 7 million more jobs than workers by 2010.

The Sociocultural Segment

Sociocultural forces influence the values, beliefs, and lifestyles of a society. Examples include a higher percentage of women in the workforce, dual-income families, increases in the number of temporary workers, greater concern for healthy diets and physical fitness, greater interest in the environment, and postponement of having children. Such forces enhance sales of products and services in many industries but depress sales in others. The increased number of women in the workforce has increased the need for business clothing merchandise but decreased the demand for baking product staples (since people would have less time to cook from scratch). A greater concern for health and fitness has had differential effects. This trend has helped industries that manufacture exercise equipment and healthful foods but harmed industries that produce unhealthful foods.

The trend toward increased educational attainment by women in the workplace has led to an increase in the number of women in upper management positions. U.S. Department of Education statistics show that women have become the dominant holders of college degrees. Based on figures of a recent graduating class, women with bachelor's degrees will outnumber their male counterparts by 27 percent. By the class of 2006–2007, the gap should surge to 38 percent. Additionally, throughout the 1990s the number of women earning MBAs increased by 29 percent compared to only 15 percent for men.[25] Given these educational attainments, it is hardly surprising that companies owned by women have been one of the driving forces of the U.S. economy; these companies (now more than 9 million in number) account for 40 percent of all U.S. businesses and have generated more than $3.6 trillion in annual revenue. In addition, women have a tremendous impact on consumer spending decisions. Not surprisingly,

Exhibit 2.3

**General Environment:
Key Trends and Events**

Demographic

- Aging population
- Rising affluence
- Changes in ethnic composition
- Geographic distribution of population
- Greater disparities in income levels

Sociocultural

- More women in the workforce
- Increase in temporary workers
- Greater concern for fitness
- Greater concern for environment
- Postponement of family formation

Political/Legal

- Tort reform
- Americans with Disabilities Act (ADA) of 1990
- Repeal of Glass-Steagall Act in 1999 (banks may now offer brokerage services)
- Deregulation of utility and other industries
- Increases in federally mandated minimum wages
- Taxation at local, state, federal levels
- Legislation on corporate governance reforms in bookkeeping, stock options, etc. (Sarbanes-Oxley Act of 2002)

Technological

- Genetic engineering
- Emergence of Internet technology
- Computer-aided design/computer-aided manufacturing systems (CAD/CAM)
- Research in synthetic and exotic materials
- Pollution/global warming
- Miniaturization of computing technologies
- Wireless communications
- Nanotechnology

Economic

- Interest rates
- Unemployment rates
- Consumer Price Index
- Trends in GDP
- Changes in stock market valuations

Global

- Increasing global trade
- Currency exchange rates
- Emergence of the Indian and Chinese economies
- Trade agreements among regional blocs (e.g., NAFTA, EU, ASEAN)
- Creation of WTO (leading to decreasing tariffs/free trade in services)

The Sarbanes-Oxley Act: A Boon for Accountants

Government regulation is often prompted as elected officials respond to voters' expectations. When faced with a crisis, voters often demand a solution and expect elected officials to provide one. If the politicians fail to deliver, they suffer in the next election. Consider some of the historical examples of how the U.S. government has reacted to ethical disasters with the blunt force of increased legislation.

- The creation of the Securities and Exchange Commission (SEC) and other legislation following the stock market crash of 1929.

- The Foreign Corrupt Practices Act of 1977, which followed Lockheed's bribes to government officials.

- In the wake of the Enron, WorldCom, and Andersen debacles, Congress passed the Sarbanes-Oxley Act on July 30, 2002. (The law was passed just 35 days

after WorldCom announced that it had overstated its revenues by at least $3.8 billion.)

Accounting firms have really benefited from the Sarbanes-Oxley Act. They had lobbied hard to keep the act from being passed. But, fortunately for them, they lost!

Companies are working hard to comply with Section 404 of the act. The provision requires publicly traded corporations to vouch for internal financial controls and remedy problems. A recent survey by Financial Executives International (FEI) finds that, on average, companies will spend $3.1 million and 30,700 hours to comply—nearly double the estimates of an earlier poll.

Much of that expense goes to privately held accounting firms. Audit fees are expected to surge more than 50 percent, according to FEI. To deal with the increased business, the Big Four accounting firms are in a hiring frenzy and logging lots of overtime. For example, KPMG has added 850 auditors in 2004, while PricewaterhouseCoopers (PWC) has hired 400 people from English-speaking foreign countries as temporary employees. "It's a scramble," say Dennis Nally, PWC's U.S. senior partner. It seems every cloud has a silver lining.

Sources: Arndt, M. 2004. A boon for bean counters. *BusinessWeek*, November 22: 13; and Thomas, T., Schermerhorn, R. R., Jr., & Dienhart, J. W. 2004. Strategic leadership of ethical behavior in business. *The Academy of Management Executive*, 18(2): 56–68.

many companies have focused their advertising and promotion efforts on female consumers. Consider, for example, Wilkesboro (North Carolina)–based Lowe's efforts to attract female shoppers: Lowe's has found that women prefer to do larger home-improvement projects with a man—be it a boyfriend, husband, or neighbor.[26] As a result, in addition to its "recipe card classes" (that explain various projects that take only one weekend), Lowe's offers co-ed store clinics for projects like sink installation. "Women like to feel they're given the same attention as a male customer," states Lowe's spokespersons Julie Valeant-Yenichek, who points out that most seminar attendees, whether male or female, are inexperienced.

Not surprisingly, Home Depot has recently spent millions of dollars to add softer lighting and brighter signs in 300 stores. Why? It is an effort to match rival Lowe's long-standing appeal to women.

The Political/Legal Segment

Political processes and legislation influence the environmental regulations with which industries must comply.[27] Some important elements of the political/legal arena include tort reform, the Americans with Disabilities Act (ADA) of 1990, the repeal of the Glass-Steagall Act in 1999 (banks may now offer brokerage services), deregulation of utilities and other industries, and increases in the federally mandated minimum wage.

Government legislation can also have a significant impact on the governance of corporations. The U.S. Congress passed the Sarbanes-Oxley Act in 2002, which greatly increases the accountability of auditors, executives, and corporate lawyers. This act was a response to the widespread perception that existing governance mechanisms have failed to protect the interests of shareholders, employees, and creditors. Perhaps it is not too surprising that Sarbanes-Oxley has also created a tremendous demand for professional accounting services. We address this trend in Strategy Spotlight 2.3.

Legislation also helps companies in the high-tech sector of the economy by expanding the number of temporary visas available for highly skilled foreign professionals. For example, a bill passed in October 2000 allows 195,000 H-1B visas in each of the next three years, up from the cap of only 115,000 in 2000. The allotment for the year 2000 was used up by March, and the cap decreased to 107,500 for 2001 and a mere 65,000 each year thereafter. Almost half of the visas are for professionals from India, and most of them are computer or software specialists.[28] For U.S. labor and workers' rights groups, however, the issue was a political hot potato.

The Technological Segment

Developments in technology lead to new products and services and improve how they are produced and delivered to the end user. Innovations can create entirely new industries and alter the boundaries of existing industries.[29] Examples of technological developments and trends are genetic engineering, Internet technology, computer-aided design/computer-aided manufacturing (CAD/CAM), research in artificial and exotic materials, and, on the downside, pollution and global warming. Firms in the petroleum and primary metals industries incur significant expenses to reduce the amount of pollution they produce. Engineering and consulting firms that work with polluting industries derive financial benefits from solving such problems.

Another important technological development is the combination of information technology (IT) and the Internet, which has played a key role in productivity improvement.[30] In the United States, for example, improvement in productivity rates is running at an all-time high. For the 20-year period ending in 1990, U.S. worker productivity grew at less than 1.7 percent annually. In contrast, from 2001 to 2005, it grew at an annual rate of 3.6 percent. In recent years, productivity around the world has also increased by, for example, nearly 6 percent in Taiwan and nearly 10 percent in South Korea. Better productivity means that more work can be done by fewer people.

Nanotechnology is becoming a very promising area of research with many potentially useful applications.[31] Nanotechnology takes place at industry's tiniest stage: one billionth of a meter. Remarkably, this is the size of 10 hydrogen atoms in a row.

Researchers have discovered that matter at such a tiny scale behaves very differently. While some of the science behind this phenomenon is still shrouded in mystery, the commercial potential is coming sharply into focus. Familiar materials—from gold to carbon soot—display startling and useful new properties. Some transmit light or electricity. Others become harder than diamonds or turn into potent chemical catalysts. What's more, researchers have found that a tiny dose of nanoparticles can transform the chemistry and nature of far bigger things, creating everything from stronger fenders to superefficient fuel cells. Exhibit 2.4 lists a few of the potential ways in which nanotechnology could revolutionize industries.

There are downsides to technology. In addition to ethical issues in biotechnology, there are threats to our environment associated with the emission of greenhouse gases. In response,

Exhibit 2.4
How Nanotechnology Might Revolutionize Various Industries

- **To fight cancer,** sensors will be able to detect a single cancer cell and will help guide nanoparticles that can burn tumors from the inside out, leaving healthy cells alone.
- **To transform energy,** nano-enhanced solar panels will feed cheap electricity onto superconducting power lines made of carbon nanotubes.
- **To replace silicon,** carbon nanotubes will take over when silicon peters out, leading to far faster chips that need less power than today's chips.
- **For space travel,** podlike crawlers will carry cargo thousands of miles up a carbon-nanotube cable to a space station for billions less than rocket launches.

Source: Baker, S. & Aston, A. 2004. Universe in a grain of sand. *BusinessWeek*, October 11: 139–140.

some firms have taken a proactive approach. BP Amoco plans to decrease its greenhouse gas emissions by giving each of its 150 business units a quota of emission permits and encouraging the units to trade them. If a unit cuts emissions and has leftover permits, it can sell them to other units that are having difficulty meeting their goals. For example, Julie Hardwick, manager at the Naperville, Illinois, petrochemical division, saved up permits by fast-tracking a furnace upgrade that allowed elimination of a second furnace.[32]

The Economic Segment

The economy has an impact on all industries, from suppliers of raw materials to manufacturers of finished goods and services, as well as all organizations in the service, wholesale, retail, government, and nonprofit sectors. Key economic indicators include interest rates, unemployment rates, the Consumer Price Index, the gross domestic product, and net disposable income. Interest-rate increases have a negative impact on the residential home construction industry but a negligible (or neutral) effect on industries that produce consumer necessities such as prescription drugs or common grocery items.

Other economic indicators are associated with equity markets. Perhaps the most watched is the Dow Jones Industrial Average (DJIA), which is composed of 30 large industrial firms. When stock market indexes increase, consumers' discretionary income rises and there is often an increased demand for luxury items such as jewelry and automobiles. But when stock valuations decrease, demand for these items shrinks.

The Global Segment

There is an increasing trend for firms to expand their operations and market reach beyond the borders of their "home" country. Globalization provides both opportunities to access larger potential markets and a broad base of production factors such as raw materials, labor, skilled managers, and technical professionals. However, such endeavors also carry many political, social, and economic risks.

Examples of key elements include currency exchange rates, increasing global trade, the economic emergence of China, trade agreements among regional blocs (e.g., North American Free Trade Agreement, European Union), and the General Agreement on Tariffs and Trade (GATT) (lowering of tariffs). Increases in trade across national boundaries also provide benefits to air cargo and shipping industries but have a minimal impact on service industries such as bookkeeping and routine medical services. The emergence of China as an economic power has benefited many industries, such as construction, soft drinks, and computers. However, it has had a negative impact on the defense industry in the United States as diplomatic relations between the two nations improve.

Few industries are as global as the automobile industry. Consider just a few examples of how some of the key players expanded their reach into Latin America during the 1990s. Fiat built a new plant in Argentina, Volkswagen retooled a plant in Mexico to launch the New Beetle, DaimlerChrysler built a new plant as a joint venture with BMW to produce engines in Brazil, and General Motors built a new car factory in Brazil. Why the interest? In addition to the region's low wage rates and declining trade barriers, the population of 400 million is very attractive. But the real bonus lies in the 9-to-1 ratio of people to cars in the region compared to a 2-to-1 ratio in developed countries. With this region's growth expected to be in the 3 to 4 percent range for the first part of the century, sales should increase at a healthy rate.[33]

Finally, consider the cost of terrorism. A recent survey indicates that for S&P 500 firms, the threat has caused direct and indirect costs of $107 billion a year. This figure includes extra spending (on insurance and redundant capacity, for instance) as well as lost revenues (from fearful consumers' decreased activity). Another finding in a 2006 survey of CFOs: Some 21 percent of U.S. companies have reduced employees' air travel since September 11 (as have 17 percent of European companies).[34]

Relationships among Elements of the General Environment

In our discussion of the general environment, we see many relationships among the various elements.[35] For example, a demographic trend in the United States, the aging of the population, has important implications for the economic segment (in terms of tax policies to provide benefits to increasing numbers of older citizens). Another example is the emergence of information technology as a means to increase the rate of productivity gains in the United States and other developed countries. Such use of IT results in lower inflation (an important element of the economic segment) and helps offset costs associated with higher labor rates.

The effects of a trend or event in the general environment vary across industries. Governmental legislation (political/legal) to permit the importation of prescription drugs from foreign countries is a very positive development for drugstores but a very negative event for U.S. drug manufacturers. Exhibit 2.5 provides other examples of how the impact of trends or events in the general environment can vary across industries.

Exhibit 2.5

The Impact of General Environmental Trends on Various Industries

Segment/Trends and Events	Industry	Positive	Neutral	Negative
Demographic				
Aging population	Health care	✓		
	Baby products			✓
Rising affluence	Brokerage services	✓		
	Fast foods			✓
	Upscale pets and supplies	✓		
Sociocultural				
More women in the workforce	Clothing	✓		
	Baking products (staples)			✓
Greater concern for health and fitness	Home exercise equipment	✓		
	Meat products			✓
Political/legal				
Tort reform	Legal services			✓
	Auto manufacturing	✓		
Americans with Disabilities Act (ADA)	Retail			✓
	Manufacturers of elevators, escalators, and ramps	✓		
Technological				
Genetic engineering	Pharmaceutical	✓		
	Publishing		✓	
Pollution/global warming	Engineering services	✓		
	Petroleum			✓
Economic				
Interest rate increases	Residential construction			✓
	Most common grocery products		✓	
Global				
Increasing global trade	Shipping	✓		
	Personal service		✓	
Emergence of China as an economic power	Soft drinks	✓		
	Defense			✓

The Internet and Digital Technologies: Affecting Many Environmental Segments

The Internet has dramatically changed the way business is conducted in every corner of the globe. According to digital economy visionary Don Tapscott:

> The Net is much more than just another technology development; the Net represents something qualitatively new—an unprecedented, powerful, universal communications medium. Far surpassing radio and television, this medium is digital, infinitely richer, and interactive. . . . Mobile computing devices, broadband access, wireless networks, and computing power embedded in everything from refrigerators to automobiles are converging into a global network that will enable people to use the Net just about anywhere and anytime.

The Internet provides a platform or staging area for the application of numerous technologies, rapid advances in knowledge, and unprecedented levels of global communication and commerce. Even technologies that don't require the Internet to function, such as wireless phones and GPS, rely on the Internet for data transfer and communications.

Growth in Internet usage has surged in recent years both among individual users as well as businesses. Exhibit 2.6 illustrates current usage levels as well as worldwide growth trends in Internet use. Business use of the Internet has become nearly ubiquitous throughout the economy. Major corporations all have a Web presence, and many companies use the Internet to interact with key stakeholders. For example, some companies have direct links with suppliers through online procurement systems that automatically reorder inventories and supplies. Companies such as Cisco Systems even interact with their own employees

Internet Users (in millions)		
Geographic Region	**2005**	**2010 (estimated)**
North America	219,650	259,390
Western Europe	215,734	319,528
Eastern Europe/Russia	70,381	130,888
Asia-Pacific	420,999	745,421
South/Central America	83,724	155,590
Middle East/Africa	64,245	146,624
Total Internet Users	1,074,733	1,785,941

Source: Computer Industry Almanac.

Exhibit 2.6 Growth in Internet Activity

using the Internet to update employment records, such as health care information and benefits.

Small and medium-sized enterprises (SMEs) are also relying on the Internet more than ever. A recent study found that 87 percent of SMEs are receiving monthly revenue from their Web site, and 42 percent derive more than a quarter of their monthly revenue from their Internet presence. According to Joel Kocher, CEO of Interland, "We are getting to the point in most small-business categories where it will soon be safe to say that if you're not online, you're not really serious about being in business."

Despite these advances, the Internet and digital technologies still face numerous challenges. For example, international standards for digital and wireless communications are still in flux. As a result, cell phones and other devices that work in the United States are often useless in many parts of Europe and Asia. And, unlike analog systems, electronic bits of data that are zooming through space can be more easily lost, stolen, or manipulated. However, even with these problems, Internet and digital technologies will continue to be a growing global phenomenon. As Andy Grove, former chairman of Intel, stated, "The world now runs on Internet time."

Sources: Anonymous. 2005. SMBs believe in the Web. *eMarketer.com,* www.emarketer.com, May 16. Downes, L. & Mui, C. 1998. *Unleashing the killer app.* Boston: Harvard Business School Press. Green, H. 2003. Wi-Fi means business. *BusinessWeek,* April 28: 86–92; McGann, R. 2005. Broadband: High speed, high spend. *ClickZ Network,* www.clickz.com, January 24; Tapscott, D. 2001. Rethinking strategy in a Networked World. *Strategy and Business,* Third Quarter: 34–41; and, Yang, C. 2003. Beyond wi-fi: A new wireless age. *BusinessWeek,* December 15: 84–88.

Before moving on, let's consider a recent event that has had a strong influence on many segments of the environment—the Internet. The Internet has been a leading and highly visible component of a broader technological phenomenon—the emergence of digital technology. These technologies are altering the way business is conducted and having an impact on nearly every business domain. Strategy Spotlight 2.4 addresses the impact of the Internet and digital technologies on the business environment.

The Competitive Environment

In addition to the general environment, managers must also consider the competitive environment (also sometimes referred to as the task or industry environment). The nature of competition in an industry, as well as the profitability of a firm, is often more directly influenced by developments in the competitive environment.

The **competitive environment** consists of many factors that are particularly relevant to a firm's strategy. These include competitors (existing or potential), customers, and suppliers. Potential competitors may include a supplier considering forward integration, such as an automobile manufacturer acquiring a rental car company, or a firm in an entirely new industry introducing a similar product that uses a more efficient technology.

In the following sections, we will discuss key concepts and analytical techniques that managers should use to assess their competitive environments. First, we examine Michael Porter's five-forces model that illustrates how these forces can be used to explain low profitability in an industry.[36] Second, we discuss how the five forces are being affected by the capabilities provided by Internet technologies. Third, we address some of the limitations, or "caveats" that managers should be familiar with when conducting industry analysis. Finally, we address the concept of strategic groups. This concept demonstrates that even within an industry it is often useful to group firms on the basis of similarities of their strategies. As we will see, competition tends to be more intense among firms *within* a strategic group than between strategic groups.

competitive environment factors that pertain to an industry and affect a firm's strategies.

Porter's Five-Forces Model of Industry Competition

The "five-forces" model developed by Michael E. Porter has been the most commonly used analytical tool for examining the competitive environment. It describes the competitive environment in terms of five basic competitive forces.[37]

1. The threat of new entrants.
2. The bargaining power of buyers.
3. The bargaining power of suppliers.
4. The threat of substitute products and services.
5. The intensity of rivalry among competitors in an industry.

Each of these forces affects a firm's ability to compete in a given market. Together, they determine the profit potential for a particular industry. The model is shown in Exhibit 2.7 on page 53. As a manager, you should be familiar with the five-forces model for several reasons. It helps you decide whether your firm should remain in or exit an industry. It provides the rationale for increasing or decreasing resource commitments. The model helps you assess how to improve your firm's competitive position with regard to each of the five forces. For example you can use insights provided by the five-forces model to create higher entry barriers that discourage new rivals from competing with you.[38] Or you may develop strong relationships with your distribution channels. You may decide to find suppliers who satisfy the price/performance criteria needed to make your product or service a top performer.

The Threat of New Entrants The threat of new entrants refers to the possibility that the profits of established firms in the industry may be eroded by new competitors.[39] The extent of the threat depends on existing barriers to entry and the combined reactions from existing competitors. If entry barriers are high and/or the newcomer can anticipate a sharp retaliation from established competitors, the threat of entry is low. These circumstances discourage new competitors. There are six major sources of entry barriers.

Economies of Scale Economies of scale refers to spreading the costs of production over the number of units produced. The cost of a product per unit declines as the absolute volume per period increases. This deters entry by forcing the entrant to come

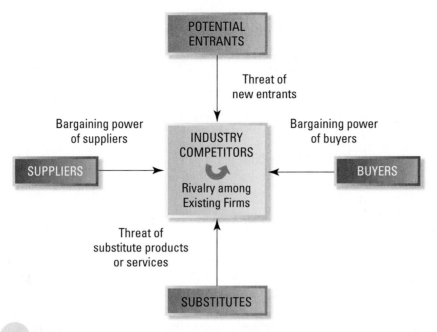

Exhibit 2.7 Porter's Five-Forces Model of Industry Competition

Source: Reprinted with permission of The Free Press, a division of Simon & Schuster Adult Publishing Group, from *Competitive Strategy: Techniques for Analyzing Industries and Competitors* by Michael E. Porter. Copyright © 1980, 1998 by The Free Press. All rights reserved.

in at a large scale and risk strong reaction from existing firms or come in at a small scale and accept a cost disadvantage. Both are undesirable options.

Product Differentiation When existing competitors have strong brand identification and customer loyalty, differentiation creates a barrier to entry by forcing entrants to spend heavily to overcome existing customer loyalties.

Capital Requirements The need to invest large financial resources to compete creates a barrier to entry, especially if the capital is required for risky or unrecoverable upfront advertising or research and development (R&D).

Switching Costs A barrier to entry is created by the existence of one-time costs that the buyer faces when switching from one supplier's product or service to another.

Access to Distribution Channels The new entrant's need to secure distribution for its product can create a barrier to entry.

Cost Disadvantages Independent of Scale Some existing competitors may have advantages that are independent of size or economies of scale. These derive from:

- Proprietary products
- Favorable access to raw materials
- Government subsidies
- Favorable government policies

In an environment where few, if any, of these entry barriers are present, the threat of new entry is high. For example, if a new firm can launch its business with a low capital investment and operate efficiently despite its small scale of operation, it is likely to be a threat. One company that failed because of low entry barriers in an industry is ProCD.[40] You probably never heard of this company. It didn't last very long. ProCD provides an example of a firm that failed because it entered an industry with very low entry barriers.

The story begins in 1986 when Nynex (a former Baby Bell company) issued the first electronic phone book, a compact disk containing all listings for the New York City area. It charged $10,000 per copy and sold the CDs to the FBI, IRS, and other large commercial and government organizations. James Bryant, the Nynex executive in charge of the project, smelled a fantastic business opportunity. He quit Nynex and set up his own firm, ProCD, with the ambitious goal of producing an electronic directory covering the entire United States.

As expected, the telephone companies, fearing an attack on their highly profitable Yellow Pages business, refused to license digital copies of their listings to this upstart. Bryant was not deterred. He traveled to Beijing and hired Chinese workers at $3.50 a day to type every listing from every U.S. telephone book into a database. The result contained more than 70 million phone numbers and was used to create a master disk that enabled ProCD to make hundreds of thousands of copies. Each CD sold for hundreds of dollars and cost less than a dollar each to produce.

It was a profitable business indeed! However, success was fleeting. Competitors such as Digital Directory Assistance and American Business Information quickly launched competing products with the same information. Since customers couldn't tell one product from the next, the players were forced to compete on price alone. Prices for the CD soon plummeted to a few dollars each. A high-priced, high-margin product just months earlier, the CD phone book became little more than a cheap commodity.

The Bargaining Power of Buyers   Buyers threaten an industry by forcing down prices, bargaining for higher quality or more services, and playing competitors against each other. These actions erode industry profitability.[41] The power of each large buyer group depends on attributes of the market situation and the importance of purchases from that group compared with the industry's overall business. A buyer group is powerful under the following conditions:

- ***It is concentrated or purchases large volumes relative to seller sales.*** If a large percentage of a supplier's sales are purchased by a single buyer, the importance of the buyer's business to the supplier increases. Large-volume buyers also are powerful in industries with high fixed costs (e.g., steel manufacturing).
- ***The products it purchases from the industry are standard or undifferentiated.*** Confident they can always find alternative suppliers, buyers play one company against the other, as in commodity grain products.
- ***The buyer faces few switching costs.*** Switching costs lock the buyer to particular sellers. Conversely, the buyer's power is enhanced if the seller faces high switching costs.
- ***It earns low profits.*** Low profits create incentives to lower purchasing costs. On the other hand, highly profitable buyers are generally less price sensitive.
- ***The buyers pose a credible threat of backward integration.*** If buyers are either partially integrated or pose a credible threat of backward integration, they are typically able to secure bargaining concessions.
- ***The industry's product is unimportant to the quality of the buyer's products or services.*** When the quality of the buyer's products is not affected by the industry's product, the buyer is more price sensitive.

At times, a firm or set of firms in an industry may increase its buyer power by using the services of a third party. FreeMarkets Online is one such third party.[42] Pittsburgh-based FreeMarkets has developed software enabling large industrial buyers to organize online auctions for qualified suppliers of semistandard parts such as fabricated components, packaging materials, metal stampings, and services. By aggregating buyers, FreeMarkets increases the buyers' bargaining power. The results are impressive. In its first 48 auctions, most participating companies saved over 15 percent; some saved as much as 50 percent.

The Bargaining Power of Suppliers   Suppliers can exert bargaining power over participants in an industry by threatening to raise prices or reduce the quality of purchased goods and services. Powerful suppliers can squeeze the profitability of firms in an industry so far that they can't recover the costs of raw material inputs.[43] The factors that make suppliers powerful tend to mirror those that make buyers powerful. A supplier group will be powerful in the following circumstances:

- *The supplier group is dominated by a few companies and is more concentrated (few firms dominate the industry) than the industry it sells to.* Suppliers selling to fragmented industries influence prices, quality, and terms.
- *The supplier group is not obliged to contend with substitute products for sale to the industry.* The power of even large, powerful suppliers can be checked if they compete with substitutes.
- *The industry is not an important customer of the supplier group.* When suppliers sell to several industries and a particular industry does not represent a significant fraction of its sales, suppliers are more prone to exert power.
- *The supplier's product is an important input to the buyer's business.* When such inputs are important to the success of the buyer's manufacturing process or product quality, the bargaining power of suppliers is high.
- *The supplier group's products are differentiated or it has built up switching costs for the buyer.* Differentiation or switching costs facing the buyers cut off their options to play one supplier against another.
- *The supplier group poses a credible threat of forward integration.* This provides a check against the industry's ability to improve the terms by which it purchases.

When considering supplier power, we focus on companies that supply raw materials, equipment, machinery, and associated services. But the supply of labor is also an important input to businesses, and labor's power varies over time and across occupations and industries. Currently, the outlook is not very good for semiskilled and unskilled laborers. When annual wage gains before inflation are taken into account—typically a good measure of workers' bargaining clout in the labor market—wages have remained in the 3 percent range for much of the 1990s.[44] When the CPI averaged around 2 percent, that provided employees with pay increases that exceeded inflation. With higher consumer prices, however, real wage gains (wage increases above the inflation rate) have been virtually nonexistent recently.

Strategy Spotlight 2.5 discusses how catfish farmers were able to enhance their bargaining power vis-à-vis their customers—large agribusiness firms—by banding together to form a cooperative.

The Threat of Substitute Products and Services   All firms within an industry compete with industries producing substitute products and services. Substitutes limit the potential returns of an industry by placing a ceiling on the prices that firms in that industry can profitably charge. The more attractive the price/performance ratio of substitute products, the tighter the lid on an industry's profits.

Identifying substitute products involves searching for other products or services that can perform the same function as the industry's offerings. This is a subtle task, one that leads a manager into businesses seemingly far removed from the industry. For example, the airline industry might not consider video cameras much of a threat. But as digital technology has improved and wireless and other forms of telecommunication have become more efficient, teleconferencing has become a viable substitute for business travel for many executives. That is, the rate of improvement in the price–performance relationship of the substitute product (or service) is high.

Teleconferencing can save both time and money, as IBM found out with its "Manager Jam" idea.[45] Currently, with 319,000 employees scattered around six continents,

Enhancing Supplier Power: The Creation of Delta Pride Catfish

The formation of Delta Pride Catfish in 1981 is an example of the power that a group of suppliers can attain if they exercise the threat of forward integration. Catfish farmers in Mississippi had historically supplied their harvest to processing plants run by large agribusiness firms such as ConAgra and Farm Fresh. When the farmers increased their production of catfish in response to growing demand in the early 1970s, they found, much to their chagrin, that processors were holding back on their plans to increase their processing capabilities in hopes of higher retail prices for catfish.

Source: Cargile, D. 2005. Personal communication. (Vice President of Sales, Delta Pride Catfish, Inc.), February 2; Anonymous. 2003. Delta Pride Catfish names Steve Osso President and CEO. www.deltabusiness.journal.com, February; and Fritz, M. 1988. Agribusiness: Catfish story. *Forbes*, December 12: 37.

What action did the farmers take? They responded by forming a cooperative, raising $4.5 million, and constructing their own processing plant, which they supplied themselves. Within two years, ConAgra's market share had dropped from 35 percent to 11 percent, and Farm Fresh's market share fell by over 20 percent.

By the late 1980s, Delta Pride controlled over 40 percent of the 280-million-pound-per-year U.S. catfish market. It has continued to grow by including value-added products such as breaded and marinated catfish products. Recently it introduced Country Crisp Catfish Strips, a bakeable, breaded product with country-style seasoning. By 2005, Delta Pride had more than 500 employees. Its approximately 100 shareholders are mostly catfish farmers who own more than 60,000 acres of catfish production ponds and produce more than 200 million pounds of live catfish each year.

---

it is one of the world's largest businesses (including 32,000 managers) and can be a pretty confusing place. The shift to an increasingly mobile workplace means many managers supervise employees they rarely see face-to-face. To enhance coordination, Samuel Palmisano, IBM's new CEO, launched one of his first big initiatives: a two-year program exploring the role of the manager in the 21st century. "Manager Jam," as the project was nicknamed, was a 48-hour real-time Web event in which managers from 50 different countries swapped ideas and strategies for dealing with problems shared by all of them, regardless of geography. Some 8,100 managers logged on to the company's intranet to participate in the discussion forums.

Renewable energy resources are also a promising substitute product and are rapidly becoming more economically competitive with fossil fuels. Strategy Spotlight 2.6 addresses this critical issue.

The Intensity of Rivalry among Competitors in an Industry   Rivalry among existing competitors takes the form of jockeying for position. Firms use tactics like price competition, advertising battles, product introductions, and increased customer service or warranties. Rivalry occurs when competitors sense the pressure or act on an opportunity to improve their position.

Some forms of competition, such as price competition, are typically highly destabilizing and are likely to erode the average level of profitability in an industry.[46] Rivals easily match price cuts, an action that lowers profits for all firms. On the other hand, advertising battles expand overall demand or enhance the level of product differentiation for the benefit of all firms in the industry. Rivalry, of course, differs across industries. In some instances it is characterized as warlike, bitter, or cutthroat, whereas in other industries it is referred to as polite and gentlemanly. Intense rivalry is the result of several interacting factors, including the following:

- ***Numerous or equally balanced competitors.*** When there are many firms in an industry, the likelihood of mavericks is great. Some firms believe they can make moves without being noticed. Even when there are relatively few firms, and they are nearly

The Growing Viability of Renewable Resources as Substitutes for Fossil Fuels

Renewable resources currently provide just over 6 percent of total U.S. energy. However, that figure could increase rapidly in the years ahead, according to a joint report issued in September 2006 by the Worldwatch Institute and the Center for Progress, entitled "American Energy: The Renewable Path to Energy Security."

The report indicates that many of the new technologies that harness renewables are, or soon will be, economically competitive with fossil fuels. Dynamic growth rates are driving down costs and spurring rapid advances in technologies. And, since 2000, global wind energy generation has more than tripled, solar cell production has risen six-fold, production of fuel ethanol from crops has more than doubled, and biodiesel production has expanded nearly four-fold. Annual global investment in

"new" renewable energy has risen almost six-fold since 1995, with cumulative investment over the period nearly $180 billion. The report claims: "With oil prices soaring, the security risks of petroleum dependence growing, and the environmental costs of today's fuels becoming more apparent, the country faces compelling reasons to put these technologies to use on a larger scale."

A November 2006 study by the RAND Corporation is consistent with the aforementioned report. It asserts that the economy of the United States would likely benefit, rather than be slowed, if the nation attained the goal of supplying 25 percent of its energy needs from renewable sources by 2025. The RAND study also says that while most renewable fuels cannot yet compete with fossil fuels, their costs of production are falling steadily. If the trend continues, America's energy mix by 2025 could be far greener and cleaner—without damaging the economy—than most analysts could have anticipated a few years ago. Such developments would also reduce U.S. dependence on oil, which would mean a substantial start on capping greenhouse gas emissions, which most scientists link to global warming.

Sources: Clayton, M. 2006. Greener, cleaner . . . and competitive. www.csmonitor.com. December 4; and, Anonymous. 2006. Renewables becoming cost-competitive with fossil fuels in the U.S. www.worldwatch.org. September 18.

equal in size and resources, instability results from fighting among companies having the resources for sustained and vigorous retaliation.

- *Slow industry growth.* Slow industry growth turns competition into a fight for market share, since firms seek to expand their sales.
- *High fixed or storage costs.* High fixed costs create strong pressures for all firms to increase capacity. Excess capacity often leads to escalating price cutting.
- *Lack of differentiation or switching costs.* Where the product or service is perceived as a commodity or near commodity, the buyer's choice is typically based on price and service, resulting in pressures for intense price and service competition. Lack of switching costs, described earlier, has the same effect.
- *Capacity augmented in large increments.* Where economies of scale require that capacity must be added in large increments, capacity additions can be very disruptive to the industry supply/demand balance.
- *High exit barriers.* Exit barriers are economic, strategic, and emotional factors that keep firms competing even though they may be earning low or negative returns on their investments. Some exit barriers are specialized assets, fixed costs of exit, strategic interrelationships (e.g., relationships between the business units and others within a company in terms of image, marketing, shared facilities, and so on), emotional barriers, and government and social pressures (e.g., governmental discouragement of exit out of concern for job loss).

Rivalry between firms is often based solely on price, but it can involve other factors. Take Pfizer's market position in the impotence treatment market. Pfizer was the first pharmaceutical firm to develop Viagra, a drug that treats impotence. International sales of Viagra were $332 million during a recent quarter. There are currently 30 million prescriptions for the drug. Pfizer would like to keep competitors from challenging this lucrative position.

In several countries, the United Kingdom among them, Pfizer faced a lawsuit by Eli Lilly & Co. and Icos Corp. challenging its patent protection. These two pharmaceutical firms recently entered into a joint venture to market Cialis, a drug to compete with Viagra. The U.K. courts agreed and lifted the patent.

This opened the door for Eli Lilly and Icos to proceed with challenging Pfizer's market position. Because Cialis has fewer side effects than Viagra, the drug has the potential to rapidly decrease Pfizer's market share in the United Kingdom if physicians switch prescriptions from Viagra to Cialis. If future patent challenges are successful, Pfizer may see its sales of Viagra erode rapidly. With projected annual sales of Cialis at $1 billion, Pfizer has reason to worry. With FDA approval, sales of Cialis could cause those of Viagra to plummet in the United States, further eroding Pfizer's market share.[47] But Pfizer is hardly standing still. It recently doubled its advertising expenditures on Viagra.

Exhibit 2.8 summarizes our discussion of industry five-forces analysis. It points out how various factors such as economies of scale and capital requirements affect each "force."

How the Internet and Digital Technologies Are Affecting the Five Competitive Forces

>LO6

How the Internet and digitally based capabilities are affecting the five competitive forces and industry profitability.

The Internet and other digital technologies are having a significant impact on nearly every industry. These technologies have fundamentally changed the ways businesses interact with each other and with consumers. In most cases, these changes have affected industry forces in ways that have created many new strategic challenges. In this section, we will evaluate Michael Porter's five-forces model in terms of the actual use of the Internet and the new technological capabilities that it makes possible.

The Threat of New Entrants   In most industries, the threat of new entrants has increased because digital and Internet-based technologies lower barriers to entry. For example, businesses that reach customers primarily through the Internet may enjoy savings on other traditional expenses such as office rent, sales-force salaries, printing, and postage. This may encourage more entrants who, because of the lower start-up expenses, see an opportunity to capture market share by offering a product or performing a service more efficiently than existing competitors. Thus, a new cyber entrant can use the savings provided by the Internet to charge lower prices and compete on price despite the incumbent's scale advantages.

Alternatively, because digital technologies often make it possible for young firms to provide services that are equivalent or superior to an incumbent, a new entrant may be able to serve a market more effectively, with more personalized services and greater attention to product details. A new firm may be able to build a reputation in its niche and charge premium prices. By so doing, it can capture part of an incumbent's business and erode profitability. Consider Voice Over Internet Protocol (VOIP), a fast growing alternative to traditional phone service, which is expected to reach 12.1 million U.S. households by 2009.[48] Savings of 20 to 30 percent are common for VOIP consumers. This is driving prices down and lowering telecom industry profits. A more sweeping implication is that it threatens the value of the phone line infrastructure that the major carriers have invested in so heavily. Clearly, VOIP represents a major new entrant threat to incumbent phone service providers.

Another potential benefit of Web-based business is access to distribution channels. Manufacturers or distributors that can reach potential outlets for their products more efficiently by means of the Internet may be encouraged to enter markets that were previously closed to them. Such access is not guaranteed, however, because of the strong barriers to entry that may exist in certain industries.[49] Nevertheless, Internet and digital technologies are providing many new entrants with more efficient and lower cost methods of accessing customers.

Threat of New Entrants Is High When:	High	Low
Economies of scale are		X
Product differentiation is		X
Capital requirements are		X
Switching costs are		X
Incumbent's control of distribution channels is		X
Incumbent's proprietary knowledge is		X
Incumbent's access to raw materials is		X
Incumbent's access to government subsidies is		X

Power of Buyers Is High When:	High	Low
Concentration of buyers relative to suppliers is	X	
Switching costs are		X
Product differentiation of suppliers is		X
Threat of backward integration by buyers is	X	
Extent of buyer's profits is		X
Importance of the supplier's input to quality of buyer's final product is		X

Power of Suppliers Is High When:	High	Low
Concentration relative to buyer industry is	X	
Availability of substitute products is		X
Importance of customer to the supplier is		X
Differentiation of the supplier's products and services is	X	
Switching costs of the buyer are	X	
Threat of forward integration by the supplier is	X	

Threat of Substitute Products Is High When:	High	Low
The differentiation of the substitute product is	X	
Rate of improvement in price–performance relationship of substitute product is	X	

Intensity of Competitive Rivalry Is High When:	High	Low
Number of competitors is	X	
Industry growth rate is		X
Fixed costs are	X	
Storage costs are	X	
Product differentiation is		X
Switching costs are		X
Exit barriers are	X	
Strategic stakes are	X	

Exhibit 2.8 Competitive Analysis Checklist

Buyer Power in the Book Industry: The Role of the Internet

The $25 billion book publishing industry illustrates some of the changes brought on by the Internet that have affected buying power among two types of buyers—end users and buyer channel intermediaries. Prior to the Internet, book publishers worked primarily through large distributors. These intermediaries such as Tennessee-based Ingram, one of the largest and most powerful distributors, exercised strong control over the movement of books from publishers to book-

stores. This power was especially strong relative to small, independent publishers who often found it difficult to get their books into bookstores and in front of potential customers.

The Internet has significantly changed these relationships. Publishers can now negotiate distribution agreements directly with online retailers such as Amazon and Books-A-Million. Such online bookstores now account for about $4 billion in annual sales. And small publishers can use the Internet to sell directly to end users and publicize new titles, without depending on buyer channel intermediaries to handle their books. By using the Internet to appeal to niche markets, 63,000 small publishers with revenues of less than $50 million each generated $14.2 billion in sales in 2005—over half of the industry's total sales.

Sources: Hoynes, M. 2002. Is it the same for book sales? *BookWeb.org*, www.bookweb.org, March 20; www.parapublishing.com; Teague, D. 2005. U.S. book production reaches new high of 195,000 titles in 2004; Fiction soars. *Bowker.com*, www.bowker.com, May 24; and Teicher, C. M. 2007. March of the small presses. *Publishers Weekly*, www.publishersweekly.com, March 26.

The Bargaining Power of Buyers   The Internet and wireless technologies may increase buyer power by providing consumers with more information to make buying decisions and by lowering switching costs. But these technologies may also suppress the power of traditional buyer channels that have concentrated buying power in the hands of a few, giving buyers new ways to access sellers. To sort out these differences, let's first distinguish between two types of buyers: end users and buyer channel intermediaries.

End users, as the name implies, are the final customers in a distribution channel. They are the consumers who actually buy a product and put it to use. Internet sales activity that is labeled "B2C"—that is, business-to-consumer—is concerned with end users. The Internet is likely to increase the power of these buyers for several reasons. First, a large amount of consumer information is available on the Internet. This gives end users the information they need to shop for quality merchandise and bargain for price concessions. The automobile industry provides an excellent example of this phenomenon. For a small fee, agencies such as Consumers Union (publishers of *Consumer Reports*) will provide customers with detailed information about actual automobile manufacturer costs.[50] This information, available online, can be used to bid down dealers' profits. Second, an end user's switching costs are also potentially much lower because of the Internet. Switching may involve only a few clicks of the mouse to find and view a competing product or service online.

In contrast, the bargaining power of distribution channel buyers may decrease because of the Internet. *Buyer channel intermediaries* are the wholesalers, distributors, and retailers who serve as intermediaries between manufacturers and end users. In some industries, they are dominated by powerful players that control who gains access to the latest goods or the best merchandise. The Internet and wireless communications, however, make it much easier and less expensive for businesses to reach customers directly. Thus, the Internet may increase the power of incumbent firms relative to that of traditional buyer channels. Strategy Spotlight 2.7 illustrates some of the changes brought on by the Internet that have affected the industry's two types of buyers.

The Bargaining Power of Suppliers   Use of the Internet and digital technologies to speed up and streamline the process of acquiring supplies is already benefiting many sectors of the economy. But the net effect of the Internet on supplier power will depend on the nature of competition in a given industry. As with buyer power, the extent to which the Internet is a benefit or a detriment may also hinge on the supplier's position along the supply chain.

The role of suppliers typically involves providing products or services to other businesses. Thus, the term "B2B"—that is, business-to-business—is often used to refer to businesses that supply or sell to other businesses. The effect of the Internet on the bargaining power of suppliers is a double-edged sword. On the one hand, suppliers may find it difficult to hold onto customers because buyers can do comparative shopping and price negotiations so much faster on the Internet and can turn to other suppliers with a few clicks of the mouse. This is especially damaging to supply-chain intermediaries, such as product distributors, who may not be able to stop suppliers from directly accessing other potential business customers. In addition, one of the greatest threats to supplier power is that the Internet inhibits the ability of suppliers to offer highly differentiated products or unique services. Most procurement technologies can be imitated by competing suppliers, and the technologies that make it possible to design and customize new products rapidly are being used by all competitors.

On the other hand, several factors may also contribute to stronger supplier power. First, the growth of new Web-based business in general may create more downstream outlets for suppliers to sell to. Second, suppliers may be able to create Web-based purchasing arrangements that make purchasing easier and discourage their customers from switching. Online procurement systems, for example, create a direct link between suppliers and customers that reduces transaction costs and paperwork.[51] Third, the use of proprietary software that links buyers to a supplier's Web site may create a rapid, low-cost ordering capability that discourages the buyer from seeking other sources of supply. Amazon.com, for example, created and patented One-Click purchasing technology that speeds up the ordering process for customers who enroll in the service.[52]

Finally, suppliers will have greater power to the extent that they can reach end users directly without intermediaries. Previously, suppliers often had to work through intermediaries who brought their products or services to market for a fee. But a process known as *disintermediation* is removing the organizations or business process layers responsible for intermediary steps in the value chain of many industries.[53] Just as the Internet is eliminating some business functions, it is creating an opening for new functions. These new activities are entering the value chain by a process known as *reintermediation*—the introduction of new types of intermediaries. Many of these new functions are affecting traditional supply chains. For example, delivery services are enjoying a boom because of the Internet. Many more consumers are choosing to have products delivered to their door rather than going out to pick them up. Electronic delivery of products such as tickets to sporting events and electronic postage stamps is also becoming common.

The Threat of Substitutes   Along with traditional marketplaces, the Internet has created a new marketplace; along with traditional channels, it has become a new channel. In general, therefore, the threat of substitutes is heightened because the Internet introduces new ways to accomplish the same tasks.

Consumers will generally choose to use a product or service until a substitute that meets the same need becomes available at a lower cost. The economies created by Internet technologies have led to the development of numerous substitutes for traditional ways of doing business. For example, a company called Conferenza is offering an alternative way to participate in conferences for people who don't want to spend the time and money to attend. The Web site provides summaries of many conference events, quality ratings using an "event intelligence" score, and schedules of upcoming events.[54]

Another example of substitution is in the realm of electronic storage. With expanded desktop computing, the need to store information electronically has increased dramatically. Until recently, the trend has been to create increasingly larger desktop storage capabilities and techniques for compressing information that create storage efficiencies. But a viable substitute has recently emerged: storing information digitally on the Internet. Companies such as My Docs Online Inc. are providing Web-based storage that firms can access simply by leasing space online. Since these storage places are virtual, they can be accessed anywhere the Web can be accessed. This makes it possible for a traveler to access important documents and files without transporting them physically from place to place. Cyberstorage is not free, but it is still cheaper and more convenient than purchasing and carrying additional disk storage.[55]

The Intensity of Competitive Rivalry   Because the Internet creates more tools and means for competing, rivalry among competitors is likely to be more intense. Only those competitors that can use digital technologies and the Web to give themselves a distinct image, create unique product offerings, or provide "faster, smarter, cheaper" services are likely to capture greater profitability with the new technology. Such gains are hard to sustain, however, because in most cases the new technology can be imitated quickly. Thus, the Internet tends to increase rivalry by making it difficult for firms to differentiate themselves and by shifting customer attention to issues of price.

Rivalry is more intense when switching costs are low and product or service differentiation is minimized. Because the Internet makes it possible to shop around with a few clicks of the mouse, it has "commoditized" products that might previously have been regarded as rare or unique. Since the Internet eliminates the importance of location, products that previously had to be sought out in geographically distant outlets are now readily available online. This makes competitors in cyberspace seem more equally balanced, thus intensifying rivalry.

The problem is made worse for marketers by the presence of shopping robots ("bots") and infomediaries that search the Web for the best possible prices. Consumer websites like mySimon and PriceSCAN seek out all the Web locations that sell similar products and provide price comparisons.[56] Obviously, this hinders a firm's ability to establish unique characteristics and focuses the consumer exclusively on price. Some shopping infomediaries, such as BizRate and CNET, not only search for the lowest prices on many different products but also rank the customer service quality of different sites that sell similarly priced items.[57] Such infomediary services are good for consumers because they give them the chance to compare services as well as price. For businesses, however, they increase rivalry by consolidating the marketing message that consumers use to make a purchase decision to a few key pieces of information over which the selling company has little control.

Exhibit 2.9 summarizes many of the ways the Internet is affecting industry structure. These influences will also change how companies develop and deploy strategies to generate above-average profits and sustainable competitive advantage.

Using Industry Analysis: A Few Caveats

For industry analysis to be valuable, a company must collect and evaluate a wide variety of information from many sources. As the trend toward globalization accelerates, information on foreign markets as well as on a wider variety of competitors, suppliers, customers, substitutes, and potential new entrants becomes more critical. Industry analysis helps a firm not only to evaluate the profit potential of an industry, but also to consider various ways to strengthen its position vis-à-vis the five forces. However, we'd like to address a few caveats. First, *managers must not always avoid low profit industries (or low profit segments in profitable industries)*. Such industries can still yield high returns for some players who

	Benefits to Industry (+)	Disadvantages to Industry (−)
Threat of New Entrants		• Lower barriers to entry increases number of new entrants. • Many Internet-based capabilities can be easily imitated.
Bargaining Power of Buyers	• Reduces the power of buyer intermediaries in many distribution channels.	• Switching costs decrease. • Information availability online empowers end users.
Bargaining Power of Suppliers	• Online procurement methods can increase bargaining power over suppliers.	• The Internet gives suppliers access to more customers and makes it easier to reach end users. • Online procurement practices deter competition and reduce differentiating features.
Threat of Substitutes	• Internet-based increases in overall efficiency can expand industry sales.	• Internet-based capabilities create more opportunities for substitution.
Intensity of Rivalry		• Since location is less important, the number of competitors increases. • Differences among competitors are harder to perceive online. • Rivalry tends to focus on price and differentiating features are minimized.

Sources: Bodily, S., & Venkataraman, S. 2004. Not walls, windows: Capturing value in the digital age. *Journal of Business Strategy,* 25(3): 15–25; Lumpkin, G. T., Droege, S. B., & Dess, G. G. 2002. E-commerce strategies: Achieving sustainable competitive advantage and avoiding pitfalls. *Organizational Dynamics,* 30 (Spring): 1–17.

Exhibit 2.9 How the Internet and Digital Technologies Influence Industry

pursue sound strategies. As examples, consider Paychex, a payroll-processing company, and WellPoint Health Network, a huge health care insurer:[58]

> Paychex, with $1.6 billion in revenues, became successful by serving small businesses. Existing firms had ignored them because they assumed that such businesses could not afford the service. When Paychex's founder, Tom Golisano, failed to convince his bosses at Electronic Accounting Systems that they were missing a great opportunity, he launched the firm. It now serves 550,000 businesses—each employing about 17 employees. Paychex's after-tax-return on sales is a stunning 28 percent.
>
> In 1986, WellPoint Health Network (when it was known as Blue Cross of California) suffered a loss of $160 million. That year, Leonard Schaeffer became CEO and challenged the conventional wisdom that individuals and small firms were money losers. (This was certainly "heresy" at the time—the firm was losing $5 million a year insuring 65,000 individuals!) However, by the early 1990s, the health insurer was leading the industry in profitability. The firm has continued to grow and outperform its rivals even during economic downturns. By 2006, its revenues and profits were nearly $60 billion and $3 billion, respectively—each figure representing an *annual* increase of over 35 percent for the most recent five-year period.

Second, five-forces analysis implicitly *assumes a zero-sum game, determining how a firm can enhance its position relative to the forces.* Yet such an approach can often be shortsighted; that is, it can overlook the many potential benefits of developing constructive win–win relationships with suppliers and customers. Establishing long-term mutually beneficial relationships with suppliers improves a firm's ability to implement just-in-time (JIT) inventory systems, which let it manage inventories better and respond quickly to market demands. A recent study found that if a company exploits its powerful position against a supplier, that action may come back to haunt the company. Consider, for example, General Motors's heavy-handed dealings with its suppliers:[60]

> GM has a reputation for particularly aggressive tactics. Although it is striving to crack down on the most egregious of these, it continues to rank dead last in the annual supplier satisfaction survey. "It's a brutal process," says David E. Cole, who is head of the Center for Automotive Research in Ann Arbor. "There are bodies lying by the side of the road."
>
> Suppliers point to one particularly nasty tactic: shopping their technology out the back door to see if rivals can make it cheaper. In one case, a GM purchasing manager showed a supplier's new brake design to Delphi Corporation. He was fired. However, in a recent survey, parts executives said they tend to bring hot new technology to other carmakers first. This is yet another reason GM finds it hard to compete in an intensely competitive industry.

Third, the five-forces analysis also has been criticized for *being essentially a static analysis*. External forces as well as strategies of individual firms are continually changing the structure of all industries. The search for a dynamic theory of strategy has led to greater use of game theory in industrial organization economics research and strategy research. Based on game-theoretic considerations, Brandenburger and Nalebuff recently introduced the concept of the value net,[61] which in many ways is an extension of the five-forces analysis. It is illustrated in Exhibit 2.10. The value net represents all the players in the game and analyzes how their interactions affect a firm's ability to generate and appropriate value. The vertical dimension of the net includes suppliers and customers. The firm has direct transactions with them. On the horizontal dimension are substitutes and complements, players with whom a firm interacts but may not necessarily transact. The concept of complementors is perhaps the single most important contribution of value net analysis and is explained in more detail below.

complements
products or services that have an impact on the value of a firm's products or services.

Complements typically are products or services that have a potential impact on the value of a firm's own products or services. Those who produce complements are usually referred to as complementors.[62] Powerful hardware is of no value to a user unless there is software that runs on it. Similarly, new and better software is possible only if the hardware on which it can be run is available. This is equally true in the video game industry, where the sales of game

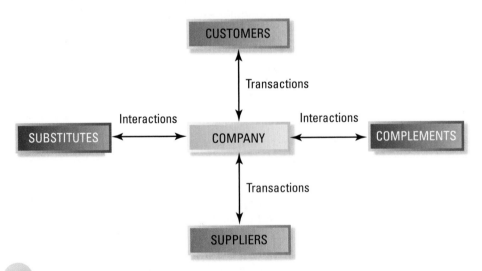

Exhibit 2.10 The Value Net

Source: Adapted and reprinted by permission of *Harvard Business Review.* Exhibit from "The Right Game: Use Game Theory to Shape Strategy," by A. Brandenburger and B. J. Nalebuff, July–August 1995. Copyright © 1995 by the Harvard Business School Publishing Corporation. All rights reserved.

strategy spotlight

Apple's iPod: Relationships with its Complementors

In 2002, Steve Jobs began his campaign to cajole the major music companies into selling tracks to iPod users through the iTunes Music Store, an online retail site. Most industry executives, after being burned by illegal file-sharing services like Napster and Kazaa, just wanted digital music to disappear. However, Jobs's passionate vision persuaded them to climb on board. He promised to reduce the risks that they faced by offering safeguards against piracy, as well as a hip product (iPod) that would drive sales.

However, Apple had a much stronger bargaining position when its contracts with the music companies came up for renewal in April 2005. By then, iTunes had captured 80 percent of the market for legal downloads. The music companies, which were receiving between 60 and 70 cents per download, wanted more. Their reasoning: If the iTunes Music Store would only charge $1.50 or $2.00 per track, they could double or triple their revenues and profits. Since Jobs knew that he could sell more iPods if the music was cheap, he was determined to keep the price of a download at 99 cents and to maintain Apple's margins. Given iTunes dominant position, the music companies had little choice but to relent.

Apple's venture into music has been tremendously successful. For the fiscal year ending September 30, 2006, iPod sales had increased to $7.4 billion, and other music-related products and services totaled $1.9 billion. These figures represent increases of 69 percent and 110 percent, respectively, over the previous year.

• A female employee sits at her desk equipped with both an iMac and an iPod. She works on a spreadsheet, uses iTunes and listens to an iPod.

Source: Apple Computer Inc. 10-K, December 29, 2006; and, Yoffie, D. B. & Kwak, M. 2006. With friends like these: The art of managing complementors. *Harvard Business Review*, 84(9): 88–98.

consoles and video games complement each other. Nintendo's success in the early 1990s was a result of their ability to manage their relationship with their complementors. They built a security chip into the hardware and then licensed the right to develop games to outside firms. These firms paid a royalty to Nintendo for each copy of the game sold. The royalty revenue enabled Nintendo to sell game consoles at close to their cost, thereby increasing their market share, which, in turn, caused more games to be sold and more royalties to be generated.[63]

Despite efforts to create win–win scenarios, conflict among complementors is inevitable.[64] After all, it is naive to expect that even the closest of partners will do you the favor of abandoning their own interests. And even the most successful partnerships are seldom trouble free. Power is a factor that comes into play as we see in Strategy Spotlight 2.8 with the example of Apple's iPod—an enormously successful product.

> **>LO7**
>
> The concept of strategic groups and their strategy and performance implications.

Strategic Groups within Industries

In an industry analysis, two assumptions are unassailable: (1) No two firms are totally different, and (2) no two firms are exactly the same. The issue becomes one of identifying groups of firms that are more similar to each other than firms that are not, otherwise known as **strategic groups**.[65] This is important because rivalry tends to be greater among firms

> **strategic groups**
> clusters of firms that share similar strategies.

that are alike. Strategic groups are clusters of firms that share similar strategies. After all, is Kmart more concerned about Nordstrom or Wal-Mart? Is Mercedes more concerned about Hyundai or BMW? The answers are straightforward.[66]

These examples are not meant to trivialize the strategic groups concept.[67] Classifying an industry into strategic groups involves judgment. If it is useful as an analytical tool, we must exercise caution in deciding what dimensions to use to map these firms. Dimensions include breadth of product and geographic scope, price/quality, degree of vertical integration, type of distribution (e.g., dealers, mass merchandisers, private label), and so on. Dimensions should also be selected to reflect the variety of strategic combinations in an industry. For example, if all firms in an industry have roughly the same level of product differentiation (or R&D intensity), this would not be a good dimension to select.

What value is the strategic groups concept as an analytical tool? *First, strategic groupings help a firm identify barriers to mobility that protect a group from attacks by other groups.*[68] Mobility barriers are factors that deter the movement of firms from one strategic position to another. For example, in the chainsaw industry, the major barriers protecting the high-quality/dealer-oriented group are technology, brand image, and an established network of servicing dealers.

The second value of strategic grouping is that it *helps a firm identify groups whose competitive position may be marginal or tenuous.* We may anticipate that these competitors may exit the industry or try to move into another group. This has been the case in recent years in the retail department store industry, where firms such as JCPenney and Sears have experienced extremely difficult times because they were stuck in the middle, neither an aggressive discount player like Wal-Mart nor a prestigious upscale player like Neiman Marcus.

Third, strategic groupings *help chart the future directions of firms' strategies.* Arrows emanating from each strategic group can represent the direction in which the group (or a firm within the group) seems to be moving. If all strategic groups are moving in a similar direction, this could indicate a high degree of future volatility and intensity of competition. In the automobile industry, for example, the competition in the minivan and sport utility segments has intensified in recent years as many firms have entered those product segments.

Fourth, strategic groups are *helpful in thinking through the implications of each industry trend for the strategic group as a whole.* Is the trend decreasing the viability of a group? If so, in what direction should the strategic group move? Is the trend increasing or decreasing entry barriers in a given group? Will the trend decrease the ability of one group to separate itself from other groups? Such analysis can help in making predictions about industry evolution. A sharp increase in interest rates, for example, would tend to have less impact on providers of higher-priced goods (e.g., Porsches) than on providers of lower-priced goods (e.g., Chevrolet Cobalt). The Chevrolet Cobalt customer base is much more price sensitive.

Exhibit 2.11 provides a strategic grouping of the worldwide automobile industry.[69] The firms in each group are representative; not all firms are included in the mapping. We have identified four strategic groups. In the top left-hand corner are high-end luxury automakers who focus on a very narrow product market. Most of the cars produced by the members of this group cost well over $100,000. Some cost many times that amount. The Ferrari F50 costs roughly $550,000 and the Lamborghini L147 $300,000[70] (in case you were wondering how to spend your employment signing bonus). Players in this market have a very exclusive clientele and face little rivalry from other strategic groups. At the other extreme, in the lower left-hand corner is a strategic group that has low-price/quality attributes and targets a narrow market. These players, Hyundai and Kia, limit competition from other strategic groups by pricing their products very low. The third group (near the middle) consists of firms high in product pricing/quality and average in their product-line breadth. The final group (at the far right) consists of firms with a broad range of products

*t*wo firms compete in the same industry and both have many strengths in a variety of functional areas: marketing, operations, logistics, and so on. However, one of these firms outperforms the other by a wide margin over a long period of time. How can this be so? This chapter endeavors to answer that question.

We begin with two sections that include frameworks for gaining key insights into a firm's internal environment: value-chain analysis and the resource-based view of the firm. In value-chain analysis, we divide a firm's activities into a series of value-creating steps. We then explore how individual activities within the firm add value, and also how *interrelationships* among activities within the firm, and between the firm and its suppliers and customers, create value.

In the resource-based view of the firm, we analyze the firm as a collection of tangible and intangible resources as well as organizational capabilities. Advantages that tend to be sustainable over time typically arise from creating *bundles* of resources and capabilities that satisfy four criteria: they are valuable, rare, difficult to imitate, and difficult to substitute. Not all of the value created by a firm will necessarily be kept (or appropriated) by the owners. We discuss the four key factors that determine how profits will be distributed between owners as well as employees and managers.

In the closing sections, we discuss how to evaluate a firm's performance and make comparisons across firms. We emphasize both the inclusion of financial resources and the interests of multiple stakeholders. Central to our discussion is the concept of the balanced scorecard, which recognizes that the interests of different stakeholders can be interrelated. We also consider how a firm's performance evolves over time and how it compares with industry norms and key competitors.

In an appendix to this chapter, we explore how Internet-based businesses and incumbent firms are using digital technologies to add value. We consider four activities—search, evaluation, problem solving, and transaction—as well as three types of content—customer feedback, expertise, and entertainment programming. Such technology-enhanced capabilities are providing new means with which firms can achieve competitive advantages.

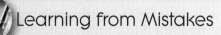 Learning from Mistakes

In the late 1980s, Goodyear Tire & Rubber Co., then the largest tire company in the world, began an organizationwide initiative to adopt the principles of total quality management (TQM).[1] Like so many other companies that embraced TQM, Goodyear's operations, logistics, procurement, and research and development were reengineered with the objective of producing "defect-free" products. So far, so good? Read on. . . .

Unfortunately, sales and distribution, which had always been central to Goodyear's success, were demoted to secondary status because TQM focused almost entirely on the manufacturing process. Not surprisingly, relationships began to sour between manufacturing people and the sales and distribution staff.

Resources to support the highly successful existing U.S. dealer network, which had taken nearly a century to develop and perfect, were reallocated to operations. With fewer resources, Goodyear had little choice but to cannibalize its existing distribution arrangement. Wholesalers became dealers and vice versa. Multiple sales outlets appeared everywhere where there had previously been only one or two Goodyear dealers for years. Thus, Goodyear's control over the sale and distribution of its products began to crumble.

For Goodyear's consumers, this was good news. They could now have Wrangler or American Eagle tires mounted on their cars while they shopped at the mall or purchased dry goods at large, powerful retailers such as Wal-Mart and Sears, which *[continued]* began selling Goodyear tires in the early 1990s. Retailers also came out ahead. Since such new retailers were not exclusive dealers, they placed Goodyear tires next to competing brands, giving their customers more choices. Not surprisingly, the price of Goodyear's tires sharply declined. And, with a large number of outlets competing for the same customer base, price wars became inevitable.

In the long run, the only loser was Goodyear and its employees. The firm's competitive position and profitability began to erode. Unable to raise its prices through a compromised distribution network, Goodyear faced inevitable plant closures. This was done to compensate for steady losses from the ill-conceived dissolution of its dealer network. By early 2003, the company was carrying a huge debt burden, and its pension fund was underfunded by $2 billion. What's worse, Goodyear's once-loyal dealers were in open revolt because the company could not even fill the orders from dealers—mainly because of the disconnect between the factories and the distributor network.

Goodyear's problems began when it failed to invest in its valuable resources in its downstream activities—sales and distribution. Instead, it "followed the herd" and became a TQM disciple by focusing its resources on improving its operations, logistics, and research and development activities. Thus, its performance suffered when its key strength began to wither. Without its superb distribution network, the firm was forced to sell its products through mass merchandisers such as Wal-Mart and Sears, and its customers began perceiving its products, in essence, as a commodity. Clearly, firms benefit from assessing the internal environment to address what value-creating activities lead to their competitive advantages and developing strategies accordingly. Overemphasizing one part of the value chain and neglecting others may result in a failure to maintain and enhance overall organizational effectiveness.[2]

value chain analysis
a strategic analysis of an organization that uses value-creating activities.

primary activities
sequential activities of the value chain that refer to the physical creation of the product or service, its sale and transfer to the buyer, and its service after sale, including inbound logistics, operations, outbound logistics, marketing and sales, and service.

Before moving ahead to value-chain analysis, let's briefly revisit SWOT analysis to discuss some of its benefits and limitations. As discussed in Chapter 2, a SWOT analysis consists of a careful listing of a firm's strengths, weaknesses, opportunities, and threats. While we believe SWOT analysis is very helpful as a starting point, it should not form the primary basis for evaluating a firm's internal strengths and weaknesses or the opportunities and threats in the environment. Strategy Spotlight 3.1 elaborates on the limitations of the traditional SWOT approach.

We will now turn to value-chain analysis. As you will see, it provides greater insights into analyzing a firm's competitive position than SWOT analysis does by itself.

Value-Chain Analysis

Value-chain analysis views the organization as a sequential process of value-creating activities. The approach is useful for understanding the building blocks of competitive advantage. Value-chain analysis was described in Michael Porter's seminal book *Competitive Advantage*.[3] In competitive terms, value is the amount that buyers are willing to pay for what a firm provides them. Value is measured by total revenue, a reflection of the price a firm's product commands and the quantity it can sell. A firm is profitable to the extent that the value it receives exceeds the total costs involved in creating its product or service. Creating value for buyers that exceeds the costs of production (i.e., margin) is a key concept used in analyzing a firm's competitive position.

Porter described two different categories of activities. First, five **primary activities**— inbound logistics, operations, outbound logistics, marketing and sales, and service— contribute to the physical creation of the product or service, its sale and transfer to

The Limitations of SWOT Analysis

SWOT analysis is a tried-and-true tool of strategic analysis. SWOT (strengths, weaknesses, opportunities, threats) analysis is used regularly in business to initially evaluate the opportunities and threats in the business environment as well as the strengths and weaknesses of a firm's internal environment. Top managers rely on SWOT to stimulate self-reflection and group discussions about how to improve their firm and position it for success.

But SWOT has its limitations. It is just a starting point for discussion. By listing the firm's attributes, managers have the raw material needed to perform more in-depth strategic analysis. However, SWOT cannot show them how to achieve a competitive advantage. They must not make SWOT analysis an end in itself, temporarily raising awareness about important issues but failing to lead to the kind of action steps necessary to enact strategic change.

Consider the ProCD example from Chapter 2, page 54. A brief SWOT analysis might include the following:

Strengths	Opportunities
First-mover advantage	Demand for electronic phone books
Low labor cost	Sudden growth in use of digital technology

Weaknesses	Threats
Inexperienced new company	Easily duplicated product
No proprietary information	Market power of incumbent firms

The combination of low production costs and an early-mover advantage in an environment where demand for CD-based phone books was growing rapidly seems to indicate that ProCD founder James Bryant had a golden opportunity. But the SWOT analysis did not reveal how to turn those strengths into a competitive advantage, nor did it highlight how rapidly the environment would change, allowing imitators to come into the market and erode his first-mover advantage. Let's look at some of the limitations of SWOT analysis.

Strengths May Not Lead to an Advantage

A firm's strengths and capabilities, no matter how unique or impressive, may not enable it to achieve a competitive advan-

Sources: Shapiro, C., & Varian, H. R. 2000. Versioning: The smart way to sell information. *Harvard Business Review,* 78(1): 99–106; and Picken, J. C., & Dess, G. G. 1997. *Mission Critical.* Burr Ridge, IL: Irwin Professional Publishing.

tage in the marketplace. It is akin to recruiting a concert pianist to join a gang of thugs—even though such an ability is rare and valuable, it hardly helps the organization attain its goals and objectives! Similarly, the skills of a highly creative product designer would offer little competitive advantage to a firm that produces low-cost commodity products. Indeed, the additional expense of hiring such an individual could erode the firm's cost advantages. If a firm builds its strategy on a capability that cannot, by itself, create or sustain competitive advantage, it is essentially a wasted use of resources. ProCD had several key strengths, but it did not translate them into lasting advantages in the marketplace.

SWOT's Focus on the External Environment Is Too Narrow

Strategists who rely on traditional definitions of their industry and competitive environment often focus their sights too narrowly on current customers, technologies, and competitors. Hence they fail to notice important changes on the periphery of their environment that may trigger the need to redefine industry boundaries and identify a whole new set of competitive relationships. Reconsider the example from Chapter 2 of *Encyclopaedia Britannica,* whose competitive position was severely eroded by a "nontraditional" competitor—CD-based encyclopedias (e.g., Microsoft *Encarta*) that could be used on home computers.

SWOT Gives a One-Shot View of a Moving Target

A key weakness of SWOT is that it is primarily a static assessment. It focuses too much of a firm's attention on one moment in time. Essentially, this is like studying a single frame of a motion picture. You may be able to identify the principal actors and learn something about the setting, but it doesn't tell you much about the plot. Competition among organizations is played out over time. As circumstances, capabilities, and strategies change, static analysis techniques do not reveal the dynamics of the competitive environment. Clearly, ProCD was unaware that its competitiveness was being eroded so quickly.

SWOT Overemphasizes a Single Dimension of Strategy

Sometimes firms become preoccupied with a single strength or a key feature of the product or service they are offering and ignore other factors needed for competitive success. For example, Food Lion, a large grocery retailer, paid a heavy price for its excessive emphasis on cost control. The resulting problems with labor and the negative publicity led to its eventual withdrawal from several markets.

SWOT analysis has much to offer, but only as a starting point. By itself, it rarely helps a firm develop competitive advantages that it can sustain over time.

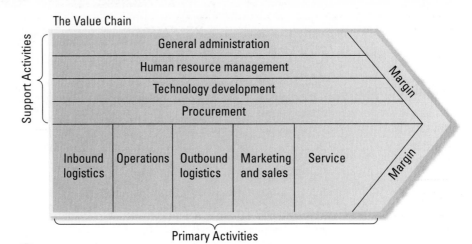

Exhibit 3.1 **The Value Chain: Primary and Support Activities**

Source: Adapted with the permission of The Free Press, a division of Simon & Schuster Adult Publishing Group, from *Competitive Advantage: Creating and Sustaining Superior Performance* by Michael E. Porter. Copyright © 1985, 1998 by Michael E. Porter. All rights reserved.

support activities
activities of the value chain that either add value by themselves or add value through important relationships with both primary activities and other support activities; including procurement, technology development, human resource management, and general administration.

the buyer, and its service after the sale. Second, **support activities**—procurement, technology development, human resource management, and general administration—either add value by themselves or add value through important relationships with both primary activities and other support activities. Exhibit 3.1 illustrates Porter's value chain.

To get the most out of value-chain analysis, you need to view the concept in its broadest context, without regard to the boundaries of your own organization. That is, place your organization within a more encompassing value chain that includes your firm's suppliers, customers, and alliance partners. Thus, in addition to thoroughly understanding how value is created within the organization, you must become aware of how value is created for other organizations that are involved in the overall supply chain or distribution channel in which your firm participates.[4]

Next, we'll describe and provide examples of each of the primary and support activities. Then, we'll provide examples of how companies add value by means of relationships among activities within the organization as well as activities outside the organization, such as those activities associated with customers and suppliers.[5]

Primary Activities

Five generic categories of primary activities are involved in competing in any industry, as shown in Exhibit 3.2. Each category is divisible into a number of distinct activities that depend on the particular industry and the firm's strategy.[6]

Inbound Logistics Inbound logistics is primarily associated with receiving, storing, and distributing inputs to the product. It includes material handling, warehousing, inventory control, vehicle scheduling, and returns to suppliers.

Just-in-time (JIT) inventory systems, for example, were designed to achieve efficient inbound logistics. In essence, Toyota epitomizes JIT inventory systems, in which parts deliveries arrive at the assembly plants only hours before they are needed. JIT systems will play a vital role in fulfilling Toyota's commitment to fill a buyer's new car order in just five days.[7] This standard is in sharp contrast to most competitors that require approximately 30 days' notice to build vehicles. Toyota's standard is three times faster than even Honda Motors, considered to be the industry's most efficient in order follow-through. The five days represent the time from the company's

Inbound Logistics	Operations	Outbound Logistics	Marketing and Sales	Service
• Location of distribution facilities to minimize shipping times. • Excellent material and inventory control systems. • Systems to reduce time to send "returns" to suppliers. • Warehouse layout and designs to increase efficiency of operations for incoming materials.	• Efficient plant operations to minimize costs. • Appropriate level of automation in manufacturing. • Quality production control systems to reduce costs and enhance quality. • Efficient plant layout and workflow design.	• Effective shipping processes to provide quick delivery and minimize damages. • Efficient finished goods warehousing processes. • Shipping of goods in large lot sizes to minimize transportation costs. • Quality material handling equipment to increase order picking.	• Highly motivated and competent sales force. • Innovative approaches to promotion and advertising. • Selection of most appropriate distribution channels. • Proper identification of customer segments and needs. • Effective pricing strategies.	• Effective use of procedures to solicit customer feedback and to act on information. • Quick response to customer needs and emergencies. • Ability to furnish replacement parts as required. • Effective management of parts and equipment inventory. • Quality of service personnel and ongoing training. • Appropriate warranty and guarantee policies.

Source: Adapted with permission of The Free Press, a division of Simon & Schuster Adult Publishing Group, from *Competitive Advantage: Creating and Sustaining Superior Performance* by Michael E. Porter. Copyright © 1985, 1998 by Michael E. Porter. All rights reserved.

Exhibit 3.2 The Value Chain: Some Factors to Consider in Assessing a Firm's Primary Activities

receipt of an order to the time the car leaves the assembly plant. Actual delivery may take longer, depending on where a customer lives. How can Toyota achieve such fast turnaround?

- Its 360 key suppliers are now linked to the company by way of computer on a virtual assembly line.
- Suppliers load parts onto trucks in the order in which they will be installed.
- Parts are stacked on trucks in the same place each time to help workers unload them quickly.
- Deliveries are required to meet a rigid schedule with as many as 12 trucks a day and no more than four hours between trucks.

Operations Operations include all activities associated with transforming inputs into the final product form, such as machining, packaging, assembly, testing, printing, and facility operations.

Creating environmentally friendly manufacturing is one way to use operations to achieve competitive advantage. Shaw Industries (now part of Berkshire Hathaway), a world-class competitor in the floor-covering industry, is well known for its concern for the environment.[8] It has been successful in reducing the expenses associated with the disposal of dangerous chemicals and other waste products from its manufacturing operations. Its environmental endeavors have multiple payoffs. Shaw has received many awards for its recycling efforts—awards that enhance its reputation.

Outbound Logistics Outbound logistics is associated with collecting, storing, and distributing the product or service to buyers. These activities include finished goods, warehousing, material handling, delivery vehicle operation, order processing, and scheduling.

Campbell Soup uses an electronic network to facilitate its continuous-replenishment program with its most progressive retailers.[9] Each morning, retailers electronically inform Campbell of their product needs and of the level of inventories in their distribution centers. Campbell uses that information to forecast future demand and to determine which products require replenishment (based on the inventory limits previously established with each retailer). Trucks leave Campbell's shipping plant that afternoon and arrive at the retailers' distribution centers the same day. The program cuts the inventories of participating retailers from about a four- to a two-weeks' supply. Campbell Soup achieved this improvement because it slashed delivery time and because it knows the inventories of key retailers and can deploy supplies when they are most needed.

The Campbell Soup example also illustrates the win–win benefits of exemplary value-chain activities. Both the supplier (Campbell) and its buyers (retailers) come out ahead. Since the retailer makes more money on Campbell products delivered through continuous replenishment, it has an incentive to carry a broader line and give the company greater shelf space. After Campbell introduced the program, sales of its products grew twice as fast through participating retailers as through all other retailers. Not surprisingly, supermarket chains love such programs. For example, Wegman's Food Markets in upstate New York has augmented its accounting system to measure and reward suppliers whose products cost the least to stock and sell.

Marketing and Sales These activities are associated with purchases of products and services by end users and the inducements used to get them to make purchases.[10] They include advertising, promotion, sales force, quoting, channel selection, channel relations, and pricing.[11]

It is not always enough to have a great product.[12] The key is to convince your channel partners that it is in their best interests not only to carry your product but also to market it in a way that is consistent with your strategy. Consider Monsanto's efforts at educating distributors to improve the value proposition of its line of Saflex® windows.[13] The products introduced in the early 1990s had a superior attribute: The window design permitted laminators to form an exceptional type of glass by sandwiching a plastic sheet interlayer between two pieces of glass. This product is not only stronger and offers better ultraviolet protection than regular glass, but also when cracked, it adheres to the plastic sheet—an excellent safety feature for both cars and homes.

Despite these benefits, Monsanto had a hard time convincing laminators and window manufacturers to carry products made with Saflex. According to Melissa Toledo, brand manager at Monsanto, "Saflex was priced at a 30 percent premium above traditional glass, and the various stages in the value chain (distributors and retailers) didn't think there would be a demand for such an expensive glass product." What was Monsanto's solution? Subsequently, it reintroduced Saflex as KeepSafe® and worked to coordinate the product's value propositions. By analyzing the experiences of all of the players in the supply chain, it was able to create marketing programs that helped each build a business aimed at selling its products. Said Toledo, "We want to know how they go about selling those types of products, what challenges they face, and what they think they need to sell our products. This helps us a lot when we try to provide them with these needs." Thus, marketing is often a key element of competitive advantage.[14]

Coach's Effective Marketing Strategy

Coach has put its leather in Lexus cars and insignias on Canon Elph digital camera cases. However, the firm has turned down offers to lend its name to hotels and athletic drinks. It calls the strategy "focus," and the firm admits that it had a rather stodgy image a decade ago. How things have changed!

Coach now has 443 stores and has made a fortune selling stylish but fairly affordable handbags. Revenue has quadrupled since the company went public in 2000. At the time, Coach bags were most often bought by women looking for well-made totes. In the year ending July 1, 2006, sales rose 23 percent to $2.1 billion, and income before interest and taxes rose 34 percent to $765 million. The company's stock also hit an all-time high of $46 in January 2007.

A key element of Coach's success is its knowledge of customers' buying habits. It spends $4 million to $5 million a year on market research, including talking to 15,000 women on the phone, in stores, or via the Internet or regular mail. Analyzing that information has enabled Coach to know that the biggest spenders visit their stores every four to five weeks. Thus, Coach rolls out its new products and store designs to keep pace with this "rhythm."

In addition to market timing, the proprietary information that it gathers provides the basis for market experiments that record the effect of changing such variables as price, features, and offers from competing brands. Based on such data, Coach quickly alters product designs, drops items that test poorly, creates new lines in a wider range of fabrics and colors, changes prices, and tailors mer-

Sources: Fass, A. 2007. Trading up. *Forbes*. January 29: 48–49; Slywotzky, A. J., & Drzik, J. 2005. Countering the biggest risk of all. *Harvard Business Review*, 83(4): 78–88; and Fass. A. 2005. Thank you for spending $300. *Forbes*. January 10: 150.

● Coach has dramatically improved its competitive position through effective marketing strategies.

chandise presentation to fit customer demographics at specific stores. Several years ago, Coach had customers preview its Hampton satchel and learned that they would willingly pay $30 more than the company had thought. In the case of another bag, Coach solicited customer feedback on the design and, learning that customers found it "tippy," responded by widening the bag's base.

Strategy Spotlight 3.2 addresses a vital aspect of marketing—marketing research. We discuss Coach, the high-end producer of leather handbags and other leather products.

At times, a firm's marketing initiatives may become overly aggressive and lead to actions that are both unethical and illegal.[15] For example:

- *Burdines.* This department store chain is under investigation for allegedly adding club memberships to its customers' credit cards without prior approval.
- *Fleet Mortgage.* This company has been accused of adding insurance fees for dental coverage and home insurance to its customers' mortgage loans without the customers' knowledge.
- *HCI Direct.* Eleven states have accused this direct-mail firm with charging for panty hose samples that customers did not order.
- *Juno Online Services.* The Federal Trade Commission brought charges against this Internet service provider for failing to provide customers with a telephone number to cancel service.

Service This primary activity includes all actions associated with providing service to enhance or maintain the value of the product, such as installation, repair, training, parts supply, and product adjustment.

Let's see how two retailers are providing exemplary customer service. At Sephora. com, a customer service representative taking a phone call from a repeat customer has instant access to what shade of lipstick she likes best. This will help the rep cross-sell by suggesting a matching shade of lip gloss. CEO Jim Wiggett expects such personalization to build loyalty and boost sales per customer. Nordstrom, the Seattle-based department store chain, goes even a step further. It offers a cyber-assist: A service rep can take control of a customer's Web browser and literally lead her to just the silk scarf that she is looking for. CEO Dan Nordstrom believes that such a capability will close enough additional purchases to pay for the $1 million investment in software.

Ritz-Carlton, the luxury hotelier and two-time winner of the prestigious Baldrige Award (1992, 1999) provides an example of exemplary customer service.[16] Its credo includes the goal of fulfilling "even the unexpected wishes and needs" of its guests. According to John Collins, Ritz-Carlton's human resource director, "If you go to a good hotel and ask for something, you get it. If you go to a great hotel, you don't even have to ask." To fulfill this goal, Ritz-Carlton uses its chainwide guest-recognition database to track guest preferences such as preferred floor and newspaper. It also gathers data from employees such as housekeepers, who track events like a guest's moving a desk to get a better view. That observation is placed on a guest recognition slip so that furniture can be arranged according to a guest's preference on his or her next visit.

Support Activities

Support activities in the value chain can be divided into four generic categories, as shown in Exhibit 3.3. As with primary activities, each category of the support activity is divisible into a number of distinct value activities that are specific to a particular industry. For example, technology development's discrete activities may include component design, feature design, field testing, process engineering, and technology selection. Similarly, procurement may be divided into activities such as qualifying new suppliers, purchasing different groups of inputs, and monitoring supplier performance.

Procurement Procurement refers to the function of purchasing inputs used in the firm's value chain, not to the purchased inputs themselves.[17] Purchased inputs include raw materials, supplies, and other consumable items as well as assets such as machinery, laboratory equipment, office equipment, and buildings.[18]

Microsoft has improved its procurement process (and the quality of its suppliers) by providing formal reviews of its suppliers. One of Microsoft's divisions has extended the review process used for employees to its outside suppliers.[19] The employee services group, which is responsible for everything from travel to 401(k) programs to the on-site library, outsources more than 60 percent of the services it provides. Unfortunately, the employee services group was not providing them with enough feedback on how well Microsoft thought they were doing. This was feedback that the suppliers wanted to get and that Microsoft wanted to give. The evaluation system that Microsoft developed helped clarify its expectations to suppliers. An executive noted: "We had one supplier—this was before the new system—that would have scored a 1.2 out of 5. After we started giving this feedback, and the supplier understood our expectations, its performance improved dramatically. Within six months, it scored a 4. If you'd asked me before we began the feedback system, I would have said that was impossible."

Technology Development Every value activity embodies technology.[20] The array of technologies employed in most firms is very broad, ranging from technologies used to prepare documents and transport goods to those embodied in processes and equipment or the product itself. Technology development related to the product and its features supports the entire value chain, while other technology development is associated with particular primary or support activities.

The 2000 merger of Allied Signal and Honeywell brought together roughly 13,000 scientists and an $870 million R&D budget that promises to lead to some innovative products and services in two major areas: performance materials and control systems. Some of the possible innovations include:

- **Performance materials.** The development of uniquely shaped fibers with very high absorption capability. When employed in the company's Fram oil filters, they capture 50 percent more particles than ordinary filters. This means that cars can travel further with fewer oil changes.
- **Control systems.** Working with six leading oil companies, Honeywell developed software using "self-learning" algorithms that predict when something might go wrong in an oil refinery before it actually does. Examples include a faulty gas valve or hazardous spillage.[21]

General Administration

- Effective planning systems to attain overall goals and objectives.
- Ability of top management to anticipate and act on key environmental trends and events.
- Ability to obtain low-cost funds for capital expenditures and working capital.
- Excellent relationships with diverse stakeholder groups.
- Ability to coordinate and integrate activities across the "value system."
- High visibility to inculcate organizational culture, reputation, and values.
- Effective information technology to integrate value-creating activities.

Human Resource Management

- Effective recruiting, development, and retention mechanisms for employees.
- Quality relations with trade unions.
- Quality work environment to maximize overall employee performance and minimize absenteeism.
- Reward and incentive programs to motivate all employees.

Technology Development

- Effective research and development activities for process and product initiatives.
- Positive collaborative relationships between R&D and other departments.
- State-of-the art facilities and equipment.
- Culture that enhances creativity and innovation.
- Excellent professional qualifications of personnel.
- Ability to meet critical deadlines.

Procurement

- Procurement of raw material inputs to optimize quality and speed, and to minimize the associated costs.
- Development of collaborative "win–win" relationships with suppliers.
- Effective procedures to purchase advertising and media services.
- Analysis and selection of alternate sources of inputs to minimize dependence on one supplier.
- Ability to make proper lease-versus-buy decisions.

Source: Reprinted with the permission of The Free Press, a division of Simon & Schuster Adult Publishing Group, from *Competitive Advantage: Creating and Sustaining Superior Performance* by Michael E. Porter. Copyright © 1985, 1998 by Michael E. Porter. All rights reserved.

Commuter Power: A New Meaning

How many Japanese commuters does it take to light a bulb? On October 16, 2006, East Japan Railway, or JR East, began testing rubber floor mats that generate electricity when walked on. The mats, which will be at several turnstiles inside Tokyo Station for two months, work by converting vibrations into energy.

Presently, they certainly don't produce much energy: just 100 milliwatts with each commuter's steps.

Source: Hall, K. 2006. Now that's commuter power. *BusinessWeek*, November 13: 10.

With about 700,000 commuters entering and leaving Tokyo Station each day, that translates to about 70 kilowatts of power—barely enough to light a 100-watt lightbulb for 10 minutes.

However, officials aren't discouraged. They claim that if the technology gets refined over the years those stomping feet could generate much more energy—providing electricity for a train station's lighting and other needs. "The mats could power machines and signs that don't require much energy," claims JR East spokesman Takaki Nemoto. "But that's far into the future."

Strategy Spotlight 3.3 addresses a unique application of technology—using rubber floor mats at a railway station to generate electricity!

Human Resource Management Human resource management consists of activities involved in the recruiting, hiring, training, development, and compensation of all types of personnel.[22] It supports both individual primary and support activities (e.g., hiring of engineers and scientists) and the entire value chain (e.g., negotiations with labor unions).

Like all great service companies, JetBlue Airways Corporation is obsessed with hiring superior employees.[23] But they found it difficult to attract college graduates to commit to careers as flight attendants. JetBlue developed a highly innovative recruitment program for flight attendants—a one-year contract that gives them a chance to travel, meet lots of people, and then decide what else they might like to do. They also introduced the idea of training a friend and employee together so that they could share a job. With such employee-friendly initiatives, JetBlue has been very successful in attracting talent.

Employees often leave a firm because they reach a plateau and begin to look for new opportunities.[24] AT&T strives to retain such people with Resource Link, an in-house temporary service that enables employees with diverse management, technical, or professional skills to market their abilities to different departments for short-term assignments. This enables professionals to broaden their experience base as well as provide a mechanism for other parts of the organization to benefit from new sources of ideas.

Jeffrey Immelt, GE's chairman, addresses the importance of effective human resource management:[25]

> Human resources has to be more than a department. GE recognized early on—50 or 60 years ago—that in a multibusiness company, the common denominators are people and culture. From an employee's first day at GE, she discovers that she's in the people-development business as much as anything else. You'll find that most good companies have the same basic HR processes that we have, but they're discrete. HR at GE is not an agenda item; it is the agenda.

Strategy Spotlight 3.4 describes how SAS Institute's innovative approach to human resources provides an insightful financial justification for the broad array of benefits it provides to employees.

General Administration General administration consists of a number of activities, including general management, planning, finance, accounting, legal and government affairs, quality management, and information systems. Administration (unlike the other support activities) typically supports the entire value chain and not individual activities.

SAS and Employee Turnover

Jeffrey Pfeffer, professor of organizational behavior at Stanford University, asked a managing partner at a San Francisco law firm about its employee turnover rate. Turnover had increased from 25 percent to 30 percent over the last few years. The law firm's solution was to increase recruitment of new employees. Pfeffer's response was, "What kind of doctor would you be if your patient was bleeding faster and faster, and your only response was to increase the rate of transfusion?"

It's not difficult to calculate the cost of a new hire, but what does it cost a firm when employees leave? Software developer SAS Institute puts the cost at around $50 million. David Russo, director of human resources at SAS, a $1.7 billion company suggested that keeping employees is not just about caring for your employees, it also provides a strong economic advantage to the company.

Consider Russo's example: Average employee turnover in the software business is 20 percent per year. SAS's turnover rate is 4 percent. SAS has 5,200 employees earning an average of $80,000 a year. The difference between turnover in the industry and turnover at SAS is 16 percent. Multiplying 16 percent by SAS's 5,200 employees at $80,000

a year, SAS has a cost savings of nearly $70 million. SAS estimates the total cost of turnover per employee to equal the employee's annual salary.

What can a firm do with an extra $70 million? SAS spends a large portion of this sum on its employees. The SAS gym, cafeteria (with pianist), on-site medical and child care, flexible work schedules, employer retirement contributions of 15 percent of an employee's pay, and a host of other family-friendly programs help keep SAS's employee turnover level well below the industry average. Even after all these perks, SAS still has money left over.

Russo's message? "This is not tree-huggery. This is money in the bank." The bottom line is it pays to retain employees.

A final note: During the 1990s go-go stock market, a privately held technology firm like SAS seemed an anachronism. For a few weeks in 1999, SAS's cofounder, Jim Goodnight (who ranks 52nd on The Forbes 400 list), considered doing an initial public offering (IPO). He was concerned about losing his top tech people to local highfliers such as Red Hat, who were doling out stock options like candy. Goodnight once said, "Morgan Stanley and Goldman Sachs called me up (about an IPO). I asked, 'What's your fee?' They said 7 percent. I said, 'Make it 0.7 percent and we'll do a deal.'" Richard Karlgaard, *Forbes'* publisher, who heard Goodnight make these comments, recalls, "Goodnight snickered at his punch line. I knew then that SAS would never go public."

Sources: Karlgaard, R. 2006. Who wants to go public? *Forbes.* October 19:31; Fisher, A. 2007. Playing for Keeps. *Fortune,* January 22:85–88; Levering, R., & Moskowitz, M. 2003. The 100 best companies to work for. *Fortune,* January 20: 127–152; and Webber, A. M. 1998. Danger: Toxic Company. *Fast Company,* November: 152–161.

Although general administration is sometimes viewed only as overhead, it can be a powerful source of competitive advantage. In a telephone operating company, for example, negotiating and maintaining ongoing relations with regulatory bodies can be among the most important activities for competitive advantage. In a similar vein, effective information systems can contribute significantly to cost position, while in some industries top management plays a vital role in dealing with important buyers.[26]

The strong and effective leadership of top executives can also make a significant contribution to an organization's success. As we discussed in Chapter 1, chief executive officers (CEOs) such as Herb Kelleher, Andrew Grove, and Jack Welch have been credited with playing critical roles in the success of Southwest Airlines, Intel, and General Electric. And Carlos Ghosn is considered one of today's top corporate leaders after his turnaround of Nissan, the Japan-based automobile manufacturer.

Information systems can also play a key role in increasing operating efficiencies and enhancing a firm's performance.[27] Consider Walgreen Co.'s introduction of Intercom Plus, a computer-based prescription management system. Linked by computer to both doctors' offices and third-party payment plans, the system automates telephone refills, store-to-store prescription transfers, and drug reordering. It also provides information on drug interactions and, coupled with revised workflows, frees up pharmacists from administrative tasks to devote more time to patient counseling.

>LO3

How value-chain analysis can help managers create value by investigating relationships among activities within the firm and between the firm and its customers and suppliers.

Interrelationships among Value-Chain Activities within and across Organizations

We have defined each of the value-chain activities separately for clarity of presentation. Managers must not ignore, however, the importance of <u>relationships</u> among value-chain activities.[28] There are two levels: (1) interrelationships among activities <u>within the firm</u> and (2) relationships among activities within the firm and <u>with other organizations</u> (e.g., customers and suppliers) that are part of the firm's expanded value chain.[29]

With regard to the first level, recall AT&T's innovative Resource Link program wherein employees who have reached their plateau may apply for temporary positions in other parts of the organization. Clearly, this program has the potential to benefit all activities within the firm's value chain because it creates opportunities for top employees to lend their expertise to all of the organization's value-creating activities.

With regard to the second level, Campbell Soup's use of electronic networks enabled it to improve the efficiency of outbound logistics.[30] However, it also helped Campbell manage the ordering of raw materials more effectively, improve its production scheduling, and help its customers better manage their inbound logistics operations.

An example of how a firm's value-creating activity can enhance customer value is provided by Ciba Specialty Chemicals (which merged with Sandoz in 1996 to form Novartis), a Swiss manufacturer of textile dyes.[31] The firm's research and development experts have created dyes that fix more readily to the fabric and therefore require less salt. How does this innovation add value for Ciba's customers? There are three ways. First, it lowers the outlays for salt. Textile companies using the new dyes are able to reduce their costs for salt by up to 2 percent of revenues, a significant drop in an industry with razor thin profit margins. Second, it reduces manufacturers' costs for water treatment. Used bathwater full of salt and unfixed dye must be treated before it is released into rivers or streams (even in low-income countries where environmental standards are typically lax). Simply put, less salt and less unfixed dye mean lower water-treatment costs. Third, the higher fixation rates of the new dyes make quality control easier, lowering the costs of rework.

We conclude this section with Strategy Spotlight 3.5. It addresses how Cardinal Health expertly integrates several value activities to create value for its suppliers and customers.

Applying the Value Chain to Service Organizations

The concepts of inbound logistics, operations, and outbound logistics suggest managing the raw materials that might be manufactured into finished products and delivered to customers. However, these three steps do not apply only to manufacturing. They correspond to any transformation process in which inputs are converted through a work process into outputs that add value. For example, accounting is a sort of transformation process that converts daily records of individual transactions into monthly financial reports. In this example, the transaction records are the inputs, accounting is the operation that adds value, and financial statements are the outputs.

What are the "operations," or transformation processes, of service organizations? These could be many different things. At times, the difference between manufacturing and service is in providing a customized solution rather than the kind of mass production that is common in manufacturing. For example, a travel agent adds value by creating an itinerary that includes transportation, accommodations, and activities that are customized to your budget and your dates of travel. A law firm renders services that are specific to a client's needs and circumstances. In both cases, the work process (operation) involves the application of specialized knowledge based on the specifics of a situation (inputs) and the outcome that the client seeks to achieve (outputs).

The application of the value chain to service organizations suggests that the value-adding process may be configured differently depending on the type of business a firm is engaged in. As the preceding discussion on support activities suggests, activities such as procurement and

Cardinal Health: Creating Value through the Extended Value Chain

Cardinal Health is a wholesale drug distributor that buys sprays, pills, and capsules from pharmaceutical companies and puts them on the shelves in pharmacies or into the hands of emergency-room nurses. Profitability is a problem in this business, because the company is caught between powerful manufacturers and cost-conscious customers. Cardinal, for example, buys pharmaceuticals from the likes of Pfizer (its biggest supplier) and sells them to the likes of CVS (its largest customer).

Cardinal responded to the profitability challenge by trying to add value for both customers and suppliers. It understood how urgent it was for one of its customer groups (hospitals) to control costs, so it began to offer services to hospital pharmacies. Rather than shipping medications to the hospitals' front door, it "followed the pill" into the hospital and right to the patient's room, offering pharmacy-management services and extending those services to customized surgical kits.

Sources: Slywotzky, A., & Wise, R. 2003. Double digit growth in no-growth times. *Fast Company,* April: 66–70; Stewart, T. 2002. Fueling drug growth during an economic drought. *Business 2.0,* May: 17–21; and Lashinsky, A. 2003. Big man in the "middle." *Fortune,* April 14: 161–162.

As the knowledgeable intermediary, Cardinal realized it could bring significant value to its suppliers (the pharmaceutical manufacturers) by providing services in drug formulation, testing, manufacturing, and packaging, freeing those companies to concentrate on the discovery of the next round of blockbuster medicines. Cardinal even used its position to develop new services for commercial pharmacies. Cardinal's drug-chain customers depend on third-party payments for most of the prescriptions it fills. It worked with a number of leading chains to develop a system called ScriptLINE that automates the reimbursement process for pharmacies and updates rates daily.

The result of this stream of innovations is a wave of growth and profits. Cardinal, with annual sales of $65 billion, has registered compound annual earnings growth of approximately 20 percent or better for the past 15 years.

The Cardinal Health story is a powerful example of extending the value chain and adding value to the many players involved—from the suppliers to the customers. The company found opportunities in an unpromising business landscape by identifying new customer needs related to the activities that surround the products it sells.

legal services are critical for adding value. Indeed, the activities that may only provide support to one company may be critical to the primary value-adding activity of another firm.

Exhibit 3.4 provides two models of how the value chain might look in service industries. In the retail industry, there are no manufacturing operations. A firm, such as Circuit City, adds value by developing expertise in the procurement of finished goods and by displaying

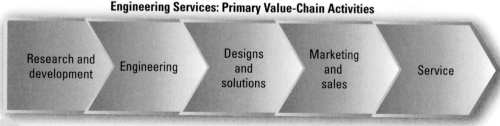

Retail: Primary Value-Chain Activities

Partnering with vendors → Purchasing goods → Managing and distributing inventory → Operating stores → Marketing and selling

Engineering Services: Primary Value-Chain Activities

Research and development → Engineering → Designs and solutions → Marketing and sales → Service

Exhibit 3.4 Some Examples of Value Chains in Service Industries

them in their stores in a way that enhances sales. Thus, the value chain makes procurement activities (i.e., partnering with vendors and purchasing goods) a primary rather than a support activity. Operations refer to the task of operating Circuit City's stores.

For an engineering services firm, research and development provides inputs, the transformation process is the engineering itself, and innovative designs and practical solutions are the outputs. Arthur D. Little, for example, is a large consulting firm with offices in 30 countries. In its technology and innovation management practice, A. D. Little strives to make the best use of the science, technology and knowledge resources available to create value for a wide range of industries and client sectors. This involves activities associated with research and development, engineering, and creating solutions as well as downstream activities such as marketing, sales, and service. These examples suggest that how the primary and support activities of a given firm are configured and deployed will often depend on industry conditions and the extent to which the company is service and/or manufacturing oriented.

Resource-Based View of the Firm

The **resource-based view (RBV) of the firm** combines two perspectives: (1) the internal analysis of phenomena within a company and (2) an external analysis of the industry and its competitive environment.[32] It goes beyond the traditional SWOT (strengths, weaknesses, opportunities, threats) analysis by integrating internal and external perspectives. The ability of a firm's resources to confer competitive advantage(s) cannot be determined without taking into consideration the broader competitive context. That is, a firm's resources must be evaluated in terms of how valuable, rare, and hard they are for competitors to duplicate. Otherwise, at best, the firm would be able to attain only competitive parity. As noted earlier in the chapter (in Strategy Spotlight 3.1), a firm's strengths and capabilities—no matter how unique or impressive—do not necessarily lead to competitive advantages in the marketplace. The criteria for whether advantages are created and whether or not they can be sustained over time will be addressed later in this section. Thus, the RBV is a very useful framework for gaining insights as to why some competitors are more profitable than others. As we will see later in the book, the RBV is also helpful in developing strategies for individual businesses and diversified firms by revealing how core competencies embedded in a firm can help it exploit new product and market opportunities.

In the two sections that follow, we will discuss the three key types of resources that firms possess (summarized in Exhibit 3.5): tangible resources, intangible resources, and organizational capabilities. Then we will address the conditions under which such assets and capabilities can enable a firm to attain a sustainable competitive advantage.[33]

It is important to note that resources by themselves typically do not yield a competitive advantage. Even if a basketball team recruited an all-star center, there would be little chance of victory if the other members of the team were continually outplayed by their opponents or if the coach's attitude was so negative that everyone, including the center, became unwilling to put forth their best efforts. And imagine how many World Series titles Joe Torre would have won as manager of the New York Yankees if none of the pitchers on his team could throw fastballs over 70 miles per hour. Although the all-star center and the baseball manager are unquestionably valuable resources, they would *not* enable the organization to attain advantages under these circumstances.

In a business context, Cardinal Health's excellent value-creating activities (e.g., logistics, drug formulation) would not be a source of competitive advantage if those activities were not integrated with other important value-creating activities such as marketing and sales. Thus, a central theme of the resource-based view of the firm is that competitive advantages are created (and sustained) through the bundling of several resources in unique combinations.

Tangible Resources

Financial	• Firm's cash account and cash equivalents. • Firm's capacity to raise equity. • Firm's borrowing capacity.
Physical	• Modern plant and facilities. • Favorable manufacturing locations. • State-of-the-art machinery and equipment.
Technological	• Trade secrets. • Innovative production processes. • Patents, copyrights, trademarks.
Organizational	• Effective strategic planning processes. • Excellent evaluation and control systems.

Intangible Resources

Human	• Experience and capabilities of employees. • Trust. • Managerial skills. • Firm-specific practices and procedures.
Innovation and creativity	• Technical and scientific skills. • Innovation capacities.
Reputation	• Brand name. • Reputation with customers for quality and reliability. • Reputation with suppliers for fairness, non–zero-sum relationships.

Organizational Capabilities

• Firm competencies or skills the firm employs to transfer inputs to outputs.
• Capacity to combine tangible and intangible resources, using organizational processes to attain desired end.

EXAMPLES:

• Outstanding customer service.
• Excellent product development capabilities.
• Innovativeness of products and services.
• Ability to hire, motivate, and retain human capital.

Source: Adapted from Barney, J. B. 1991. Firm resources and sustained competitive advantage. *Journal of Management:* 17: 101; Grant, R. M. 1991. *Contemporary Strategy Analysis:* 100–102. Cambridge England: Blackwell Business and Hitt, M. A., Ireland, R. D., & Hoskisson, R. E. 2001. *Strategic management: Competitiveness and globalization* (4th ed.). Cincinnati: South-Western College Publishing.

Types of Firm Resources

We define firm resources to include all assets, capabilities, organizational processes, information, knowledge, and so forth, controlled by a firm that enable it to develop and implement value-creating strategies.

Tangible Resources   **Tangible resources** are assets that are relatively easy to identify. They include the physical and financial assets that an organization uses to create value for its

tangible resources
organizational assets that are relatively easy to identify, including physical assets, financial resources, organizational resources, and technological resources.

customers. Among them are financial resources (e.g., a firm's cash, accounts receivable, and its ability to borrow funds); physical resources (e.g., the company's plant, equipment, and machinery as well as its proximity to customers and suppliers); organizational resources (e.g., the company's strategic planning process and its employee development, evaluation, and reward systems); and technological resources (e.g., trade secrets, patents, and copyrights).

Many firms are finding that high-tech, computerized training has dual benefits: It develops more effective employees and reduces costs at the same time. Employees at FedEx take computer-based job competency tests every 6 to 12 months.[34] The 90-minute computer-based tests identify areas of individual weakness and provide input to a computer database of employee skills—information the firm uses in promotion decisions.

intangible resources organizational assets that are difficult to identify and account for and are typically embedded in unique routines and practices, including human resources, innovation resources, and reputation resources.

Intangible Resources Much more difficult for competitors (and, for that matter, a firm's own managers) to account for or imitate are **intangible resources,** which are typically embedded in unique routines and practices that have evolved and accumulated over time. These include human resources (e.g., experience and capability of employees, trust, effectiveness of work teams, managerial skills), innovation resources (e.g., technical and scientific expertise, ideas), and reputation resources (e.g., brand name, reputation with suppliers for fairness and with customers for reliability and product quality). A firm's culture may also be a resource that provides competitive advantage.[35]

For example, you might not think that motorcycles, clothes, toys, and restaurants have much in common. Yet Harley-Davidson has entered all of these product and service markets by capitalizing on its strong brand image—a valuable intangible resource.[36] It has used that image to sell accessories, clothing, and toys, and it has licensed the Harley-Davidson Café in New York City to provide further exposure for its brand name and products.

organizational capabilities the competencies and skills that a firm employs to transform inputs into outputs.

Organizational Capabilities **Organizational capabilities** are not specific tangible or intangible assets, but rather the competencies or skills that a firm employs to transform inputs into outputs.[37] In short, they refer to an organization's capacity to deploy tangible and intangible resources over time and generally in combination, and to leverage those capabilities to bring about a desired end.[38] Examples of organizational capabilities are outstanding customer service, excellent product development capabilities, superb innovation processes, and flexibility in manufacturing processes.[39]

Gillette's capability to combine several technologies has been one of the keys to its unparalleled success in the wet-shaving industry. Key technologies include its expertise concerning the physiology of facial hair and skin, the metallurgy of blade strength and sharpness, the dynamics of a cartridge moving across skin, and the physics of a razor blade severing the hair—highly specialized areas for which Gillette has unique capabilities. Combining these technologies has helped the company to develop innovative products such as the Excel, Sensor Excel, MACH 3, and Fusion shaving systems.

In 1984, Michael Dell started Dell Inc. in a University of Texas dorm room with an investment of $1,000. By 2006, Dell had attained annual revenues of $56 billion and a net income of $3.5 billion. Dell achieved this meteoric growth by differentiating itself through the direct sales approach that it pioneered. Its user-configurable products enabled it to satisfy the diverse needs of its corporate and institutional customer base. Exhibit 3.6 summarizes the Dell recipe for its remarkable success by integrating its tangible resources, intangible resources, and organizational capabilities.

Dell has continued to maintain this competitive advantage by further strengthening its value-chain activities and interrelationships that are critical to satisfying the largest market opportunities. They achieved this by (1) implementing e-commerce direct sales and support processes that accounted for the sophisticated buying habits of the largest markets and (2) matching their operations to the purchase options by adopting flexible assembly processes, while leaving inventory management to its extensive supplier network. Dell has sustained these advantages by investing in intangible resources such as proprietary assembly methods

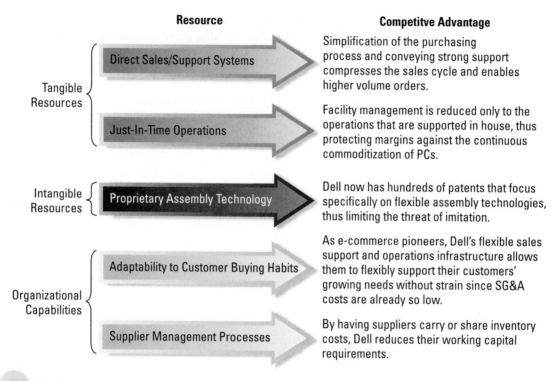

Resource

Competitve Advantage

Tangible Resources

Direct Sales/Support Systems — Simplification of the purchasing process and conveying strong support compresses the sales cycle and enables higher volume orders.

Just-In-Time Operations — Facility management is reduced only to the operations that are supported in house, thus protecting margins against the continuous commoditization of PCs.

Intangible Resources

Proprietary Assembly Technology — Dell now has hundreds of patents that focus specifically on flexible assembly technologies, thus limiting the threat of imitation.

Organizational Capabilities

Adaptability to Customer Buying Habits — As e-commerce pioneers, Dell's flexible sales support and operations infrastructure allows them to flexibly support their customers' growing needs without strain since SG&A costs are already so low.

Supplier Management Processes — By having suppliers carry or share inventory costs, Dell reduces their working capital requirements.

Exhibit 3.6 Dell's Tangible Resources, Intangible Resources, and Organizational Capabilities

and packaging configurations that help to protect against the threat of imitation. Dell recognizes that the PC is a complex product with components sourced from several different technologies and manufacturers. Thus, in working backwards from the customer's purchasing habits, Dell saw that they could build valuable solutions by organizing their resources and capabilities around the build-to-specification tastes, making both the sales and integration processes flexible, and passing on overhead expenses to their suppliers. As the PC industry has become further commoditized, Dell has been one of the few competitors that has retained solid margins. They have accomplished this by adapting their manufacturing and assembly capabilities to match the PC market's trend toward user compatibility.

Firm Resources and Sustainable Competitive Advantages

As we have mentioned, resources alone are not a basis for competitive advantages, nor are advantages sustainable over time. In some cases, a resource or capability helps a firm to increase its revenues or to lower costs but the firm derives only a temporary advantage because competitors quickly imitate or substitute for it. Many e-commerce businesses in the early 2000s have seen their profits seriously eroded because new (or existing) competitors easily duplicated their business model. For example, Priceline.com, expanded its offerings from enabling customers to place bids online for airline tickets to a wide variety of other products. However, it was easy for competitors (e.g., a consortium of major airlines) to duplicate Priceline's products and services. Ultimately, its market capitalization had plummeted roughly 98 percent from its all-time high.

For a resource to provide a firm with the potential for a sustainable competitive advantage, it must have four attributes.[40] First, the resource must be valuable in the sense that it exploits opportunities and/or neutralizes threats in the firm's environment. Second, it must be rare among the firm's current and potential competitors. Third, the resource must be difficult for competitors to imitate. Fourth, the resource must have no strategically equivalent

>LO5

The four criteria that a firm's resources must possess to maintain a sustainable advantage and how value created can be appropriated by employees and managers.

Is the resource or capability . . .	Implications
Valuable?	• Neutralize threats and exploit opportunities
Rare?	• Not many firms possess
Difficult to imitate?	• Physically unique
	• Path dependency (how accumulated over time)
	• Causal ambiguity (difficult to disentangle what it is or how it could be re-created)
	• Social complexity (trust, interpersonal relationships, culture, reputation)
Difficult to substitute?	• No equivalent strategic resources or capabilities

substitutes. These criteria are summarized in Exhibit 3.7. We will now discuss each of these criteria. Then, we will examine how Dell's competitive advantage, which seemed secure just a few years ago, has eroded.

Is the Resource Valuable?   Organizational resources can be a source of competitive advantage only when they are valuable. Resources are valuable when they enable a firm to formulate and implement strategies that improve its efficiency or effectiveness. The SWOT framework suggests that firms improve their performance only when they exploit opportunities or neutralize (or minimize) threats.

The fact that firm attributes must be valuable in order to be considered resources (as well as potential sources of competitive advantage) reveals an important complementary relationship among environmental models (e.g., SWOT and five-forces analyses) and the resource-based model. Environmental models isolate those firm attributes that exploit opportunities and/or neutralize threats. Thus, they specify what firm attributes may be considered as resources. The resource-based model then suggests what additional characteristics these resources must possess if they are to develop a sustained competitive advantage.

Is the Resource Rare?   If competitors or potential competitors also possess the same valuable resource, it is not a source of a competitive advantage because all of these firms have the capability to exploit that resource in the same way. Common strategies based on such a resource would give no one firm an advantage. For a resource to provide competitive advantages, it must be uncommon, that is, rare relative to other competitors.

This argument can apply to bundles of valuable firm resources that are used to formulate and develop strategies. Some strategies require a mix of multiple types of resources—tangible assets, intangible assets, and organizational capabilities. If a particular bundle of firm resources is not rare, then relatively large numbers of firms will be able to conceive of and implement the strategies in question. Thus, such strategies will not be a source of competitive advantage, even if the resource in question is valuable.

Can the Resource Be Imitated Easily?   Inimitability (difficulty in imitating) is a key to value creation because it constrains competition.[41] If a resource is inimitable, then any profits generated are more likely to be sustainable. Having a resource that competitors can easily copy generates only temporary value. This has important implications. Since managers often fail to apply this test, they tend to base long-term strategies on resources that are imitable. IBP (Iowa Beef Processors) became the first meatpacking company in the United States to modernize by building a set of assets (automated plants located in cattle-producing states) and capabilities (low-cost "disassembly" of carcasses) that earned returns on assets of 1.3 percent in the 1970s. By the late 1980s, however, ConAgra and Cargill had imitated these resources, and IBP's profitability fell by nearly 70 percent, to 0.4 percent.

Monster.com entered the executive recruiting market by providing, in essence, a substitute for traditional bricks-and-mortar headhunting firms. Although Monster.com's resources are rare and valuable, they are subject to imitation by new rivals—other dot-com firms. Why? There are very low entry barriers for firms wanting to try their hand at recruitment. For example, many job search dot-coms have emerged in recent years, including jobsearch.com, headhunter.com, nationjob.com, and hotjobs.com. In all, there are approximately 30,000 online job boards available to job seekers. It would be most difficult for a firm to attain a sustainable advantage in this industry.

Clearly, an advantage based on inimitability won't last forever. Competitors will eventually discover a way to copy most valuable resources. However, managers can forestall them and sustain profits for a while by developing strategies around resources that have at least one of the following four characteristics.[42]

Physical Uniqueness The first source of inimitability is physical uniqueness, which by definition is inherently difficult to copy. A beautiful resort location, mineral rights, or Pfizer's pharmaceutical patents simply cannot be imitated. Many managers believe that several of their resources may fall into this category, but on close inspection, few do.

Path Dependency A greater number of resources cannot be imitated because of what economists refer to as **path dependency.** This simply means that resources are unique and therefore scarce because of all that has happened along the path followed in their development and/or accumulation. Competitors cannot go out and buy these resources quickly and easily; they must be built up over time in ways that are difficult to accelerate.

path dependency a characteristic of resources that is developed and/or accumulated through a unique series of events.

The Gerber Products Co. brand name for baby food is an example of a resource that is potentially inimitable. Re-creating Gerber's brand loyalty would be a time-consuming process that competitors could not expedite, even with expensive marketing campaigns. Similarly, the loyalty and trust that Southwest Airlines employees feel toward their firm and its cofounder, Herb Kelleher, are resources that have been built up over a long period of time. Also, a crash R&D program generally cannot replicate a successful technology when research findings cumulate. Clearly, these path-dependent conditions build protection for the original resource. The benefits from experience and learning through trial and error cannot be duplicated overnight.

Causal Ambiguity The third source of inimitability is termed **causal ambiguity.** This means that would-be competitors may be thwarted because it is impossible to disentangle the causes (or possible explanations) of either what the valuable resource is or how it can be re-created. What is the root of 3M's innovation process? You can study it and draw up a list of possible factors. But it is a complex, unfolding (or folding) process that is hard to understand and would be hard to imitate.

casual ambiguity a characteristic of a firm's resources that is costly to imitate because a competitor cannot determine what the resource is and/or how it can be re-created.

Often, causally ambiguous resources are organizational capabilities, involving a complex web of social interactions that may even depend on particular individuals. When Continental and United tried to mimic the successful low-cost strategy of Southwest Airlines, the planes, routes, and fast gate turnarounds were not the most difficult aspects for them to copy. Those were all rather easy to observe and, at least in principle, easy to duplicate. However, they could not replicate Southwest's culture of fun, family, frugality, and focus since no one can clearly specify exactly what that culture is or how it came to be.

Social Complexity A firm's resources may be imperfectly inimitable because they reflect a high level of **social complexity.** Such phenomena are typically beyond the ability of firms to systematically manage or influence. When competitive advantages are based on social complexity, it is difficult for other firms to imitate them.

social complexity a characteristic of a firm's resources that is costly to imitate because the social engineering required is beyond the capability of competitors, including interpersonal relations among managers, organizational culture, and reputation with suppliers and customers.

A wide variety of firm resources may be considered socially complex. Examples include interpersonal relations among the managers in a firm, its culture, and its reputation with its suppliers and customers. In many of these cases, it is easy to specify how these socially complex resources add value to a firm. Hence, there is little or no causal ambiguity surrounding the link between them and competitive advantage. But an understanding that certain firm attributes, such as quality relations among managers, can improve a firm's efficiency does not necessarily lead to systematic efforts to imitate them. Such social engineering efforts are beyond the capabilities of most firms.

Although complex physical technology is not included in this category of sources of imperfect inimitability, the exploitation of physical technology in a firm typically involves the use of socially complex resources. That is, several firms may possess the same physical technology, but only one of them may have the social relations, culture, group norms, and so on to fully exploit the technology in implementing its strategies. If such complex social resources are not subject to imitation (and assuming they are valuable and rare and no substitutes exist), this firm may obtain a sustained competitive advantage from exploiting its physical technology more effectively than other firms.

Are Substitutes Readily Available?   The fourth requirement for a firm resource to be a source of sustainable competitive advantage is that there must be no strategically equivalent valuable resources that are themselves not rare or inimitable. Two valuable firm resources (or two bundles of resources) are strategically equivalent when each one can be exploited separately to implement the same strategies.

Substitutability may take at least two forms. First, though it may be impossible for a firm to imitate exactly another firm's resource, it may be able to substitute a similar resource that enables it to develop and implement the same strategy. Clearly, a firm seeking to imitate another firm's high-quality top management team would be unable to copy the team exactly. However, it might be able to develop its own unique management team. Though these two teams would have different ages, functional backgrounds, experience, and so on, they could be strategically equivalent and thus substitutes for one another.

● Dell's competitive position in personal computers—including desktops and laptops—has eroded in recent years.

Second, very different firm resources can become strategic substitutes. For example, Internet booksellers such as Amazon.com compete as substitutes for bricks-and-mortar booksellers such as B. Dalton. The result is that resources such as premier retail locations become less valuable. In a similar vein, several pharmaceutical firms have seen the value of patent protection erode in the face of new drugs that are based on different production processes and act in different ways, but can be used in similar treatment regimes. The coming years will likely see even more radical change in the pharmaceutical industry as the substitution of genetic therapies eliminates certain uses of chemotherapy.[43]

To recap this section, recall that resources and capabilities must be rare and valuable as well as difficult to imitate or substitute in order for a firm to attain competitive advantages that are sustainable over time.[44] Exhibit 3.8 illustrates the relationship among the four criteria of sustainability and shows the competitive implications.

In firms represented by the first row of Exhibit 3.8, managers are in a difficult situation. When their resources and capabilities do not meet any of the four criteria, it would be difficult to develop any type of competitive advantage, in the short or long term. The resources and capabilities they possess enable the firm neither to exploit environmental opportunities nor neutralize environmental threats. In the second and third rows, firms have resources and capabilities that are valuable as well as rare, respectively. However, in both cases the resources and capabilities are not difficult for competitors to imitate or substitute. Here, the firms could attain some level of competitive parity. They could perform on par with equally endowed rivals or attain a temporary competitive advantage. But their advantages would be easy for competitors

Is a resource or capability . . .				
Valuable?	Rare?	Difficult to Imitate?	Without Substitutes?	Implications for Competitiveness?
No	No	No	No	Competitive disadvantage
Yes	No	No	No	Competitive parity
Yes	Yes	No	No	Temporary competitive advantage
Yes	Yes	Yes	Yes	Sustainable competitive advantage

Source: Adapted from Barney, J. B. 1991. Firm resources and sustained competitive advantage. *Journal of Management*, 17: 99–120.

to match. It is only in the fourth row, where all four criteria are satisfied, that competitive advantages can be sustained over time.

Revisiting Dell   For many years, it looked as if Dell's competitive advantage over its rivals would be sustainable for a very long period of time. However, by early 2007, Dell was falling behind its rivals in market share. This led to a significant decline in its stock price—followed by a complete shake-up of the top management team. But what led to Dell's competitive decline in the first place?[45]

- Dell had become so focused on cost that it failed to pay attention to the design of the brand. Customers increasingly began to see the product as a commodity.
- Much of the growth in the PC industry today is in laptops. Customers demand a sleeker, better-designed machine instead of just the cheapest laptop. Also, they often want to see the laptop before they buy it.
- When Dell outsourced its customer service function to foreign locations, it led to a decline in customer support. This eroded Dell's brand value.
- Dell's efforts to replicate its made-to-order, no middleman strategy to other products such as printers and storage devices proved to be a failure because customers saw very little need for customization of these products. Meanwhile, rivals such as Hewlett-Packard have been improving their product design and reducing their costs. Thus, they now have cost parity with Dell, while enjoying a better brand image and the support of an extensive dealer network.

The Generation and Distribution of a Firm's Profits: Extending the Resource-Based View of the Firm

Many scholars would agree that the resource-based view of the firm has been useful in determining when firms will create competitive advantages and enjoy high levels of profitability. However, it has not been developed to address how a firm's profits (often referred to as "rents" by economists) will be distributed to a firm's management and employees.[46] This becomes an important issue because firms may be successful in creating competitive advantages that can be sustainable for a period of time but much of the profits can be retained (or "appropriated") by its employees and managers instead of flowing to the owners of the firm (i.e., the stockholders).*

Consider Viewpoint DataLabs International, a Salt Lake City–based company that makes sophisticated three-dimensional models and textures for film production houses,

---

* Economists define rents as profits (or prices) in excess of what is required to provide a normal return.

video games, and car manufacturers. This example will help to show how employees are often able to obtain (or "appropriate") a high proportion of a firm's profits:

> Walter Noot, head of production, was having trouble keeping his highly skilled Generation X employees happy with their compensation. Each time one of them was lured away for more money, everyone would want a raise. "We were having to give out raises every six months—30 to 40 percent—then six months later they'd expect the same. It was a big struggle to keep people happy."[47]

At Viewpoint DataLabs, it is apparent that much of the profits are being generated by the highly skilled professionals working together on a variety of projects. They are able to exercise their power by successfully demanding more financial compensation. In part, management has responded favorably because they are united in their demands, and their work involves a certain amount of social complexity and causal ambiguity—given the complex, coordinated efforts that their work entails.

Four factors help explain the extent to which employees and managers will be able to obtain a proportionately high level of the profits that they generate:[48]

- ***Employee Bargaining Power.*** If employees are vital to forming a firm's unique capability, they will earn disproportionately high wages. For example, marketing professionals may have access to valuable information that helps them to understand the intricacies of customer demands and expectations, or engineers may understand unique technical aspects of the products or services. Additionally, in some industries such as consulting, advertising, and tax preparation, clients tend to be very loyal to individual professionals employed by the firm, instead of to the firm itself. This enables them to "take the clients with them" if they leave. This enhances their bargaining power.
- ***Employee Replacement Cost.*** If employees' skills are idiosyncratic and rare (a source of resource-based advantages), they should have high bargaining power based on the high cost required by the firm to replace them. For example, Raymond Ozzie, the software designer who was critical in the development of Lotus Notes, was able to dictate the terms under which IBM acquired Lotus.
- ***Employee Exit Costs.*** This factor may tend to reduce an employee's bargaining power. An individual may face high personal costs when leaving the organization. Thus, that individual's threat of leaving may not be credible. In addition, some of an employee's expertise may be firm-specific, that is, of limited value to other firms. A related factor is that of causal ambiguity, which would make it difficult for the employee to explain his or her specific contribution to a given project. Thus, a rival firm might be less likely to pay a high wage premium since it would be unsure of the employee's unique contribution.
- ***Manager Bargaining Power.*** Like other members of the firm, managers' power would be based on how well they create resource-based advantages. They are generally charged with creating value through the process of organizing, coordinating, and leveraging employees as well as other forms of capital such as plant, equipment, and financial capital (issues that we will address in more detail in Chapter 4). Such activities provide managers with sources of information that may not be readily available to others. Thus, although managers may not know as much about the specific nature of customers and technologies, they are in a position to have a more thorough, integrated understanding of the total operation.

Chapter 9 addresses the conditions under which top-level managers (such as CEOs) of large corporations have been, at times, able to obtain levels of total compensation that would appear to be significantly disproportionate to their contributions to wealth generation as well as to top executives in peer organizations. Here, corporate governance becomes a critical control mechanism. For example, William Esrey and Ronald T. LeMay (the former two top executives at

Sprint Corporation) were able to earn more than $130 million in stock options primarily because of "cozy" relationships with members of their board of directors, who tended to approve with little debate huge compensation packages.[49] Such diversion of profits from the owners of the business to top management is far less likely when the board does not consist of a high proportion of the firm's management and board members are truly independent outsiders (i.e., they do not have close ties to management). In general, given the external market for top talent, the level of compensation that executives receive is based on factors similar to the ones just discussed that determine the level of their bargaining power.[50]

Evaluating Firm Performance: Two Approaches

This section addresses two approaches to use when evaluating a firm's performance. The first is financial ratio analysis, which, generally speaking, identifies how a firm is performing according to its balance sheet, income statement, and market valuation. As we will discuss, when performing a financial ratio analysis, you must take into account the firm's performance from a historical perspective (not just at one point in time) as well as how it compares with both industry norms and key competitors.[51]

The second perspective takes a broader stakeholder view. Firms must satisfy a broad range of stakeholders, including employees, customers, and owners, to ensure their long-term viability. Central to our discussion will be a well-known approach—the balanced scorecard—that has been popularized by Robert Kaplan and David Norton.[52]

Financial Ratio Analysis

The beginning point in analyzing the financial position of a firm is to compute and analyze five different types of financial ratios:

- Short-term solvency or liquidity
- Long-term solvency measures
- Asset management (or turnover)
- Profitability
- Market value

Exhibit 3.9 summarizes each of these five ratios.

The Appendix to Chapter 13 (the Case Analysis chapter) provides detailed definitions for and discussions of each of these types of ratios as well as examples of how each is calculated. Refer to pages 470 to 484.

A meaningful ratio analysis must go beyond the calculation and interpretation of financial ratios.[53] It must include an analysis of how ratios change over time as well as how they are interrelated. For example, a firm that takes on too much long-term debt to finance operations will see an immediate impact on its indicators of long-term financial leverage. The additional debt will also have a negative impact on the firm's short-term liquidity ratio (i.e., current and quick ratios) since the firm must pay interest and principal on the additional debt each year until it is retired. Additionally, the interest expenses must be deducted from revenues, reducing the firm's profitability.

>LO6
The usefulness of financial ratio analysis, its inherent limitations, and how to make meaningful comparisons of performance across firms.

A firm's financial position should not be analyzed in isolation. Important reference points are needed. We will address some issues that must be taken into account to make financial analysis more meaningful: historical comparisons, comparisons with industry norms, and comparisons with key competitors.

Historical Comparisons   When you evaluate a firm's financial performance, it is very useful to compare its financial position over time. This provides a means of evaluating trends. For example, Microsoft reported revenues of $44.3 billion and net income of $12.6 billion in 2006. Almost all firms—except a few of the largest and most profitable companies

I. Short-term solvency, or liquidity, ratios

$$\text{Current ratio} = \frac{\text{Current assets}}{\text{Current liabilities}}$$

$$\text{Quick ratio} = \frac{\text{Current assets} - \text{Inventory}}{\text{Current liabilities}}$$

$$\text{Cash ratio} = \frac{\text{Cash}}{\text{Current liabilities}}$$

II. Long-term solvency, or financial leverage, ratios

$$\text{Total debt ratio} = \frac{\text{Total assets} - \text{Total equity}}{\text{Total assets}}$$

$$\text{Debt-equity ratio} = \text{Total debt/Total equity}$$

$$\text{Equity multiplier} = \text{Total assets/Total equity}$$

$$\text{Times interest earned ratio} = \frac{\text{EBIT}}{\text{Interest}}$$

$$\text{Cash coverage ratio} = \frac{\text{EBIT} + \text{Depreciation}}{\text{Interest}}$$

III. Asset utilization, or turnover, ratios

$$\text{Inventory turnover} = \frac{\text{Cost of goods sold}}{\text{Inventory}}$$

$$\text{Days' sales in inventory} = \frac{365 \text{ days}}{\text{Inventory turnover}}$$

$$\text{Receivables turnover} = \frac{\text{Sales}}{\text{Accounts receivable}}$$

$$\text{Days' sales in receivables} = \frac{365 \text{ days}}{\text{Receivables turnover}}$$

$$\text{Total asset turnover} = \frac{\text{Sales}}{\text{Total assets}}$$

$$\text{Capital intensity} = \frac{\text{Total assets}}{\text{Sales}}$$

IV. Profitability ratios

$$\text{Profit margin} = \frac{\text{Net income}}{\text{Sales}}$$

$$\text{Return on assets (ROA)} = \frac{\text{Net income}}{\text{Total assets}}$$

$$\text{Return on equity (ROE)} = \frac{\text{Net income}}{\text{Total equity}}$$

$$\text{ROE} = \frac{\text{Net income}}{\text{Sales}} \times \frac{\text{Sales}}{\text{Assets}} \times \frac{\text{Assets}}{\text{Equity}}$$

V. Market value ratios

$$\text{Price-earnings ratio} = \frac{\text{Price per share}}{\text{Earnings per share}}$$

$$\text{Market-to-book ratio} = \frac{\text{Market value per share}}{\text{Book value per share}}$$

Exhibit 3.9 A Summary of Five Types of Financial Ratios.

in the world—would be very happy with such financial success. These figures reflect an annual growth in revenue and net income of 10 percent and 24 percent, respectively for the 2004 to 2006 time period. Clearly, had Microsoft's revenues and net income in 2006 been $35 billion and $10 billion, respectively, it would still be a very large and highly profitable enterprise. However, such performance would have resulted in significant damage to Microsoft's market valuation and reputation as well as to the careers of many of its executives. Exhibit 3.10 illustrates a 10-year period of return on sales (ROS) for a hypothetical company. As indicated by the dotted trend lines, the rate of growth (or decline) differs substantially over time periods.

Comparison with Industry Norms   When you are evaluating a firm's financial performance, remember also to compare it with industry norms. A firm's current ratio or profitability may appear impressive at first glance. However, it may pale when compared with industry standards or norms.

By comparing your firm with all other firms in your industry, you can assess relative performance. Banks often use such comparisons when evaluating a firm's creditworthiness. Exhibit 3.11 includes a variety of financial ratios for three industries: semiconductors, grocery stores, and skilled-nursing facilities. Why is there such variation among the financial ratios for these three industries? There are several reasons. With regard to the collection period, grocery stores operate mostly on a cash basis, hence a very short collection period. Semiconductor manufacturers sell their output to other manufacturers (e.g., computer makers) on terms such as 2/15 net 45, which means they give a 2 percent discount on bills paid within

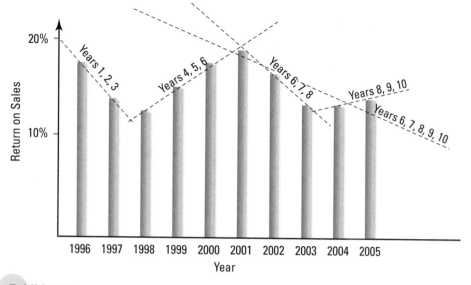

Exhibit 3.10 Historical Trends: Return on Sales (ROS) for a Hypothetical Company

15 days and start charging interest after 45 days. Skilled-nursing facilities would also have a longer collection period than grocery stores because they typically rely on payments from insurance companies.

The industry norms for return on sales also highlight some differences among these industries. Grocers, with very slim margins, have a lower return on sales than either skilled-nursing facilities or semiconductor manufacturers. But how might we explain the differences between skilled-nursing facilities and semiconductor manufacturers? Health care facilities, in general, are limited in their pricing structures by Medicare/Medicaid regulations and by insurance reimbursement limits, but semiconductor producers have pricing structures determined by the market. If their products have superior performance, semiconductor manufacturers can charge premium prices.

Comparison with Key Competitors   Recall from Chapter 2 that firms with similar strategies are members of a strategic group in an industry. Furthermore, competition tends to be more intense among competitors within groups than across groups. Thus, you can gain valuable insights into a firm's financial and competitive position if you make comparisons between a firm and its most direct rivals. Consider Procter & Gamble's ill-fated efforts to enter

Exhibit 3.11

How Financial Ratios Differ across Industries

Financial Ratio	Semiconductors	Grocery Stores	Skilled-Nursing Facilities
Quick ratio (times)	1.9	0.5	1.1
Current ratio (times)	4.0	1.6	1.6
Total liabilities to net worth (%)	30.7	92.0	163.5
Collection period (days)	49.6	2.9	31.2
Assets to sales (%)	187.8	20.2	101.6
Return on sales (%)	5.8	0.8	1.6

Source: Dun & Bradstreet. *Industry Norms and Key Business Ratios, 2003–2004*. One Year Edition, SIC #2000-3999 (Semiconductors); SIC #5200-5499 (Grocery Stores); SIC #6100-8999 (Skilled-Nursing Facilities). New York: Dun & Bradstreet Credit Services.

Exhibit 3.12

Comparison of Procter &
Gamble's and Key
Competitors' Drug
Revenues and R&D
Expenditures

Company (or division)	Sales* ($ billions)	R&D Budget ($ billions)
P&G Drug Division	$ 0.8	$0.38
Bristol-Myers Squibb	20.2	1.80
Pfizer	27.4	4.00
Merck	32.7	2.10

Source: Berner, R. 2000. Procter & Gamble: Just say no to drugs. *BusinessWeek,*
October 9: 128; data courtesy of Lehman Brothers and Procter & Gamble.

*Data: Lehman Brothers, Procter & Gamble Co.

the highly profitable pharmaceutical industry. Although P&G is a giant in consumer products, its efforts over two decades have produced nominal profits at best. In 1999 P&G spent $380 million on R&D in drugs—22 percent of its total corporate R&D budget. However, its drug unit produced only 2 percent of the company's $40 billion sales. Why? While $380 million is hardly a trivial amount of capital, its key competitors dwarf P&G. Consider the drug revenues and R&D budgets of P&G compared to its main rivals as shown in Exhibit 3.12. *BusinessWeek*'s take on P&G's chances in an article entitled "Just Say No to Drugs" was this: "Don't bet on it. P&G may be a giant in detergent and toothpaste, but the consumer-products maker is simply outclassed by the competition."[54]

Integrating Financial Analysis and Stakeholder Perspectives: The Balanced Scorecard

It is useful to see how a firm is performing over time in terms of the several ratios. However, such traditional approaches to performance assessments can be a double-edged sword.[55] Many important transactions that managers make—investments in research and development, employee training and development, and, advertising and promotion of key brands—may greatly expand a firm's market potential and create significant long-term shareholder value. But such critical investments are not reflected positively in short-term financial reports. Why? Because financial reports typically measure expenses, not the value created. Thus, managers may be penalized for spending money in the short term to improve their firm's long-term competitive viability!

Now consider the other side of the coin. A manager may be destroying the firm's future value by operating in a way that makes customers dissatisfied, depletes the firm's stock of good products coming out of R&D, or damages the morale of valued employees. Such budget cuts, however, may lead to very good short-term financials. The manager may look good in the short run and even receive credit for improving the firm's performance. In essence, such a manager has mastered "denominator management," whereby decreasing investments makes the return on investment (ROI) ratio larger, even though the actual return remains constant or shrinks.

> **>LO7**
>
> The value of the "balanced scorecard" in recognizing how the interests of a variety of stakeholders can be interrelated.

balanced scorecard
a method of evaluating a firm's performance using performance measures from the customers', internal, innovation and learning, and financial perspectives.

The Balanced Scorecard: Description and Benefits   To provide a meaningful integration of the many issues that come into evaluating a firm's performance, Kaplan and Norton developed a **"balanced scorecard."**[56] This is a set of measures that provide top managers with a fast but comprehensive view of the business. In a nutshell, it includes financial measures that reflect the results of actions already taken, but it complements these indicators with operational measures of customer satisfaction, internal processes, and the organization's innovation and improvement activities—operational measures that drive future financial performance.

Exhibit 3.13
The Balanced
Scorecard's Four
Perspectives

- How do customers see us? (customer perspective)
- What must we excel at? (internal business perspective)
- Can we continue to improve and create value? (innovation and learning perspective)
- How do we look to shareholders? (financial perspective)

The balanced scorecard enables managers to consider their business from four key perspectives: customer, internal, innovation and learning, and financial. These are briefly described in Exhibit 3.13.

Customer Perspective Clearly, how a company is performing from its customers' perspective is a top priority for management. The balanced scorecard requires that managers translate their general mission statements on customer service into specific measures that reflect the factors that really matter to customers. For the balanced scorecard to work, managers must articulate goals for four key categories of customer concerns: time, quality, performance and service, and cost. For example, lead time may be measured as the time from the company's receipt of an order to the time it actually delivers the product or service to the customer.

Internal Business Perspective Although customer-based measures are important, they must be translated into indicators of what the firm must do internally to meet customers' expectations. Excellent customer performance results from processes, decisions, and actions that occur throughout organizations in a coordinated fashion, and managers must focus on those critical internal operations that enable them to satisfy customer needs. The internal measures should reflect business processes that have the greatest impact on customer satisfaction. These include factors that affect cycle time, quality, employee skills, and productivity. Firms also must identify and measure the key resources and capabilities they need to ensure continued strategic success.

Innovation and Learning Perspective Given the rapid rate of markets, technologies, and global competition, the criteria for success are constantly changing. To survive and prosper, managers must make frequent changes to existing products and services as well as introduce entirely new products with expanded capabilities. A firm's ability to improve, innovate, and learn is tied directly to its value. Simply put, only by developing new products and services, creating greater value for customers, and increasing operating efficiencies can a company penetrate new markets, increase revenues and margins, and enhance shareholder value. A firm's ability to do well from an innovation and learning perspective is more dependent on its intangible than tangible assets. Three categories of intangible assets are critically important: human capital (skills, talent, and knowledge), information capital (information systems, networks), and organization capital (culture, leadership).

Financial Perspective Measures of financial performance indicate whether the company's strategy, implementation, and execution are indeed contributing to bottom-line improvement. Typical financial goals include profitability, growth, and shareholder value. Periodic financial statements remind managers that improved quality, response time, productivity, and innovative products benefit the firm only when they result in improved sales, increased market share, reduced operating expenses, or higher asset turnover.[57]

We now provide an example that illustrates the causal relationships among the multiple perspectives in the model. Sears, the huge retailer, found a strong causal relationship between employee attitudes, customer attitudes, and financial outcomes.[58] Through an ongoing study, Sears developed (and continues to refine) what it calls its total performance indicators, or TPI—a set of indicators that shows how well the company is doing with customers, employees, and investors. Sears's quantitative model has shown that a 5.0 percent improvement in employee attitudes leads to a 1.3 percent improvement in customer satisfaction, which in turn will drive a 0.5 percent improvement in revenue. Thus, if a single store improved its employee attitude by 5.0 percent on a survey scale, Sears could predict with confidence that if the revenue growth in the district as a whole were 5.0 percent, the revenue growth in this particular store would be 5.5 percent. Interestingly, Sears's managers consider such numbers as rigorous as any others that they work with every year. The company's accounting firm audits management as closely as it audits the financial statements.

A key implication of the balanced scorecard is that managers do not need to look at their job as primarily balancing stakeholder demands. They need to avoid the following mind-set: "How many units in employee satisfaction do I have to give up to get some additional units of customer satisfaction or profits?" Instead, when done properly, the balanced scorecard provides a win–win approach—a means of simultaneously increasing satisfaction among a wide variety of organizational stakeholders, including employees (at all levels), customers, and stockholders.

Limitations and Potential Downsides of the Balanced Scorecard   There is general agreement that there is nothing inherently wrong with the concept of the balanced scorecard.[59] The key limitation is that some executives may view it as a "quick fix" that can be easily installed in their organization. However, implementing a balanced metrics system is an evolutionary process. It is not a one-time task that can be quickly checked off as "completed." If managers do not recognize this from the beginning and fail to commit to it long term, the organization will be disappointed with the results. Poor execution becomes the cause of such performance outcomes. And organizational scorecards must be aligned with individuals' scorecards to turn the balanced scorecards into a powerful tool for sustained organizational performance.

In a recent study of 50 Canadian medium-size and large organizations, the number of users expressing skepticism about scorecard performance was much greater than the number claiming positive results. However, the overwhelming perspective was that balanced scorecards can be worthwhile in clarifying an organization's strategy, and if this can be accomplished, better results will follow. A few companies stated categorically that scorecards have improved their firm's financial results. For example, one respondent claimed that, "We did not meet our financial goals previously, but since implementing our balanced scorecard, we have now met our goals three years running."

On the other hand, a greater number of respondents agreed with the statement, "Balanced scorecards don't really work." Some representative comments included: "It became just a number-crunching exercise by accountants after the first year," "It is just the latest management fad and is already dropping lower on management's list of priorities as all fads eventually do," and, "If scorecards are supposed to be a measurement tool, why is it so hard to measure their results?" Few would argue that there is much work to do before scorecards can become a viable framework for the measurement of sustained strategic performance.

Problems often occur in the balanced scorecard implementation efforts when there is an insufficient commitment to learning and the inclusion of employees' personal ambitions. If there is not a set of rules for employees that address continuous process improvement and the personal improvement of individual employees, there will be limited employee buy-in and insufficient cultural change. Thus, many improvements may be temporary and superficial. Often, scorecards that failed to attain alignment and improvements

---

* Building on the concepts that are the foundation of the balanced scorecard approach, Kaplan and Norton have recently developed a useful tool called the strategy map. Strategy maps show the cause and effect links by which specific improvements in different areas lead to a desired outcome. Strategy maps also help employees see how their jobs are related to the overall objectives of the organization. They also help us understand how an organization can convert its assets—both tangible and intangible—into tangible outcomes. Refer to Kaplan, R. S., & Norton, D. P. 2000. Having trouble with your strategy? Then map it. *Harvard Business Review*, 78(10): 167–176.

Exhibit 3.14
Potential Limitations of the Balanced Scorecard

Most agree that the balanced scorecard concept is a useful and an appropriate management tool. However, there are many design and implementation issues that may short circuit its value, including the following:

- **Lack of a Clear Strategy.** A scorecard can be developed without the aid of a strategy. However, it then becomes a key performance indicator or stakeholder system, lacking in many of the attributes offered from a true balanced scorecard.
- **Limited or Ineffective Executive Sponsorship.** Although training and education is important, without tenacious leadership and support of a scorecard project, the effort is most likely doomed.
- **Too Much Emphasis on Financial Measures Rather than Nonfinancial Measures.** This leads to measures that do not connect to the drivers of the business and are not relevant to performance improvement.
- **Poor Data on Actual Performance.** This can negate most of the effort invested in defining performance measures because a company can't monitor actual changes in results from changes in behavior.
- **Inappropriate Links of Scorecard Measures to Compensation.** Although this can focus managerial and employee attention, exercising it too soon can produce many unintended side effects such as dysfunctional decision making by managers looking to cash in.
- **Inconsistent or Inappropriate Terminology.** Everyone must speak the same language if measurement is to be used to guide change within an organization. Translating strategy into measures becomes even more difficult if everyone cannot agree on (or understand) the same language and terminology.

Sources: Angel, R., & Rampersad, H. 2005. Do scorecards add up? *Camagazine.com*. May: np; and Niven, P. 2002. *Balanced scorecard step by step: Maximizing performance and maintaining results*. New York: John Wiley & Sons.

dissipated very quickly. And, in many cases, management's efforts to improve performance were seen as divisive. That is, it was viewed by employees as aimed at benefiting senior management compensation which fostered a "what's in it for me?" attitude among employees. Exhibit 3.14 summarizes some of the primary limitations and potential downsides of the balanced scorecard.

Reflecting on Career Implications . . .

- *The Value Chain:* Carefully analyze where you can add value in your firm's value chain. How might your firm's support activities (e.g., information technology, human resource practices) help you accomplish your assigned tasks more effectively?
- *The Value Chain:* Consider important relationships among activities both within your firm as well as between your firm and its suppliers, customers, and alliance partners.
- *Resource Based View of the Firm:* Are your skills and talents rare, valuable, difficult to imitate, and have few substitutes? If so, you are in a better position to add value for your firm—and earn rewards and incentives. How can your skills and talents be enhanced to help satisfy these criteria to a greater extent? More training? Change positions within the firm? Consider career options at other organizations?
- *Balanced Scorecard:* In your decision making, strive to "balance" the four perspectives: customer, internal business, innovation and learning, and financial. Do not focus too much on short-term profits. Do your personal career goals provide opportunities to develop your skills in all four directions?

Summary

In the traditional approaches to assessing a firm's internal environment, the primary goal of managers would be to determine their firm's relative strengths and weaknesses. Such is the role of SWOT analysis, wherein managers analyze their firm's strengths and weaknesses as well as the opportunities and threats in the external environment. In this chapter, we discussed why this may be a good starting point but hardly the best approach to take in performing a sound analysis. There are many limitations to SWOT analysis, including its static perspective, its potential to overemphasize a single dimension of a firm's strategy, and the likelihood that a firm's strengths do not necessarily help the firm create value or competitive advantages.

We identified two frameworks that serve to complement SWOT analysis in assessing a firm's internal environment: value-chain analysis and the resource-based view of the firm. In conducting a value-chain analysis, first divide the firm into a series of value-creating activities. These include primary activities such as inbound logistics, operations, and service as well as support activities such as procurement and human resources management. Then analyze how each activity adds value as well as how *interrelationships* among value activities in the firm and among the firm and its customers and suppliers add value. Thus, instead of merely determining a firm's strengths and weaknesses per se, you analyze them in the overall context of the firm and its relationships with customers and suppliers—the value system.

The resource-based view of the firm considers the firm as a bundle of resources: tangible resources, intangible resources, and organizational capabilities. Competitive advantages that are sustainable over time generally arise from the creation of bundles of resources and capabilities. For advantages to be sustainable, four criteria must be satisfied: value, rarity, difficulty in imitation, and difficulty in substitution. Such an evaluation requires a sound knowledge of the competitive context in which the firm exists. The owners of a business may not capture all of the value created by the firm. The appropriation of value created by a firm between the owners and employees is determined by four factors: employee bargaining power, replacement cost, employee exit costs, and manager bargaining power.

An internal analysis of the firm would not be complete unless you evaluate its performance and make the appropriate comparisons. Determining a firm's performance requires an analysis of its financial situation as well as a review of how well it is satisfying a broad range of stakeholders, including customers, employees, and stockholders. We discussed the concept of the balanced scorecard, in which four perspectives must be addressed: customer, internal business, innovation and learning, and financial. Central to this concept is the idea that the interests of various stakeholders can be interrelated. We provide examples of how indicators of employee satisfaction lead to higher levels of customer satisfaction, which in turn lead to higher levels of financial performance. Thus, improving a firm's performance does not need to involve making trade-offs among different stakeholders. Assessing the firm's performance is also more useful if it is evaluated in terms of how it changes over time, compares with industry norms, and compares with key competitors.

In the Appendix to Chapter 3, we discuss how Internet and digital technologies have created new opportunities for firms to add value. Four value-adding activities that have been enhanced by Internet capabilities are search, evaluation, problem solving, and transaction. These four activities are supported by three different types of content that Internet businesses often use—customer feedback, expertise, and entertainment programming. Seven business models have been identified that are proving successful for use by Internet firms. These include commission, advertising, markup, production, referral, subscription, and fee-for-service–based models. Firms also are finding that combinations of these business models can contribute to greater success.

Summary Review Questions

1. SWOT analysis is a technique to analyze the internal and external environment of a firm. What are its advantages and disadvantages?

2. Briefly describe the primary and support activities in a firm's value chain.

3. How can managers create value by establishing important relationships among the value-chain activities both within their firm and between the firm and its customers and suppliers?

4. Briefly explain the four criteria for sustainability of competitive advantages.

5. Under what conditions are employees and managers able to appropriate some of the value created by their firm?

6. What are the advantages and disadvantages of conducting a financial ratio analysis of a firm?

7. Summarize the concept of the balanced scorecard. What are its main advantages?

Key Terms

Experiential Exercise

Dell Computer is a leading firm in the personal computer industry, with annual revenues of $56 billion during its 2006 fiscal year. Dell has created a very strong competitive position via its "direct model," whereby it manufactures its personal computers to detailed customer specifications.

Below we address several questions that focus on Dell's value-chain activities and interrelationships among them as well as whether they are able to attain sustainable competitive advantage(s). (We discuss Dell in this chapter on pages 90–91.)

1. Where in Dell's value chain are they creating value for their customer?

Value-Chain Activity	Yes/No	How Does Dell Create Value for the Customer?
Primary:		
Inbound logistics		
Operations		
Outbound logistics		
Marketing and sales		
Service		
Support:		
Procurement		
Technology development		
Human resource management		
General administration		

2. What are the important relationships among Dell's value-chain activities? What are the important inter-dependencies? For each activity, identify the relationships and interdependencies.

	Inbound logistics	Operations	Outbound logistics	Marketing and sales	Service	Procurement	Technology development	Human resource management	General administration
Inbound logistics									
Operations									
Outbound logistics									
Marketing and sales									
Service									
Procurement									
Technology development									
Human resource management									
General administration									

3. What resources, activities, and relationships enable Dell to achieve a sustainable competitive advantage?

Resource/Activity	Is It Valuable?	Is It Rare?	Are There Few Substitutes?	Is It Difficult to Make?
Inbound logistics				
Operations				
Outbound logistics				
Marketing and sales				
Service				
Procurement				
Technology development				
Human resource management				
General administration				

Application Questions Exercises

1. Using published reports, select two CEOs who have recently made public statements regarding a major change in their firm's strategy. Discuss how the successful implementation of such strategies requires changes in the firm's primary and support activities.

2. Select a firm that competes in an industry in which you are interested. Drawing upon published financial reports, complete a financial ratio analysis. Based on changes over time and a comparison with industry norms, evaluate the firm's strengths and weaknesses in terms of its financial position.

3. How might exemplary human resource practices enhance and strengthen a firm's value-chain activities?

4. Using the Internet, look up your university or college. What are some of its key value-creating activities that provide competitive advantages? Why?

Ethics Questions

1. What are some of the ethical issues that arise when a firm becomes overly zealous in advertising its products?

2. What are some of the ethical issues that may arise from a firm's procurement activities? Are you aware of any of these issues from your personal experience or businesses you are familiar with?

References

1. Thomas, A. R., & Wilkinson, T. J. 2006. The outsourcing compulsion. *MIT Sloan Management Review,* 48(1): 10–14; and Fahey, J. 2005. Rolling, rolling, rolling. *Forbes.com.* November 28: np.

2. As a postscript, the Goodyear story does have the making of a happy ending. In early 2003, Robert Keegan, a former president of Eastman Kodak, replaced 37-year veteran Samir Gibara as chief executive officer at Goodyear. At the time, Goodyear's stock was struggling at around $5 per share (reaching a low of $3.57 on February 3 of that year). Keegan began a restructuring plan to reposition the company as a consumer-products firm rather than a rust belt manufacturer. For years, Goodyear had chased volume, selling low-margin tires to auto manufacturers and replacement tires to the middle of the market. In contrast, under Keegan's leadership the firm began developing expensive tires aimed at performance and luxury-car drivers. Production of low-end tires was being moved offshore to Goodyear plants in lower-wage countries in Latin America, Asia, and Eastern Europe. Says Jonathan Rich, head of North American operations: "We owned the wrong real estate." After a long period of losses for 2001 through 2004, Goodyear turned a net profit of $228 million in 2005. And, in the beginning of 2007, its stock is back up to more than $21 per share—far above the level it was at when Keegan took over. Source: Fahey, J. 2005. Rolling, rolling, rolling. Forbes.com, November 28.

3. Our discussion of the value chain will draw on Porter, M. E. 1985. *Competitive advantage:* chap. 2. New York: Free Press.

4. Dyer, J. H. 1996. Specialized supplier networks as a source of competitive advantage: Evidence from the auto industry. *Strategic Management Journal,* 17: 271–291.

5. For an insightful perspective on value-chain analysis, refer to Stabell, C. B., & Fjeldstad, O. D. 1998. Configuring value for competitive advantage: On chains, shops, and networks. *Strategic Management Journal,* 19: 413–437. The authors develop concepts of value chains, value shops, and value networks to extend the value-creation logic across a broad range of industries. Their work builds on the seminal contributions of Porter, 1985, op. cit., and others who have addressed how firms create value through key interrelationships among value-creating activities.

6. Ibid.

7. Maynard, M. 1999. Toyota promises custom order in 5 days. *USA Today,* August 6: B1.

8. Shaw Industries. 1999. Annual report: 14–15.

9. Fisher, M. L. 1997. What is the right supply chain for your product? *Harvard Business Review,* 75(2): 105–116.

10. Jackson. M. 2001. Bringing a dying brand back to life. *Harvard Business Review,* 79(5): 53–61.

11. Anderson, J. C., & Nmarus, J. A. 2003. Selectively pursuing more of your customer's business. *MIT Sloan Management Review,* 44(3): 42–50.

12. An insightful discussion of the role of identity marketing—that is, the myriad labels that people use to express who they are—in successful marketing activities is found in Reed, A., II, & Bolton, L. E. 2005. The complexity of identify. *MIT Sloan Management Review,* 46(3): 18–22.

13. Berggren, E., & Nacher, T. 2000. Why good ideas go bust. *Management Review,* February: 32–36.

14. For an insightful perspective on creating effective brand portfolios, refer to Hill, S., Ettenson, R., & Tyson, D. 2005. Achieving the ideal brand portfolio. *MIT Sloan Management Review,* 46(2): 85–90.

15. Haddad, C., & Grow, B. 2001. Wait a second—I didn't order that! *BusinessWeek,* July 16: 45.

16. Berman, B. 2005. How to delight your customers. *California Management Review,* 48(1): 129–151.

17. For a scholarly discussion on the procurement of technology components, read Hoetker, G. 2005. How much you know versus how well I know you: Selecting a supplier for a technically innovative component. *Strategic Management Journal,* 26(1): 75–96.

18. For a discussion on criteria to use when screening suppliers for back-office functions, read Feeny, D., Lacity, M., & Willcocks, L. P. 2005. Taking the measure of outsourcing providers. *MIT Sloan Management Review,* 46(3): 41–48.

19. Imperato, G. 1998. How to give good feedback. *Fast Company,* September: 144–156.

20. Bensaou, B. M., & Earl, M. 1998. The right mindset for managing information technology. *Harvard Business Review,* 96(5): 118–128.

21. Donlon, J. P. 2000. Bonsignore's bid for the big time. *Chief Executive,* March: 28–37.

22. Ulrich, D. 1998. A new mandate for human resources. *Harvard Business Review,* 96(1): 124–134.

23. Wood, J. 2003. Sharing jobs and working from home: The new face of the airline industry. *AviationCareer. net,* February 21.

24. Follow AT&T's lead in this tactic to retain "plateaued" employees. n.d. *Recruitment & Retention:* 1.

25. Green, S., Hasan, F., Immelt, J. Marks, M., & Meiland, D. 2003. In search of global leaders. *Harvard Business Review,* 81(8): 38–45.

26. For a cautionary note on the use of IT, refer to McAfee, A. 2003. When too much IT knowledge is a dangerous thing. *MIT Sloan Management Review,* 44(2): 83–90.

27. Walgreen Co. 1996. *Information technology and Walgreens: Opportunities for employment,* January; and Dess, G. G., & Picken, J. C. 1997. *Beyond productivity.* New York: AMACOM.

28. For an interesting perspective on some of the potential downsides of close customer and supplier relationships, refer to Anderson, E., & Jap, S. D. 2005. The dark side of close relationships. *MIT Sloan Management Review,* 46(3): 75–82.

29. Day, G. S. 2003. Creating a superior customer-relating capability. *MIT Sloan Management Review,* 44(3): 77–82.

30. To gain insights on the role of electronic technologies in enhancing a firm's connections to outside suppliers and customers, refer to Lawrence, T. B., Morse, E. A., & Fowler, S. W. 2005. Managing your portfolio of connections. *MIT Sloan Management Review,* 46(2): 59–66.

31. Reinhardt, F. L. 1999. Bringing the environment down to earth. *Harvard Business Review,* 77(4): 149–157.

32. Collis, D. J., & Montgomery, C. A. 1995. Competing on resources: Strategy in the 1990's. *Harvard Business Review,* 73(4): 119–128; and Barney, J. 1991. Firm resources and sustained competitive advantage. *Journal of Management,* 17(1): 99–120.

33. For recent critiques of the resource-based view of the firm, refer to: Sirmon, D. G., Hitt, M. A., & Ireland, R. D. 2007. Managing firm resources in dynamic environments to create value: Looking inside the black box. *Academy of Management Review,* 32(1): 273–292; and Newbert, S. L. Empirical research on the resource-based view of the firm: An assessment and suggestions for future research. *Strategic Management Journal,* 28(2): 121–146.

34. Henkoff, R. 1993. Companies that train the best. *Fortune,* March 22: 83; and Dess & Picken, *Beyond productivity,* p. 98.

35. Barney, J. B. 1986. Types of competition and the theory of strategy: Towards an integrative framework. *Academy of Management Review,* 11(4): 791–800.

36. Harley-Davidson. 1993. Annual report.

37. For a rigorous, academic treatment of the origin of capabilities, refer to Ethiraj, S. K., Kale, P., Krishnan, M. S., & Singh, J. V. 2005. Where do capabilities come from and how do they matter? A study of the software services industry. *Strategic Management Journal,* 26(1): 25–46.

38. For an academic discussion on methods associated with organizational capabilities, refer to Dutta, S., Narasimhan, O., & Rajiv, S. 2005. Conceptualizing and measuring capabilities: Methodology and empirical application. *Strategic Management Journal,* 26(3): 277–286.

39. Lorenzoni, G., & Lipparini, A. 1999. The leveraging of interfirm relationships as a distinctive organizational capability: A longitudinal study. *Strategic Management Journal,* 20: 317–338.

40. Barney, J. 1991. Firm resources and sustained competitive advantage. *Journal of Management,* 17(1): 99–120.

41. Barney, 1986, op. cit. Our discussion of inimitability and substitution draws upon this source.

42. Deephouse, D. L. 1999. To be different, or to be the same? It's a question (and theory) of strategic balance. *Strategic Management Journal,* 20: 147–166.

43. Yeoh, P. L., & Roth, K. 1999. An empirical analysis of sustained advantage in the U.S. pharmaceutical industry: Impact of firm resources and capabilities. *Strategic Management Journal,* 20: 637–653.

44. Robins, J. A., & Wiersema, M. F. 2000. Strategies for unstructured competitive environments: Using scarce resources to create new markets. In Bresser, R. F., et al., (Eds.), *Winning strategies in a deconstructing world:* 201–220. New York: John Wiley.

45. Byrnes, N., & Burrows, P. 2007. Where Dell went wrong. *BusinessWeek,* February 18: 62–63; and Smith, A. D. 2007. Dell's moves create buzz. *Dallas Morning News.* Februrary 21: D1.

46. Amit, R., & Schoemaker, J. H. 1993. Strategic assets and organizational rent. *Strategic Management Journal,* 14(1): 33–46; Collis, D. J., & Montgomery, C. A. 1995. Competing on resources: Strategy in the 1990's. *Harvard Business Review,* 73(4): 118–128; Coff, R. W. 1999. When competitive advantage doesn't lead to performance: The resource-based view and stakeholder bargaining power. *Organization Science,* 10(2): 119–133; and Blyler, M., & Coff, R. W. 2003. Dynamic capabilities, social capital, and rent appropriation: Ties that split pies. *Strategic Management Journal,* 24: 677–686.

47. Munk, N. 1998. The new organization man. *Fortune,* March 16: 62–74.

48. Coff, op. cit.

49. Lavelle, L. 2003. Sprint's board needs a good sweeping, too. *BusinessWeek,* February 24: 40; Anonymous. 2003. Another nail in the coffin. *The Economist,* February 15: 69–70; and Byrnes, N., Dwyer, P., & McNamee, M. 2003. Hacking away at tax shelters, *BusinessWeek,* February 24: 41.

50. We have focused our discussion on how internal stakeholders (e.g., employees, managers, and top executives) may appropriate a firm's profits (or rents). For an interesting discussion of how a firm's innovations may be appropriated by external stakeholders (e.g., customers, suppliers) as well as competitors, refer to Grant, R. M. 2002. *Contemporary strategy analysis* (4th ed.): 335–340. Malden, MA: Blackwell.

51. Luehrman, T. A. 1997. What's it worth? A general manager's guide to valuation. *Harvard Business Review,* 45(3): 132–142.

52. See, for example, Kaplan, R. S., & Norton, D. P. 1992. The balanced scorecard: Measures that drive performance. *Harvard Business Review,* 69(1): 71–79.

53. Hitt, M. A., Ireland, R. D., & Stadter, G. 1982. Functional importance of company performance: Moderating effects of grand strategy and industry type. *Strategic Management Journal,* 3: 315–330.

54. Berner, R. 2000. Procter & Gamble: Just say no to drugs. *BusinessWeek,* October 9: 128.

55. Kaplan & Norton, op. cit.

56. Ibid.

57. For a discussion of the relative value of growth versus increasing margins, read Mass, N. J. 2005. The relative value of growth. *Harvard Business Review,* 83(4): 102–112.

58. Rucci, A. J., Kirn, S. P., & Quinn, R. T. 1998. The employee-customer-profit chain at Sears. *Harvard Business Review,* 76(1): 82–97.

59. Our discussion draws upon: Angel, R., & Rampersad, H. 2005. Do scorecards add up? *camagazine.com.* May: np.; and Niven, P. 2002. *Balanced scorecard step by step: Maximizing performance and maintaining results.* New York: John Wiley & Sons.

Appendix to Chapter 3

How the Internet and Digital Technologies Add Value

The Internet has changed the way business is conducted. By providing new ways to interact with customers and using digital technologies to streamline operations, the Internet is helping companies create new value propositions. Let's take a look at several ways these changes have added new value. Exhibit 3A.1 illustrates four related activities that are being revolutionized by the Internet—search, evaluation, problem solving, and transactions.[1]

>LO8

How firms are using Internet technologies to add value and achieve unique advantages. (Appendix)

Search Activities

Search refers to the process of gathering information and identifying purchase options. The Internet has enhanced both the speed of information gathering and the breadth of information that can be accessed. This enhanced search capability is one of the key reasons the Internet has lowered switching costs—by

[1]The ideas in this section draw on several sources, including Zeng, M., & Reinartz, W. 2003. Beyond online search: The road to profitability. *California Management Review,* Winter: 107–130; and Stabell, C. B., & Fjeldstad, O. D. 1998. Configuring value for competitive advantage: On chains, shops, and networks. *Strategic Management Journal,* 19: 413–437.

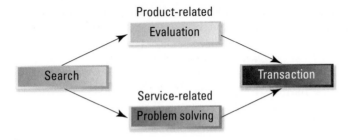

Exhibit 3A.1 Internet Activities that Add Value

Sources: Adapted from Zeng, M., & Reinartz, W. 2003. Beyond online search: The road to profitability. *California Management Review.* Winter: 107–130; and Stabell, C. B., & Fjeldstad, O. D. 1998. Configuring value for competitive advantage: On chains, shops, and networks. *Strategic Management Jounral,* 19: 413–437.

decreasing the cost of search. These efficiency gains have greatly benefited buyers. Suppliers also have benefited. Small suppliers that had difficulty getting noticed can be found more easily, and large suppliers can publish thousands of pages of information for a fraction of the cost that hard-copy catalogs once required. Additionally, online search engines have accelerated the search process to incredible speeds. Consider the example of Google:

> Google, a search engine developed as a project by two graduate students, became the number one search service in just four years. Why? Because it is capable of incredible things. Using over 10,000 networked computers, it searches 3 billion Web pages in an average of 500 milliseconds. To do the same search manually, by thumbing through 3 billion pages at the rate of one minute per page, would take 5,707 years. This ability has made Google an essential tool for many businesses. As a result, Google has built a powerful advertising business. Mark Kini, who runs a small limousine service in Boston, spends 80 percent of his advertising budget on Google and other search engines. "It's how we survive," says Kini.[2]

Evaluation Activities

Evaluation refers to the process of considering alternatives and comparing the costs and benefits of various options. Online services that facilitate comparative shopping, provide product reviews, and catalog customer evaluations of performance have made the Internet a valuable resource.[3] For example, BizRate.com offers extensive product ratings that can help evaluate products. Sites such as CNET that provide comparative pricing have helped lower prices even for quality products that have traditionally maintained premium prices. Opinion-based sites such as ePinions.com and PlanetFeedback.com provide reports of consumer experiences with various vendors.

Many Internet businesses, according to digital business experts Ming Zeng and Werner Reinartz, could improve their performance by making a stronger effort to help buyers evaluate purchases.[4] Even so, only certain types of products can be evaluated online. Products such as CDs that appeal primarily to the sense of sound sell well on the Internet. But products that appeal to multiple senses are harder to evaluate online. This explains why products such as furniture and fashion have never been strong online sellers. It's one thing to look at a leather sofa, but to be able to sit on it, touch, and smell the leather online are impossible.

Problem-Solving Activities

Problem solving refers to the process of identifying problems or needs and generating ideas and action plans to address those needs. Whereas evaluation is primarily product-related, problem solving is typically used in the context of services. Customers usually have unique problems that are handled one at a time. For example, online travel services such as Travelocity help customers select from many options to form a unique travel package. Furthermore, problem solving often involves providing

[2]Hardy, Q. 2003. All eyes on Google. *Forbes,* May 26, www.forbes.com.
[3]For an interesting discussion of how successful Internet-based companies are using evaluation to add value see Weiss, L. M., Capozzi, M. M., & Prusak, L. 2004. Learning from the Internet giants. *Sloan Management Review,* 45(4): 79–84.
[4]Zeng & Reinartz, *op.cit.*

answers immediately (compared to the creation of a new product). Firms in industries such as medicine, law, and engineering are using the Internet and digital technologies to deliver many new solutions.

Many products involve both a service and a product component; therefore, both problem solving and evaluation may be needed. Dell Computer's website is an example of a site that has combined the benefits of both. By creating a website that allows for customization of individual computers, they address the unique concerns of customers "one computer at a time." But the site also features a strong evaluative component because it allows users to compare the costs and features of various options. Shoppers can even compare their customized selection to refurbished Dell computers that are available at a substantially lower cost.

Transaction Activities

Transaction refers to the process of completing the sale, including negotiating and agreeing contractually, making payments, and taking delivery. Numerous types of Internet-enabled activities have contributed to lowering this aspect of overall transaction costs. Auctions of various sorts, from raw materials used in manufacturing to collectibles sold on eBay, facilitate the process of arriving at mutually agreed-on prices. Services such as PayPal provide a third-party intermediary that facilitates transactions between parties who never have (and probably never will) meet. Amazon.com's One-Click technology allows for very rapid purchases, and Amazon's overall superiority in managing order fulfillment has made its transactions process rapid and reliable. Amazon's success today can be attributed to a large extent to its having sold this transaction capability to other companies such as Target, Toys "R" Us and even Borders (another bookseller!).[5]

Other Sources of Competitive Advantage

There are other factors that can be important sources of competitive advantage. One of the most important of these is content. The Internet makes it possible to capture vast amounts of content at a very low cost. Three types of content can improve the value proposition of a Web site—customer feedback, expertise, and entertainment programming.

- ***Customer Feedback.*** Buyers often trust what other buyers say more than a company's promises. One type of content that can enhance a Web site is customer testimonials. Remember the leather sofa online? The testimonials of other buyers can build confidence and add to the chances that the purchaser will buy online sight unseen. This is one way that content can be a source of competitive advantage. Being able to interact with like-minded customers by reading their experiences or hearing how they have responded to a new product offering builds a sense of belonging that is otherwise hard to create.
- ***Expertise.*** The Internet has emerged as a tremendously important learning tool. Fifty-one percent of users compare the Internet to a library.[6] The prime reason many users go to the Web is to gain expertise. Web sites that provide new knowledge or unbiased information are highly valuable. Additionally the problem-solving function often involves educating consumers regarding options and implications of various choices. For example, LendingTree.com, the online loan company, provides a help center that includes extensive information and resources about obtaining loans, maintaining good credit, and so forth. Further, the expertise function is not limited to consumer sites. In the case of B2B businesses, Web sites that facilitate sharing expert knowledge help build a sense of community in industry or professional groups.
- ***Entertainment Programming.*** The Internet is being used by more and more people as an entertainment medium. With technologies such as streaming media, which allows the Internet to send televisionlike images and sound, computers can provide everything from breaking news to video games to online movies. A study by the Pew Internet and American Life Project indicates that among people using high-speed broadband service, TV viewing is down and online activity has increased. One reason is that the technology is interactive, which means that viewers don't just passively watch, but they use the Web to create art or play online games. Businesses have noticed this trend, of course, and are creating Web content that is not just informative but entertaining.

These three types of content—customer feedback, expertise, and entertainment programming—are potential sources of competitive advantage. That is, they create advantages by making the value creation process even stronger. Or, if they are handled poorly, they diminish performance.

[5]Bayers, C. 2002. The last laugh. *Business 2.0,* September: 86–93.
[6]Greenspan, R. 2003. Internet not for everyone. *CyberAtlas,* April 16, www.cyberatlas.com.

Business Models

The Internet provides a unique platform or staging area for business activity, which has become, in some ways, like a new marketplace. How do firms conduct business in this new arena? One way of addressing this question is by describing various Internet business models. A business model is a method and a set of assumptions that explain how a business creates value and earns profits in a competitive environment. Some of these models are quite simple and traditional even when applied in an Internet context. Others have features that are unique to the digitally networked, online environment. In this section, we discuss seven Internet business models that account for the vast majority of business conducted online.[7]

- *Commission-Based* **Models** are used by businesses that provide services for a fee. The business is usually a third-party intermediary, and the commission charged is often based on the size of the transaction. The most common type is a brokerage service, such as a stock-broker (e.g., Schwab.com), real estate broker (e.g., Remax.com), or transaction broker (e.g., PayPal.com). This category also includes auction companies such as eBay. In exchange for putting buyers and sellers together, eBay earns a commission.
- *Advertising-Based* **Models** are used by companies that provide content and/or services to visitors and sell advertising to businesses that want to reach those visitors. It is similar to the broadcast television model, in which viewers watch shows produced with advertising dollars. A key difference is that online visitors can interact with both the ads and the content. Large portals such as Yahoo.com are in this category as well as specialty portals such as iNest.com, which provides services for buyers of newly constructed homes. Epinions.com, a recommender system, is just one example of the many types of content that are often available.
- *Markup-Based* **Models** are used by businesses that add value in marketing and sales (rather than production) by acquiring products, marking up the price, and reselling them at a profit. Also known as the merchant model, it applies to both wholesalers and retailers. Amazon.com is the best-known example in this category. It also includes bricks-and-mortar companies such as Wal-Mart, which has a very successful online operation, and vendors whose products are purely digital such as Fonts.com, which sells downloadable fonts and photographs.
- *Production-Based* **Models** are used by companies that add value in the production process by converting raw materials into value-added products. Thus, it is also referred to as the manufacturing model. The Internet adds value to this model in two key ways. First, it lowers marketing costs by enabling direct contact with end users. Second, such direct contact facilitates customization and problem solving. Dell's online ordering system is supported by a state-of-the-art customized manufacturing process. Travelocity uses its rich database of travel options and customer profiles to identify, produce, and deliver unique solutions.
- *Referral-Based* **Models** are used by firms that steer customers to another company for a fee. One type is the affiliate model, in which a vendor pays an affiliate a fee each time a visitor clicks through the affiliate's Web site and makes a purchase from the vendor. Many name-brand companies use affiliate programs. For example, WeddingChannel.com, which provides a bridal registry where wedding guests can buy gifts from companies such as Tiffany's, Macy's, or Crate & Barrel, receives a fee each time a sale is made through its Web Site. Another referral-based example is Yesmail.com, which generates leads using e-mail marketing.
- *Subscription-Based* **Models** are used by businesses that charge a flat fee for providing either a service or proprietary content. Internet service providers are one example of this model. Companies such as America Online and Earthlink supply Internet connections for fees that are charged whether buyers use the service or not. Subscription-based models are also used by content creators such as the *Economist* or the *New York Times*. Although these recognizable brands often provide free content, only a small portion is available free. The *Economist,* for example, advertises that 70 percent of its content is available only to subscribers.
- *Fee-For-Service–Based* **Models** are used by companies that provide ongoing services similar to a utility company. Unlike the commission-based model, the fee-for-service model involves a pay-as-you-go system. That is, activities are metered and companies pay only for the amount of service

---

[7]Afuah, A., & Tucci, C.L. 2003. *Internet business models and strategies* (2nd ed). New York: McGraw-Hill; and, Timmers, P. 1999. *Electronic commerce.* New York: Wiley.

used. Application service providers fall in this category. For example, eProject.com provides virtual work space where people in different physical locations can collaborate online. Users essentially rent Internet space, and a host of tools that make it easy to interact, for a fee based on their usage.

Exhibit 3A.2 summarizes the key feature of each Internet business model, suggest what role content may play in the model, and addresses how the four value-adding activities—search, evaluation, problem solving, and transaction—can be sources of competitive advantage.

Exhibit 3A.2
Internet Business Models

Type	Features and Content	Sources of Competitive Advantage
Commission-Based	Charges commissions for brokerage or intermediary services. Adds value by providing expertise and/or access to a wide network of alternatives.	Search Evaluation Problem solving Transaction
Advertising-Based	Web content paid for by advertisers. Adds value by providing free or low-cost content—including customer feedback, expertise, and entertainment programming—to audiences that range from very broad (general content) to highly targeted (specialized content).	Search Evaluation
Markup-Based	Resells marked-up merchandise. Adds value through selection, through distribution efficiencies, and by leveraging brand image and reputation. May use entertainment programming to enhance sales.	Search Transaction
Production-Based	Sells manufactured goods and custom services. Adds value by increasing production efficiencies, capturing customer preferences, and improving customer service.	Search Problem solving
Referral-Based	Charges fees for referring customers. Adds value by enhancing a company's product or service offering, tracking referrals electronically, and generating demographic data. Expertise and customer feedback often included with referral information.	Search Problem solving Transaction
Subscription-Based	Charges fees for unlimited use of service or content. Adds value by leveraging strong brand name, providing high-quality information to specialized markets, or providing access to essential services. May consist entirely of entertainment programming.	Evaluation Problem solving
Fee-for-service–Based	Charges fees for metered services. Adds value by providing service efficiencies, expertise, and practical outsourcing solutions.	Problem solving Transaction

Sources: Afuah, A., & Tucci, C. L. 2003. *Internet business models and strategies* (2nd ed). New York: McGraw-Hill; Rappa, M. 2005. *Business models on the Web*, digitalenterprise.org/models/models.html; and Timmers, P. 1999. *Electronic commerce*. New York: Wiley.

chapter 4

Recognizing a Firm's Intellectual Assets:

Moving beyond a Firm's Tangible Resources

>learning objectives

After reading this chapter, you should have a good understanding of:

LO1 Why the management of knowledge professionals and knowledge itself are so critical in today's organizations.

LO2 The importance of recognizing the interdependence of attracting, developing, and retaining human capital.

LO3 The key role of social capital in leveraging human capital within and across the firm.

LO4 The importance of social networks in knowledge management and in promoting career success.

LO5 The vital role of technology in leveraging knowledge and human capital.

LO6 Why "electronic" or "virtual" teams are critical in combining and leveraging knowledge in organizations and how they can be made more effective.

LO7 The challenge of protecting intellectual property and the importance of a firm's dynamic capabilities.

LO8 How leveraging human capital is critical to strategy formulation for business-level, corporate-level, international, and entrepreneurial strategies.

One of the most important trends that managers must consider is the significance of the knowledge worker in today's economy. Managers must both recognize the importance of top talent and provide mechanisms to leverage human capital to innovate and, in the end, develop products and services that create value.

The first section addresses the increasing role of knowledge as the primary means of wealth generation in today's economy. A company's value is not derived solely from its physical assets, such as plant, equipment, and machinery. Rather, it is based on knowledge, know-how, and intellectual assets—all embedded in people.

The second section discusses the key resource itself, human capital, which is the foundation of intellectual capital. We explore ways in which the organization can attract, develop, and retain top talent—three important, interdependent activities. With regard to attracting human capital, we address issues such as "hiring for attitude, training for skill." One of the issues regarding developing human capital is encouraging widespread involvement throughout the organization. Our discussion on retaining human capital addresses issues such as the importance of having employees identify with an organization's mission and values. We also address the value of a diverse workforce.

The attraction, development, and retention of human capital are necessary but not sufficient conditions for organizational success. In the third section we address social capital—networks of relationships among a firm's members. This is especially important where collaboration and sharing information are critical. In this section we address why social capital can be particularly important in attracting human capital and making teams effective. We also address the vital role of social networks—both in improving knowledge management and in promoting career success.

The fourth section addresses the role of technology in leveraging human capital. Examples range from e-mail and the use of networks to facilitate collaboration among individuals to more complex forms of technologies, such as sophisticated knowledge management systems. We discuss how electronic teams can be effectively managed. We also address how technology can help to retain knowledge.

The fifth section discusses the differences between protection of physical property and intellectual property. We suggest that the development of dynamic capabilities may be one of the best ways that a firm can protect its intellectual property.

The sixth and final section discusses how leveraging human capital is vital to each of the four levels of strategy formulation—business, corporate, international, and Internet.

Learning from Mistakes

Some companies excel in attracting top talent and leveraging such talent. This often leads to positive relationships among individuals within the firm, promoting a social infrastructure that is critical for gaining consensus on major decisions, sharing information, and promoting cooperation. However, at times, hiring top talent or "stars" can have a big downside. Consider the experience of The Wildflower Group, a New York–based licensing and marketing group that represents the trademark owners of such products as home furnishings, giftware, and popular characters, including ALF and Newton's Law (a small bear extremely popular in Great Britain).

To Michael Carlisle, one of Wildflower's partners, it seemed like the coup of a lifetime.[1] Although his firm was just three years old and had only 10 employees, it was able to recruit a highly regarded salesperson from one of the industry's largest and *[continued]* most prestigious companies. She was a bona fide superstar, with a blue-chip resume, a Rolodex brimming with contacts, and a track record for landing top-dollar clients. The excited Carlisle remembers thinking, "She could do a lot for us."

But that was then . . . and things didn't work out as planned. The new employee was accustomed to the comforts and amenities of a large corporation. She became testy and unpleasant when asked to, for example, troubleshoot her own computer problems or alter her travel plans to take advantage of cheaper airfares. And she hardly created warm, positive feelings among her co-workers by trying to fob off administrative chores such as sending faxes. To make matters worse, she was not bringing in new business for Wildflower. Finally, and not too surprisingly, she did not take direction very well. Carlisle would lay out Wildflower's sales plan, and she'd argue about it.

Carlisle and his partner, Fred Paprin, spent many unproductive hours discussing how to best salvage the situation. However, as the complaints mounted, Carlisle began to worry about losing other employees. The final straw came when Carlisle noticed that several younger employees were beginning to emulate the star's poor behavior. The partners agreed it was time for the company to cut its losses. Wildflower's big "hiring coup" lasted less than 10 months.

Managers are always hunting for stellar employees who can raise the organization to the next level. Unfortunately, as Carlisle discovered, bulletproof credentials are far from a "happily ever after" guarantee. Just the opposite may come true instead.

We will discuss how attracting, developing, and retaining talent is a necessary but not sufficient condition for success. Many firms have experienced problems leveraging talent and technologies into successful products and services. In today's knowledge economy, it doesn't matter too much how big your stock of resources is—whether it be top talent, physical resources, or financial capital. Rather, the question becomes: How good is the organization at attracting top talent and leveraging that talent to produce a stream of products and services valued by the marketplace?

The Central Role of Knowledge in Today's Economy

Central to our discussion is an enormous change that has accelerated over the past few decades and its implications for the strategic management of organizations.[2] That is, for most of the 20th century, managers were primarily concerned with tangible resources such as land, equipment, and money as well as intangibles such as brands, image, and customer loyalty. Most efforts were directed more toward the efficient allocation of labor and capital—the two traditional factors of production.

How times have changed. Today, more than 50 percent of the gross domestic product (GDP) in developed economies is knowledge-based; that is, it is based on intellectual assets and intangible people skills.[3] In the United States, intellectual and information processes create most of the value for firms in large service industries (e.g., software, medical care, communications, and education), which make up 76 percent of the U.S. GDP. In the manufacturing sector, intellectual activities like R&D, process design, product design, logistics, marketing, or technological innovation produce the preponderance of value added.[4] To drive home the point, consider the perspective of Gary Hamel and C. K. Prahalad, two leading writers in strategic management:

> The machine age was a physical world. It consisted of things. Companies made and distributed things (physical products). Management allocated things (capital budgets); management invested in things (plant and equipment).

In the machine age, people were ancillary, and things were central. In the information age, things are ancillary, knowledge is central. A company's value derives not from things, but from knowledge, know-how, intellectual assets, competencies—all embedded in people.[5]

In the **knowledge economy,** wealth is increasingly created through the effective management of knowledge workers instead of by the efficient control of physical and financial assets. The growing importance of knowledge, coupled with the move by labor markets to reward knowledge work, tells us that someone who invests in a company is, in essence, buying a set of talents, capabilities, skills, and ideas—intellectual capital—not physical and financial resources.[6]

Let's provide a few examples. People don't buy Microsoft's stock because of its software factories; it doesn't own any. Rather, the value of Microsoft is bid up because of its ability to set standards for personal-computing software, exploit the value of its name, and forge alliances with other companies. Similarly, Merck didn't become the "Most Admired" company, for seven consecutive years in *Fortune*'s annual survey, because it can manufacture pills, but because its scientists can discover medicines. P. Roy Vagelos, who was CEO of Merck, the $22 billion pharmaceutical giant, during its long run atop the "Most Admired" survey, said, "A low-value product can be made by anyone anywhere. When you have knowledge no one else has access to—that's dynamite. We guard our research even more carefully than our financial assets."[7]

To apply some numbers to our arguments, let's ask, What's a company worth?[8] Start with the "big three" financial statements: income statement, balance sheet, and statement of cash flow. If these statements tell a story that investors find useful, then a company's market value* should roughly (but not precisely, because the market looks forward and the books look backward) be the same as the value that accountants ascribe to it—the book value of the firm. However, this is not the case. A study compared the market value with the book value of 3,500 U.S. companies over a period of two decades. In 1978 the two were similar: Book value was 95 percent of market value. However, market values and book values have diverged significantly. By 1998, book value was just 28 percent of market value. A colorful commentary comes from Robert A. Howell, an expert on the changing role of finance and accounting, "The big three financial statements . . . are about as useful as an 80-year-old Los Angeles road map."

The gap between a firm's market value and book value is far greater for knowledge-intensive corporations than for firms with strategies based primarily on tangible assets. Exhibit 4.1 shows the ratio of market-to-book value for some well-known companies. In firms where knowledge and the management of knowledge workers are relatively important contributors to developing products and services—and physical resources are less critical—the ratio of market-to-book value tends to be much higher. Many writers have defined **intellectual capital** as the difference between a firm's market value and book value—that is, a measure of the value of a firm's intangible assets.[9] This broad definition includes assets such as reputation, employee loyalty and commitment, customer relationships, company values, brand names, and the experience and skills of employees.[10] Thus, simplifying, we have:

Intellectual capital = Market value of firm − Book value of the firm

The issue becomes: How do companies create value in the knowledge-intensive economy? As we stated above, the general answer is to attract and leverage human capital effectively through mechanisms that create products and services of value over time. Let's articulate a few of the basic concepts that we will be talking about in this chapter.

---

* The market value of a firm is equal to the value of a share of its common stock times the number of shares outstanding. The book value of a firm is primarily a measure of the value of its tangible assets. It can be calculated by the formula: total assets − total liabilities.

>LO1
Why the management of knowledge professionals and knowledge itself are so critical in today's organizations.

knowledge economy an economy where wealth is created through the effective management of knowledge workers instead of by the efficient control of physical and financial assets.

intellectual capital the difference between the market value of the firm and the book value of the firm, including assets such as reputation, employee loyalty and commitment, customer relationships, company values, brand names, and the experience and skills of employees.

Exhibit 4.1

Ratio of Market Value to Book Value for Selected Companies

Company	Annual Sales ($ billions)	Market Value ($ billions)	Book Value ($ billions)	Ratio of Market to Book Value
Genentech	9.3	86.5	9.5	9.1
Google	10.7	142.5	17.0	8.4
Yahoo!	6.4	42.5	9.2	4.6
eBay	6.0	45.4	10.9	4.2
Southwest Airlines	9.1	11.6	6.4	1.8
Union Pacific (Railroad)	15.6	27.5	15.3	1.8
General Motors	192.6	17.3	14.6	1.2

Note: The data on market valuations are as of March 30, 2007. All other financial data is based on the most recently available balance sheets and income statements.

human capital the individual capabilities, knowledge, skills, and experience of a company's employees and managers.

First, consider human capital. **Human capital** is the "*individual* capabilities, knowledge, skills, and experience of the company's employees and managers."[11] This is knowledge that is relevant to the task at hand, as well as the capacity to add to this reservoir of knowledge, skills, and experience through learning.[12]

Second, **social capital** can be defined as "the network of relationships that individuals have throughout the organization." Such relationships are critical in sharing and leveraging knowledge and in acquiring resources.[13] Social capital also can extend beyond the organizational boundaries to include relationships between the firm and its suppliers, customers, and alliance partners.[14]

social capital the network of relationships that individuals have both inside and outside the organization.

Third is the concept of "knowledge," which comes in two different forms. First, there is **explicit knowledge** that is codified, documented, easily reproduced, and widely distributed. Examples include engineering drawings, software code, and patents.[15] The other type of knowledge is **tacit knowledge.** That is, in essence, in the minds of employees and is based on their experiences and backgrounds.[16] Tacit knowledge is shared only with the consent and participation of the individual.

explicit knowledge knowledge that is codified, documented, easily reproduced, and widely distributed.

New knowledge is constantly being created. It involves the continual interaction of explicit and tacit knowledge. Consider, for example, two software engineers working together on a computer code. The computer code is the explicit knowledge. However, through their sharing of ideas based on each individual's experience—that is, their tacit knowledge—new knowledge is created when they make modifications to the code. Another important issue is the role of "socially complex processes," which include leadership, culture, and trust.[17] These processes play a central role in the creation of knowledge.[18] They represent the "glue" that holds the organization together and helps to create a working environment where individuals are more willing to share their ideas, work in teams, and, in the end, create products and services of value. In a later section, we will address the importance of social capital in the value creation process.

tacit knowledge knowledge that is in the minds of employees and is based on their experiences and backgrounds.

Numerous books have been written on the subject of knowledge management and the central role that it has played in creating wealth in organizations and countries throughout the developed world.[19] Here, we focus on some of the key issues that organizations must address to compete through knowledge.

We will now turn our discussion to the central resource itself—human capital—and some guidelines on how it can be attracted/selected, developed, and retained. Tom Stewart, editor of the *Harvard Business Review*, noted that organizations must also undergo significant efforts to protect their human capital. A firm may "diversify the ownership of vital knowledge by emphasizing teamwork, guard against obsolescence by developing learning programs, and shackle key people with golden handcuffs."[20] In addition, people are less likely to leave an organization if there are effective structures to promote teamwork and information sharing, strong leadership that encourages innovation, and cultures that demand excellence and ethical behavior. Such issues are also central to the topic of this chapter. Although we touch on these issues throughout this chapter, we provide more detail in later chapters. We discuss organizational controls (culture, rewards, and boundaries) in Chapter 9, organization structure and design in Chapter 10, and a variety of leadership and entrepreneurship topics in Chapters 11 and 12.

Human Capital: The Foundation of Intellectual Capital

Organizations must recruit talented people—employees at all levels with the proper sets of skills and capabilities coupled with the right values and attitudes. Such skills and attitudes must be continually developed, strengthened, and reinforced, and each employee must be motivated and her efforts focused on the organization's goals and objectives.

The rise to prominence of the knowledge worker as a vital source of competitive advantage is changing the balance of power in today's organization. Knowledge workers place professional development and personal enrichment (financial and otherwise) above company loyalty. Attracting, recruiting, and hiring the "best and the brightest," is a critical first step in the process of building intellectual capital. At a symposium for CEOs, Bill Gates said, "The thing that is holding Microsoft back . . . is simply how [hard] we find it to go out and recruit the kind of people we want to grow our research team."[21]

Hiring is only the first of three key processes in which all successful organizations must engage to build and leverage their human capital. Firms must also *develop* employees at all levels and specialties to fulfill their full potential to maximize their joint contributions. Finally, the first two processes are for naught if firms can't provide the working environment and intrinsic and extrinsic rewards to *retain* their best and brightest.[22]

These three activities are highly interrelated. We would like to suggest the imagery of a three-legged stool (see Exhibit 4.2).[23] If one leg is weak or broken, the stool collapses.

To illustrate such interdependence, poor hiring impedes the effectiveness of development and retention processes. In a similar vein, ineffective retention efforts place additional

>LO2

The importance of recognizing the interdependence of attracting, developing, and retaining human capital.

Exhibit 4.2 Human Capital: Three Interdependent Activities

burdens on hiring and development. Consider the following anecdote, provided by Jeffrey Pfeffer of the Stanford University Business School:

> Not long ago, I went to a large, fancy San Francisco law firm—where they treat their associates like dog doo and where the turnover is very high. I asked the managing partner about the turnover rate. He said, "A few years ago, it was 25 percent, and now we're up to 30 percent." I asked him how the firm had responded to that trend. He said, "We increased our recruiting." So I asked him, "What kind of doctor would you be if your patient was bleeding faster and faster, and your only response was to increase the speed of the transfusion?"[24]

Clearly, stepped-up recruiting is a poor substitute for weak retention. Although there are no simple, easy-to-apply answers, we can learn from what leading-edge firms are doing to attract, develop, and retain human capital in today's highly competitive and rapidly changing marketplace. Let's begin by discussing hiring and selection practices.

Attracting Human Capital

> All we can do is bet on the people we pick. So my whole job is picking the right people.
>
> **Jack Welch,** former chairman, General Electric Company[25]

The first step in the process of building superior human capital is input control: attracting and selecting the right person. Many human resource professionals still approach employee selection from a "lock and key" mentality—that is, fit a key (a job candidate) into a lock (the job). Such an approach involves a thorough analysis of both the person and the job. Only then can the right decision be made as to how well the two will fit together. How can you fail, the theory goes, if you get a precise match of knowledge, ability, and skill profiles? Frequently, however, the precise matching approach places its emphasis on task-specific skills (e.g., motor skills, specific information processing capabilities, and communication skills) and puts less emphasis on the broad general knowledge and experience, social skills, values, beliefs, and attitudes of employees.

Many have questioned the precise matching approach. Instead, they argue that firms can identify top performers by focusing on key employee mind-sets, attitudes, social skills, and general orientations. These firms reason that if they get these elements right, the task-specific skills can be learned in relatively short order. (This does not imply, however, that task-specific skills are unimportant; rather, it suggests that the requisite skill sets must be viewed as a necessary but not sufficient condition.) This leads us to a popular phrase today and serves as the title of the next section.

"Hire for Attitude, Train for Skill"   Organizations are increasingly placing their emphasis on the general knowledge and experience, social skills, values, beliefs, and attitudes of employees. Consider Southwest Airlines's hiring practices, with their strong focus on employee values and attitudes. Given its strong team orientation, Southwest uses an "indirect" approach. For example, the interviewing team asks a group of employees to prepare a five-minute presentation about themselves. During the presentations, the interviewers observe which candidates are enthusiastically supporting their peers and which candidates are focused on polishing their own presentations while the others are presenting.[26] The former are, of course, favored.

Alan Cooper, president of Cooper Software, Inc., in Palo Alto, California, goes further. He cleverly *uses technology* to hone in on the problem-solving ability of his applicants and their attitudes before an interview even takes place. He has devised a "Bozo Filter," a test administered online (see Strategy Spotlight 4.1) that can be applied to any industry. Before you spend time figuring out whether job candidates will work out satisfactorily, find out how their minds work. Cooper advised, "Hiring was a black hole. I don't talk to bozos anymore because 90 percent of them turn away when they see our test. It's a self-administering bozo filter."[27]

Cooper Software's "Bozo Filter"

Hiring is often easier than firing. Even when unemployment rates are low and labor is scarce, it's still easier to find employees than it is to get them out the door if they don't work out. Not only do poor employees affect the morale of better talent, but they also cost the company money in lost productivity.

Cooper Software has found an innovative way to prevent the problem of hiring bad employees. CEO Alan Cooper asks job applicants to visit the company's Web site, where the applicants will find a test that takes between two and five hours to complete. The test asks questions designed to see how prospective employees approach problem-solving tasks. For example, one key question asks software engineer applicants to design a new table-creation software program for Microsoft Word. Candidates provide pencil sketches and a description of the new user interface. Another question is used for design communicators. They are asked to develop a marketing strategy for a new touch-tone phone—directed at consumers in the year 1850. Candidates e-mail their answers back to the company, and the answers are circulated around the firm to solicit feedback. Only candidates with the highest marks get interviews.

Jonathan Korman, a design communicator, suggested that the test "told me more about real job duties than any description could." Josh Seiden, a software designer, is even more positive: "It was a fun puzzle—much more engaging than most of what I was doing at my previous job."

That's exactly the kind of attitude Cooper wants. "We get e-mail from some people saying, 'Before I take this test, is the position still open?' I say no, because I don't want anybody who sees it as an effort," claims Cooper. "People who really care take the test and love it. Other people say it's hard. We don't want those people."

Sources: Cardin, R. 1997. Make your own bozo filter. *Fast Company*, October–November: 56; Coop, A. 1997. Getting design across. Unpublished manuscript, November 23: 1–8; and www.cooper.com.

Sound Recruiting Approaches and Networking   Companies that take hiring seriously must also take recruiting seriously. The number of jobs that successful knowledge-intensive companies must fill is astonishing. Ironically, many companies still have no shortage of applicants. Southwest Airlines typically gets 150,000 résumés a year, yet hires only about 5,000 new employees. And, Google, named in 2007 as the "Best Company to Work For" by *Fortune* magazine, gets an astounding 1,300 résumés a *day*![28] Netscape (now part of Time Warner) reviews 60 résumés for every hire.[29] The challenge becomes having the right job candidates, not the greatest number of them.

GE Medical Systems, which builds CT scanners and magnetic resonance imaging (MRI) systems, relies extensively on networking. They have found that current employees are the best source for new ones. Recently, Steven Patscot, head of staffing and leadership development, made a few simple changes to double the number of referrals. First, he simplified the process—no complex forms, no bureaucracy, and so on. Second, he increased incentives. Everyone referring a qualified candidate received a gift certificate from Sears. For referrals who were hired, the "bounty" was increased to $2,000 (or $3,000 if the referral was a software engineer). Although this may sound like a lot of money, it is "peanuts" compared to the $15,000 to $20,000 fees that GE typically pays to headhunters for each person hired.[30] Also, when someone refers a former colleague or friend for a job, his or her credibility is on the line. Thus, employees will tend to be careful in recommending people for employment unless they are reasonably confident that these people are good candidates. This provides a good "screen" for the firm in deciding whom to hire. After all, hiring the right people makes things a lot easier: fewer rules and regulations, less need for monitoring and hierarchy, and greater internalization of organizational norms and objectives.

Before moving on, it is useful to point out some of the approaches that companies are currently using to recruit and retain young talent. As more of the baby boomers retire,

Exhibit 4.3

What Companies are
Doing to Attract and Keep
Young Talent

Here are some "best practices" that companies are using to help recruit and retain today's high-maintenance Millennials. This generation has also been termed "Generation Y" or "Echo Boom" and includes people born after 1982:

- ***Don't Fudge the Sales Pitch.*** High-tech presentations and one-on-one attention may be attractive to undergrads, but the pitch better match the experience. Today's ultra-connected students can get the lowdown on a company by spending five minutes on a social networking site.

- ***Let Them Have a Life.*** Wary of their parents' 80-hour workweeks, Millennials strive for more balance, so liberal vacations are a must. They also want assurances they'll be able to use it. At KPMG, 80 percent of employees used 40 hours of paid time off in the six months through May 2006.

- ***No Time Clocks, Please.*** Recent grads don't mind long hours if they can work them on their own time. Lockheed Martin and its comptroller of the currency allow employees to work nine-hour days and take every other Friday off.

- ***Give Them Responsibility.*** A chance to work on fulfilling projects and develop ones of their own is important to Millennials. Google urges entry-level employees to spend 20 percent of their time developing new ideas. PepsiCo allows promising young employees to manage small teams in six months.

- ***Feedback and More Feedback.*** Career planning advice and frequent performance appraisals are keys to holding on to young hires. Lehman Brothers provides new hires with two mentors—a slightly older peer to help them get settled and a senior employee to give long-term guidance.

- ***Giving Back Matters.*** Today's altruistic young graduates expect to have opportunities for community service. Wells Fargo encourages its employees to teach financial literacy classes in the community. Accenture and Bain allow employees to consult for nonprofits.

Source: Gerdes, L. 2006. The top 50 employers for new college grads. *BusinessWeek,* September 18: 64–81.

people in this demographic group are becoming more and more important in today's workforce. We address this issue in Exhibit 4.3.

Developing Human Capital

It is not enough to hire top-level talent and expect that the skills and capabilities of those employees remain current throughout the duration of their employment. Rather, training and development must take place at all levels of the organization.[31] For example, Solectron assembles printed circuit boards and other components for its Silicon Valley clients.[32] Its employees receive an average of 95 hours of company-provided training each year. Chairman Winston Chen observed, "Technology changes so fast that we estimate 20 percent of an engineer's knowledge becomes obsolete each year. Training is an obligation we owe to our employees. If you want high growth and high quality, then training is a big part of the equation." Although the financial returns on training may be hard to calculate, most experts believe it is not only real, but also essential. One company that has calculated the benefit from training is Motorola. This high-technology firm has calculated that every dollar spent on training returns $30 in productivity gains over the following three years.

In addition to the importance of training and developing human capital, let's now discuss three other related topics: encouraging widespread involvement, monitoring and tracking employee development, and evaluating human capital.[33]

Encouraging Widespread Involvement   Developing human capital requires the active involvement of leaders at all levels. It won't be successful if it is viewed only as the responsibility of the human resources department. Each year at General Electric, 200 facilitators, 30 officers, 30 human resource executives, and many young managers actively participate in GE's orientation program at Crotonville, its training center outside New York City. Topics include global competition, winning on the global playing field, and personal examination of the new employee's core values vis-à-vis GE's values. As a senior manager once commented, "There is nothing like teaching Sunday school to force you to confront your own values."

Transferring Knowledge   Often in our lives, we need to either transfer our knowledge to someone else (a child, a junior colleague, a peer) or access accumulated bits of wisdom—someone else's tacit knowledge.[34] A vital aspect of developing human capital is transferring unique and specialized knowledge. However, before we can even begin to plan such a transfer, we need to understand how our brains process incoming information. According to Dorothy A. Leonard of Harvard University:

> Our existing tacit knowledge determines how we assimilate new experiences. Without receptors—hooks on which to hang new information—we may not be able to perceive and process the information. It is like being sent boxes of documents but having no idea how they could or should be organized.

This cognitive limitation also applies to the organizational level as well. For example, when GE Healthcare sets up or transfers operations from one location to another, it appoints an experienced manager to be the "pitcher" and a team in the receiving plant to be the "catcher." These two teams work together, often over a period of years—first at the pitcher's location and then at the catcher's. In order to ensure a smooth transition, the pitching team needs to be sensitive to the catching team's level of experience and familiarity with GE Healthcare procedures.

Strategy Spotlight 4.2 discusses Intel's Mentoring Program. It is a very effective way to share information throughout an organization.

Monitoring Progress and Tracking Development   Whether a firm uses on-site formal training, off-site training (e.g., universities), or on-the-job training, tracking individual progress—and sharing this knowledge with both the employee and key managers—becomes essential. At Citibank (part of Citigroup, the large financial services organization), a talent inventory program keeps track of roughly 10,000 employees worldwide—how they're doing, what skills they need to work on, and where else in the company they might thrive. Larry Phillips, head of human resources, considers the program critical to the company's global growth.[35]

Like many leading-edge organizations, GlaxoSmithKline places strong emphasis on broader experiences over longer time periods. Dan Phelan, senior vice president and director of human resources, explained, "We ideally follow a two-plus-two-plus-two formula in developing people for top management positions." This reflects the belief that SmithKline's best people should gain experience in two business units, two functional units (such as finance and marketing), in two countries.

Evaluating Human Capital   In today's competitive environment, collaboration and interdependence have become vital to organizational success. Individuals must share their knowledge and work together constructively to achieve collective, not just individual, goals. However, traditional evaluation systems evaluate performance from a single perspective (i.e., "top down") and generally don't address the "softer" dimensions of communications and social skills, values, beliefs, and attitudes.[36]

To address the limitations of the traditional approach, many organizations have begun to use 360-degree evaluation and feedback systems.[37] Here, superiors, direct reports, colleagues, and even internal and external customers rate a person's performance. Managers also rate themselves in order to have a personal benchmark. The 360-degree feedback system complements teamwork, employee involvement, and organizational flattening.

strategy spotlight

How Intel Shares Information through Its Mentoring Program

Mentor relationships are often stereotyped as one-way transfers from older experienced employees to the young for the purposes of professional development and career advancement. However, that's not the case at Intel, where the partner may outrank the mentor. Thus, an administrative assistant who is an expert at navigating informal internal networks may be selected to mentor an executive. Or a young technology-savvy employee may be chosen to share his knowledge with an older, more senior employee.

Intel's mentoring program began in a chip-making factory in New Mexico in 1997. At the time, Intel was growing rapidly and many of the factory's managers were being transferred to new locations. The company needed to develop new experts in a variety of fields. Thus, the factory's top managers started matching partners with mentors who had the needed skills and knowledge.

Sources: Morrison, R., Erickson, T., & Dychtwald, K. 2006. Managing middlescence. *Harvard Business Review,* 84(3): 78–86; Hill, R. P., & Stephens, D. L. 2003. The compassionate organization of the 21st century. *Organizational Dynamics,* 32(4): 331–341; www.intel.com; and Warner, R. 2002. Inside Intel's mentoring movement. *Fast Company,* April: 67–69.

Today Intel's program uses an intranet-based questionnaire to match partners with the right mentor, creating relationships that stretch across state lines and national boundaries. The system works by having potential mentors list their top skills at Circuit, Intel's internal employee site. Partners click on topics they want to master. Then an algorithm computes all of the variables and the database hashes out a list of possible matches. Once a match is made, an automatic e-mail goes to the mentor asking her to set up a time to meet and talk. The mentor and partner learn and follow some simple guidelines:

1. The partner controls the relationship.
2. A mentoring contract is drawn up to outline what needs to be accomplished by the end of the mentoring.
3. Both the partner and the mentor decide what to talk about.

Unlike many corporations, Intel does not use its mentoring for career advancement. Its style is all about learning and sharing the knowledge pool of someone whom you have probably never met.

As organizations continue to push responsibility downward, traditional top-down appraisal systems become insufficient. For example, a manager who previously managed the performance of 3 supervisors might now be responsible for 10 and might be less likely to have the in-depth knowledge needed to appraise and develop them adequately. Exhibit 4.4 provides a portion of GE's 360-degree evaluation system.

Evaluation systems must also ensure that a manager's success does not come at the cost of compromising the organization's core values. Clearly, such behavior generally leads to only short-term wins for both the manager and the organization. The organization typically suffers long-term losses in terms of morale, turnover, productivity, and so on. Accordingly, Merck's chairman, Ray Gilmartin, told his employees, "If someone is achieving results but not demonstrating the core values of the company, at the expense of our people, that manager does not have much of a career here."

Retaining Human Capital

It has been said that talented employees are like "frogs in a wheelbarrow."[38] They can jump out at any time! By analogy, the organization can either try to force employees to stay in the firm or try to keep them from wanting to jump out by creating incentives. In other words, today's leaders can either provide the work environment and incentives to keep productive employees and management from wanting to bail out, or they can rely on legal means such as employment contracts and noncompete clauses.[39] Clearly, firms must provide mechanisms that prevent the transfer of valuable and sensitive information outside the organization. Failure to do so would be the neglect of a leader's fiduciary responsibility to shareholders. However, greater efforts should be directed at the former (e.g., good work

Vision	• Has developed and communicated a clear, simple, customer-focused vision/direction for the organization.
	• Forward-thinking, stretches horizons, challenges imaginations.
	• Inspires and energizes others to commit to Vision. Captures minds. Leads by example.
	• As appropriate, updates Vision to reflect constant and accelerating change affecting the business.

Exhibit 4.4

An Excerpt from General Electric's 360-Degree Leadership Assessment Chart

Customer/Quality Focus

Integrity

Accountability/Commitment

Communication/Influence

Shared Ownership/Boundaryless

Team Builder/Empowerment

Knowledge/Expertise/Intellect

Initiative/Speed

Global Mind-Set

Source: Adapted from Slater, R. 1994. *Get better or get beaten:* 152–155. Burr Ridge, IL: Irwin Professional Publishing.

Note: This evaluation system consists of 10 "characteristics"—Vision, Customer/Quality Focus, Integrity, and so on. Each of these characteristics has four "performance criteria." For illustrative purposes, the four performance criteria of "Vision" are included.

environment and incentives), but, as we all know, the latter (e.g., employment contracts and noncompete clauses) have their place.[40]

Identifying with an Organization's Mission and Values   People who identify with and are more committed to the core mission and values of the organization are less likely to stray or bolt to the competition. Consider Medtronic, Inc., an $11 billion medical products firm based in Minneapolis.[41] Former CEO Bill George stated, "Shareholder value is a hollow notion as the sole source of employee motivation. If you do business that way, you'll end up like ITT." What motivates its workers to go well beyond Medtronic's excellent financial performance? Simply put, it's helping sick people get well. The company's motto is "Restoring patients to full life," and its symbol is an image of a supine human rising toward upright wellness. That sounds good, but how does the "resurrection" imagery come to life?

> Each December, at the company's holiday party, patients, their families, and their doctors are flown in to tell their survival stories. It's for employees—who are moved to tears year after year—and journalists are generally not invited. President Art Collins, a strapping guy with a firm handshake who is not prone to crying fits, said, "I remember my first holiday party and someone asked me if I had brought my Kleenex. I assumed I'd be fine, but these parents got up with their daughter who was alive because of our product. Even surgeons who see this stuff all the time were crying." Collins calls it "our most important meeting of the year."

So much for the all-consuming emphasis on profits.

In addition to identifying with the organization, "tribal loyalty" is another key factor that links people to the organization.[42] A tribe is not the organization as a whole (unless it is very small). Rather, it is teams, communities of practice, and other groups within an organization or occupation.

Brian Hall, CEO of Values Technology in Santa Cruz, California, documented a shift in people's emotional expectations from work. From the 1950s on, a "task first" relationship—"tell me what the job is, and let's get on with it"—dominated employee attitudes. Emotions and personal life were checked at the door. In the past few years, a "relationship-first" set of values has challenged the task orientation. Hall believes that it will become dominant. Employees want to share attitudes and beliefs as well as workspace.

Challenging Work and a Stimulating Environment   Arthur Schawlow, winner of the 1981 Nobel Prize in physics, was asked what made the difference between highly creative and less creative scientists. His reply: "The labor of love aspect is very important. The most successful scientists often are not the most talented. But they are the ones impelled by curiosity. They've got to know what the answer is."[43] Such insights highlight the importance of intrinsic motivation: the motivation to work on something because it is exciting, satisfying, or personally challenging.[44]

One way successful firms keep highly mobile employees motivated and challenged is through an internal market for opportunities that lower the barriers to an employee's mobility within a company. For example, Shell Oil Company has created an "open sourcing" model for talent. Jobs are listed on Shell's intranet, and, with a two-month notice, employees can go to work on anything that interests them. Monsanto[45] has developed a similar approach. According to one executive:

> Because we don't have a lot of structure, people will flow toward where success and innovation are taking place. We have a free-market system where people can move, so you have an outflow of people in areas where not much progress is being made. Before, the HR function ran processes like management development and performance evaluation. Now it also facilitates this movement of people.

Exhibit 4.5 lists some of the best practices that leading-edge organizations are using to create a challenging and stimulating work environment to help attract and retain top young

Exhibit 4.5

Creating a Challenging and Stimulating Workplace: *BusinessWeek*'s "Best Places to Launch a Career"

Company (Industry)	Comments
Lockheed Martin (Defense)	Offers leadership programs in communications, engineering, finance, human resources, information systems, and operations.
Enterprise Rent-a-Car (Transportation)	Management training program amounts to an MBA crash course for executive wannabes. New hires get to run their own business.
Verizon Wireless (Telecommunications)	Verizon Wireless recently launched a retail training program where participants work in as many as three locations over two years.
National Instruments (Technology)	NI puts its money where its mouth is, spending over $30,000 a year to train each participant in its engineering leadership program.
L'Oreal (Consumer Goods)	Rising entry-level marketing stars are put through a fast-paced training program that lasts between 18 months and two years.
Vanguard (Financial Services)	Four extensive rotational training and development programs range from 12 to 24 months in length with three to six rotations.

Source: Gerdes, L. 2006. The top 50 employers for new college grads. *BusinessWeek,* September 18: 64–81.

talent. It draws upon an in-depth study conducted by *BusinessWeek* to identify the "Best Places to Launch a Career."

Financial and Nonfinancial Rewards and Incentives Without a doubt, financial rewards are a vital organizational control mechanism (as we will discuss in Chapter 9). Money—whether in the form of salary, bonus, stock options, and so forth—can mean many different things to people. For some it might mean security, to others recognition, and to still others, a sense of freedom and independence.

Paying people more is seldom the most important factor in attracting and retaining human capital.[46] Most surveys show that money is not the most important reason why people take or leave jobs, and that money, in some surveys, is not even in the top 10. Consistent with these findings, Tandem Computers (now part of Hewlett-Packard) typically doesn't tell people being recruited what their salaries would be. People who asked were told that their salaries were competitive. If they persisted along this line of questioning, they would not be offered a position. Why? Tandem realized a rather simple idea: People who come for money will leave for money. Clearly, money can't be ignored, but it shouldn't be the primary mechanism to attract and retain talent.

Another nonfinancial reward involves accommodating working families with children. Coping with the conflicting demands of family and work is a problem at some point for virtually all employees.

Strategy Spotlight 4.3 discusses some of the challenges (and solutions) with the use of flextime. With this popular employment practice, flextime allows employees greater flexibility in when and where they do their work.

Enhancing Human Capital: The Role of Diversity in the Workforce

Today, a combination of demographic trends and accelerating globalization of business has made the management of cultural differences a critical issue.[47] Workforces, which reflect demographic changes in the overall population, will be increasingly heterogeneous along dimensions such as gender, race, ethnicity, and nationality. For example, demographic trends in the United States indicate a growth in Hispanic Americans from 6.9 million in 1960 to over 35 million in 2000. This figure also is expected to increase to over 55 million by 2020. Similarly, the Asian-American population should grow to 20 million in 2020 from 12 million in 2000 and only 1.5 million in 1970. And the African-American population is becoming more ethnically heterogeneous. Census estimates project that by 2010 as many as 10 percent of Americans of African descent will be immigrants from Africa or the Caribbean.[48]

Such demographic changes have implications not only for the labor pool but also for customer bases, which are also becoming more diverse. This creates important organizational challenges and opportunities.

The effective management of diversity can enhance the social responsibility goals of an organization.[49] However, there are many other benefits as well. Six other areas where sound management of diverse workforces can improve an organization's effectiveness and competitive advantages are: (1) cost, (2) resource acquisition, (3) marketing, (4) creativity, (5) problem-solving, and (6) organizational flexibility.

- ***Cost Argument.*** As organizations become more diverse, firms effective in managing diversity will have a cost advantage over those that are not.
- ***Resource Acquisition Argument.*** Firms with excellent reputations as prospective employers for women and ethnic minorities will have an advantage in the competition for top talent. As labor pools shrink and change in composition, such advantages will become even more important.

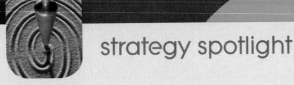

Solving the Challenges of Flextime

A recently study by Hewitt Associates, a human resources consulting firm, found that 75 percent of companies offered some kind of flexible work arrangement. However, these policies have earned mixed results. Working remotely can leave employees feeling isolated and managers feeling they lack control. Further, flextimers often find themselves squeezed into policies that are anything but flexible. "The work–life movement has always had a heavy layer of one-size-fits-all-ism," says Stewart D. Friedman, head of the Work/Life Integration Project and the Wharton School at the University of Pennsylvania.

Such a complaint is prompting many organizations to change their policies, says Hewitt's Carol Sladek, who heads the firm's work–life practice. Now more and more managers are using a template of questions to help them design their most fitting arrangement. "There's definitely a focus away from the structure of rigid flextime policies" says Sladek.

In a sense, flexibility is becoming more flexible. At Deloitte & Touche, years of stagnant enrollment in formal flexibility programs have led managers to help teams create flexible schedules among themselves. Staffers fill out a survey that helps them set goals as a group (reducing the number of times they interrupt co-workers off-hours, for instance) and jointly keep track of people's schedules so they know, say, when someone has reserved time with their kids. Deloitte is also experimenting with something called "mass career customization" that redefines flexibility over the course of a career rather than by the hours in a week. This helps employees to adjust their pace, workload, schedule, and work roles during various life stages.

Below are some suggested best practices or tips for making flextime programs work:

Source: Conlin, M. 2006. Smashing the clock. *BusinessWeek*, December 11: 60–68.

● Flextime and telecommuting can be an effective way to attract and retain talent. Here a man works from home on his laptop.

- **Measure.** Before unplugging workers, metrics are key to ensuring that productivity, engagement, and turnover improve.

- **Tailor.** Imposing new work rules rarely pays because managers and workers need to tailor schedules to their needs.

- **Trust.** Inevitably, some untethered workers will slack off. Managers need to trust, then rely on data to assess performance.

- **Educate.** Location-agnostic work is a hard concept to grasp. Thus, refresher courses are a must for managers and workers.

- **Gather.** When workers are nomads, regular gatherings, in person or by videoconference, help retain a team dynamic.

- ***Marketing Argument.*** For multinational firms, the insight and cultural sensitivity that members with roots in other countries bring to marketing efforts will be very useful. A similar rationale applies to subpopulations within domestic operations.
- ***Creativity Argument.*** Less emphasis on conformity to norms of the past and a diversity of perspectives will improve the level of creativity.
- ***Problem-Solving Argument.*** Heterogeniety in decision-making and problem-solving groups potentially produces better decisions because of a wider range of perspectives as well as more thorough and critical analysis of issues. To illustrate, Jim Schiro, CEO of PriceWaterhouseCoopers, explains, "When you make a genuine commitment

MTV: Benefiting from a Diverse Workforce

Managers know that heterogeneous workforces are rich seedbeds for ideas. However, companies seldom tap employees for insights and experiences specific to their cultures. Further, barriers of language, geography, and association often prevent diverse employees from collaborating on innovation efforts.

Chief Diversity Officers (CDOs) are probably more familiar with the cultural breadth and variety of their companies' talent than anyone. Consequently, they are in an excellent position to bring together different groups to produce innovation.

On October 28, 2006, MTV Networks, a unit of Viacom International Inc. announced that Billy Dexter was appointed the firm's first Executive Vice President and Chief Diversity Officer. He will lead MTV's global initiatives to foster the highest levels of diversity throughout every aspect of the business.

Source: Johansson, F. 2005. Masters of the multicultural. *Harvard Business Review,* 83(10): 18–19; and Anonymous. 2006. MTV Networks names Billy Dexter as Chief Diversity Officer. *PRNewswire.* October 28. np.

Judy McGrath, Chairman and CEO of MTV Networks states:

> We are completely committed to diversity and inclusion, because it's the most creative and vibrant thing we can do for our future. The audience for our content is increasingly global, diverse in thought, demographic, and lifestyle. Over the years, no other initiative has so enriched MTV Networks, or made us more relevant and successful.

How has MTV Networks benefited from their diversity?

One cross-cultural group discovered marketing opportunities in the similarities between North American country music and Latin American music, which use many of the same instruments, feature singers with similar vocal styles, and—in the U.S. Sunbelt—appeal to much the same audience. Other groups have influenced the multicultural content of Nickelodeon's children's programming. Says Tom Freston, MTV's former CEO, "Those teams are diverse by design to generate innovation. The probability that you will get a good, original, innovative idea with that type of chemistry is simply much higher."

---

to diversity, you bring a greater diversity of ideas, approaches, and experiences and abilities that can be applied to client problems. After all, six people with different perspectives have a better shot at solving complex problems than sixty people who all think alike."[50]

- *System Flexibility Argument.* With effective programs to enhance workplace diversity, systems become less determinant, less standardized, and therefore more fluid. Such fluidity should lead to greater flexibility to react to environmental changes. Reactions should be faster and less costly.

In the past, the role of the diversity officer was mostly to ensure compliance with EEOC (Equal Employment Opportunity Commission) requirements or, at best, to make minimal efforts to produce the appearance of diversity. Today many companies are realizing that the role of the Chief Diversity Officer (CDO) can add real value to a company. Strategy Spotlight 4.4 discusses how the role of the CDO at MTV Networks (part of Viacom) has evolved and how its business has benefited from a diverse workforce.

The Vital Role of Social Capital

>LO3

The key role of social capital in leveraging human capital within and across the firm.

Successful firms are well aware that the attraction, development, and retention of talent *is a necessary but not sufficient condition* for creating competitive advantages.[51] In the knowledge economy, it is not the stock of human capital that is important, but the extent to which it is combined and leveraged. In a sense, developing and retaining human capital becomes less important as key players (talented professionals, in particular) take the role of "free agents" and bring with them the requisite skill in many cases. Rather, the development of social capital (that is, the friendships and working relationships among talented individuals) gains importance, because it helps tie knowledge workers to a given firm.[52] Knowledge workers often exhibit greater loyalties to their colleagues and their profession than their employing organization, which may be "an amorphous, distant, and sometimes threatening entity."[53] Thus, a firm must find ways to create "ties" among its knowledge workers.

To illustrate, let's look at a hypothetical example. Two pharmaceutical firms are fortunate enough to hire Nobel Prize–winning scientists.[54] In one case, the scientist is offered a very attractive salary, outstanding facilities and equipment, and told to "go to it!" In the second case, the scientist is offered approximately the same salary, facilities, and equipment plus one additional ingredient. He or she will be working in a laboratory with 10 highly skilled and enthusiastic scientists. Part of the job is to collaborate with these peers and jointly develop promising drug compounds. There is little doubt as to which scenario will lead to a higher probability of retaining the scientist. Clearly, the interaction, sharing, and collaboration will create a situation in which the scientist will develop firm-specific ties and be less likely to "bolt" for a higher salary offer. Such ties are critical because knowledge-based resources tend to be more tacit in nature, as we mentioned early in this chapter. Therefore, they are much more difficult to protect against loss (i.e., the individual quitting the organization) than other types of capital, such as equipment, machinery, and land.

Another way to view this situation is in terms of the resource-based view of the firm that we discussed in Chapter 3. That is, competitive advantages tend to be harder for competitors to copy if they are based on "unique bundles" of resources.[55] So, if employees are working effectively in teams and sharing their knowledge and learning from each other, not only will they be more likely to add value to the firm, but they also will be less likely to leave the organization, because of the loyalties and social ties that they develop over time.

Next, we'll address a key concept in the New Economy—the Pied Piper Effect. Here, groups of professionals join (or leave) organizations en masse, not one at a time. Then, we will discuss the vital role of social networks in promoting knowledge management and enhancing career success.

How Social Capital Helps Attract and Retain Talent

The importance of social ties among talented professionals is creating a significant challenge (and opportunity) for organizations today. In *The Wall Street Journal,* Bernard Wysocki described the increasing prevalence of a type of "Pied Piper Effect," in which teams or networks of people are leaving one company for another.[56] The trend is to recruit job candidates at the crux of social relationships in organizations, particularly if they are seen as having the potential to bring with them a raft of valuable colleagues. This is a process that is referred to as "hiring via personal networks." Let's look at one instance of this practice.

> Gerald Eickhoff, founder of an electronic commerce company called Third Millennium Communications, tried for 15 years to hire Michael Reene. Why? Mr. Eickhoff says that he has "these Pied Piper skills." Mr. Reene was a star at Andersen Consulting in the 1980s and at IBM in the 1990s. He built his businesses and kept turning down overtures from Mr. Eickhoff.
>
> However, in early 2000, he joined Third Millennium as chief executive officer, with a salary of just $120,000 but with a 20 percent stake in the firm. Since then, he has brought in a raft of former IBM colleagues and Andersen subordinates. One protégé from his time at Andersen, Mary Goode, was brought on board as executive vice president. She promptly tapped her own network and brought along a half-dozen friends and former colleagues.

Company	What It Does	Defectors from Microsoft
Crossgain	Builds software around XML computer language	23 of 60 employees
ViAir	Makes software for wireless providers	Company declines to specify
CheckSpace	Builds online payment service for small businesses	Company says "a good chunk" of its 30 employees
digiMine	Sells data mining service	About 15% of 62 employees in addition to the 3 founders
Avogadro	Builds wireless notification software	8 of 25 employees
Tellme Networks	Offers information like stock quotes and scores over the phone	About 40 of 250 employees; another 40 from the former Netscape

Source: Buckman, R. 2000. "Tech Defectors from Microsoft Resettle Together," *The Wall Street Journal,* Eastern Edition, 2000. Copyright © 2000 by Dow Jones & Company, Inc. Reproduced with permission of Dow Jones & Company, Inc. via Copyright Clearance Center.

Wysocki considers the Pied Piper effect one of the underappreciated factors in the war for talent today. This is because one of the myths of the New Economy is rampant individualism, wherein individuals find jobs on the Internet career sites and go to work for complete strangers. Perhaps, instead of Me Inc., the truth is closer to We Inc.[57]

Another example of social relationships causing human capital mobility is the emigration of talent from an organization to form start-up ventures. Microsoft is perhaps the best-known example of this phenomenon.[58] Professionals have frequently left Microsoft en masse to form venture capital and technology start-ups built around teams of software developers. One example is Ignition Corporation, of Bellevue, Washington, which was formed by Brad Silverberg, a former Microsoft senior vice president. Eight former Microsoft executives, among others, founded the company. Exhibit 4.6 provides a partial listing of other companies that have been formed by groups of former Microsoft employees.

Social relationships can provide an important mechanism for obtaining both resources and information from individuals and organizations outside the boundary of a firm.[59] Strategy Spotlight 4.5 touts the benefits of firms' alumni programs. It describes how eBay's general counsel became an excellent source of business for his prior employer.

Social Networks: Implications for Knowledge Management and Career Success

Today, managers face a myriad of challenges driven by such factors as rapid changes in globalization and technology. Clearly, leading a successful company is more than a one-person job. As Tom Malone recently put it in *The Future of Work,* "As managers, we need to shift our thinking from command and control to coordinate and cultivate—the best way to gain power is sometimes to give it away." The move away from top-down bureaucratic control to more open, decentralized network models of organization makes it more difficult for managers to understand how work is actually getting done, who is interacting with whom both within and outside the organization, and the consequences of these

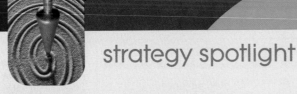
Alumni Programs: A Great Way to Stay in Touch

Michael Jacobson had worked in securities practices at Cooley Godward, a Palo Alto, California law firm, for a dozen years. Nobody was happy when he gave notice in 1998. Everyone felt that it would be difficult to get along without him.

However, a few months later, Cooley Godward's managers couldn't have been happier. Why? Jacobson's new job was as general counsel at a little-known online auction site called eBay! When the site needed outside counsel, Jacobsen tapped his former employer. A few months later, Cooley Godward was lead counsel for eBay's record-breaking $1.3 billion initial public offering. "It's a great relationship," says Mark Pitchford, partner and chief operating officer of the firm.

With such a "lucky break," Cooley Godward no longer leaves such matters to chance. In January 2004, it launched an alumni program to help the firm stay in touch with its former attorneys. Such programs are not particularly new to corporate America. Firms such as McKinsey & Company, Ernst & Young, and Procter & Gamble have had them in place for years. However, as partners at Cooley Godward have found, smaller firms can also benefit from alumni initiatives. "Former employees are a resource," says John Izzo, president of Izzo Consulting, a firm based in Vancouver, Washington. The firm advises small businesses on employee training and retention issues.

Despite the potential benefits of maintaining active contact with former employees, many employers treat them as just another name in the Rolodex—or even worse, as a competitive threat. Izzo warns that this can be a big mistake. Often, he claims, former staffers can act as goodwill ambassadors for their former employers, helping to refer new talent and clients. They may even return at a later point and will requiring little training. And with the job market now showing signs of improvement and many employees more likely to move on, alumni programs could become very important, especially at firms that have a hard time recruiting and retaining qualified professionals.

Source: Rich, L. 2005. Don't be a stranger. *Inc.*, January: 32–33.

>LO4

The importance of social networks in knowledge management and in promoting career success.

social network analysis analysis of the pattern of social interactions among individuals.

interactions for the long-term health of the organization. In short, coordination, cultivation, and collaboration are increasingly becoming the mode of work at every level throughout organizations.[60]

But how can this be done? One approach that has provided valuable insights is social network analysis.[61] **Social network analysis** depicts the pattern of interactions among individuals and helps to diagnose effective and ineffective patterns. It can be used to help identify groups or clusters of individuals that comprise the network, individuals who link the clusters, and other network members. It helps diagnose communication patterns and, consequently, communication effectiveness.[62] Such analysis of communication patterns is helpful because the configuration of group members' social ties within and outside the group affects the extent to which members connect to individuals who:

- convey needed resources,
- have the opportunity to exchange information and support,
- have the motivation to treat each other in positive ways, and,
- have the time to develop trusting relationships that might improve the groups' effectiveness.

However, such relationships don't "just happen."[63] Developing and protecting social capital requires interdependence among members in a group. Social capital erodes when people in the network become more independent of each other. And increased interactions between members aid in the development and maintenance of mutual obligations in a social network.

Let's take a brief look at a simplified network analysis to get a grasp of the key ideas. In Exhibit 4.7, the links are used to depict informal relationships among individuals

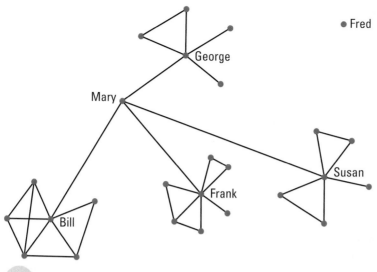

Exhibit 4.7 A Simplified Social Network

involving communication flows, personal support, and advice networks. There may be some individuals with literally no linkages, such as Fred. These individuals are typically labeled "isolates." However, most people do have some linkages with others.

To simplify, there are two primary types of mechanisms through which social capital will flow: *closure relationships* (depicted by Bill, Frank, George, and Susan) and *bridging relationships* (depicted by Mary). As we can see, in the former relationships one member is central to the communication flows in a group. In contrast, in the latter relationship, one person "bridges" or brings together groups that would have been otherwise unconnected.

Both closure and bridging relationships have important implications for the effective flow of information in organizations and for the management of knowledge. We will now briefly discuss each of these types of relationships. We will also address some of the implications that understanding social networks has for one's career success.

Closure   With **closure,** each group has a high level of connectedness. That is, many members have relationships (or ties) with other members. As indicated in Exhibit 4.7, Bill's group would have a higher level of closure than Frank, Susan, or George's groups because more group members are connected to each other. Through closure, group members develop strong relationships with each other, high levels of trust, and greater solidarity. High levels of trust help to ensure that informal norms in the group will be more easily enforced and there will tend to be less "free riding." Social pressure will prevent people from withholding effort or shirking their responsibilities. In addition, people in the network are more willing to extend favors and "go the extra mile" on a colleague's behalf because they are confident that their efforts will be reciprocated by another member in their group. Another benefit of a network with closure is that there is a high level of emotional support. This becomes particularly valuable when setbacks occur that may destroy morale or an unexpected tragedy happens that might cause the group to lose its focus. Social support helps the group to rebound from misfortune and get back on track.

But high levels of closure often come with a price. Groups that become too closed can become insular. They cut themselves off from learning about what is happening in the rest of the organization and fail to share what they are learning from people outside their group. Research shows that while managers need to encourage closure up to a point, if there is too much closure, they need to encourage people to open up their groups and infuse new ideas through bridging relationships.[64]

closure the degree to which all members of a social network have relationships (or ties) with other group members.

Bridging Relationships   The closure perspective rests on an assumption that there is a high level of similarity among group members. However, members can be quite heterogeneous with regard to their positions in either the formal or informal structures of the group or the organization. Such heterogeneity exists because of, for example, vertical boundaries (different levels in the hierarchy) and horizontal boundaries (different functional areas).

bridging relationships

relationships in a social network that connect otherwise disconnected people.

structural holes

social gaps between groups in a social network where there are few relationships bridging the groups.

Bridging relationships, in contrast to closure, stresses the importance of ties connecting heterogeneous people. Employees who bridge otherwise disconnected people tend to receive timely, diverse information because of their access to a wide range of heterogeneous information flows. Such bridging relationships can serve to span a number of different types of boundaries within an organization.

The University of Chicago's Ron Burt originally coined the term **"structural holes"** to refer to the social gap between two groups. Structural holes are common in organizations. When they occur in business, managers typically refer to them as "silos" or "stovepipes." Sales and engineering are a classic example of two groups whose members traditionally interact with their peers rather than across groups.

Let's briefly review a study that Burt conducted at Raytheon, a $20 billion U.S. electronics company and military contractor, that provides further insight into the benefits of bridging.[65]

> Burt studied several hundred managers within Raytheon's supply chain group and asked each manager to write down ideas to improve the company's supply chain management. Then he asked two Raytheon executives to rate the ideas. The conclusion: *The best suggestions consistently came from managers who discussed ideas outside their regular work group.*
>
> Burt found that Raytheon managers were good at thinking of ideas but bad at developing them. Too often, Burt said, the managers discussed their ideas with colleagues already in their informal discussion network. Instead, he said, they should have had discussions outside their typical contacts, particularly with an informal boss, or someone with enough power to be an ally but not an actual supervisor.

Strategy Spotlight 4.6 addresses the value of informal friendships as an effective source of social capital. Interestingly, it also discusses the downside of insular, self-reliant groups.

Before we address the implications of social network theory for managers' career success, one might ask: Which is the more valuable mechanism to develop and nurture social capital—closure or bridging relationships? As with many aspects of strategic management, the answer becomes: "It all depends." So let's consider a few contingent issues.[66] First, consider firms in competitive environments characterized by rapidly changing technology and market factors. These firms should bridge relationships across networks because they need a wide variety of timely sources of information. Also, innovation is facilitated if there are multiple, interdisciplinary perspectives. On the other hand, firms competing in a stable environment would typically face a rather small amount of unpredictability. Thus, the cohesive ties associated with network closure would help to ensure the timely and effective implementation of strategies.

A second contingent factor would be the type of business strategies that a firm may choose to follow (a topic that we address next in Chapter 5). Managers with social networks characterized by closure would be in a preferred position if their firm is following an overall low cost strategy.[67] Here, there is a need for control and coordination to implement strategies that are rather constrained by pressures to reduce costs. Alternatively, the uncertainties generally associated with differentiation strategies (i.e., creating products that are perceived by customers as unique and highly valued) would require a broad range of information sources and inputs. Social networks characterized by bridging relationships across groups would access the diverse informational sources needed to deal with more complex, multifaceted strategies.

A caveat: In both contingencies that we have discussed—competitive environment and business strategy—closure and bridging relationships across groups are necessary. Our purpose is to address where one type should be more dominant.

strategy spotlight

The Value (and Limitations) of Informal Friendships in Organizations

Rope courses and Outward Bound-type activities help white-collar workers develop corporate collegiality through socializing, sweating and sharing stressful situations. People go in as co-workers and come out as friends. However, wholesale congeniality can actually make teams *less* effective.

Recently, Joe Labianca (now at the University of Kentucky) and two colleagues studied 60 teams in 11 companies representing a wide variety of industries. In the most effective teams, about half of the relationships among members were close enough to be considered friendships. However, in teams where the number of friendships approached 100 percent, performance dropped dramatically. Why? Such groups suffered because they were insular, impermeable to outside influences, and unhealthily self-reliant. Members may have developed a high level of trust and commitment with each other but they were too dependent on their own members for new insights and initiatives. At times, those problems can be avoided by brainstorming or by assigning someone in the group to be a devil's advocate. But where friendships are especially close, even those techniques are unlikely to produce dramatically differing perspectives.

Sources: Labianca, J. 2004. The ties that bind. *Harvard Business Review*, 82(10): 19; Oh, H. Chung, M., & Labianca, G. 2004. Group social capital and group effectiveness: The role of informal socializing ties. *Academy of Management Journal*, 47(6): 86–875; and Labianca, J. 2007. Personal communication. February 28.

The friendships that benefit teams most are formed *outside the group*. Business-centered relationships with people in other parts of the company are important for transmitting simple work flow information. But even more important are relationships that extend into the social sphere—to lunches and dinners and after-work drinks. Such interactions are especially valuable sources of social capital. Team members who socialize in this way, particularly with top managers and with leaders of other teams play a key role in bridging groups and individuals who otherwise would be unconnected to their own group. This enables them to bring back to their groups strategic information, task-related advice, and political and social support.

Higher-level managers can't require employees to befriend people outside their own domains. However, they can encourage it. Team leaders should be told that developing a broad social network is part of their job. Managers should set aside funds for cross-functional social activities and create opportunities for employees to bond around common hobbies or pursuits. When composing teams, leaders should consider whom—as well as what—potential members know. And mentoring programs should aim to place company fledglings beneath the wings of veterans from other departments rather than with people they work with every day.

To sum up, there is nothing wrong with Outward Bound activities. However, instead of braving the wilderness, teams should venture into the far corners of their own organization!

Implications for Career Success Clearly, effective social networks can provide many advantages for an organization. They can also play a key role in an individual's career advancement and success. From an individual's perspective, social networks deliver three unique advantages: private information, access to diverse skill sets, and power.[68] Managers see these advantages at work every day but might not pause to consider how their networks regulate them.

Private Information When we make judgments, we use both public and private information. Today, public information is easily available from a variety of sources, including the Internet. However, since it is so accessible, public information offers significantly less competitive advantage than it used to.

In contrast, private information is gathered from personal contacts who can offer something unique that cannot be found in publicly available sources, such as the release date of a new product or knowledge about what a particular interviewer looks for in candidates. Private information, therefore, can give managers an edge, though it is more subjective than public information since it cannot be easily verified by independent sources, such as Dunn & Bradstreet. Consequently the value of your private information to others—and the value of others' private information to you—depends on how much trust exists in the network of relationships.

Access to Diverse Skill Sets Linus Pauling, one of only two people to win a Nobel Prize in two different areas and considered one of the towering geniuses of the 20th century, attributed his creative success not to his immense brainpower or luck but to his diverse contacts. He said, "The best way to have a good idea is to have a lot of ideas."

While expertise has become more specialized during the past 15 years, organizational, product, and marketing issues have become more interdisciplinary. This means that success is tied to the ability to transcend natural skill limitations through others. Highly diverse network relationships, therefore, can help you develop more complete, creative, and unbiased perspectives on issues. And when you trade information or skills with people whose experiences differ from your own, you provide one another with unique, exceptionally valuable resources. It is common for people in relationships to share their problems with each other. If you know enough people, you will begin to see how the problems that another person is struggling with can be solved by the solutions being developed by others. If you can bring together problems and solutions, it will greatly benefit your career.

Power Traditionally, a manager's power was embedded in a firm's hierarchy. But, when corporate organizations became flatter, more like pancakes than pyramids, that power was repositioned in the network's brokers (people who bridged multiple networks), who could adapt to changes in the organization, develop clients, and synthesize opposing points of view. Such brokers weren't necessarily at the top of the hierarchy or experts in their fields, but they linked specialists in the firm with trustworthy and informative relationships.

Most personal networks are highly clustered; that is, an individual's friends are likely to be friends with one another as well. Most corporate networks are made up of several clusters that have few links between them. Brokers are especially powerful because they connect separate clusters, thus stimulating collaboration among otherwise independent specialists.

The Potential Downside of Social Capital

We'd like to close our discussion of social capital by addressing some of its limitations; that is, how social capital can impede an organization's effectiveness. First, some firms have been adversely affected by very high levels of social capital because it may breed **"groupthink"**—a tendency not to question shared beliefs.[69] Such thinking may occur in networks with high levels of closure where there is little input from people outside of the network. In effect, too many warm and fuzzy feelings among group members prevent people from rigorously challenging each other with tough questions. People are discouraged from engaging in the "creative abrasion" that Dorothy Leonard of Harvard University describes as a key source of innovation.[70] Two firms that were well known for their collegiality, strong sense of employee membership, and humane treatment—Digital Equipment (now part of Hewlett-Packard) and Polaroid—suffered greatly from market misjudgments and strategic errors. The aforementioned aspects of their culture contributed to their problems.

The second potential limitation is an outcome of the first one. If there are deeprooted mindsets, there would be a tendency to develop dysfunctional human resource practices. That is, the organization (or group) would continue to hire, reward, and promote like-minded people who tend to further intensify organizational inertia and erode innovation. Such homogeneity would increase over time and decrease the effectiveness of decision-making processes.

Third, the socialization processes (orientation, training, etc.) can be expensive in terms of both financial resources and managerial commitment. Such investments can represent a

groupthink a tendency in an organization for individuals not to question shared beliefs.

significant opportunity cost that should be evaluated in terms of the intended benefits. If such expenses become excessive, profitability would be adversely affected.

Finally, individuals may use the contacts they develop to pursue their own interests and agendas that may be inconsistent with the organization's goals and objectives. Thus, they may distort or selectively use information to favor their preferred courses of action or withhold information in their own self-interest to enhance their power in the organization to the detriment of the common good. Drawing on our discussion of social networks, this is particularly true in an organization that has too many bridging relationships but not enough closure relationships. When people are involved in high closure groups, it is easy for them to watch each other to make certain that illegal or unethical acts don't occur. By contrast, bridging relationships make it easier for a person to play one group or individual off on another, with no one being the wiser.[71] We will discuss some behavioral control mechanisms in Chapter 9 (rewards, control, boundaries) that serve to reduce such dysfunctional behaviors and actions.[72]

Using Technology to Leverage Human Capital and Knowledge

Sharing knowledge and information throughout the organization can be a means of conserving resources, developing products and services, and creating new opportunities. In this section we will discuss how technology can be used to leverage human capital and knowledge within organizations as well as with customers and suppliers beyond their boundaries.

>LO5
The vital role of technology in leveraging knowledge and human capital.

Using Networks to Share Information

As we all know, e-mail is an effective means of communicating a wide variety of information. It is quick, easy, and almost costless. Of course, it can become a problem when employees use it extensively for personal reasons. And we all know how fast jokes or rumors can spread within and across organizations!

Below is an example of how a CEO curbed what he felt was excessive e-mail use in his firm.[73]

> Scott Dockter, CEO of PBD Worldwide Fulfillment Services in Alpharetta, Georgia, launched "no e-mail Friday." Why? He suspected that overdependence on e-mail at PBD, which offers services such as call center management and distribution, was hurting productivity and, perhaps, sales. Accordingly, he instructed his 275 employees to pick up the phone or meet in person each Friday, and reduce e-mail use the rest of the time.
>
> That was tough to digest, especially for the younger staffers. "We discovered a lot of introverts . . . who had drifted into a pattern of communicating by e-mail," says Dockter. However, in less than four months, the simple directive resulted in quicker problem-solving, better teamwork, and, best of all, happier customers." "Our relationship with PBD is much stronger," says Cynthia Fitzpatrick of Crown Financial Ministries. "You can't get to know someone through e-mail."

E-mail can, however, be a means for top executives to communicate information efficiently. For example, Martin Sorrell, chairman of WPP Group PLC, a $2.4 billion advertising and public relations firm, is a strong believer in the use of e-mail.[74] He e-mails all of his employees once a month to discuss how the company is doing, address specific issues, and offer his perspectives on hot issues, such as new business models for the Internet. He believes that it keeps people abreast of what he is working on.

Technology can also enable much more sophisticated forms of communication in addition to knowledge sharing. Buckman Laboratories is a $300 million specialty chemicals company based in Memphis, Tennessee, with approximately 1,300 employees in over

100 countries. Buckman has successfully used its global knowledge sharing network—known as K'Netix—to enhance its competitive advantages:[75]

> Here's an example of how the network can be applied. One of Buckman's paper customers in Michigan realized that the peroxide it was adding to remove ink from old magazines was no longer working. A Buckman sales manager presented this problem to the knowledge network. Within two days, salespeople from Belgium and Finland identified a likely cause: Bacteria in the paper slurry was producing an enzyme that broke down the peroxide. The sales manager recommended a chemical to control the bacteria, solving the problem. You can imagine how positive the customer felt about Buckman. And with the company and the customer co-creating knowledge, a new level of trust and value can emerge.

Electronic Teams: Using Technology to Enhance Collaboration

>LO6

Why "electronic" or "virtual" teams are critical in combining and leveraging knowledge in organizations and how they can be made more effective.

The use of technology has also enabled professionals to work as part of electronic, or virtual, teams to enhance the speed and effectiveness with which products are developed. For example, Microsoft has concentrated much of its development on **electronic teams** (or e-teams) that are networked together throughout the company.[76] This helps to accelerate design and testing of new software modules that use the Windows-based framework as their central architecture. Microsoft is able to foster specialized technical expertise while sharing knowledge rapidly throughout the organization. This helps the firm learn how its new technologies can be applied rapidly to new business ventures such as cable television, broadcasting, travel services, and financial services.

electronic teams a team of individuals that completes tasks primarily through e-mail communication.

What are electronic teams (or e-teams)? There are two key differences between e-teams and more traditional teams.[77] First, e-team members either work in geographically separated work places or they may work in the same space but at different times. E-teams may have members working in different spaces and time zones, as is the case with many multinational teams. Second, most of the interactions among members of e-teams occur through electronic communication channels such as fax machines and groupware tools such as e-mail, bulletin boards, chat, and videoconferencing.

E-teams have expanded exponentially in recent years.[78] Organizations face increasingly high levels of complex and dynamic change. E-teams are also effective in helping businesses cope with global challenges. Most e-teams perform very complex tasks and most knowledge-based teams are charged with developing new products, improving organizational processes, and satisfying challenging customer problems. For example, Eastman Kodak's e-teams design new products, Hewlett Packard's e-teams solve clients' computing problems, and Sun Microsystems' e-teams generate new business models.

Advantages There are multiple advantages of e-teams.[79] In addition to the rather obvious use of technology to facilitate communications, the potential benefits parallel the other two major sections in this chapter—human capital and social capital. First, e-teams are less restricted by the geographic constraints that are placed on face-to-face teams. Thus, e-teams have the potential to acquire a broader range of "human capital" or the skills and capacities that are necessary to complete complex assignments. So, e-team leaders can draw upon a greater pool of talent to address a wider range of problems since they are not constrained by geographic space. Once formed, e-teams can be more flexible in responding to unanticipated work challenges and opportunities because team members can be rotated out of projects when demands and contingencies alter the team's objectives.

Second, e-teams can be very effective in generating "social capital"—the quality of relationships and networks that leaders and team members form. Such capital is a key lubricant in work transactions and operations. Given the broader boundaries associated with e-teams, members and leaders generally have access to a wider range of social contacts than would be typically available in more traditional face-to-face teams. Such contacts are often connected to a broader scope of clients, customers, constituents, and other key stakeholders.

Challenges However, there are challenges associated with making e-teams effective. Successful action by both traditional teams and e-teams requires that:

- Members *identify* who among them can provide the most appropriate knowledge and resources, and,
- E-team leaders and key members know how to *combine* individual contributions in the most effective manner for a coordinated and appropriate response.

Group psychologists have termed such activities "identification and combination" activities and teams that fail to perform them face a "process loss."[80] Process losses prevent teams from reaching high levels of performance because of inefficient interaction dynamics among team members. Such poor dynamics require that some collective energy, time, and effort be devoted to dealing with team inefficiencies, thus diverting the team away from its objectives. For example, if a team member fails to communicate important information at critical phases of a project, other members may waste time and energy. This can lead to conflict and resentment as well as to decreased motivation to work hard to complete tasks. Clearly, team leaders and other members must expend collective energy to repair the breach, resulting in a process loss.

The potential for process losses tends to be more prevalent in e-teams than in traditional teams because the geographical dispersion of members increases the complexity of establishing effective interaction and exchanges. Generally, teams suffer process loss because of low cohesion, low trust among members, a lack of appropriate norms or standard operating procedures, or a lack of shared understanding among team members about their tasks. With e-teams, members are more geographically or temporally dispersed, and the team becomes more susceptible to the risk factors that can create process loss. Such problems can be exacerbated when team members have less than ideal competencies and social skills. This can erode problem-solving capabilities as well as the effective functioning of the group as a social unit.

Codifying Knowledge for Competitive Advantage

As we discussed early in this chapter, there are two different kinds of knowledge. Tacit knowledge is embedded in personal experience and shared only with the consent and participation of the individual. Explicit (or codified) knowledge, on the other hand, is knowledge that can be documented, widely distributed, and easily replicated. One of the challenges of knowledge-intensive organizations is to capture and codify the knowledge and experience that, in effect, resides in the heads of its employees. Otherwise, they will have to constantly "reinvent the wheel," which is both expensive and inefficient. Also, the "new wheel" may not necessarily be superior to the "old wheel."[81]

Once a knowledge asset (e.g., a software code or processes, routines for a consulting firm) is developed and paid for, it can be reused many times at very low cost, assuming that it doesn't have to be substantially modified each time. Let's take the case of a consulting company, such as Accenture (formerly Andersen Consulting).[82] Since the knowledge of its consultants has been codified and stored in electronic repositories, it can be employed in many jobs by a huge number of consultants. Additionally, since the work has a high level of standardization (i.e., there are strong similarities across the numerous client engagements), there generally tends to be a rather high ratio of consultants to partners. For example, the ratio of consultants to partners is roughly 30, which is quite high. As one might expect, there must be extensive training of the newly hired consultants for such an approach to work. The recruits are trained at Accenture's Center for Professional Education, a 150-acre campus in St. Charles, Illinois. Using the center's knowledge-management respository, the consultants work through many scenarios designed to improve business processes. In effect, the information technologies enable the consultants to be "implementers, not inventors."

Access Health, a call-in medical center, also uses technology to capture and share knowledge. When someone calls the center, a registered nurse uses the company's "clinical decision architecture" to assess the caller's symptoms, rule out possible conditions, and

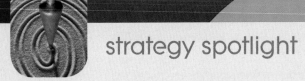
How Context Integration Developed an Effective Knowledge Management System

Bruce Strong, founder and CEO of Context Integration, a Web consulting firm, decided to develop a knowledge-management system. Six months and a half million dollars later, he unveiled IAN (Intellectual Assets Network). The objective was to provide a medium for his consultants to share ideas, ask questions, and trace earlier journeys on similar projects. In theory it was fine. But Strong was disappointed with the lack of involvement by his employees. Why didn't the consultants embrace IAN? There were many reasons:

- Consultants saw depositing notes or project records into the database as one more task in a busy day.

- The task didn't appear to have any urgency.

- Consultants generally did not like to admit that they couldn't solve a problem.

- They resented management trying to impose what consultants perceived as a rigid structure on their work.

What did Strong decide to do? He began to reinforce the many benefits of the system, such as providing better and more consistent service. He also publicly recognized people who stood out as strong IAN contributors, and he made this part of everyone's job description. Perhaps most important, he began paying people to use it. He assigned points when people used the system—for example, one point for posting a résumé on the system, five points for creating a project record, and so on. The results were tallied every three months and the score accounted for 10 percent of a consultant's quarterly bonus. Over a two-month period, overall IAN usage almost doubled. However, more importantly, many consultants became enthusiastic converts once they had a positive experience with IAN. Not only does IAN continue to help many of them provide excellent service to their clients, but it also allows the firm to retain some of their knowledge when they leave.

Bruce Strong's initial disappointment was hardly surprising. According to Carla O'Dell, president of the American Productivity and Quality Center, of the companies trying knowledge management, fewer than 10 percent succeeded in making it part of their culture. She suggests:

Technology plays a laggard role, not a leadership role. You need to establish relationships, the communities, the networks, the habits of sharing, the agreements about what we're going to share, and why it's important. All of that has to be working first before you automate it.

Sources: O'Dell, C. 2005. Knowledge Management: Identify, capture, share, and reuse key information. *EMA Communicator*. Fall: 4–5; and Koudsi, S. 2000. Actually, it is brain surgery. *Fortune*. March 20: 233.

recommend a home remedy, doctor's visit, or trip to the emergency room. The company's knowledge repository contains algorithms of the symptoms of more than 500 illnesses. According to CEO Joseph Tallman, "We are not inventing a new way to cure disease. We are taking available knowledge and inventing processes to put it to better use." The software algorithms were very expensive to develop, but the investment has been repaid many times over. The first 300 algorithms that Access Health developed have each been used an average of 8,000 times a year. Further, the company's paying customers—insurance companies and provider groups—save money because many callers would have made expensive trips to the emergency room or the doctor's office had they not been diagnosed over the phone.

Motivation is often a key issue in making knowledge management systems effective. That is, what are the incentives for people to contribute their knowledge? Some organizations have found that such systems work best when they are incorporated into the firm's evaluation and reward systems. Strategy Spotlight 4.7 discusses some of the challenges faced by Context Integration's CEO in developing his firm's knowledge management system.

We close this section with a series of questions managers should consider in determining (1) how effective their organization is in attracting, developing, and retaining human capital and (2) how effective they are in leveraging human capital through social capital and technology. These questions, included in Exhibit 4.8, summarize some of the key issues addressed in this chapter.

Human Capital

Recruiting "Top-Notch" Human Capital

- Does the organization assess attitude and "general makeup" instead of focusing primarily on skills and background in selecting employees at all levels?
- How important are creativity and problem-solving ability? Are they properly considered in hiring decisions?
- Do people throughout the organization engage in effective networking activities to obtain a broad pool of worthy potential employees? Is the organization creative in such endeavors?

Enhancing Human Capital through Employee Development

- Does the development and training process inculcate an "organizationwide" perspective?
- Is there widespread involvement, including top executives, in the preparation and delivery of training and development programs?
- Is the development of human capital effectively tracked and monitored?
- Are there effective programs for succession at all levels of the organization, especially at the top-most levels?
- Does the firm effectively evaluate its human capital? Is a 360-degree evaluation used? Why? Why not?
- Are mechanisms in place to assure that a manager's success does not come at the cost of compromising the organization's core values?

Retaining the Best Employees

- Are there appropriate financial rewards to motivate employees at all levels?
- Do people throughout the organization strongly identify with the organization's mission?
- Are employees provided with a stimulating and challenging work environment that fosters professional growth?
- Are valued amenities provided (e.g., flex time, child-care facilities, telecommuting) that are appropriate given the organization's mission, strategy, and how work is accomplished?
- Is the organization continually devising strategies and mechanisms to retain top performers?

Social Capital

- Are there positive personal and professional relationships among employees?
- Is the organization benefiting (or being penalized) by hiring (or by voluntary turnover) en masse?
- Does an environment of caring and encouragement rather than competition enhance team performance?
- Do the social networks within the organization have the appropriate levels of closure and bridging relationships?
- Does the organization minimize the adverse effects of excessive social capital, such as excessive costs and "groupthink"?

Technology

- Has the organization used technologies such as e-mail and networks to develop products and services?
- Does the organization effectively use technology to transfer best practices across the organization?
- Does the organization use technology to leverage human capital and knowledge both within the boundaries of the organization and among its suppliers and customers?
- Has the organization effectively used technology to codify knowledge for competitive advantage?
- Does the organization try to retain some of the knowledge of employees when they decide to leave the firm?

Source: Adapted from Dess, G. G., & Picken, J. C. 1999. *Beyond Productivity:* 63–64. New York: AMACON.

Exhibit 4.8   Issues to Consider in Creating Value through Human Capital, Social Capital, and Technology

Protecting the Intellectual Assets of the Organization: Intellectual Property and Dynamic Capabilities

>LO7

The challenge of protecting intellectual property and the importance of a firm's dynamic capabilities.

In today's dynamic and turbulent world, unpredictability and fast change dominate the business environment. Economic prosperity rests upon the useful application of knowledge. Firms can use technology, attract human capital, or tap into research and design networks to get access to pretty much the same information as their competitors. So what would give firms a sustainable competitive advantage?[83] Protecting a firm's intellectual property requires a concerted effort on the part of the company. After all, employees become disgruntled and patents expire. The management of intellectual property involves, besides patents, contracts with confidentiality and noncompete clauses, copyrights, and the development of trademarks. Moreover, developing dynamic capabilities is the only avenue providing firms with the ability to reconfigure their knowledge and activities to achieve a sustainable competitive advantage.

Intellectual property rights are more difficult to define and protect than property rights for physical assets (e.g., plant, equipment, and land). However, if intellectual property rights are not reliably protected by the state, no individuals will have the incentive to develop new products and services. Property rights have been enshrined in constitutions and rules of law in many countries. In the information era, though, adjustments need to be made to accommodate the new realities of knowledge. Knowledge and information are fundamentally different assets from the physical ones that property rights have been designed to protect.

The protection of intellectual rights raises unique issues, compared to physical property rights. Much of the production of intellectual property is characterized by significant development costs and very low marginal costs. Indeed, it may take a substantial investment to develop a software program, an idea, or a digital music tune. Once developed, though, their reproduction and distribution cost may be almost zero, especially if the Internet is used. Effective protection of intellectual property is necessary before any investor will finance such an undertaking. Appropriation of their returns is harder to police since possession and deployment are not as readily observable. Unlike physical assets, intellectual property can be stolen by simply broadcasting it. Recall Napster and MP3 as well as the debates about counterfeit software, music CDs, and DVDs coming from developing countries such as China. Part of the problem is that using an idea does not prevent others from simultaneously using it for their own benefit, which is typically impossible with physical assets. Moreover, new ideas are frequently built on old ideas and are not easily traceable. Strategy Spotlight 4.8 describes the many legal battles fought by a Canadian firm, Research in Motion of Waterloo, the developer of the popular Blackberry. This example illustrates the high stakes that ride on intellectual property rights.

Countries are attempting to pass new legislation to cope with developments in such diverse fields as new pharmaceutical compounds, stem cell research, and biotechnology. However, a firm that is faced with this challenge today cannot wait for the legislation to catch up. It has to embark on the next technological development, drug, software solution, electronic game, online service, or any of a myriad of other products and services to contribute to our economic prosperity and the creation of wealth for those entrepreneurs who have the idea first and risk bringing it to the market.

Related to the above, dynamic capabilities entail the capacity to build and protect a competitive advantage. This rests on knowledge, assets, competencies, and complementary assets and technologies as well as the ability to sense and seize new opportunities, generate new knowledge, and reconfigure existing assets and capabilities. According to

Research in Motion, Maker of the Blackberry, Loses an Intellectual Property Lawsuit

Research in Motion (RIM) is a Waterloo, Ontario–based company that is best known for developing the Blackberry, a wireless device that integrates the functionalities of a cell phone with the ability to receive e-mail messages. During its brief history, it has beccome one of the fastest growing companies in North America. Founded by Mike Lazaridis, a former University of Waterloo student in 1984, Research in Motion was a competent but obscure technology firm until 1999 when the first Blackberry was released. Through the development of integrated hardware, software, and services that support multiple wireless network standards, the Blackberry has enabled RIM to grow from less than $50 million in sales revenue in 1999 to $2 billion by 2006. Even more impressive, by 2007 the company can boast a market capitalization in excess of $25 billion. RIM's commitment to their slogan "always on, always connected" has won them a legion of dedicated followers around the globe.

Interestingly, legal challenges have been the biggest obstacles that Research in Motion has faced in the eight years since the introduction of the first Blackberry. In 2002, Virginia-based NTP sued the company alleging patent infringement. Although RIM tried to demonstrate that NTP's patents were invalid because wireless e-mail technology existed prior to NTP's filing of patent applications, the court found them guilty of willfully infringing NTP's patents. While the appeal process dragged on through higher courts, the fear that the court might issue an injunction against Blackberry greatly slowed the growth of RIM's subscriber base. Given the need to allay the anxieties of the subscribers, who could not imagine life without their Blackberries, RIM decided to settle its dispute with NTP in March, 2006. The settlement amount was a staggering $612.5 million in "full and final settlement of all claims"!

In a bizarre postscript to the settlement with NTP, in May 2006, RIM was sued by Redwood Shores, California–based Visto for infringement of its patents. Visto has a history of suing, and occasionally winning, patent infringement lawsuits against companies such as Good Technology, Microsoft, and Seven. Interestingly, NTP holds an equity stake in Visto!

Sources: Hesseldahl, A. 2006. RIM's latest patent problem. *BusinessWeek Online,* May 2: np; Anonymous. 2006. Settlement reached in Blackberry patent case. (The Associated Press) MSNBC.Com. March 3: np; and Wolk, M. 2006. RIM pays up, taking "one for the team." MSNBC.Com. March 3.

● Research in Motion (RIM) has faced litigation over its highly acclaimed Blackberry.

David Teece, an economist at the University of California at Berkeley, dynamic capabilities are related to the entrepreneurial side of the firm and are built within a firm through its environmental and technological "sensing" apparatus, its choices of organizational form, and its collective ability to strategize. Dynamic capabilities are about the ability of an organization to challenge the conventional wisdom within its industry and market, learn and innovate, adapt to the changing world, and continuously adopt new ways to serve the evolving needs of the market.

The Central Role of Leveraging Human Capital in Strategy Formulation

>LO8

How leveraging human capital is critical to strategy formulation for business-level, corporate-level, international, and entrepreneurial strategies.

In this chapter we have emphasized the importance of human capital and how such intangible assets can create the greatest value in today's successful organizations. As we have noted throughout the chapter, attracting top talent is a necessary, but not a sufficient, condition for competitive advantage. It must be not only developed and retained, but also leveraged through effective use of social capital and technology. In this section we will discuss how leveraging human capital is vital to each of the levels of strategy that we will address in the next four chapters (5, 6, 7, and 8) of the book.

Leveraging Human Capital and Business-Level Strategy

At the business level (Chapter 5), firms strive to create advantages that are sustainable over time. To do this, managers must integrate the primary and support activities in their firm's value chain (discussed in Chapter 3). We will discuss how FedEx has provided its drivers with handheld computers—a valuable technology—to help them effectively track customer packages. The FedEx example points out how technology can help a firm enhance business-level strategies by leveraging its human capital.

Leveraging Human Capital and Corporate-Level Strategy

In Chapter 6 on corporate-level strategy, we will discuss how firms can create value by managing their business to create synergy; that is, how more value can be created by working together across business units than if they were freestanding units. Managers must determine what important relationships (products, markets, technologies) exist across businesses and how they can be leveraged. For such knowledge transfer to occur, managers must be aware of not only their human capital (tacit knowledge), but also their organization's codified knowledge and relationships among key professionals and across business units.

Leveraging Human Capital and International-Level Strategy

In Chapter 7 we will address how companies create value by leveraging resources and knowledge across national boundaries. Here firms are faced with two opposing forces: how to achieve economies of scale and how to adapt to local market needs. We will discuss how some leading-edge firms are able to successfully attain a "transnational strategy" wherein not only do the firms achieve lower costs through economies of scale, but also they are able to adapt successfully to local markets. To do so, firms must facilitate the flow of information and knowledge between business units in different countries. This requires not only attracting, developing, and retaining superior talent, but also leveraging their knowledge and skills through effective working relationships (i.e., social capital) and use of technology.

Leveraging Human Capital and Entrepreneurial Strategies

One of the key resources that entrepreneurial firms use to foster new value creation is technology. Technology knowledge provides managers who use it with the ability to lower costs, enhance customer service, and improve performance. Human resources and knowledge are also used to exploit market uncertainties and launch preemptive strategies aimed at achieving first-mover advantages. Such competitive actions require sophisticated knowledge by talented professionals as well as strong, positive working relationships between managers and technology experts. We provide the example of SkyTower Telecommunications, a pioneering entrepreneurial firm that received NASA backing and $80 million in investment capital for combining unmanned aircraft technology with knowledge of wireless communications to create solar-powered, flying wing-style airplanes designed to replace the radio towers and satellites presently being used to send out Internet, mobile phone, and high-definition TV signals.

Reflecting on Career Implications . . .

- **Human Capital:** Does your organization effectively attract, develop, and retain talent? If not, you may have fewer career opportunities to enhance your human capital at your organization. Take advantage of your organization's human resource programs such as tuition reimbursement, mentoring, etc.
- **Human Capital:** Does your organization value diversity? What kinds of diversity seems to be encouraged (e.g., age-based or ethnicity-based)? If not, there may be limited perspectives on strategic and operational issues and a career at this organization may be less attractive to you.
- **Social Capital:** Does your organization have effective programs to build and develop social capital such that professionals develop strong "ties" to the organization? Alternatively, is social capital so strong that you see effects occur such as "groupthink"? From your perspective, how might you better leverage social capital towards pursuing other career opportunities?
- **Technology:** Does your organization provide and effectively use technology (e.g., groupware, knowledge management systems) to help you leverage your talents and expand your knowledge base?

Summary

Firms throughout the industrial world are recognizing that the knowledge worker is the key to success in the marketplace. However, we also recognize that human capital, although vital, is still only a necessary, but not a sufficient, condition for creating value. We began the first section of the chapter by addressing the importance of human capital and how it can be attracted, developed, and retained. Then we discussed the role of social capital and technology in leveraging human capital for competitive success. We pointed out that intellectual capital—the difference between a firm's market value and its book value—has increased significantly over the past few decades. This is particularly true for firms in knowledge-intensive industries, especially where there are relatively few tangible assets, such as software development.

The second section of the chapter addressed the attraction, development, and retention of human capi-

tal. We viewed these three activities as a "three-legged stool"—that is, it is difficult for firms to be successful if they ignore or are unsuccessful in any one of these activities. Among the issues we discussed in *attracting* human capital were "hiring for attitude, training for skill" and the value of using social networks to attract human capital. In particular, it is important to attract employees who can collaborate with others, given the importance of collective efforts such as teams and task forces. With regard to *developing* human capital, we discussed the need to encourage widespread involvement throughout the organization, monitor progress and track the development of human capital, and evaluate human capital. Among the issues that are widely practiced in evaluating human capital is the 360-degree evaluation system. Employees are evaluated by their superiors, peers, direct reports, and even internal and external customers. We also addressed the value of maintaining a diverse workforce. Finally, some mechanisms for retaining human capital are employees' identification with the organization's mission and values, providing challenging work and a stimulating environment, the importance of financial and nonfinancial rewards and incentives, and providing flexibility and amenities. A key issue here is that a firm should not overemphasize financial rewards. After all, if individuals join an organization for money, they also are likely to leave for money. With money as the primary motivator, there is little chance that employees will develop firm-specific ties to keep them with the organization.

The third section of the chapter discussed the importance of social capital in leveraging human capital. Social capital refers to the network of relationships that individuals have throughout the organization as well as with customers and suppliers. Such ties can be critical in obtaining both information and resources. With regard to recruiting, for example, we saw how some firms are able to hire en masse groups of individuals who are part of social networks. Social relationships can also be very important in the effective functioning of groups. Finally, we discussed some of the potential downsides of social capital. These include the expenses that firms may bear when promoting social and working relationships among individuals as well as the potential for "groupthink," wherein individuals are reluctant to express divergent (or opposing) views on an issue because of social pressures to conform. We also introduced the concept of social networks. The relative advantages of being central in a network versus bridging multiple networks was discussed. We addressed the key role that social networks can play in both improving knowledge management and promoting career success.

The fourth section addressed the role of technology in leveraging human capital. We discussed relatively simple means of using technology, such as e-mail and networks where individuals can collaborate by way of personal computers. We provided suggestions and guidelines on how electronic teams can be effectively managed. We also addressed more sophisticated uses of technology, such as sophisticated management systems. Here knowledge can be codified and reused at very low cost, as we saw in the examples of firms in the consulting, health care, and high-technology industries.

In the fifth section we discussed the increasing importance of protecting a firm's intellectual property. Although traditional approaches such as patents, copyrights, and trademarks are important, the development of

dynamic capabilities may be the best protection in the long run.

The final section addressed how the leveraging of human capital is critical in strategy formulation at all levels. This includes business-level, corporate-level, international, and entrepreneurial strategies.

Summary Review Questions

1. Explain the role of knowledge in today's competitive environment.

2. Why is it important for managers to recognize the interdependence in the attraction, development, and retention of talented professionals?

3. What are some of the potential downsides for firms that engage in a "war for talent"?

4. Discuss the need for managers to use social capital in leveraging their human capital both within and across their firm.

5. Discuss the key role of technology in leveraging knowledge and human capital.

Key Terms

knowledge economy, 117
intellectual capital, 117
human capital, 118
social capital, 118
explicit knowledge, 118
tacit knowledge, 118

social network analysis, 132
closure, 133
bridging relationships, 134
structural holes, 134
groupthink, 136
electronic teams, 138

Experiential Exercise

Johnson & Johnson, a leading health care firm with $47 billion in 2004 revenues, is often rated as one of *Fortune*'s "Most Admired Firms." It is also considered an excellent place to work and has generated high return to shareholders. Clearly, they value their human capital. Using the Internet and/or library resources, identify some of the actions/strategies Johnson & Johnson has taken to attract, develop, and retain human capital. What are their implications?

Activity	Actions/Strategies	Implications
Attracting human capital		
Developing human capital		
Retaining human capital		

Application Questions Exercises

1. Look up successful firms in a high-technology industry as well as two successful firms in more traditional industries such as automobile manufacturing and retailing. Compare their market values and book values. What are some implications of these differences?
2. Select a firm for which you believe its social capital—both within the firm and among its suppliers and customers—is vital to its competitive advantage. Support your arguments.
3. Choose a company with which you are familiar. What are some of the ways in which it uses technology to leverage its human capital?
4. Using the Internet, look up a company with which you are familiar. What are some of the policies and procedures that it uses to enhance the firm's human and social capital?

Ethics Questions

1. Recall an example of a firm that recently faced an ethical crisis. How do you feel the crisis and management's handling of it affected the firm's human capital and social capital?
2. Based on your experiences or what you have learned in your previous classes, are you familiar with any companies that used unethical practices to attract talented professionals? What do you feel were the short-term and long-term consequences of such practices?

References

1. Wellner, A. S. 2004. The perils of hiring stars. *Inc.,* August: 32–33; Molaro, R. 2005. Bear season. *The Art of Licensing,* Winter: S-11–S13; and personal communication with Michael Carlisle and the authors, February 10, 2005.
2. Parts of this chapter draw upon some of the ideas and examples from Dess, G. G., & Picken, J. C. 1999. *Beyond Productivity.* New York: AMACOM.
3. An acknowledged trend: The world economic survey. 1996. *The Economist,* September 28: 25–28.
4. Quinn, J. B., Anderson, P., & Finkelstein, S. 1996. Leveraging intellect. *Academy of Management Executive,* 10(3): 7–27.
5. Hamel, G., & Prahalad, C. K. 1996. Competing in the new economy: Managing out of bounds. *Strategic Management Journal,* 17: 238.
6. Stewart, T. A. 1997. *Intellectual capital: The new wealth of organizations.* New York: Doubleday/ Currency.
7. Leif Edvisson and Michael S. Malone have a similar, more detailed definition of *intellectual capital:* "the combined knowledge, skill, innovativeness, and ability to meet the task at hand." They consider intellectual capital to equal human capital plus structural capital. *Structural capital* is defined as "the hardware, software, databases, organization structure, patents, trademarks, and everything else of organizational capability that supports those employees' productivity—in a word, everything left at the office when the employees go home." Edvisson, L., &

Malone, M. S. 1997. *Intellectual capital: Realizing your company's true value by finding its hidden brainpower:* 10–14. New York: HarperBusiness.

8. Stewart, T. A. 2001. Accounting gets radical. *Fortune,* April 16: 184–194.

9. Thomas Stewart has suggested this formula in his book *Intellectual Capital.* He provides an insightful discussion on pages 224–225, including some of the limitations of this approach to measuring intellectual capital. We recognize, of course, that during the late 1990s and in early 2000, there were some excessive market valuations of high-technology and Internet firms. For an interesting discussion of the extraordinary market valuation of Yahoo!, an Internet company, refer to Perkins, A. B. 2001. The Internet bubble encapsulated: Yahoo! *Red Herring,* April 15: 17–18.

10. Roberts, P. W., & Dowling, G. R. 2002. Corporate reputation and sustained superior financial performance. *Strategic Management Journal,* 23(12): 1077–1095.

11. For a recent study on the relationships between human capital, learning, and sustainable competitive advantage, read Hatch, N. W., & Dyer, J. H. 2005. Human capital and learning as a source of sustainable competitive advantage. *Strategic Management Journal,* 25: 1155–1178.

12. One of the seminal contributions on knowledge management is Becker, G. S. 1993. *Human capital: A theoretical and empirical analysis with special reference to education* (3rd ed.). Chicago: University of Chicago Press.

13. For an excellent overview of the topic of social capital, read Baron, R. A. 2005. Social capital. In Hitt, M. A., & Ireland, R. D. (Eds.), *The Blackwell encyclopedia of management* (2nd ed.): 224–226. Malden, MA: Blackwell.

14. For an excellent discussion of social capital and its impact on organizational performance, refer to Nahapiet, J., & Ghoshal, S. 1998. Social capital, intellectual capital, and the organizational advantage. *Academy of Management Review,* 23: 242–266.

15. An interesting discussion of how knowledge management (patents) can enhance organizational performance can be found in Bogner, W. C., & Bansal, P. 2007. Knowledge management as the basis of sustained high performance. *Journal of Management Studies,* 44(1): 165–188.

16. Polanyi, M. 1967. *The tacit dimension.* Garden City, NY: Anchor Publishing.

17. Barney, J. B. 1991. Firm resources and sustained competitive advantage. *Journal of Management,* 17: 99–120.

18. For an interesting perspective of empirical research on how knowledge can adversely affect performance, read Haas, M. R., & Hansen, M. T. 2005. When using knowledge can hurt performance: The value of organizational capabilities in a management consulting company. *Strategic Management Journal,* 26(1): 1–24.

19. Some of the notable books on this topic include Edvisson & Malone, op. cit.; Stewart, op. cit.; and Nonaka, I., & Takeuchi, I. 1995. *The knowledge creating company.* New York: Oxford University Press.

20. Stewart, T. A. 2000. Taking risk to the marketplace. *Fortune,* March 6: 424.

21. Dutton, G. 1997. Are you technologically competent? *Management Review,* November: 54–58.

22. For a discussion of attracting, developing, and retaining top talent, refer to Goffee, R., & Jones, G. 2007. Leading clever people. *Harvard Business Review,* 85(3): 72–89.

23. Dess & Picken, op. cit.: 34.

24. Webber, A. M. 1998. Danger: Toxic company. *Fast Company,* November: 152–161.

25. Morris, B. 1997. Key to success: People, people, people. *Fortune,* October 27: 232.

26. Martin, J. 1998. So, you want to work for the best. . . . *Fortune,* January 12: 77.

27. Cardin, R. 1997. Make your own Bozo Filter. *Fast Company,* October–November: 56.

28. Lavering, R., & Muskowitz. M. 2007. In good company. *Fortune,* January 22: 94–114.

29. Martin, op. cit.; Henkoff, R. 1993. Companies that train best. *Fortune,* March 22: 53–60.

30. Ibid.

31. An interesting perspective on developing new talent rapidly when they join an organization can be found in Rollag, K., Parise, S., & Cross, R. 2005. Getting new hires up to speed quickly. *MIT Sloan Management Review,* 46(2): 35–41.

32. Stewart, T. A. 1998. Gray flannel suit? moi? *Fortune,* March 18: 80–82.

33. An interesting perspective on how Cisco Systems develops its talent can be found in Chatman, J., O'Reilly, C., & Chang, V. 2005. Cisco Systems: Developing a human capital strategy. *California Management Review,* 47(2): 137–166.

34. This section is based on Leonard, D. A., & Swap, W. 2004. Deep smarts. *Harvard Business Review,* 82(9): 88–97.

35. Morris, B. op. cit.

36. For an innovative perspective on the appropriateness of alternate approaches to evaluation and rewards, refer to Seijts, G. H., & Lathan, G. P. 2005. Learning versus performance goals: When should each be used? *Academy of Management Executive,* 19(1): 124–132.

37. The discussion of the 360-degree feedback system draws on the article UPS. 1997. 360-degree feedback: Coming from all sides. *Vision* (a UPS Corporation internal company publication), March: 3; Slater, R. 1994. *Get better or get beaten: Thirty-one leadership secrets from Jack Welch.* Burr Ridge, IL: Irwin; Nexon, M. 1997. General Electric: The secrets of the finest company in the world. *L'Expansion,* July 23: 18–30; and Smith, D. 1996. Bold new directions for human resources. *Merck World* (internal company publication), October: 8.

38. Kets de Vries, M. F. R. 1998. Charisma in action: The transformational abilities of Virgin's Richard Branson and ABB's Percy Barnevik. *Organizational Dynamics,* Winter: 20.

39. We have only to consider the most celebrated case of industrial espionage in recent years, wherein José Ignacio Lopez was indicted in a German court for stealing sensitive product planning documents from his former employer, General Motors, and sharing them with his executive colleagues at Volkswagen. The lawsuit was dismissed by the German courts, but Lopez and his colleagues were investigated by the U.S. Justice Department. Also consider the recent litigation involving noncompete employment contracts and confidentiality clauses of *International Paper v. Louisiana-Pacific, Campbell Soup v. H. J. Heinz Co.,* and *PepsiCo v. Quaker Oats's Gatorade.* In addition to retaining valuable human resources and often their valuable network of customers, firms must also protect proprietary information and knowledge. For interesting insights, refer to Carley, W. M. 1998. CEO gets hard lesson in how not to keep his lieutenants. *The Wall Street Journal,* February 11: A1, A10; and Lenzner, R., & Shook, C. 1998. Whose Rolodex is it, anyway? *Forbes,* February 23: 100–103.

40. For an insightful discussion of retention of knowledge workers in today's economy, read Davenport, T. H. 2005. *The care and feeding of the knowledge worker.* Boston, MA: Harvard Business School Press.

41. Lieber, R. B. 1998, Why employees love these companies. *Fortune,* January 12: 72–74.

42. Stewart, T. A. 2001. *The wealth of knowledge.* New York: Currency.

43. Amabile, T. M. 1997. Motivating creativity in organizations: On doing what you love and loving what you do. *California Management Review,* Fall: 39–58.

44. For an insightful perspective on alternate types of employee–employer relationships, read Erickson, T. J., & Gratton, L. 2007. What it means to work here. *Harvard Business Review,* 85(3): 104–112.

45. Monsanto has been part of Pharmacia since 2002. *Hoover's Handbook of Am. Bus. 2004:* 562.

46. Pfeffer, J. 2001. Fighting the war for talent is hazardous to your organization's health. *Organizational Dynamics,* 29(4): 248–259.

47. Cox, T. L. 1991. The multinational organization. *Academy of Management Executive,* 5(2): 34–47. Without doubt, a great deal has been written on the topic of creating and maintaining an effective diverse workforce. Some excellent, recent books include: Harvey, C. P., & Allard, M. J. 2005. *Understanding and managing diversity: Readings, cases, and exercises.* (3rd ed.). Upper Saddle River, NJ: Pearson Prentice-Hall; Miller, F. A., & Katz, J. H. 2002. *The inclusion breakthrough: Unleashing the real power of diversity.* San Francisco: Berrett Koehler; and Williams, M. A. 2001. *The 10 lenses: Your guide to living and working in a multicultural world.* Sterling, VA: Capital Books.

48. www.rand.org/publications/RB/RB/5050.

49. This section, including the six potential benefits of a diverse workforce, draws on Cox, T. H., & Blake, S. 1991. Managing cultural diversity: Implications for organizational competitiveness. *Academy of Management Executive,* 5(3): 45–56.

50. www.pwcglobal.com/us/eng/careers/diversity/index.html.

51. This discussion draws on Dess, G. G., & Lumpkin, G. T. 2001. Emerging issues in strategy process research. In Hitt, M. A., Freeman, R. E., & Harrison, J. S. (Eds.). *Handbook of strategic management:* 3–34. Malden, MA: Blackwell.

52. Adler, P. S., & Kwon, S. W. 2002. Social capital: Prospects for a new concept. *Academy of Management Review,* 27(1): 17–40.

53. Capelli, P. 2000. A market-driven approach to retaining talent. *Harvard Business Review,* 78(1): 103–113.

54. This hypothetical example draws on Peteraf, M. 1993. The cornerstones of competitive advantage. *Strategic Management Journal,* 14: 179–191.

55. Wernerfelt, B. 1984. A resource-based view of the firm. *Strategic Management Journal,* 5: 171–180.

56. Wysocki, B., Jr. 2000. Yet another hazard of the new economy: The Pied Piper Effect. *The Wall Street Journal,* March 20: A1–A16.

57. Ibid.

58. Buckman, R. C. 2000. Tech defectors from Microsoft resettle together. *The Wall Street Journal,* October: B1–B6.

59. An insightful discussion of the interorganizational aspects of social capital can be found in Dyer, J. H., & Singh, H. 1998. The relational view: Cooperative strategy and sources of interorganizational competitive advantage. *Academy of Management Review,* 23: 66–79.

60. Hoppe, B. 2005. Structural holes, Part one. connectedness.blogspot.com. January 18: np.

61. There has been a tremendous amount of theory building and empirical research in recent years in the area of social network analysis. Unquestionably, two of the major contributors to this domain have been Ronald Burt and J. S. Coleman. For excellent background discussions, refer to: Burt, R. S. 1992. *Structural holes: The social structure of competition.* Cambridge, MA: Harvard University Press; Coleman, J. S. 1990. *Foundations of social theory.* Cambridge, MA: Harvard University Press; and Coleman, J. S. 1988. Social capital in the creation of human capital. *American Journal of Sociology.* 94: S95–S120. For a more recent review and integration of current thought on social network theory, consider: Burt, R. S. 2005. *Brokerage & closure: An introduction to social capital.* Oxford Press: New York.

62. Our discussion draws on the concepts developed by Burt, 1992, op. cit.; Coleman, 1990, op. cit.; Coleman, 1988, op. cit.; and Oh, H., Chung, M. & Labianca, G. 2004. Group social capital and group effectiveness: The role of informal socializing ties. *Academy of Management Journal,* 47(6): 860–875. We would like to thank Joe Labianca (University of Kentucky) for his helpful feedback and ideas in our discussion of social networks.

63. Arregle, J. L., Hitt, M. A., Sirmon, D. G., & Very, P. 2007. The development of organizational social capital: Attributes of family firms. *Journal of Management Studies,* 44(1): 73–95.

64. Oh, et. al., op. cit.

65. Hoppe, op. cit.

66. The discussion of these two contingent factors draws on Dess, G. G., & Shaw, J. D. 2001. Voluntary turnover, social capital, and organizational performance. *Academy of Management Review,* 26(3): 446–456.

67. The business-level strategies of overall low cost and differentiation draws upon Michael E. Porter's classic work and will be discussed in more detail in Chapter 5. Source: Porter, M. E. 1985. *Competitive advantage.* Free Press: New York.

68. Our discussion of the three advantages of social networks draws on Uzzi, B., & Dunlap. S. 2005. How to build your network. *Harvard Business Review,* 83(12): 53–60. For a recent, excellent review on the research exploring the relationship between social capital and managerial performance, read Moran, P. 2005. Structural vs. relational embeddedness: Social capital and managerial performance. *Strategic Management Journal,* 26(12): 1129–1151.

69. Prusak, L., & Cohen, D. 2001. How to invest in social capital. *Harvard Business Review,* 79(6): 86–93.

70. Leonard, D., & Straus, S. 1997. Putting your company's whole brain to work. *Harvard Business Review,* 75(4): 110–122.

71. For an excellent discussion of public (i.e., the organization) versus private (i.e., the individual manager) benefits of social capital, refer to Leana, C. R., & Van Buren, H. J. 1999. Organizational social capital and employment practices. *Academy of Management Review,* 24(3): 538–555.

72. The authors would like to thank Joe Labianca, University of Kentucky, and John Lin, University of Texas at Dallas, for their very helpful input in our discussion of social network theory and its practical implications.

73. Brady, D. 2006. *!#?@ the e-mail. Can we talk?. *BusinessWeek,* December 4: 109.

74. Taylor, W. C. 1999. Whatever happened to globalization? *Fast Company,* December: 228–236.

75. Prahalad, C. K., & Ramaswamy, V. 2004. *The future of competition: Co-creating value with customers.* Boston: Harvard Business School Press.

76. Lei, D., Slocum, J., & Pitts, R. A. 1999. Designing organizations for competitive advantage: The power of unlearning and learning. *Organizational Dynamics,* Winter: 24–38.

77. This section draws upon Zaccaro, S. J., & Bader, P. 2002. E-Leadership and the challenges of leading

e-teams: Minimizing the bad and maximizing the good. *Organizational Dynamics,* 31(4): 377–387.

78. Kirkman, B. L., Rosen, B., Tesluk, P. E., & Gibson, C. B. 2004. The impact of team empowerment on virtual team performance: The moderating role of face-to-face interaction. *Academy of Management Journal,* 47(2): 175–192.

79. The discussion of the advantages and challenges associated with e-teams draws on Zacarro & Bader, op. cit.

80. For a recent study exploring the relationship between team empowerment, face-to-face interaction, and performance in virtual teams, read Kirkman, Rosen, Tesluk, & Gibson, op. cit.

81. For an innovative study on how firms share knowledge with competitors and the performance implications, read Spencer, J. W. 2003. Firms' knowledge sharing strategies in the global innovation system: Empirical evidence from the flat panel display industry. *Strategic Management Journal,* 24(3): 217–235.

82. The examples of Andersen Consulting and Access Health draw upon Hansen, M. T., Nohria, N., & Tierney, T. 1999. What's your strategy for managing knowledge? *Harvard Business Review,* 77(2): 106–118.

83. This discussion draws on Conley, J. G. 2005. Intellectual capital management, Kellogg School of Management and Schulich School of Business, York University, Toronto, KS 2003; Conley, J. G., & Szobocsan, J. 2001. Snow White shows the way. *Managing Intellectual Property,* June: 15–25; Greenspan, A. 2004. Intellectual property rights, The Federal Reserve Board, Remarks by the chairman, February 27; and Teece, D. J. 1998. Capturing value from knowledge assets, *California Management Review,* 40(3): 54–79. The authors would like to thank Professor Theo Peridis, York University, for his contribution to this section.

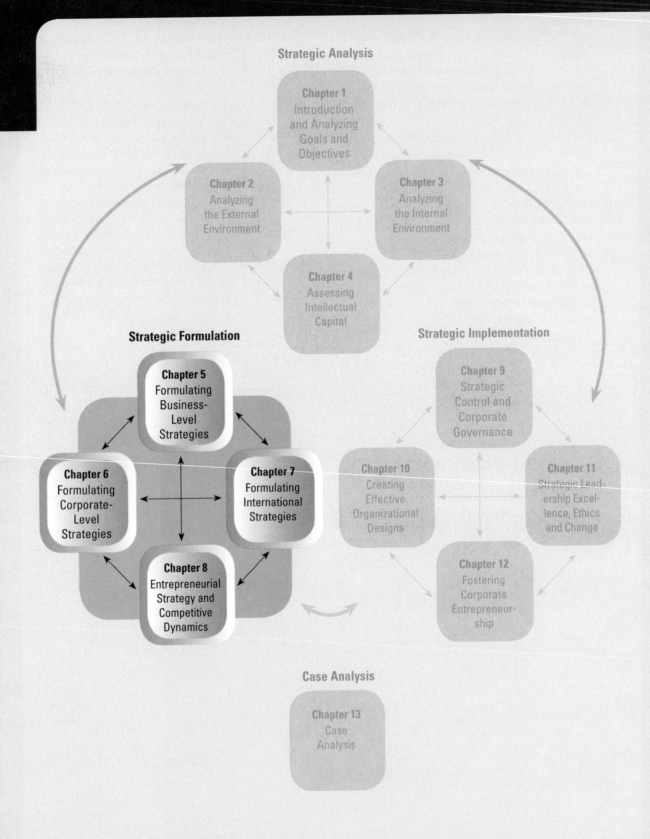

Strategic Analysis

Chapter 1
Introduction and Analyzing Goals and Objectives

Chapter 2
Analyzing the External Environment

Chapter 3
Analyzing the Internal Environment

Chapter 4
Assessing Intellectual Capital

Strategic Formulation

Chapter 5
Formulating Business-Level Strategies

Chapter 6
Formulating Corporate-Level Strategies

Chapter 7
Formulating International Strategies

Chapter 8
Entrepreneurial Strategy and Competitive Dynamics

Strategic Implementation

Chapter 9
Strategic Control and Corporate Governance

Chapter 10
Creating Effective Organizational Designs

Chapter 11
Strategic Leadership Excellence, Ethics and Change

Chapter 12
Fostering Corporate Entrepreneurship

Case Analysis

Chapter 13
Case Analysis

Strategic Formulation

chapter 5

Business-Level Strategy:

Creating and Sustaining Competitive Advantages

>learning objectives

After reading this chapter, you should have a good understanding of:

LO1 The central role of competitive advantage in the study of strategic management.

LO2 The three generic strategies: overall cost leadership, differentiation, and focus.

LO3 How the successful attainment of generic strategies can improve a firm's relative power vis-à-vis the five forces that determine an industry's average profitability.

LO4 The pitfalls managers must avoid in striving to attain generic strategies.

LO5 How firms can effectively combine the generic strategies of overall cost leadership and differentiation.

LO6 How Internet-enabled business models are being used to improve strategic positioning.

LO7 The importance of considering the industry life cycle to determine a firm's business-level strategy and its relative emphasis on functional area strategies and value-creating activities.

LO8 The need for turnaround strategies that enable a firm to reposition its competitive position in an industry.

*b*ow firms compete with each other and how they attain and sustain competitive advantages go to the heart of strategic management. In short, the key issue becomes: Why do some firms outperform others and enjoy such advantages over time? This subject, business-level strategy, is the focus of Chapter 5.

The first part of the chapter draws on Michael Porter's framework of generic strategies. He identifies three strategies—overall cost leadership, differentiation, and focus—that firms may apply to outperform their rivals in an industry. We begin by describing each of these strategies and providing examples of firms that have successfully attained them as a means of outperforming competitors in their industry. Next, we address how these strategies help a firm develop a favorable position vis-à-vis the "five forces" (Chapter 2). We then suggest some of the pitfalls that managers must avoid if they are to successfully pursue these generic strategies and discuss the conditions under which firms may effectively combine generic strategies to outperform rivals. We close this section by addressing how competitive strategies should be revised and redeployed in light of the shifts in industry and competitive forces caused by Internet and digital strategies. Here, combination strategies are the most solid because they integrate the new capabilities with sound principles.

The second part of Chapter 5 discusses a vital consideration in the effective use of business-level strategies: industry life cycles. The four stages of the industry life cycle—introduction, growth, maturity, and decline—are indicative of an evolving management process that affects factors such as the market growth rate and the intensity of competition. Accordingly, the stages of an industry's life cycle are an important contingency that managers should take into account when making decisions concerning the optimal overall business-level strategies and the relative emphasis to place on functional capabilities and value-creating activities. At times, firms are faced with performance declines and must find ways to revitalize their competitive positions. The actions followed to do so are referred to as turnaround strategies, which may be needed at any stage of the industry life cycle. However, they occur more frequently during the maturity and decline stages.

Learning from Mistakes

Few companies have been as successful as Starbucks. What began in 1985 as a small coffee shop in Seattle's Pike Place Market has emerged as a megabrand, with almost $8 billion in revenues and more than 13,000 retail outlets worldwide. And, by early 2007, its market capitalization was approaching that of Ford and General Motors *combined*.[1] By doing what? Selling cups of consistent, although richly priced coffee. But as we will see below, even hugely successful companies can stumble.

> Starbucks's strategy is driven by innovation—a promise that is implicit in its well-known and complicated menu. To spur growth, Starbucks places a tremendous amount of effort and expense in developing new products. Also, it continually researches various metrics to determine customer attitudes about new beverages.
>
> However, Starbucks found that there was an unexpected cost to such complex, innovative offerings. Such added complexity increased the time required to serve customers. And, not too surprisingly, demand for its labor-intensive customized drinks declined. *[continued]*

According to Starbucks's research, a "highly satisfied customer" spent $4.42 on average during each visit and visited an average of 7.2 times a month. In contrast, although "unsatisfied customers" spent about the same amount per visit ($3.88), they only averaged about half as many visits (3.9) each month. Further, the company's research found that 75 percent of customers valued friendly, fast, convenient service, while only 15 percent considered new, innovative beverages to be highly important. Clearly, although innovation is a key part of Starbucks's strategy, it loses its value if people must wait too long.*

Since all firms endeavor to enjoy above-average returns (or profits), the question of how management should go about this is a core issue in strategic management. Organizations that have created sustainable competitive advantages don't rely too much on a single strength—as Starbucks apparently did with its overemphasis on innovation. Instead they strive for well-rounded strategies that recognize the tradeoffs associated with their competitive positions. Tradeoffs occur when activities are incompatible (e.g., innovation and fast customer service).[2] Managers who recognize tradeoffs in their strategies and activities enhance the chance that their firm's advantages will be more lasting, or sustainable.

Starbucks's competitive advantage is based on the unique "Starbucks experience"—a superior product served by a knowledgeable salesperson in a friendly social environment with short wait times. Obviously, it is this uniqueness that enables the company to charge a premium price.

In this chapter, we address several forms that competitive advantage may take: overall cost leadership, differentiation, and focus. Next we discuss how Michael Porter's three generic strategies contribute to a firm's competitive advantage and how firms can successfully combine multiple strategies.

Types of Competitive Advantage and Sustainability

>LO1
The central role of competitive advantage in the study of strategic management.

>LO2
The three generic strategies: overall cost leadership, differentiation, and focus.

Michael Porter presented three generic strategies that a firm can use to overcome the five forces and achieve competitive advantage.[3] Each of Porter's generic strategies has the potential to allow a firm to outperform rivals in their industry. The first, *overall cost leadership,* is based on creating a low-cost-position. Here, a firm must manage the relationships throughout the value chain and lower costs throughout the entire chain. On the other hand, *differentiation* requires a firm to create products and/or services that are unique and valued. Here, the primary emphasis is on "nonprice" attributes for which customers will gladly pay a premium. Finally, with a *focus* strategy, firms must direct their attention (or "focus") toward narrow product lines, buyer segments, or targeted geographic markets and they must attain advantages either through differentiation or cost leadership. Whereas the overall cost leadership and differentiation strategies strive to attain advantages industrywide, focusers build their strategy with a narrow target market in mind. Exhibit 5.1 illustrates these three strategies on two dimensions: competitive advantage and strategic target.

Both casual observation and research support the notion that firms that identify with one or more of the forms of competitive advantage outperform those that do not.[4] There has been a rich history of strategic management research addressing this topic. One study analyzed 1,789 strategic business units and found that businesses combining multiple

---

*As one would expect, Starbucks promptly took corrective action. It streamlined its artisan approach to making drinks by automating and standardizing various elements of the latte manufacturing process. Further, the firm spent $40 million adding staff to cut wait times. It also introduced the Starbucks Card to speed payment. The result: 85 percent of customers were served within three minutes (compared to the prior 54 percent), and customer satisfaction levels increased 20 percent.

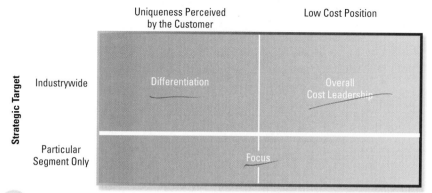

Exhibit 5.1 **Three Generic Strategies**

Source: Adepted with the permission of The Free Press, a division of Simon & Schuster Adult Publishing Group, from *Competitive Strategy: Techniques for Analyzing Industries and Competitors* by Michael E. Porter. Copyright © 1980, 1998 by The Free Press. All rights reserved.

forms of competitive advantage (differentiation and overall cost leadership) outperformed businesses that used only a single form. The lowest performers were those that did not identify with any type of advantage. They were classified as "stuck in the middle." Results of this study are presented in Exhibit 5.2.[5]

Overall Cost Leadership

The first generic strategy is overall cost leadership. Overall cost leadership requires a tight set of interrelated tactics that include:

- Aggressive construction of efficient-scale facilities.
- Vigorous pursuit of cost reductions from experience.
- Tight cost and overhead control.
- Avoidance of marginal customer accounts.
- Cost minimization in all activities in the firm's value chain, such as R&D, service, sales force, and advertising.

overall cost leadership a firm's generic strategy based on appeal to the industrywide market using a competitive advantage based on low cost.

Exhibit 5.3 draws on the value-chain concept (see Chapter 3) to provide examples of how a firm can attain an overall cost leadership strategy in its primary and support activities.

	Competitive Advantage					
	Differentiation and Cost	Differentiation	Cost	Differentiation and Focus	Cost and Focus	Stuck in the Middle
Performance						
Return on investment (%)	35.5	32.9	30.2	17.0	23.7	17.8
Sales growth (%)	15.1	13.5	13.5	16.4	17.5	12.2
Gain in market share (%)	5.3	5.3	5.5	6.1	6.3	4.4
Sample size	123	160	100	141	86	105

Exhibit 5.2 **Competitive Advantage and Business Performance**

Firm infrastructure	Few management layers to reduce overhead costs.			Standardized accounting practices to minimize personnel required.	
Human resource management	Minimize costs associated with employee turnover through effective policies.			Effective orientation and training programs to maximize employee productivity.	
Technology development	Effective use of automated technology to reduce scrappage rates.			Expertise in process engineering to reduce manufacturing costs.	
Procurement	Effective policy guidelines to ensure low-cost raw materials (with acceptable quality levels).			Shared purchasing operations with other business units.	
	Effective layout of receiving dock operations.	Effective use of quality control inspectors to minimize rework on the final product.	Effective utilization of delivery fleets.	Purchase of media in large blocks. Sales force utilization is maximized by territory management.	Thorough service repair guidelines to minimize repeat maintenance calls. Use of single type of repair vehicle to minimize costs.
	Inbound logistics	Operations	Outbound logistics	Marketing and sales	Service

Exhibit 5.3 Value-Chain Activities: Examples of Overall Cost Leadership

Source: Adapted with the permission of The Free Press, a division of Simon & Schuster Adult Publishing Group, from *Competitive Advantage: Creating and Sustaining Superior Performance* by Michael E. Porter. Copyright © 1985, 1998 by Michael E. Porter. All rights reserved.

An important concept related to an overall cost leadership strategy is the experience curve, which refers to how business "learns" to lower costs as it gains experience with production processes. That is, with experience, unit costs of production decline as output increases in most industries. The experience curve concept is discussed in Strategy Spotlight 5.1 and Exhibit 5.4 (page 160).

To generate above-average performance, a firm following an overall cost leadership position must attain **competitive parity** on the basis of differentiation relative to competitors. In other words, a firm achieving parity is similar to its competitors, or "on par," with respect to differentiated products.[6] Competitive parity on the basis of differentiation permits a cost leader to translate cost advantages directly into higher profits than competitors. Thus, the cost leader earns above-average returns.[7]

The failure to attain parity on the basis of differentiation can be illustrated with an example from the automobile industry—the ill-fated Yugo. Below is an excerpt from a speech by J. W. Marriott, Jr., Chairman of the Marriott Corporation:[8]

> . . . money is a big thing. But it's not the only thing. In the 1980s, a new automobile reached North America from behind the Iron Curtain. It was called the Yugo, and its main attraction was price. About $3,000 each. But the only way they caught on was as the butt of jokes. Remember the guy who told his mechanic, "I want a gas cap for my Yugo." "OK," the mechanic replied, "that sounds like a fair trade."

competitive parity a firm's achievement of similarity, or being "on par," with competitors with respect to low cost, differentiation, or other strategic product characteristic.

The Experience Curve

The experience curve, developed by the Boston Consulting Group in 1968, is a way of looking at efficiencies developed through a firm's cumulative experience. In its basic form, the experience curve relates production costs to production output. As output doubles, costs decline by 10 percent to 30 percent. For example, if it costs $1 per unit to produce 100 units, the per unit cost will decline to between 70 to 90 cents as output increases to 200 units.

What factors account for this increased efficiency? First, the success of an experience curve strategy depends on the industry life cycle for the product. Early stages of a product's life cycle are typically characterized by rapid gains in technological advances in production efficiency. Most experience curve gains come early in the product life cycle.

Second, the inherent technology of the product offers opportunities for enhancement through gained experience. High-tech products give the best opportunity for gains in production efficiencies. As technology is developed, "value engineering" of innovative production processes is implemented, driving down the per unit costs of production.

Third, a product's sensitivity to price strongly affects a firm's ability to exploit the experience curve. Cutting the price of a product with high demand elasticity—where demand increases when price decreases—rapidly creates consumer purchases of the new product. By cutting prices, a firm can increase demand for its product. The increased demand in turn increases product manufacture, thus increasing the firm's experience in the manufacturing process. So by decreasing price and increasing demand, a firm gains manufacturing experience in that particular product, which drives down per unit production costs.

Fourth, the competitive landscape factors into whether or not a firm might benefit from an experience curve strategy. If other competitors are well positioned in the market, have strong capital resources, and are known to promote their product lines aggressively to gain market share, an experience curve strategy may lead to nothing more than a price war between two or more strong competitors. But if a company is the first to market with the product and has good financial backing, an experience curve strategy may be successful.

In an article in the *Harvard Business Review,* Pankaj Ghemawat recommended answering several questions when considering an experience curve strategy.

- Does my industry exhibit a significant experience curve?
- Have I defined the industry broadly enough to take into account interrelated experience?
- What is the precise source of cost reduction?
- Can my company keep cost reductions proprietary?
- Is demand sufficiently stable to justify using the experience curve?
- Is cumulated output doubling fast enough for the experience curve to provide much strategic leverage?
- Do the returns from an experience curve strategy warrant the risks of technological obsolescence?
- Is demand price-sensitive?
- Are there well-financed competitors who are already following an experience curve strategy or are likely to adopt one if my company does?

Michael Porter suggested, however, that the experience curve is not useful in all situations. Whether or not to base strategy on the experience curve depends on what specifically causes the decline in costs. For example, if costs drop from efficient production facilities and not necessarily from experience, the experience curve is not helpful. But as Sharon Oster pointed out in her book on competitive analysis, the experience curve can help managers analyze costs when efficient learning, rather than efficient machinery, is the source of cost savings.

Sources: Ghemawat, P. 1985. Building strategy on the experience curve. *Harvard Business Review,* March–April: 143–149; Porter, M. E. 1996. *On competition.* Boston: Harvard Business Review Press; and Oster, S. M. 1994. *Modern competitive analysis* (2nd ed.). New York: Oxford University Press.

Yugo was offering a lousy value proposition. The cars literally fell apart before your eyes. And the lesson was simple. Price is just one component of value. No matter how good the price, the most cost-sensitive consumer won't buy a bad product.

Next, we discuss some examples of how firms enhance cost leadership position.

While other managed care providers were having a string of weak years, WellPoint, based in Thousand Oaks, California, has had a number of banner years and recently enjoyed an annual profit growth of over 50 percent to $3.1 billion over the past three years.[9] Chairman Leonard Schaeffer credits the company's focus on innovation for both

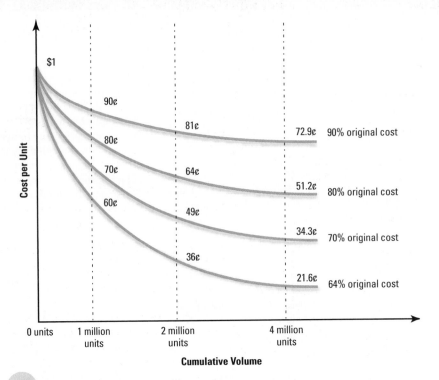

Exhibit 5.4 Comparing Experience Curve Effects

expanding revenues and cutting costs. Recently, for example, WellPoint asked the Food and Drug Administration (FDA) to make the allergy drug Claritin available over the counter. Surprisingly, this may be the first time that an insurer has approached the FDA with this type of request. Schaeffer claimed, "They were kind of stunned," but the FDA agreed to consider it. It was a smart move for WellPoint. If approved as an over-the-counter drug, Claritin would reduce patient visits to the doctor and eliminate the need for prescriptions—two reimbursable expenses for which WellPoint would otherwise be responsible.

Stephen Sanger, CEO of General Mills, recently came up with an idea that helped his firm cut costs.[10] To improve productivity, he sent technicians to watch pit crews during a NASCAR race. That experience inspired the techies to figure out how to reduce the time it takes to switch a plant line from five hours to 20 minutes. This provided an important lesson: Many interesting benchmarking examples can take place far outside of an industry. Often, process improvements involve identifying the best practices in other industries and adapting them for implementation in your own firm. After all, when firms benchmark competitors in their own industry, the end result is often copying and playing catch-up.[11]

A business that strives for a low-cost advantage must attain an absolute cost advantage relative to its rivals. This is typically accomplished by offering a no-frills product or service to a broad target market using standardization to derive the greatest benefits from economies of scale and experience. However, such a strategy may fail if a firm is unable to attain parity on important dimensions of differentiation such as quick responses to customer requests for services or design changes. Strategy Spotlight 5.2 discusses Ryanair—a firm that has developed a very unique overall cost leadership strategy. One might say that it "one upped" Southwest Airlines!

Ryanair: A Highly Effective Overall Cost Leadership Strategy

Michael O'Leary, CEO of Ryanair Holdings PLC, makes no apologies for his penny-pinching. Want to check luggage? You'll pay up to $9.50 per bag for the privilege. Expecting free drinks and snacks? You'll be disappointed. Even a bottle of water will cost you $3.40. And it is not just the passengers who are affected. Flight crews buy their own uniforms, and staff at Ryanair's Spartan Dublin Airport headquarters must supply their own pens. After a customer sued Ryanair for charging $34 for the use of a wheelchair, the company added a 63 cent "wheelchair levy" to every ticket!

Low-fare U.S. carriers have taken the opposite approach of Ryanair by adding perks such as leather seats, live television, and business class. "All of the low-cost carriers' costs have gotten a little out of control," says Tim Sieber, general manager of The Boyd Group, an Evergreen (Colorado) aviation consultant. Clearly Ryanair hasn't followed its industry peers.

Ryanair has been extremely successful. For 2006, its revenues were $2.1 billion—only one-seventh the size of British Airways (BA). However, its operating margins are 22.7 percent—three times as large as BA's. Not too surprisingly, Ryanair's market capitalization of nearly $14 billion (in early 2007) is more than that of British Airways ($12.5 billion), and, incidentally, even more than Southwest Airlines

($12.1 billion). The latter, of course, has been the industry role model of low-cost strategies.

What is O'Leary's secret? He thinks like a retailer and charges for every little thing. Imagine the seat as a cell phone: It comes free, or nearly free, but its owner winds up spending money on all sorts of services.

However, what O'Leary loses in seat revenue he more than makes up by turning both his planes and the Ryanair Web site into stores brimming with irresistible goodies, even as he charges for such "perks" as priority boarding and assigned seating.

Sounds outrageous? Probably so, but the strategy is clearly working. Although its average fare is $53, compared with $92 for Southwest Airlines, Ryanair's net margins are, at 18 percent—more than double the 7 percent achieved by Southwest. Says Nick van den Brul, an aviation analyst: "Ryanair is Wal-Mart with wings." As O'Leary says, "You want luxury? Go somewhere else."

A few other Ryanair practices include:

- Flight attendants sell digital cameras ($137.50) and iPocket MP3 players ($165). Soon-to-come is on-board gaming and cell-phone service.

- The seats don't recline, seat-back pockets have been removed to cut cleaning time and speed turn-around of the planes, there's no entertainment, and seat-back trays will soon carry ads.

- Ryanair sells more than 98 percent of its tickets online. Its Web site offers insurance, hotels, car rentals, and more—even online bingo.

Sources: Capell, K. 2006. Wal-Mart with Wings. *BusinessWeek.* November 27: 44–45; Kumar, N. 2006. Strategies to fight low-cost rivals. *Harvard Business Review,* 84(12): 104–113; and, *Ryanair Annual Report,* 2006.

Overall Cost Leadership: Improving Competitive Position vis-à-vis the Five Forces   An overall low-cost position enables a firm to achieve above-average returns despite strong competition. It protects a firm against rivalry from competitors, because lower costs allow a firm to earn returns even if its competitors eroded their profits through intense rivalry. A low-cost position also protects firms against powerful buyers. Buyers can exert power to drive down prices only to the level of the next most efficient producer. Also, a low-cost position provides more flexibility to cope with demands from powerful suppliers for input cost increases. The factors that lead to a low-cost position also provide substantial entry barriers from economies of scale and cost advantages. Finally, a low-cost position puts the firm in a favorable position with respect to substitute products introduced by new and existing competitors.

A few examples will illustrate these points. Ryanair's close attention to costs helps to protect them from buyer power and intense rivalry from competitors. Thus, they are able to drive down costs and enjoy relatively high power over their customers. By increasing its productivity and lowering unit costs, General Mills (and its competitors in that industry) enjoy greater scale economies and erect higher entry barriers for others who want to enter the industry. Finally, as competitors such as WellPoint lower costs through means such as

>LO3

How the successful attainment of generic strategies can improve a firm's relative power vis-à-vis the five forces that determine an industry's average profitability.

petitioning the FDA to make certain drugs available over the counter, they become less vulnerable to substitutes such as Internet-based competitors.

Potential Pitfalls of Overall Cost Leadership Strategies

Potential pitfalls of overall cost leadership strategy include:

- ***Too much focus on one or a few value-chain activities.*** Would you consider a person to be astute if he cancelled his newspaper subscription and quit eating out to save money, but then "maxed out" several credit cards, requiring him to pay hundreds of dollars a month in interest charges? Of course not. Similarly, firms need to pay attention to all activities in the value chain. Too often managers make big cuts in operating expenses, but don't question year-to-year spending on capital projects. Or managers may decide to cut selling and marketing expenses but ignore manufacturing expenses. Managers should explore *all* value-chain activities, including relationships among them, as candidates for cost reductions.

- ***All rivals share a common input or raw material.*** Here, firms are vulnerable to price increases in the factors of production. Since they're competing on costs, they are less able to pass on price increases, because customers can take their business to rivals who have lower prices. Consider the hardship experienced by fertilizer producers in early 2001 when energy prices spiked.[12] A quadrupling of prices to $10 per thousand cubic feet of natural gas forced firms to shut down nearly half of their production capacity. Why? Natural gas accounts for over 70 percent of the fertilizer's cost. According to Betty-Ann Hegge, senior vice president of Potash Corporation of Saskatchewan, Inc., North America's second largest producer, "Many companies are not even covering their cash costs at these prices."

- ***The strategy is imitated too easily.*** One of the common pitfalls of a cost-leadership strategy is that a firm's strategy may consist of value-creating activities that are easy to imitate.[13] Such was the case with online brokers in recent years.[14] As of early 2001, there were about 140 online brokers, hardly symbolic of an industry where imitation is extremely difficult. But according to Henry McVey, financial services analyst at Morgan Stanley, "We think you need five to ten" online brokers.

  What are some of the dynamics? First, although online brokers were geared up to handle 1.2 million trades a day, volume had shrunk to about 834,000—a 30 percent drop. Thus, competition for business intensified. Second, when the stock market is down, many investors trust their instincts less and seek professional guidance from brokerages that offer differentiated services. Eric Rajendra of A. T. Kearney, an international consulting company, claimed, "The current (online broker) model is inadequate for the pressures the industry is facing now."

- ***A lack of parity on differentiation.*** As noted earlier, firms striving to attain cost leadership advantages must obtain a level of parity on differentiation. Organizations providing online degree programs to adults working full-time may offer low prices. However, they may not be successful unless they can offer instruction that is perceived as comparable to traditional providers. For them, parity can be achieved on differentiation dimensions such as reputation and quality and through signaling mechanisms such as national and regional accreditation agencies.

- ***Erosion of cost advantages when the pricing information available to customers increases.*** This is becoming a more significant challenge as the Internet dramatically increases both the quantity and volume of information available to consumers about pricing and cost structures. Life insurance firms offering whole life insurance provide an interesting example.[15] One study found that for each 10 percent increase in consumer use of the Internet, there is a corresponding reduction in insurance prices to consumers of 3 to 5 percent. Recently, the nationwide savings (or, alternatively, reduced revenues to providers) was between $115 and $125 million annually.

Differentiation

As the name implies, a **differentiation strategy** consists of creating differences in the firm's product or service offering by creating something that is perceived *industrywide* as unique and valued by customers. Differentiation can take many forms:

- Prestige or brand image (Adam's Mark hotels, BMW automobiles).[16]
- Technology (Martin guitars, Marantz stereo components, North Face camping equipment).
- Innovation (Medtronic medical equipment, Nokia cellular phones).
- Features (Cannondale mountain bikes, Honda Goldwing motorcycles).
- Customer service (Nordstrom department stores, Sears lawn equipment retailing).
- Dealer network (Lexus automobiles, Caterpillar earthmoving equipment).

differentiation strategy a firm's generic strategy based on creating differences in the firm's product or service offering by creating something that is perceived *industrywide* as unique and valued by customers.

Exhibit 5.5 draws on the concept of the value chain as an example of how firms may differentiate themselves in primary and support activities.

Firms may differentiate themselves along several different dimensions at once. For example, BMW is known for its high prestige, superior engineering, and high-quality automobiles. And, Harley-Davidson differentiates on image and dealer services.[17]

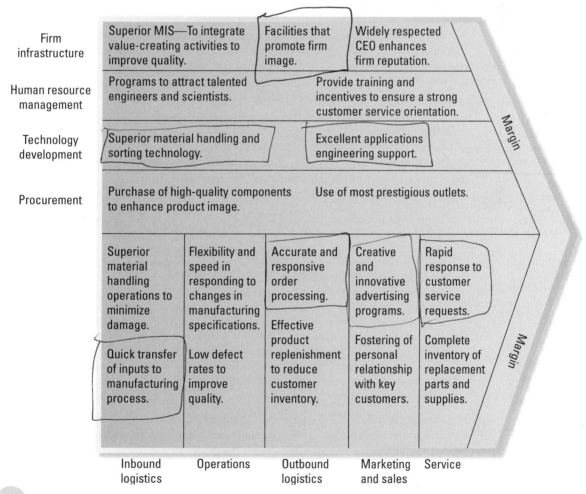

Exhibit 5.5 Value-Chain Activities: Examples of Differentiation

Source: Adapted with the permission of The Free Press, a division of Simon & Schuster Adult Publishing Group, from *Competitive Advantage: Creating and Sustaining Superior Performance* by Michael E. Porter. Copyright © 1985, 1998 by Michael E. Porter. All rights reserved.

● Through effective advertising, Intel strives to further differentiate its products. This advertisement touts Apple's use of its processors in their newest line of computers. An Apple store is behind the ad.

Firms achieve and sustain differentiation advantages and attain above-average performance when their price premiums exceed the extra costs incurred in being unique.[18] For example, both BMW and Harley-Davidson must increase consumer costs to offset added marketing expenses. Thus, a differentiator will always seek out ways of distinguishing itself from similar competitors to justify price premiums greater than the costs incurred by differentiating. Clearly, a differentiator cannot ignore costs. After all, its premium prices would be eroded by a markedly inferior cost position. Therefore, it must attain a level of cost *parity* relative to competitors. Differentiators can do this by reducing costs in all areas that do not affect differentiation. Porsche, for example, invests heavily in engine design—an area in which its customers demand excellence—but it is less concerned and spends fewer resources in the design of the instrument panel or the arrangement of switches on the radio.[19]

Many companies successfully follow a differentiation strategy.[20] For example, FedEx's CEO and founder, Fred Smith, claims that the key to his firm's success is innovation.[21] He contends his management team didn't understand their real goal when they started the firm in 1971: "We thought that we were selling the transportation of goods; in fact, we were selling peace of mind." To that end, they now provide each driver with a handheld computer and a transmitting device that makes it possible for customers to track their packages right from their desktop PCs.

Lexus, a division of Toyota, provides an example of how a firm can strengthen its differentiation strategy by *achieving integration at multiple points along the value chain.*[22] Although the luxury car line was not introduced until the late 1980s, by the early 1990s the cars had already soared to the top of J. D. Power & Associates's customer satisfaction ratings.

> In the spirit of benchmarking, one of Lexus's competitors hired Custom Research Inc. (CRI), a marketing research firm, to find out why Lexus owners were so satisfied. CRI conducted a series of focus groups in which Lexus drivers eagerly offered anecdotes about the special care they experienced from their dealers. It became clear that, although Lexus was manufacturing cars with few mechanical defects, it was the extra care shown by the sales and service staff that resulted in satisfied customers. Such pampering is reflected in the feedback from one customer who claimed she never had a problem with her Lexus. However, upon further probing, she said, "Well, I suppose you could call the four times they had to replace the windshield a 'problem.' But frankly, they took care of it so well and always gave me a loaner car, so I never really considered it a problem until you mentioned it now." An insight gained in CRI's research is that perceptions of product quality (design, engineering, and manufacturing) can be strongly influenced by downstream activities in the value chain (marketing and sales, service).

Strategy Spotlight 5.3 discusses how three firms have been successful through effective differentiation strategies. Similar to Starbucks, these firms have taken commodity-type products and converted them to high-priced goods.

Differentiation: Improving Competitive Position vis-à-vis the Five Forces   Differentiation provides protection against rivalry since brand loyalty lowers customer sensitivity to price and raises customer switching costs. By increasing a firm's margins, differentiation also avoids the need for a low-cost position. Higher entry barriers result because of customer

Successful Differentiators Who Follow the Starbucks Model

Starbucks has been extremely successful in turning the purchase of coffee into a gourmet event. Others have copied the model and several café concepts have sprung up. Here are three of them:

- Ten high-end **Ethel's Chocolate Lounges** located in the Chicago area now sell individual chocolates with flavors such as mojito, expresso, and cinna-swirl for $1.50 apiece. When customers visit the frilly pink-and-chocolate-brown cafes, they can spend $15 for a chocolate fondue for two or enjoy tea and truffles. Some of the cache might erode if customers knew that Ethel's was owned by M&M maker Mars Inc.

- **Sprinkles Cupcakes** opened a chic, minimalist store in Beverly Hills, California. It sells flavors like lemon coconut and chai latte for $3.25 a cupcake. Here, the ingredients are not low-priced commodities—the vanilla is not just vanilla but rather Madagascar Bourbon Vanilla. The cupcakes were featured on "The Oprah Winfrey Show." The next day, cupcake sales increased 50 percent!

- **Cereality,** a new chain with locations in Illinois, Pennsylvania, and Arizona has happily found that people are willing to pay $3.50 for a bowl of breakfast cereal. For that, its pajama-clad employees will serve you two scoops of cereal, one topping (fruit, nuts, marshmallows, etc.) and milk. The cereal is blended to order and is served in containers similar to Chinese food-style paper cartons. The most popular blend is a $4 concoction of Life cereal, almonds, bananas, and honey.

Sources: Danigelis, A. 2006. Customers find local hereo: Cereality. www.fastcompany.com. np; Caplan, J. 2006. In a real crunch. *Inside Business*, July: A37–A38; Luna, N. 2006. Sprinkles bakery to open in Corona del Mar. *The Orange County Register*, May 18, np; and Gottfried, M. 2006. What hath Starbucks wrought? *Forbes*. April 10: 52.

loyalty and the firm's ability to provide uniqueness in its products or services. Differentiation also provides higher margins that enable a firm to deal with supplier power. And it reduces buyer power, because buyers lack comparable alternatives and are therefore less price sensitive. Supplier power is also decreased because there is a certain amount of prestige associated with being the supplier to a producer of highly differentiated products and services. Last, differentiation enhances customer loyalty, thus reducing the threat from substitutes.

Our examples illustrate these points. Lexus has enjoyed enhanced power over buyers because its top J. D. Power ranking makes buyers more willing to pay a premium price. This lessens rivalry, since buyers become less price-sensitive. The prestige associated with its brand name also lowers supplier power since margins are high. Suppliers would probably desire to be associated with prestige brands, thus lessening their incentives to drive up prices. Finally, the loyalty and "peace of mind" associated with a service provider such as FedEx makes such firms less vulnerable to rivalry or substitute products and services.

Potential Pitfalls of Differentiation Strategies   Potential pitfalls of differentiation strategy include:

- *Uniqueness that is not valuable.* A differentiation strategy must provide unique bundles of products and/or services that customers value highly. It's not enough just to be "different." An example is Gibson's Dobro bass guitar. Gibson came up with a unique idea: Design and build an acoustic bass guitar with sufficient sound volume so that amplification wasn't necessary. The problem with other acoustic bass guitars was that they did not project enough volume because of the low-frequency bass notes. By adding a resonator plate on the body of the traditional acoustic bass, Gibson increased the sound volume. Gibson believed this product would serve a particular niche market—bluegrass and folk artists who played in small group "jams" with other acoustic musicians. Unfortunately, Gibson soon discovered that its targeted market was content with their existing options: an upright bass amplified with a microphone or an acoustic electric guitar. Thus, Gibson developed a unique product, but it was not perceived as valuable by its potential customers.[23]

- **Too much differentiation.** Firms may strive for quality or service that is higher than customers desire. Thus, they become vulnerable to competitors who provide an appropriate level of quality at a lower price. For example, consider the expensive Mercedes-Benz S-Class, which ranges in price between $75,000 and $125,000.[24] *Consumer Reports* described it as "sumptuous," "quiet and luxurious," and a "delight to drive." The magazine also considered it to be the least reliable sedan available in the United States. According to David Champion, who runs their testing program, the problems are electronic. "The engineers have gone a little wild," he says. "They've put every bell and whistle that they think of, and sometimes they don't have the attention to detail to make these systems work." Some features include: a computer-driven suspension that reduces body roll as the vehicle whips around a corner; cruise control that automatically slows the car down if it gets too close to another car; and seats that are adjustable 14 ways and that are ventilated by a system that uses eight fans.

- **Too high a price premium.** This pitfall is quite similar to too much differentiation. Customers may desire the product, but they are repelled by the price premium. For example, Duracell (a division of Gillette) recently charged too much for batteries.[25] The firm tried to sell consumers on its superior quality products, but the mass market wasn't convinced. Why? The price differential was simply too high. At a CVS drugstore just one block from Gillette's headquarters, a four-pack of Energizer AA batteries was on sale at $2.99 compared with a Duracell four-pack at $4.59. Duracell's market share dropped 2 percent in a recent two-year period, and its profits declined over 30 percent. Clearly, the price/performance proposition Duracell offered customers was not accepted.

- **Differentiation that is easily imitated.** As we noted in Chapter 3, resources that are easily imitated cannot lead to sustainable advantages. Similarly, firms may strive for, and even attain, a differentiation strategy that is successful for a time. However, the advantages are eroded through imitation. In Strategy Spotlight 5.3 we discussed Cereality's innovative differentiation strategy of offering a wide variety of cereals.[26] As one would expect, once their idea proved successful, competitors entered the market because much of the initial risk had already been taken. Rivals include an Iowa City restaurant named the Cereal Cabinet, the Cereal Bowl in Miami, and Bowls: A Cereal Joint in Gainesville, Florida. Says David Roth, one of Cereality's founders: "With any good business idea, you're faced with people who see you've cracked the code and who try to cash in on it."

- **Dilution of brand identification through product-line extensions.** Firms may erode their quality brand image by adding products or services with lower prices and less quality. Although this can increase short-term revenues, it may be detrimental in the long run. Consider Gucci.[27] In the 1980s Gucci wanted to capitalize on its prestigious brand name by launching an aggressive strategy of revenue growth. It added a set of lower-priced canvas goods to its product line. It also pushed goods heavily into department stores and duty-free channels and allowed its name to appear on a host of licensed items such as watches, eyeglasses, and perfumes. In the short term, this strategy worked. Sales soared. However, the strategy carried a high price. Gucci's indiscriminate approach to expanding its products and channels tarnished its sterling brand. Sales of its high-end goods (with higher profit margins) fell, causing profits to decline.

- **Perceptions of differentiation may vary between buyers and sellers.** The issue here is that "beauty is in the eye of the beholder." Companies must realize that although they may perceive their products and services as differentiated, their customers may view them as commodities. Indeed, in today's marketplace, many products and services have been reduced to commodities.[28] Thus, a firm could overprice its offerings and lose margins altogether if it has to lower prices to reflect market realities.

Overall Cost Leadership:

- Too much focus on one or a few value-chain activities.
- All rivals share a common input or raw material.
- The strategy is imitated too easily.
- A lack of parity on differentiation.
- Erosion of cost advantages when the pricing information available to customers increases.

Differentiation:

- Uniqueness that is not valuable.
- Too much differentiation.
- The price premium is too high.
- Differentiation that is easily imitated.
- Dilution of brand identification through product-line extensions.
- Perceptions of differentiation may vary between buyers and sellers.

Exhibit 5.6 summarizes the pitfalls of overall cost leadership and differentiation strategies. In addressing the pitfalls associated with these two generic strategies there is one common, underlying theme. Managers must be aware of the dangers associated with concentrating so much on one strategy that they fail to attain parity on the other.

Focus

A **focus strategy** is based on the choice of a narrow competitive scope within an industry. A firm following this strategy selects a segment or group of segments and tailors its strategy to serve them. The essence of focus is the exploitation of a particular market niche. As you might expect, narrow focus itself (like merely "being different" as a differentiator) is simply not sufficient for above-average performance. The focus strategy, as indicated in Exhibit 5.1, has two variants. In a cost focus, a firm strives to create a cost advantage in its target segment. In a differentiation focus, a firm seeks to differentiate in its target market. Both variants of the focus strategy rely on providing better service than broad-based competitors who are trying to serve the focuser's target segment. Cost focus exploits differences in cost behavior in some segments, while differentiation focus exploits the special needs of buyers in other segments.

focus strategy a firm's generic strategy based on appeal to a narrow market segment within an industry.

Let's look at examples of two firms that have successfully implemented focus strategies. Network Appliance (NA) has developed a more cost-effective way to store and distribute computer files.[29] Its larger rival, EMC, makes mainframe-style products priced over $1 million that store files and accommodate Internet traffic. NA makes devices that cost under $200,000 for particular storage jobs such as caching (temporary storage) of Internet content. Focusing on such narrow segments has certainly paid off for NA; it has posted a remarkable 20 straight quarters of revenue growth.

Bessemer Trust competes in the private banking industry.[30] A differentiation focuser, it targets families with a minimum of $5 million in assets, who desire both capital preservation and wealth accumulation. In other words, these are not people who want to put all their "eggs in a dot-com basket." Bessemer configures its activities for highly personalized service by assigning one account officer for every 14 families. Meetings are more likely to be held at a client's ranch or yacht than in Bessemer's office. Bessemer offers a wide range of customized services, such as investment management, estate administration, oversight of oil and gas investments, and accounting for race horses and aircraft. Despite the industry's most generous compensation of account officers and the highest personnel cost as a percentage of operating expenses, Bessemer's focused differentiation strategy is estimated to yield the highest return on equity in the industry.

Focus: Improving Competitive Position vis-à-vis the Five Forces   Focus requires that a firm either have a low-cost position with its strategic target, high differentiation, or both. As we discussed with regard to cost and differentiation strategies, these positions provide defenses against each competitive force. Focus is also used to select niches that are least vulnerable to substitutes or where competitors are weakest.

Let's look at our examples to illustrate some of these points. First, Bessemer Trust experienced less rivalry and lower buyer bargaining power by providing products and services to a targeted market segment that was less price-sensitive. New rivals would have difficulty attracting customers away from Bessemer based only on lower prices. Similarly, the brand image and quality that this brand evoked heightened rivals entry barriers. Additionally, we could reasonably speculate that Bessemer Trust enjoyed some protection against substitute products and services because of their relatively high reputation, brand image, and customer loyalty. With regard to the strategy of cost focus, Network Appliances, the successful rival to EMC in the computer storage industry, was better able to absorb pricing increases from suppliers as a result of its lower cost structure, reducing supplier power.

Potential Pitfalls of Focus Strategies   Potential pitfalls of focus strategies include:

- *Erosion of cost advantages within the narrow segment.* The advantages of a cost focus strategy may be fleeting if the cost advantages are eroded over time. For example, Dell's pioneering direct selling model in the personal computer industry, while still the industry standard, is constantly being challenged and eroded by rivals such as Hewlett Packard as they gain experience with Dell's distribution method. Similarly, other firms have seen their profit margins drop as competitors enter their product segment.

- *Even product and service offerings that are highly focused are subject to competition from new entrants and from imitation.* Some firms adopting a focus strategy may enjoy temporary advantages because they select a small niche with few rivals. However, their advantages may be short-lived. A notable example is the multitude of dot-com firms that specialize in very narrow segments such as pet supplies, ethnic foods, and vintage automobile accessories. The entry barriers tend to be low, there is little buyer loyalty, and competition becomes intense. And since the marketing strategies and technologies employed by most rivals are largely nonproprietary, imitation is easy. Over time, revenues fall, profits margins are squeezed, and only the strongest players survive the shakeout.

- *Focusers can become too focused to satisfy buyer needs.* Some firms attempting to attain competitive advantages through a focus strategy may have too narrow a product or service. Examples include many retail firms. Hardware chains such as Ace and True Value are losing market share to rivals such as Lowe's and Home Depot who offer a full line of home and garden equipment and accessories. And given the enormous purchasing power of the national chains, it would be difficult for such specialty retailers to attain parity on costs.

Combination Strategies: Integrating Overall Low Cost and Differentiation

>LO5

How firms can effectively combine the generic strategies of overall cost leadership and differentiation.

There has been ample evidence—in the popular press and in research studies—about the strategic benefits of combining generic strategies. In the beginning of this section, we provided some evidence from a study of nearly 1,800 strategic business units (see Exhibit 5.2) to support this contention. As you will recall, the highest performers were businesses that attained both cost and differentiation advantages, followed by those that had either one or the other. Those strategic business units that had the lowest performance identified with neither generic strategy; that is, they were "stuck in the middle." Results from other studies are consistent with these findings across a wide variety of industries including low-profit industries, the paints and allied products industry, the Korean electronics industry, the apparel industry, and the screw machine products industry.[31]

Perhaps the primary benefit to firms that integrate low-cost and differentiation strategies is that it is generally harder for rivals to duplicate or imitate. This strategy enables a firm to provide two types of value to customers: differentiated attributes (e.g., high quality, brand identification, reputation) and lower prices (because of the firm's lower costs in value-creating activities). The goal becomes one of providing unique value to customers in an efficient manner.[32] Some firms are able to attain both types of advantages simultaneously. For example, superior quality can lead to lower costs because of less need for rework in manufacturing, fewer warranty claims, a reduced need for customer service personnel to resolve customer complaints, and so forth. Thus, the benefits of combining advantages can be additive, instead of merely involving trade-offs. Next, we consider three approaches to combining overall low-cost and differentiation.

Automated and Flexible Manufacturing Systems   Given the advances in manufacturing technologies such as CAD/CAM (computer aided design and computer aided manufacturing) as well as information technologies, many firms have been able to manufacture unique products in relatively small quantities at lower costs—a concept known as "mass customization."[33]

Let's consider Andersen Windows of Bayport, Minnesota—a $1 billion manufacturer of windows for the building industry.[34] Until about 20 years ago, Andersen was a mass producer, in small batches, of a variety of standard windows. However, to meet changing customer needs, Andersen kept adding to its product line. The result was catalogs of ever-increasing size and a bewildering set of choices for both homeowners and contractors. Over a 6-year period, the number of products tripled, price quotes took several hours, and the error rate increased. This not only damaged the company's reputation, but also added to its manufacturing expenses.

To bring about a major change, Andersen developed an interactive computer version of its paper catalogs that it sold to distributors and retailers. Salespersons can now customize each window to meet the customer's needs, check the design for structural soundness, and provide a price quote. The system is virtually error free, customers get exactly what they want, and the time to develop the design and furnish a quotation has been cut by 75 percent. Each showroom computer is connected to the factory, and customers are assigned a code number that permits them to track the order. The manufacturing system has been developed to use some common finished parts, but it also allows considerable variation in the final products. Despite its huge investment, Andersen has been able to lower costs, enhance quality and variety, and improve its response time to customers.

Below are some other examples of how flexible production systems have enabled firms to successfully engage in mass customization for their customers:[35]

- At Nikeid.com, customers can design an athletic or casual shoe to their specifications online, selecting almost every element of the shoe from the material of the sole to the color of the shoelace.
- Eleuria sells custom perfumes. Each product is created in response to a user profile constructed from responses to a survey about habits and preferences. Eleuria provides a sample at modest cost to verify fit.
- Lands' End offers customized shirts and pants. Consumers specify style parameters, measurements, and fabrics through the company's Web site. These settings are saved so that returning users can easily order a duplicate item.
- Cannondale permits consumers to specify the parameters that define a road bike frame, including custom colors and inscriptions. The user specifies the parameters on the company's Web site and then arranges for delivery through a dealer.

Exploiting the Profit Pool Concept for Competitive Advantage   A profit pool can be defined as the total profits in an industry at all points along the industry's value chain.[36] Although the concept is relatively straightforward, the structure of the profit pool

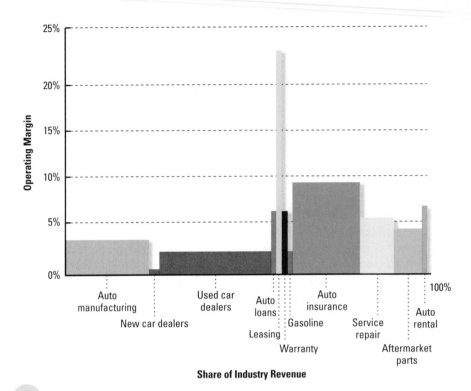

Exhibit 5.7 The U.S. Automobile Industry's Profit Pool

Source: Adapted and reprinted by permission of *Harvard Business Review,* Exhibit from "Profit Pools: A Fresh Look at Strategy," by O. Gadiesh and J. L. Gilbert, May–June 1998. Copyright © 1999 by the Harvard Business School Publishing Corporation; all rights reserved.

can be complex. The potential pool of profits will be deeper in some segments of the value chain than in others, and the depths will vary within an individual segment. Segment profitability may vary widely by customer group, product category, geographic market, or distribution channel. Additionally, the pattern of profit concentration in an industry is very often different from the pattern of revenue generation.

Consider the automobile industry profit pool in Exhibit 5.7. Here we see little relationship between the generation of revenues and capturing of profits. While manufacturing generates most of the revenue, this value activity is far smaller profitwise than other value activities such as financing and extended warranty operations. So while a car manufacturer may be under tremendous pressure to produce cars efficiently, much of the profit (at least proportionately) can be captured in the aforementioned downstream operations. Thus, a carmaker would be ill-advised to focus solely on manufacturing and leave downstream operations to others through outsourcing.

Coordinating the "Extended" Value Chain by Way of Information Technology
Many firms have achieved success by integrating activities throughout the "extended value chain" by using information technology to link their own value chain with the value chains of their customers and suppliers. As noted in Chapter 3, this approach enables a firm to add value not only through its own value-creating activities, but also for its customers and suppliers.

Such a strategy often necessitates redefining the industry's value chain. A number of years ago, Wal-Mart took a close look at its industry's value chain and decided to reframe the competitive challenge.[37] Although its competitors were primarily focused on retailing—merchandising and promotion—Wal-Mart determined that it was not so much in the retailing industry as in the transportation logistics and communications industries. Here, linkages in the extended value chain became central. That became Wal-Mart's chosen battleground. By redefining the rules of competition that played to its strengths, Wal-Mart has attained competitive advantages and dominates its industry.

Integrated Overall Low-Cost and Differentiation Strategies: Improving Competitive Position vis-à-vis the Five Forces   Firms that successfully integrate both differentiation and cost advantages create an enviable position. For example, Wal-Mart's integration of information systems, logistics, and transportation helps it to drive down costs and provide outstanding product selection. This dominant competitive position, serves to erect high entry barriers to potential competitors that have neither the financial nor physical resources to compete head-to-head. Wal-Mart's size—$316 billion in 2006 sales—provides the chain with enormous bargaining power over suppliers. Its low pricing and wide selection reduce the power of buyers (its customers), because there are relatively few competitors that can provide a comparable cost/value proposition. This reduces the possibility of intense head-to-head rivalry, such as protracted price wars. Finally, Wal-Mart's overall value proposition makes potential substitute products (e.g., Internet competitors) a less viable threat.

Pitfalls of Integrated Overall Cost Leadership and Differentiation Strategies   The pitfalls of integrated overall cost leadership and differentiation include:

- *Firms that fail to attain both strategies may end up with neither and become "stuck in the middle."* A key issue in strategic management is the creation of competitive advantages that enable a firm to enjoy above-average returns. Some firms may become "stuck in the middle" if they try to attain both cost and differentiation advantages. An example that we are all familiar with would be the Big 3 U.S. automobile makers. They are plagued by very expensive "legacy costs" associated with pension and health care obligations. And, they suffer from long-term customer perceptions of mediocre quality—inferior to their European and Japanese rivals. The troubling quality perceptions persist despite the fact that the Big 3 has attained approximate parity with their Japanese and European competitors in recent J. D. Power surveys.

- *Underestimating the challenges and expenses associated with coordinating value-creating activities in the extended value chain.* Successfully integrating activities across a firm's value chain with the value chain of suppliers and customers involves a significant investment in financial and human resources. Managers must not underestimate the expenses linked to technology investment, managerial time and commitment, and the involvement and investment required by the firm's customers and suppliers. The firm must be confident that it can generate a sufficient scale of operations and revenues to justify all associated expenses.

- *Miscalculating sources of revenue and profit pools in the firm's industry.* Firms may fail to accurately assess sources of revenue and profits in their value chain. This can occur for several reasons. For example, a manager may be biased due to his or her functional area background, work experiences, and educational background. If the manager's background is in engineering, he or she might perceive that proportionately greater revenue and margins were being created in manufacturing, product, and process design than a person whose background is in a "downstream" value-chain activity such as marketing and sales. Or politics could make managers "fudge" the numbers to favor their area of operations. This would make them responsible for a greater proportion of the firm's profits, thus improving their bargaining position.

A related problem is directing an overwhelming amount of managerial time, attention, and resources to value-creating activities that produce the greatest margins—to the detriment of other important, albeit less profitable, activities. For example, car manufacturer may focus too much on downstream activities, such as warranty fulfillment and financing operations, to the detriment of differentiation and cost of the cars themselves.

How the Internet and Digital Technologies Are Affecting the Competitive Strategies

>LO6

How Internet-enabled business models are being used to improve strategic positioning.

Internet and digital technologies have swept across the economy and now have an impact on how nearly every company conducts its business. These changes have created new cost efficiencies and avenues for differentiation that never existed before. However, the presence of these technologies is so widespread that it is questionable how any one firm can use them effectively in ways that genuinely set them apart from rivals. Thus, to stay competitive, firms must update their strategies to reflect the new possibilities and constraints that these phenomena represent. In this section, we address both the opportunities and the pitfalls that Internet and digital technologies offer to companies using overall cost leadership, differentiation, and focus strategies. We also briefly consider two major impacts that the Internet is having on business: lowering transaction costs and enabling mass customization.

Overall Cost Leadership

The Internet and digital technologies are creating new opportunities for firms to achieve low-cost advantages by enabling them to manage costs and achieve greater efficiencies. Managing costs, and even changing the cost structures of certain industries, is a key feature of the new digital economy. Most analysts agree that the Internet's ability to lower transaction costs is transforming business. Broadly speaking, *transaction costs* refer to all the various expenses associated with conducting business. It applies not just to buy/sell transactions but to the costs of interacting with every part of a firm's value chain, within and outside the firm. Think about it. Hiring new employees, meeting with customers, ordering supplies, addressing government regulations—all of these exchanges have some costs associated with them. Because business can be conducted differently on the Internet, new ways of saving money are changing the competitive landscape.

Other factors also help to lower transaction costs. The process of disintermediation, described briefly in Chapter 2, has a similar effect. Each time intermediaries are used in a transaction, additional costs are added. Removing those intermediaries lowers transaction costs. The Internet reduces the costs of traveling to a location to search for a product or service, whether it is a retail outlet (as in the case of consumers) or a trade show (as in the case of business-to-business shoppers). Not only is the need for travel eliminated but so is the need to maintain a physical address, whether it's a permanent retail location or a temporary presence at a trade show.

Exhibit 5.8 identifies several types of cost leadership strategies that are made possible by Internet and digital technologies. These cost savings are available throughout a firm's value chain, in both primary and support activities.

Exhibit 5.8
Internet-Enabled Low Cost Leader Strategies

- Online bidding and order processing are eliminating the need for sales calls and are minimizing sales force expenses.
- Online purchase orders are making many transactions paperless, thus reducing the costs of procurement and paper.
- Direct access to progress reports and the ability for customers to periodically check work in progress is minimizing rework.
- Collaborative design efforts using Internet technologies that link designers, materials suppliers, and manufacturers are reducing the costs and speeding the process of new product development.

Potential Internet-Related Pitfalls for Low-Cost Leaders   One of the biggest threats to low-cost leaders is imitation. This problem is intensified for business done on the Internet. Most of the advantages associated with contacting customers directly, and even capabilities that are software driven (e.g., customized ordering systems or real-time access to the status of work in progress), can be duplicated quickly and without threat of infringement on proprietary information. Another pitfall relates to companies that become overly enamored with using the Internet for cost-cutting. Companies that do so may suffer if they place too much attention on one business activity and ignore others. They may jeopardize customer relations or neglect other cost centers, such as providing services or controlling turnover and recruiting expenses, which then dig into their cost advantages.

Differentiation

For many companies, Internet and digital technologies have enhanced their ability to build brand, promote a favorable reputation, offer quality products and services, and achieve other differentiation advantages. Among the most striking trends that the new technologies foster are new ways to interact with consumers. In particular, the Internet is creating new ways of differentiating by enabling *mass customization,* which improves the response of companies to customer wishes. Mass customization is not a new phenomenon; it has been growing for years as flexible manufacturing systems have made manufacturing more adaptable and electronic data interchange has made communications more direct. But the Internet has generated a giant leap forward in the amount of control customers can have in influencing the process. Such capabilities are changing the way companies develop unique product and service offerings, build their reputation, and preserve their brand image.

Methods like mass customization, which are changing the way companies go to market, are challenging some of the tried-and-true techniques of differentiation. Traditionally, companies reached customers using high-end catalogs, the showroom floor, the personal sales calls and made products more inviting using prestige packaging, celebrity endorsements, and charity sponsorships. All of these avenues are still available and may still be effective, depending on a firm's competitive environment. But many customers now judge the quality and uniqueness of a product or service by their ability to be involved in its planning and design, combined with speed of delivery and reliable results. Internet and digitally based capabilities are thus changing the way differentiators make exceptional products and achieve superior service. And these improvements are being made at a reasonable cost, allowing firms to achieve parity on the basis of overall cost leadership relative to competitors.

Exhibit 5.9 identifies differentiation activities that are made possible by Internet and digital technologies. Opportunities to differentiate are available in all parts of a company's value chain—both primary and support activities.

Exhibit 5.9
Internet-Enabled Differentiation Strategies

- Personalized online access provides customers with their own "site within a site" in which their prior orders, status of current orders, and requests for future orders are processed directly on the supplier's website.
- Online access to real-time sales and service information is being used to empower the sales force and continually update R&D and technology development efforts.
- Internet-based knowledge management systems that link all parts of the organization are shortening response times and accelerating organization learning.
- Quick online responses to service requests and rapid feedback to customer surveys and product promotions are enhancing marketing efforts.

Potential Internet-Related Pitfalls for Differentiators   Traditional differentiation strategies such as building strong brand identity and prestige pricing have been undermined by Internet-enabled capabilities such as the ability to compare product features side-by-side or bid online for competing services. As applications of these technologies become part of the mainstream, it will become harder to use the Web to differentiate. The sustainability of Internet-based gains from differentiation will deteriorate if companies offer differentiating features that customers don't want or create a sense of uniqueness that customers don't value. The result can be a failed value proposition—the value companies thought they were offering, does not translate into sales. Other problems can result from overpricing products and services or developing brand extensions that dilute a company's image or reputation.

Focus

A focus strategy involves targeting a narrow market segment with customized products and/or specialized services. For companies that pursue focus strategies, the Internet offers new avenues in which to compete because they can access markets less expensively (low cost) and provide more services and features (differentiation). Some claim that the Internet has opened up a new world of opportunities for niche players who seek to access small markets in a highly specialized fashion.[38] Niche businesses are among the most active users of digital technologies and e-business solutions. According to the ClickZ.com division of Jupitermedia Corporation, 77 percent of small businesses agree that a Web site is essential for small business success. Small businesses also report that the Internet has helped them grow (58 percent), made them more profitable (51 percent), and helped reduce business costs (49 percent).[39] Clearly niche players and small businesses are using the Internet and digital technologies to create more viable focus strategies.

Many aspects of the Internet economy favor focus strategies because niche players and small firms have been able to extend their reach and effectively compete with larger competitors using Internet and digital technologies. For example, niche firms have been quicker than Fortune 1000 firms to adopt blogging as a way to create a community and gather customer feedback.[40] Effective use of blogs is a good example of how focusers are using the new technology to provide the kinds of advantages that have been the hallmark of a focus strategy in the past—specialized knowledge, rapid response, and strong customer service. Thus, the Internet has provided many companies that pursue focus strategies with new tools for creating competitive advantages.

Exhibit 5.10 outlines several approaches to strategic focusing that are made possible by Internet and digital technologies. Both primary and support activities can be enhanced using the kind of singlemindedness that is characteristic of a focus strategy.

Exhibit 5.10
Internet-Enabled Focus Strategies

- Permission marketing techniques are focusing sales efforts on specific customers who opt to receive advertising notices.
- Niche portals that target specific groups are providing advertisers with access to viewers with specialized interests.
- Virtual organizing and online "officing" are being used to minimize firm infrastructure requirements.
- Procurement technologies that use Internet software to match buyers and sellers are highlighting specialized buyers and drawing attention to smaller suppliers.

Potential Internet-Related Pitfalls for Focusers A key danger for focusers using the Internet relates to correctly assessing the size of the online marketplace. Focusers may misstep if they misread the scope and interests of their target markets. This can cause them to focus on segments that are too narrow to be profitable or to lose their uniqueness by going after overly broad niches, making them vulnerable to imitators or new entrants. What happens when an e-business focuser tries to overextend its niche? Efforts to appeal to a broader audience by carrying additional inventory, developing additional content, or offering additional services can cause it to lose the cost advantages associated with a limited product or service offering. Conversely, when focus strategies become too narrow, the e-business may have trouble generating enough activity to justify the expense of operating the Web site.

Are Combination Strategies the Key to E-Business Success?

Because of the changing dynamics presented by digital and Internet-based technologies, new strategic combinations that make the best use of the competitive strategies just described may hold the greatest promise for future success.[41] Many experts agree that the net effect of the digital economy is fewer rather than more opportunities for sustainable advantages.[42] This means strategic thinking is even more important in the Internet age.

More specifically, the Internet has provided all companies with greater tools for managing costs. So it may be that cost management and control will become more important management tools. In general, this may be good if it leads to an economy that makes more efficient use of its scarce resources. However, for individual companies, it may shave critical percentage points off profit margins and create a climate that makes it impossible to survive, much less achieve sustainable above-average profits.

Many differentiation advantages are also diminished by the Internet. The ability to comparison shop—to check product reviews and inspect different choices with a few clicks of the mouse—is depriving some companies, such as auto dealers, of the unique advantages that were the hallmark of their success in a previous time. Differentiating is still an important strategy, of course. But how firms achieve it may change, and the best approach may be to combine a differentiation strategy with other competitive strategies.

Perhaps the greatest beneficiaries are the focusers who can use the Internet to capture a niche that previously may have been inaccessible. Even this is not assured, however, because the same factors that make it possible for a small niche player to be a contender may make that same niche attractive to a big company. That is, an incumbent firm that previously thought a niche market was not worth the effort may use Internet technologies to enter that segment for a lower cost than in the past. The larger firm can then bring its market power and resources to bear in a way that a smaller competitor cannot match.

A combination strategy, by definition, challenges a company to carefully blend alternative strategic approaches and remain mindful of the impact of different decisions on the firm's value-creating processes and its extended value-chain activities. Strong leadership is needed to maintain a bird's-eye perspective on a company's overall approach and to coordinate the multiple dimensions of a combination strategy.

Strategy Spotlight 5.4 describes the efforts of Liberty Mutual, a company that used Internet and digital technologies to successfully combine both differentiation and overall low-cost advantages.

strategy spotlight

5.4

Liberty Mutual's Electronic Invoice System: Combining Low Cost and Differentiation Advantages

Boston-based Liberty Mutual Group is a leading global insurer and the sixth largest property and casualty insurer in the United States. Its largest line of business is personal automobile insurance. Liberty Mutual has $85.5 billion in assets and $23.5 billion in annual revenues—ranking the firm 102nd on the Fortune 500 list of the largest corporations.

In 2000, Liberty Mutual became one of the first companies to experiment with electronic invoices. It set up a pilot program with a few law firms to submit its bills through a secured Web site. These firms, for the most part, handle claims litigation for Liberty, defending its policyholders in lawsuits. Its success with this program convinced Liberty that it could achieve significant cost savings and also pass along differentiating features to its customers and strategic partners. Liberty now processes nearly 400,000 electronic legal-services invoices a year—70 percent of the total invoices that the firm receives.

As expected, the initial transition was quite expensive. The company invested nearly $1 million in the first four years. However, Liberty estimates that the electronic invoice program saves the company $750,000 a year in direct costs by streamlining the distribution, payment, storage, and retrieval of invoices. E-invoices enable Liberty to move from intake to payment with half the staff that it had taken to process paper invoices. The firm has also created new efficiencies by cutting costs resulting from data entry errors, late payments, and overpayments. As a relatively minor issue, Liberty saves more than $20,000 per year on postage, photocopying, archiving, and retrieval costs.

The legal invoices are organized by litigation phase or task—for example, taking a deposition or reporting a witness statement. Work is diced into tiny increments of six minutes

or less. A single invoice that covers a month of complex litigation, for example, can include well over 1,000 lines. However, by building and mining a database of law firm billing practices, Liberty is able to generate a highly granular report card about law firm activities and performance. The new knowledge generated by this system not only increases internal effectiveness but also allows Liberty to provide detailed feedback to clients and other external stakeholders.

Online invoicing has also helped speed up both processing and response time. Liberty can instantaneously see how firms deploy and bill for partners, paralegals, and other staff, how they compare with each other on rates, hours, and case outcomes; and whether, how, and how often they send duplicate invoices or charge for inappropriate services. The system also allows Liberty to instantly review all of the time billed for a particular attorney across many cases, enabling the firm to reconstruct the total time billed to Liberty during a single day. More than once they have found that attorneys have billed more than 24 hours in a day. Liberty is also able to easily expose prohibited formula billing patterns (wherein, for example, they are billed a set amount for a service instead of actual time spent). In two cases in which formula billing was used, Liberty found that there were more than $28,000 in suspected overcharges.

Liberty Mutual is in the process of developing a large database of law firms' billing practices on different types of cases. The database should eventually enable Liberty to evaluate a law firm's billing activities and compare them to the norms of all of its partner firms. With such intelligence, it will be a rather straightforward matter to rate each firm's cost effectiveness in handling certain types of cases and match firms with cases accordingly.

Liberty's decision to use electronic invoices was initially based on the potential for cost savings. But the differentiating advantages it has achieved in terms of rapid feedback, decreased response time, and a knowledge trove in databases that can be electronically mined has provided the company with a fruitful combination of Internet-based strategic advantages.

Sources: Coyle, M., & Angevine, R. 2007. Liberty Mutual Group reports fourth quarter 2006 results. February 26, www.libertymutual.com; and Smunt, T. L., & Sutcliffe, C. L., 2004. There's gold in them bills. *Harvard Business Review*, 82(9): 24–25.

Industry Life Cycle Stages: Strategic Implications

> **industry life cycle**
> the stages of introduction, growth, maturity, and decline that typically occur over the life of an industry.

The **industry life cycle** refers to the stages of introduction, growth, maturity, and decline that occur over the life of an industry. In considering the industry life cycle, it is useful to think in terms of broad product lines such as personal computers, photocopiers, or long-distance telephone service. Yet the industry life cycle concept can be explored from several levels, from the life cycle of an entire industry to the life cycle of a single variation or model of a specific product or service.

Why is it important to consider industry life cycles?[43] The emphasis on various generic strategies, functional areas, value-creating activities, and overall objectives varies over the course of an industry life cycle. Managers must become even more aware of their firm's strengths and weaknesses in many areas to attain competitive advantages. For example, firms depend on their research and development (R&D) activities in the introductory stage of the life cycle. R&D is the source of new products and features that everyone hopes will appeal to customers. Firms develop products and services to stimulate consumer demand. Later, during the maturity phase, the functions of the product have been defined, more competitors have entered the market, and competition is intense. Managers then place greater emphasis on production efficiencies and process (as opposed to the product) engineering in order to lower manufacturing costs. This helps to protect the firm's market position and to extend the product life cycle because the firm's lower costs can be passed on to consumers in the form of lower prices, and price-sensitive customers will find the product more appealing.

Exhibit 5.11 illustrates the four stages of the industry life cycle and how factors such as generic strategies, market growth rate, intensity of competition, and overall objectives change over time. As we noted earlier, managers must strive to emphasize the key functional areas during each of the four stages and to attain a level of parity in all functional areas and value-creating activities. For example, even though controlling production costs may be a primary concern during the maturity stage, managers should not totally ignore other functions such as marketing and R&D. If they do, they can become so focused on lowering costs that they miss market trends or fail to incorporate important product or process designs. In such cases, the firm may attain low-cost products that have limited market appeal.

It is important to point out a caveat. While the life cycle idea is analogous to a living organism (i.e., birth, growth, maturity, and death), the comparison does have limitations.[44] Products and services go through many cycles of innovation and renewal. For the most part, only fad products have a single life cycle. Maturity stages of an industry can be "transformed" or followed by a stage of rapid growth if consumer tastes change, technological innovations take place, or new developments occur in the general environment. The cereal industry is a good example. When medical research indicated that oat consumption reduced a person's cholesterol, sales of Quaker Oats increased dramatically.[45]

Next we discuss each stage of the industry life cycle. Then, we will discuss turnaround strategies—that is, strategies that are necessary in order to reverse performance erosion and regain competitive position.

Strategies in the Introduction Stage

In the **introduction stage,** products are unfamiliar to consumers.[46] Market segments are not well defined, and product features are not clearly specified. The early development of an industry typically involves low sales growth, rapid technological change, operating losses, and the need for strong sources of cash to finance operations. Since there are few players and not much growth, competition tends to be limited.

Success requires an emphasis on research and development and marketing activities to enhance awareness. The challenge becomes one of (1) developing the product and finding a way to get users to try it, and (2) generating enough exposure so the product emerges as the "standard" by which all other rivals' products are evaluated.

There's an advantage to being the "first mover" in a market.[47] Consider Coca-Cola's success in becoming the first soft-drink company to build a recognizable global brand. Moving first enabled Caterpillar to get a lock on overseas sales channels and service capabilities. Being a first mover allowed Matsushita to establish Video Home Source (VHS) as the global standard for videocassette recorders.

>LO7

The importance of considering the industry life cycle to determine a firm's business-level strategy and its relative emphasis on functional area strategies and value-creating activities.

introduction stage the first stage of the industry life cycle characterized by (1) new products that are not known to customers, (2) poorly defined market segments, (3) unspecified product features, (4) low sales growth, (5) rapid technological change, (6) operating losses, and (7) a need for financial support.

Stage / Factor	Introduction	Growth	Maturity	Decline
Generic strategies	Differentiation	Differentiation	Differentiation Overall cost leadership	Overall cost leadership Focus
Market growth rate	Low	Very large	Low to moderate	Negative
Number of segments	Very few	Some	Many	Few
Intensity of competition	Low	Increasing	Very intense	Changing
Emphasis on product design	Very high	High	Low to moderate	Low
Emphasis on process design	Low	Low to moderate	High	Low
Major functional area(s) of concern	Research and development	Sales and marketing	Production	General management and finance
Overall objective	Increase market awareness	Create consumer demand	Defend market share and extend product life cycles	Consolidate, maintain, harvest, or exit

Exhibit 5.11 Stages of the Industry Life Cycle

However, there can also be a benefit to being a "late mover." Target carefully thought out the decision to delay its Internet strategy. Compared to its competitors Wal-Mart and Kmart, Target was definitely the industry laggard. But things certainly turned out well for Target:[48]

By waiting, Target gained a late mover advantage. The store was able to use competitors' mistakes as its own learning curve. This saved money, and customers didn't seem to mind the wait: When Target finally opened its Web site, it quickly captured market share from both Kmart and Wal-Mart Internet shoppers. Forrester Research Internet analyst Stephen Zrike commented, "There's no question, in our mind, that Target has a far better understanding of how consumers buy online."

Examples of products currently in the introductory stages of the industry life cycle include electric vehicles, digital cameras, and high-definition television (HDTV).

Strategies in the Growth Stage

The **growth stage** is characterized by strong increases in sales. The potential for strong sales (and profits) attracts other competitors. In the growth stage, the primary key to success is to build consumer preferences for specific brands. This requires strong brand recognition, differentiated products, and the financial resources to support a variety of value-chain activities such as marketing and sales, customer service, and research and development. Whereas marketing and sales initiatives were mainly directed at spurring *aggregate* demand—that is, demand for all such products in the introduction stage—efforts in the growth stage are directed toward stimulating *selective* demand, in which a firm's product offerings are chosen instead of those of its rivals.

Revenues in the growth stage increase at an accelerating rate because (1) new consumers are trying the product and (2) a growing proportion of satisfied consumers are making repeat purchases.[49] In general, as a product moves through its life cycle, the proportion of repeat buyers to new purchasers increases. Conversely, new products and services often fail if there are relatively few repeat purchases. This is especially true with many consumer products that are characterized by relatively low price and frequent purchase. For example, Alberto-Culver introduced Mr. Culver's Sparklers, which were solid air fresheners that looked like stained glass. Although the product quickly went from the introductory to the growth stage, sales then plummeted. Why? Unfortunately, there were few repeat purchasers because buyers treated them as inexpensive window decorations, left them there, and felt little need to purchase new ones. Examples of products currently in the growth stage of the industry life cycle include Internet servers and personal digital assistants (e.g., Palm Pilots).

growth stage the second stage of the product life cycle characterized by (1) strong increases in sales; (2) growing competition; (3) developing brand recognition; and (4) a need for financing complementary value-chain activities such as marketing, sales, customer service, and research and development.

Strategies in the Maturity Stage

In the **maturity stage** aggregate industry demand begins to slow. Since markets are becoming saturated, there are few opportunities to attract new adopters. It's no longer possible to "grow around" the competition, so direct competition becomes predominant.[50] With few attractive prospects, marginal competitors begin to exit the market. At the same time, rivalry among existing rivals intensifies because there is often fierce price competition at the same time that expenses associated with attracting new buyers are rising. Advantages based on efficient manufacturing operations and process engineering become more important for keeping costs low as customers become more price sensitive. It also becomes more difficult for firms to differentiate their offerings, because users have a greater understanding of products and services.

An article in *Fortune* magazine that addressed the intensity of rivalry in mature markets was aptly titled "A Game of Inches." It stated, "Battling for market share in a slowing industry can be a mighty dirty business. Just ask laundry soap archrivals Unilever and Procter & Gamble."[51] These two firms have been locked in a battle for market share since 1965. Why is the competition so intense? There is not much territory to gain. In 2000, total sales for the industry were flat at $6 billion a year. A Lehman Brothers analyst noted, "People aren't getting any dirtier." Thus, the only way to win is to take market share from the competition. To increase its share, Procter & Gamble (P&G) spends $100 million a year promoting its Tide brand on television, billboards, subways, buses, magazines, and the Internet. But Unilever isn't standing still. Armed with a new $80 million budget, it recently launched a soap tablet product named Wisk Dual Action Tablets. For example, it delivered samples of this product to 24 million U.S. homes in Sunday newspapers, followed by a series of TV ads. P&G launched a counteroffensive with Tide

maturity stage the third stage of the product life cycle characterized by (1) slowing demand growth, (2) saturated markets, (3) direct competition, (4) price competition, and (5) strategic emphasis on efficient operations.

Rapid Action Tablets ads showed in side-by-side comparisons of the two products dropped into beakers of water. In the promotion, P&G claimed that its product is superior because it dissolves faster than Unilever's product. A minor point, but Unilever is challenging P&G in court. And the beat goes on. . . .

Although this is only one example, many product classes and industries, including consumer products such as beer, automobiles, and televisions, are in the maturity stage.

Studies have shown that firms do not need to be "held hostage" to the life-cycle curve. By positioning or repositioning their products in unexpected ways, firms can change how customers mentally categorize them. Thus, firms are able to rescue products floundering in the maturity phase of their life cycles and return them to the growth phase.

Two positioning strategies that managers can use to affect consumers' mental shifts are **reverse positioning,** which strips away "sacred" product attributes while adding new ones, and **breakaway positioning,** which associates the product with a radically different category.[52] We discuss each of these positioning strategies below and then provide an example of each in Strategy Spotlight 5.5.

Reverse Positioning   Reverse positioning assumes that although customers don't desire more than the baseline product, they also don't necessarily want an endless list of features. Such companies make the creative decision to step off the augmentation treadmill and shed product attributes that the rest of the industry considers sacred. Then, once a product is returned to its baseline state, reverse positioners supplement the stripped-down product with one or more carefully selected attributes that would usually be found only in a highly augmented product. Such an unconventional combination of attributes allows the product to assume a new competitive position within the category and move backwards from maturity into a growth position on the life-cycle curve.

Breakaway Positioning   As noted above, with reverse positioning, a product establishes a unique position in its category but retains a clear category membership. However, with breakaway positioning, a product escapes its category by deliberately associating with a different one. Thus, managers leverage the new category's conventions to change both how products are consumed and with whom they compete. Instead of merely seeing the breakaway product as simply an alternative to others in its category, consumers perceive it as altogether different.

When a breakaway product is successful in leaving its category and joining a new one, it is able to redefine its competition. Similar to reverse positioning, this strategy permits the product to shift backward on the life-cycle curve, moving from the rather dismal maturity phase to a thriving growth opportunity.

Strategy Spotlight 5.5 provides examples of reverse and breakaway positioning.

Strategies in the Decline Stage

Although all decisions in the phases of an industry life cycle are important, they become particularly difficult in the **decline stage.** Hard choices must be made, and firms must face up to the fundamental strategic choices of either exiting or staying and attempting to consolidate their position in the industry.[53]

The decline stage occurs when industry sales and profits begin to fall. Typically, changes in the business environment are at the root of an industry or product group entering this stage.[54] Changes in consumer tastes or a technological innovation can push a product into decline. Typewriters have entered into the decline stage because of the word processing capabilities of personal computers. Compact disks have forced cassette

---

reverse positioning a break in industry tendency to continuously augment products, characteristic of the product life cycle, by offering products with fewer product attributes and lower prices.

breakaway positioning a break in industry tendency to incrementally improve products along specific dimensions, characteristic of the product life cycle, by offering products that are still in the industry but that are perceived by customers as being different.

decline stage the fourth stage of the product life cycle characterized by (1) falling sales and profits, (2) increasing price competition, and (3) industry consolidation.

Reverse and Breakaway Positioning: How to Avoid Being Held Hostage to the Life-Cycle Curve

When firms adopt a reverse or breakaway positioning strategy, there is typically no pretense about what they are trying to accomplish. In essence, they subvert convention through unconventional promotions, prices, and attributes. That becomes a large part of their appeal—a cleverly positioned product offering. Next we discuss Commerce Bank's reverse positioning and Swatch's breakaway positioning.

Commerce Bank

While most banks offer dozens of checking and savings accounts and compete by trying to offer the highest interest rates, Commerce Bank takes a totally different approach. It pays among the lowest rates in its market. Further, it offers a very limited product line—just four checking accounts, for example. One would think that such a stingy approach would seem to scare off customers. However, Commerce Bank has been very successful. Between 1999 and 2005, it expanded from 120 to 373 branches and its total assets have soared from $5.6 billion to $39 billion.

How has it been so successful? It has stripped away all of what customers expect—lots of choices and peak interest rates and it has *reverse positioned* itself as "the most convenient bank in America." It's open seven days a week, including evenings until 8 p.m. You can get a debit card while you wait. And, when it rains, an escort with an umbrella will escort you to your car. Further, the bank offers free coffee,

Sources: Moon, Y. 2005. Break free from the product life cycle. *Harvard Business Review*, 83(5): 87–94; Commerce Bancorp, Inc. www.hoovers.com; Swatch. en.wikipedia.org; and, www.commercebank.com.

newspapers, and most of the branches have free coin-counting machines that customers love (in one recent week, customers fed the machines a total of $28 million in loose change). Not too surprisingly, despite the inferior rates and few choices, new customers are flocking to the bank.

Swatch

Interestingly, the name "Swatch" is often misconstrued as a contraction of the words *Swiss watch*. However, Nicholas Hayek, Chairman, affirms that the original contraction was "Second Watch"—the new watch was introduced as a new concept of watches as casual, fun, and relatively disposable accessories. And therein lies Swatch's *breakaway positioning*.

When Swatch was launched in 1983, Swiss watches were marketed as a form of jewelry. They were serious, expensive, enduring, and discreetly promoted. Once a customer purchased one, it lasted a lifetime. Swatch changed all of that by defining its watches as playful fashion accessories which were showily promoted. They inspired impulse buying—customers would often purchase half a dozen in different designs. Their price—$40 when the brand was introduced—expanded Swatch's reach beyond its default category (watches as high-end jewelry) and moved it into the fashion accessory category, where it has different customers and competitors. Swatch was the official timekeeper of the 1996, 2000, and 2004 Summer Olympics.

Today, The Swatch Group is the largest watch company in the world. It has acquired many brands over the years including Omega, Longines, Calvin Klein, and Hamilton. Revenues have grown to $3.6 billion in 2005 and net income has increased to $500 million. And it remains on a roll. As of February 2007, its stock had soared 42 percent over the prior 52-week period.

tapes into decline in the prerecorded music industry, and digital video disks (DVDs) are replacing compact disks. About 20 years earlier, of course, cassette tapes had led to the demise of long-playing records (LPs).

When a product enters the decline stage, it often consumes a large share of management time and financial resources relative to its potential worth. Not only are sales and profits declining, but also competitors may start drastically cutting their prices to raise cash and remain solvent in the short term. The situation is further aggravated by the wholesale liquidation of assets, including inventory, of some of the competitors that have failed. This further intensifies price competition.

In the decline stage, a firm's strategic options become dependent on the actions of rivals. If many competitors decide to leave the market, sales and profit opportunities increase. On the other hand, prospects are limited if all competitors remain.[55] If some

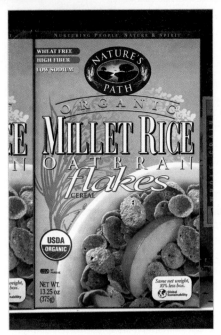

• Many consumer food products such as cereal are in the mature stage of the product life cycle. However, some organic products are enjoying high rates of growth.

competitors merge, their increased market power may erode the opportunities for the remaining players. Managers must carefully monitor the actions and intentions of competitors before deciding on a course of action.

Four basic strategies are available in the decline phase: *maintaining, harvesting, exiting,* or *consolidating.*[56]

- *Maintaining* refers to keeping a product going without significantly reducing marketing support, technological development, or other investments, in the hope that competitors will eventually exit the market. Many offices, for example, still use typewriters for filling out forms and other purposes that cannot be completed on a personal computer. In some rural areas, rotary (or dial) telephones persist because of the older technology used in central switching offices. Thus, if a firm remains in the business and others exit, there may still be the potential for revenues and profits.

- *Harvesting* involves obtaining as much profit as possible and requires that costs be reduced quickly. Managers should consider the firm's value-creating activities and cut associated budgets. Value-chain activities to consider are primary (e.g., operations, sales and marketing) and support (e.g., procurement, technology development). The objective is to wring out as much profit as possible.

- *Exiting the market* involves dropping the product from a firm's portfolio. Since a residual core of consumers may still use the product, eliminating it should be considered carefully. If the firm's exit involves product markets that affect important relationships with other product markets in the corporation's overall portfolio, an exit could have repercussions for the whole corporation. For example, it may involve the loss of valuable brand names or human capital with a broad variety of expertise in many value-creating activities such as marketing, technology, and operations.

- *Consolidation* involves one firm acquiring at a reasonable price the best of the surviving firms in an industry. This enables firms to enhance market power and acquire valuable assets. One example of a consolidation strategy took place in the defense industry in the early 1990s. As the cliché suggests, "peace broke out" at the end of the Cold War and overall U.S. defense spending levels plummeted.[57] Many companies that make up the defense industry saw more than 50 percent of their market disappear. Only one-quarter of the 120,000 companies that once supplied the Department of Defense still serve in that capacity; the others have shut down their defense business or dissolved altogether. But one key player, Lockheed Martin, became a dominant rival by pursuing an aggressive strategy of consolidation. During the 1990s, it purchased 17 independent entities, including General Dynamics's tactical aircraft and space systems divisions, GE Aerospace, Goodyear Aerospace, and Honeywell ElectroOptics. These combinations enabled Lockheed Martin to emerge as the top provider to three governmental customers: the Department of Defense, the Department of Energy, and NASA. Despite several downsizing initiatives, the firm was ranked for the first time in the Fortune 25 (the largest 25 industrial concerns in the United States). Clearly, the prospects for industry prosperity have increased in the aftermath of the September 11, 2001, terrorist attacks, the wars in Iraq and Afghanistan, and the "War on Terror."

Examples of products currently in the decline stage of the industry life cycle include automotive spark plugs (replaced by electronic fuel ignition), videocassette recorders (replaced by digital video disk recorders), and personal computer zip drives (replaced by compact disk read-write drives). As we mentioned previously, compact disks are being replaced by digital video disks (DVDs).

Turnaround Strategies

A **turnaround strategy** involves reversing a firm's decline in performance and reinvigorating it back to growth and profitability. A need for turnaround may occur at any stage in the life cycle. However, it is more likely to occur during the maturity or decline stage.

turnaround strategy
a strategy that reverses a firm's decline in performance and returns it to growth and profitability.

Most turnarounds require a firm to carefully analyze the external and internal environments.[58] The external analysis leads to identification of market segments or customer groups that may still find the product attractive. Internal analysis results in actions aimed at reduced costs and higher efficiency. Typically, a firm needs to undertake a mix of both internally and externally oriented actions to effect a turnaround.[59]

A study of 260 mature businesses in need of a turnaround identified three strategies used by successful companies.[60]

- *Asset and cost surgery.* Very often, mature firms tend to have assets that do not produce any returns. These include real estate, buildings, etc. Outright sales or sale and leaseback free up considerable cash and improve returns. Investment in new plants and equipment can be deferred. Firms in turnaround situations try to aggressively cut administrative expenses and inventories and speed up collection of receivables. Costs also can be reduced by outsourcing production of various inputs for which market prices may be cheaper than in-house production costs.

>LO8
The need for turnaround strategies that enable a firm to reposition its competitive position in an industry.

- *Selective product and market pruning.* Most mature or declining firms have many product lines that are losing money or are only marginally profitable. One strategy is to discontinue these product lines and focus all resources on a few core profitable areas. For example, in the early 1980s, faced with possible bankruptcy, Chrysler Corporation sold off all its nonautomotive businesses as well as all its production facilities abroad. Focus on the North American market and identification of a profitable niche—namely, minivans—were keys to their eventual successful turnaround.
- *Piecemeal productivity improvements.* There are hundreds of ways in which a firm can eliminate costs and improve productivity. Although individually these are small gains, they cumulate over a period of time to substantial gains. Improving business processes by reengineering them, benchmarking specific activities against industry leaders, encouraging employee input to identify excess costs, reducing R&D and marketing expenses, increasing capacity utilization, and improving employee productivity lead to a significant overall gain.

The turnaround of software maker Intuit is an interesting case of a quick but well-implemented turnaround strategy. After stagnating and stumbling during the dot-com boom, Intuit, which is known for its Quickbook and Turbotax software, hired Stephen M. Bennett, a 22-year GE veteran, in 1999. He immediately discontinued Intuit's online finance, insurance, and bill-paying operations that were losing money. Instead, he focused on software for small businesses that employ less than 250 people. He also instituted a performance-based reward system that greatly improved employee productivity. Within a few years, Intuit was once again making substantial profits and its stock was up 42 percent.[61]

Mitchell Caplan's Successful Turnaround at E*Trade

Mitchell Caplan is an optimist. He was confident that E*Trade Financial Corporation would survive and prosper. However, such optimism seemed to be misplaced given the fact that the shares of the online broker and bank had plunged from $60 at the peak of the Internet frenzy to a low of $3 in 2002. In 2001 and 2002, the firm lost a total of $428 million.

Fortunately for E*Trade (and their shareholders), Mr. Caplan was elevated to the CEO position in 2003, and he initiated what became a very successful turnaround. Let's take a look at how he did it.

First, Caplan had to change the firm's general approach to business. E*Trade had traditionally ignored the red ink as long as the stock price climbed. However, Caplan realized that he had to cut costs and sell off unrelated businesses. This included sharply reducing marketing and advertising expenses. E*Trade no longer splurges on $2 million Super Bowl commercials. In fact, one year, the company spent $500 million on marketing—more than the entire U.S. liquor industry! Now it only spends about $140 million a year. There are also fewer employees—down to about 4,000 now from a peak of 5,000. He also sold off businesses and assets that were unrelated to E*Trade's core. This included a national ATM network, kiosks in Target stores, a palatial New York retail branch that sold

Source: Weber, J. 2005. E*Trade rises from the ashes. *BusinessWeek,* January 17: 58–59; and Schmerken, I. 2004. Innovation in motion. *Wall Street & Technology,* October: 22–26.

E*Trade souvenirs, and a TV business-news service. In addition, new ventures, such as a string of small storefront offices in major cities, are now rigorously analyzed for profitability. Notes Caplan, "I am adamant—and as a team we are adamant—about financial returns."

Mitch Caplan also felt that he needed to change the organization's culture and instill more discipline. He moved the headquarters from Menlo Park, California, to New York City. In effect, he left behind the propeller beanies, rubber chickens, and geeky props that made the firm's atmosphere rather loose. In its place are jackets and ties.

In addition to cutting costs and changing the culture, Caplan also focused E*Trade on leveraging its core banking operations. Here, it had a clear edge over rivals Charles Schwab Corp. and Ameritrade Inc. By offering banking products such as checking accounts and loans at reduced rates to customers who had brokerage accounts, E*Trade has built the nation's eighth-largest thrift. It also has become a big profit center, accounting for 40 percent of all revenues and 48 percent of profits. Now the company has about 632,000 bank accounts and 2.9 million active brokerage accounts—up from 170,00 bank accounts and 2.4 million brokerage accounts in early 2000.

By focusing on its core business, E*Trade's revenues were only $1.6 billion for the year 2004, which is less than the roughly $2 billion for the years 2003, 2002, 2001. However, profits have soared to $389 million in 2004 compared to an average *loss* of about $75 million for the three previous years. And E*Trade was recently recognized by *Information-Week* as one of the 40 top firms in the financial services industry for delivering IT solutions to solve business problems.

Even when an industry is in overall decline, pockets of profitability remain. These are segments with customers who are relatively price insensitive. For example, the replacement demand for vacuum tubes affords its manufacturers an opportunity to earn above normal returns although the product itself is technologically obsolete. Surprisingly, within declining industries, there may still be segments that are either stable or growing. Cigars and chewing tobacco are examples of profitable segments within the tobacco industry. Although fountain pens ceased to be the writing instrument of choice a long time ago, the fountain pen industry has successfully reconceptualized the product as a high margin luxury item that signals accomplishment, success, and appreciation of the finer things in life. In the final analysis, every business has the potential for rejuvenation. But it takes creativity, persistence, and most of all a clear strategy to translate that potential into reality.

Strategy Spotlight 5.6 summarizes how Mitchell Caplan conducted a successful turnaround at E*Trade. He was able to effectively cut costs and sell off unrelated businesses, change the firm's general approach to business and its culture, and leverage its core banking operations.

Summary

How and why firms outperform each other goes to the heart of strategic management. In this chapter, we identified three generic strategies and discussed how firms are able not only to attain advantages over competitors, but also to sustain such advantages over time. Why do some advantages become long-lasting while others are quickly imitated by competitors?

The three generic strategies—overall cost leadership, differentiation, and focus—form the core of this chapter. We began by providing a brief description of each generic strategy (or competitive advantage) and furnished examples of firms that have successfully implemented these strategies. Successful generic strategies invariably enhance a firm's position vis-à-vis the five forces of that industry—a point that we stressed and illustrated with examples. However, as we pointed out, there are pitfalls to each of the generic strategies. Thus, the sustainability of a firm's advantage is always challenged because of imitation or substitution by new or existing rivals. Such competitor moves erode a firm's advantage over time.

We also discussed the viability of combining (or integrating) overall cost leadership and generic differentiation strategies. If successful, such integration can enable a firm to enjoy superior performance and improve its competitive position. However, this is challenging, and managers must be aware of the potential downside risks associated with such an initiative.

The way companies formulate and deploy strategies is changing because of the impact of the Internet and digital technologies in many industries. Further, Internet technologies are enabling the mass customization capabilities of greater numbers of competitors. Focus strategies are likely to increase in importance because the Internet provides highly targeted and lower-cost access to narrow or specialized markets. These strategies are not without their pitfalls, however, and firms need to understand the dangers as well as the potential benefits of Internet-based approaches.

The concept of the industry life cycle is a critical contingency that managers must take into account in striving to create and sustain competitive advantages. We identified the four stages of the industry life cycle—introduction, growth, maturity, and decline—and suggested how these stages can play a role in decisions that managers must make at the business level. These include overall strategies as well as the relative emphasis on functional areas and value-creating activities.

When a firm's performance severely erodes, turnaround strategies are needed to reverse its situation and enhance its competitive position. We have discussed three approaches—asset cost surgery, selective product and market pruning, and piecemeal productivity improvements.

Summary Review Questions

1. Explain why the concept of competitive advantage is central to the study of strategic management.
2. Briefly describe the three generic strategies—overall cost leadership, differentiation, and focus.
3. Explain the relationship between the three generic strategies and the five forces that determine the average profitability within an industry.

4. What are some of the ways in which a firm can attain a successful turnaround strategy?
5. Describe some of the pitfalls associated with each of the three generic strategies.
6. Can firms combine the generic strategies of overall cost leadership and differentiation? Why or why not?
7. Explain why the industry life cycle concept is an important factor in determining a firm's business-level strategy.

Key Terms

overall low-cost leadership, 157
competitive parity, 158
differentiation strategy, 163
focus strategy, 167
industry life cycle, 176
introduction stage, 177
growth stage, 179
maturity stage, 179
decline stage, 180
reverse positioning, 180
breakaway positioning, 180
turnaround strategy, 183

Experiential Exercise

What are some examples of primary and support activities that enable Nucor, an $11 billion steel manufacturer, to achieve a low-cost strategy?

Application Questions Exercises

1. Go to the Internet and look up www.walmart.com. How has this firm been able to combine overall cost leadership and differentiation strategies?
2. Choose a firm with which you are familiar in your local business community. Is the firm successful in following one (or more) generic strategies? Why or why not? What do you think are some of the challenges it faces in implementing these strategies in an effective manner?
3. Think of a firm that has attained a differentiation focus or cost focus strategy. Are their advantages sustainable? Why? Why not? (*Hint:* Consider its position vis-à-vis Porter's five forces.)
4. Think of a firm that successfully achieved a combination overall cost leadership and differentiation strategy. What can be learned from this example? Are these advantages sustainable? Why? Why not? (*Hint:* Consider its competitive position vis-à-vis Porter's five forces.)

Value-Chain Activity	Yes/No	How Does Nucor Create Value for the Customer?
Primary:		
Inbound logistics		
Operations		
Outbound logistics		
Marketing and sales		
Service		
Support:		
Procurement		
Technology development		
Human resource management		
General administration		

Ethics Questions

1. Can you think of a company that suffered ethical consequences as a result of an overemphasis on a cost leadership strategy? What do you think were the financial and nonfinancial implications?

2. In the introductory stage of the product life cycle, what are some of the unethical practices that managers could engage in to enhance their firm's market position? What could be some of the long-term implications of such actions?

References

1. The Starbucks example draws upon the following sources: Crane, M. 2007. How to run a restaurant: Best role model. www.forbes.com. February 2: np.; McGovern, G. J., Court, D., Quelch, J. A., & Crawford, B. 2004. Bringing customers into the boardroom. *Harvard Business Review*, 82(11): 70–80; Gottfrendson, M., & Aspinall, K. 2005. Innovation and complexity. *Harvard Business Review*, 83(11); 62–71; and Francis, D. 2005. The secret of successful marketing. *Financial Post*. November 25: FP2.

2. For a seminal discussion on competitive advantage and the importance of recognizing tradeoffs, refer to Porter, M. 1996. What is strategy? *Harvard Business Review*, 74(6): 61–78.

3. For a recent perspective by Porter on competitive strategy, refer to Porter, M. E. 1996. What is strategy? *Harvard Business Review*, 74(6): 61–78.

4. Some useful ideas on maintaining competitive advantages can be found in Ma, H., & Karri, R. 2005. Leaders beware: Some sure ways to lose your competitive advantage. *Organizational Dynamics*, 343(1): 63–76.

5. Miller, A., & Dess, G. G. 1993. Assessing Porter's model in terms of its generalizability, accuracy, and simplicity. *Journal of Management Studies*, 30(4): 553–585.

6. For a scholarly discussion and analysis of the concept of competitive parity, refer to Powell, T. C. 2003. Varieties of competitive parity. *Strategic Management Journal*, 24(1): 61–86.

7. Rao, A. R., Bergen, M. E., & Davis, S. 2000. How to fight a price war. *Harvard Business Review*, 78(2): 107–120.

8. Marriot, J. W. Jr. Our competitive strength: Human capital. A speech given to the Detroit Economic Club on October 2, 2000.

9. Whalen, C. J., Pascual, A. M., Lowery, T., & Muller, J. 2001. The top 25 managers. *BusinessWeek*, January 8: 63.

10. Ibid.

11. For an interesting perspective on the need for creative strategies, refer to Hamel, G., & Prahalad, C. K. 1994. *Competing for the Future*. Boston: Harvard Business School Press.

12. Symonds, W. C., Arndt, M., Palmer, A. T., Weintraub, A., & Holmes, S. 2001. Trying to break the choke hold. *BusinessWeek*, January 22: 38–39.

13. For a perspective on the sustainability of competitive advantages, refer to Barney, J. 1995. Looking inside for competitive advantage. *Academy of Management Executive*, 9(4): 49–61.

14. Thornton, E., 2001, Why e-brokers are broker and broker. *BusinessWeek*, January 22: 94.

15. Koretz, G. 2001. E-commerce: The buyer wins. *BusinessWeek*, January 8: 30.

16. For an interesting perspective on the value of corporate brands and how they may be leveraged, refer to Aaker, D. A. 2004, *California Management Review*, 46(3): 6–18.

17. MacMillan, I., & McGrath, R. 1997. Discovering new points of differentiation. *Harvard Business Review*, 75(4): 133–145; Wise, R., & Baumgarter, P. 1999. Beating the clock: Corporate responses to rapid change in the PC industry. *California Management Review*, 42(1): 8–36.

18. For a discussion on quality in terms of a company's software and information systems, refer to Prahalad, C. K., & Krishnan, M. S. 1999. The new meaning of quality in the information age. *Harvard Business Review*, 77(5): 109–118.

19. Taylor, A., III. 2001. Can you believe Porsche is putting its badge on this car? *Fortune*, February 19: 168–172.

20. Ward, S., Light, L., & Goldstine, J. 1999. What high-tech managers need to know about brands. *Harvard Business Review*, 77(4): 85–95.

21. Rosenfeld, J. 2000. Unit of one. *Fast Company*, April: 98.

22. Markides, C. 1997. Strategic innovation. *Sloan Management Review*, 38(3): 9–23.

23. The authors would like to thank Scott Droege, a faculty member at Western Kentucky University, for providing this example.

24. Flint, J. 2004. Stop the nerds. *Forbes*, July 5: 80; and, Fahey, E. 2004. Over-engineering 101. *Forbes*, December 13: 62.

25. Symonds, W. C. 2000. Can Gillette regain its voltage? *BusinessWeek,* October 16: 102–104.

26. Caplan, J. 2006. In a real crunch. *Inside Business,* July: A37–A38.

27. Gadiesh, O., & Gilbert, J. L. 1998. Profit pools: A fresh look at strategy. *Harvard Business Review,* 76(3): 139–158.

28. Colvin, G. 2000. Beware: You could soon be selling soybeans. *Fortune,* November 13: 80.

29. Whalen et al., op. cit.: 63.

30. Porter, M. E. 1996. What is Strategy? *Harvard Business Review,* 74(6): 61–78.

31. Hall, W. K. 1980. Survival strategies in a hostile environment, *Harvard Business Review,* 58: 75–87; on the paint and allied products industry, see Dess, G. G., & Davis, P. S. 1984. Porter's (1980) generic strategies as determinants of strategic group membership and organizational performance. *Academy of Management Journal,* 27: 467–488; for the Korean electronics industry, see Kim, L., & Lim, Y. 1988. Environment, generic strategies, and performance in a rapidly developing country: A taxonomic approach. *Academy of Management Journal,* 31: 802–827; Wright, P., Hotard, D., Kroll, M., Chan, P., & Tanner, J. 1990. Performance and multiple strategies in a firm: Evidence from the apparel industry. In Dean, B. V., & Cassidy, J. C. (Eds.). *Strategic management: Methods and studies:* 93–110. Amsterdam: Elsevier-North Holland; and Wright, P., Kroll, M., Tu, H., & Helms, M. 1991. Generic strategies and business performance: An empirical study of the screw machine products industry. *British Journal of Management,* 2: 1–9.

32. Gilmore, J. H., & Pine, B. J., II. 1997. The four faces of customization. *Harvard Business Review,* 75(1): 91–101.

33. Ibid. For interesting insights on mass customization, refer to Cattani, K., Dahan, E., & Schmidt, G. 2005. Offshoring versus "spackling." *MIT Sloan Management Review,* 46(3): 6–7.

34. Goodstein, L. D., & Butz, H. E. 1998. Customer value: The linchpin of organizational change. *Organizational Dynamics,* Summer: 21–34.

35. Randall, T., Terwiesch, C., & Ulrich, K. T. 2005. Principles for user design of customized products. *California Management Review,* 47(4): 68–85.

36. Gadiesh & Gilbert, op. cit.: 139–158.

37. This example draws on Dess & Picken. 1997. op. cit.

38. Seybold, P. 2000. Niches bring riches. *Business 2.0,* June 13: 135.

39. Greenspan, R. 2004. Net drives profits to small biz. *ClickZ.com,* March 25, www.clickz.com. Greenspan, R. 2002. Small biz benefits from Internet tools. *ClickZ.com,* March 28, www.clickz.com.

40. Burns, E. 2006. Executives slow to see value of corporate blogging. *ClickZ.com,* May 9, www.clickz.com

41. Empirical support for the use of combination strategies in an e-business context can be found in Kim, E., Nam, D., & Stimpert, J. L. 2004. The applicability of Porter's generic strategies in the Digital Age: Assumptions, conjectures, and suggestions. *Journal of Management,* 30(5): 569–589.

42. Porter, M. E. 2001. Strategy and the Internet. *Harvard Business Review,* 79: 63–78.

43. For an interesting perspective on the influence of the product life cycle and rate of technological change on competitive strategy, refer to Lei, D., & Slocum, J. W. Jr. 2005. Strategic and organizational requirements for competitive advantage. *Academy of Management Executive,* 19(1): 31–45.

44. Dickson, P. R. 1994. *Marketing Management:* 293. Fort Worth, TX: Dryden Press; Day, G. S. 1981. The product life cycle: Analysis and application. *Journal of Marketing Research,* 45: 60–67.

45. Bearden, W. O., Ingram, T. N., & LaForge, R. W. 1995. *Marketing principles and practices.* Burr Ridge, IL: Irwin.

46. MacMillan, I. C. 1985. Preemptive strategies. In Guth, W. D. (Ed.). *Handbook of Business Strategy:* 9-1–9-22. Boston: Warren, Gorham & Lamont; Pearce, J. A., & Robinson, R. B. 2000. *Strategic management* (7th ed.). New York: McGraw-Hill; Dickson, op. cit.: 295–296.

47. Bartlett, C. A., & Ghoshal, S. 2000. Going global: Lessons for late movers. *Harvard Business Review,* 78(2): 132–142.

48. Neuborne, E. 2000. E-tailers hit the relaunch key. *BusinessWeek,* October 17: 62.

49. Berkowitz, E. N., Kerin, R. A., & Hartley, S. W. 2000. *Marketing* (6th ed.). New York: McGraw-Hill.

50. MacMillan, op. cit.

51. Brooker, K. 2001. A game of inches. *Fortune,* February 5: 98–100.

52. Our discussion of reverse and breakaway positioning draws on Moon, Y. 2005. Break free from the product life cycle. *Harvard Business Review,* 83(5): 87–94. This article also discusses stealth positioning as a means of overcoming consumer resistance and advancing a product from the introduction to the growth phase.

53. MacMillan, op. cit

53. Berkowitz et al., op. cit.

55. Bearden et al., op. cit.

56. The discussion of these four strategies draws on MacMillan, op. cit.; Berkowitz et al., op. cit.; and Bearden et al., op. cit.

57. Augustine, N. R. 1997. Reshaping an industry: Lockheed Martin's survival story. *Harvard Business Review,* 75(3): 83–94.

58. A study that draws on the resource-based view of the firm to investigate successful turnaround strategies is: Morrow, J. S., Sirmon, D. G., Hitt, M. A., & Holcomb, T. R. 2007. *Strategic Management Journal,* 28(3): 271–284.

59. For some useful ideas on effective turnarounds and handling downsizings, refer to Marks, M. S., & De Meuse, K. P. 2005. Resizing the organization: Maximizing the gain while minimizing the pain of layoffs, divestitures and closings. *Organizational Dynamics,* 34(1): 19–36.

60. Hambrick, D. C., & Schecter, S. M. 1983. Turnaround strategies for mature industrial product business units. *Academy of Management Journal,* 26(2): 231–248.

61. Mullaney, T. J. 2002. The wizard of Intuit. *BusinessWeek,* October 28: 60–63.

chapter 6

Corporate-Level Strategy:
Creating Value through Diversification

>learning objectives

After reading this chapter, you should have a good understanding of:

LO1 The reasons for the failure of many diversification efforts.

LO2 How managers can create value through diversification initiatives.

LO3 How corporations can use related diversification to achieve synergistic benefits through economies of scope and market power.

LO4 How corporations can use unrelated diversification to attain synergistic benefits through corporate restructuring, parenting, and portfolio analysis.

LO5 The various means of engaging in diversification—mergers and acquisitions, joint ventures/strategic alliances, and internal development.

LO6 Managerial behaviors that can erode the creation of value.

orporate-level strategy addresses two related issues: (1) what businesses should a corporation compete in, and (2) how can these businesses be managed so they create "synergy"—that is, more value by working together than if they were freestanding units? As we will see, these questions present a key challenge for today's managers. Many diversification efforts fail or, in many cases, provide only marginal returns to shareholders. Thus, determining how to create value through entering new markets, introducing new products, or developing new technologies is a vital issue in strategic management.

We begin by discussing why diversification initiatives, in general, have not yielded the anticipated benefits. Then, in the next three sections of the chapter, we explore the two key alternative approaches: related and unrelated diversification. With related diversification, corporations strive to enter product markets that share some resources and capabilities with their existing business units or increase their market power. Here we suggest four means of creating value: leveraging core competencies, sharing activities, pooled negotiating power, and vertical integration. With unrelated diversification, there are few similarities in the resources and capabilities among the firm's business units, but value can be created in multiple ways. These include restructuring, corporate parenting, and portfolio analysis approaches. Whereas the synergies to be realized with related diversification come from *horizontal relationships* among the business units, the synergies from unrelated diversification are derived from *hierarchical relationships* between the corporate office and the business units.

The last two sections address (1) the various means that corporations can use to achieve diversification and (2) managerial behaviors (e.g., self-interest) that serve to erode shareholder value. We address merger and acquisitions (M&A), divestitures, joint ventures/strategic alliances, and internal development. Each of these involves the evaluation of important trade-offs. Detrimental managerial behaviors, often guided by a manager's self-interest, are "growth for growth's sake," egotism, and antitakeover tactics. Some of these behaviors raise ethical issues because managers, in some cases, are not acting in the best interests of a firm's shareholders.

 ## Learning from Mistakes

In what *Fortune* magazine claimed was the second biggest merger and acquisition blunder of all time (next only to AOL/Time Warner), Boston Scientific acquired Guidant for $27.3 billion in late 2006. Why did Boston Scientific offer such a huge amount for what at best was a "dubious prize"? In retrospect, this seems like a classic case of the "winner's curse," where in the heat of a bidding war, the winner ends up paying a price that is well above the rest of the market's valuation of an asset. The chances are that the market is right and the winner is wrong.[1] Let's take a brief look at what happened.[2]

On a warm August 2006 evening in Manhattan, the former leaders of medical-device maker Guidant joined their investment bankers in a private room at the tony Bouley restaurant to celebrate the sale of their company to Boston Scientific. Sipping rare Bordeaux, they marveled over the wild bidding war between Boston Scientific and rival Johnson & Johnson, which had netted them $27.3 billion, a premium price for their company—at the time reeling from a series of damaging product failures and lawsuits. (Astonishingly, about nine months earlier, on November 15, 2005, Johnson & Johnson and Guidant had agreed on a much lower price of $21.5 billion! But at that point Boston Scientific entered the fray and a bidding war began.) *[continued]*

Boston Scientific had held its own bash on May 1, 2006, just after the deal had closed (on April 21). Boston Scientific's investment bankers, Merrill Lynch and Bank of America, organized the feast at the St. Regis Hotel in New York City. However, the day of the event, thunderstorms in the New York area played havoc with the arriving flight schedules. Boston Scientific co-founder Pete Nicholas, CEO Jim Tobin, and CFO Larry Best sat for hours in a drafty hanger on Hanscomb Field in Bedford, Massachusetts, while their lawyers and investment bankers, as well as lower-level executives, partied into the night. The stormy weather turned out to be an omen: While the lawyers and bankers were, of course, well paid for their efforts, the deal turned into to a deluge of bad days for Boston Scientific's top executives.

About two months later, in late June, Boston Scientific issued recalls or warnings on almost 50,000 Guidant cardiac devices and acknowledged that it could take as long as two years to fix the safety problems. Then, on September 21, Boston issued a profit warning that shocked Wall Street, sending its already beaten-down shares plunging another 9.2 percent in a single day.

Since it announced the bid for Guidant on December 2005, Boston's stock had dropped a stunning 46 percent, wiping out $18 billion in shareholder value in a matter of months.

Indeed the deal is arguably the second-worst ever, trailing only the spectacular AOL Time Warner debacle. "It's like the movie The Money Pit," Matthew Dodds, an analyst at Citigroup, says of Boston Scientific's handling of the deal. "Once you've put enough in, you'll go all the way till it's done, regardless of the value."

Boston Scientific is not alone in having a disappointing experience with an acquisition. Many large multinational firms and recent big acquirers have also failed to effectively integrate their acquisitions, paid too high a premium for the target's common stock, or were unable to understand how the acquired firm's assets would fit with their own lines of business. And, at times, top executives may not have acted in the best interests of shareholders. That is, the motive for the acquisition may have been to enhance the executives' power and prestige rather than to improve shareholder returns. At times, the only other people who may have benefited were the shareholders of the *acquired* firms—or the investment bankers who advise the acquiring firm because they collect huge fees upfront regardless of what happens afterwards!

There have been several studies that were conducted over a variety of time periods that show how disappointing acquisitions have typically turned out. For example:

- A study evaluated the stock market reaction of 600 acquisitions over the period between 1975 and 1991. The results indicated that the acquiring firms suffered an average 4 percent drop in market value (after adjusting for market movements) in the three months following the acquisitions announcement.[3]
- In a study by Solomon Smith Barney of U.S. companies acquired since 1997 in deals for $15 billion or more, the stocks of the acquiring firms have, on average, underperformed the S&P stock index by 14 percentage points and underperformed their peer group by 4 percentage points after the deals were announced.[4]

Exhibit 6.1 lists some well-known examples of failed acquisitions and mergers.

Many acquisitions ultimately result in divestiture—an admission that things didn't work out as planned. In fact, some years ago, a writer for *Fortune* magazine lamented, "Studies show that 33 percent to 50 percent of acquisitions are later divested, giving corporate marriages a divorce rate roughly comparable to that of men and women."[5]

Admittedly, we have been rather pessimistic so far. Clearly, many diversification efforts have worked out very well—whether through mergers and acquisitions, strategic alliances and joint ventures, or internal development. We will discuss many success stories throughout this chapter. Next, we will discuss the primary rationales for diversification.

The chapter began with Boston Scientific's acquisition of Guidant. Here are examples of some other very expensive blunders:

- AOL paid $114 billion to acquire Time Warner in 2001. Over the next two years, AOL Time Warner lost $150 billion in market valuation.

- Conseco paid $5.8 billion to buy Green Tree, a mobile home mortgage lender, in 1998 though the company's net worth was not even $1 billion. In the next two years, Conseco lost 90 percent of its market value!

- Quaker Oats' acquisition of the once high-flying Snapple for $1.8 billion in 1994 was followed by its divestment for $300 million three years later.

- AT&T bought computer equipment maker NCR for $7.4 billion in 1991, only to spin it off for $3.4 billion six years later.

- Sony acquired Columbia Pictures in 1989 for $4.8 billion although it had no competencies in movie production. Five years later, Sony was forced to take a $2.7 billion write-off on the acquisition.

Source: Tully, S. 2006. The (second) worst deal ever. *Fortune*. October 16: 102–119.

Making Diversification Work: An Overview

Clearly, not all diversification moves, including those involving mergers and acquisitions, erode performance. For example, acquisitions in the oil industry, such as British Petroleum's purchases of Amoco and Arco, are performing well as is the Exxon-Mobil merger. In the automobile industry, the Renault-Nissan alliance, under CEO Carlos Ghosn's leadership, has led to a quadrupling of its collective market capitalization—from $20.4 billion to $84.9 billion—by the end of 2006.[6] Many leading high-tech firms such as Microsoft, Cisco Systems, and Intel have dramatically enhanced their revenues, profits, and market values through a wide variety of diversification initiatives, including acquisitions, strategic alliances, and joint ventures, as well as internal development.*

So the question becomes: Why do some diversification efforts pay off and others produce disappointing results? In this chapter we will address this question. Whereas Chapter 5 focused on business-level strategy—that is, how to achieve sustainable advantages in a given business or product market—this chapter addresses two related issues: (1) What businesses should a corporation compete in? and (2) How should these businesses be managed to jointly create more value than if they were freestanding units?

Diversification initiatives—whether through mergers and acquisitions, strategic alliances and joint ventures, or internal development—must be justified by the creation of value for shareholders. But this is not always the case. As noted earlier, acquiring firms typically pay high premiums when they acquire a target firm. For example, in 2006 Freeport-McMoran paid a 30 percent premium to acquire Phelps Dodge in order to create the largest metals and mining concern in the United States. In contrast, you and I, as private investors, can diversify our portfolio of stocks very cheaply. With

>LO2
How managers can create value through diversification initiatives.

---

* Many high-tech firms, such as Motorola, IBM, Qualcomm, and Intel have also diversified through company-owned venture capital arms. Intel Capital, for example, has invested $4 billion in 1,000 companies over 15 years. Some 160 of those companies have been sold to other firms, while another 150 of them have been publicly listed. In 2006, Intel Capital's investments added $214 million to the parent company's net income. For an insightful discussion of how Apple might benefit from a venture capital initiative, refer to Hesseldahl, A. 2007. What to do with Apple's cash. *BusinessWeek*, March 19: 80.

an intensely competitive online brokerage industry, we can acquire hundreds (or thousands) of shares for a transaction fee of as little as $10.00 or less—a far cry from the 30 to 40 percent (or higher) premiums that corporations typically must pay to acquire companies.

Given the seemingly high inherent downside risks and uncertainties, it might be reasonable to ask why companies should even bother with diversification initiatives. The answer, in a word, is *synergy,* derived from the Greek word *synergos,* which means "working together." This can have two different, but not mutually exclusive, meanings. First, a firm may diversify into *related* businesses. Here, the primary potential benefits to be derived come from *horizontal relationships;* that is, businesses sharing intangible resources (e.g., core competences such as marketing) and tangible resources (e.g., production facilities, distribution channels). Additionally, firms can enhance their market power through pooled negotiating power and vertical integration. For example, Procter & Gamble enjoys many synergies from having businesses that share distribution resources.

Second, a corporation may diversify into *unrelated* businesses. In these instances, the primary potential benefits are derived largely from *hierarchical relationships;* that is, value creation derived from the corporate office. Examples of the latter would include leveraging some of the support activities in the value chain that we discussed in Chapter 3, such as information systems or human resource practices. Cooper Industries has followed a successful strategy of unrelated diversification. There are few similarities in the products it makes or the industries in which it competes. However, the corporate office adds value through such activities as superb human resource practices as well as planning and budgeting systems.

Please note that the aforementioned benefits derived from horizontal (related diversification) and hierarchical (unrelated diversification) relationships are not mutually exclusive. Many firms that diversify into related areas benefit from information technology expertise in the corporate office. Similarly, firms diversifying into unrelated areas often benefit from the "best practices" of sister businesses even though their products, markets, and technologies may differ dramatically.

Exhibit 6.2 provides an overview of how we will address the various means by which firms create value through both related and unrelated diversification and also include a summary of some examples that we will address in this chapter.[7]

Related Diversification: Economies of Scope and Revenue Enhancement

As discussed earlier, **related diversification** enables a firm to benefit from horizontal relationships across different businesses in the diversified corporation by leveraging core competencies and sharing activities (e.g., production facilities and distribution facilities). This enables a corporation to benefit from economies of scope. **Economies of scope** refers to cost savings from leveraging core competencies or sharing related activities among businesses in the corporation. A firm can also enjoy greater revenues if two businesses attain higher levels of sales growth combined than either company could attain independently.

For example, a sporting goods store with one or several locations may acquire retail stores carrying other product lines. This enables it to leverage, or reuse, many of its key resources—favorable reputation, expert staff and management skills, efficient purchasing operations—the basis of its competitive advantage(s), over a larger number of stores.[8] Let's next address how to create value by leveraging core competencies.

related diversification
a firm entering a different business in which it can benefit from leveraging core competencies, sharing activities, or building market power.

economies of scope
cost savings from leveraging core competencies or sharing related activities among businesses in a corporation.

>LO3
How corporations can use related diversification to achieve synergistic benefits through economies of scope and market power.

Exhibit 6.2
Creating Value through
Related and Unrelated
Diversification

Related Diversification: Economies of Scope

Leveraging core competences
- 3M leverages its competencies in adhesives technologies to many industries, including automotive, construction, and telecommunications.

Sharing activities
- McKesson, a large distribution company, sells many product lines, such as pharmaceuticals and liquor, through its superwarehouses.

Related Diversification: Market Power

Pooled negotiating power
- The Times Mirror Company increases its power over customers by providing "one-stop shopping" for advertisers to reach customers through multiple media—television and newspapers—in several huge markets such as New York and Chicago.

Vertical integration
- Shaw Industries, a giant carpet manufacturer, increases its control over raw materials by producing much of its own polypropylene fiber, a key input to its manufacturing process.

Unrelated Diversification: Parenting, Restructuring, and Financial Synergies

Corporate restructuring and parenting
- The corporate office of Cooper Industries adds value to its acquired businesses by performing such activities as auditing their manufacturing operations, improving their accounting activities, and centralizing union negotiations.

Portfolio management
- Novartis, formerly Ciba-Geigy, uses portfolio management to improve many key activities, including resource allocation and reward and evaluation systems.

Leveraging Core Competencies

The concept of core competencies can be illustrated by the imagery of the diversified corporation as a tree.[9] The trunk and major limbs represent core products; the smaller branches are business units; and the leaves, flowers, and fruit are end products. The core competencies are represented by the root system, which provides nourishment, sustenance, and stability. Managers often misread the strength of competitors by looking only at their end products, just as we can fail to appreciate the strength of a tree by looking only at its leaves. Core competencies may also be viewed as the "glue" that binds existing businesses together or as the engine that fuels new business growth.

Core competencies reflect the collective learning in organizations—how to coordinate diverse production skills, integrate multiple streams of technologies, and market and merchandise diverse products and services. The theoretical knowledge necessary to put a radio on a chip does not in itself assure a company of the skill needed to produce a miniature radio approximately the size of a business card. To accomplish this, Casio, a giant electronic products producer, must synthesize know-how in miniaturization, microprocessor design, material science, and ultrathin precision castings. These are the same skills that it applies in its miniature card calculators, pocket TVs, and digital watches.

core competencies
a firm's strategic resources that reflect the collective learning in the organization.

For a core competence to create value and provide a viable basis for synergy among the businesses in a corporation, it must meet three criteria.[10]

- *The core competence must enhance competitive advantage(s) by creating superior customer value.* It must enable the business to develop strengths relative to the competition. Every value-chain activity has the potential to provide a viable basis for building on a core competence.[11] At Gillette, for example, scientists developed the Fusion and Mach 3 after the introduction of the tremendously successful Sensor System because of a thorough understanding of several phenomena that underlie shaving. These include the physiology of facial hair and skin, the metallurgy of blade strength and sharpness, the dynamics of a cartridge moving across skin, and the physics of a razor blade severing hair. Such innovations are possible only with an understanding of such phenomena and the ability to combine such technologies into innovative products. Customers have consistently been willing to pay more for such technologically differentiated products.

- *Different businesses in the corporation must be similar in at least one important way related to the core competence.* It is not essential that the products or services themselves be similar. Rather, at least one element in the value chain must require similar skills in creating competitive advantage if the corporation is to capitalize on its core competence. At first glance you might think that cars and houses have little in common. However, Strategy Spotlight 6.1 discusses how Toyota creates synergies in a business—manufactured homes—that has little to do with its core business—automobiles.

- *The core competencies must be difficult for competitors to imitate or find substitutes for.* As we discussed in Chapter 5, competitive advantages will not be sustainable if the competition can easily imitate or substitute them. Similarly, if the skills associated with a firm's core competencies are easily imitated or replicated, they are not a sound basis for sustainable advantages. Consider Sharp Corporation, a $26 billion consumer electronics giant.[12] It has a set of specialized core competencies in optoelectronics technologies that are difficult to replicate and contribute to its competitive advantages in its core businesses. Its most successful technology has been liquid crystal displays (LCDs) that are critical components in nearly all of Sharp's products. Its expertise in this technology enabled Sharp to succeed in videocassette recorders (VCRs) with its innovative LCD viewfinder and led to the creation of its Wizard, a personal electronic organizer.

Sharing Activities

As we saw above, leveraging core competencies involves transferring accumulated skills and expertise across business units in a corporation. When carried out effectively, this leads to advantages that can become quite sustainable over time. Corporations also can achieve synergy by **sharing activities** across their business units. These include value-creating activities such as common manufacturing facilities, distribution channels, and sales forces. As we will see, sharing activities can potentially provide two primary payoffs: cost savings and revenue enhancements.

sharing activities having activities of two or more businesses' value chains done by one of the businesses.

Deriving Cost Savings through Sharing Activities Typically, this is the most common type of synergy and the easiest to estimate. Peter Shaw, head of mergers and acquisitions at the British chemical and pharmaceutical company ICI, refers to cost savings as "hard synergies" and contends that the level of certainty of their achievement is quite high. Cost savings come from many sources, including elimination of jobs, facilities, and related expenses that are no longer needed when functions are consolidated, or from economies of scale in purchasing. Cost savings are generally highest when one company acquires another from the same industry in the same country. Shaw Industries, recently acquired by

Toyota's Diversification into Home Manufacturing

Looking for the biggest Toyota on the market? It's not the Tundra pickups and Sequoia SUVs down at your local dealer. Instead, you'll have to travel to the Toyota factory in Kasugai, a city of 300,000 about three hours west of Tokyo. There you won't see much in the way of horsepower or acceleration. But they are very roomy—as in multiple bedrooms, a living room, kitchen, bath, and patio.

At Kasugai, Toyota's houses are 85 percent completed at the plant before being transported by road and built in just six hours. To improve efficiency, Toyota borrows know-how from its fabled Toyota Production System with its principles of just-in-time delivery and *kaizen*, or continuous improvement. Using methods adopted from car production, anticorrosive paint is applied evenly to the houses' steel frames. Just as in all of Toyota's Japan automobile factories, a banner proclaiming "good thinking, good products" hangs from the roof. "We follow the Toyota way in housing," says Senta Morioka, a managing officer at Toyota.

Source: Rowley, I. 2006. Way, way, off-road. *BusinessWeek*, July 17: 36–37.

● Toyota is a world-class automobile producer. Above is a Scion, one of its popular products. Toyota has also diversified into many areas, including manufactured homes.

Toyota currently builds about 5,000 prefabricated houses a year. And, in 2005, it took a 13 percent stake in Misawa Homes, another maker of prefabs.

Berkshire Hathaway, is the nation's largest carpet producer. Over the years, it has dominated the competition through a strategy of acquisition which has enabled Shaw, among other things, to consolidate its manufacturing operations in a few, highly efficient plants and to lower costs through higher capacity utilization.

Sharing activities inevitably involve costs that the benefits must outweigh such as the greater coordination required to manage a shared activity. Even more important is the need to compromise on the design or performance of an activity so that it can be shared. For example, a salesperson handling the products of two business units must operate in a way that is usually not what either unit would choose if it were independent. If the compromise erodes the unit's effectiveness, then sharing may reduce rather than enhance competitive advantage.

Enhancing Revenue and Differentiation through Sharing Activities   Often an acquiring firm and its target may achieve a higher level of sales growth together than either company could on its own. Shortly after Gillette acquired Duracell, it confirmed its expectation that selling Duracell batteries through Gillette's existing channels for personal care products would increase sales, particularly internationally. Gillette sold Duracell products in 25 new markets in the first year after the acquisition and substantially increased sales in established international markets. Also, a target company's distribution channel can be used to escalate the sales of the acquiring company's product. Such was the case when Gillette acquired Parker Pen. Gillette estimated that it could gain an additional $25 million in sales of its own Waterman pens by taking advantage of Parker's distribution channels.

Firms also can enhance the effectiveness of their differentiation strategies by means of sharing activities among business units. A shared order-processing system, for example, may permit new features and services that a buyer will value. Also, sharing can reduce the cost of differentiation. For instance, a shared service network may make more advanced, remote service technology economically feasible. To illustrate the potential for enhanced differentiation though sharing, consider $7 billion VF Corporation—producer of such well-known brands as Lee, Wrangler, Vanity Fair, and Jantzen.

> VF's acquisition of Nutmeg Industries and H. H. Cutler provided it with several large customers that it didn't have before, increasing its plant utilization and productivity. But more importantly, Nutmeg designs and makes licensed apparel for sports teams and organizations, while Cutler manufactures licensed brand-name children's apparel, including Walt Disney kids' wear. Such brand labeling enhances the differentiation of VF's apparel products. According to VF President Mackey McDonald, "What we're doing is looking at value-added knitwear, taking our basic fleece from Basset-Walker [one of its divisions], embellishing it through Cutler and Nutmeg, and selling it as a value-added product." Additionally, Cutler's advanced high-speed printing technologies will enable VF to be more proactive in anticipating trends in the fashion-driven fleece market. Claims McDonald, "Rather than printing first and then trying to guess what the customer wants, we can see what's happening in the marketplace and then print it up."[13]

As a cautionary note, managers must keep in mind that sharing activities among businesses in a corporation can have a negative effect on a given business's differentiation. For example, with the merger of Chrysler and Daimler-Benz, many consumers may lower their perceptions of Mercedes's quality and prestige because they felt that common production components and processes were being used across the two divisions. And Ford's Jaguar division was adversely affected as consumers came to understand that it shared many components with its sister divisions at Ford, including Lincoln.

Strategy Spotlight 6.2 discusses how Freemantle Media leverages its hit television show *American Idol* through its core competences and shared activities to create multiple revenue streams.

Related Diversification: Market Power

In the previous section, we explained how leveraging core competencies and sharing activities help firms create economies of scale and scope through related diversification. In this section, we discuss how companies achieve related diversification through **market power.** We also address the two principal means by which firms achieve synergy through market power: *pooled negotiating power* and *vertical integration.* It is important to recognize that managers have limits on their ability to use market power for diversification, because government regulations can sometimes restrict the ability of a business to gain very large shares of a particular market.

market power firms' abilities to profit through restricting or controlling supply to a market or coordinating with other firms to reduce investment.

When General Electric announced a $41 billion bid for Honeywell, the European Union stepped in. GE's market clout would have expanded significantly with the deal: GE would supply over one-half the parts needed to build several aircraft engines. The commission's concern, causing them to reject the acquisition, was that GE could use its increased market power to dominate the aircraft engine parts market and crowd out rivals.[14] Thus, while managers need to be aware of the strategic advantages of market power, they must at the same time be aware of regulations and legislation.

Pooled Negotiating Power

Similar businesses working together or the affiliation of a business with a strong parent can strengthen an organization's bargaining position relative to suppliers and customers and enhance its position vis-à-vis competitors. Compare, for example, the position of an independent food manufacturer with the same business within Nestlé. Being part of Nestlé

American Idol: Far More than Just a Television Show

American Idol is one of several of FremantleMedia's (FM) hit television shows. FM is a division of German media giant Bertlesmann, which has approximately $26 billion in revenues. Some of FM's other well-known television shows are *The Apprentice, The Swan,* and at a ripe old age of 48—*The Price Is Right.*

First shown in the United States in June 2002, *American Idol* became a tremendous overnight success. Although the show may be crass and occasionally cruel, it is undeniably brilliant. It's become the ultimate testament to a singular business achievement: FM has become extremely successful at creating truly global programming. In part, that is due to the creative minds at Fremantle. It has some of the best professionals in the business who have a talent for developing shows that appeal to huge populations with different backgrounds and circumstances.

Amazingly, FM, which created *Pop Idol* in Britain in 2001, is now rolling out the show in its 30th country. There's *Belgium Idol, Portugal Idolos, Deutschland Sucht den SuperStar* (Germany), *SuperStar KZ* (Kazakhstan), and of course, the largest and best-known show, *American Idol,* in the United States. *American Idol* is the primary reason that Fremantle's revenue is up 9 percent to more than $1 billion since the show was launched. According to Fremantle's CEO Tony Cohen, "*Idol* has become a national institution in lots of countries." To illustrate, fans cast more than 65 million votes for the *American Idol* finale in May, 2004—that is two-thirds as many people as voted in the 2004 U.S. presidential election.

The real key to Fremantle's success is not just adapting its television hits to other countries, but systematically

leveraging its core product—television shows—to create multiple revenue streams. In essence, the "Fremantle Way" holds lessons not just for show business but for all business. It enables a company to use its core competence of making products of mass appeal and then to customize them for places with widely varying languages, cultures, and mores. It then milks the hits for every penny through tie-ins, spinoffs, innovative uses of technology, and marketing masterstrokes.

The *Idol* franchise has created a wide variety of new revenue streams for Fremantle's German parent, Bertelsmann. Here's how much *American Idol* has generated in its first two years since its June 2002 launch:

- *Products ($50 million).* Brand extensions range from videogames and fragrances to a planned microphone-shaped soap-on-a-rope. Fremantle receives a licensing fee from manufacturers.

- *TV Licensing ($75 million).* For its rights fee, Fox gets to broadcast the show and, in turn, sell ads and lucrative sponsorships.

- *Compact Discs (CDs) ($130 million).* The most successful performers on the *Idols* shows have sold millions of CDs; more than one-third of the revenue goes to BMG, which, like Fremantle, is an affiliate of Bertelsmann.

- *Concerts ($35 million).* Although artists and their management get the bulk of the take, concerts sell records and merchandise and promote the next *Idol* show.

In addition, Fremantle Licensing Worldwide signed Warner Brothers Publications to produce and distribute *Idol* audition books with CDs for the United States, Canada, United Kingdom, and Australia. The new books/CDs—*Pop Idol* (UK), *Australian Idol,* and *Canadian Idol*—join the *American Idol* book/CD.

Sources: Sloan, P. 2004. The reality factory. *Business 2.0,* August: 74–82; Cooney, J. 2004. In the news. *License!,* March: 48; and, Anonymous. 2005. Fox on top in Feb; NBC languishing at the bottom. www.indiantelevision.com, March 2.

Corporation provides the business with significant clout—greater bargaining power with suppliers and customers—since it is part of a firm that makes large purchases from suppliers and provides a wide variety of products to its customers. Access to the parent's deep pockets increases the business's strength relative to rivals. Further, the Nestlé unit enjoys greater protection from substitutes and new entrants. Not only would rivals perceive the unit as a more formidable opponent, but the unit's association with Nestlé would also provide greater visibility and improved image.

Consolidating an industry can also increase a firm's market power. This is clearly an emerging trend in the multimedia industry.[15] All of these mergers and acquisitions have a common goal: to control and leverage as many news and entertainment channels as possible. In total, more than $261 billion in mergers and acquisitions in the media industry were announced in 2000—up 12 percent from 1999. For example, consider the Tribune Company's $8 billion purchase of the Times Mirror Company.

> The merger doubled the size of the Tribune and secured its position among the top tier of major media companies. The enhanced scale and scope helped it to compete more effectively and grow more rapidly in two consolidating industries—newspaper and television broadcasting. The combined company would increase its power over customers by providing a "one-stop shop" for advertisers desiring to reach consumers through multiple media in enormous markets such as Chicago, Los Angeles, and New York. The company had estimated its incremental revenue from national and cross-media advertising will grow from $40 to $50 million in 2001 to $200 million over four years. The combined company should also increase its power relative to its suppliers. The company's enhanced size is expected to lead to increased efficiencies when purchasing newsprint and other commodities.[16]

When acquiring related businesses, a firm's potential for pooled negotiating power vis-à-vis its customers and suppliers can be very enticing. However, managers must carefully evaluate how the combined businesses may affect relationships with actual and potential customers, suppliers, and competitors. For example, when PepsiCo diversified into the fast-food industry with its acquisitions of Kentucky Fried Chicken, Taco Bell, and Pizza Hut (now part of Yum! Brands), it clearly benefited from its position over these units that served as a captive market for its soft-drink products. However, many competitors such as McDonald's have refused to consider PepsiCo as a supplier of its own soft-drink needs because of competition with Pepsi's divisions in the fast-food industry. Simply put, McDonald's did not want to subsidize the enemy! Thus, although acquiring related businesses can enhance a corporation's bargaining power, it must be aware of the potential for retaliation.

Strategy Spotlight 6.3 discusses how 3M's actions to increase its market power led to a lawsuit (which 3M lost) by a competitor.

Vertical Integration

vertical integration
an expansion or extension of the firm by integrating preceding or successive production processes.

Vertical integration occurs when a firm becomes its own supplier or distributor. That is, it represents an expansion or extension of the firm by integrating preceding or successive production processes.[17] The firm incorporates more processes toward the original source of raw materials (backward integration) or toward the ultimate consumer (forward integration). For example, an automobile manufacturer might supply its own parts or make its own engines to secure sources of supply. Or it might control its own system of dealerships to ensure retail outlets for its products. Similarly, an oil refinery might secure land leases and develop its own drilling capacity to ensure a constant supply of crude oil. Or it could expand into retail operations by owning or licensing gasoline stations to guarantee customers for its petroleum products.

Clearly, vertical integration can be a viable strategy for many firms. Strategy Spotlight 6.4 discusses Shaw Industries, a carpet manufacturer that has attained a dominant position in the industry via a strategy of vertical integration. Shaw has successfully implemented strategies of both forward and backward integration. Exhibit 6.3 depicts the stages of Shaw's vertical integration.

Benefits and Risks of Vertical Integration   Although vertical integration is a means for an organization to reduce its dependence on suppliers or its channels of distribution to end users, it represents a major decision that an organization must carefully consider. The benefits associated with vertical integration—backward or forward—must be carefully weighed against the risks.[18]

The *benefits* of vertical integration include (1) a secure supply of raw materials or distribution channels that cannot be "held hostage" to external markets where costs can

How 3M's Efforts to Increase its Market Power Backfired

In the spring and summer of 2006, 3M found itself in court facing three class-action lawsuits launched by consumers and retailers of transparent and invisible adhesive tape (often generically known as "Scotch tape"). The suits all alleged that 3M had unlawfully bullied its way into a monopoly position in the tape market and that, as a result, consumers had been deprived of their rightful amount of choice and often paid up to 40 percent too much for their tape.

One rival that is particularly interested in these cases is LaPage's Inc. of North York, Ontario—3M's only significant competitor in the home and office adhesive tape market. LaPage's has everything to gain from court penalties against 3M's selling practices. This includes greater access to the lucrative North American market. The Canadian company started 3M's legal travails in the first place: all of the current class-action suits were initiated by LePage's.

Back in 1997, LePage's (then based in Pittsburgh) filed a complaint in the Pennsylvania District Court against 3M's practice of selling its various tape products using what was called "bundled rebates." LePage's argued that it

violated the Sherman Act, the century-old U.S. legislation that limited monopoly power. 3M's bundled rebate program offered significant rebates—sometimes in the millions of dollars—to retailers as a reward for selling targeted amounts of six product lines. LePage's claimed that such selling targets were so large that retailers could only meet them by excluding competing products—in this case LePage's tape—from store shelves. For example, LePage's argued that Kmart, which had constituted 10% of LePage's sales dropped the account when 3M started offering the discount chain $1 million in rebates in return for selling more than $15 million worth of 3M products each year. Further, LePage's offered its own conspiracy theory: 3M introduced rebates not simply to grow its sales, but to eliminate LePage's—its only significant competitor.

A jury awarded LePage's $68.5 million in damages (the amount after trebling)—almost 15 percent of the 3M Consumer and Office Business unit's operating income in 2000. The Court of Appeals for the Third Circuit rejected 3M's appeal and upheld the judgment. It concluded that rebate bundling, even if above cost, may exclude equally efficient competitors from offering product (in this case, tape). In the ruling, Judge Dolores K. Sloviter wrote that "they may foreclose portions of the market to a potential competitor who does not manufacture an equally diverse group of products and who therefore cannot make a comparable offer." Therefore, the bundled rebates were judged to be an exploitation of 3M's monopoly power.

Sources: Bush, D., & Gelb, B. D. 2005. When marketing practices raise antitrust concerns. *MIT Sloan Management Review,* 46(4): 73–81; Campbell, C. 2006. Tale of the tape. *Canadian Business.* April 24: 39–40; and Bergstrom, B. 2003. $68M jury award upheld against 3M in antitrust case. *The Associated Press:* March 26.

---

fluctuate over time, (2) protection and control over assets and services required to produce and deliver valuable products and services, (3) access to new business opportunities and new forms of technologies, and (4) simplified procurement and administrative procedures since key activities are brought inside the firm, eliminating the need to deal with a wide variety of suppliers and distributors.

Winnebago, the leader in the market for drivable recreational vehicles with a 19.3 percent market share, illustrates some of vertical integration's benefits.[19] The word Winnebago means "big RV" to most Americans. And the firm has a sterling reputation for great quality.

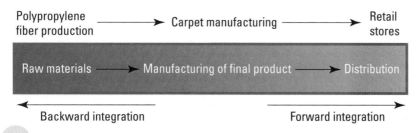

Exhibit 6.3 Simplified Stages of Vertical Integration: Shaw Industries

strategy spotlight

Vertical Integration at Shaw Industries

Shaw Industries (now part of Berkshire Hathaway) is an example of a firm that has followed a very successful strategy of vertical integration. By relentlessly pursuing both backward and forward integration, Shaw has become the dominant manufacturer of carpeting products in the United States. According to CEO Robert Shaw, "We want to be involved with as much of the process of making and selling carpets as practical. That way, we're in charge of costs." For example, Shaw acquired Amoco's polypropylene fiber manufacturing facilities in Alabama and Georgia. These new plants provide carpet fibers for internal use and for sale to other manufacturers. With this backward integration, fully one-quarter of Shaw's carpet fiber needs are now met in-house. In early 1996 Shaw began to integrate forward, acquiring seven floor-covering retailers in a move that suggested a strategy to consolidate the fragmented industry and increase its influence over retail pricing. Exhibit 6.3 provides a simplified depiction of the stages of vertical integration for Shaw Industries.

Sources: White, J. 2003. Shaw to home in on more with Georgia Tufters deal. *HFN: The Weekly Newspaper for the Home Furnishing Network,* May 5: 32; Shaw Industries. 1993, 2000. Annual reports; and Server, A. 1994. How to escape a price war. *Fortune,* June 13: 88.

The firm's huge northern Iowa factories do everything from extruding aluminum for body parts to molding plastics for water and holding tanks to dashboards. Such vertical integration at the factory may appear to be outdated and expensive, but it guarantees excellent quality. The Recreational Vehicle Dealer Association started giving a quality award in 1996, and Winnebago has won it every year.

The *risks* of vertical integration include (1) the costs and expenses associated with increased overhead and capital expenditures to provide facilities, raw material inputs, and distribution channels inside the organization; (2) a loss of flexibility resulting from the inability to respond quickly to changes in the external environment because of the huge investments in vertical integration activities that generally cannot be easily deployed elsewhere; (3) problems associated with unbalanced capacities or unfilled demand along the value chain; and (4) additional administrative costs associated with managing a more complex set of activities. Exhibit 6.4 summarizes the benefits and risks of vertical integration.

Exhibit 6.4
Benefits and Risks of Vertical Integration

Benefits

- A secure source of raw materials or distribution channels.
- Protection of and control over valuable assets.
- Access to new business opportunities.
- Simplified procurement and administrative procedures.

Risks

- Costs and expenses associated with increased overhead and capital expenditures.
- Loss of flexibility resulting from large investments.
- Problems associated with unbalanced capacities along the value chain.
- Additional administrative costs associated with managing a more complex set of activities.

In making vertical integration decisions, six issues should be considered.[20]

1. *Is the company satisfied with the quality of the value that its present suppliers and distributors are providing?* If the performance of organizations in the vertical chain—both suppliers and distributors—is satisfactory, it may not, in general, be appropriate for a company to perform these activities themselves. Firms in the athletic footwear industry such as Nike and Reebok have traditionally outsourced the manufacture of their shoes to countries such as China and Indonesia where labor costs are low. Since the strengths of these companies are typically in design and marketing, it would be advisable to continue to outsource production operations and continue to focus on where they can add the most value.

2. *Are there activities in the industry value chain presently being outsourced or performed independently by others that are a viable source of future profits?* Even if a firm is outsourcing value-chain activities to companies that are doing a credible job, it may be missing out on substantial profit opportunities. To illustrate, consider the automobile industry's profit pool. As you may recall from Chapter 5, there is much more potential profit in many downstream activities (e.g., leasing, warranty, insurance, and service) than in the manufacture of automobiles. Not surprising, carmakers such as Ford and General Motors are undertaking forward integration strategies to become bigger players in these high-profit activities.

3. *Is there a high level of stability in the demand for the organization's products?* High demand or sales volatility would not be conducive to a vertical integration strategy. With the high level of fixed costs in plant and equipment as well as operating costs that accompany endeavors toward vertical integration, widely fluctuating sales demand can either strain resources (in times of high demand) or result in unused capacity (in times of low demand). The cycles of "boom and bust" in the automobile industry are a key reason why the manufacturers have increased the amount of outsourced inputs in recent years.

4. *How high is the proportion of additional production capacity actually absorbed by existing products or by the prospects of new and similar products?* The smaller the proportion of production capacity to be absorbed by existing or future products, the lower is the potential for achieving scale economies associated with the increased capacity—either in terms of backward integration (toward the supply of raw materials) or forward integration (toward the end user). Alternatively, if there is excess capacity in the near term, the strategy of vertical integration may be viable if there is the anticipation of future expansion of products.

5. *Does the company have the necessary competencies to execute the vertical integration strategies?* As many companies would attest, successfully executing strategies of vertical integration can be very difficult. For example, Unocal, a major petroleum refiner, which once owned retail gas stations, was slow to capture the potential grocery and merchandise side of the business that might have resulted from customer traffic to its service stations. Unocal lacked the competencies to develop a separate retail organization and culture. The company eventually sold the assets and brand to Tosco (now part of Phillips Petroleum).

6. *Will the vertical integration initiative have potential negative impacts on the firm's stakeholders?* Managers must carefully consider the impact that vertical integration may have on existing and future customers, suppliers, and competitors. After Lockheed Martin, a dominant defense contractor, acquired Loral Corporation, an electronics supplier, for $9.1 billion, it had an unpleasant and unanticipated surprise. Loral, as a captive supplier of Lockheed, is now viewed as a rival by many of its previous customers. Thus, before Lockheed Martin can realize any net synergies from this acquisition, it must make up for the substantial business that it has lost.

transaction cost perspective a perspective that the choice of a transaction's governance structure, such as vertical integration or market transaction, is influenced by transaction costs, including search, negotiating, contracting, monitoring, and enforcement costs, associated with each choice.

Analyzing Vertical Integration: The Transaction Cost Perspective Another approach that has proved very useful in understanding vertical integration is the **transaction cost perspective**.[21] According to this perspective, every market transaction involves some *transaction costs.* First, a decision to purchase an input from an outside source leads to *search* costs (i.e., the cost to find where it is available, the level of quality, etc.). Second, there are costs associated with *negotiating*. Third, a *contract* needs to be written spelling out future possible contingencies. Fourth, parties in a contract have to *monitor* each other. Finally, if a party does not comply with the terms of the contract, there are *enforcement* costs. Transaction costs are thus the sum of search costs, negotiation costs, contracting costs, monitoring costs, and enforcement costs. These transaction costs can be avoided by internalizing the activity, in other words, by producing the input in-house.

A related problem with purchasing a specialized input from outside is the issue of *transaction-specific investments.* For example, when an automobile company needs an input specifically designed for a particular car model, the supplier may be unwilling to make the investments in plant and machinery necessary to produce that component for two reasons. First, the investment may take many years to recover but there is no guarantee the automobile company will continue to buy from them after the contract expires, typically in one year. Second, once the investment is made, the supplier has no bargaining power. That is, the buyer knows that the supplier has no option but to supply at ever-lower prices because the investments were so specific that they cannot be used to produce alternative products. In such circumstances, again, vertical integration may be the only option.

Vertical integration, however, gives rise to a different set of costs. These costs are referred to as *administrative costs.* Coordinating different stages of the value chain now internalized within the firm causes administrative costs to go up. Decisions about vertical integration are, therefore, based on a comparison of transaction costs and administrative costs. If transaction costs are lower than administrative costs, it is best to resort to market transactions and avoid vertical integration. For example, McDonald's may be the world's biggest buyer of beef, but they do not raise cattle. The market for beef has low transaction costs and requires no transaction-specific investments. On the other hand, if transaction costs are higher than administrative costs, vertical integration becomes an attractive strategy. Most automobile manufacturers produce their own engines because the market for engines involves high transaction costs and transaction-specific investments.

Unrelated Diversification: Financial Synergies and Parenting

>LO4
How corporations can use unrelated diversification to attain synergistic benefits through corporate restructuring, parenting, and portfolio analysis.

With unrelated diversification, unlike related diversification, few benefits are derived from *horizontal relationships*—that is, the leveraging of core competencies or the sharing of activities across business units within a corporation. Instead, potential benefits can be gained from *vertical (or hierarchical) relationships*—the creation of synergies from the interaction of the corporate office with the individual business units. There are two main sources of such synergies. First, the corporate office can contribute to "parenting" and restructuring of (often acquired) businesses. Second, the corporate office can add value by viewing the entire corporation as a family or "portfolio" of businesses and allocating resources to optimize corporate goals of profitability, cash flow, and growth. Additionally, the corporate office enhances value by establishing appropriate human resource practices and financial controls for each of its business units.

Corporate Parenting and Restructuring

So far, we have discussed how firms can add value through related diversification by exploring sources of synergy *across* business units. Here, we will discuss how value can be created *within* business units as a result of the expertise and support provided by the corporate office. Thus, we look at these as *hierarchical* sources of synergy.

Parenting   The positive contributions of the corporate office have been referred to as the **"parenting advantage."**[22] Many firms have successfully diversified their holdings without strong evidence of the more traditional sources of synergy (i.e., horizontally across business units). Diversified public corporations such as BTR, Emerson Electric, and Hanson and leveraged buyout firms such as Kohlberg, Kravis, Roberts & Company, and Clayton, Dublilier & Rice are a few examples.[23] These parent companies create value through management expertise. How? They improve plans and budgets and provide especially competent central functions such as legal, financial, human resource management, procurement, and the like. Additionally, they help subsidiaries make wise choices in their own acquisitions, divestitures, and new internal development decisions. Such contributions often help business units to substantially increase their revenues and profits. Consider Texas-based Cooper Industries' acquisition of Champion International, the spark plug company, as an example of corporate parenting:[24]

> Cooper applies a distinctive parenting approach designed to help its businesses improve their manufacturing performance. New acquisitions are "Cooperized"—Cooper audits their manufacturing operations; improves their cost accounting systems; makes their planning, budgeting, and human resource systems conform with its systems; and centralizes union negotiations. Excess cash is squeezed out through tighter controls and reinvested in productivity enhancements, which improve overall operating efficiency. As one manager observed, "When you get acquired by Cooper, one of the first things that happens is a truckload of policy manuals arrives at your door." Such active parenting has been effective in enhancing the competitive advantages of many kinds of manufacturing businesses.

Restructuring   **Restructuring** is another means by which the corporate office can add substantial value to a business.[25] The central idea can be captured in the real estate phrase "buy low and sell high." Here, the corporate office tries to find either poorly performing firms with unrealized potential or firms in industries on the threshold of significant, positive change. The parent intervenes, often selling off parts of the business; changing the management; reducing payroll and unnecessary sources of expenses; changing strategies; and infusing the company with new technologies, processes, reward systems, and so forth. When the restructuring is complete, the firm can either "sell high" and capture the added value or keep the business in the corporate family and enjoy the financial and competitive benefits of the enhanced performance.[26]

Loews Corporation, a conglomerate with $18 billion in revenues competes in such industries as oil and gas, tobacco, watches, insurance, and hotels. It provides an exemplary example of how firms can successfully "buy low and sell high" as part of their corporate strategy.[27]

> Energy accounts for 33 percent of Loews' $30 billion in total assets. In the 1980s it bought six oil tankers for only $5 million each during a sharp slide in oil prices. The downside was limited. After all these huge hulks could easily have been sold as scrap steel. However, that didn't have to happen. Eight years after Loews purchased the tankers, they sold them for $50 million each.
>
> Loews was also extremely successful with its next energy play—drilling equipment. Although wildcatting for oil is very risky, selling services to wildcatters is not, especially if the assets are bought during a down cycle. Loews did just that. It purchased 10 offshore drilling rigs for $50 million in 1989 and formed Diamond Offshore Drilling. In 1995 Loews received $338 million after taking a 30 percent piece of this operation public!

For the restructuring strategy to work, the corporate management must have both the insight to detect undervalued companies (otherwise the cost of acquisition would be too high) or businesses competing in industries with a high potential for transformation.[28] Additionally,

parenting advantage the positive contributions of the corporate office to a new business as a result of expertise and support provided and not as a result of substantial changes in assets, capital structure, or management.

restructuring the intervention of the corporate office in a new business that substantially changes the assets, capital structure, and/or management, including selling off parts of the business, changing the management, reducing payroll and unnecessary sources of expenses, changing strategies, and infusing the new business with new technologies, processes, and reward systems.

of course, they must have the requisite skills and resources to turn the businesses around, even if they may be in new and unfamiliar industries.

Restructuring can involve changes in assets, capital structure, or management.

- *Asset restructuring* involves the sale of unproductive assets, or even whole lines of businesses, that are peripheral. In some cases, it may even involve acquisitions that strengthen the core business.
- *Capital restructuring* involves changing the debt-equity mix, or the mix between different classes of debt or equity. Although the substitution of equity with debt is more common in buyout situations, occasionally the parent may provide additional equity capital.
- *Management restructuring* typically involves changes in the composition of the top management team, organizational structure, and reporting relationships. Tight financial control, rewards based strictly on meeting short- to medium-term performance goals, and reduction in the number of middle-level managers are common steps in management restructuring. In some cases, parental intervention may even result in changes in strategy as well as infusion of new technologies and processes.

Hanson, plc, a British conglomerate, made numerous such acquisitions in the United States in the 1980s, often selling these firms at significant profits after a few years of successful restructuring efforts. Hanson's acquisition and subsequent restructuring of the SCM group is a classic example of the restructuring strategy. Hanson acquired SCM, a diversified manufacturer of industrial and consumer products (including Smith-Corona typewriters, Glidden paints, and Durkee Famous Foods), for $930 million in 1986 after a bitter takeover battle. In the next few months, Hanson sold SCM's paper and pulp operations for $160 million, the chemical division for $30 million, Glidden paints for $580 million, and Durkee Famous Foods for $120 million, virtually recovering the entire original investment. In addition, Hanson also sold the SCM headquarters in New York for $36 million and reduced the headquarters staff by 250. They still retained several profitable divisions, including the titanium dioxide operations and managed them with tight financial controls that led to increased returns.[29]

Exhibit 6.5 summarizes the three primary types of restructuring activities.

Portfolio Management

During the 1970s and early 1980s, several leading consulting firms developed the concept of **portfolio management** to achieve a better understanding of the competitive position of an overall portfolio (or family) of businesses, to suggest strategic alternatives for each of the businesses, and to identify priorities for the allocation of resources. Several studies have reported widespread use of these techniques among American firms.[30]

Description and Potential Benefits   The key purpose of portfolio models is to assist a firm in achieving a balanced portfolio of businesses.[31] This consists of businesses whose profitability, growth, and cash flow characteristics complements each other and adds up to a satisfactory overall corporate performance. Imbalance, for example, could be caused either by excessive cash generation with too few growth opportunities or by insufficient cash

portfolio management a method of a) assessing the competitive position of a portfolio of businesses within a corporation, b) suggesting strategic alternatives for each business, and c) to identify priorities for the allocation of resources across the businesses.

Exhibit 6.5
The Three Primary Types of Restructuring Activities

Asset Restructuring: The sale of unproductive assets, or even whole lines of businesses, that are peripheral.

Capital Restructuring: Changing the debt-equity mix, or the mix between different classes of debt or equity.

Management Restructuring: Changes in the composition of the top management team, organization structure, and reporting relationships.

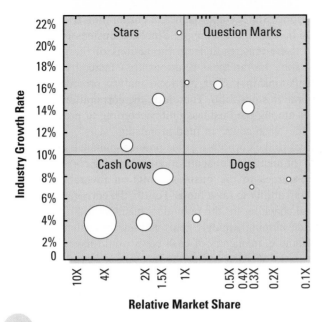

Exhibit 6.6 The Boston Consulting Group (BCG) Portfolio Matrix

generation to fund the growth requirements in the portfolio. Monsanto, for example, used portfolio planning to restructure its portfolio, divesting low-growth commodity chemicals businesses and acquiring businesses in higher-growth industries such as biotechnology.

The Boston Consulting Group's (BCG) growth/share matrix is among the best known of these approaches.[32] In the BCG approach, each of the firm's strategic business units (SBUs) is plotted on a two-dimensional grid in which the axes are relative market share and industry growth rate. The grid is broken into four quadrants. Exhibit 6.6 depicts the BCG matrix. Following are a few clarifications:

1. Each circle represents one of the corporation's business units. The size of the circle represents the relative size of the business unit in terms of revenues.
2. Relative market share, measured by the ratio of the business unit's size to that of its largest competitor, is plotted along the horizontal axis.
3. Market share is central to the BCG matrix. This is because high relative market share leads to unit cost reduction due to experience and learning curve effects and, consequently, superior competitive position.

Each of the four quadrants of the grid has different implications for the SBUs that fall into the category:

- **Stars** are SBUs competing in high-growth industries with relatively high market shares. These firms have long-term growth potential and should continue to receive substantial investment funding.
- **Question Marks** are SBUs competing in high-growth industries but having relatively weak market shares. Resources should be invested in them to enhance their competitive positions.
- **Cash Cows** are SBUs with high market shares in low-growth industries. These units have limited long-run potential but represent a source of current cash flows to fund investments in "stars" and "question marks."
- **Dogs** are SBUs with weak market shares in low-growth industries. Because they have weak positions and limited potential, most analysts recommend that they be divested.

In using portfolio strategy approaches, a corporation tries to create synergies and shareholder value in a number of ways.[33] Since the businesses are unrelated, synergies that develop are those that result from the actions of the corporate office with the individual units (i.e., hierarchical relationships) instead of among business units (i.e., horizontal relationships). First, portfolio analysis provides a snapshot of the businesses in a corporation's portfolio. Therefore, the corporation is in a better position to allocate resources among the business units according to prescribed criteria (e.g., use cash flows from the "cash cows" to fund promising "stars"). Second, the expertise and analytical resources in the corporate office provide guidance in determining what firms may be attractive (or unattractive) acquisitions. Third, the corporate office is able to provide financial resources to the business units on favorable terms that reflect the corporation's overall ability to raise funds. Fourth, the corporate office can provide high-quality review and coaching for the individual businesses. Fifth, portfolio analysis provides a basis for developing strategic goals and reward/evaluation systems for business managers. For example, managers of cash cows would have lower targets for revenue growth than managers of stars, but the former would have higher threshold levels of profit targets on proposed projects than the managers of star businesses. Compensation systems would also reflect such realities. Cash cows understandably would be rewarded more on the basis of cash that their businesses generate than would managers of star businesses. Similarly, managers of star businesses would be held to higher standards for revenue growth than managers of cash cow businesses.

To see how companies can benefit from portfolio approaches, consider Ciba-Geigy.

In 1994 Ciba-Geigy adopted portfolio planning approaches to help it manage its business units, which competed in a wide variety of industries, including chemicals, dyes, pharmaceuticals, crop protection, and animal health.[34] It placed each business unit in a category corresponding to the BCG matrix. The business unit's goals, compensation programs, personnel selection, and resource allocation were strongly associated with the category within which the business was placed. For example, business units classified as "cash cows" had much higher hurdles for obtaining financial resources (from the corporate office) for expansion than "question marks" since the latter were businesses for which Ciba-Geigy had high hopes for accelerated future growth and profitability. Additionally, the compensation of a business unit manager in a cash cow would be strongly associated with its success in generating cash to fund other businesses, whereas a manager of a question mark business would be rewarded on his or her ability to increase revenue growth and market share. The portfolio planning approaches appear to be working. In 2006, Ciba-Geigy's (now Novartis) revenues and net income stood at $26 billion and $8 billion, respectively. This represents a 22 percent increase in revenues and a most impressive 40 percent growth in net income over the past two years.

Limitations Despite the potential benefits of portfolio models, there are also some notable downsides. First, they compare SBUs on only two dimensions, making the implicit but erroneous assumption that (1) those are the only factors that really matter and (2) every unit can be accurately compared on that basis. Second, the approach views each SBU as a stand-alone entity, ignoring common core business practices and value-creating activities that may hold promise for synergies across business units. Third, unless care is exercised, the process becomes largely mechanical, substituting an oversimplified graphical model for the important contributions of the CEO's (and other corporate managers's) experience and judgment. Fourth, the reliance on "strict rules" regarding resource allocation across SBUs can be detrimental to a firm's long-term viability. For example, according to one study, over one-half of all the businesses that should have been cash users (based on the BCG matrix) were instead cash providers.[35]

Finally, while colorful and easy to comprehend, the imagery of the BCG matrix can lead to some troublesome and overly simplistic prescriptions. According to one author:

> The dairying analogy is appropriate (for some cash cows), so long as we resist the urge to oversimplify it. On the farm, even the best-producing cows eventually begin to dry up. The farmer's solution to this is euphemistically called "freshening" the cow: The farmer arranges a date for the cow with a bull, she has a calf, the milk begins flowing again. Cloistering the cow—isolating her from everything but the feed trough and the milking machines—assures that she will go dry.[36]

To see what can go wrong, consider Cabot Corporation.

> Cabot Corporation supplies carbon black for the rubber, electronics, and plastics industries. Following the BCG matrix, Cabot moved away from its cash cow, carbon black, and diversified into stars such as ceramics and semiconductors in a seemingly overaggressive effort to create more revenue growth for the corporation. Predictably, Cabot's return on assets declined as the firm shifted away from its core competence to unrelated areas. The portfolio model failed by pointing the company in the wrong direction in an effort to spur growth—away from their core business. Recognizing its mistake, Cabot Corporation returned to its mainstay carbon black manufacturing and divested unrelated businesses. Today the company is a leader in its field with $2.5 billion in 2006 revenues.[37]

● "Cows" in the BCG matrix as well as "live" cows need nourishment to be productive. Corporations will falter if they "milk" their cows excessively and fail to invest in these business units.

Exhibit 6.7 summarizes the limitations of portfolio model analysis.

Caveat: Is Risk Reduction a Viable Goal of Diversification?

Analysts and academics have suggested that one of the purposes of diversification is to reduce the risk that is inherent in a firm's variability in revenues and profits over time. In essence, the argument is that if a firm enters new products or markets that are affected differently by seasonal or economic cycles, its performance over time will be more stable. For example, a firm manufacturing lawn mowers may diversify into snow blowers to even out its annual sales. Or a firm manufacturing a luxury line of household furniture may introduce a lower-priced line since affluent and lower-income customers are affected differently by economic cycles.

At first glance the above reasoning may make sense, but there are some problems with it. First, a firm's stockholders can diversify their portfolios at a much lower cost than a corporation. As we have noted in this chapter, individuals can purchase their shares with almost no premium (e.g., only a small commission is paid to a discount broker), and they don't have to worry about integrating the acquisition into their portfolio. Second, economic cycles as well as their impact on a given industry (or firm) are difficult to predict with any degree of accuracy.

- They are overly simplistic; consisting of only two dimensions (growth and market share).
- They view each business as separate, ignoring potential synergies across businesses.
- The process may become overly largely mechanical, minimizing the potential value of managers' judgment and experience.
- The reliance on strict rules for resource allocation across SBUs can be detrimental to a firm's long-term viability.
- The imagery (e.g., cash cows, dogs) while colorful, may lead to troublesome and overly simplistic prescriptions.

Exhibit 6.7

Limitations of Portfolio Models

Notwithstanding the above, some firms have benefited from diversification by lowering the variability (or risk) in their performance over time. Consider Emerson Electronic.

Emerson Electronic is a $16 billion manufacturer that has enjoyed an incredible run—43 consecutive years of earnings growth![38] It produces a wide variety of products, including measurement devices for heavy industry, temperature controls for heating and ventilation systems, and power tools sold at Home Depot. Recently, many analysts questioned Emerson's purchase of companies that sell power systems to the volatile telecommunications industry. Why? This industry is expected to experience, at best, minimal growth. However, CEO David Farr maintained that such assets could be acquired inexpensively because of the aggregate decline in demand in this industry. Additionally, he argued that the other business units, such as the sales of valves and regulators to the now-booming oil and natural gas companies, were able to pick up the slack. Therefore, while net profits in the electrical equipment sector (Emerson's core business) sharply decreased, Emerson's overall corporate profits increased 1.7 percent.

In summary, risk reduction in and of itself is rarely viable as a means to create shareholder value. It must be undertaken with a view of a firm's overall diversification strategy.

The Means to Achieve Diversification

>LO5
The various means of engaging in diversification—mergers and acquisitions, joint ventures/strategic alliances, and internal development.

In the prior two sections, we have addressed the types of diversification (e.g., related and unrelated) that a firm may undertake to achieve synergies and create value for its shareholders. In this section, we address the means by which a firm can go about achieving these desired benefits.

We will address three basic means. First, through acquisitions or mergers, corporations can directly acquire a firm's assets and competencies. Although the terms *mergers* and *acquisitions* are used quite interchangeably, there are some key differences. With **acquisitions,** one firm buys another either through a stock purchase, cash, or the issuance of debt. **Mergers,** on the other hand, entail a combination or consolidation of two firms to form a new legal entity. Mergers are relatively rare and entail a transaction among two firms on a relatively equal basis. Despite such differences, we consider both mergers and acquisitions to be quite similar in terms of their implications for a firm's corporate-level strategy.

Second, corporations may agree to pool the resources of other companies with their resource base, commonly known as a joint venture or strategic alliance. Although these two forms of partnerships are similar in many ways, there is an important difference. Joint ventures involve the formation of a third-party legal entity where the two (or more) firms each contribute equity, whereas strategic alliances do not.

Third, corporations may diversify into new products, markets, and technologies through internal development. This approach, sometimes called corporate entrepreneurship, involves the leveraging and combining of a firm's own resources and competencies to create synergies and enhance shareholder value.

acquisitions the incorporation of one firm into another through purchase.

mergers the combining of two or more firms into one new legal entity.

Mergers and Acquisitions

The rate of mergers and acquisitions (M&A) had dropped off beginning in 2001. This trend was largely a result of a recession, corporate scandals, and a declining stock market. However, the situation has changed dramatically. Recently, several large mergers and acquisitions were announced. These include:[39]

- Mittal Steel's acquisition of Arcelor for $33 billion.
- Freeport-McMoRan's acquisition of Phelps Dodge for $26 billion.
- BellSouth's acquisition of AT&T for $86.0 billion.
- Sprint's merger with Nextel for $39 billion.
- Boston Scientific's $27 billion acquisition of medical device maker Guidant.

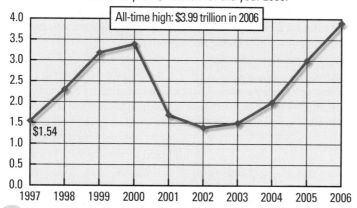

Global Value of Mergers and Acquisitions

Global mergers and acquisitions soared past their previous record and nearly hit $4 trillion for the year 2006.

All-time high: $3.99 trillion in 2006

$1.54

Exhibit 6.8 Global Value of Mergers and Acquistions

Source: Bloomberg; Dealogic.

- Exelon's acquisition of Public Service Enterprise Group for $12 billion.
- Procter & Gamble's purchase of Gillette for $54 billion.
- Kmart Holding Corp.'s acquisition of Sears, Roebuck & Co. for $11 billion.

Exhibit 6.8 illustrates the dramatic increase in worldwide merger and acquisition activity in the United States in the past few years. Several factors help to explain the recent rise. First, there is the robust economy and the increasing corporate profits that have boosted stock prices and cash. For example, the Standard & Poor's 500 stock index companies, including financial companies, have a record of over $2 trillion in cash and other short-term assets, according to S&P Compustat.

Second, the weak U.S. dollar makes U.S. assets more attractive to other countries. That is, from the perspective of a foreign acquirer, compared to any other period in recent memory, U.S. companies are "cheap" today. For example, a Euro which was worth only 80 cents in 1999 was worth $1.35 by mid 2007. This makes U.S. companies a relative bargain for a European acquirer. And third, stricter governance standards are requiring poorly performing CEOs and boards of directors to consider unsolicited offers. In essence, top executives and board members are less likely to be protected by anti-takeover mechanisms such as greenmail, poison pills and golden parachutes (which we will discuss at the end of the chapter).

Next, we will address some of the motives and potential benefits of mergers and acquisitions as well as their potential limitations.

Motives and Benefits Growth through mergers and acquisitions has played a critical role in the success of many corporations in a wide variety of high-technology and knowledge-intensive industries. Here, market and technology changes can occur very quickly and unpredictably.[40] Speed—speed to market, speed to positioning, and speed to becoming a viable company—is critical in such industries. For example, Alex Mandl, then AT&T's president, was responsible for the acquisition of McCaw Cellular. Although many industry experts felt the price was too steep, he believed that cellular technology was a critical asset for the telecommunications business and that it would have been extremely difficult to build that business from the ground up. Mandl claimed, "The plain fact is that acquiring is much faster than building."[41]

As we discussed earlier in the chapter, mergers and acquisitions also can be a means of *obtaining valuable resources that can help an organization expand its product offerings and services.* For example, Cisco Systems, a dominant player in networking equipment, acquired more than 70 companies over a recent seven-year period.[42] This provides Cisco with access to the latest in networking equipment. Then it uses its excellent sales force to market the new technology to its corporate customers and telephone companies. Cisco also provides strong incentives to the staff of acquired companies to stay on. In order to realize the greatest value from its acquisitions, Cisco also has learned to integrate acquired companies efficiently and effectively.[43]

Mergers and acquisitions also can *provide the opportunity for firms to attain the three bases of synergy that were addressed earlier in the chapter—leveraging core competencies, sharing activities, and building market power.* Consider Procter & Gamble's $57 billion acquisition of Gillette.[44] First, it helps Procter & Gamble to leverage its core competencies in marketing and product positioning in the area of grooming and personal care brands. For example, P&G has experience in repositioning brands such as Old Spice in this market (which recently passed Gillette's Right Guard brand to become No. 1 in the deodorant market). Gillette has very strong brands in razors and blades. Thus, P&G's marketing expertise enhances its market position. Second, there are opportunities to share value-creating activities. Gillette will benefit from P&G's stronger distribution network in developing countries where the potential growth rate for the industry's products remains higher than in the United States, Europe, or Japan. Consider the insight of A. F. Lafley, P&G's CEO:

> When I was in Asia in the 90s, we had already gone beyond the top 500 cities in China. Today, we're way down into the rural areas. So we add three, four, five Gillette brands, and we don't even have to add a salesperson.

Third, the addition of Gillette increases P&G's market power. In recent years, the growth of powerful global retailers such as Wal-Mart, Carrefour, and Costco has eroded much of the consumer goods industry's pricing power. A central part of P&G's recent strategy has been to focus its resources on enhancing its core brands. Today, 16 of its brands (each with revenues of over $1 billion) account for $30 billion of the firm's $51.4 billion in total revenues. Gillette, with $10.5 billion in total revenues, adds five brands which also have revenues of over $1 billion. P&G anticipates that its growing stable of "superbrands" will help it to weather the industry's tough pricing environment and enhance its power relative to large, powerful retailers such as Wal-Mart and Target.

Merger and acquisition activity also can *lead to consolidation within an industry and can force other players to merge.*[45] In the pharmaceutical industry, the patents for many top-selling drugs are expiring and M&A activity is expected to heat up.[46] For example, a few years ago SG Cowen Securities predicted that between 2000 and 2005, U.S. patents would expire on pharmaceutical products with annual domestic sales of approximately $34.6 billion. Clearly, this is an example of how the political—legal segment of the general environment (discussed in Chapter 2) can affect a corporation's strategy and performance. Although health care providers and patients are happy about the lower-cost generics that will arrive, drug firms are being pressed to make up for lost revenues. Combining top firms such as Pfizer Inc. and Warner-Lambert Co. as well as Glaxo Wellcome and SmithKline Beecham has many potential long-term benefits. They not only promise significant postmerger cost savings, but also the increased size of the combined companies brings greater research and development possibilities.

Two other industries where consolidation is the primary rationale are telecommunications and software.[47] In 2004, Cingular Wireless became number one in the industry by acquiring AT&T Wireless Communications. Subsequently, Sprint agreed to buy Nextel to form a stronger number three. In software, the primary motive for mergers is to offer customers a fuller portfolio of products. Many niche players are selling out to serial buyers like Oracle Corp., which recently acquired PeopleSoft Inc. after a long and heated struggle. Symantec Corp. agreed to acquire Veritas Software Corporation for $13.5 billion. Such consolidation raises questions about whether smaller players such as McAfee, BEA Systems, and Siebel Systems are big enough to remain independent. According to Joseph M. Tucci, president and CEO of data-storage giant EMC, "This is going to be a big boys' game. They're going to move very aggressively and quickly."

Corporations can also *enter new market segments by way of acquisitions.* Although Charles Schwab & Co. is best known for providing discount trading services for middle America, it clearly is interested in other target markets.[48] In late 2000 Schwab surprised its rivals by paying $2.7 billion to acquire (divested in 2006) U.S. Trust Corporation, a 147-year-old financial services institution that is a top estate planner for the wealthy. However, Schwab is in no way ignoring its core market. The firm also purchased Cybercorp Inc., a Texas brokerage company, for $488 million. That firm offers active online traders sophisticated quotes and stock-screening tools.

Potential Limitations   As noted in the previous section, mergers and acquisitions provide a firm with many potential benefits. However, at the same time, there are many potential drawbacks or limitations to such corporate activity.[49]

First, *the takeover premium that is paid for an acquisition is very high.* Two times out of three, the stock price of the acquiring company falls once the deal is made public. Since the acquiring firm often pays a 30 percent to 40 percent premium for the target company, the acquirer must create synergies and scale economies that result in sales and market gains exceeding the premium price. Firms paying higher premiums set the performance hurdle even higher. For example, Household International paid an 82 percent premium to buy Beneficial, and Conseco paid an 83 percent premium to acquire Green Tree Financial. Historically, paying a high premium over the stock price has been a largely unprofitable strategy.

Second, *competing firms often can imitate any advantages realized or copy synergies that result from the M&A.* Thus, a firm can often see its advantages quickly evaporate if it plans to achieve competitive advantage through M&A activity. Unless the advantages are sustainable and difficult to copy, investors will not be willing to pay a high premium for the stock. Similarly, the time value of money must be factored into the stock price. M&A costs are paid up front. Conversely, firms pay for research and development, ongoing marketing, and capacity expansion over time. This stretches out the payments needed to gain new competencies. The M&A argument is that a large initial investment is worthwhile because it creates long-term advantages. However, stock analysts want to see immediate results from such a large cash outlay. If the acquired firm does not produce results quickly, investors often sell the stock, driving the price down.

Third, *managers' credibility and ego can sometimes get in the way of sound business decisions.* If the M&A does not perform as planned, managers who pushed for the deal find that their reputation may be at stake. Sometimes, this can lead these managers to protect their credibility by funneling more money, or escalating their commitment, into an inevitably doomed operation. Further, when a merger fails and a firm tries to unload the acquisition, managers often find that they must sell at a huge discount. These problems further compound the costs and weaken the stock price.

Fourth, *there can be many cultural issues that may doom the intended benefits from M&A endeavors.* Consider, for example, the insights of Joanne Lawrence, who played an important role as vice president and director of communications and investor relations at SmithKline Beecham, in the merger between SmithKline and the Beecham Group, a diversified consumer-oriented group headquartered in the United Kingdom.[50]

> The key to a strategic merger is to create a new culture. This was a mammoth challenge during the SmithKline Beecham merger. We were working at so many different cultural levels, it was dizzying. We had two national cultures to blend—American and British—that compounded the challenge of selling the merger in two different markets with two different shareholder bases. There were also two different business cultures: One was very strong, scientific, and academic; the other was much more commercially oriented. And then we had to consider within both companies the individual businesses, each of which has its own little culture.[51]

Divestment: The Other Side of the "M&A Coin"   When firms acquire other businesses it typically generates quite a bit of "press" in business publications such as *The Wall Street Journal, BusinessWeek,* and *Fortune.* It makes for exciting news and one thing is for sure—large acquiring firms automatically improve their standing in the Fortune 500 rankings (since it is based solely on total revenues). However, managers must also carefully consider the strategic implications of exiting businesses.

divestment the exit of a business from a firm's portfolio.

Divestments, the exit of a business from a firm's portfolio, are quite common. One study found that large, prestigious U.S. companies divested more acquisitions than they had kept.[52] Well-known divestitures in business history include (1) Novell's purchase of WordPerfect for stock valued at $1.4 billion and later sold to Corel for $124 million, and (2) Quaker Oats unloading of the Snapple Beverage Company to Triarc for only $300 million in 1997—three years after it had bought it for $1.8 billion! Also, in early 2007, DaimlerChrysler announced that they are looking for a buyer for its Chrysler unit, which they had acquired a decade earlier.[53]

Divesting a business can accomplish many different objectives.* As the examples above demonstrate, it can be used to help a firm reverse an earlier acquisition that didn't work out as planned. Often, this is simply to help "cut their losses." Other objectives include: (1) enabling managers to focus their efforts more directly on the firm's core businesses,[54] (2) providing the firm with more resources to spend on more attractive alternatives; and, (3) raising cash to help fund existing businesses.

In summary, divesting can enhance a firm's competitive position only to the extent that it reduces its tangible (e.g., maintenance, investments, etc.) or intangible (e.g., opportunity costs, managerial attention) costs without sacrificing a current competitive advantage or the seeds of future advantages.[55] To be effective, divesting requires a thorough understanding of a business unit's current ability and future potential to contribute to a firm's value creation. However, since such decisions involve a great deal of uncertainty, it is very difficult to make such evaluations. In addition, because of managerial self-interests and organizational inertia, firms often delay divestments of underperforming businesses.

Strategy Spotlight 6.5 addresses how Royal Philips Electronics NV, a bastion of European business with $35 billion in revenues, has gone about divesting businesses over the past several years.

Strategic Alliances and Joint Ventures

strategic alliances a cooperative relationship between two or more firms.

A **strategic alliance** is a cooperative relationship between two (or more) firms. Alliances may be either informal or formal—that is, involving a written contract. **Joint ventures** represent a special case of alliances, wherein two (or more) firms contribute equity to form a new legal entity.

Strategic alliances and joint ventures are assuming an increasingly prominent role in the strategy of leading firms, both large and small.[56] Such cooperative relationships have many potential advantages.[57] Among these are entering new markets, reducing manufacturing (or other) costs in the value chain, and developing and diffusing new technologies.[58]

joint ventures new entities formed within a strategic alliance in which two or more firms, the parents, contribute equity to form the new legal entity.

Entering New Markets   Often a company that has a successful product or service wants to introduce it into a new market. However, it may not have the requisite marketing

---

* Firms can divest their businesses in a number of ways. Sell-offs, spin-offs, equity carve-outs, asset sales/ dissolution, and split-ups are some such modes of divestment. In a sell-off, the divesting firm privately negotiates with a third party to divest a unit/subsidiary for cash/stock. In a spin-off, a parent company distributes shares of the unit/subsidiary being divested pro-rata to its existing shareholders and a new company is formed. Equity carve-outs are similar to spin-offs except that shares in the unit/subsidiary being divested are offered to new shareholders. Dissolution involves sale of redundant assets, not necessarily as an entire unit/subsidiary as in sell-offs but a few bits at a time. A split-up, on the other hand, is an instance of divestiture where the parent company is split into two or more new companies and the parent ceases to exist. Shares in the parent company are exchanged for shares in new companies and the exact distribution varies case by case.

Philips Divests Some of its Businesses

Royal Philips Electronics NV started making lightbulbs in Eindhoven in the Netherlands in 1891. In the first half of the 20th century it produced X-ray machines and radio equipment, and in the 1970s it moved into the record business. By 2007, it employed 122,000 people in 60 countries in its diversified businesses.

Until recently, however, Philips wasn't like most big companies. It was a huge, unwieldy conglomerate that made everything from lightbulbs, consumer electronics, mobile phones, microprocessors, and electric shavers to less-well-known products such as defibrillators and MRI machines. In fact, at one time, Philips was even in the music business, with internationally known artists like Sting and Elton John recording on its PolyGram label. Not surprisingly, the company even confused analysts. "Can You Tell What It Is Yet?" asked Citigroup's Simon Smith in a report on Philips that touted the company as "one of the last great misunderstood conglomerates of Europe."

Sources: Anonymous. 2007. Home and abroad. *The Economist*. February 10: 7–8; Sterling, T. 2007. Philips 4Q doubles, sales slip, bizyahoo.com. January 22; Schwartz, N. D. 2007. Europe businessman of the year: Gerard Kleisterlee. Money.cnn.com. January 12; and Reihardt, A. 2004. Philips: Back on the beam. www.businessweek.com. May 3.

In recent years, Philips has been undergoing an endless round of restructuring in an effort to make it more competitive. Things came to a head in the 2001 recession when the company suffered huge losses and had to shed 55,000 jobs—about one-fourth of its workforce. Thirty separate divisions were reduced to only five—domestic appliances, lighting, medical, consumer electronics, and semiconductors. A net loss of $4.2 billion in 2002 turned into a net profit of $3.6 billion by 2004.

Philips has continued its effective divestment strategy. It has been steadily exiting electronics markets where it doesn't hold a first- or second-place position—most notably divesting its mobile phones operation after being eclipsed by Nokia Corp.

Its biggest divestiture was its sale of its microprocessor division for $5.6 billion in August 2006 to a consortium of private investors led by Kohlberg Kravis Roberts & Co. The proceeds were used to focus on faster growing lines like lighting and medical devices and to reward investors with a multibillion-dollar share buyback. The streamlined company's goal is now to refocus on its fastest-growing and most profitable sectors, such as medical systems. "No question, it's a much more focused company," says Rene Verhaef of Fortis Bank in Amsterdam.

Philip's performance has continued to soar. Its 2006 earnings hit $7 billion on revenues of $35 billion.

expertise because it does not understand customer needs, know how to promote the product, or have access to the proper distribution channels.

The partnerships formed between Time-Warner, Inc., and three African American–owned cable companies in New York City are examples of joint ventures created to serve a domestic market. Time-Warner built a 185,000-home cable system in the city and asked the three cable companies to operate it. Time-Warner supplied the product, and the cable companies supplied the knowledge of the community and the know-how to market the cable system. Joining with the local companies enabled Time-Warner to win the acceptance of the cable customers and to benefit from an improved image in the black community.

Reducing Manufacturing (or Other) Costs in the Value Chain   Strategic alliances (or joint ventures) often enable firms to pool capital, value-creating activities, or facilities in order to reduce costs. For example, Molson Companies and Carling O'Keefe Breweries in Canada formed a joint venture to merge their brewing operations. Although Molson had a modern and efficient brewery in Montreal, Carling's was outdated. However, Carling had the better facilities in Toronto. In addition, Molson's Toronto brewery was located on the waterfront and had substantial real estate value. Overall, the synergies gained by using their combined facilities more efficiently added $150 million of pretax earnings during the initial year of the venture. Economies of scale were realized and facilities were better utilized.

Developing and Diffusing New Technologies   Strategic alliances also may be used to build jointly on the technological expertise of two or more companies in order to develop products technologically beyond the capability of the companies acting independently. STMicroelectronics (ST) is a high-tech company based in Geneva, Switzerland, that has thrived—largely due to the success of its strategic alliances.[59] The firm develops and manufactures computer chips for a variety of applications such as mobile phones, set-top boxes, smart cards, and flash memories. In 1995 it teamed up with Hewlett-Packard to develop powerful new processors for various digital applications that are now nearing completion. Another example was its strategic alliance with Nokia to develop a chip that would give Nokia's phones a longer battery life. Here, ST produced a chip that tripled standby time to 60 hours—a breakthough that gave Nokia a huge advantage in the marketplace.

The firm's CEO, Pasquale Pistorio, was among the first in the industry to form R&D alliances with other companies. Now ST's top 12 customers, including HP, Nokia, and Nortel, account for 45 percent of revenues. According to Pistorio, "Alliances are in our DNA." Such relationships help ST keep better-than-average growth rates, even in difficult times. That's because close partners are less likely to defect to other suppliers. ST's financial results are most impressive. During 2000 its revenues grew 55 percent—nearly double the industry average.

Potential Downsides   Despite their promise, many alliances and joint ventures fail to meet expectations for a variety of reasons.[60] First, without the proper partner, a firm should never consider undertaking an alliance, even for the best of reasons. Each partner should bring the desired complementary strengths to the partnership. Ideally, the strengths contributed by the partners are unique; thus synergies created can be more easily sustained and defended over the longer term. The goal must be to develop synergies between the contributions of the partners, resulting in a win–win situation for both. Moreover, the partners must be compatible and willing to trust each other. Unfortunately, often little attention is given to nurturing the close working relationships and interpersonal connections that bring together the partnering organizations. The human or people factors are not carefully considered or, at worst, they are dismissed as an unimportant consideration.

Internal Development

Firms can also diversify by means of corporate entrepreneurship and new venture development. **In today's economy, internal development is such an important means by which companies expand their businesses that we have devoted a whole chapter to it (see Chapter 12).** Sony and the Minnesota Mining & Manufacturing Co. (3M), for example, are known for their dedication to innovation, R&D, and cutting-edge technologies. For example, 3M has developed its entire corporate culture to support its ongoing policy of generating at least 25 percent of total sales from products created within the most recent four-year period. During the 1990s, 3M exceeded this goal by achieving about 30 percent of sales per year from new internally developed products.

Many companies use some form of internal development to extend their product lines or add to their service offerings. This approach to internal development is used by many large publicly held corporations as well as small firms. An example of the latter is Rosa Verde, a small but growing business serving the health care needs of San Antonio, Texas.

This small company began with one person who moved from Mexico to San Antonio, Texas, to serve the health care needs of inner-city residents.[61] Beginning as a sole proprietor, Dr. Lourdes Pizana started Rosa Verde Family Health Care Group in 1995 with only $10,000 obtained from credit card debt. She has used a strategy of internal development to propel the company to where it is today—six clinics, 30 doctors, and a team of other health care professionals.

How was Dr. Pizana able to accomplish this in such a short time? She emphasizes the company's role in the community, forging links with community leaders. In addition, she hires nearly all her professional staff as independent contractors to control

The Ritz-Carlton Leadership Center: A Successful Internal Venture

Companies worldwide often strive to be the "Ritz-Carlton" of their industries. Ritz-Carlton, the large luxury hotel chain, is the only service company to have won the prestigious Malcolm Baldrige National Quality Award twice—in 1992 and 1999 (one year after being acquired by Marriott). It also has placed first in guest satisfaction among luxury hotels in the most recent J.D. Power & Associates hotel survey.

Until a few years ago, being "Ritz-Carlton-like" was just a motivational simile. However, in 2000, the company launched the Ritz-Carlton Leadership Center, where it offers 12 leadership development programs for its employees and seven benchmarking seminars and workshops to outside companies. It also conducts 35 off-site presentations on such topics as "Creating a Dynamic Employee Orientation," and "The Key to Retaining and Selecting Talented Employees." (Incidentally, Ritz-Carlton's annual turnover rate among nonmanagement employees is 25 percent— roughly half the average rate for U.S. luxury hotels.)

Within its first four years of operation, 800 different companies from such industries as health care, banking and finance, hospitality, and the automotive industries have participated in the Leadership Center's programs. And to date it has generated over $2 million in revenues. Ken Yancey, CEO of the nonprofit small-business consultancy, Score, says the concepts he learned, like "the three steps of service," apply directly to his business. "Hotels are about service to a client," he says. "And we are too."

To give a few specifics on one of the Leadership Center's programs, consider its "Legendary Service I" course. The topics that are covered include empowerment, using customer recognition to boost loyalty, and Ritz-Carlton's approach to quality. The course lasts two days and costs $2,000 per attendee. Well-known companies that have participated include Microsoft, Morgan Stanley, and Starbucks.

Sources: McDonald, D. 2004. Roll out the blue carpet. *Business 2.0,* May: 53; and Johnson, G. 2003. Nine tactics to take your corporate university from good to GREAT. *Training,* July/August: 38–41.

---

costs. These professionals are paid based on the volume of work they do rather than a set salary; Pizana splits her revenue with them, thus motivating them to work efficiently. Her strategy is to grow the company from the inside out through high levels of service, commitment to the community she serves, and savvy leadership. By committing to a solid plan, Pizana has proven that internal growth and development can be a successful strategy.

The luxury hotel chain Ritz-Carlton has long been recognized for its exemplary service. In fact, it is the only service company ever to win two Malcolm Baldrige National Quality Awards. It has built on this capability by developing a highly successful internal venture to offer leadership development programs—both to its employees as well as to outside companies. We address this internal venture in Strategy Spotlight 6.6.

Compared to mergers and acquisitions, firms that engage in internal development are able to capture the value created by their own innovative activities without having to "share the wealth" with alliance partners or face the difficulties associated with combining activities across the value chains of several companies or merging corporate cultures. Another advantage is that firms can often develop new products or services at a relatively lower cost and thus rely on their own resources rather than turning to external funding. There are also potential disadvantages. Internal development may be time consuming; thus, firms may forfeit the benefits of speed that growth through mergers or acquisitions can provide. This may be especially important among high-tech or knowledge-based organizations in fast-paced environments where being an early mover is critical. Thus, firms that choose to diversify through internal development must develop capabilities that allow them to move quickly from initial opportunity recognition to market introduction.

How Managerial Motives Can Erode Value Creation

>LO6

Managerial behaviors that can erode the creation of value.

Thus far in the chapter we have implicitly assumed that CEOs and top executives are "rational beings"; that is, they act in the best interests of shareholders to maximize long-term shareholder value. In the real world, however, this is not the case. Frequently, they may act in their own self-interest. Next, we address some managerial motives that can serve to erode, rather than enhance, value creation. These include "growth for growth's sake," excessive egotism, and the creation of a wide variety of antitake-over tactics.

Growth for Growth's Sake

There are huge incentives for executives to increase the size of their firm, and many of these are hardly consistent with increasing shareholder wealth. Top managers, including the CEO, of larger firms typically enjoy more prestige, higher rankings for their companies on the Fortune 500 list (which is based on revenues, not profits), greater incomes, more job security, and so on. There is also the excitement and associated recognition of making a major acquisition. As noted by Harvard's Michael Porter, "There's a tremendous allure to mergers and acquisitions. It's the big play, the dramatic gesture. With one stroke of the pen you can add billions to size, get a front-page story, and create excitement in markets."[62]

In recent years many high-tech firms have suffered from the negative impact of their uncontrolled growth. Consider, for example, Priceline.com's ill-fated venture into an online service to offer groceries and gasoline.[63] A myriad of problems—perhaps most importantly, a lack of participation by manufacturers—caused the firm to lose more than $5 million a *week* prior to abandoning these ventures. Similarly, many have questioned the profit potential of Amazon.com's recent ventures into a variety of products such as tools and hardware, cell phones, and service. Such initiatives are often little more than desperate moves by top managers to satisfy investor demands for accelerating revenues. Unfortunately, the increased revenues often fail to materialize into a corresponding hike in earnings.

At times, executives' overemphasis on growth can result in a plethora of ethical lapses, which can have disastrous outcomes for their companies. A good example (of bad practice) is Joseph Bernardino's leadership at Andersen Worldwide. Bernardino had a chance early on to take a hard line on ethics and quality in the wake of earlier scandals at clients such as Waste Management and Sunbeam. Instead, according to former executives, he put too much emphasis on revenue growth. Consequently, the firm's reputation quickly eroded when it audited and signed off on the highly flawed financial statements of such infamous firms as Enron, Global Crossing, and WorldCom. WorldCom, in fact, is recognized as the biggest financial fraud of all time. Bernardino ultimately resigned in disgrace in March 2002, and his firm was dissolved later that year.[64]

Egotism

Most would agree that there is nothing wrong with ego, per se. After all, a healthy ego helps make a leader confident, clearheaded, and able to cope with change. CEOs, by their very nature, are typically fiercely competitive people in the office as well as on the tennis court or golf course. However, sometimes when pride is at stake, individuals will go to great lengths to win. Such behavior, of course, is not a new phenomenon. We discuss the case of Cornelius Vanderbilt, one of the original American moguls, in Strategy Spotlight 6.7.

Egos can get in the way of a "synergistic" corporate marriage. Few executives (or lower-level managers) are exempt from the potential downside of excessive egos. Consider, for

Cornelius Vanderbilt: Going to Great Lengths to Correct a Wrong!

Cornelius Vanderbilt's legendary ruthlessness set a bar for many titans to come. Back in 1853, the Commodore took his first vacation, an extended voyage to Europe aboard his yacht. He was in for a big surprise when he returned. Two of his associates had taken the power of attorney that

he had left them and sold his interest in his steamship concern, Accessory Transit Company, to themselves.

"Gentlemen," he wrote, in a classic battle cry, "you have undertaken to cheat me. I won't sue you, for the law is too slow. I'll ruin you." He converted his yacht to a passenger ship to compete with them and added other vessels. He started a new line, appropriately named *Opposition*. Before long, he bought his way back in and regained control of the company.

Source: McGregor, J. 2007. Sweet revenge. *BusinessWeek*, January 22: 64–70.

example, the reflections of General Electric's former CEO Jack Welch, considered by many to be the world's most admired executive. He admitted to his regrettable decision for GE to acquire Kidder Peabody.[65] According to Welch, "My hubris got in the way in the Kidder Peabody deal. [He was referring to GE's buyout of the soon-to-be-troubled Wall Street firm.] I got wise advice from Walter Wriston and other directors who said, 'Jack, don't do this.' But I was bully enough and on a run to do it. And I got whacked right in the head." In addition to poor financial results, Kidder Peabody was wracked by a widely publicized trading scandal that tarnished the reputations of both GE and Kidder Peabody. Welch ended up selling Kidder in 1994.

The business press has included many stories of how egotism and greed have infiltrated organizations. Some incidents are considered rather astonishing, such as Tyco's former (and now convicted) CEO Dennis Kozlowski's well-chronicled purchase of a $6,000 shower curtain and vodka-spewing, full-size replica of Michaelangelo's David.[66] Other well-known examples of power grabs and extraordinary consumption of compensation and perks include executives at Enron, the Rigas family who were convicted of defrauding Adelphia of roughly $1 billion, former CEO Bernie Ebbers's $408 million loan from WorldCom, and so on. However, executives in the United States clearly don't have a monopoly on such deeds. Consider, for example, Jean-Marie Messier, former CEO of Vivendi Universal.[67]

> In striving to convert a French utility into a global media conglomerate, Messier seldom passed up a chance for self-promotion. Although most French executives have a preference for discreet personal lives, Messier hung out with rock stars and moved his family into a $17.5 million Park Avenue spread paid for by Vivendi. He pushed the company to the brink of collapse by running up $19 billion in debt from an acquisition spree and confusing investors with inconsistent financial transactions which are now under investigation by authorities in both the United States and France. Not one to accept full responsibility, less than five months after his forced resignation, he published a book, *My True Diary*, that blames a group of French business leaders for plotting against him. And his ego is clearly intact: At a recent Paris press conference, he described his firing as a setback for French capitalism!

Antitakeover Tactics

Unfriendly or hostile takeovers can occur when a company's stock becomes undervalued. A competing organization can buy the outstanding stock of a takeover candidate in sufficient quantity to become a large shareholder. Then it makes a tender offer to gain full

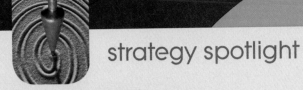

strategy spotlight

6.8

Poison Pills: How Antitakeover Strategies Can Raise Ethical Issues

Poison pills are almost always good for managers but not always so good for shareholders. They present managers with an ethical dilemma: How can they balance their own interests with their fiduciary responsibility to shareholders?

Here's how poison pills work. In the event of a take-over bid, existing shareholders have the option to buy additional shares of stock at a discount to the current market price. This action is typically triggered when a new shareholder rapidly accumulates more than a set percentage of ownership (usually 20 percent) through stock purchases. When this happens, managers fear that the voting rights and increased proportional ownership of the new shareholder might be a ploy to make a takeover play.

To protect existing shareholders, stock is offered at a discount, but only to existing shareholders. As the existing owners buy the discounted stock, the stock is diluted (i.e., there are now more shares, each with a lower value). If there has been a takeover offer at a set price per share,

Sources: Vicente, J. P. 2001. Toxic treatment: Poison pills proliferate as Internet firms worry they've become easy marks. *Red Herring*, May 1 and 15: 195; Chakraborty, A., & Baum, C. F. 1998. Poison pills, optimal contracting and the market for corporate control: Evidence from Fortune 500 firms. *International Journal of Finance*, 10(3): 1120–1138; Sundaramurthy, C. 1996. Corporate governance within the context of antitakeover provisions. *Strategic Management Journal*, 17: 377–394.

the overall price for the company immediately goes up since there are now more shares. This assures stockholders of receiving a fair price for the company.

Sounds good, but here's the problem. Executives on the company's board of directors retain the right to allow the stock discount. The discounted stock price for existing shareholders may or may not be activated when a takeover is imminent. This brings in the issue of motive: Why did the board enact the poison pill provision in the first place? At times, it may have been simply to protect the existing shareholders. At other times, it may have been to protect the interests of those on the board of directors. In other words, the board may have enacted the rule not to protect shareholders, but to protect their own jobs.

When the board receives a takeover offer, the offering company will be aware of the poison pill provision. This gives negotiating power to board members of the takeover target. They may include as part of the negotiation that the new company keep them as members of the board. In exchange, the board members would not enact the discounted share price; existing stockholders would lose, but the jobs of the board members would be protected.

When a company offers poison pill provisions to shareholders, the shareholders should keep in mind that things are not always as they seem. The motives may reflect concern for shareholders. But on the other hand....

control of the company. If the shareholders accept the offer, the hostile firm buys the target company and either fires the target firm's management team or strips them of their power. For this reason, antitakeover tactics are common. Three of these are greenmail, golden parachutes, and poison pills.[68]

The first, *greenmail,* is an effort by the target firm to prevent an impending takeover. When a hostile firm buys a large block of outstanding target company stock and the target firm's management feels that a tender offer is impending, they offer to buy the stock back from the hostile company at a higher price than the unfriendly company paid for it. The positive side is that this often prevents a hostile takeover. On the downside, the same price is not offered to preexisting shareholders. However, it protects the jobs of the target firm's management.

The second strategy is a *golden parachute.* A golden parachute is a prearranged contract with managers specifying that, in the event of a hostile takeover, the target firm's managers will be paid a significant severance package. Although top managers lose their jobs, the golden parachute provisions protect their income.

Strategy Spotlight 6.8 illustrates how poison pills are used to prevent takeovers. *Poison pills* are means by which a company can give shareholders certain rights in the event of a takeover by another firm. In addition to "poison pills," they are also known as shareholder rights plans.

As you can see, antitakeover tactics can often raise some interesting ethical issues.

Reflecting on Career Implications . . .

- *Corporate-level strategy:* Be aware of your firm's corporate-level strategy. Can you come up with an initiative that will create value both within and across business units?
- *Core Competencies:* What do you see as your core competencies? How can you leverage them both within your business unit as well as across other business units?
- *Sharing Infrastructures:* What infrastructure activities and resources (e.g., information systems, legal) are available in the corporate office that would help you add value for your business unit—or other business units?
- *Diversification:* From your career perspective, what actions can you take to diversify your employment risk (e.g., coursework at a local university, obtain professional certification such as a C.P.A., networking through professional affiliation, etc.)? For example, in periods of retrenchment, such actions will provide you with a greater number of career options.

Summary

A key challenge for today's managers is to create "synergy" when engaging in diversification activities. As we discussed in this chapter, corporate managers do not, in general, have a very good track record in creating value in such endeavors when it comes to mergers and acquisitions. Among the factors that serve to erode shareholder values are paying an excessive premium for the target firm, failing to integrate the activities of the newly acquired businesses into the corporate family, and undertaking diversification initiatives that are too easily imitated by the competition.

We addressed two major types of corporate-level strategy: related and unrelated diversification. With *related diversification* the corporation strives to enter into areas in which key resources and capabilities of the corporation can be shared or leveraged. Synergies come from horizontal relationships between business units. Cost savings and enhanced revenues can be derived from two major sources. First, economies of scope can be achieved from the leveraging of core competencies and the sharing of activities. Second, market power can be attained from greater, or pooled, negotiating power and from vertical integration.

When firms undergo *unrelated diversification* they enter product markets that are dissimilar to their present businesses. Thus, there is generally little opportunity to either leverage core competencies or share activities across business units. Here, synergies are created from vertical relationships between the corporate office and the individual business units. With unrelated diversification, the primary ways to create value are corporate restructuring and parenting, as well as the use of portfolio analysis techniques.

Corporations have three primary means of diversifying their product markets—mergers and acquisitions, joint ventures/strategic alliances, and internal development. There are key trade-offs associated with each of these. For example, mergers and acquisitions are typically the quickest means to enter new markets and provide the corporation with a high level of control over the acquired business. However, with the expensive premiums that often need to be paid to the shareholders of the target firm and the challenges associated with integrating acquisitions, they can also be quite expensive. Not surprisingly, many poorly performing acquisitions are subsequently divested. At times, however, divestitures can help firms refocus their efforts and generate resources. Strategic alliances and joint ventures between two or more firms, on the other hand, may be a means of reducing risk since they involve the sharing and combining of resources. But such joint initiatives also provide a firm with less control (than it would have with an acquisition) since governance is shared between two independent entities. Also, there is a limit to the potential upside for each partner because returns must be shared as well. Finally, with internal development, a firm is able to capture all of the value from its initiatives (as opposed to sharing it with a merger or alliance partner). However, diversification by means of internal development can be very time-consuming—a disadvantage that becomes even more important in fast-paced competitive environments.

Finally, some managerial behaviors may serve to erode shareholder returns. Among these are "growth for growth's sake," egotism, and antitakeover tactics. As we discussed, some of these issues—particularly antitakeover tactics—raise ethical considerations because the managers of the firm are not acting in the best interests of the shareholders.

Summary Review Questions

1. Discuss how managers can create value for their firm through diversification efforts.
2. What are some of the reasons that many diversification efforts fail to achieve desired outcomes?
3. How can companies benefit from related diversification? Unrelated diversification? What are some of the key concepts that can explain such success?
4. What are some of the important ways in which a firm can restructure a business?
5. Discuss some of the various means that firms can use to diversify. What are the pros and cons associated with each of these?
6. Discuss some of the actions that managers may engage in to erode shareholder value.

Key Terms

related diversification, 194
economies of scope, 194
core competencies, 195
sharing activities, 196
market power, 198
vertical integration, 200
transaction cost
   perspective, 204

parenting advantage, 205
restructuring, 205
portfolio management, 206
acquisitions, 210
mergers, 210
divestment, 214
strategic alliances, 214
joint ventures, 214

Experiential Exercise

Time Warner (formerly AOL Time Warner) is a firm that follows a strategy of related diversification. Evaluate its success (or lack thereof) with regard to how well it has: (1) built on core competencies, (2) shared infrastructures, and (3) increased market power.

Application Questions Exercises

1. What were some of the largest mergers and acquisitions over the last two years? What was the rationale for these actions? Do you think they will be successful? Explain.
2. Discuss some examples from business practice in which an executive's actions appear to be in his or her self-interest rather than the corporation's well-being.
3. Discuss some of the challenges that managers must overcome in making strategic alliances successful. What are some strategic alliances with which you are familiar? Were they successful or not? Explain.
4. Use the Internet and select a company that has recently undertaken diversification into new product markets. What do you feel were some of the reasons for this diversification (e.g., leveraging core competencies, sharing infrastructures)?

Ethics Questions

1. In recent years there has been a rash of corporate downsizing and layoffs. Do you feel that such actions raise ethical considerations? Why or why not?
2. What are some of the ethical issues that arise when managers act in a manner that is counter to their firm's best interests? What are the long-term implications for both the firms and the managers themselves?

Rationale for Related Diversification	Successful/Unsuccessful?	Why?
1. Build on core competencies		
2. Share infrastructures		
3. Increase market power		

References

1. For a detailed discussion of the phenomenon of winner's curse, refer to Thaler, R. H. 1992. *The Winner's Curse*. The Free Press: New York.

2. This example draws upon Tully, S. 2006. The (second) worst deal ever. *Fortune,* October 2006: 102–119; and Levenson, E. 2006. Buyer's remorse. *Fortune,* October 16: 12.

3. Dr. G. William Schwert, University of Rochester study cited in Pare, T. P. 1994. The new merger boom. *Fortune*. November 28: 96.

4. Lipin, S. & Deogun, N. 2000. Big mergers of the 1990's prove disappointing to shareholders. *The Wall Street Journal*. October 30: C1.

5. Pare, T. P. 1994. The new merger boom. *Fortune,* November 28: 96.

6. Ghosn, C. 2006. Inside the alliance: The win–win nature of a unique business mode. *Address to the Detroit Economic Club,* November 16.

7. Our framework draws upon a variety of sources, including Goold, M., & Campbell, A. 1998. Desperately seeking synergy. *Harvard Business Review,* 76(5): 131–143; Porter, M. E. 1987. From advantage to corporate strategy. *Harvard Business Review,* 65(3): 43–59; and Hitt, M. A., Ireland, R. D., & Hoskisson, R. E. 2001. *Strategic management: competitiveness and globalization* (4th ed.). Cincinnati, OH: South-Western.

8. Collis, D. J., & Montgomery, C. A. 1987. *Corporate strategy: Resources and the scope of the firm.* New York: McGraw-Hill.

9. This imagery of the corporation as a tree and related discussion draws on Prahalad, C. K., & Hamel, G. 1990. The core competence of the corporation. *Harvard Business Review,* 68(3): 79–91. Parts of this section also draw on Picken, J. C., & Dess, G. G. 1997. *Mission critical:* chap. 5. Burr Ridge, IL: Irwin Professional Publishing.

10. This section draws on Prahalad & Hamel, op. cit.; and Porter, op. cit.

11. A recent study that investigates the relationship between a firm's technology resources, diversification, and performance can be found in Miller, D. J. 2004. Firms' technological resources and the performance effects of diversification. A longitudinal study. *Strategic Management Journal,* 25: 1097–1119.

12. Collis & Montgomery, op. cit.

13. Henricks, M. 1994. VF seeks global brand dominance. *Apparel Industry Magazine,* August: 21–40; VF Corporation. 1993. First quarter corporate summary report. *1993 VF Annual Report.*

14. Hill, A., & Hargreaves, D. 2001. Turbulent times for GE-Honeywell deal. *Financial Times,* February 28: 26.

15. Lowry, T. 2001. Media. *BusinessWeek,* January 8: 100–101.

16. The Tribune Company. 1999. *Annual report.*

17. This section draws on Hrebiniak, L. G., & Joyce, W. F. 1984. *Implementing strategy.* New York: MacMillan; and Oster, S. M. 1994. *Modern competitive analysis.* New York: Oxford University Press.

18. The discussion of the benefits and costs of vertical integration draws on Hax, A. C., & Majluf, N. S. 1991. *The strategy concept and process: A pragmatic approach:* 139. Englewood Cliffs, NJ: Prentice Hall.

19. Fahey, J. 2005. Gray winds. *Forbes*. January 10: 143.

20. This discussion draws on Oster, op. cit.; and Harrigan, K. 1986. Matching vertical integration strategies to competitive conditions. *Strategic Management Journal,* 7(6): 535–556.

21. For a scholarly explanation on how transaction costs determine the boundaries of a firm, see Oliver E. Williamson's pioneering books *Markets and Hierarchies: Analysis and Antitrust Implications* (New York: Free Press, 1975) and *The Economic Institutions of Capitalism* (New York: Free Press, 1985).

22. Campbell, A., Goold, M., & Alexander, M. 1995. Corporate strategy: The quest for parenting advantage. *Harvard Business Review,* 73(2): 120–132; and Picken & Dess, op. cit.

23. Anslinger, P. A., & Copeland, T. E. 1996. Growth through acquisition: A fresh look. *Harvard Business Review,* 74(1): 126–135.

24. Campbell et al., op. cit.

25. This section draws on Porter, op. cit.; and Hambrick, D. C. 1985. Turnaround strategies. In Guth, W. D. (Ed.). *Handbook of business strategy:* 10-1–10-32. Boston: Warren, Gorham & Lamont.

26. There is an important delineation between companies that are operated for a long-term profit and those that are bought and sold for short-term gains. The latter are sometimes referred to as "holding companies" and are generally more concerned about financial issues than strategic issues.

27. Lenzner, R. 2007. High on Loews. *Forbes,* February 26: 98–102.

28. Casico. W. F. 2002. Strategies for responsible restructuring. *Academy of Management Executive,* 16(3): 80–91; and Singh, H. 1993. Challenges in researching

corporate restructuring. *Journal of Management Studies,* 30(1): 147–172.

29. Cusack, M. 1987. *Hanson Trust: A review of the company and its prospects.* London: Hoare Govett.

30. Hax & Majluf, op. cit. By 1979, 45 percent of Fortune 500 companies employed some form of portfolio analysis, according to Haspelagh, P. 1982. Portfolio planning: Uses and limits. *Harvard Busines Review,* 60: 58–73. A later study conducted in 1993 found that over 40 percent of the respondents used portfolio analysis techniques, but the level of usage was expected to increase to more than 60 percent in the near future: Rigby, D. K. 1994. Managing the management tools. *Planning Review,* September–October: 20–24.

31. Goold, M., & Luchs, K. 1993. Why diversify? Four decades of management thinking. *Academy of Management Executive,* 7(3): 7–25.

32. Other approaches include the industry attractiveness–business strength matrix developed jointly by General Electric and McKinsey and Company, the life-cycle matrix developed by Arthur D. Little, and the profitability matrix proposed by Marakon. For an extensive review, refer to Hax & Majluf, op. cit.: 182–194.

33. Porter, op. cit.: 49–52.

34. Collis, D. J. 1995. Portfolio planning at Ciba-Geigy and the Newport investment proposal. Harvard Business School Case No. 9-795-040. Novartis AG was created in 1996 by the merger of Ciba-Geigy and Sandoz.

35. Buzzell, R. D., & Gale, B. T. 1987. *The PIMS Principles: Linking Strategy to Performance.* New York: Free Press; and Miller, A., & Dess, G. G. 1996. *Strategic Management,* (2nd ed.). New York: McGraw-Hill.

36. Seeger, J. 1984. Reversing the images of BCG's growth share matrix. *Strategic Management Journal,* 5(1): 93–97.

37. Picken & Dess, op. cit.; Cabot Corporation. 2001. 10-Q filing, Securities and Exchange Commission, May 14.

38. Koudsi, S. 2001. Remedies for an economic hangover. *Fortune,* June 25: 130–139.

39. Coy, P., Thornton, E., Arndt, M., & Grow, B. 2005. Shake, rattle, and merge. *BusinessWeek,* January 10: 32–35; and Anonymous. 2005. Love is in the air. *Economist,* February 5: 9.

40. For an interesting study of the relationship between mergers and a firm's product-market strategies, refer to Krisnan, R. A., Joshi, S., & Krishnan, H. 2004. The influence of mergers on firms' product-mix strategies. *Strategic Management Journal,* 25: 587–611.

41. Carey, D., moderator. 2000. A CEO roundtable on making mergers succeed. *Harvard Business Review,* 78(3): 146.

42. Shinal, J. 2001. Can Mike Volpi make Cisco sizzle again? *BusinessWeek,* February 26: 102–104; Kambil, A. Eselius, E. D., & Monteiro, K. A. 2000. Fast venturing: The quick way to start Web businesses. *Sloan Management Review,* 41(4): 55–67; and Elstrom, P. 2001. Sorry, Cisco: The old answers won't work. *BusinessWeek,* April 30: 39.

43. Like many high-tech firms during the economic slump that began in mid-2000, Cisco Systems has experienced declining performance. On April 16, 2001, it announced that its revenues for the quarter closing April 30 would drop 5 percent from a year earlier—and a stunning 30 percent from the previous three months—to about $4.7 billion. Furthermore, Cisco announced that it would lay off 8,500 employees and take an enormous $2.5 billion charge to write down inventory. By late October 2002, its stock was trading at around $10, down significantly from its 52-week high of $70. Elstrom, op. cit.: 39.

44. Coy, P., Thornton, E., Arndt, M. & Grow, B. 2005, Shake, rattle, and merge. *BusinessWeek,* January 10: 32–35; and, Anonymous. 2005. The rise of the superbrands. *Economist.* February 5: 63–65; and, Sellers, P. 2005. It was a no-brainer. *Fortune,* February 21: 96–102.

45. For a discussion of the trend toward consolidation of the steel industry and how Lakshmi Mittal is becoming a dominant player, read Reed, S., & Arndt, M. 2004. The Raja of steel. *BusinessWeek,* December 20: 50–52.

46. Barrett, A. 2001. Drugs. *BusinessWeek,* January 8: 112–113.

47. Coy, P., et al. 2005, op. cit.

48. Whalen, C. J., Pascual, A. M., Lowery, T., & Muller, J. 2001. The top 25 managers. *BusinessWeek,* January 8: 63.

49. This discussion draws upon Rappaport, A., & Sirower, M. L. 1999. Stock or cash? The trade-offs for buyers and sellers in mergers and acquisitions. *Harvard Business Review,* 77(6): 147–158; and Lipin, S., & Deogun, N. 2000. Big mergers of 90s prove disappointing to shareholders. *Wall Street Journal,* October 30: C1.

50. Mouio, A. (Ed.). 1998. Unit of one. *Fast Company,* September: 82.

51. Ibid.

52. Porter, M. E. 1987. From competitive advantage to corporate strategy. *Harvard Business Review,* 65(3): 43.

53. This was originally termed a "merger of equals." However, as noted in *The Economist* and elsewhere, it has turned out to be "just another disastrous car-industry takeover." For an interesting, recent discussion, see Anonymous. 2007. Dis-assembly. *The Economist.* February 17: 63–64.

54. The divestiture of a business which is undertaken in order to enable managers to better focus on its core business has been termed "downscoping." Refer to Hitt, M. A., Harrison, J. S., & Ireland, R. D. 2001. *Mergers and acquisitions: A guide to creating value for stakeholders*. Oxford Press: New York.

55. Sirmon, D. G., Hitt, M. A., & Ireland, R. D. 2007. Managing firm resources in dynamic environments to create value: Looking inside the black box. *Academy of Management Review,* 32(1): 273–292.

56. For scholarly perspectives on the role of learning in creating value in strategic alliances, refer to Anard, B. N., & Khanna, T. 2000. Do firms learn to create value? *Strategic Management Journal,* 12(3): 295–317; and Vermeulen, F., & Barkema, H. P. 2001. Learning through acquisitions. *Academy of Management Journal,* 44(3): 457–476.

57. For a detailed discussion of transaction cost economics in strategic alliances, read Reuer, J. J., & Arno, A. 2007. Strategic alliance contracts: Dimensions and determinants of contractual complexity. *Strategic Management Journal,* 28(3): 313–330.

58. This section draws on Hutt, M. D., Stafford, E. R., Walker, B. A., & Reingen, P. H. 2000. Case study: Defining the strategic alliance. *Sloan Management Review,* 41(2): 51–62; and Walters, B. A., Peters, S., & Dess, G. G. 1994. Strategic alliances and joint ventures: Making them work. *Business Horizons,* 4: 5–10.

59. Edmondson, G., & Reinhardt, A. 2001. From niche player to Goliath. *BusinessWeek,* March 12: 94–96.

60. For an institutional theory perspective on strategic alliances, read: Dacin, M. T., Oliver, C., & Roy, J. P. 2007. The legitimacy of strategic alliances: An institutional perspective. *Strategic Management Journal,* 28(2): 169–187.

61. Clayton, V. 2000. Lourdes Pizana's passions: Confessions and lessons of an accidental business owner. *E-Merging Business,* Fall–Winter: 73–75.

62. Porter, op. cit.: 43–59.

63. Angwin, J. S., & Wingfield, N. 2000. How Jay Walker built WebHouse on a theory that he couldn't prove. *The Wall Street Journal,* October 16: A1, A8.

64. *BusinessWeek.* 2003. The fallen. January 13: 80–82.

65. The Jack Welch example draws upon Sellers, P. 2001. Get over yourself. *Fortune,* April 30: 76–88.

66. Polek, D. 2002. The rise and fall of Dennis Kozlowski. *BusinessWeek,* December 23: 64–77.

67. *BusinessWeek.* 2003. op. cit.: 80.

68. This section draws on Weston, J. F., Besley, S., & Brigham, E. F. 1996. *Essentials of Managerial Finance* (11th ed.): 18–20. Fort Worth, TX: Dryden Press, Harcourt Brace.

chapter 7

International Strategy:

Creating Value in Global Markets

>learning objectives

After reading this chapter, you should have a good understanding of:

LO1 The importance of international expansion as a viable diversification strategy.

LO2 The sources of national advantage; that is, why an industry in a given country is more (or less) successful than the same industry in another country.

LO3 The motivations (or benefits) and the risks associated with international expansion, including the emerging trend for greater offshoring and outsourcing activity.

LO4 The two opposing forces—cost reduction and adaptation to local markets—that firms face when entering international markets.

LO5 The advantages and disadvantages associated with each of the four basic strategies: international, global, multidomestic, and transnational.

LO6 The difference between regional companies and truly global companies.

LO7 The four basic types of entry strategies and the relative benefits and risks associated with each of them.

*t*he global marketplace provides many opportunities for firms to increase their revenue base and their profitability. Furthermore, in today's knowledge-intensive economy, there is the potential to create advantages by leveraging firm knowledge when crossing national boundaries to do business. At the same time, however, there are pitfalls and risks that firms must avoid in order to be successful. In this chapter we will provide insights on how to be successful and create value when diversifying into global markets.

After some introductory comments on the global economy, we address the question: What explains the level of success of a given industry in a given country? To provide a framework for analysis, we draw on Michael Porter's "diamond of national advantage," in which he identified four factors that help to explain performance differences.

In the second section of the chapter, we shift our focus to the level of the firm and discuss some of the major motivations and risks associated with international expansion. Recognizing such potential benefits and risks enables managers to better assess the growth and profit potential in a given country. We also address important issues associated with a topic of growing interest in the international marketplace—offshoring and outsourcing.

Next, in the third section—the largest in this chapter—we address how firms can attain competitive advantages in the global marketplace. We discuss two opposing forces firms face when entering foreign markets: cost reduction and local adaptation. Depending on the intensity of each of these forces, they should select among four basic strategies: international, global, multidomestic, and transnational. We discuss both the strengths and limitations of each of these strategies. We also present a recent perspective which posits that even the largest multinational firms are more regional than global even today.

The final section addresses the four categories of entry strategies that firms may choose in entering foreign markets. These strategies vary along a continuum from low investment, low control (exporting) to high investment, high control (wholly owned subsidiaries and greenfield ventures). We discuss the pros and cons associated with each.

Learning from Mistakes

Wal-Mart, the world's largest retailer, certainly didn't have a good year in 2006.[1] There were executive turnover problems, such as the resignation of Sam's Clubs marketing head Mark Goodman and the embarrassing firing of Julie Roehm, the young advertising whiz who Wal-Mart had hired away from DaimlerChrysler. Also, there were ongoing legal problems—a Philadelphia jury ordered Wal-Mart to pay $78 million to a class of 185,000 workers who claimed that they were denied breaks and forced to work off the clock.

There were also business setbacks: same-store sales were only up 1.6 percent (while those of Costco and Target were up 9 percent and 4.1 percent, respectively). Wal-Mart's stock was flat in an otherwise strong year for equities. In fact, from January 2000 (when Lee Scott took over for David Glass as CEO) to early 2007, the stock has fallen 22 percent. *[continued]*

The company has also had its share of setbacks overseas. Wal-Mart suffered a $900 million loss after its forays into Germany and South Korea failed. Let's take a closer look at what might explain its 2006 exit from South Korea—a market it entered in 1998.

Wal-Mart was never successful in South Korea. They were slow in opening stores—failing not only to win customers but also to build enough market share to press suppliers on pricing. The core of their problem was an inability to adapt to local markets. As noted by Na Hong Seok, an analyst in Seoul: "Wal-Mart is a typical example of a global giant who has failed to localize its operations in South Korea."

Wal-Mart put off South Korean consumers by sticking to Western marketing strategies that concentrated on dry goods, from electronics to clothing. Their rivals, on the other hand, focused on food and beverages, the segment that specialists say attracts South Koreans to hypermarkets. In South Korea, fresh, quality food is a key ingredient of success. It typically generates half of a store's revenues. To make matters worse, one of Wal-Mart's competitors, E-Mart, even owned its own farms that supplied its stores.

Wal-Mart also ran into problems with a membership approach that was similar to the one used by its Sam's warehouses. According to Song Kye-Hyon, a financial analyst: "It turned out to be a strategic flaw of Wal-Mart when it first adopted the Western policy of the membership where customers were required to pay a membership fee for shopping privileges."

Further, Wal-Mart had difficulty overcoming mechanisms that some of its rivals had developed to create greater customer loyalty. Some employed green-capped young men who helped bring the shopping carts to the customers' cars in the parking lot. Further, rivals operated shuttle buses to go through neighborhoods to pick up customers and drop them off at their homes after they completed their shopping. Simply put, Wal-Mart did not adapt to the local market conditions by investing the resources necessary to achieve some level of parity on such customer-service initiatives.

In the end, Wal-Mart continued to flounder until it sold all 16 of its South Korean outlets in May 2006 to Shinsgae, a local retailer. Consistent with its long-term problems in the South Korean market, Wal-Mart lost $10.4 million on revenues of $787 million in 2005—its last full year of operations in South Korea. Wal-Mart's vice chairman, Michael Duke, summed up the situation quite well: "As we continue to focus our efforts where we have the greatest impact on our growth strategy, it became increasingly clear that in South Korea's environment it would be difficult for us to reach the scale we desired."

In this chapter we discuss how firms can create value and achieve competitive advantage in the global marketplace. We also discuss how firms can avoid pitfalls such as those experienced by Wal-Mart in South Korea. In addition, we address factors that can influence a nation's success in a particular industry. In our view, this is an important context in determining how well firms might eventually do when they compete beyond their nation's boundaries.

The Global Economy: A Brief Overview

>LO1
The importance of international expansion as a viable diversification strategy.

Managers face many opportunities and risks when they diversify abroad.[2] The trade among nations has increased dramatically in recent years and it is estimated that by 2015, the trade *across* nations will exceed the trade within nations. In a variety of industries such as semiconductors, automobiles, commercial aircraft, telecommunications, computers, and consumer electronics, it is almost impossible to survive unless firms scan the world for competitors, customers, human resources, suppliers, and technology.[3]

GE's wind energy business illustrates the benefits of tapping into talent around the world. The firm has built research centers in China, Germany, India, and the United States.

"We did it," says CEO Jeffrey Immelt, "to access the best brains everywhere in the world." All four centers have played a key role in GE's development of huge 92-ton turbines. How did each contribute?[4]

- Chinese researchers in Shanghai designed the microprocessors that control the pitch of the blade.
- Mechanical engineers from India (Bangladore) devised mathematical models to maximize the efficiency of materials in the turbine.
- Power-systems experts in the United States (Niskayuna, New York), which has researchers from 55 countries, do the design work.
- Technicians in Munich, Germany have created a "smart" turbine that can calculate wind speeds and signal sensors in other turbines to pitch their blades to produce maximum electricity.

The rise of globalization—meaning the rise of market capitalism around the world—has undeniably contributed to the economic boom in America's New Economy, where knowledge is the key source of competitive advantage and value creation. It is estimated that it has brought phone service to about 300 million households in developing nations and a transfer of nearly $2 trillion from rich countries to poor countries through equity, bond investments, and commercial loans.[5]

Without doubt, there have been extremes in the effect of global capitalism on national economies and poverty levels around the world.[6] Clearly, the economies of East Asia have attained rapid growth, but there has been comparatively little progress in other areas of the world. For example, income in Latin America grew by only 6 percent in the past two decades when the continent was opening up to global capitalism. Average incomes in sub-Saharan Africa and the old Eastern European bloc have actually declined. Indeed, the World Bank estimates that the number of people living on $1 per day has *increased* to 1.3 billion over the past decade.

Such disparities in wealth among nations raise an important question: Why do some countries and their citizens enjoy the fruits of global capitalism while others are mired in poverty? Or why do some governments make the best use of inflows of foreign investment and know-how and others do not? There are many explanations. Among these are the need of governments to have track records of business-friendly policies to attract multinationals and local entrepreneurs to train workers, invest in modern technology, and nurture local suppliers and managers. Also, it means carefully managing the broader economic factors in an economy, such as interest rates, inflation, and unemployment, as well as a good legal system that protects property rights, strong educational systems, and a society where prosperity is widely shared.

The above policies are the type that East Asia—in locations such as Hong Kong, Taiwan, South Korea, and Singapore—has employed to evolve from the sweatshop economies of the 1960s and 1970s to industrial powers today. On the other hand, many countries have moved in the other direction. For example, in Guatemala only 52.0 percent of males complete fifth grade and an astonishing 39.8 percent of the population subsists on less than $1 per day.[7] (By comparison, the corresponding numbers for South Korea are 98 percent and less than 2 percent, respectively.)

Strategy Spotlight 7.1 provides an interesting perspective on global trade—marketing to the "bottom of the pyramid." This refers to the practice of a multinational firm targeting its goods and services to the nearly 5 billion poor people in the world who inhabit developing countries. Collectively, this represents a very large market with $14 trillion in purchasing power.

Next, we will address in more detail the question of why some nations and their industries are more competitive. This establishes an important context or setting for the remainder of the chapter. After we discuss why some *nations and their industries* outperform others, we will be better able to address the various strategies that *firms* can take to create competitive advantage when they expand internationally.

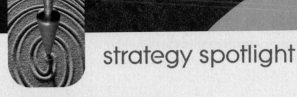

Marketing to the "Bottom of the Pyramid"

Many executives wrongly believe that profitable opportunities to sell consumer goods exist only in countries where income levels are high. Even when they expand internationally, they often tend to limit their marketing to only the affluent segments within the developing countries. Such narrow conceptualizations of the market cause them to ignore the vast opportunities that exist at "the bottom of the pyramid," according to University of Michigan professor C. K. Prahalad. The *bottom of the pyramid* refers to the nearly 5 billion poor people who inhabit the developing countries. Surprisingly, they represent $14 trillion in purchasing power! And they are looking for products and services that can improve the quality of their lives such as clean energy, personal-care products, lighting, and medicines. Multinationals are missing out on growth opportunities if they ignore this vast segment of the market.

Other innovative firms have found creative ways to serve the poor and still make a profit. Grameen Bank in Bangladesh is very different from the money center banks of London or New York. Pioneers of the concept of microcredit, Grameen Bank (whose founder, Muhammad Yunus, won the 2006 Nobel Peace Prize) extends small loans— sometimes as small as $20—to thousands of struggling micro-entrepreneurs who have no collateral to offer. The value of microcredit loans has soared from $4 million to $1.3 billion between 1996 and 2006. Not only are their loan recovery rates comparable to big banks, but they are also changing the lives of thousands of people while making a profit as well. Casas Bahias, the Brazilian retailer, has built a $2.5 billion-a-year chain selling to the poor who live in the *favelas,* the illegal shanty towns. Another amazing example is Aravind Eye Care, an Indian hospital that specializes in cataract surgeries. Today, they are the largest eye care facility in the world, performing more than 200,000 surgeries per year. The secret of their volume: The surgeries cost only about $25! A comparable surgery in the West costs $3,000. And best of all, Aravind has a return on equity of more than 75 percent!

As the above examples demonstrate, in order to sell to the bottom of the pyramid, managers must rethink their costs, quality, scale of operations, and even their use of capital. What prevents managers from selling to this vast market? Often they are victims of their own false assumptions. First, they think that the poor have no purchasing power. But $14 trillion can buy a lot. Second, they assume that poor people have no need for new technologies. We only have to see the demand for cell phones from entrepreneurs who run microbusinesses in villages in India to dispel this myth. Third, they assume that the poor have no use for their products and services. Shampoo, detergents, and banking satisfy universal needs, not just the needs of the rich. Fourth, they assume that managers may not be excited about working in these markets. Recent experience shows that this may be a more exciting environment than dogs fighting for fractions of market shares in the mature markets of the developed countries.

No one is helped by viewing the poor as the wretched of the earth. Instead, they are the latest frontier of opportunity for those who can meet their needs. A vast market that is barely tapped, the bottom of the pyramid offers enormous opportunities.

Sources: Miller, C. C. 2006. Easy money. *Forbes,* November 27: 134–138; Prahalad, C. K. 2004. Why selling to the poor makes for good business. *Fortune,* 150(9): 32–33; Overholt, A. 2005. A new path to profit. *Fast Company,* January: 25–26; and Prahalad, C. K. 2005. *The fortune at the bottom of the pyramid: Eradicating poverty through profits.* Philadelphia: Wharton School Publishing.

---

factor conditions (national advantage)
a nation's position in factors of production.

demand conditions (national advantage)
the nature of home-market demand for the industry's product or service.

Factors Affecting a Nation's Competitiveness

Michael Porter of Harvard University conducted a four-year study in which he and a team of 30 researchers looked at the patterns of competitive success in 10 leading trading nations. He concluded that there are four broad attributes of nations that individually, and as a system, constitute what is termed "the diamond of national advantage." In effect, these attributes jointly determine the playing field that each nation establishes and operates for its industries. These factors are:

- *Factor conditions.* The nation's position in factors of production, such as skilled labor or infrastructure, necessary to compete in a given industry.
- *Demand conditions.* The nature of home-market demand for the industry's product or service.

- *Related and supporting industries.* The presence or absence in the nation of supplier industries and other related industries that are internationally competitive.
- *Firm strategy, structure, and rivalry.* The conditions in the nation governing how companies are created, organized, and managed, as well as the nature of domestic rivalry.

We will now briefly discuss each of these factors.[8] Then we will provide an integrative example—the Indian software industry—to demonstrate how these attributes interact to explain India's high level of competitiveness in this industry.

>LO2
The sources of national advantage; that is, why an industry in a given country is more (or less) successful than the same industry in another country.

Factor Conditions[9]

Classical economics suggests that factors of production such as land, labor, and capital are the building blocks that create usable consumer goods and services.[10] But this tells only part of the story when we consider the global aspects of economic growth. Companies in advanced nations seeking competitive advantage over firms in other nations *create* many of the factors of production. For example, a country or industry dependent on scientific innovation must have a skilled human resource pool to draw upon. This resource pool is not inherited; it is created through investment in industry-specific knowledge and talent. The supporting infrastructure of a country—that is, its transportation and communication systems as well as its banking system—are also critical.

To achieve competitive advantage, factors of production must be developed that are industry and firm specific. In addition, the pool of resources a firm or a country has at its disposal is less important than the speed and efficiency with which these resources are deployed. Thus, firm-specific knowledge and skills created within a country that are rare, valuable, difficult to imitate, and rapidly and efficiently deployed are the factors of production that ultimately lead to a nation's competitive advantage.

For example, the island nation of Japan has little land mass, making the warehouse space needed to store inventory prohibitively expensive. But by pioneering just-in-time inventory management, Japanese companies managed to create a resource from which they gained advantage over companies in other nations that spent large sums to warehouse inventory.

related and supporting industries (national advantage) the presence, absence, and quality in the nation of supplier industries and other related industries that supply services, support, or technology to firms in the industry value chain.

Demand Conditions

Demand conditions refer to the demands that consumers place on an industry for goods and services. Consumers who demand highly specific, sophisticated products and services force firms to create innovative, advanced products and services to meet the demand. This consumer pressure presents challenges to a country's industries. But in response to these challenges, improvements to existing goods and services often result, creating conditions necessary for competitive advantage over firms in other countries.

Demanding consumers push firms to move ahead of companies in other countries where consumers are less demanding and more complacent. Countries with demanding consumers drive firms in that country to meet high standards, upgrade existing products and services, and create innovative products and services. Thus, the conditions of consumer demand influence how firms view a market, with more demanding consumers stimulating advances in products and services. This, in turn, helps a nation's industries to better anticipate future global demand conditions and proactively respond to product and service requirements.

Denmark, for instance, is known for its environmental awareness. Demand from consumers for environmentally safe products has spurred Danish manufacturers to become leaders in water pollution control equipment—products it successfully exported.

firm strategy, structure, and rivalry (national advantage) the conditions in the nation governing how companies are created, organized, and managed, as well as the nature of domestic rivalry.

Related and Supporting Industries

Related and supporting industries enable firms to manage inputs more effectively. For example, countries with a strong supplier base benefit by adding efficiency to downstream activities. A competitive supplier base helps a firm obtain inputs using cost-effective, timely methods, thus reducing manufacturing costs. Also, close working relationships with suppliers provide the potential to develop competitive advantages through joint research and development and the ongoing exchange of knowledge.

Related industries offer similar opportunities through joint efforts among firms. In addition, related industries create the probability that new companies will enter the market, increasing competition and forcing existing firms to become more competitive through efforts such as cost control, product innovation, and novel approaches to distribution. Combined, these give the home country's industries a source of competitive advantage.

In the Italian footwear industry the supporting industries show how they can lead to national competitive advantage. In Italy, shoe manufacturers are geographically located near their suppliers. The manufacturers have ongoing interactions with leather suppliers and learn about new textures, colors, and manufacturing techniques while a shoe is still in the prototype stage. The manufacturers are able to project future demand and gear their factories for new products long before companies in other nations become aware of the new styles. Similarly, geographic proximity of industries related to the pharmaceutical industry (e.g., the dye industry) in Switzerland has given that nation a leadership position in this market, with firms such as Novartis, Hoffman LaRoche, and Sandoz using dyes from local manufacturers in many pharmaceutical products.

Firm Strategy, Structure, and Rivalry

Rivalry is particularly intense in nations with conditions of strong consumer demand, strong supplier bases, and high new entrant potential from related industries. This competitive rivalry in turn increases the efficiency with which firms develop, market, and distribute products and services within the home country. Domestic rivalry thus provides a strong impetus for firms to innovate and find new sources of competitive advantage.

Interestingly, this intense rivalry forces firms to look outside their national boundaries for new markets, setting up the conditions necessary for global competitiveness. Among all the points on Porter's diamond of national advantage, domestic rivalry is perhaps the strongest indicator of global competitive success. Firms that have experienced intense domestic competition are more likely to have designed strategies and structures that allow them to successfully compete in world markets.

In the United States, for example, intense rivalry has spurred companies such as Dell Computer to find innovative ways to produce and distribute its products. This is largely a result of competition from IBM and Hewlett-Packard.

Strategy Spotlight 7.2 discusses India's software industry. It provides an integrative example of how Porter's "diamond" can help to explain the relative degree of success of an industry in a given country. Exhibit 7.1 illustrates India's "software diamond."

Concluding Comment on Factors Affecting a Nation's Competitiveness

Porter drew his conclusions based on case histories of firms in more than 100 industries. Despite the differences in strategies employed by successful global competitors, a common theme emerged: Firms that succeeded in global markets had first succeeded in intensely competitive home markets. We can conclude that competitive advantage for global firms typically grows out of relentless, continuing improvement, and innovation.

Now that we have talked about the important role that nations play in international strategy, let's turn to the level of the individual firm.[11] In the next section, we will discuss a company's motivations and the risks associated with international expansion.

India and the Diamond of National Advantage

Consider the following facts:

- SAP, the German software company, has developed new applications for notebook PCs at its 500-engineer Bangalore facility.

- General Electric plans to invest $100 million and hire 2,600 scientists to create the world's largest research and development lab in Bangalore, India.

- Microsoft plans to invest $400 million in new research partnerships in India.

- Over one-fifth of Fortune 1000 companies outsource their software requirements to firms in India.

Sources: Kripalani, M. 2002. Calling Bangalore: Multinationals are making it a hub for high-tech research *BusinessWeek*, November 25: 52–54; Kapur, D., & Ramamurti, R. 2001. India's emerging competitive advantage in services. 2001. *Academy of Management Executive*, 15(2): 20–33; World Bank. *World development report:* 6. New York: Oxford University Press. Reuters. 2001. Oracle in India push, taps software talent. *Washington Post Online*, July 3.

- McKinsey & Co. projects that the Indian software and services industry will be an $87 billion business by 2008; $50 billion of this will be exported.

- For the past decade, the Indian software industry has grown at a 50 percent annual rate.

- More than 800 firms in India are involved in software services as their primary activity.

- Software and information technology firms in India are projected to employ 2.2 million people by 2008.

What is causing such global interest in India's software services industry? Porter's diamond of national advantage helps clarify this question. See Exhibit 7.1.

First, *factor conditions* are conducive to the rise of India's software industry. Through investment in human resource development with a focus on industry-specific knowledge, India's universities and software firms have literally created this essential factor of production. For example, India produces the second largest annual output of scientists and engineers in the world, behind only the United States. In a knowledge-intensive industry *(continued)*

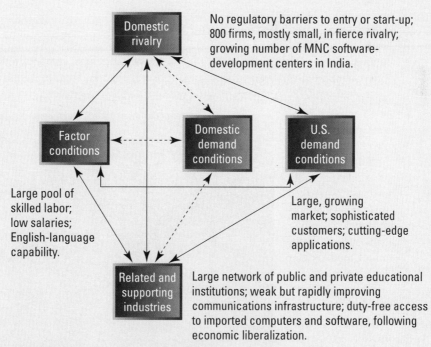

No regulatory barriers to entry or start-up; 800 firms, mostly small, in fierce rivalry; growing number of MNC software-development centers in India.

Large pool of skilled labor; low salaries; English-language capability.

Large, growing market; sophisticated customers; cutting-edge applications.

Large network of public and private educational institutions; weak but rapidly improving communications infrastructure; duty-free access to imported computers and software, following economic liberalization.

Note: Dashed lines represent weaker interactions.

Exhibit 7.1 India's Diamond in Software

Source: From Kampur D. and Ramamurti R., "India's Emerging Competition Advantage in Services," *Academy of Management Executive: The Thinking Manager's Source.* Copyright © 2001 by Academy of Management. Reproduced with permission of Academy of Management via Copyright Clearance Center.

(continued) such as software, development of human resources is fundamental to both domestic and global success.

Second, *demand conditions* require that software firms stay on the cutting edge of technological innovation. India has already moved toward globalization of its software industry; consumer demand conditions in developed nations such as Germany, Denmark, parts of Southeast Asia, and the United States created the consumer demand necessary to propel India's software makers toward sophisticated software solutions.*

Third, India has the *supplier base as well as the related industries* needed to drive competitive rivalry and enhance competitiveness. In particular, information technology (IT)

* Although India's success cannot be explained in terms of its home market demand (according to Porter's model), the nature of the industry enables software to be transferred among different locations simultaneously by way of communications links. Thus, competitiveness of markets outside India can be enhanced without a physical presence in those markets.

hardware prices declined rapidly in the 1990s. Furthermore, rapid technological change in IT hardware meant that latecomers like India were not locked into older-generation technologies. Thus, both the IT hardware and software industries could "leapfrog" older technologies. In addition, relationships among knowledge workers in these IT hardware and software industries offer the social structure for ongoing knowledge exchange, promoting further enhancement of existing products. Further infrastructure improvements are occurring rapidly.

Fourth, with over 800 firms in the software services industry in India, *intense rivalry forces firms to develop competitive strategies and structures.* Although firms like TCS, Infosys, and Wipro have become large, they were quite small only five years ago. And dozens of small and midsized companies are aspiring to catch up. This intense rivalry is one of the primary factors driving Indian software firms to develop overseas distribution channels, as predicted by Porter's diamond of national advantage.

International Expansion: A Company's Motivations and Risks

Motivations for International Expansion

There are many motivations for a company to pursue international expansion. The most obvious one is to *increase the size of potential markets* for a firm's products and services.[12] By early 2007, the world's population exceeded 6.5 billion, with the United States representing less than 5 percent. Exhibit 7.2 lists the population of the United States compared to other major markets abroad.

Many multinational firms are intensifying their efforts to market their products and services to countries such as India and China as the ranks of their middle class have increased over the past decade. These include Procter & Gamble's success in achieving a 50 percent share in China's shampoo market as well as

● Starbucks, based in Seattle, Washington, has aggressively expanded its international operations. By 2007 it had several thousand coffeehouses in 36 countries outside of the United States. Above is one of its coffeehouses in Bangkok, Thailand.

Exhibit 7.2
**Populations of Selected
Nations and the World**

Country	March 2007 (in millions) (estimated)
China	1,320
India	1,107
United States	300
Japan	127
Germany	82
World Total	6,580

Source: www.geohive.com/global/pop_data2.php.

PepsiCo's impressive inroads in the Indian soft-drink market.[13] Let's take a brief look at China's emerging middle class:[14]

- China's middle class has finally attained a critical mass—between 35 million and 200 million people, depending on what definition is used. The larger number is preferred by Fan Gong, director of China's National Economic Research Institute, who fixes the lower boundary of "middle" as a family income of $10,000.
- The central government's emphasis on science and technology has boosted the rapid development of higher education, which is the incubator of the middle class.
- China may be viewed as a new example of economies of scale. Many American companies already have factories in China exporting goods. Now that there is a domestic market to go along with the export market, those factories can increase their output with little additional cost. That is one reason why many foreign companies' profits in China have been so strong in recent years.

Expanding a firm's global presence also automatically increases its scale of operations, providing it with a larger revenue and asset base. As we noted in Chapter 5 in discussing overall cost leadership strategies, such an increase in revenues and asset base potentially enables a firm to *attain economies of scale.* This provides multiple benefits. One advantage is the spreading of fixed costs such as research and development over a larger volume of production. Examples include the sale of Boeing's commercial aircraft and Microsoft's operating systems in many foreign countries.

A second advantage would be *reducing the costs of research and development as well as operating costs.* Recall, Microsoft's software development operations and other firms in talent-rich India (see Strategy Spotlight 7.2). A final advantage would be the attainment of greater purchasing power by pooling purchases. For example, as McDonald's increases the number of outlets it has all over the world, it can place larger orders for equipment and supplies, thus increasing its bargaining power with suppliers.

International expansion can also *extend the life cycle of a product* that is in its maturity stage in a firm's home country but that has greater demand potential elsewhere. As we noted in Chapter 5, products (and industries) generally go through a four-stage life cycle of introduction, growth, maturity, and decline. In recent decades, U.S. soft-drink producers such as Coca-Cola and PepsiCo have aggressively pursued international markets to attain levels of growth that simply would not be available in the United States. Similarly, personal computer manufacturers such as Dell and Hewlett-Packard have sought out foreign markets to offset the growing saturation in the U.S. market.

Finally, international expansion can enable a firm to *optimize the physical location for every activity in its value chain.* Recall from our discussions in Chapters 3 and 5 that the value chain represents the various activities in which all firms must engage to produce products and services. They include primary activities, such as inbound logistics, operations, and marketing, as well as support activities, such as procurement, research and development, and human resource management. All firms have to make critical decisions as to where each activity will take place.[15] Optimizing the location for every activity in the value chain can yield one or more of three strategic advantages: performance enhancement, cost reduction, and risk reduction. We will now discuss each of these.

Performance Enhancement   Microsoft's decision to establish a corporate research laboratory in Cambridge, England, is an example of a location decision that was guided mainly by the goal of building and sustaining world-class excellence in selected value-creating activities.[16] This strategic decision provided Microsoft with access to outstanding technical and professional talent. Location decisions can affect the quality with which any activity is performed in terms of the availability of needed talent, speed of learning, and the quality of external and internal coordination.

Cost Reduction   Two location decisions founded largely on cost-reduction considerations are (1) Nike's decision to source the manufacture of athletic shoes from Asian countries such as China, Vietnam, and Indonesia, and (2) the decision of many multinational companies to set up production operations just south of the United States–Mexico border to access lower-cost labor. These operations are called *maquiladoras*. Such location decisions can affect the cost structure in terms of local manpower and other resources, transportation and logistics, and government incentives and the local tax structure.

Performance enhancement and cost-reduction benefits parallel the business-level strategies (discussed in Chapter 5) of differentiation and overall cost leadership. They can at times be attained simultaneously. Consider our example in the previous section on the Indian software industry. When Oracle set up a development operation in that country, the company benefited both from lower labor costs and operational expenses as well as from performance enhancements realized through the hiring of superbly talented professionals.

Managing across borders can lead to challenging ethical dilemmas. One issue that has received a good deal of attention in the recent business press is the issue of child labor. Strategy Spotlight 7.3 discusses how two multinational companies have taken different approaches to address this issue.

Risk Reduction   Given the erratic swings in the exchange ratios between the U.S. dollar and the Japanese yen (in relation to each other as well as other major currencies), an important basis for cost competition between Ford and Toyota has been their relative ingenuity at managing currency risks. One of the ways for such competitors to manage currency risks has been to spread the high-cost elements of their manufacturing operations across a few select and carefully chosen locations around the world. Location decisions such as these can affect the overall risk profile of the firm with respect to currency, economic, and political risks.[17]

Potential Risks of International Expansion

When a company expands its international operations, it does so to increase its profits or revenues. As with any other investment, however, there are also potential risks.[18] To help companies assess the risk of entering foreign markets, rating systems have been developed to evaluate political, economic, and financial and credit risks.[19] *Euromoney* magazine publishes a semiannual "Country Risk Rating" that evaluates political, economic, and other risks that entrants potentially face. Exhibit 7.3 depicts a sample of country risk ratings, published by the World Bank, from the 178 countries that *Euromoney* evaluates. Note that the lower the score, the higher the country's expected level of risk.

strategy spotlight

Child Labor: How Two Companies Have Addressed This Issue

It is interesting to consider how multinational companies have taken different approaches to address the issue of child labor in their overseas operations. Nike, for example, has revised its code of conduct a few times since 1992, including increasing the minimum age from 14 to 18 years for footwear factory workers and from 14 to 16 for equipment and apparel, which is quite a bit higher than other company codes and the International Labor Organization's (ILO) convention. The company also has started an internal compliance program, supplemented with external monitoring. However, this does not seem to have silenced the staunchest critics. Nike's Web site reflects the way in which the company tries to openly address this critique, providing ample information about the monitoring of facili-

Source: Kolk, A., & Tulder, R. V. 2004. Ethics in international business: Multinational approaches to child labor. *Journal of World Business*, 39: 49–60.

ties and the dilemmas the company faces after the introduction of its latest code.

Chiquita Banana almost completely follows the SA 8000 standard, including all references to international conventions, but with a few modifications, primarily to take account of workplace issues specific to agriculture. (The SA 8000 standard is developed by the Council on Economic Priorities Accreditation Agency and is widely recognized and accepted. It is based on ILO and United Nations conventions.) The company's strict child labor provisions do not apply to family farms or to small-scale holdings in the seasonal, nonbanana business, which do not regularly employ hired workers. This is also meant to allow for employment of a farmer's own children in seasonal activities. In line with its standard, Chiquita Banana tries to address the problem associated with children found to be working in supplying factories by giving "adequate support to enable such children to attend and remain in school until no longer a child."

Next we will discuss the four main types of risk: political risk, economic risk, currency risk, and management risk.

Political and Economic Risk   Generally speaking, the business climate in the United States is very favorable. However, some countries around the globe may be hazardous to

Rank	Country	Total Risk Assessment	Economic Performance	Political Risk	Total of Debt Indicators	Total of Credit and Access to Finance Indicators
1	Luxembourg	99.51	25.00	24.51	20.00	30.00
2	Switzerland	98.84	23.84	25.00	20.00	30.00
3	United States	98.37	23.96	24.41	20.00	30.00
40	China	71.27	18.93	16.87	19.73	15.74
55	Poland	57.12	18.56	13.97	9.36	15.23
63	Vietnam	52.04	14.80	11.91	18.51	6.82
86	Russia	42.62	11.47	8.33	17.99	4.83
114	Albania	34.23	8.48	5.04	19.62	1.09
161	Mozambique	21.71	3.28	2.75	13.85	1.83
178	Afghanistan	3.92	0.00	3.04	0.00	0.88

Source: Adapted from worldbank.org/html/prddr/trans/so96/art7.htm.

Exhibit 7.3

A Sample of International Country Risk Rankings

Piracy: A Key Threat to World Trade

Counterfeiting has grown up and has become a major threat to multinational corporations. "We've seen a massive increase in the last five years, and there is a risk that it will spiral out of control," claims Anthony Simon, marketing chief of Unilever Bestfoods. "It is no longer a cottage industry."

The figures are astounding. The World Customs Organization estimates that counterfeiting accounts for about 5 percent to 7 percent of global merchandise trade—equivalent to as much as $512 billion. Seizures of fakes by United States customs jumped 46 percent last year as counterfeiters boosted exports to Western markets. Unilever Groups says that knockoffs of its shampoos, soaps, and teas are growing at a rate of 30 percent annually.

Such counterfeiting can also have health and safety implications as well. The World Health Organization says up to 10 percent of medicines worldwide are counterfeit—a deadly hazard that could be costing the pharmaceutical industry $46 billion a year. "You won't die from purchasing a pair of counterfeit blue jeans or a counterfeit golf club.

Source: Engardio, P., & Yang, C. 2006. The runaway trade giant. *BusinessWeek.* April 24: 30–32; Letzing, J. 2007. Antipiracy group make's list of worst-offendor nations. www.marketwatch. February 12: np. Balfour, F. 2005. Fake! *Business-Week,* February 7: 54–64; Anonymous. 2005. Editorial. *BusinessWeek,* February 7: 96; and Simon, B. 2004. The world's greatest fakes. www.cbsnews. com, August 8.

You can die from taking counterfeit pharmaceutical products. And there's no doubt that people have died in China from bad medicine," says John Theirault, head of global security for American pharmaceutical giant, Pfizer. And, sadly, cases like the one in China, where fake baby formula recently killed 60 infants, have investigators stepping up enforcement at U.S. ports. Injuries from overheating counterfeit cell phone batteries purchased right on Verizon store shelves sparked a recall. According to Hal Stratton, of the Consumer Product Safety Commission, "We know of at least one apartment fire that's occurred. We know of at least one burn situation of someone's face that's occurred." And bogus car parts are a $12 billion market worldwide. "Counterfeiting has gone from a local nuisance to a global threat," says Hanns Glatz, DaimlerChrysler's point man on intellectual property.

China is the key to any solution. Given the country's economic power, its counterfeiting is turning into quite the problem itself, accounting for nearly two-thirds of all fake and pirated goods worldwide. Dan Chow, a law professor at Ohio State University who specializes in Chinese counterfeiting provides some perspective: "We have never seen a problem of this size and magnitude in world history. There's more counterfeiting going on in China now than we've ever seen anywhere. We know that 15 to 20 percent of all goods in China are counterfeit."

---

political risk
potential threat to a firm's operations in a country due to ineffectiveness of the domestic political system.

economic risk
potential threat to a firm's operations in a country due to economic policies and conditions, including property rights laws and enforcement of those laws.

the health of corporate initiatives because of **political risk.**[20] Forces such as social unrest, military turmoil, demonstrations, and even violent conflict and terrorism can pose serious threats.[21] Consider, for example, the ongoing tension and violence in the Middle East between Israelis and Palestinians, and the social and political unrest in Indonesia.[22] Because such conditions increase the likelihood of destruction of property and disruption of operations as well as nonpayment for goods and services, countries that are viewed as high risk are less attractive for most types of business. Typical exceptions include providers of munitions and counterintelligence services.

The laws, and the enforcement of laws, associated with the protection of intellectual property rights can be a major potential **economic risk** in entering new countries.[23] Microsoft, for example, has lost billions of dollars in potential revenue through piracy of its software products in many countries, including China. Other areas of the globe, such as the former Soviet Union and some eastern European nations, have piracy problems as well. Firms rich in intellectual property have encountered financial losses as imitations of their products have grown due to a lack of law enforcement of intellectual property rights.[24]

Strategy Spotlight 7.4 discusses a problem that presents a severe threat to global trade—piracy. As we will see, estimates are that counterfeiting accounts for between 5 percent and 7 percent of global merchandise trade—the equivalent of as much as $512 billion a year. And the potential corrosive effects include health and safety, not just economic, damage.

Currency Risks Currency fluctuations can pose substantial risks. A company with operations in several countries must constantly monitor the exchange rate between its own currency and that of the host country to minimize **currency risks.** Even a small change in the exchange rate can result in a significant difference in the cost of production or net profit when doing business overseas. When the U.S. dollar appreciates against other currencies, for example, U.S. goods can be more expensive to consumers in foreign countries. At the same time, however, appreciation of the U.S. dollar can have negative implications for American companies that have branch operations overseas. The reason for this is that profits from abroad must be exchanged for dollars at a more expensive rate of exchange, reducing the amount of profit when measured in dollars. For example, consider an American firm doing business in Italy. If this firm had a 20 percent profit in euros at its Italian center of operations, this profit would be totally wiped out when converted into U.S. dollars if the euro had depreciated 20 percent against the U.S. dollar. (U.S. multinationals typically engage in sophisticated "hedging strategies" to minimize currency risk. The discussion of this is beyond the scope of this section.)

It is important to note that even when government intervention is well intended, the macroeconomic effects of such action can be very negative for multinational corporations. Such was the case in 1997 when Thailand suddenly chose to devalue its currency, the baht, after months of trying to support it at an artificially high level. This, in effect, made the baht worthless compared to other currencies. And in 1998 Russia not only devalued its ruble but also elected not to honor its foreign debt obligations.

Management Risks **Management risks** may be considered the challenges and risks that managers face when they must respond to the inevitable differences that they encounter in foreign markets. These take a variety of forms: culture, customs, language, income levels, customer preferences, distribution systems, and so on.[25] As we will note later in the chapter, even in the case of apparently standard products, some degree of local adaptation will become necessary.

Differences in cultures across countries can also pose unique challenges for managers.[26] Cultural symbols can evoke deep feelings.[27] For example, in a series of advertisements aimed at Italian vacationers, Coca-Cola executives turned the Eiffel Tower, Empire State Building, and the Tower of Pisa into the familiar Coke bottle. So far, so good. However, when the white marble columns of the Parthenon that crowns the Acropolis in Athens were turned into Coke bottles, the Greeks became outraged. Why? Greeks refer to the Acropolis as the "holy rock," and a government official said the Parthenon is an "international symbol of excellence" and that "whoever insults the Parthenon insults international culture." Coca-Cola apologized for the ad. Below are a few examples of how culture varies across nations and some of the implications for business.[28]

- *Ecuador.* Dinners at Ecuadorian homes last for many hours. Expect drinks and appetizers around 8:00 p.m., with dinner not served until 11:00 p.m. or midnight. You will dismay your hosts if you leave as early as 1:00 a.m. A party at an Ecuadorian home will begin late and end around 4:00 a.m. or 5:00 a.m. Late guests may sometimes be served breakfast before they leave.
- *France.* Words in French and English may have the same roots but different meanings or connotations. For example, a French person might "demand" something because demander in French means "to ask."
- *Hong Kong.* Negotiations occur over cups of tea. Always accept an offer of tea whether you want it or not. When you are served, wait for the host to drink first.
- *Singapore.* Singaporeans associate all of the following with funerals, so do not give them as gifts: straw sandals, clocks, a stork or crane, handkerchiefs, or gifts or wrapping paper where the predominant color is white, black, or blue.

currency risk
potential threat to a firm's operations in a country due to fluctuations in the local currency's exchange rate.

management risk
potential threat to a firm's operations in a country due to the problems that managers have making decisions in the context of foreign markets.

How a Local Custom Can Affect a Manufacturing Plant's Operations

At times, a lack of understanding and awareness of local customs can provide some frustrating and embarrassing situations. Such customs can raise issues that must be taken into account in order to make good decisions.

For example, consider the unique problem that Larry Henderson, plant manager, and John Lichthental, manager

Source: Harvey, M., & Buckley, M. R. 2002. Assessing the "conventional wisdoms" of management for the 21st century organization. *Organizational Dynamics*, 30(4): 368–378.

of human resources, were faced with when they were assigned by Celanese Chemical Corp. to build a new plant in Singapore. The $125 million plant was completed in July, but according to local custom, a plant should only be christened on "lucky" days. Unfortunately, the next "lucky" day was not until September 3.

Henderson and Lichthental had to convince executives at Celanese's Dallas headquarters to delay the plant opening. It wasn't easy. But after many heated telephone conversations and flaming e-mails, the president agreed to open the new plant on the "lucky" day— September 3.

Strategy Spotlight 7.5 addresses a rather humorous example of how a local custom can affect operations at a manufacturing plant.

We have addressed several of the motivations and risks associated with international expansion. A major recent trend has been the dispersion of the value chains of multinational corporations across different countries; that is, the various activities that constitute the value chain of a firm are now spread across several countries and continents. Such dispersion of value occurs mainly through increasing offshoring and outsourcing. We now address some of the primary associated benefits and costs.

Global Dispersion of Value Chains: Outsourcing and Offshoring

A report issued by the World Trade Organization describes the production of a particular U.S. car as follows: "30 percent of the car's value goes to Korea for assembly, 17.5 percent to Japan for components and advanced technology, 7.5 percent to Germany for design, 4 percent to Taiwan and Singapore for minor parts, 2.5 percent to U.K. for advertising and marketing services, and 1.5 percent to Ireland and Barbados for data processing. This means that only 37 percent of the production value is generated in the U.S."[29] Similarly, in the production of a Barbie doll, Mattel purchases plastic and hair from Taiwan and Japan, the molds from the United States, the doll clothing from China, and paint from the U.S. and assembles the product in Indonesia and Malaysia for sales worldwide. In today's economy these are not isolated examples. Instead, we are increasingly witnessing two interrelated trends: outsourcing and offshoring.

Outsourcing occurs when a firm decides to utilize other firms to perform value-creating activities that were previously performed in-house.[30] In some cases, it may be a new activity that the firm is perfectly capable of doing, but it still chooses to have someone else perform the function for cost or quality reasons. Outsourcing can be to either a domestic company or a foreign firm.

Offshoring takes place when a firm decides to shift an activity that they were previously performing in a domestic location to a foreign location. For example, both Microsoft and Intel now have R&D facilities in India, employing a large number of Indian scientists and engineers. In many cases, offshoring and outsourcing go together; that is, a firm

outsourcing using other firms to perform value-creating activities that were previously performed in-house.

offshoring shifting a value-creating activity from a domestic location to a foreign location.

may outsource an activity to a foreign supplier, thereby causing the work to be off-shored as well.

Spending on offshore information technology will nearly triple between 2004 and 2010 to $60 billion, according to research firm Gartner.[31] And offshore employment in information technology (IT), banking, and six other areas will double to 1.2 million from 2003 to 2008, says the McKinsey Global Institute.

The recent explosion in the volume of outsourcing and offshoring is due to a variety of factors. Up until the 1960s, for most companies, the entire value chain was in one location. Further, the production took place close to where the customers were in order to keep transportation costs under control. In the case of service industries, it was generally believed that offshoring was not possible because the producer and consumer had to be present at the same place at the same time. After all, a haircut could not be performed if the barber and the client were separated!

In the case of manufacturing industries, the rapid decline in transportation and coordination costs has enabled firms to disperse their value chains over different locations. For example, Nike's R&D takes place in the United States, raw materials are procured from a multitude of countries, actual manufacturing takes place in China or Indonesia, advertising is produced in the United States, and sales and service take place in practically all the countries. Each value-creating activity is performed in the location where the cost is the lowest or the quality is the best. Without finding optimal locations for each activity and the resultant dispersion of the value chain, Nike could not have attained its position as the world's largest shoe company.

The experience of the manufacturing sector was repeated in the service sector as well by the mid-1990s. A trend that began with the outsourcing of low-level programming and data entry work to countries such as India and Ireland suddenly grew manyfold, encompassing a variety of white collar and professional activities ranging from call-centers to R&D. Now, the technical support lines of a large number of U.S. firms are answered from call centers in faraway locations. The cost of a long distance call from the United States to India has decreased from about $3 to $0.03 in the last 20 years, thereby making it possible to have call centers located in countries like India where a combination of low labor costs and English proficiency presents an ideal mix of factor conditions. Bangalore, India, in recent years, has emerged as a location where more and more U.S. tax returns are prepared. In India, U.S.–trained and licensed radiologists interpret chest X-rays and CT scans from U.S. hospitals for half the cost. The advantages from offshoring go beyond mere cost savings today. In many specialized occupations in science and engineering, there is a shortage of qualified professionals in developed countries whereas countries like India, China, and Singapore have what seems like an inexhaustible supply.[32]

For most of the 20th century, domestic companies catered to the needs of local populations. However, with the increasing homogenization of customer needs around the world and the institutionalization of free trade and investment as a global ideology (especially after the creation of the WTO), competition has become truly global. Each company has to keep its costs low in order to survive. They also must find the best suppliers and the most skilled workers as well as locate each stage of the value chain in places where factor conditions are most conducive. Thus, outsourcing and offshoring are no longer mere options to consider, but an imperative for competitive survival.

While there is a compelling logic for companies to engage in offshoring, there are many pitfalls associated with it. Strategy Spotlight 7.6 discusses the experience of Misiu Systems, a U.S. alarm systems manufacturer that found out the hard way that offshoring is not for everyone.

Let's now look at how firms can attain competitive advantages when they move beyond the boundaries of their home nation.

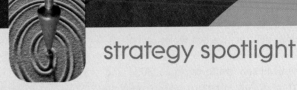

strategy spotlight

7.6

Misiu Systems: Outsourcing Is Not for Everyone

When Todd Hodgen, CEO of Misiu Systems, a Bothell, Washington–based manufacturer of alarm systems, learned that he could save 65 percent of his design costs by outsourcing it to a Taiwanese firm, he was really excited. In addition to cost savings, an added bonus was that the Taiwanese engineers would be working after Misiu's engineers had gone home because of the time differences. This meant that the product development cycle could be greatly accelerated. For a start-up financed mostly with loans from friends and family, the twin advan-

tages of cost savings and reduced cycle time were too much to resist.

After several months of discussions with the contractor and a visit to Taiwan, Hodgen signed the outsourcing agreement. However, things did not quite work out as he had expected. His feedback to the design team in Taiwan often went unheeded. The design was eventually delivered eight months late and the quality fell well short of expectations. Why? The Taiwanese engineers who were supposed to be working solely for him were also working for other clients. Business from a small firm like Misiu was not given the same priority that was given to bigger clients. Eventually Hodgen ended up terminating the agreement with the Taiwanese firm and hiring a U.S. firm to finish the project!

Source: Wahlgren, E. 2004. The outsourcing dilemma. *Inc.*, April: 41–43.

Achieving Competitive Advantage in Global Markets

We now discuss the two opposing forces that firms face when they expand into global markets: cost reduction and adaptation to local markets. Then we address the four basic types of international strategies that they may pursue: international, global, multidomestic, and transnational. The selection of one of these four types of strategies is largely dependent on a firm's relative pressure to address each of the two forces.

Two Opposing Pressures: Reducing Costs and Adapting to Local Markets

>LO4

The two opposing forces—cost reduction and adaptation to local markets—that firms face when entering international markets.

Many years ago, the famed marketing strategist Theodore Levitt advocated strategies that favored global products and brands. That is, he suggested that firms should standardize all of their products and services for all of their worldwide markets. Such an approach would help a firm lower its overall costs by spreading its investments over as large a market as possible. Levitt's approach rested on three key assumptions:

1. Customer needs and interests are becoming increasingly homogeneous worldwide.
2. People around the world are willing to sacrifice preferences in product features, functions, design, and the like for lower prices at high quality.
3. Substantial economies of scale in production and marketing can be achieved through supplying global markets.[33]

However, there is ample evidence to refute these assumptions.[34] Regarding the first assumption—the increasing worldwide homogeneity of customer needs and interests—consider the number of product markets, ranging from watches and handbags to soft drinks and fast foods. Here, companies have successfully identified global customer segments and developed global products and brands targeted to those segments. In addition, many other companies adapt lines to idiosyncratic country preferences and develop local brands targeted to local market segments. For example, Nestlé's line of pizzas marketed in the United Kingdom includes cheese with ham and pineapple topping on a French bread crust. Similarly, Coca-Cola in Japan markets Georgia (a tonic drink) as well as Classic Coke and Hi-C.

Consider the second assumption—the sacrifice of product attributes for lower prices. While there is invariably a price-sensitive segment in many product markets, there is no indication that this is increasing. In contrast, in many product and service markets—ranging from watches, personal computers, and household appliances, to banking and insurance—there is a growing interest in multiple product features, product quality, and service.

Finally, the third assumption is that significant economies of scale in production and marketing could be achieved for global products and services. Although standardization may lower manufacturing costs, such a perspective does not consider three critical and interrelated points. First, as we discussed in Chapter 5, technological developments in flexible factory automation enable economies of scale to be attained at lower levels of output and do not require production of a single standardized product. Second, the cost of production is only one component, and often not the critical one, in determining the total cost of a product. Third, a firm's strategy should not be product-driven. It should also consider other activities in the firm's value chain, such as marketing, sales, and distribution.

Based on the above, we would have a hard time arguing that it is wise to develop the same product or service for all markets throughout the world. While there are some exceptions, such as Harley-Davidson motorcycles and some of Coca-Cola's soft-drink products, managers must also strive to tailor their products to the culture of the country in which they are attempting to do business. Few would argue that "one size fits all" generally applies.

What we have briefly discussed so far are two opposing pressures that managers face when they compete in markets beyond their national boundaries. These forces place conflicting demands on firms as they strive to be competitive.[35] On the one hand, competitive pressures require that firms do what they can to *lower unit costs* so that consumers will not perceive their product and service offerings as too expensive. This may lead them to consider locating manufacturing facilities where labor costs are low and developing products that are highly standardized across multiple countries.

In addition to responding to pressures to lower costs, managers also must strive to be *responsive to local pressures* in order to tailor their products to the demand of the local market in which they do business. This requires differentiating their offerings and strategies from country to country to reflect consumer tastes and preferences and making changes to reflect differences in distribution channels, human resource practices, and governmental regulations. However, since the strategies and tactics to differentiate products and services to local markets can involve additional expenses, a firm's costs will tend to rise.

The two opposing pressures result in four different basic strategies that companies can use to compete in the global marketplace: international, global, multidomestic, and transnational. The strategy that a firm selects depends on the degree of pressure that it is facing for cost reductions and the importance of adapting to local markets. Exhibit 7.4 shows the conditions under which each of these strategies would be most appropriate. As we would expect, there are advantages and disadvantages associated with each of these strategies. In the following sections we will summarize each strategy, discuss where each is most appropriate, and identify relative advantages and disadvantages.

It is important to note that we consider these strategies to be "basic" or "pure"; that is, in practice, all firms will tend to have some elements of international, global, multidomestic, and transnational strategies.

International Strategy

There are a small number of industries in which pressures for both local adaptation and lowering costs are rather low. An extreme example of such an industry is the "orphan" drug industry. These are medicines for diseases that are severe but affect only a small number of people. Diseases such as the Gaucher disease and Fabry disease fit into this category. Companies such as Genzyme and Oxford GlycoSciences are active in this segment of the drug industry. There is virtually no need to adapt their products to the local markets. And the

>LO5
The advantages and disadvantages associated with each of the four basic strategies: international, global, multidomestic, and transnational.

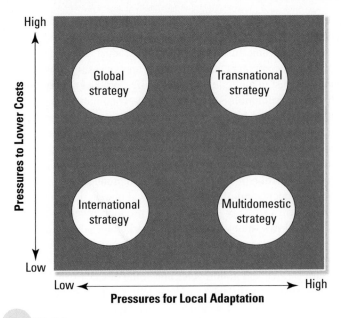

Exhibit 7.4 Opposing Pressures and Four Strategies

pressures to reduce costs are low; even though only a few thousand patients are affected, the revenues and margins are significant because patients are charged up to $100,000 per year.

An international strategy is based on diffusion and adaptation of the parent company's knowledge and expertise to foreign markets. Country units are allowed to make some minor adaptations to products and ideas coming from the head office, but they have far less independence and autonomy compared to multidomestic companies. The primary goal of the strategy is worldwide exploitation of the parent firm's knowledge and capabilities. All sources of core competencies are centralized.

For most of its history, Ericsson, a Swedish telecommunications firm, has followed this strategy. Because its home market (Sweden) was too small to support the required R&D effort, Ericsson built its strategy on its ability to transfer and adapt its innovative products and process technologies to international markets. This strategy of sequential diffusion of innovation developed at home helped it compete successfully against NEC, which followed a global strategy, and ITT, which followed a multidomestic strategy.[36]

The majority of large U.S. multinationals pursued the international strategy in the decades following World War II. These companies centralized R&D and product development but established manufacturing facilities as well as marketing organizations abroad. Companies such as McDonald's and Kellogg are examples of firms following such a strategy. Although these companies do make some local adaptations, they are of a very limited nature. With increasing pressures to reduce costs due to global competition, especially from low-cost countries, opportunities to successfully employ international strategy are becoming more limited. This strategy is most suitable in situations where a firm has distinctive competencies that local companies in foreign markets lack.

Risks and Challenges   Below, are some of the risks and challenges associated with an international strategy.

- Different activities in the value chain typically have different optimal locations. That is, R&D may be optimally located in a country with an abundant supply of scientists and engineers, whereas assembly may be better conducted in a low-cost location. Nike, for example, designs its shoes in the United States, but all the manufacturing is

Exhibit 7.5

Strengths and
Limitations of
International Strategies
in the Global
Marketplace

Strengths	Limitations
• Leverage and diffusion of a parent firm's knowledge and core competencies. • Lower costs because of less need to tailor products and services.	• Limited ability to adapt to local markets • Inability to take advantage of new ideas and innovations occurring in local markets.

done in countries like China or Thailand. The international strategy, with its tendency to concentrate most of its activities in one location, fails to take advantage of the benefits of an optimally distributed value chain.

- The lack of local responsiveness may result in the alienation of local customers. Worse still, the firm's inability to be receptive to new ideas and innovation from its foreign subsidiaries may lead to missed opportunities.

Exhibit 7.5 summarizes the strengths and weaknesses of international strategies in the global marketplace.

Global Strategy

As indicated in Exhibit 7.4, a firm whose emphasis is on lowering costs tends to follow a global strategy. Competitive strategy is centralized and controlled to a large extent by the corporate office. Since the primary emphasis is on controlling costs, the corporate office strives to achieve a strong level of coordination and integration across the various businesses.[37] Firms following a global strategy strive to offer standardized products and services as well as to locate manufacturing, R&D, and marketing activities in only a few locations.[38]

A global strategy emphasizes economies of scale due to the standardization of products and services, and the centralization of operations in a few locations. As such, one advantage may be that innovations that come about through efforts of either a business unit or the corporate office can be transferred more easily to other locations. Although costs may be lower, the firm following a global strategy may, in general, have to forgo opportunities for revenue growth since it does not invest extensive resources in adapting product offerings from one market to another.

Consistent with Exhibit 7.4, a global strategy is most appropriate when there are strong pressures for reducing costs and comparatively weak pressures for adaptation to local markets. Identifying potential economies of scale becomes an important consideration.[39] Advantages to increased volume may come not only from larger production plants or runs but also from more efficient logistics and distribution networks. Worldwide volume is also especially important in supporting high levels of investment in research and development. As we would expect, many industries requiring high levels of R&D, such as pharmaceuticals, semiconductors, and jet aircraft, follow global strategies.

Another advantage of a global strategy is that it can enable a firm to create a standard level of quality throughout the world. Let's look at what Tom Siebel, chairman of Siebel Systems (now part of Oracle), the $2 billion developer of e-business application software, has to say about global standardization.

> Our customers—global companies like IBM, Zurich Financial Services, and Citicorp—expect the same high level of service and quality, and the same licensing policies, no matter where we do business with them around the world. Our human resources and legal departments help us create policies that respect local cultures and requirements worldwide, while at the same time maintaining the highest standards. We have one brand, one image, one set of corporate colors, and one set of messages, across every place on the planet. An organization needs central quality control to avoid surprises.[40]

Exhibit 7.6

Strengths and Limitations of Global Strategies

Strengths	Limitations
• Strong integration across various businesses.	• Limited ability to adapt to local markets.
• Standardization leads to higher economies of scale, which lowers costs.	• Concentration of activities may increase dependence on a single facility.
• Helps create uniform standards of quality throughout the world.	• Single locations may lead to higher tariffs and transportation costs.

Risks and Challenges   There are, of course, some risks associated with a global strategy.[41]

- A firm can enjoy scale economies only by concentrating scale-sensitive resources and activities in one or few locations. Such concentration, however, becomes a "double-edged sword." For example, if a firm has only one manufacturing facility, it must export its output (e.g., components, subsystems, or finished products) to other markets, some of which may be a great distance from the operation. Thus, decisions about locating facilities must weigh the potential benefits from concentrating operations in a single location against the higher transportation and tariff costs that result from such concentration.
- The geographic concentration of any activity may also tend to isolate that activity from the targeted markets. Such isolation may be risky since it may hamper the facility's ability to quickly respond to changes in market conditions and needs.
- Concentrating an activity in a single location also makes the rest of the firm dependent on that location. Such dependency implies that, unless the location has world-class competencies, the firm's competitive position can be eroded if problems arise. A European Ford executive, reflecting on the firm's concentration of activities during a global integration program in the mid-1990s, lamented, "Now if you misjudge the market, you are wrong in 15 countries rather than only one."

Exhibit 7.6 summarizes the strengths and weaknesses of global strategies.

Multidomestic Strategy

According to Exhibit 7.4, a firm whose emphasis is on differentiating its product and service offerings to adapt to local markets follows a multidomestic strategy. Decisions evolving from a multidomestic strategy tend to be decentralized to permit the firm to tailor its products and respond rapidly to changes in demand. This enables a firm to expand its market and to charge different prices in different markets. For firms following this strategy, differences in language, culture, income levels, customer preferences, and distribution systems are only a few of the many factors that must be considered. Even in the case of relatively standardized products, at least some level of local adaptation is often necessary. Consider, for example, Honda motorcycles.

> Although we could argue that a good product knows no national boundaries, there are subtle differences in ways that a product is used and what customers expect of it. Thus, while Honda uses a common basic technology, it must develop different types of motorcycles for different regions of the world. For example, North Americans primarily use motorcycles for leisure and sports; thus aggressive looks and high horsepower are key. Southeast Asians provide a counterpoint. Here, motorcycles are a basic means of transportation. Thus, they require low cost and ease of maintenance. And, in Australia and New Zealand, shepherds use motorcycles to herd sheep. Therefore, they demand low-speed torque, rather than high speed and maintenance.[42]

Dealing with Bribery Abroad

Most multinational firms experience difficult dilemmas when it comes to the question of adapting rules and guidelines, both formal and informal, while operating in foreign countries. A case in point is the Foreign Corrupt Practices Act of 1977, which makes it illegal for U.S. companies to bribe foreign officials to gain business or facilitate approvals and permissions. Unfortunately, in many parts of the world, bribery is a way of life, with large payoffs to government officials and politicians the norm to win government contracts. At a lower level, goods won't clear customs unless routine illegal, but well-accepted, payments, are made to officials. What is an American company to do in such situations?

Source: Begley, T. M., & Boyd, D. P. 2003. The need for a corporate global mind-set. *MIT Sloan Management Review*, Winter: 25–32.

Intel follows a strict rule-based definition of bribery as "a thing of value given to someone with the intent of obtaining favorable treatment from the recipient." The company strictly prohibits payments to expedite a shipment through customs if the payment did not "follow applicable rules and regulations, and if the agent gives money or payment in kind to a government official for personal benefit." Texas Instruments, on the other hand, follows a middle approach. They require employees to "exercise good judgment" in questionable circumstances "by avoiding activities that could create even the appearance that our decisions could be compromised." And Analog Devices has set up a policy manager as a consultant to overseas operations. The policy manager does not make decisions for country managers. Instead, the policy manager helps country managers think through the issues and provides information on how the corporate office has handled similar situations in the past.

In addition to the products themselves, how they are packaged must sometimes be adapted to local market conditions. Some consumers in developing countries are likely to have packaging preferences very different from western consumers. For example, single-serve packets, or sachets, are very popular in India.[43] They permit consumers to purchase only what they need, experiment with new products, and conserve cash. Products as varied as detergents, shampoos, pickles, and cough syrup are sold in sachets in India. It is estimated that they make up 20 percent to 30 percent of the total sold in their categories. In China, sachets are spreading as a marketing device for such items as shampoos. This reminds us of the importance of considering all activities in a firm's value chain (discussed in Chapters 3 and 5) in determining where local adaptations may be required.

Cultural differences may also require a firm to adapt its personnel practices when it expands internationally.[44] For example, some facets of Wal-Mart stores have been easily "exported" to foreign operations, while others have required some modifications.[45] When the retailer entered the German market in 1997, it took along the company "cheer"—Give me a W! Give me an A! Give me an L! Who's Number One? The Customer!—which suited German employees. However, Wal-Mart's 10-Foot Rule, which requires employees to greet any customer within a 10-foot radius, was not so well received in Germany, where employees and shoppers alike weren't comfortable with the custom. (As noted in this chapter's opening case, Wal-Mart exited the German market in 2006.)

Strategy Spotlight 7.7 describes how U.S. multinationals have adapted to the problem of bribery in various countries while adhering to strict federal laws on corrupt practices abroad.

Risks and Challenges   As you might expect, there are some risks associated with a multidomestic strategy. Among these are the following:

- Typically, local adaptation of products and services will increase a company's cost structure. In many industries, competition is so intense that most firms can ill afford any competitive disadvantages on the dimension of cost. A key challenge of managers is to determine the trade-off between local adaptation and its cost structure. For example, cost considerations led Procter & Gamble to standardize its diaper design across all European markets. This was done despite research data indicating that

Exhibit 7.7
Strengths and Limitations of Multidomestic Strategies

Strengths	Limitations
• Ability to adapt products and services to local market conditions.	• Decreased ability to realize cost savings through scale economies.
• Ability to detect potential opportunities for attractive niches in a given market, enhancing revenue.	• Greater difficulty in transferring knowledge across countries.
	• May lead to "overadaptation" as conditions change.

Italian mothers, unlike those in other countries, preferred diapers that covered the baby's navel. Later, however, P&G recognized that this feature was critical to these mothers, so the company decided to incorporate this feature for the Italian market despite its adverse cost implications.

- At times, local adaptations, even when well intentioned, may backfire. When the American restaurant chain TGI Fridays entered the South Korean market, it purposely incorporated many local dishes, such as kimchi (hot, spicy cabbage), in its menu. This responsiveness, however, was not well received. Company analysis of the weak market acceptance indicated that Korean customers anticipated a visit to TGI Fridays as a visit to America. Thus, finding Korean dishes was inconsistent with their expectations.

- Consistent with other aspects of global marketing, the optimal degree of local adaptation evolves over time. In many industry segments, a variety of factors, such as the influence of global media, greater international travel, and declining income disparities across countries, may lead to increasing global standardization. On the other hand, in other industry segments, especially where the product or service can be delivered over the Internet (such as music), the need for even greater customization and local adaptation may increase over time. Firms must recalibrate the need for local adaptation on an ongoing basis; excessive adaptation extracts a price as surely as underadaptation.

Exhibit 7.7 summarizes the strengths and limitations of multidomestic strategies.

Transnational Strategy

A *transnational strategy* strives to optimize the trade-offs associated with efficiency, local adaptation, and learning.[46] It seeks efficiency not for its own sake, but as a means to achieve global competitiveness. It recognizes the importance of local responsiveness but as a tool for flexibility in international operations.[47] Innovations are regarded as an outcome of a larger process of organizational learning that includes the contributions of everyone in the firm.[48] Also, a core tenet of the transnational model is that a firm's assets and capabilities are dispersed according to the most beneficial location for each activity. Thus, managers avoid the tendency to either concentrate activities in a central location (a global strategy) or disperse them across many locations to enhance adaptation (a multidomestic strategy). Peter Brabeck, CEO of Nestlé, the giant food company, provides such a perspective.

> We believe strongly that there isn't a so-called global consumer, at least not when it comes to food and beverages. People have local tastes based on their unique cultures and traditions—a good candy bar in Brazil is not the same as a good candy bar in China. Therefore, decision making needs to be pushed down as low as possible in the organization, out close to the markets. Otherwise, how can you make good brand decisions? That said, decentralization has its limits. If you are too decentralized, you can become too complicated—you get too much complexity in your production system. The closer we come to the consumer, in branding, pricing, communication, and product adaptation, the more we decentralize. The more we are dealing with production, logistics, and supply-chain management, the more centralized decision making becomes. After all, we want to leverage Nestlé's size, not be hampered by it.[49]

The Nestlé example illustrates a common approach in determining whether or not to centralize or decentralize a value-chain activity. Typically, primary activities that are "downstream" (e.g., marketing, sales, and service), or closer to the customer, tend to require more decentralization in order to adapt to local market conditions. On the other hand, primary activities that are "upstream" (e.g., logistics and operations), or further away from the customer, tend to be centralized. This is because there is less need for adapting these activities to local markets and the firm can benefit from economies of scale. Additionally, many support activities, such as information systems and procurement, tend to be centralized in order to increase the potential for economies of scale.

A central philosophy of the transnational organization is enhanced adaptation to all competitive situations as well as flexibility by capitalizing on communication and knowledge flows throughout the organization.[50] A principal characteristic is the integration of unique contributions of all units into worldwide operations. Thus, a joint innovation by headquarters and by one of the overseas units can lead potentially to the development of relatively standardized and yet flexible products and services that are suitable for multiple markets.

Asea Brown Boveri (ABB) is a firm that successfully follows a transnational strategy. ABB, with its home bases in Sweden and Switzerland, illustrates the trend toward cross-national mergers that lead firms to consider multiple headquarters in the future. It is managed as a flexible network of units, and one of management's main functions is the facilitation of information and knowledge flows between units. ABB's subsidiaries have complete responsibility for product categories on a worldwide basis. Such a transnational strategy enables ABB to benefit from access to new markets and the opportunity to utilize and develop resources wherever they may be located.

Risks and Challenges   As with the other strategies, there are some unique risks and challenges associated with a transnational strategy.

- *The choice of a seemingly optimal location cannot guarantee that the quality and cost of factor inputs (i.e., labor, materials) will be optimal.* Managers must ensure that the relative advantage of a location is actually realized, not squandered because of weaknesses in productivity and the quality of internal operations. Ford Motor Co., for example, has benefited from having some of its manufacturing operations in Mexico. While some have argued that the benefits of lower wage rates will be partly offset by lower productivity, this does not always have to be the case. Since unemployment in Mexico is higher than in the United States, Ford can be more selective in its hiring practices for its Mexican operations. And, given the lower turnover among its Mexican employees, Ford can justify a high level of investment in training and development. Thus, the net result can be not only lower wage rates but also higher productivity than in the United States.
- *Although knowledge transfer can be a key source of competitive advantage, it does not take place "automatically."* For knowledge transfer to take place from one subsidiary to another, it is important for the source of the knowledge, the target units, and the corporate headquarters to recognize the potential value of such unique know-how. Given that there can be significant geographic, linguistic, and cultural distances that typically separate subsidiaries, the potential for knowledge transfer can become very difficult to realize. Firms must create mechanisms to systematically and routinely uncover the opportunities for knowledge transfer.

Exhibit 7.8 summarizes the relative advantages and disadvantages of transnational strategies.

Global or Regional? A Second Look at Globalization

Thus far, we have suggested four possible strategies from which a firm must choose once it has decided to compete in the global marketplace. In recent years, many writers have asserted that the process of globalization has caused national borders to become increasingly

>LO6

The difference between regional companies and truly global companies.

Exhibit 7.8

Strengths and Limitations of Transnational Strategies

Strengths	Limitations
• Ability to attain economies of scale. • Ability to adapt to local markets. • Ability to locate activities in optimal locations. • Ability to increase knowledge flows and learning.	• Unique challenges in determining optimal locations of activities to ensure cost and quality. • Unique managerial challenges in fostering knowledge transfer.

irrelevant. However, some scholars have recently questioned this perspective, and they have argued that it is unwise for companies to rush into full scale globalization.[51]

Before answering questions about the extent of firms' globalization, let's try to clarify what "globalization" means. Traditionally, a firm's globalization is measured in terms of its foreign sales as a percentage of total sales. However, this measure can be misleading. For example, consider a U.S. firm that has expanded its activities into Canada. Clearly, this initiative is qualitatively different from achieving the same sales volume in a distant country such as China. Similarly, if a Malaysian firm expands into Singapore or a German firm starts selling its products in Austria, this would represent an expansion into a geographically adjacent country. Such nearby countries would often share many common characteristics in terms of language, culture, infrastructure, and customer preferences. In other words, this is more a case of regionalization than globalization.

Extensive analysis of the distribution data of sales across different countries and regions led Alan Rugman and Alain Verbeke to conclude that there is a stronger case to be made in favor of regionalization than globalization. According to their study, a company would have to have at least 20 percent of its sales in each of the three major economic regions—North America, Europe, and Asia—to be considered a global firm. However, they found that only nine of the world's 500 largest firms met this standard! Even when they relaxed the criterion to 20 percent of sales each in at least two of the three regions, the number only increased to 25. *Thus, most companies are regional or, at best, biregional—not global—even today.* Exhibit 7.9 provides a listing of the large firms that met each of these two criteria.

One might ask: In a world of instant communication, rapid transportation, and governments that are increasingly willing to open up their markets to trade and investment, why are so few firms "global"? The most obvious answer is that distance still matters. After all, it is easier to do business in a neighboring country than in a far away country, all else being equal. Distance, in the final analysis, may be viewed as a concept with many dimensions, not just a measure of geographical distance. For example, both Canada and Mexico are the same distance from the United States. However, U.S. companies find it easier to expand operations into Canada than into Mexico. Why? Canada and the United States share many commonalities in terms of language, culture, economic development, legal and political systems, and infrastructure development. Thus, if we view distance as having many dimensions, the United States and Canada are very close, whereas there is greater distance between the United States and Mexico. Similarly, when we look at what we might call the "true" distance between the United States and China, the effects of geographic distance is multiplied by distance in terms of culture, language, religion, and legal and political systems between the two countries. On the other hand, although United States and Australia are geographically distant, the "true" distance is somewhat less when one considers distance along the other dimensions.

Another reason for regional expansion is the rise of the trading blocs. The European Union originally started in the 1950s as a regional trading bloc. However, recently it has achieved a large degree of economic and political integration in terms of common currency

Exhibit 7.9

Global or Regional?
Sales Distribution of
the *Fortune* Global
500 Firms

Firms with at least 20 percent sales in Asia, Europe, and North America each but with less than 50 percent sales in any one region:

IBM	Nokia	Coca-Cola
Sony	Intel	Flextronics
Philips	Canon	LVMH

Firms with at least 20 percent sales in at least two of the three regions (Asia, Europe, North America) but with less than 50 percent sales in any one region:

BP Amoco	Alstom	Michelin
Toyota	Aventis	Kodak
Nissan	Daigeo	Electrolux
Unilever	Sun Microsystems	BAE
Motorola	Bridgestone	Alcan
GlaxoSmithKline	Roche	L'Oreal
EADS	3M	Lafarge
Bayer	Skanska	
Ericsson	McDonald's	

Sources: Peng, M.W. 2006. *Global strategy:* 387. Mason, OH: Thomson Southwestern; and Rugman, A.M., & Verbeke, A. 2004. A perspective on regional and global strategies of multinational enterprises. *Journal of International Business Studies.* 35: 3–18.

and common standards that many thought infeasible, if not impossible, only 20 years ago. The resulting economic benefits have led other regions also to consider similar moves. For example, the North American Free Trade Agreement (NAFTA) has the eventual abolition of all barriers to the free movement of goods and services among Canada, the United States, and Mexico as its goal. Other regional trading blocks include MERCOSUR (consisting of Argentina, Brazil, Paraguay, and Uruguay) and the Association of Southeast Asian Nations (ASEAN) (consisting of about a dozen Southeast Asian countries).

Regional economic integration has progressed at a faster pace than global economic integration and the trade and investment patterns of the largest companies reflect this reality. After all, regions represent the outcomes of centuries of political and cultural history that results not only in commonalities but also mutual affinity. For example, stretching from Algeria and Morocco in the West to Oman and Yemen in the East, more than 30 countries share the Arabic language and the Muslim religion, making these countries a natural regional bloc. Similarly, the countries of South and Central America share the Spanish language (except Brazil), Catholic religion, and a shared history of Spanish colonialism. No wonder firms find it easier and less risky to expand within their region than to other regions.

Let's now turn to the types of entry modes that companies may use to enter international markets.

Entry Modes of International Expansion

A firm has many options available to it when it decides to expand into international markets. Given the challenges associated with such entry, many firms first start on a small scale and then increase their level of investment and risk as they gain greater experience with the overseas market in question.[52]

Exhibit 7.10 illustrates a wide variety of modes of foreign entry, including exporting, licensing, franchising, joint ventures, strategic alliances, and wholly owned subsidiaries.[53]

>LO7
The four basic types of entry strategies and the relative benefits and risks associated with each of them.

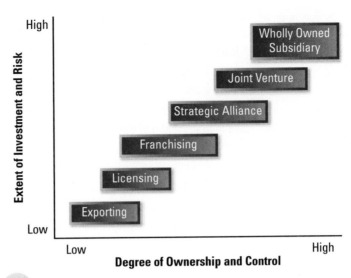

Exhibit 7.10 Entry Modes for International Expansion

As the exhibit indicates, the various types of entry form a continuum ranging from exporting (low investment and risk, low control) to a wholly owned subsidiary (high investment and risk, high control).[54]

There can be frustrations and setbacks as a firm evolves its international entry strategy from exporting to more expensive types, including wholly owned subsidiaries. For example, according to the CEO of a large U.S. specialty chemical company:

> In the end, we always do a better job with our own subsidiaries; sales improve, and we have greater control over the business. But we still need local distributors for entry, and we are still searching for strategies to get us through the transitions without battles over control and performance.[55]

Let's discuss each of these international entry modes.[56]

Exporting

exporting producing goods in one country to sell to residents of another country.

Exporting consists of producing goods in one country to sell in another. This entry strategy enables a firm to invest the least amount of resources in terms of its product, its organization, and its overall corporate strategy. Many host countries dislike this entry strategy because it provides less local employment than other modes of entry.[57]

Multinationals often stumble onto a stepwise strategy for penetrating markets, beginning with the exporting of products. This often results in a series of unplanned actions to increase sales revenues. As the pattern recurs with entries into subsequent markets, this approach, named a "beachhead strategy," often becomes official policy.

Benefits Such an approach definitely has its advantages. After all, firms start from scratch in sales and distribution when they enter new markets. Because many foreign markets are nationally regulated and dominated by networks of local intermediaries, firms need to partner with local distributors to benefit from their valuable expertise and knowledge of their own markets. Multinationals, after all, recognize that they cannot master local business practices, meet regulatory requirements, hire and manage local personnel, or gain access to potential customers without some form of local partnership.

In addition to the need to partner with local firms, multinationals also want to minimize their own risk. They do this by hiring local distributors and investing very little in the undertaking. In essence, the firm gives up control of strategic marketing decisions to the local partners—much more control than they would be willing to give up in their home market.

Risks and Limitations As we might expect, exporting is a relatively inexpensive way to enter foreign markets. However, it can still have significant downsides. In a study of 250 instances in which multinational firms used local distributors to implement their exporting entry strategy, the results were dismal. In the vast majority of the cases, the distributors were bought (to increase control) by the multinational firm or fired. In contrast, successful distributors shared two common characteristics:

- They carried product lines that complemented, rather than competed with, the multinational's products.
- They behaved as if they were business partners with the multinationals. They shared market information with the corporations, they initiated projects with distributors in neighboring countries, and they suggested initiatives in their own or nearby markets. Additionally, these distributors took on risk themselves by investing in areas such as training, information systems, and advertising and promotion in order to increase the business of their multinational partners.

The key point is the importance of developing collaborative, win–win relationships.

To ensure more control over operations without incurring significant risks, many firms have used licensing and franchising as a mode of entry. Let's now discuss these and their relative advantages and disadvantages.

Licensing and Franchising

Licensing and franchising are both forms of contractual arrangements. **Licensing** enables a company to receive a royalty or fee in exchange for the right to use its trademark, patent, trade secret, or other valuable item of intellectual property.[58]

Franchising contracts generally include a broader range of factors in an operation and have a longer time period during which the agreement is in effect. Franchising remains a primary form of American business. According to a recent survey, more than 400 U.S. franchisers have international exposure.[59] This is greater than the combined totals of the next four largest franchiser home countries—France, the United Kingdom, Mexico, and Austria.

Benefits In international markets, an advantage of licensing is that the firm granting a license incurs little risk, since it does not have to invest any significant resources into the country itself. In turn, the licensee (the firm receiving the license) gains access to the trademark, patent, and so on, and is able to potentially create competitive advantages. In many cases, the country also benefits from the product being manufactured locally. For example, Yoplait yogurt is licensed by General Mills from Sodima, a French cooperative, for sale in the United States. The logos of college and professional athletic teams in the United States are another source of trademarks that generate significant royalty income domestically and internationally.

Franchising has the advantage of limiting the risk exposure that a firm has in overseas markets. At the same time, the firm is able to expand the revenue base of the company.

● While Australia is geographically distant from the United States, it is much closer when other dimensions are considered such as income levels, language, culture, and political/legal systems.

licensing a contractual arrangement in which a company receives a royalty or fee in exchange for the right to use its trademark, patent, trade secret, or other valuable intellectual property.

franchising a contractual arrangement in which a company receives a royalty or fee in exchange for the right to use its intellectual property; it usually involves a longer time period than licensing and includes other factors, such as monitoring of operations, training, and advertising.

Risks and Limitations   There are, of course, some important disadvantages with this type of entry. For example, the licensor gives up control of its product and forgoes potential revenues and profits. Furthermore, the licensee may eventually become so familiar with the patent and trade secrets that it may become a competitor; that is, the licensee may make some modifications to the product and manufacture and sell it independently of the licensor without having to pay a royalty fee. This potential situation is aggravated in countries that have relatively weak laws to protect intellectual property. Additionally, if the licensee selected by the multinational firm turns out to be a poor choice, the brand name and reputation of the product may be tarnished.[60]

With franchising, the multinational firm receives only a portion of the revenues, in the form of franchise fees. Had the firm set up the operation itself (e.g., a restaurant through direct investment), it would have had the entire revenue to itself.

Companies often desire a closer collaboration with other firms in order to increase revenue, reduce costs, and enhance their learning—often through the diffusion of technology. To achieve such objectives, they enter into strategic alliances or joint ventures, two entry modes we will discuss next.

Strategic Alliances and Joint Ventures

Joint ventures and strategic alliances have recently become increasingly popular. These two forms of partnership differ in that joint ventures entail the creation of a third-party legal entity, whereas strategic alliances do not. In addition, strategic alliances generally focus on initiatives that are smaller in scope than joint ventures.

Benefits   As we discussed in Chapter 6, these strategies have been effective in helping firms increase revenues and reduce costs as well as enhance learning and diffuse technologies. These partnerships enable firms to share the risks as well as the potential revenues and profits. Also, by gaining exposure to new sources of knowledge and technologies, such partnerships can help firms develop core competencies that can lead to competitive advantages in the marketplace.[61] Finally, entering into partnerships with host country firms can provide very useful information on local market tastes, competitive conditions, legal matters, and cultural nuances.[62]

Joint ventures can often include more than two different parties. Strategy Spotlight 7.8 discusses a joint venture that involved companies from the United States, China, and India.

Risks and Limitations   Managers must be aware of the risks associated with strategic alliances and joint ventures and how they can be minimized.[63] First, there needs to be a clearly defined strategy that is strongly supported by the organizations that are party to the partnership. Otherwise, the firms may work at cross-purposes and not achieve any of their goals. Second, and closely allied to the first issue, there must be a clear understanding of capabilities and resources that will be central to the partnership. Without such clarification, there will be fewer opportunities for learning and developing competencies that could lead to competitive advantages. Third, trust is a vital element. Phasing in the relationship between alliance partners permits them to get to know each other better and develop trust. According to Philip Benton, Jr., former president of Ford Motor Co. (which has been involved in multiple international partnerships over the years), "The first time two companies work together, the chances of succeeding are very slight. But once you find ways to work together, all sorts of opportunities arise." Without trust, one party may take advantage of the other by, for example, withholding its fair share of resources and gaining access to privileged information through unethical (or illegal) means. Fourth, cultural issues that can potentially lead to conflict and dysfunctional behaviors need to be addressed. An organization's culture is the set of values,

A Joint Venture with Partners from Three Countries

A joint venture has been formed with partners from China, India, and the United States. In December 2006, Tata Consulting Services (TCS), India's largest information technology outsourcing company, joined forces with three Chinese state-owned companies and Microsoft to form a new software development center based in Beijing, China.

The development has been hailed as one of the most striking steps forward in bilateral IT relations between India and China, which for many years have been marred by mutual suspicions. Political leaders, especially in India, have traditionally been skeptical about the export of technology skills from India to China. Why? India had concerns about assisting an economic rival.

One sign of the complexities in establishing such a partnership in China is the time that it has taken to set up

TCS China: The parties had signed the initial agreement to go ahead with the project 17 months earlier in June 2005. Under the agreement, TCS will hold 65 percent of the venture while the three Chinese partners will hold 25 percent. Microsoft will hold the remaining 10 percent. The three Chinese partners are organized under the National Development and Reform Commission, the powerful central government planning agency.

The joint venture will leverage the complementary strengths of the investing parties in technology, software development management, and talent training. Of particular value will be TCS's best processes and practices as well as its experience in handling large and industrial-scale projects. It will also benefit from the resources of the Chinese partners, which run the national software development parks.

Microsoft should also benefit. According to Jonathan Spira, chief analyst of a Basex, an IT research firm: "Microsoft is a global company so it makes sense for them to invest and participate in global partnerships, especially in markets as large as China's. China is a region where Microsoft does not have anything close to resembling a foothold."

Sources: Leahy, J. 2006. Asian partnership takes off. www.ft.com, December 5: 3; Anonymous. 2005. TCS and Microsoft intend to establish joint venture with Chinese firms. Microsoft Press Release. June 30, np.; and Anonymous. 2005. Microsoft sets up JV with Tata. www.basex.com. July 1, np.

beliefs, and attitudes that influence the behavior and goals of its employees. Thus, recognizing cultural differences as well as striving to develop elements of a "common culture" for the partnership is vital. Without a unifying culture, it will become difficult to combine and leverage resources that are increasingly important in knowledge-intensive organizations (discussed in Chapter 4).[64]

As we know, not all partnerships are successful, for a variety of reasons. One of the most famous in recent business history was the joint venture formed by General Motors and Daewoo Motor Co.

In the mid-1980s General Motors sought cheap labor in Korea while Daewoo (of Korea) wanted to export automobiles. Thus, the two companies joined forces in 1986 to manufacture the ill-fated Pontiac LeMans. Things did not work out as planned. The LeMans experienced a sales decline of 39 percent from 1988 to 1990 and further declines in 1990 until the partnership was dissolved shortly thereafter.

What went wrong? The first cars had quality problems: GM sent engineers to Korea to correct them. Korea's cheap labor didn't materialize because of economic improvement, devaluation of the dollar, and increasingly strong demands from the newly formed labor unions for higher wages. However, the biggest problem was the differing goals of the two firms. While Daewoo wanted to upgrade the models to gain a larger share of the domestic market, GM wanted to keep costs down.

In effect, the alliance failed from the start, due to minimal understanding of each other's objectives and a lack of effort to reevaluate plans when problems appeared.[65]

Finally, the success of a firm's alliance should not be left to chance.[66] To improve their odds of success, many companies have carefully documented alliance-management knowledge by creating guidelines and manuals to help them manage specific aspects of the entire alliance life cycle (e.g., partner selection and alliance negotiation and contracting). For example, Lotus Corp. (part of IBM) created what it calls its "35 rules of thumb" to manage each phase of an alliance from formation to termination. Hewlett-Packard developed 60 different tools and templates, which it placed in a 300-page manual for guiding decision making. The manual included such tools as a template for making the business case for an alliance, a partner evaluation form, a negotiation template outlining the roles and responsibilities of different departments, a list of the ways to measure alliance performance, and an alliance termination checklist.

When a firm desires the highest level of control, it develops wholly owned subsidiaries. Although wholly owned subsidiaries can generate the greatest returns, they also have the highest levels of investment and risk. We will now discuss them.

Wholly Owned Subsidiaries

A **wholly owned subsidiary** is a business in which a multinational company owns 100 percent of the stock. Two ways a firm can establish a wholly owned subsidiary are to (1) acquire an existing company in the home country or (2) develop a totally new operation (often referred to as a "greenfield venture").

Benefits   Establishing a wholly owned subsidiary is the most expensive and risky of the various entry modes. However, it can also yield the highest returns. In addition, it provides the multinational company with the greatest degree of control of all activities, including manufacturing, marketing, distribution, and technology development.[67]

Wholly owned subsidiaries are most appropriate where a firm already has the appropriate knowledge and capabilities that it can leverage rather easily through multiple locations in many countries. Examples range from restaurants to semiconductor manufacturers. To lower costs, for example, Intel Corporation builds semiconductor plants throughout the world—all of which use virtually the same blueprint. In establishing wholly owned subsidiaries, knowledge can be further leveraged by the hiring of managers and professionals from the firm's home country, often through hiring talent from competitors.

Risks and Limitations   As noted, wholly owned subsidiaries are typically the most expensive and risky of the various entry modes. With franchising, joint ventures, or strategic alliances, the risk is shared with the firm's partners. With wholly owned subsidiaries, the entire risk is assumed by the parent company. The risks associated with doing business in a new country (e.g., political, cultural, and legal) can be lessened by hiring local talent.

For example, Wendy's was saved from committing two separate blunders in Germany by hiring locals to its advertising staff.[68] In one case, the firm wanted to promote its "old-fashioned" qualities. However, a literal translation would have resulted in the company promoting itself as "outdated." In another situation, Wendy's wanted to emphasize that its hamburgers could be prepared 256 ways. The problem? The German word that Wendy's wanted to use for "ways" usually meant "highways" or "roads." Although such errors may sometimes be entertaining to the public, it is certainly preferable to catch these mistakes before they confuse the consumer or embarrass the company.

In this closing section, we have addressed entry strategies as a progression from exporting through the creation of wholly owned subsidiaries. However, we must point out that many firms do not follow such an evolutionary approach. Instead, such firms follow rather unique entry strategies; see the discussion of Häagen-Dazs in Strategy Spotlight 7.9.

Häagen-Dazs's Unique Entry Strategy

The ice-cream and frozen yogurt company Häagen-Dazs (now a subsidiary of General Mills) has taken a unique route for cross-border entry. Rather than follow traditional entry modes, the Bronx, New York–based company has an unconventional way of moving beyond the boundaries of the United States.

The company uses a three-step process. First, it uses high-end retailers to introduce the brand. Next, it finds high-traffic areas to build company-owned stores. The last step is to sell Häagen-Dazs products in convenience stores and supermarkets.

Häagen-Dazs is quick to adapt to local needs. For instance, freezers in some European stores are notorious for their unreliability. Clearly, a freezer malfunction would ruin a store's stock of Häagen-Dazs products. So Häagen-Dazs buys high-quality freezers for stores willing to carry its brand. Small sacrifices such as this have grown the company from a small ice-cream manufacturer in the Bronx to a worldwide franchiser with 650 stores in 55 countries, including Belgium, France, Japan, and the United Kingdom.

Sources: Meremenot, M. 1991. Screaming for Häagen-Dazs. *BusinessWeek*, October 14: 121; Häagen-Dazs. 2001. Information for franchisees. Häagen-Dazs company document: 1–24.

Reflecting on Career Implications . . .

- *International Strategy:* Be aware of your organization's international strategy. What percentage of the total firm activity is international? What skills are needed to enhance your company's international efforts? How can you get more involved in your organization's international strategy? For your career, what conditions in your home country might cause you to seek careers abroad?
- *Outsourcing and Offshoring:* What activities in your organization can/should be outsourced or offshored? Be aware that you are competing in the global marketplace for employment and professional advancement. Continually take inventory of your talents, skills, and competencies.
- *International Career Opportunities:* Work assignments in other countries can often provide a career boost. Be proactive in pursuing promising career opportunities in other countries. Anticipate how such opportunities will advance your short- and long-term career aspirations.
- *Management Risks:* Develop cultural sensitivity. This applies, of course, to individuals from different cultures in your home-based organization as well as in your overseas experience.

Summary

We live in a highly interconnected global community where many of the best opportunities for growth and profitability lie beyond the boundaries of a company's home country. Along with the opportunities, of course, there are many risks associated with diversification into global markets.

The first section of the chapter addressed the factors that determine a nation's competitiveness in a particular industry. The framework was developed by Professor Michael Porter of Harvard University and was based on a four-year study that explored the competitive success of 10 leading trading nations. The four factors, collectively termed the "diamond of national advantage," were factor conditions, demand characteristics, related and supporting industries, and firm strategy, structure, and rivalry.

The discussion of Porter's "diamond" helped, in essence, to set the broader context for exploring competitive advantage at the firm level. In the second section, we discussed the primary motivations and the potential risks associated with international expansion. The primary motivations included increasing the size of the potential market for the firm's products and services, achieving economies of scale, extending the life cycle of the firm's products, and optimizing the location for every activity in the value chain. On the other hand, the key risks included political and economic risks, currency risks, and management risks. Management risks are the challenges associated with responding to the inevitable differences that exist across countries such as customs, culture, language, customer preferences, and distribution systems. We also addressed some of the managerial challenges and opportunities associated with offshoring and outsourcing.

Next, we addressed how firms can go about attaining competitive advantage in global markets. We began by discussing the two opposing forces—cost reduction and adaptation to local markets—that managers must contend with when entering global markets. The relative importance of these two factors plays a major part in determining which of the four basic types of strategies to select: international, global, multidomestic, or transnational. The chapter covered the benefits and risks associated with each type of strategy. We also presented a recent perspective by Alan Rugman who argues that despite all the talk of globalization, most of the large multinationals are regional or at best biregional (in terms of geographical diversification of sales) rather than global.

The final section discussed the four types of entry strategies that managers may undertake when entering international markets. The key trade-off in each of these strategies is the level of investment or risk versus the level of control. In order of their progressively greater investment/risk and control, the strategies range from exporting to licensing and franchising, to strategic alliances and joint ventures, to wholly owned subsidiaries. The relative benefits and risks associated with each of these strategies were addressed.

Summary Review Questions

1. What are some of the advantages and disadvantages associated with a firm's expansion into international markets?

2. What are the four factors described in Porter's diamond of national advantage? How do the four factors explain why some industries in a given country are more successful than others?

3. Explain the two opposing forces—cost reduction and adaptation to local markets—that firms must deal with when they go global.

4. There are four basic strategies—international, global, multidomestic, and transnational. What are the advantages and disadvantages associated with each?

5. What is the basis of Alan Rugman's argument that most multinationals are still more regional than global? What factors inhibit firms from becoming truly global?

6. Describe the basic entry strategies that firms have available when they enter international markets. What are the relative advantages and disadvantages of each?

Key Terms

factor conditions (national advantage), 230
demand conditions (national advantage), 230
related and supporting industries (national advantage), 231
firm strategy, structure, and rivalry (national advantage), 231
political risk, 238
economic risk, 238
currency risk, 239
management risk, 239
outsourcing, 240
offshoring, 240
exporting, 252
licensing, 253
franchinsing, 253
wholly owned subsidiary, 256

Experiential Exercise

The United States is considered a world leader in the motion picture industry. Using Porter's diamond framework for national competitiveness, explain the success of this industry.

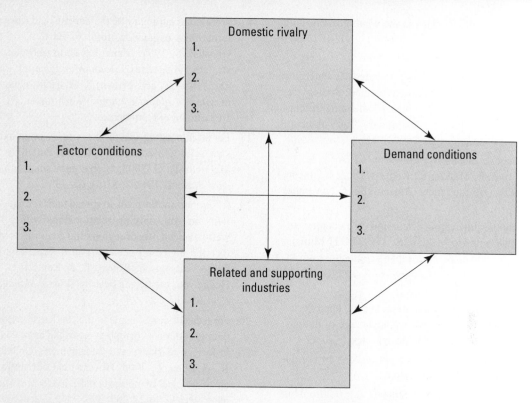

Domestic rivalry
1.
2.
3.

Factor conditions
1.
2.
3.

Demand conditions
1.
2.
3.

Related and supporting industries
1.
2.
3.

Application Questions Exercises

1. Data on the "competitiveness of nations" can be found at www.imd.ch/wcy/ranking/. This Web site provides a ranking on a variety of criteria for 49 countries. How might Porter's diamond of national advantage help to explain the rankings for some of these countries for certain industries that interest you?

2. The Internet has lowered the entry barriers for smaller firms that wish to diversify into international markets. Why is this so? Provide an example.

3. Many firms fail when they enter into strategic alliances with firms that link up with companies based in other countries. What are some reasons for this failure? Provide an example.

4. Many large U.S.–based management consulting companies such as McKinsey and Company and the BCG Group have been very successful in the international marketplace. How can Porter's diamond explain their success?

Ethics Questions

1. Over the past few decades, many American firms have relocated most or all of their operations from the United States to countries such as Mexico and China that pay lower wages. What are some of the ethical issues that such actions may raise?

2. Business practices and customs vary throughout the world. What are some of the ethical issues concerning payments that must be made in a foreign country to obtain business opportunities?

References

1. Birger, J. 2007. The unending woes of Lee Scott. *Fortune.* January 27: 118, 122; Berner, R. 2007. My year at Wal-Mart. *BusinessWeek,* February 12: 70–74; Anonymous. 2006. Wal-Mart in Japan sees losses. www.sptimes.com, August 23, np; and Mi-Young, A. 2000. Wal-Mart has to adapt to the South Korean customer. *Deutsche Presse-Agentur.* November 8: 1–3.

2. For a recent discussion on globalization by one of international business's most respected authors, read Ohmae, K. 2005. *The next global stage: Challenges and opportunities in our borderless world.* Philadelphia: Wharton School Publishing.

3. Our discussion of globalization draws upon Engardio, P., & Belton, C. 2000. Global capitalism: Can it be made to work better? *BusinessWeek,* November 6: 72–98.

4. Sellers, P. 2005. Blowing in the wind. *Fortune,* July 25: 63.

5. Engardio & Belton, op. cit.

6. For insightful perspectives on strategy in emerging economies, refer to the article entitled: Strategy research in emerging economies: Challenging the conventional wisdom in the January 2005 issue of *Journal of Management Studies,* 42(1).

7. The above discussion draws on Clifford, M. L., Engardio, P., Malkin, E., Roberts, D., & Echikson, W. 2000. Up the ladder. *BusinessWeek,* November 6: 78–84.

8. For another interesting discussion on a country perspective, refer to Makino, S. 1999. MITI Minister Kaora Yosano on reviving Japan's competitive advantages. *Academy of Management Executive,* 13(4): 8–28.

9. The following discussion draws heavily upon Porter, M. E. 1990. The competitive advantage of nations. *Harvard Business Review,* March–April: 73–93.

10. Landes, D. S. 1998. *The wealth and poverty of nations.* New York: W. W. Norton.

11. A recent study that investigates the relationship between international diversification and firm performance is Lu, J. W., & Beamish, P. W. 2004. International diversification and firm performance: The s-curve hypothesis. *Academy of Management Journal,* 47(4): 598–609.

12. Part of our discussion of the motivations and risks of international expansion draws upon Gregg, F. M. 1999. International strategy. In Helms, M. M. (Ed.). *Encyclopedia of management:* 434–438. Detroit: Gale Group.

13. These two examples are discussed, respectively, in Dawar, N., & Frost, T. 1999. Competing with giants: Survival strategies for local companies in emerging markets. *Harvard Business Review,* 77(2): 119–129; and Prahalad, C. K., & Lieberthal, K. 1998. The end of corporate imperialism. *Harvard Business Review,* 76(4): 68–79.

14. Meredith, R. 2004. Middle kingdom, middle class. *Forbes,* November 15: 188–192; and Anonymous. 2004. Middle class becomes rising power in China. www.Chinadaily.com. November 6.

15. This discussion draws upon Gupta, A. K., & Govindarajan, V. 2001. Converting global presence into global competitive advantage. *Academy of Management Executive,* 15(2): 45–56.

16. Stross, R. E. 1997. Mr. Gates builds his brain trust. *Fortune,* December 8: 84–98.

17. For a good summary of the benefits and risks of international expansion, refer to Bartlett, C. A., & Ghoshal, S. 1987. Managing across borders: New strategic responses. *Sloan Management Review,* 28(5): 45–53; and Brown, R. H. 1994. *Competing to win in a global economy.* Washington, DC: U.S. Department of Commerce.

18. For an interesting insight into rivalry in global markets, refer to MacMillan, I. C., van Putten, A. B., & McGrath, R. G. 2003. Global gamesmanship. *Harvard Business Review,* 81(5): 62–73.

19. It is important for firms to spread their foreign operations and outsourcing relationships with a broad, well-balanced mix of regions and countries to reduce risk and increase potential reward. For example, refer to Vestring, T., Rouse, T., & Reinert, U. 2005. Hedge your offshoring bets. *MIT Sloan Management Review,* 46(3): 27–29.

20. For a discussion of some of the challenges associated with government corruption regarding entry strategies in foreign markets, read Rodriguez, P., Uhlenbruck, K., & Eden, L. 2005. Government corruption and entry strategies of multinationals. *Academy of Management Review,* 30(2): 383–396.

21. For a discussion of the political risks in China for United States companies, refer to Garten, J. E. 1998. Opening the doors for business in China. *Harvard Business Review,* 76(3): 167–175.

22. Shari, M. 2001. Is a holy war brewing in Indonesia? *BusinessWeek,* October 15: 62.

23. For an interesting perspective on the relationship between diversification and the development of a nation's institutional environment, read Chakrabarti, A., Singh, K., & Mahmood, I. 2007. Diversification and performance: Evidence from East Asian firms. *Strategic Management Journal,* 28(2): 101–120.

24. Gikkas, N. S. 1996. International licensing of intellectual property: The promise and the peril. *Journal of Technology Law & Policy,* 1(1): 1–26.

25. For an excellent theoretical discussion of how cultural factors can affect knowledge transfer across national boundaries, refer to Bhagat, R. S., Kedia, B. L., Harveston, P. D., & Triandis, H. C. 2002. Cultural variations in the cross-border transfer of organizational knowledge: An integrative framework. *Academy of Management Review,* 27(2): 204–221.

26. To gain insights on the role of national and regional cultures on knowledge management models and frameworks, read Pauleen, D. J., & Murphy, P. 2005.

In praise of cultural bias. *MIT Sloan Management Review,* 46(2): 21–22.

27. Berkowitz, E. N. 2000. *Marketing* (6th ed.). New York: McGraw-Hill.

28. Morrison, T. Conaway, W., & Borden, G. 1994. *Kiss, bow, or shake hands.* Avon, MA: Adams Media; and www.executiveplanet.com/business-culture.

29. World Trade Organization. *Annual Report 1998.* Geneva: World Trade Organization.

30. Lei, D. 2005. Outsourcing. In Hitt, M. A., & Ireland, R. D. (Eds.). *The Blackwell encyclopedia of management.* Entrepreneurship: 196–199. Malden, MA: Blackwell.

31. Dolan, K.A. 2006. Offshoring the offshorers. *Forbes.* April 17: 74–78.

32. The discussion above draws from Colvin, J. 2004. Think your job can't be sent to India? Just watch. *Fortune,* December 13: 80; Schwartz, N. D. 2004. Down and out in white collar America. *Fortune,* June 23: 321–325; Hagel, J. 2004. Outsourcing is not just about cost cutting. *The Wall Street Journal,* March 18: A3.

33. Levitt, T. 1983. The globalization of markets. *Harvard Business Review,* 61(3): 92–102.

34. Our discussion of these assumptions draws upon Douglas, S. P., & Wind, Y. 1987. The myth of globalization. *Columbia Journal of World Business,* Winter: 19–29.

35. Ghoshal, S. 1987. Global strategy: An organizing framework. *Strategic Management Journal,* 8: 425–440.

36. Bartlett, C. A., & Ghoshal, S. 1989. *Managing across borders: The transnational solution.* Boston: Harvard Business School Press.

37. For insights on global branding, refer to Aaker, D. A., & Joachimsthaler, E. 1999. The lure of global branding. *Harvard Business Review,* 77(6): 137–146.

38. For an interesting perspective on how small firms can compete in their home markets, refer to Dawar & Frost, op. cit.: 119–129.

39. Hout, T., Porter, M. E., & Rudden, E. 1982. How global companies win out. *Harvard Business Review,* 60(5): 98–107.

40. Fryer, B. 2001. Tom Siebel of Siebel Systems: High tech the old-fashioned way. *Harvard Business Review,* 79(3): 118–130.

41. The risks that are discussed for the global, multidomestic, and transnational strategies draw upon Gupta & Govindarajan, op. cit.

42. Sigiura, H. 1990. How Honda localizes its global strategy. *Sloan Management Review,* 31: 77–82.

43. Prahalad & Lieberthal, op. cit.: 68–79. Their article also discusses how firms may have to reconsider their brand management, costs of market building, product design, and approaches to capital efficiency when entering foreign markets.

44. Hofstede, G. 1980. *Culture's consequences: International differences in work-related values.* Beverly Hills, CA: Sage; Hofstede, G. 1993. Cultural constraints in management theories. *Academy of Management Executive,* 7(1): 81–94; Kogut, B., & Singh, H. 1988. The effect of national culture on the choice of entry mode. *Journal of International Business Studies,* 19: 411–432; and Usinier, J. C. 1996. *Marketing across cultures.* London: Prentice Hall.

45. McCune, J. C. 1999. Exporting corporate culture. *Management Review,* December: 53–56.

46. Prahalad, C. K., & Doz, Y. L. 1987. *The multinational mission: Balancing local demands and global vision.* New York: Free Press.

47. Kidd, J. B., & Teramoto, Y. 1995. The learning organization: The case of Japanese RHQs in Europe. *Management international review,* 35 (Special Issue): 39–56.

48. Gupta, A. K., & Govindarajan, V. 2000. Knowledge flows within multinational corporations. *Strategic Management Journal,* 21(4): 473–496.

49. Wetlaufer, S. 2001. The business case against revolution: An interview with Nestlé's Peter Brabeck. *Harvard Business Review,* 79(2): 112–121.

50. Nobel, R., & Birkinshaw, J. 1998. Innovation in multinational corporations: Control and communication patterns in international R&D operations. *Strategic Management Journal,* 19(5): 461–478.

51. This section draws upon Ghemawat, P. 2005. Regional strategies for global leadership. *Harvard Business Review.* 84(12): 98–108; Ghemawat, P. 2006. Apocalypse now? *Harvard Business Review.* 84(12): 32; Ghemawat, P. 2001. Distance still matters: The hard reality of global expansion. *Harvard Business Review,* 79(8): 137–147; Peng, M.W. 2006. *Global strategy:* 387. Mason, OH: Thomson Southwestern; and Rugman, A. M., & Verbeke, A. 2004. A perspective on regional and global strategies of multinational enterprises. *Journal of International Business Studies.* 35: 3–18.

52. For a rigorous analysis of performance implications of entry strategies, refer to Zahra, S. A., Ireland, R. D., & Hitt, M. A. 2000. International expansion by new venture firms: International diversity, modes of entry, technological learning, and performance. *Academy of Management Journal,* 43(6): 925–950.

53. Li, J. T. 1995. Foreign entry and survival: The effects of strategic choices on performance in international markets. *Strategic Management Journal,* 16: 333–351.

54. For a discussion of how home-country environments can affect diversification strategies, refer to Wan, W. P., & Hoskisson, R. E. 2003. Home country environments, corporate diversification strategies, and firm performance. *Academy of Management Journal,* 46(1): 27–45.

55. Arnold, D. 2000. Seven rules of international distribution. *Harvard Business Review,* 78(6): 131–137.

56. Sharma, A. 1998. Mode of entry and ex-post performance. *Strategic Management Journal,* 19(9): 879–900.

57. This section draws upon Arnold, op. cit.: 131–137; and Berkowitz, op. cit.

58. Kline, D. 2003. Strategic licensing. *MIT Sloan Management Review,* 44(3): 89–93.

59. Martin, J. 1999. Franchising in the Middle East. *Management Review.* June: 38–42.

60. Arnold, op. cit.; and Berkowitz, op. cit.

61. Manufacturer–supplier relationships can be very effective in global industries such as automobile manufacturing. Refer to Kotabe, M., Martin, X., & Domoto, H. 2003. Gaining from vertical partnerships: Knowledge transfer, relationship duration, and supplier performance improvement in the U.S. and Japanese automotive industries. *Strategic Management Journal,* 24(4): 293–316.

62. For a good discussion, refer to Merchant, H., & Schendel, D. 2000. How do international joint ventures create shareholder value? *Strategic Management Journal,* 21(7): 723–738.

63. This discussion draws upon Walters, B. A., Peters, S., & Dess, G. G. 1994. Strategic alliances and joint ventures: Making them work. *Business Horizons,* 37(4): 5–11.

64. For a rigorous discussion of the importance of information access in international joint ventures, refer to Reuer, J. J., & Koza, M. P. 2000. Asymmetric information and joint venture performance: Theory and evidence for domestic and international joint ventures. *Strategic Management Journal,* 21(1): 81–88.

65. Treece, J. 1991. Why Daewoo wound up on the road to nowhere. *BusinessWeek,* September 23: 55.

66. Dyer, J. H., Kale, P., & Singh, H. 2001. How to make strategic alliances work. *MIT Sloan Management Review,* 42(4): 37–43.

67. For a discussion of some of the challenges in managing subsidiaries, refer to O'Donnell, S. W. 2000. Managing foreign subsidiaries: Agents of headquarters, or an independent network? *Strategic Management Journal,* 21(5): 525–548.

68. Ricks, D. 2006. *Blunders in international business* (4th ed.). Malden, MA: Blackwell Publishing.

Entrepreneurial Strategy and Competitive Dynamics

>learning objectives

After reading this chapter, you should have a good understanding of:

LO1 The role of new ventures and small businesses in the U.S. economy.

LO2 The role of opportunities, resources, and entrepreneurs in successfully pursuing new ventures.

LO3 Three types of entry strategies—pioneering, imitative, and adaptive—commonly used to launch a new venture.

LO4 How the generic strategies of overall cost leadership, differentiation, and focus are used by new ventures and small businesses.

LO5 How competitive actions, such as the entry of new competitors into a marketplace, may launch a cycle of actions and reactions among close competitors.

LO6 The components of competitive dynamics analysis—new competitive action, threat analysis, motivation and capability to respond, types of competitive actions, and likelihood of competitive reaction.

*n*ew technologies, shifting social and demographic trends, and sudden changes in the business environment create opportunities for entrepreneurship. New ventures, which often emerge under such conditions, face unique strategic challenges if they are going to survive and grow. Young and small businesses, which are a major engine of growth in the U.S. economy because of their role in job creation and innovation, must rely on sound strategic principles to be successful.

This chapter addresses how new ventures and entrepreneurial firms can achieve competitive advantages. It also examines how entrepreneurial activity influences a firm's strategic priorities and intensifies the rivalry among an industry's close competitors.

In the first section, we discuss the role of opportunity recognition in the process of new venture creation. Three factors that are important in determining whether a value-creating opportunity should be pursued are highlighted—the nature of the opportunity, the resources available to undertake it, and the characteristics of the entrepreneur(s) pursuing it.

The second section addresses three different types of new entry strategies—pioneering, imitative, and adaptive. Then, the generic strategies (discussed in Chapter 5) as well as combination strategies are addressed in terms of how they apply to new ventures and entrepreneurial firms. Additionally, some of the pitfalls associated with each of these strategic approaches are presented.

In section three, we explain how new entrants and other competitors often set off a series of actions and reactions that affect the competitive dynamics of an industry. In determining how to react to a competitive action, firms must analyze whether they are seriously threatened by the action, how important it is for them to respond, and what resources they can muster to mount a response. They must also determine what type of action is appropriate—strategic or tactical—and whether their close competitors are likely to counterattack. Taken together, these actions often have a strong impact on the strategic choices and overall profitability of an industry.

Learning from Mistakes

The success of an entrepreneurial venture—whether it is undertaken by a small start-up or a major corporation—depends on many factors. The right combination of resources, know-how, and strategic action can lead to above-average profitability and value-creating advantages. However, many things can go wrong. To see how a firm's efforts to launch an entrepreneurial new entry can turn sour, consider the example of ESPN's foray into the cell phone business.[1]

ESPN, the giant sports network, has grown to an impressive $5 billion-a-year business since it was launched just 27 years ago. Today it shows up everywhere in the world of sports and seems as if it has been around forever. That impression stems in part from ESPN's great ability to know sports fans and to deliver what its customers want. The company has leveraged its brand "with the ferocity of a linebacker on steroids" according to *BusinessWeek* media expert Tom Lowry.[2] The result has been a number of successful brand extensions including *ESPN Magazine* with a circulation of nearly 2 million, ESPN Zone Restaurants, and ESPN2, a second cable TV station that scrolls sports scores and plays rock music.

With such an impressive track record, it's no surprise that ESPN, the high-flying unit of the Walt Disney Co., would attempt to extend its reach into the fast-growing world of wireless communications. On Super Bowl Sunday 2006, ESPN *[continued]*

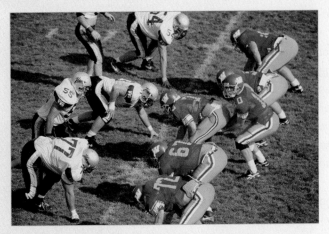

● Football is one of many sports that ESPN has aggressively promoted through its broadcasts.

announced that it was launching its own cell phone service, Mobile ESPN. The service was targeted at sports fanatics—the kind who can't stand to miss "Sports Center" or not know the latest scores. Through an expensive $40 million ad campaign that ran on ESPN.com as well as TV and radio stations, Mobile ESPN promised unique sports content on a 24/7 basis.

The effort was troubled from the start. Despite extensive advertising, ". . . it was tough to tell where you could get their phones," observed wireless industry expert Peter Gorham in *Red Herring*.[3] The phones, which critics described as "very plain," cost up to $199, and monthly service ran from $65 to as much as $225 for premium content. Except for the sports content, no incentives were offered to customers who were being asked to switch carriers and abandon their family calling plans.

Behind the scenes, the hurdles facing ESPN's new entry proved insurmountable. Although ESPN was primarily targeting existing customers, the move into cell phones represented entry into a new industry where it was one of 175 MVNOs (mobile virtual network operators) in the United States. To make this move, it had to pay Sprint to lease its network infrastructure. In addition, because ESPN is a secondary rights holder to most sports content, it has to pay the leagues for the clips it broadcasts. It was this "double whammy" of expenses that led ESPN to charge such high fees.

In the end, the cost of switching was too high and only 30,000 users signed up for the service. ESPN had projected that 500,000 were needed to break even so after just eight months, it pulled the plug. Overall, the experiment cost ESPN nearly $150 million.

Despite ESPN's large base of dedicated customers, the company misread how easy it would be to leverage its brand. The entrepreneurial entry it attempted involved using its strong reputation and differentiated content to attract users of its new service. But unlike other ESPN brand extensions such as clothing and publications, cell phones are more of a necessity than a luxury for millions of users. ESPN did not recognize that most customers would prefer reliable service at competitive prices over highly specialized content at premium prices. ESPN also failed to assess the competitive environment correctly. The sports network was simply no match for well-known, reliable MVNO companies capable of offering multiple phone plans, buyer incentives, and 24/7 customer service.[4] Given that ESPN had to pay for both sports content and network access to offer the service, its profit margin was too narrow to react to these competitive pressures. To its credit, ESPN cut its losses and got out quickly once it realized its new venture was failing.

The ESPN case illustrates how important it is for new entrepreneurial entrants—whether they are start-ups or incumbents—to think and act strategically. Even with a strong resource base and good track record, an ill-conceived strategy and strong competitive forces may prevent what seems like a good idea from taking off.

In this chapter we address entrepreneurial strategies. The previous three chapters have focused primarily on the business-level, corporate-level, and international strategies of incumbent firms. Here we ask: What about the strategies of those entering into a market or industry for the first time? Whether it's a small, young start-up or an existing company seeking growth opportunities such as ESPN, new entrants need effective strategies. In the first part of this chapter, we discuss how companies recognize opportunities and improve their chances of success by effectively using entrepreneurial strategy.

Companies wishing to launch new ventures must also be aware that, consistent with the five forces model in Chapter 2, new entrants are a threat to existing firms in an industry. Entry into a new market arena is intensely competitive from the perspective of incumbents in that arena. Therefore, new entrants can nearly always expect a competitive response from other companies in the industry it is entering. Knowledge of the competitive dynamics that are at work in the business environment is an aspect of entrepreneurial new entry that will be addressed later in this chapter.

Before moving on, it is important to highlight the role that entrepreneurial start-ups and small business play in entrepreneurial value creation. Young and small firms are responsible for more innovations and more new job creation than any other type of business.[5] As such, they are the primary users of entrepreneurial strategies. Strategy Spotlight 8.1 addresses some of the reasons why small business and entrepreneurship are viewed favorably in the United States.

>LO1
The role of new ventures and small businesses in the U.S. economy.

Recognizing Entrepreneurial Opportunities

Defined broadly, **entrepreneurship** refers to new value creation. As noted earlier, even though entrepreneurial activity is usually associated with start-up companies, new value can be created in many different contexts including:

- *Start-up ventures*
- *Major corporations*
- *Family-owned businesses*
- *Non-profit organizations*
- *Established institutions*

entrepreneurship
the creation of new value by an existing organization or new venture that involves the assumption of risk.

For an entrepreneurial venture to create new value, three factors must be present—an entrepreneurial opportunity, the resources to pursue the opportunity, and an entrepreneur or entrepreneurial team willing and able to undertake the opportunity.[6] The entrepreneurial strategy that an organization uses will depend on these three factors. Thus, beyond merely identifying a venture concept, the opportunity recognition process also involves organizing the key people and resources that are needed to go forward. Exhibit 8.2 on page 269 depicts the three factors that are needed to successfully proceed—opportunity, resources, and entrepreneur(s). In the sections that follow, we address each of these factors.

>LO2
The role of opportunities, resources, and entrepreneurs in successfully pursuing new ventures.

Entrepreneurial Opportunities

The starting point for any new venture is the presence of an entrepreneurial opportunity. Where do opportunities come from? For new business start-ups, opportunities come from many sources—current or past work experiences, hobbies that grow into businesses or lead to inventions, suggestions by friends or family, or a chance event that makes an entrepreneur aware of an unmet need. For established firms, new business opportunities come from the needs of existing customers, suggestions by suppliers, or technological developments that lead to new advances.[7] For all firms, there is a major, overarching factor behind all viable opportunities that emerge in the business landscape: change. Change creates opportunities. Entrepreneurial firms make the most of changes brought about by new technology, sociocultural trends, and shifts in consumer demand.

strategy spotlight

The Contribution of Small Businesses to the U.S. Economy

In the late 1970s, MIT professor David Birch launched a study to explore the sources of business growth. "I wasn't really looking for anything in particular," says Birch. But the findings surprised him: Small businesses create the most jobs. Since then, Birch and others have shown that it's not just big companies that power the economy. Small business and entrepreneurship have become a major component of new job creation.

Sources: Small Business Administration. 2005. *The small business economy.* Washington, DC: U.S. Government Printing Office; Small Business Administration. 2006. Small business by the numbers. *SBA Office of Advocacy,* June, www.sba.gov/advo/; *Inc.* 2001. Small business 2001: Where we are now? May 29: 18–19; Minniti, M., & Bygrave, W. D. 2004. *Global entrepreneurship monitor—National entrepreneurship assessment: United States of America 2004, executive report.* Kansas City, MO: Kauffman Center for Entrepreneurial Leadership; and *Fortune.* 2001. The heroes: A portfolio. October 4: 74.

Here are the facts:

- In the United States, there are approximately 5.6 million companies with fewer than 100 employees. Another 100,000 companies have 100 to 500 employees. In addition, approximately 17.0 million individuals are nonemployer sole proprietors.

- Small businesses create the majority of new jobs. According to recent data, small business created three-quarters of U.S. net new jobs in a recent period (2.5 million of the 3.4 million total). A small percentage of the fastest growing entrepreneurial firms (5 to 15 percent) account for a majority of the new jobs created.

- Small businesses (fewer than 500 employees) employ more than half of the private sector workforce (56 million in 2002) and account for more than 50 percent of nonfarm private gross domestic product (GDP). *(continued)*

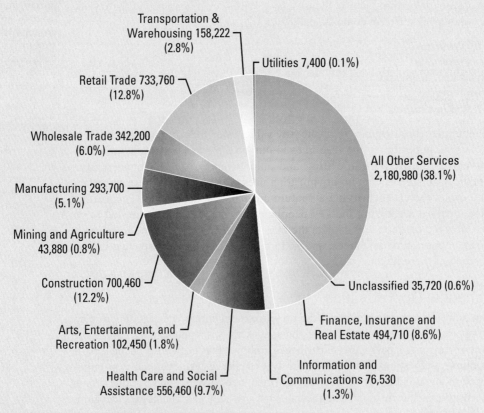

Exhibit 8.1 All U.S. Small Companies by Industry*

*Businesses with 500 or fewer employees in 2002.

Source: Small Business Administration's Office of Advocacy, based on data provided by the U.S. Census Bureau, statistics of U.S. businesses. (Percentages don't add to 100% because of rounding.)

- Small firms produce 13 to 14 times more patents per employee than large patenting firms and employ 39 percent of high-tech workers (such as scientists and engineers). In addition, smaller entrepreneurial firms account for 55 percent of all innovations.

- Small businesses make up 97 percent of all U.S. exporters and accounted for 29 percent of known U.S. export value in 2001.

Exhibit 8.1 shows the number of small businesses in the United States and how they are distributed through different sectors of the economy.

How do changes in the external environment lead to new business creation? They spark creative new ideas and innovation. Businesspeople often have ideas for entrepreneurial ventures. However, not all such ideas are good ideas—that is, viable business opportunities. To determine which ideas are strong enough to become new ventures, entrepreneurs must go through a process of identifying, selecting, and developing potential opportunities. This is the process of **opportunity recognition.**[8]

Opportunity recognition refers to more than just the "Eureka!" feeling that people sometimes experience at the moment they identify a new idea. Although such insights are often very important, the opportunity recognition process involves two phases of activity—discovery and evaluation—that lead to viable new venture opportunities.[9]

The discovery phase refers to the process of becoming aware of a new business concept.[10] Many entrepreneurs report that their idea for a new venture occurred to them in an instant, as a sort of "Aha!" experience—that is, they had some insight or epiphany, often based on their prior knowledge, that gave them an idea for a new business. This may occur unintentionally, because the discovery of new opportunities is often spontaneous and unexpected. For example, Howard Schultz, CEO of Starbucks, was in Milan, Italy, when he suddenly realized that the coffee-and-conversation café model that was common in Europe would work in the United States as well. According to Schultz, he didn't need to do research to find out if Americans would pay $3 for a

opportunity recognition the process of discovering and evaluating changes in the business environment, such as a new technology, socio-cultural trends, or shifts in consumer demand, that can be exploited.

Exhibit 8.2 Opportunity Analysis Framework

Sources: Based on Timmons, J. A., & Spinelli, S. 2004. *New venture creation* (6th ed.). New York: McGraw-Hill/Irwin; and Bygrave, W. D. 1997. The entrepreneurial process. In W. D. Bygrave (Ed.), *The portable MBA in entrepreneurship* (2nd ed.). New York: Wiley.

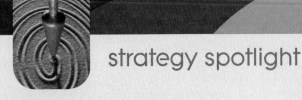
Opportunity Recognition: Great Businesses that Started with a Simple Idea

In the founding of a business, there is always a moment when the opportunity is first recognized. The recognition may unfold in tiny steps over time or appear suddenly as an Aha! experience. When founding entrepreneurs act on such realizations, the rest, as they say, is history. And speaking of history, here are a few examples of the initial sparks that eventually resulted in some very big businesses.

Carl Westcott, founder of 1-800-Flowers

While visiting Los Angeles in 1979, Carl Westcott decided to send flowers back home to his wife. It was late but he finally found a florist that was open. The only problem was, it wouldn't take his credit card over the phone. "Bottom line," recalls Westcott, "I didn't send the flowers." While trying to get the florist to take his order, however, he noticed that the word "flowers" had seven digits. The next day he dialed 1-800-356-9377. The backhaul trucker that answered wasn't too surprised—he had already heard from FTD. But Westcott persisted and offered the man $15,000 and 3 percent of the 1-800-FLOWERS business. Both the trucker and Westcott made out pretty well when he sold the business for $4 million just 18 months later.

David Cook, founder of TollTags

When David Cook heard that the Los Alamos National Laboratories in New Mexico was going to implant miniaturized radio frequency chips under the skin of cattle to track their

Sources: Hall, C. 2004. The big ideas that started here. *Dallas Morning News*, December 26: 1D–6D. www.eds.com; www.hoovers.com; and, www.ntta.org.

location, he laughed and thought, "That's just insane—and tough to market." Soon after, while driving on a toll road, he realized the same technology could be used to enable drivers to pay tolls automatically. To prove that TollTags would work, he raised $6 million from investors to build an electronic payment system on a toll road in Dallas, Texas, with the agreement that the tollway authority could scrap the system with just 24 hours notice. "It was by far the riskiest thing I've ever done in my life," recalls Cook. But it paid off. Today the North Texas Tollway Authority sells nearly 1 million TollTags annually. As for opportunity recognition, Cook says, "You have to believe in your idea and your ability to take your accumulated knowledge and intuition and apply that as you build your business."

Ross Perot, founder of Electronic Data Systems (EDS)

Ross Perot was a salesman at IBM when he had his epiphany: Computer customers don't especially care about computer hardware. What they really need is computing *power.* "It was obvious to me . . . that people wanted a system that worked, which included the computer, the software, the whole package," recalls Perot. He took the idea to his bosses who weren't interested. At the time, 80 cents of every dollar spent on computing was for hardware and IBM dominated the market. But Perot knew he was onto something. "I was sitting in a barbershop reading an old *Reader's Digest* that had a quote from Thoreau that said, 'The mass of men lead lives of quiet desperation.' That's when I made the decision that I had to try it." With $1,000 of his wife's money, he launched EDS in 1962. Today, this provider of information technology and business process outsourcing services enjoys annual revenues of about $20 billion.

cup of coffee—he just *knew*. Starbucks was just a small business at the time but Schultz began literally shaking with excitement about growing it into a bigger business.[11] Strategy Spotlight 8.2 tells how three other highly successful entrepreneurs identified their business opportunities.

Opportunity discovery also may occur as the result of a deliberate search for new venture opportunities or creative solutions to business problems. New venture ideas often emerge only after a concerted effort to identify good opportunities or realistic solutions. It is very similar to a creative process, which may be unstructured and "chaotic" at first but eventually leads to a practical solution or business innovation. To stimulate the discovery of new opportunities, companies often encourage creativity, out-of-the-box thinking, and brainstorming.

Opportunity evaluation, which occurs after an opportunity has been identified, involves analyzing an opportunity to determine whether it is viable and strong enough to be developed into a full-fledged new venture. Ideas that have been developed by new-product groups or in brainstorming sessions are tested by various methods, including talking to potential target customers and discussing operational requirements with production or logistics managers. A technique known as feasibility analysis is used to evaluate these and other critical success factors. This type of analysis often leads to the decision that a new venture project should be discontinued. If the venture concept continues to seem viable, a more formal business plan may be developed.

Among the most important factors to evaluate is the market potential for the product or service. Established firms tend to operate in established markets. They have to adjust to market trends and to shifts in consumer demand, of course, but they usually have a customer base for which they are already filling a marketplace need. New ventures, in contrast, must first determine whether a market exists for the product or service they are contemplating. Thus, a critical element of opportunity recognition is assessing to what extent the opportunity is viable *in the marketplace.*

For an opportunity to be viable, it needs to have four qualities.[12]

- *Attractive.* The opportunity must be attractive in the marketplace; that is, there must be market demand for the new product or service.
- *Achievable.* The opportunity must be practical and physically possible.
- *Durable.* The opportunity must be attractive long enough for the development and deployment to be successful; that is, the window of opportunity must be open long enough for it to be worthwhile.
- *Value creating.* The opportunity must be potentially profitable; that is, the benefits must surpass the cost of development by a significant margin.

If a new business concept meets these criteria, two other factors must be considered before the opportunity is launched as a business: the resources available to undertake it, and the characteristics of the entrepreneur(s) pursuing it. In the next section, we address the issue of entrepreneurial resources; following that, we address the importance of entrepreneurial leaders and teams.

Entrepreneurial Resources

As Exhibit 8.2 indicates, resources are an essential component of a successful entrepreneurial launch. For start-ups, the most important resource is usually money because a new firm typically has to expend substantial sums just to start the business. However, financial resources are not the only kind of resource a new venture needs. Human capital and social capital are also important. Many firms also rely on government resources to help them thrive. In this section we will address some of the resource requirements of entrepreneurial firms and how they can meet their needs.

Financial Resources   Hand-in-hand with the importance of markets (and marketing) to new-venture creation, entrepreneurial firms must also have financing. In fact, the level of available financing is often a strong determinant of how the business is launched and its eventual success. Cash finances are, of course, highly important. But access to capital, such as a line of credit or favorable payment terms with a supplier, can also help a new venture succeed.

In general, financial resources will take one of two forms—debt or equity. Exhibit 8.3 highlights the differences between debt and equity funding and provides examples of each.

The types of financial resources that may be needed depend on two factors: the stage of venture development and the scale of the venture.[13] Entrepreneurial firms that are starting from scratch—start-ups—are at the earliest stage of development. Most start-ups also begin on a relatively small scale. The funding that is available to young and small firms tends to be

Exhibit 8.3

Sources of Venture Financing

Type	Definition	Examples
Equity	Funds invested in ownership shares such as stock. The value of equity funding increases or decreases depending on firm performance. To obtain it usually requires that business founders give up some ownership and control of the business.	• Personal savings • Investments by family and friends • Private investors • Venture capital • Public stock offerings
Debt	Borrowed funds such as interest-bearing loans. In general, debt funding must be repaid regardless of firm performance. To obtain it usually requires that some business or personal assets be used as collateral.	• Bank loans • Credit cards • Loans by family and friends • Mortgaged property • Supplier financing • Public financing

Sources: Comaford-Lynch, C. 2007. Show me the money, part I. *BusinessWeek,* www.businessweek.com, March 12; and Fraser, J. A. 1998. A hitchhiker's guide to capital resources. *Inc.,* February: 74–82.

quite limited. In fact, the vast majority of new firms are low-budget start-ups launched with personal savings and the contributions of family and friends.[14] Even among firms included in the *Entrepreneur* list of the 100 fastest-growing new businesses in a recent year, 61 percent reported that their start-up funds came from personal savings.[15] Although bank financing, public financing, and venture capital are important sources of small business finance, these types of financial support are typically available only after a company has started to conduct business and generate sales. Therefore, the founders usually carry the initial burden of financing most new firms. And the burdens are many: renting space, buying inventory, installing phones and equipment, obtaining insurance, and paying salaries. Strategy Spotlight 8.3 identifies a technique known as bootstrapping that helps start-ups minimize their need for financial resources.

Once a young venture has established itself as a going concern, other sources of financing become readily available.[16] Later-stage financing is also readily available to incumbents that launch entrepreneurial initiatives. Banks, for example, are more likely to loan funds to companies with a track record of sales or other cash-generating activity.

Even "angel" investors—private individuals who provide equity investments for seed capital during the early stages of a new venture—favor companies that already have a winning business model and dominance in a market niche.[17] According to Cal Simmons, coauthor of *Every Business Needs an Angel,* "I would much rather talk to an entrepreneur who has already put his money and his effort into proving the concept.[18]

Start-ups that involve large capital investments or extensive development costs—such as manufacturing or engineering firms that are trying to commercialize an innovative product—may have high cash requirements soon after they are founded. Others need financing only when they are on the brink of rapid growth. To obtain such funding, entrepreneurial firms often seek venture capital. Venture capital is a form of private equity financing through which entrepreneurs raise money by selling shares in the new venture. In contrast to angel investors, who are actively engaged in investing their own money, venture capital companies are organized to place the funds of private investors into lucrative business opportunities. Venture capitalists nearly always have high performance expectations

How Stacy's Pita Chip Co. Bootstrapped Its Way to a Big Pay-off

How does a cash-strapped entrepreneur make ends meet? One way is by *bootstrapping*. This term is used to describe a company that relies on the owner's personal resources and resourcefulness to succeed. Applied to entrepreneurs, it refers to techniques used to minimize borrowing and avoid selling parts of a business to investors or venture capitalists. For the young start-up, this involves getting the most out of every dollar and doing without anything but the bare necessities. It may mean buying used equipment, operating out of a basement, or forgoing a new car purchase in order to reinvest in the business.

To successfully bootstrap, a new firm may have to get cash-generating products or services to market quickly in order to jump start cash flow. Consider the example of Stacy's Pita Chip Co.:

In 1996, founders Mark and Stacy Andrus were operating a successful pita-wrap sandwich business that was ready to grow. But customers kept asking for the baked chips they made every night from leftover pita bread and handed out free to customers waiting in line. "We thought we could get bigger faster with the chips," said Stacy. The couple, who were still paying off six-figure student loans, decided to take their chips nationwide. The business they created is a model of bootstrapping efficiency. The paper sign on the door, folding tables, and used dining room chairs are the first signs of their spartan approach to business. They also saved over $250,000 buying used equipment. "Everything goes into the business," said Stacy, who takes home a scavenger-level salary.

Has it paid off? Absolutely. Within just a few years, their baked pita chips were generating annual revenues over $1.3 million with sales in 37 states. In 2006, just 10 years after starting, the company was acquired by snack food giant PepsiCo for $60 million.

Sources: Anonymous. 2006. PepsiCo completes acquisition of Stacy's Pita Chip. *Boston Business Journal*, www.bizjournals.com/boston, January 13; Stuart, A. 2001. The pita principle. *Inc. Magazine*, August: 58–64; and www.stacyssnacks.com.

from the companies they invest in, but they also provide important managerial advice, and links to key contacts in an industry.

Despite the importance of venture capital to many fast-growing firms, the vast majority of external funding for young and small firms comes from informal sources such as family and friends. Exhibit 8.4, based on the *Global Entrepreneurship Monitor* survey of entrepreneurial firms, demonstrates this dramatic difference. A closer look, however, reveals an interesting fact: Firms that obtain venture capital receive funding of about $2.6 million each. In contrast, companies that obtain funding from informal sources typically receive only about $10,000 each. Although relatively few companies receive venture funding, they are attractive to venture capitalists because their profit potential and impact on innovation, job growth, and wealth creation tends to be much greater.

Clearly, financial resources are essential for entrepreneurial ventures.[19] But other types of resources are also vitally important. Next we address the role of human capital, social capital, and government resources in the entrepreneurial value creation process.

Human Capital   Bankers, venture capitalists, and angel investors who invest in entrepreneurial firms and small businesses agree that the most important asset an entrepreneurial firm can have is strong and skilled management. According to Stephen Gaal, founding member of Walnut Venture Associates, venture investors do not invest in businesses; instead "We invest in people . . . very smart people with very high integrity." Managers need to have a strong base of experience and extensive domain knowledge, as well as an ability to make rapid decisions and change direction as shifting circumstances may require. In the case of start-ups, more is better. New ventures that are started by teams of three, four, or five entrepreneurs are more likely to succeed in the long run than are ventures launched by "lone wolf" entrepreneurs.[20]

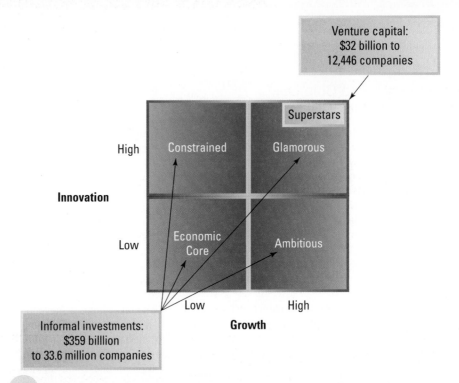

Exhibit 8.4 How Different Types of New Ventures Are Financed:
Informal Investment versus Venture Capital

Source: Reynolds, P. D., Bygrave, W. D., & Autio, E. 2004. *Global Entrepreneurship Monitor: 2003 executive report*. Babson College, London Business School, and the Kauffman Foundation. The classification of the company system used by GEM is based on Kirchhoff, B. 1994. *Entrepreneurship and dynamic capitalism*. London: Praeger.

Social Capital   New ventures founded by entrepreneurs who have extensive social contacts are more likely to succeed than are ventures started without the support of a social network.[21] Even though a venture may be new, if the founders have contacts who will vouch for them, they gain exposure and build legitimacy faster.[22] This support can come from several sources: prior jobs, industry organizations, and local business groups such as the chamber of commerce. These contacts can all contribute to a growing network that provides support for the entrepreneurial firm. Janina Pawlowski, cofounder of the online lending company E-Loan, attributes part of her success to the strong advisors she persuaded to serve on her board of directors, including Tim Koogle, former CEO of Yahoo![23]

Strategic alliances represent a type of social capital that can be especially important to young and small firms.[24] Strategy Spotlight 8.4 presents a few examples of alliances and some potential pitfalls of using alliances.

Government Resources   In the United States, the federal government provides support for entrepreneurial firms in two key arenas—financing and government contracting. The Small Business Administration (SBA) has several loan guarantee programs designed to support the growth and development of entrepreneurial firms. The government itself does not lend money but underwrites loans made by banks to small businesses, thus reducing the risk associated with lending to firms with unproven records. The SBA also offers training, counseling, and support services through its local offices and Small Business Development Centers.[25] State and local governments also

Strategic Alliances:
A Key Entrepreneurial Resource

Strategic alliances provide a key avenue for growth by entrepreneurial firms. By partnering with other companies, young or small firms can expand or give the appearance of entering numerous markets and/or handling a range of operations. Here are several types of alliances that have been used to extend or strengthen entrepreneurial firms:

Technology Alliances

Tech-savvy entrepreneurial firms often benefit from forming alliances with older incumbents. The alliance allows the larger firm to enhance its technological capabilities and expands the revenue and reach of the smaller firm.

Manufacturing Alliances

The use of outsourcing and other manufacturing alliances by small firms has grown dramatically in recent years. Internet-enabled capabilities such as collaborating online about delivery and design specifications has greatly simplified doing business, even with foreign manufacturers.

Sources: Copeland, M. V., & Tilin, A. 2005. Get someone to build it. *Business 2.0*, 6(5): 88–90; Monahan, J. 2005. All systems grow. *Entrepreneur*, March: 78–82; Prince, C. J. 2005. Foreign affairs. *Entrepreneur*, March: 56; and, Weaver, K. M., & Dickson, P. 2004. Strategic alliances. In W. J. Dennis, Jr. (Ed.), *NFIB national small business poll*. Washington, DC: National Federation of Independent Business.

Retail Alliances

Licensing agreements allow one company to sell the products and services of another in different markets, including overseas. Specialty products—the types sometimes made by entrepreneurial firms—often seem more exotic when sold in another country.

According to the National Federation of Independent Business (NFIB), nearly two-thirds of small businesses currently hold or have held some type of alliance. Strategic alliances among entrepreneurial firms can take many different forms. Exhibit 8.5 shows the different types of partnering that small businesses and small manufacturers in the NFIB study often use.

Although such alliances often sound good, there are also potential pitfalls. Lack of oversight and control is one danger of partnering with foreign firms. Problems with product quality, timely delivery, and receiving payments can also sour an alliance relationship if it is not carefully managed. With technology alliances, there is a risk that big firms may take advantage of the technological know-how of their entrepreneurial partners. However, even with these potential problems, strategic alliances provide a good means for entrepreneurial firms to develop and grow.

Type of Alliance and/or Long-Term Agreement*	Small Manufacturers	Small Businesses
Licensing	20.0%	32.5%
Export/Import	14.4%	7.3%
Franchise	5.0%	5.3%
Marketing	18.0%	25.2%
Distribution	20.1%	20.5%
Production	26.5%	11.3%
Product/Services R&D	12.2%	12.6%
Process R&D	6.7%	5.3%
Purchaser/Supplier	23.5%	13.9%
Outside Contracting	23.2%	28.5%

*Columns add to over 100 percent because firms may use multiple alliances.

Exhibit 8.5 Use of Strategic Alliances by Small Businesses and Small Manufacturers

Source: From Weaver, K. M., & Dickson, P. 2004. Strategic Alliances. In W. J. Dennis, Jr. (Ed.), *NFIB National Small Business Poll*. Washington, DC: National Federation of Independent Business. Reprinted with permission.

have hundreds of programs to provide funding, contracts, and other support for new ventures and small businesses.

Another key area of support is in government contracting. Programs sponsored by the SBA and other government agencies ensure that small businesses have the opportunity to bid on contracts to provide goods and services to the government. Although working with the government sometimes has its drawbacks in terms of issues of regulation and time-consuming decision making, programs to support small businesses and entrepreneurial activity constitute an important resource for entrepreneurial firms.

Entrepreneurial Leadership

Whether a venture is launched by an individual entrepreneur or an entrepreneurial team, effective leadership is needed. Launching a new venture requires a special kind of leadership. It involves courage, belief in one's convictions, and the energy to work hard even in difficult circumstances. Yet these are the very challenges that motivate most business owners. Entrepreneurs put themselves to the test and get their satisfaction from acting independently, overcoming obstacles, and thriving financially. To do so, they must embody three characteristics of leadership—vision, dedication and drive, and commitment to excellence—and pass these on to all those who work with them:

- *Vision.* This may be an entrepreneur's most important asset. Entrepreneurs envision realities that do not yet exist. Not all new businesses succeed. But without a vision, most entrepreneurs would never even get their venture off the ground. With a vision, entrepreneurs are able to exercise a kind of transformational leadership that creates something new and, in some way, changes the world. Just having a vision, however, is not enough. To develop support, get financial backing, and attract employees, entrepreneurial leaders must share their vision with others.
- *Dedication and drive.* Dedication and drive are reflected in hard work. Drive involves internal motivation; dedication calls for an intellectual commitment that keeps an entrepreneur going even in the face of bad news or poor luck. They both require patience, stamina, and a willingness to work long hours. However, a business built on the heroic efforts of one person may suffer in the long run. That's why the dedicated entrepreneur's enthusiasm is also important—like a magnet, it attracts others to the business to help with the work.
- *Commitment to excellence.* Excellence requires entrepreneurs to develop a commitment to knowing the customer, providing quality goods and services, paying attention to details, and continuously learning. Entrepreneurs who achieve excellence are sensitive to how these factors work together and devote themselves to surpassing the performance of competitors. However, entrepreneurs may flounder if they think they are the only ones who can create excellent results. The most successful, by contrast, often report that they owe their success to hiring people smarter than themselves.

In his book *Good to Great,* Jim Collins makes another important point about entrepreneurial leadership: Ventures that are built on the charisma of a single person may have trouble growing "from good to great" once that person leaves.[26] Thus, the leadership that is needed to build a great organization is usually exercised by a team of dedicated people working together rather than a single leader. Another aspect of this team approach is attracting team members who fit with the company's culture, goals, and work ethic. "Those people who do not share the company's core values," Collins says, "find themselves surrounded by corporate antibodies and ejected like a virus."[27] Thus, for a venture's leadership to be a valuable resource and not a liability it must be cohesive in its vision, drive and dedication, and commitment to excellence.

Once an opportunity has been recognized, and an entrepreneurial team and resources have been assembled, a new venture must craft a strategy. Prior chapters have addressed the strategies of incumbent firms. In the next section, we highlight the types of strategies and strategic considerations faced by new entrants.

Entrepreneurial Strategy

Successfully creating new ventures requires several ingredients. As indicated in Exhibit 8.2, three factors are necessary—a viable opportunity, sufficient resources, and a skilled and dedicated entrepreneur or entrepreneurial team. Once these elements are in place, the new venture needs a strategy. In this section, we consider several different strategic factors that are unique to new ventures and also how the generic strategies introduced in Chapter 5 can be applied to entrepreneurial firms. We also indicate how combination strategies might benefit entrepreneurial firms and address the potential pitfalls associated with launching new venture strategies.

To be successful new ventures must evaluate industry conditions, the competitive environment, and market opportunities in order to position themselves strategically. However, a traditional strategic analysis may have to be altered somewhat to fit the entrepreneurial situation. For example, five-forces analysis (as discussed in Chapter 2) is typically used by established firms. It can also be applied to the analysis of new ventures to assess the impact of industry and competitive forces. But you may ask: How does a new entrant evaluate the threat of other new entrants?

First, the new entrant needs to examine barriers to entry. If the barriers are too high, the potential entrant may decide not to enter or to gather more resources before attempting to do so. Compared to an older firm with an established reputation and available resources, the barriers to entry may be insurmountable for an entrepreneurial start-up. Therefore, understanding the force of these barriers is critical in making a decision to launch.

A second factor that may be especially important to a young venture is the threat of retaliation by incumbents. In many cases, entrepreneurial ventures *are* the new entrants that pose a threat to incumbent firms. Therefore, in applying the five-forces model to new ventures, the threat of retaliation by established firms needs to be considered.

Part of any decision about what opportunity to pursue is a consideration of how a new entrant will actually enter a new market. The concept of entry strategies provides a useful means of addressing the types of choices that new ventures have, and that is the subject we turn to next.

Entry Strategies

As suggested earlier, one of the most challenging aspects of launching a new venture is finding a way to begin doing business that generates cash flow, builds credibility, attracts good employees, and overcomes the liability of newness. One aspect of that effort is the initial decision about how to get a foothold in the market. The idea of an entry strategy or "entry wedge" describes several approaches that firms may take.[28] Several factors discussed earlier will affect this decision.

- Does the venture founder prefer control or growth?
- Is the product/service high-tech or low-tech?
- What resources are available for the initial launch?
- What are the industry and competitive conditions?
- What is the overall market potential?

In some respects, any type of entry into a market for the first time may be considered entrepreneurial. But the entry strategy will vary depending on how risky and innovative the new business concept is.[29] New-entry strategies typically fall into one of three categories—pioneering new entry, imitative new entry, or adaptive new entry.

Pioneering New Entry

New entrants with a radical new product or highly innovative service may change the way business is conducted in an industry. This kind of breakthrough—creating new ways to solve old problems or meeting customer's needs in a unique new way—is referred to as a **pioneering new entry.** If the product or service is unique enough, a pioneering new entrant may actually have little direct competition. The first personal computer was a pioneering product; there had never been anything quite like it and it revolutionized computing. The first Internet browser provided a type of pioneering service. These breakthroughs created whole new industries and changed the competitive landscape. And breakthrough innovations continue to inspire pioneering entrepreneurial efforts. Consider the example of SkyTower Telecommunications, a year 2000 start-up that is hoping to take wireless communications to new heights:

> Wireless communications systems have only three ways to get to your cell phone or computer—radio towers that are often not tall enough, satellites that cost $50 million to $400 million to launch, and short-range Wi-Fi transmitters. SkyTower proposes a fourth alternative: unmanned, solar-powered airplanes that look like flying wings and send out Internet, mobile phone, and high-definition TV signals. The planes have already been successfully tested over Hawaii. They are able to fly at an altitude of 12 miles in a tight 2,000-foot-wide circle for six months at a time without landing. Designed as private communication systems for both businesses and consumers, they are able to deliver Internet service for about a third of the cost of DSL or cable. SkyTower has already received the backing of NASA and $80 million in investment capital. Its target customers are major Internet Service Providers (ISPs). The plan is not without problems, however. For one thing, the Federal Aviation Administration (FAA) currently prohibits the launch of unpiloted planes. Even so, SkyTower's flying wing satellite is a breakthrough technology that addresses the increasing demand for cost-effective wireless communications.[30]

The pitfalls associated with a pioneering new entry are numerous. For one thing, there is a strong risk that the product or service will not be accepted by consumers. The history of entrepreneurship is littered with new ideas that never got off the launching pad. Take, for example, Smell-O-Vision, an invention designed to pump odors into movie theatres from the projection room at preestablished moments in a film. It was tried only once (for the film *Scent of a Mystery*) before it was declared a major flop. Innovative? Definitely. But hardly a good idea at the time.[31]

A pioneering new entry is disruptive to the status quo of an industry. It is likely based on a technological breakthrough such as the one proposed by SkyTower. If it is successful, other competitors will rush in to copy it. This can create issues of sustainability for an entrepreneurial firm, especially if a larger company with greater resources introduces a similar product. For a new entrant to sustain its pioneering advantage, therefore, it may be necessary to protect its intellectual property, advertise heavily to build brand recognition, form alliances with businesses that will adopt its products or services, and offer exceptional customer service.

Imitative New Entry

Whereas pioneers are often inventors or tinkerers with new technology, imitators usually have a strong marketing orientation. They look for opportunities to capitalize on proven market successes. An **imitative new entry** strategy is used by entrepreneurs who see products or business concepts that have been successful in one market niche or physical locale and introduce the same basic product or service in another segment of the market.

Sometimes the key to success with an imitative strategy is to fill a market space where the need had previously been filled inadequately. This was the approach used by Fixx Services, Inc., a restaurant and retail store maintenance service.

Maintenance and repairs is hardly a new business concept. But Mark Bucher found that restaurants and retail stores were poorly served. He provides a facility management service designed to alleviate the headaches associated with keeping everything running. "Customers want one number to call if their oven breaks or if someone throws a brick through their front window," says Bucher. Founded in 1999, home-based and self-funded for the first three years, Fixx Services now has 12 employees and annual sales of nearly $10 million.[32]

Entrepreneurs are also prompted to be imitators when they realize that they have the resources or skills to do a job better than an existing competitor. This can actually be a serious problem for entrepreneurial start-ups if the imitator is an established company. Consider the example of Hugger Mugger Yoga Products, a Salt Lake City producer of yoga apparel and equipment such as yoga mats for practitioners of the ancient exercise art, with sales of $7.5 million annually.

● Yoga's rising popularity has increased demand for related apparel and equipment. Both small players as well as multinational giants such as Nike and Reebok have entered the market.

> When founder Sara Chambers started the business in the mid-1980s, there was little competition. But once yoga went mainstream and became the subject of celebrity cover stories, other competitors saw an opportunity to imitate. Then Nike and Reebok jumped into the business with their own mats, clothes, and props. Hugger Mugger was a leading provider and had enjoyed 50 percent annual growth. But even after introducing a mass market line for stores such as Linens 'n' Things and hiring 50 independent sales reps, its growth rate has leveled off.[33]

Recall from Chapter 3 that the quality "difficult to imitate" was viewed as one of the keys to building sustainable advantages.[34] A strategy that can be imitated, therefore, seems like a poor way to build a business. In essence, this is true. But then consider the example of a franchise. Clearly, franchising is built on the idea of copying what another business has already done. If a business format is so easy to imitate, can it possibly have any competitive advantages? In the minds of many consumers of franchise products and services, the advantage is *because of* imitation. That is, consumers have confidence in franchises because they are familiar with them. "As time has gone by, the public has come to embrace franchising because they're familiar with the successful franchises and brand," claims Tony DeSio, founder of Mail Boxes Etc. "They know that, from one location to another, they can rely on product consistency." Thus, imitation is one of the central reasons why franchises are successful.

Adaptive New Entry   Most new entrants use a strategy somewhere between "pure" imitation and "pure" pioneering. That is, they offer a product or service that is somewhat new and sufficiently different to create new value for customers and capture market share. Such firms are adaptive in the sense that they are aware of marketplace conditions and conceive entry strategies to capitalize on current trends.

According to business creativity coach Tom Monahan, "Every new idea is merely a spin of an old idea. [Knowing that] takes the pressure off from thinking [you] have to be totally creative. You don't. Sometimes it's one slight twist to an old idea that makes all the difference."[35] Thus, an **adaptive new entry** approach does not involve "reinventing the wheel," nor is it merely imitative either. It involves taking an existing idea and adapting it to a particular situation. Let's look at the example of Under Armour:

adaptive new entry
a firm's entry into an industry by offering a product or service that is somewhat new and sufficiently different to create value for customers by capitalizing on current market trends.

> When Kevin Plank played football for the University of Maryland, it bothered him that the hard hitting game left him literally dripping wet. He knew that athletes such as competitive

strategy spotlight

8.5

AltiTunes: Success through Adaptation

"Darwin said it is not the strongest or fastest that survive but those that can adapt quickly," says Thomas Barry, chief investment officer at Bjurman, Barry & Associates. That's what Amy Nye Wolf learned when she launched her AltiTunes Partners LP business. She had been listening to the same music over and over during a six-week backpacking trip through Europe. At the end of the trip, she was elated to find a store selling music at London's Heathrow Airport. "I was so sick of the music I had, and I was just happy to see it."

About five years later, after finishing college and working as an investment banker, Wolf remembered her experience in the airport. She realized that selling CDs

was not an original idea but she thought there might be a need anyway. "I stole the idea," says Wolf, "and then did some serious adapting." Airports, she figured, constituted a unique market niche. She estimated that if she could sell just 30 CDs per day, she could keep the business afloat. Naming her business AltiTunes, Wolf took the plunge.

Today, AltiTunes sells 3,000 to 4,000 CDs per day at 27 stores in 20 airports and one train station. Sales of CDs and products such as portable stereos and computer games now exceed $15 million annually. And Wolf is still adapting. Her latest innovation is a gadget that lets shoppers roam around the store and sample any CD on the racks. It's a PDA-sized device developed by a company named MusiKube, LLC, that shoppers use by scanning a CD bar code to hear selections of music. It's just the latest improvement in Wolf's plan to stay cutting edge by continually adapting what she calls her "small format, extraordinary-location," music retailing business.

Sources: Barrett, A., & Foust, D. 2003. Hot growth companies. *Business-Week*, June 9: 74–77; Goldsmith, G. 2003. Retailers try new devices to make CD purchasing more enjoyable. *The Wall Street Journal*, June 12, www.wsj.com; Williams, G. 2002. Looks like rain. *Entrepreneur*, September: 104–111; and www.altitunes.com.

cyclists had started using moisture-wicking gear to stay drier. So Plank bought some sweat-wicking synthetic fabric and paid a tailor $460 to make seven shirts. When his teammates tried the shirts, they wanted their own. Plank had hundreds of samples made and began sending them to his football-playing friends. "I set out to build a better football undershirt," says Plank. By adapting a new fabric to an old problem, the Under Armour founder was on his way to building one of the hottest athletic apparel brands going. Between 2002 and 2005, the company grew an average of 78.3 percent per year, with 2005 sales of $310.6 million.[36]

There are several pitfalls that might limit the success of an adaptive new entrant. First, the value proposition set forth by the new entrant firm must be perceived as unique. Unless potential customers believe a new product or service does a superior job of meeting their needs, they will have little motivation to try it. Second, there is nothing to prevent a close competitor from mimicking the new firm's adaptation as a way to hold on to its customers. Third, once an adaptive entrant achieves initial success, the challenge is to keep the idea fresh. If the attractive features of the new business are copied, the entrepreneurial firm must find ways to adapt and improve the product or service offering. Strategy Spotlight 8.5 describes how adaptive new entrant Amy Nye Wolf has continually improved her venture to hold her customers' interest and grow her business.

Considering these choices, an entrepreneur or entrepreneurial team might ask, Which new entry strategy is best? As noted in Chapter 5, not one of the strategies is inherently more likely to succeed or generate profits than another. The choice depends on many competitive, financial, and marketplace considerations. Nevertheless, research indicates that the greatest opportunities may stem from being willing to enter new markets rather than seeking growth only in existing markets. A recent study found that companies that ventured into arenas that were new to the world or new to the company earned total profits of 61 percent for their efforts. In contrast, companies that made only incremental improvements, such as extending an existing product line, grew total profits by only 39 percent.[37]

These findings led W. Chan Kim and Renee Mauborgne in their new book *Blue Ocean Strategy* to conclude that companies that are willing to venture into market spaces where there is little or no competition—labeled "blue oceans"—will outperform those firms that limit growth to incremental improvements in competitively crowded industries—labeled "red oceans." Companies that identify and pursue blue ocean strategies follow somewhat different rules than those that are "bloodied" by the competitive practices in red oceans. Consider the following elements of a blue ocean strategy:

- *Create uncontested market space.* By seeking opportunities where they are not threatened by existing competitors, blue ocean firms can focus on customers rather than on competition.
- *Make the competition irrelevant.* Rather than using the competition as a benchmark, blue ocean firms cross industry boundaries to offer new and different products and services.
- *Create and capture new demand.* Rather than fighting over existing demand, blue ocean companies seek opportunities in uncharted territory.
- *Break the value/cost trade-off.* Blue ocean firms reject the idea that a trade-off between value and cost is inevitable and instead seek opportunities in areas that benefit both their cost structure and their value proposition to customers.
- *Pursue differentiation and low cost simultaneously.* By integrating the range of a firm's utility, price, and cost activities, blue ocean companies align their whole system to create sustainable strategies.

The essence of blue ocean strategy is not just to find an uncontested market, but to create one. Some blue oceans arise because new technologies create new possibilities, such as eBay's online auction business. Yet technological innovation is not a defining feature of a blue ocean strategy. Most blue oceans are created from within red oceans by companies that push beyond the existing industry boundaries. Thus, any of the new entry strategies described earlier could be used to pursue a blue ocean strategy. Strategy Spotlight 8.6 describes how Cirque du Soleil created a new market for circus entertainment by making traditional circus acts more like theatrical productions.

Once created, a blue ocean strategy is difficult to imitate. If customers flock to blue ocean creators, firms rapidly achieve economies of scale, learning advantages, and synergies across their organizational systems. Body Shop, for example chartered new territory by refusing to focus solely on beauty products. Traditional competitors such as Estee Lauder and L'Oreal, whose brands are based on promises of eternal youth and beauty, found it difficult to imitate this approach without repudiating their current images.

These factors suggest that blue ocean strategies provide an avenue by which firms can pursue an entrepreneurial new entry. Such strategies are not without risks, however. A new entrant must decide not only the best way to enter into business but also what type of strategic positioning will work best as the business goes forward. Those strategic choices can be informed by the guidelines suggested for the generic strategies. We turn to that subject next.

Generic Strategies

>LO4
How the generic strategies of overall cost leadership, differentiation, and focus are used by new ventures and small businesses.

Typically, an entrepreneurial firm begins with a single business model that is equivalent in scope to a business-level strategy (Chapter 5). In this section we address how overall low cost, differentiation, and focus strategies can be used by new ventures to achieve competitive advantages.

Overall Cost Leadership   One of the ways entrepreneurial firms achieve success is by doing more with less. That is, by holding down costs or making more efficient use of resources than larger competitors, new ventures are often able to offer lower prices and still be profitable. Thus, under the right circumstances, a low-cost leader strategy is a viable

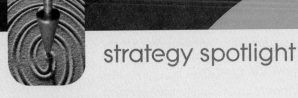

Cirque du Soleil's Blue Ocean Strategy

The blue ocean strategy of Cirque du Soleil is a prime example of creating new market space within a declining industry. The promotional tagline that the Canadian-based circus company sometimes uses explains how they did it: "We reinvent the circus." By altering the industry boundaries that had traditionally defined the circus concept, Cirque has created a new type of circus experience that audiences have enthusiastically embraced. Since 1984, when it was founded by a group of street performers, Cirque du Soleil has staged a variety of different productions that have been seen by over 40 million people in some 90 cities around the world.

How did they do it? One of the keys to redefining the circus business was to challenge conventional thinking and create a new vision of circus entertainment. Since the days of Ringling Bros. and Barnum & Bailey, the circus had consisted of animal acts, star performers, and Bozo-like clowns. Cirque questioned this formula and sought to understand what its audiences really wanted. It found that interest in animal acts was declining in part because of public concerns over the treatment of circus animals. Since managing animals—and the celebrity trainers who performed with them—created a heavy economic burden, Cirque eliminated them.

Instead Cirque has focused on three elements of the classic circus tent event that still captivated audiences: acrobatic acts, clowns, and the tent itself. Elegant acrobatics became a central feature of its performances, and clown humor became more sophisticated and less slapstick. Cirque also preserved the image of the tent by creating exotic facades that captured the symbolic elements of the traditional tent.

For Cirque to sail into a blue ocean, however, it had to make even bigger changes. It did so by introducing theatrical elements into its circus acts. Each production provides a range of features more commonly found in theatres than in circus tents—from using theatrical story lines to replacing hard benches with comfortable seating. Rather than displaying three different acts simultaneously, as in the classic three-ring circus, Cirque offers multiple productions giving audiences a reason to go to the circus more often. Each production has a different theme and its own original musical score.

As it has rolled out all of these changes, Cirque has kept its eye on the bottom line. In fact, a key motivator for many of its changes was to find ways to lower costs and increase revenues in the declining circus industry. Cutting the cost of animal acts and star performers as well as boosting revenues by offering a variety of productions has allowed it to achieve both low cost and differentiation advantages. Such a strategy creates value for both the company and its customers. The essence of its success, however, lies not in the extent to which it has outperformed competitors, but in how it has surpassed them by redefining the circus concept and becoming a prime mover in the market space it created.

Sources: Kim, W. C., & Mauborgne, R. 2004. Blue ocean strategy. *Harvard Business Review*, 82(10): 76–84; and Tischler, L. 2005. Join the circus. *Fast Company*, 96: 52–58; and www.cirquedusoleil.com.

alternative for some new ventures. The way most companies achieve low-cost leadership, however, is typically different for young or small firms.

Recall from Chapter 5 that three of the features of a low-cost approach included operating at a large enough scale to spread costs over many units of production (i.e., economies of scale), making substantial capital investments in order to increase scale economies, and using knowledge gained from experience to make cost-saving improvements. These elements of a cost-leadership strategy may be unavailable to new ventures. Because new ventures are typically small, they usually don't have high economies of scale relative to competitors. Because they are usually cash strapped, they can't make large capital investments to increase their scale advantages. And because many are young, they often don't have a wealth of accumulated experience to draw on to achieve cost reductions.

Given these constraints, how can new ventures successfully deploy cost-leader strategies? Compared to large firms, new ventures often have simple organizational structures that make decision making both easier and faster. The smaller size also helps young firms change more quickly when upgrades in technology or feedback from the marketplace indicate that improvements are needed. New ventures are also able to make decisions at the time they are founded that help them deal with the issue of controlling costs. For example, they may source materials from a supplier that provides them more cheaply or set up manufacturing facilities in another country where labor costs are especially low. Thus, new firms have several avenues for achieving low cost leadership.

Consider the example of UTStarcom, a fast-growing wireless phone service being marketed in mainland China:

> Taiwan-born founder Hong Liang Lu was an executive at Japan's Kyocera Corp. when he made his first visit to China in 1990. He found a population that badly needed decent phone service. "Before that trip, I hadn't really thought about doing business in China. Afterward, I felt it made no sense to do business anywhere else." Using Personal Access System (PAS), a technology that had never caught on in Japan, he created a low-cost service that uses existing copper networks as its backbone. The service costs only $100 per subscriber to deploy, about half the price of cellular-based systems. Customers pay nothing for incoming calls and outgoing ones are 25 percent of the cellular rate. Competing against the big telecom providers was difficult at first, but once they marketed the "Little Smart" as a low cost alternative to cellular, sales took off. Average annual revenues have grown 73 percent since 1999, and 2003 sales reached $1.96 billion. Says CEO Lu, "Our biggest problem is keeping up with demand."[38]

Whatever methods young firms use to achieve a low-cost advantage, this has always been a way that entrepreneurial firms take business away from incumbents—by offering a comparable product or service at a lower price.

Differentiation   Both pioneering and adaptive entry strategies involve some degree of differentiation. That is, the new entry is based on being able to offer a differentiated value proposition. Clearly, in the case of pioneers, the new venture is attempting to do something strikingly different, either by using a new technology or deploying resources in a way that radically alters the way business is conducted. Often, entrepreneurs do both.

Amazon founder Jeff Bezos set out to use Internet technology to revolutionize the way books are sold. He garnered the ire of other booksellers and the attention of the public by making bold claims about being the "earth's largest bookseller." As a bookseller, Bezos was not doing anything that had not been done before. But two key differentiating features—doing it on the Internet and offering extraordinary customer service—have made Amazon a differentiated success.

Even though the Internet and new technologies have provided many opportunities for entrepreneurs, differentiators don't have to be highly sophisticated to succeed. Consider the example of Spry Learning Co., a Portland, Oregon, start-up begun in 2000.

> Founders Sarah Chapman and Devin Williams believed that older people would benefit from using computers and surfing the Internet—if they only knew how. Working with gerontologists and instructional designers, they designed a computer-skills curriculum aimed at seniors. After piloting the program at two retirement communities, they successfully launched the differentiated service and, after just a few years, projected annual revenues over $4 million.[39]

There are several factors that make it more difficult for new ventures to be successful as differentiators. For one thing, the strategy is generally thought to be expensive to enact. For example, differentiation is often associated with strong brand identity, and establishing a brand is usually considered to be expensive because of the cost of advertising and promotion, paid endorsements, exceptional customer service, as well as other expenses typically associated with building brand. Differentiation successes are sometimes built on superior innovation or use of technology. These are also factors where it may be challenging for young firms to excel relative to established competitors.

Nevertheless all of these areas—innovation, technology, customer service, distinctive branding—are also arenas where new ventures have sometimes made a name for themselves even though they must operate with limited resources and experience. To be successful, according to Garry Ridge, CEO of the WD-40 Company, "You need to have a great product, make the end user aware of it, and make it easy to buy."[40] It sounds simple, but it is a difficult challenge for new ventures with differentiation strategies.

Strategic Focusing at Corporate Interns, Inc.

When Jason Engen was an undergraduate student at the University of St. Thomas in St. Paul, Minnesota, he learned the value of internships in which students worked for local companies. He wrote a business plan for one of his classes about forming an internship placement service in which he would screen students and match them with local companies. "[It's] a win–win situation," said Engen.

Sources: Torres, N. L. 2003. A perfect match. *Entrepreneur*, July: 112–114; and www.corporateinterns.com.

"The student gets the experience, and the company gets eager talent." The interest in his idea was great, and a week after graduation he started Corporate Interns, Inc.

It was difficult at first, however, because companies handle internships differently than other placement activities. But as Engen learned more, he realized this difference was an advantage: By positioning himself only in the college intern market, he avoided competing directly with large staffing companies. "Specialization is important," says Engen. "You have to stay focused on that niche." For Engen, that niche now generates $2 million in annual revenues.

Focus Focus strategies are often associated with small businesses because there is a natural fit between the narrow scope of the strategy and the small size of the firm. As we learned earlier, a focus strategy may include elements of differentiation and overall cost leadership, as well as combinations of these approaches. But to be successful within a market niche, the key strategic requirement is to stay focused. Here's why:

Despite all the attention given to fast-growing new industries, most start-ups enter industries that are mature.[41] In mature industries, growth in demand tends to be slow and there are often many competitors. Therefore, if a start-up wants to get a piece of the action, it often has to take business away from an existing competitor. If a start-up enters a market with a broad or aggressive strategy, it is likely to evoke retaliation from a more powerful competitor. Therefore, young firms can often succeed best by finding a market niche where they can get a foothold and make small advances that erode the position of existing competitors.[42] From this position, they can build a name for themselves and grow. Strategy Spotlight 8.7 considers the example of Corporate Interns, Inc.

As the Corporate Interns example indicates, many new ventures are very successful even though their share of the market is quite small. Giant companies such as Procter & Gamble and Ford are often described in terms of their market share—that is, their share of sales in a whole market. But many of the industries that small firms participate in have thousands of participants that are not direct competitors. For example, auto repair shops in California don't compete with those in Michigan or Georgia. These industries are considered "fragmented" because no single company is strong enough to have power over other competitors. Therefore, small firms focus on the market share only in their trade area. This may be defined as a geographical area or a small segment of a larger product group.

Consider, for example, the "Miniature Editions" line of books launched by Running Press, a small Philadelphia publisher. The books are palm-sized minibooks positioned at bookstore cash registers as point-of-sale impulse items costing about $4.95. Beginning with just 10 titles in 1993, Running Press grew rapidly and within 10 years had sold over 20 million copies. Even though these books represent just a tiny fraction of total sales in the $23 billion publishing industry, they have been a mainstay for Running Press.[43]

Although each of the three strategies holds promise, and pitfalls, for new ventures, firms that can make unique combinations of the generic approaches may have the greatest chances of success. It is that subject we address next.

Combination Strategies

One of the best ways for young and small businesses to achieve success is by pursuing combination strategies. By combining the best features of low-cost, differentiation, and focus strategies, new ventures can often achieve something truly distinctive.

Entrepreneurial firms are often in a strong position to offer a combination strategy because they have the flexibility to approach situations uniquely. For example, holding down expenses can be difficult for big firms because each layer of bureaucracy adds to the cost of doing business across the boundaries of a large organization. Consider how The Nartron Corporation manages this problem:

> To get a part made, or to outsource it, may be complicated and expensive for many large firms. By contrast, The Nartron Corporation, a small engineering firm whose innovations include the first keyless automobile entry system, solves that problem by building everything itself. By engineering its own products from its own designs, it not only saves money but also creates better parts. "Our parts look different from other people's because we keep adding functionality," says Nartron CEO Norman Rautiola. According to Rautiola, this capability allows the company to "run rings" around its competitors, which include Texas Instruments and Motorola.[44]

A similar argument could be made about entrepreneurial firms that differentiate. Large firms often find it difficult to offer highly specialized products or superior customer services. Entrepreneurial firms, by contrast, can often create high-value products and services through their unique differentiating efforts.

For nearly all new entrants, one of the major dangers is that a large firm with more resources will copy what they are doing. That is, well-established incumbents that observe the success of a new entrant's product or service will copy it and use their market power to overwhelm the smaller firm. Although this happens often, the threat may be lessened for firms that use combination strategies. Because of the flexibility of entrepreneurial firms, they can often enact combination strategies in ways that the large firms cannot copy. This makes the new entrant's strategies much more sustainable.

Perhaps more threatening than large competitors for many entrepreneurial firms are other firms that are close competitors. Because they have similar structural features that help them adjust quickly and be flexible in decision making, close competitors are often a danger to new ventures. Here again, a carefully crafted and executed combination strategy may be the best way for an entrepreneurial firm to thrive in a competitive environment. Nevertheless, competition among rivals is a key determinant of new venture success. To address this, we turn next to the topic of competitive dynamics.

Competitive Dynamics

New entry into markets, whether by start-ups or by incumbent firms, nearly always threatens existing competitors. This is true in part because, except in very new markets, nearly every market need is already being met, either directly or indirectly, by existing firms. As a result, the competitive actions of a new entrant are very likely to provoke a competitive response from companies that feel threatened. This, in turn, is likely to evoke a reaction to the response. As a result, a competitive dynamic—action and response—begins among the firms competing for the same customers in a given marketplace.

Competitive dynamics—intense rivalry among similar competitors—has the potential to alter a company's strategy. New entrants, for example, may be forced to change their strategies or develop new ones to survive competitive challenges by incumbent rivals. Indeed, new entry is among the most common reasons why a cycle of competitive actions and reactions gets started. But it's not the only reason. It might also occur because of threatening actions among existing competitors, such as aggressive cost cutting. Thus,

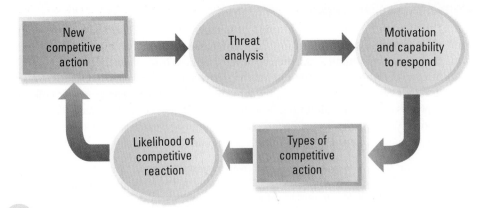

Exhibit 8.6 Model of Competitive Dynamics

Sources: Adapted from Chen, M. J. 1996. Competitor analysis and interfirm rivalry: Toward a theoretical integration. *Academy of Management Review,* 21(1): 100–134; Ketchen, D. J., Snow, C. C., & Hoover, V. L. 2004. Research on competitive dynamics: Recent accomplishments and future challenges. *Journal of Management,* 30(6): 779–804; and Smith, K. G., Ferrier, W. J., & Grimm, C. M. 2001. King of the hill: Dethroning the industry leader. *Academy of Management Executive,* 15(2): 59–70.

>LO6

The components of competitive dynamics analysis—new competitive action, threat analysis, motivation and capability to respond, types of competitive actions, and likelihood of competitive reaction.

studying competitive dynamics helps explain why strategies evolve and reveals how, why, and when to respond to the actions of close competitors.

Exhibit 8.6 identifies the factors that competitors need to consider when determining how to respond to a competitive act. In the sections below, we will review the elements that contribute to a competitor's decision to launch a competitive attack.

New Competitive Action

Entry into a market by a new competitor is a good starting point to begin describing the cycle of actions and responses characteristic of a competitive dynamic process.[45] However, new entry is only one type of competitive action. Price cutting, imitating successful products, or expanding production capacity are other examples of competitive acts that might provoke competitors to react.

Why do companies launch new competitive actions? There are several reasons:

- Improve market position
- Capitalize on growing demand
- Expand production capacity
- Provide an innovative new solution
- Obtain first mover advantages

Underlying all of these reasons is a desire to strengthen financial outcomes, capture some of the extraordinary profits that industry leaders enjoy, and grow the business. Some companies are also motivated to launch competitive challenges because they want to build their reputation for innovativeness or efficiency. For example, Southwest Airlines, once an upstart airline with only a few routes, has become phenomenally successful and an industry leader. For years it went virtually unchallenged. But Southwest's costs have crept up, and now start-up airlines such as JetBlue are challenging the industry leader with their own low-cost strategies.[46] This is indicative of the competitive dynamic cycle. As former Intel Chairman Andy Grove stated, "Business success contains the seeds of its own destruction. The more successful you are, the more people want a chunk of your business and then another chunk and then another until there is nothing left."[47]

When a company enters into a market for the first time, it is like an attack on existing competitors. As indicated earlier in the chapter, any of the entry strategies can be used to take competitive action. But competitive attacks come from many sources besides new entrants. Some of the most intense competition is among incumbent rivals intent on gaining strategic advantages. "Winners in business play rough and don't apologize for it," according to Boston Consulting Group authors George Stalk, Jr. and Rob Lachenauer in their book *Hardball: Are You Playing to Play or Playing to Win.*[48] Exhibit 8.7 outlines their five strategies for improving competitive position and consolidating gains in preparation for another attack.

The likelihood that a competitor will launch an attack depends on many factors. In the remaining sections, we discuss factors such as competitor analysis, market conditions, types of strategic actions, and the resource endowments and capabilities companies need to take competitive action.

Threat Analysis

Prior to actually observing a competitive action, companies may need to become aware of potential competitive threats. That is, companies need to have a keen sense of who their closest competitors are and the kinds of competitive actions they might be planning.[49] This may require some environmental scanning and monitoring of the sort described in Chapter 2. Awareness of the threats posed by industry rivals allows a firm to understand what type of competitive response, if any, may be necessary.

For example, Netflix founder and CEO Reed Hastings has faced numerous competitive threats since launching the online movie rental company in 1997. According to Hastings, however, not all potential threats need to be taken seriously:

> We have to recognize that now there are tens and maybe hundreds of start-ups who think that they are going to eat Netflix's lunch. The challenge for a management team is to figure out which are real threats and which aren't. . . . It's conventional to say, "only the paranoid survive" but that's not true. The paranoid die because the paranoid take all threats as serious and get very distracted.
>
> There are markets that aren't going to get very big, and then there are markets that are going to get big, but they're not directly in our path. In the first camp we have small companies like Movielink—a well-run company but not an attractive model for consumers, sort of a $4-download to watch a movie. We correctly guessed when it launched four years ago that this was not a threat and didn't react to it.
>
> The other case I brought up is markets that are going to be very large markets, but we're just not the natural leader. Advertising supported online video, whether that's at CBS.com or You Tube— great market, kind of next door to us. But we don't do advertising-supported video, we do sub-scription, so it would be a huge competence expansion for us. And it's not a threat to movies."

Being aware of competitors and cognizant of whatever threats they might pose is the first step in assessing the level of competitive threat. Once a new competitive action becomes apparent, companies must determine how threatening it is to their business. Competitive dynamics are likely to be most intense among companies that are competing for the same customers or who have highly similar sets of resources.[50] Two factors are used to assess whether or not companies are close competitors:

- **Market commonality**—In other words, whether or not competitors are vying for the same customers and how many markets they share in common. For example, aircraft manufacturers Boeing and Airbus have a high degree of market commonality because they make very similar products and have many buyers in common.
- **Resource similarity**—In other words, the degree to which rivals draw on the same types of resources to compete. For example, the home pages of Google and Yahoo! may look very different but behind the scenes, they both rely on the talent pool of high-caliber software engineers to create the cutting-edge innovations that help them compete.

When any two firms have both a high degree of market commonality and highly similar resource bases, a stronger competitive threat is present. Such a threat, however, may not lead to competitive action. On the one hand, a market rival may be hesitant to attack a company that it shares a high degree of market commonality with because it could lead to an intense battle. On the other hand, once attacked, rivals with high market commonality will be much

market commonality the extent to which competitors are vying for the same customers in the same markets.

resource similarity the extent to which rivals draw from the same types of strategic resources.

Strategy	Description	Examples
Devastate rivals' profit sanctuaries	Not all business segments generate the same level of profits for a company. Through focused attacks on a rival's most profitable segments, a company can generate maximum leverage with relatively smaller-scale attacks. Recognize, however, that companies closely guard the information needed to determine just what their profit sanctuaries are.	In 2005, Wal-Mart began offering low-priced extended warranties on home electronics after learning that its rivals Best Buy and Circuit City derived most of their profits from extended warranties.
Plagiarize with pride	Just because a close competitor comes up with an idea first does not mean it cannot be successfully imitated. Second movers, in fact, can see how customers respond, make improvements, and launch a better version without all the market development costs. Successful imitation is harder than it may appear and requires the imitating firm to keep its ego in check.	Blockbuster copied the online DVD rental strategy of its rival Netflix. Not only does Blockbuster continue to struggle even after this imitation, but also Netflix sued Blockbuster for patent violations.
Deceive the competition	A good gambit sends the competition off in the wrong direction. This may cause the rivals to miss strategic shifts, spend money pursuing dead ends, or slow their responses. Any of these outcomes support the deceiving firms' competitive advantage. Companies must be sure to not cross ethical lines during these actions.	Boeing spent several years touting its plans for a new high-speed airliner. After it became clear the customer valued efficiency over speed, Boeing quietly shifted its focus. When Boeing announced its new 7e7 (now 787) Dreamliner, its competitor, Airbus Industries, was surprised and caught without an adequate response, which helped the 787 set new sales records.
Unleash massive and overwhelming force	While many hardball strategies are subtle and indirect, this one is not. This is a full-frontal attack where a firm commits significant resources to a major campaign to weaken rivals' positions in certain markets. Firms must be sure they have the mass and stamina required to win before they declare war against a rival.	Southwest Airlines took on US Airways in Baltimore and drove US Airway's market share from over 50 percent to 10 percent. Southwest recently began flying to Philadelphia and Pittsburgh as well—additional key markets for US Airways.
Raise competitors' costs	If a company has superior insight into the complex cost and profit structure of the industry, it can compete in a way that steers its rivals into relatively higher cost/lower profit arenas. This strategy uses deception to make the rivals think they are winning, when in fact they are not. Again, companies using this strategy must be confident that they understand the industry better than their rivals.	Ecolab, a company that sells cleaning supplies to businesses, encouraged a leading competitor, Diversity, to adopt a strategy to go after the low-volume, high-margin customers. What Ecolab knew that Diversity didn't is that the high servicing costs involved with this segment make the segment unprofitable—a situation Ecolab assured by bidding high enough to lose the contracts to Diversity but low enough to ensure the business lost money for Diversity.

Sources: Berner, R. 2005. Watch out, Best Buy and Circuit City. *BusinessWeek,* November 10; Halkias, M. 2006. Blockbuster strikes back at Netflix suit. *Dallas Morning News,* June 14; McCartney, S. 2007. Southwest makes inroads at hubs. *The Wall Street Journal,* May 1, page D3; Stalk, G. Jr. 2006. Curveball strategies to fool the competition. *Harvard Business Review,* 84(9): 114–121; and Stalk, Jr., G., & Lachenauer, R. 2004. *Hardball: Are you playing to play or playing to win?* Cambridge, MA: Harvard Business School Press. Reprinted by permission of Harvard Business School Press from G. Stalk, Jr. and R. Lachenauer. Copyright 2004 by the Harvard Business School Publishing Corporation; all rights reserved.

Exhibit 8.7 Five "Hardball" Strategies

AMD and Intel: Related Rivals

Few business battles are as intensely reported as the one between chipmakers Intel and Advanced Micro Devices (AMD). For years, Intel aggressively advertised its brand by pushing its "Intel Inside" logo to average consumers. In an effort to develop a stronger presence among consumers, AMD launched a successful initiative labeled internally, "War in the Store" to promote sales of AMD-based computers in retailers such as Best Buy and CompUSA. The effort prompted a retaliation by Intel that lowered the cost of chips enough to decrease PC prices $200. Meanwhile, AMD won a recent round when Dell announced it would start using AMD chips in its servers.

Why is the battle between the two companies so intense? Because they are so much alike. Both companies were founded in the late 1960s in Silicon Valley and were partners during their early history. But in 1986, Intel cancelled a key licensing agreement with AMD to manufacture microprocessors and refused to turn over technical details. AMD sued and, after years of litigation, the Supreme Court of California forced Intel to pay AMD over $1 billion in compensation for violations of the contract. The two companies have been battling ever since.

Consider how comparable the two companies are in terms of markets and resources.

Market Commonality

A key issue facing the two chipmakers is that to continue growing, they have had to enter each other's market space.

Sources: Edwards, C. 2006. AMD: Chipping away at Intel's lead. *BusinessWeek*, June 12: 72–73; Edwards, C. 2006. Intel sharpens its offensive game. *BusinessWeek*, July 31: 60. Gonsalves, A. 2007. AMD pays the price in awakening Intel Goliath. *InformationWeek*, www.informationweek.com, April 9; Gaudin, S. 2006. AMD cracks top 10 chip ranking, Intel sales slump. *InformationWeek*, www.informationweek.com, December 5; and www.wikipedia.org.

This is a major reason why the competition has become so heated. For example, Intel dominated that high-end server business in 2003. Now AMD holds 26 percent of the U.S. server chip business and supplies a 48 percent share of the multicore processors (which feature two or more chips on one slice of silicon). To maintain its status as the number one supplier, Intel launched a new family of processors called Core 2 Duo in 2007 that combines the performance of the Pentium 4 with the energy saving features of its notebook computer processors. "We intend to energetically compete for every single microprocessor opportunity," said Intel Executive Vice President Sean M. Maloney.

Resource Similarity

Intel is the world's number one supplier of semiconductors and is expected to have five manufacturing plants by the end of 2007. Because of new manufacturing techniques at three of its plants, it can squeeze more transistors onto a chip and its processors cost less to make than AMD's. By contrast, AMD has just two manufacturing plants but it has moved aggressively to match Intel's muscle. In 2005, it paid $5.4 billion to acquire graphics chipmaker ATI Technologies and has outsourced more manufacturing to Chartered Semiconductors. One result has been that AMD, now the number two maker of processors and graphic cards, increased semiconductor sales by 90 percent in 2006.

The battle between the two companies has been costly in recent years. When Intel retaliated for AMD's rapid gains, the result was slower sales for AMD and first quarter 2006 revenues of $1.23 billion rather than the $1.55 billion analysts expected. Meanwhile, Intel was hurt when Dell decided to begin installing AMD chips in its servers after years of using Intel exclusively. "The competitive dynamics have been more intense than we expected," commented Kevin B. Rollins, Dell's former CEO.

---

more motivated to launch a competitive response. This is especially true in cases where the shared market is an important part of a company's overall business.

How strong a response an attacked rival can mount will be determined by their strategic resource endowments. In general, the same set of conditions holds true with regard to resource similarity. That is, companies that have highly similar resource bases will be hesitant to launch an initial attack but pose a serious threat if required to mount a competitive response.[51] Greater strategic resources increase a firm's capability to respond.

In the next section, we look at the types of motivations and capabilities that a company needs to consider when evaluating its response to a competitive attack. First, Strategy Spotlight 8.8 addresses how the dynamics of market commonality and resource similarity have shaped the battle between chipmakers Intel and AMD and intensified their competitive rivalry.

Motivation and Capability to Respond

Once attacked, competitors are faced with deciding how to respond. Before deciding, however, they need to evaluate not only how they will respond, but also their reasons for responding and their capability to respond. Companies need to be clear about what problems a competitive response is expected to address and what types of problems it might create.[52] There are several factors to consider.

First, how serious is the impact of the competitive attack to which they are responding? For example, a large company with a strong reputation that is challenged by a small or unknown company may elect to simply keep an eye on the new competitor rather than quickly react or overreact. Part of the story of online retailer Amazon's early success is attributed to Barnes & Noble's over-reaction to Amazon's claim that it was "earth's biggest bookstore" Because Barnes & Noble was already using the phrase "world's largest bookstore," it sued Amazon, but lost. The confrontation made it to the front pages of *The Wall Street Journal* and Amazon was on its way to becoming a household name.[53]

Companies planning to respond to a competitive challenge must also understand their motivation for responding. What is the intent of the competitive response? Is it merely to blunt the attack of the competitor or is it an opportunity to enhance its competitive position?

Sometimes the most a company can hope for is to minimize the damage caused by a competitive action. Consider the recent price war among the top three U.S. automakers:

> When GM announced its "employee pricing" program in June, 2005, it had an immediate effect in terms of driving buyers into showrooms and increasing sales. Within days, Ford and Chrysler responded with their own incentive programs. In late summer, when GM extended its program until the end of September, so did Ford and Chrysler. All three automakers got a short-term payoff from the employee discount price war: the July 2005 sales of 1.8 million cars and light trucks was the biggest single month of sales in auto industry history. By late 2005, however, the reduced margins that the incentives caused led to lower profits and contributed to plans by GM and Ford to layoff 30,000 employees each. Early in 2007, DaimlerChrysler announced its Chrysler division was for sale.

A company that seeks to improve its competitive advantage may be motivated to launch an attack rather than merely respond to one. For example, Wal-Mart is known for its aggressive efforts to live up to its "everyday low prices" corporate motto. Strategy Spotlight 8.9 describes the retailer's recent assault on rivals Circuit City and Best Buy.

Another factor a company must consider when planning a competitive challenge involves assessing its capability to respond. What strategic resources can be deployed to fend off a competitive attack? Does the company have an array of internal strengths it can draw on, or is it operating from a position of weakness?

Consider, for example, the role of firm age and size in calculating a company's ability to respond. Most entrepreneurial new ventures start out small. The smaller size makes them more nimble compared to large firms so they can respond quickly to competitive attacks. Because they are not well-known, start-ups also have have the advantage of the element of surprise in how and when they attack. Innovative uses of technology, for example, allow small firms to deploy resources in unique ways.

Because they are young, however, start-ups may not have the financial resources needed to follow through with a competitive response. In contrast, older and larger firms may have more resources and a repertoire of competitive techniques they can use in a counterattack. Large firms, however, tend to be slower to respond. Older firms tend to be predictable in their responses because they often lose touch with the competitive environment and rely on strategies and actions that have worked in the past.

Other resources may also play a role in whether a company is equipped to retaliate. For example, one avenue of counterattack may be launching product enhancements or new product/service innovations. For that approach to be successful, it requires a company to

Wal-Mart's Cutthroat Pricing Schemes

Wal-Mart has a reputation as a relentless competitor in its pursuit of an overall cost leader strategy. Most of that reputation has come from its efforts to drive down costs in its dealings with suppliers. Wal-Mart sometimes goes on the offensive with rivals as well by driving down prices.

Recently, the retail giant took on Circuit City and Best Buy who it competes with head-on in the consumer electronics market. First Wal-Mart made big improvements in the electronics departments of 1,300 of its 3,100 U.S. stores by spiffing-up displays and adding high-end products such as Apple iPods, Toshiba laptops, and Sony liquid-crystal-display televisions. Then it delivered the two rivals a proverbial one-two punch—offering low-cost extended warranties and slashing prices on flat-panel TVs.

- **Extended warranties.** These are the multiyear protection plans that salespeople offer at the close of a sale on items such as TVs and computers. For both Circuit City and Best Buy, they are one of the most profitable segments of their business accounting for at least a third of their operating profits. In late 2005, Wal-Mart launched its own extended warranty program at prices nearly 50 percent lower than Best Buy and Circuit City.

- **Flat-panel TVs.** This includes both liquid crystal display and big-screen plasma models that, until the 2006 holiday season, had never sold below $1,000. Wal-Mart broke that barrier by offering a 42-inch flat-panel TV for $998. The cuts were not limited to lesser-known brands such as Viore TV. Wal-Mart also lowered the 42-inch Panasonic high-definition TV by $500 to $1,294. The response was immediate. Circuit City lowered the price on the same Panasonic TV to $1,299 and Best Buy began offering a 42-inch Westinghouse LCD for $999.

Circuit City was among the hardest hit by this cutthroat competition. In early 2007, it closed 70 stores and laid off 3,400 employees. Best Buy, the largest electronic retailer, did a better job of absorbing the shock. Still, its stock fell 9 percent during the first quarter of 2007. Other retailers were also hit hard by the audacious pricing that has been labeled the "Wal-Mart effect" including CompUSA, which is shuttering 126 of its 229 stores, and Tweeter's, which is closing 49 of its 153 stores and laying off 650 workers.

Sources: Berner, R. 2005. Watch out, Best Buy and Circuit City. *Business-Week Online*, www.businessweek.com, November 10; and Gogoi, P. 2007. How Wal-Mart's TV prices crushed rivals. *BusinessWeek*, www.businessweek.com, April 27.

have both the intellectual capital to put forward viable innovations and the teamwork skills to prepare a new product or service and get it to market. Resources such as cross-functional teams and the social capital that makes teamwork production effective and efficient represent the type of human capital resources that enhance a company's capability to respond.

Types of Competitive Actions

Once an organization determines whether it is willing and able to launch a competitive action, it must determine what type of action is appropriate. Clearly, the actions taken will be determined by both its resource capabilities and its motivation for responding. There are also marketplace considerations. Managers must ask: What types of actions are likely to be most effective given a company's internal strengths and weaknesses as well as market conditions?

Two broadly defined types of competitive action include strategic actions and tactical actions. **Strategic actions** represent major commitments of distinctive and specific resources. Examples include launching a breakthrough innovation, building a new production facility, or merging with another company. Such actions require significant planning and resources and, once initiated, are difficult to reverse.

Tactical actions include refinements or extensions of strategies. Examples of tactical actions include cutting prices, improving gaps in service, or strengthening marketing efforts. Such actions typically draw on general resources and can be implemented quickly. Exhibit 8.8 identifies several types of strategic and tactical competitive actions.

Some competitive actions take the form of frontal assaults, that is, actions aimed directly at taking business from another company or capitalizing on industry weaknesses.

strategic actions
major commitments of distinctive and specific resources to strategic initiatives.

tactical actions
refinements or extensions of strategies usually involving minor resource commitments.

	Actions	Examples
Strategic Actions	• Entering new markets	• Make geographical expansions • Expand into neglected markets • Target rivals' markets • Target new demographics
	• New product introductions	• Imitate rivals' products • Address gaps in quality • Leverage new technologies • Leverage brand name with related products • Protect innovation with patents
	• Changing production capacity	• Create overcapacity • Tie up raw materials sources • Tie up preferred suppliers and distributors • Stimulate demand by limiting capacity
	• Mergers/Alliances	• Acquire/partner with competitors to reduce competition • Tie up key suppliers through alliances • Obtain new technology/intellectual property • Facilitate new market entry
Tactical Actions	• Price cutting (or increases)	• Maintain low price dominance • Offer discounts and rebates • Offer incentives (e.g., frequent flyer miles) • Enhance offering to move upscale
	• Product/service enhancements	• Address gaps in service • Expand warranties • Make incremetal product improvements
	• Increased marketing efforts	• Use guerilla marketing • Conduct selective attacks • Change product packaging • Use new marketing channels
	• New distribution channels	• Access suppliers directly • Access customers directly • Develop multiple points of contact with customers • Expand Internet presence

Sources: Chen, M. J. & Hambrick, D. 1995. Speed, stealth, and selective attack: How small firms differ from large firms in competitive behavior. *Academy of Management Journal,* 38: 453–482; Davies, M. 1992. Sales promotions as a competitive strategy. *Management Decision,* 30(7): 5–10; Ferrier, W., Smith, K., & Grimm, C. 1999. The role of competitive action in market share erosion and industry dethronement: A study of industry leaders and challengers. *Academy of Management Journal,* 42(4): 372–388; and Garda, R. A. 1991. Use tactical pricing to uncover hidden profits. *Journal of Business Strategy,* 12(5): 17–23.

Exhibit 8.8 Strategic and Tactical Competitive Actions

This can be especially effective when firms use a low-cost strategy. The airline industry provides a good example of this head-on approach. When Southwest Airlines began its no-frills, no-meals, no-reserved seating strategy in the late-1960s, it represented a direct assault on the major carriers of the day. Now Southwest is the target of bids by entrepreneurial airlines such as JetBlue to provide a low-cost alternative. In Europe, Ryanair has directly challenged the traditional carriers with an overall cost leadership strategy. Founded in 1985, Ryanair is one-seventh the size of British Airways in terms of revenues, but in 2006, due to cost-cutting measures that significantly improved operating margins, it had a higher market capitalization of $7.6 billion compared to BA's $7.3 billion.[54]

Guerilla offensives and selective attacks provide an alternative for firms with fewer resources.[55] These efforts are designed to draw attention to products or services by creating buzz or generating enough shock value to get some free publicity. For example, the open source software movement, which has been gaining momentum as major corporations become aware of its potential, still lacks the market power and omnipresence that software giant Microsoft enjoys.[56] Loyal users of open source software such as Linux stay connected and share software through online blogs. They also pull the occasional publicity stunt. Recently, users of Firefox, the open source browser developed by the Mozilla Corporation created a crop circle in Oregon based on the Firefox logo. The effort made the local news and garnered thousands of mentions on open source blogs and Internet news organizations.

Some companies limit their competitive response to defensive actions. Such actions rarely improve a company's competitive advantage, but a credible defensive action can lower the risk of being attacked and deter new entry. This may be especially effective during periods such as an industry shake-up, when pricing levels or future demand for a product line become highly uncertain. At such times, tactics such as lowering prices on products that are easily duplicated, buying up the available supply of goods or raw materials, or negotiating exclusive agreements with buyers and/or suppliers can insulate a company from a more serious attack.

Several of the factors discussed earlier in the chapter, such as types of entry strategies and the use of cost leadership versus differentiation strategies, can guide the decision about what types of competitive actions to take. Before launching a given strategy, however, assessing the likely response of competitors is a vital step.

Likelihood of Competitive Reaction

The final step before initiating a competitive response is to evaluate what a competitor's reaction is likely to be. Recall that the logic of competitive dynamics suggests that once competitive actions are initiated, it is likely they will be met with competitive responses.[57] Therefore, the last step before mounting an attack is to evaluate how competitors are likely to respond. Evaluating potential competitive reactions helps companies plan for future counterattacks. It may also lead to a decision to hold off—that is, not to take any competitive action at all because of the possibility that a misguided or poorly planned response will generate a devastating competitive reaction.

How a competitor is likely to respond will depend on three factors: market dependence, competitor's resources, and the reputation of the firm that initiates the action (actor's reputation). The implications of each of these is described briefly in the following sections.

Market Dependence If a company has a high concentration of its business in a particular industry, it has more at stake because it must depend on that industry's market for its sales. Thus, single-industry businesses or those where one industry dominates its activities are more likely to mount a competitive response. Young and small firms, even though they may have a high degree of market dependence, may be limited in how they respond due to resource constraints. JetBlue, itself an aggressive competitor, is unable to match some of the perks its bigger rivals can offer, such as first-class seats or international travel benefits.

Competitor's Resources Previously, we examined the internal resource endowments that a company must evaluate when assessing its capability to respond. Here, it is the competitor's resources that need to be considered. For example, a small firm may be unable to mount a serious attack due to lack of resources. As a result, it is more likely to react to tactical actions such as incentive pricing or enhanced service offerings because they are less costly to attack than large-scale strategic actions. In contrast, a firm with financial "deep pockets" may be able to mount and sustain a costly counterattack. As a way to combat these differences in market power, young firms can strengthen their resource positions by forming strategic alliances. Yahoo!, for example, pressed hard by its young but powerful rival Google, allied itself with a group of seven newspaper chains that publish a total of 176 U.S. daily papers in a content sharing arrangement. Both Yahoo! and the newspaper chains are trying to stay ahead of Google now that it is moving aggressively beyond ads on its search pages.

Actor's Reputation   Whether a company should respond to a competitive challenge will also depend on who launched the attack against it. In previous examples, we have noted that companies such as Wal-Mart and Intel are capable of bold offenses. These competitive actors also have the ability and motivation to mount overwhelming counterattacks. Compared to relatively smaller firms with less market power, competitors are more likely to respond to competitive moves by market leaders. Another consideration is how successful prior attacks have been. For example, price-cutting by the big automakers usually has the desired result—increased sales to price-sensitive buyers—at least in the short run. Given that history, when GM offers discounts or incentives, rivals Ford and Chrysler cannot afford to ignore the challenge and quickly follow suit.

Choosing Not to React: Forbearance and Co-opetition

The above discussion suggests that there may be many circumstances in which the best reaction is no reaction at all. This is known as forbearance—refraining from reacting at all as well as holding back from initiating an attack. For example, none of the Japanese automakers attempted to match the employee discount pricing war that cost the big U.S. automakers heavily in terms of lower profits and lost jobs. Yet, during the same period, Honda, Toyota and Nissan enjoyed substantial sales increases over the previous year. Exhibit 8.9 shows the U.S. sales performance of major automakers during a month when GM, Ford, and Chrysler were engaged in a major price war from which Honda, Toyota, and Nissan abstained. Thus, the Japanese rivals were able to enjoy higher margins.

Related to forbearance is the concept of "co-opetition." This is a term that was coined by network software company Novell's founder and former CEO Raymond Noorda to suggest that companies often benefit most from a combination of competing and co-operating.[58] Close competitors that differentiate themselves in the eyes of consumers may work together behind the scenes to achieve industrywide efficiencies.[59] For example, breweries in Sweden cooperate in recycling used bottles but still compete for customers on the basis of taste and variety. As long as the benefits of cooperating are enjoyed by all participants in a co-opetition system, the practice can aid companies in avoiding intense and damaging competition.[60]

Exhibit 8.9

U.S. Sales of Cars and Light Trucks in July 2005 and the Percentage Change from the Previous Year

Brand	Sales	Change	Employee Pricing
General Motors	524,218	15.2%	Yes
Ford Motor	365,329	28.5%	Yes
DaimlerChrysler	260,972	25.1%	Yes
Toyota Motor	216,417	8.1%	No
Honda	143,217	10.3%	No
Nissan	107,300	15.0%	No

Sources: Sender, I. 2006. Car incentives: More pain than gain? *BusinessWeek*, www.businessweek.com, June 29; and Woodyard, C. 2005. Employee pricing helps Big 3's July auto sales hit record. *USA Today*, www.usatoday.com, August 2.

XM, Sirius, and Satellite Radio's Uncertain Future

Satellite radio providers XM and Sirius have been doing battle for years. Both new entrants have grown steadily as the pay-to-listen business model has gained acceptance. But their ongoing rounds of attacks and counterattacks may have cost them their future. Consider some of the key moves in the six years since satellite operations were launched:

- XM launches ahead of Sirius and gets a huge first mover advantage.
- Sirius outbids XM for a 7-year, $220 million deal to broadcast NFL football games.
- Sirius outbids XM again by signing radio shock jock Howard Stern to a five-year, $500 million contract.
- XM retaliates by signing Major League Baseball to an 11-year, $650 million deal to broadcast games.
- Sirius signs Martha Stewart, Jimmy Buffett, and Bruce Springsteen.
- XM signs the National Hockey League, Bob Dylan, and Oprah.

These high-profile signings have come at a high price. Instead of exercising a little forbearance, XM and Sirius

Sources: Kharif, O. 2007. Satellite static: The XM-Sirius merger. *Business-Week,* www.businessweek.com, February 21; Lowry, T., & Lehman, P. 2006. Grudge match. *BusinessWeek,* August 21/28: 86–87. Lowry, T., & Lehman, P. 2007. XM & Sirius: What a merger won't fix. *BusinessWeek,* www.business-week.com, March 5; and Rosenbush, S. 2007. New conditions may ease XM-Sirius merger. *BusinessWeek,* www.businessweek.com, February 28.

have spent themselve into the red. Both reported heavy losses in 2005, and their combined 2006 losses are expected to hit $1.7 billion. Subscriber rates were nearly 2 million fewer than projected at the end of 2006. More realistic forecasts, which could have been anticipated, might have curbed their enthusiasm for such a competitive spending spree.

To salvage the situation, the two rivals did an about face: They proposed a merger. The problem is that a merger would create a satellite radio monopoly. However, when the FCC first granted satellite radio licenses, it called for two competitive nationwide systems and clearly stated that any future merger of the two should be prohibited. The National Association of Broadcasters, which represents land-based radio stations, called on the FCC to block it.

To counter the appearance of collusion, the two companies argued that radiolike content is being delivered through many different media. The debate has turned to the role of MP3 players, Web radio, and multimedia wireless phones as competition for satellite radio. If these alternatives are truly rivals, it is curious that XM and Sirius did not take them more seriously earlier—it might have prevented them from spending so aggressively and overestimating subscriptions. Meanwhile, if the merger goes through, many analysts question the long-term viability of satellite radio. Their current satellites are expected to be obsolete in 10 to 15 years and alternatives such as high-definition terrestrial radio may bring this high-flying phenomen back down to earth.

Despite the potential benefits of co-opetition, companies need to guard against co-operating to such a great extent that their actions are perceived as collusion, a practice that has legal ramifications in the United States. Satellite radio competitors XM and Sirius faced several challenges recently related to whether it is better to cooperate or compete. Strategy Spotlight 8.10 describes the kinds of problems that can arise from too much co-opetition and too little forbearance.

Once a company has evaluated a competitor's likelihood of responding to a competitive challenge, it can decide what type of action is most appropriate. As we have seen, competitive actions can take many forms: the entry of a start-up into a market for the first time, an attack by a lower-ranked incumbent on an industry leader, or the launch of a breakthrough innovation that disrupts the industry structure. Such actions forever change the competitive dynamics of a marketplace. Thus, the cycle of actions and reactions that occur in business every day is a vital aspect of entrepreneurial strategy that leads to continual new value creation and the ongoing advancement of economic well-being.

Reflecting on Career Implications . . .

- *Opportunity Recognition:* What ideas for new business activities are actively discussed in your work environment? Could you apply the four characteristics of an opportunity to determine whether they are viable opportunities?
- *Entrepreneurial New Entry:* Are there opportunities to launch new products or services that might add value to the organization? What are the best ways for you to bring these opportunities to the attention of key managers? Or, might this provide an opportunity for you to launch your own entrepreneurial venture?
- *Entrepreneurial Strategy:* Does your organization face competition from new ventures? If so, how are those young firms competing: Low cost? Differentiation? Focus? What could you do to help your company to address those competitive challenges?
- *Competitive Dynamics:* Is your organization "on the offense" with its close competitors or "playing defense"? What types of strategic and/or tactical actions have been taken by your close rivals recently to gain competitive advantages?

Summary

New ventures and entrepreneurial firms that capitalize on marketplace opportunities make an important contribution to the U.S. economy. They are leaders in terms of implementing new technologies and introducing innovative products and services. Yet entrepreneurial firms face unique challenges if they are going to survive and grow.

To successfully launch new ventures or implement new technologies, three factors must be present: an entrepreneurial opportunity, the resources to pursue the opportunity, and an entrepreneur or entrepreneurial team willing and able to undertake the venture. Firms must develop a strong ability to recognize viable opportunities. Opportunity recognition is a process of determining which venture ideas are, in fact, promising business opportunities.

In addition to strong opportunities, entrepreneurial firms need resources and entrepreneurial leadership to thrive. The resources that start-ups need include financial resources as well as human and social capital. Many firms also benefit from government programs that support new venture development and growth. New ventures thrive best when they are led by founders or owners who have vision, drive and dedication, and a commitment to excellence.

Once the necessary opportunities, resources, and entrepreneur skills are in place, new ventures still face numerous strategic challenges. Decisions about the strategic positioning of new entrants can benefit from conducting strategic analyses and evaluating the requirements of niche markets. Entry strategies used by new ventures take several forms, including pioneering new entry, imitative new entry, and adaptive new entry. Entrepreneurial firms can benefit from using overall low cost, differentiation, and focus strategies although each of these approaches has pitfalls that are unique to young and small firms. Entrepreneurial firms are also in a strong position to benefit from combination strategies.

The entry of a new company into a competitive arena is like a competitive attack on incumbents in that arena. Such actions often provoke a competitive response, which may, in turn, trigger a reaction to the response. As a result, a competitive dynamic—action and response—begins among close competitors. In deciding whether to attack or counterattack, companies must analyze the seriousness of the competitive threat, their ability to mount a competitive response, and the type of action—strategic or tactical—that the situation requires. At times, competitors find it is better not to respond at all or to find avenues to cooperate with, rather than challenge, close competitors.

Summary Review Questions

1. Explain how the combination of opportunities, resources, and entrepreneurs helps determine the character and strategic direction of an entrepreneurial firm.

2. What is the difference between discovery and evaluation in the process of opportunity recognition? Give an example of each.

3. What are the differences between debt and equity sources of funding for entrepreneurial ventures?

4. Describe the three characteristics of entrepreneurial leadership: vision, dedication and drive, and commitment to excellence.

5. Briefly describe the three types of entrepreneurial entry strategies: pioneering, imitative, and adaptive.

6. Explain why entrepreneurial firms are often in a strong position to use combination strategies.

7. What does the term *competitive dynamics* mean?

8. Explain the difference between strategic actions and tactical actions and provide examples of each.

Key Terms

entrepreneurship, 267
opportunity recognition, 269
pioneering new entry, 278
imitative new entry, 278
adaptive new entry, 279

competitive dynamics, 285
market commonality, 287
resource similarity, 287
strategic actions, 291
tactical actions, 291

Applications Questions and Answers

1. E-Loan and Lending Tree are two young firms that offer lending services over the Internet. Evaluate the features of these two companies and, for each company:

a. Evaluate their characteristics and assess the extent to which they are comparable in terms of market commonality and resource similarity.

Company	Market Commonality	Resource Similarity
E-Loan		
Lending Tree		

b. Based on your analysis, what strategic and/or tactical actions might these companies take to improve their competitive position? Could E-Loan and Lending Tree improve their performance more through co-opetition rather than competition? Explain your rationale.

Company	Strategic Actions	Tactical Actions
E-Loan		
Lending Tree		

2. Using the Internet, research the Small Business Administration's Web site (www.sba.gov). What different types of financing are available to small firms? Besides financing, what other programs are available to support the growth and development of small businesses?

3. Think of an entrepreneurial firm that has been successfully launched in the last 10 years. What kind of entry strategy did it use—pioneering, imitative, or adaptive? Since the firm's initial entry, how has it used or combined overall low cost, differentiation and/or focus strategies?

4. Select an entrepreneurial firm you are familiar with in your local community. Research the company and discuss how it has positioned itself relative to its close competitors. Does it have a unique strategic advantage? Disadvantage? Explain.

Ethics Questions

1. Imitation strategies are based on the idea of copying another firm's idea and using it for your own purposes. Is this unethical or simply a smart business practice? Discuss the ethical implications of this practice (if any).

2. Intense competition such as price wars are an accepted practice in the United States, but cooperation between companies has legal ramifications because of antitrust laws. Should price wars that drive small businesses or new entrants out of business be illegal? What ethical considerations are raised (if any)?

References

1. The ESPN example is based on Lowry, T. 2006. ESPN's cell-phone fumble. *BusinessWeek,* October 30: 26; Medford, C. 2006. Final bell for Mobile ESPN. *Red Herring,* September 28, www.redherring.com; Seybold, A. M. 2006. Post-mortem of an MVNO. *Outlook 4Mobility,* www.outlook4mobility.com; and Zimmermann, K. 2006. ESPN Mobile failure: Bad news for mobile media in U.S. *Search Views,* September 28, www.searchviews.com.

2. Lowry, op. cit.

3. Medford, op. cit.

4. Seybold, op. cit.

5. Small Business Administration. 2004. *The small business economy* Washington, D.C.: U.S. Government Printing Office.

6. Timmons, J. A., & Spinelli, S. 2004. *New venture creation* (6th ed.). New York: McGraw-Hill/Irwin; and Bygrave, W. D. 1997. The entrepreneurial process. In W. D. Bygrave (Ed.), *The portable MBA in entrepreneurship* (2nd ed.). New York: Wiley.

7. Fromartz, S. 1998. How to get your first great idea. *Inc. Magazine,* April 1: 91–94; and, Vesper, K. H. 1990. *New venture strategies,* 2nd ed. Englewood Cliffs, NJ: Prentice-Hall.

8. For an interesting perspective on the nature of the opportunity recognition process, see Baron, R. A. 2006. Opportunity recognition as pattern recognition: How entrepreneurs 'connect the dots' to identify new business opportunities. *Academy of Management Perspectives,* February: 104–119.

9. Gaglio, C. M. 1997. Opportunity identification: Review, critique and suggested research directions. In J. A. Katz, ed. *Advances in entrepreneurship, firm emergence and growth,* vol. 3. Greenwich, CT: JAI Press: 139–202; Lumpkin, G. T., Hills, G. E., & Shrader, R. C. 2004. Opportunity recognition. In Harold L. Welsch, (Ed.), *Entrepreneurship: The Road Ahead,* pp. 73–90.

London: Routledge; and, Long, W. & McMullan, W. E. 1984. Mapping the new venture opportunity identification process. *Frontiers of Entrepreneurship Research, 1984.* Wellesley, MA: Babson College: 567–90.

10. For an interesting discussion of different aspects of opportunity discovery, see Shepherd, D. A., & De Tienne, D. R. 2005. Prior knowledge, potential financial reward, and opportunity identification. *Entrepreneurship Theory & Practice,* 29(1): 91–112; and Gaglio, C. M. 2004. The role of mental simulations and counterfactual thinking in the opportunity identification process. *Entrepreneurship Theory & Practice,* 28(6): 533–552.

11. Stewart, T. A. 2002. How to think with your gut. *Business 2.0,* November: 99–104.

12. Timmons, J. A. 1997. Opportunity recognition. In W. D. Bygrave, ed. *The portable MBA in entrepreneurship,* 2nd ed. New York: John Wiley: 26–54.

13. Bhide, A. V. 2000. *The origin and evolution of new businesses.* New York: Oxford University Press.

14. Anonymous. 2001. Small Business 2001: Where are we now? *Inc. Magazine,* May 29: 18–19; and, Zacharakis, A. L., Bygrave, W. D., & Shepherd, D.A. 2000. *Global entrepreneurship monitor—National entrepreneurship assessment: United States of America 2000 Executive Report.* Kansas City, MO: Kauffman Center for Entrepreneurial Leadership.

15. Cooper, S. 2003. Cash cows. *Entrepreneur,* June: 36.

16. Bhide, op. cit.

17. Seglin, J. L. 1998. What angels want. *Inc. Magazine,* 20 (7): 43–44.

18. Torres, N.L. 2002. Playing an angel. *Entrepreneur,* May: 130–138.

19. For more on how different forms of organizing entrepreneurial firms as well as different stages of new firm growth and development affect financing, see Cassar, G. 2004. The financing of business start-ups. *Journal of Business Venturing,* 19(2): 261–283.

20. Eisenhardt, K. M., & Schoonhoven, C. B. 1990. Organizational growth: Linking founding team, strategy, environment, and growth among U.S. semiconductor ventures, 1978–1988. *Administrative Science Quarterly,* 35: 504–529.

21. Dubini, P., & Aldrich, H. 1991. Personal and extended networks are central to the entrepreneurship process. *Journal of Business Venturing,* 6(5): 305–333.

22. For more on the role of social contacts in helping young firms build legitimacy, see Chrisman, J. J., & McMullan, W. E. 2004. Outside assistance as a knowledge resource for new venture survival. *Journal of Small Business Management,* 42(3): 229–244.

23. Vogel, C. 2000. Janina Pawlowski. *Working Woman,* June: 70

24. For a recent perspective on entrepreneurship and strategic alliances, see Rothaermel, F. T., & Deeds, D. L. 2006. Alliance types, alliance experience and alliance management capability in high-technology ventures. *Journal of Business Venturing,* 21(4): 429–460; and Lu, J. W., & Beamish, P. W. 2006. Partnering strategies and performance of SMEs' international joint ventures. *Journal of Business Venturing,* 21(4): 461–486.

25. For more information, go to the Small Business Administration Web site at www.sba.gov.

26. Collins, J. 2001. *Good to great.* New York: Harper-Collins.

27. Collins, op. cit.

28. The idea of entry wedges was discussed by Vesper, K. 1990. *New venture strategies* (2nd ed.). Englewood Cliffs, NJ: Prentice-Hall; and, Drucker, P. F. 1985. *Innovation and entrepreneurship.* New York: Harper-Business.

29. See Dowell, G., & Swaminathan, A. 2006. Entry timing, exploration, and firm survival in the early U.S. bicycle industry. *Strategic Management Journal,* 27: 1159–1182, for a recent study of the timing of entrepreneurial new entry.

30. Frauenfelder, M. 2002. Look! Up in the sky! It's a flying cell phone tower! *Business 2.0,* November: 108–112.

31. Maiello, M. 2002. They almost changed the world. *Forbes,* December 22: 217–220.

32. Pedroza, G. M. 2003. Blanket statement. *Entrepreneur,* March: 92.

33. Gull, N. 2003. Just say om. *Inc. Magazine,* July: 42–44.

34. More on the role of imitation strategies is addressed in a recent article: Lieberman, M. B., & Asaba, S. 2006. Why do firms imitate each other? *Academy of Management Review,* 31(2): 366–385.

35. Williams, G. 2002. Looks like Rain. *Entrepreneur,* September: 104–111.

36. Carey, J. 2006. Perspiration inspiration. *BusinessWeek,* June 5: 64;

37. Pedroza, G. M. 2002. Tech tutors. *Entrepreneur,* September: 120.

38. Barrett, A. 2003. Hot growth companies. *BusinessWeek,* June 9: 74–77.

39. Dennis, Jr. W. J. 1997. *Business starts and stops.* Washington, DC: National Federation of Independent Business; and, Anonymous. 1992. *The state of small business: A report of the President, 1992.* Washington, DC: U.S. Government Printing Office: 65–90.

40. Romanelli, E. 1989. Environments and strategies of organization start-up: Effects on early survival. *Administrative Science Quarterly,* 34(3): 369–87.

41. Wallace, B. 2000. Brothers. *Philadelphia Magazine,* April: 66–75.

42. Buchanan, L. 2003. The innovation factor: A field guide to innovation. *Forbes,* April 21, www.forbes.com.

43. Kim, W. C., & Mauborgne, R. 2005. *Blue ocean strategy.* Boston: Harvard Business School Press.

44. Burrows, P. 2003. Ringing off the hook in China. *BusinessWeek,* June 9: 80–82.

45. Smith, K. G., Ferrier, W. J., & Grimm, C. M. 2001. King of the hill: Dethroning the industry leader. *Academy of Management Executive,* 15(2): 59–70.

46. Kumar, N. 2006. Strategies to fight low-cost rivals. *Harvard Business Review,* December: 104–112.

47. Grove, A. 1999. *Only the paranoid survive: How to exploit the crises points that challenge every company.* New York: Random House.

48. Stalk, Jr., G., & Lachenauer, R. 2004. *Hardball: Are you playing to play or playing to win?* Cambridge, MA: Harvard Business School Press.

49. Peteraf, M. A., & Bergen, M. A. 2003. Scanning competitive landscapes: A market-based and resource-based framework. *Strategic Management Journal,* 24: 1027–1045.

50. Chen, M. J. 1996. Competitor analysis and interfirm rivalry: Toward a theoretical integration. *Academy of Management Review,* 21(1): 100–134.

51. Chen, 1996, op.cit.

52. Chen, M. J., Su, K. H, & Tsai, W. 2007. Competitive tension: The awareness-motivation-capability perspective. *Academy of Management Journal,* 50(1): 101–118.

53. St. John, W. 1999. Barnes & Noble's Epiphany. *Wired,* www.wired.com, June.

54. Kumar 2006, op. cit.

55. Chen, M. J., & Hambrick, D. 1995. Speed, stealth, and selective attack: How small firms differ from large firms in competitive behavior. *Academy of Management Journal,* 38: 453–482.

56. Lyons, D. 2006. The cheap revolution. *Forbes,* September 18: 102–111.

57. Smith, K. G., Ferrier, W. J., & Ndofor, H. 2001. Competitive dynamics research: Critique and future directions. In M. A. Hitt, R. E. Freeman, & J. S. Harrison (Eds.), *The Blackwell handbook of strategic management,* pp. 315–361. Oxford, UK: Blackwell.

58. Gee, P. 2000. Co-opetition: The new market milieu. *Journal of Healthcare Management,* 45: 359–363.

59. Ketchen, D. J., Snow, C. C., & Hoover, V. L. 2004. Research on competitive dynamics: Recent accomplishments and future challenges. *Journal of Management,* 30(6): 779–804.

60. Khanna, T., Gulati, R., & Nohria, N. 2000. The economic modeling of strategy process: Clean models and dirty hands. *Strategic Management Journal,* 21: 781–790.

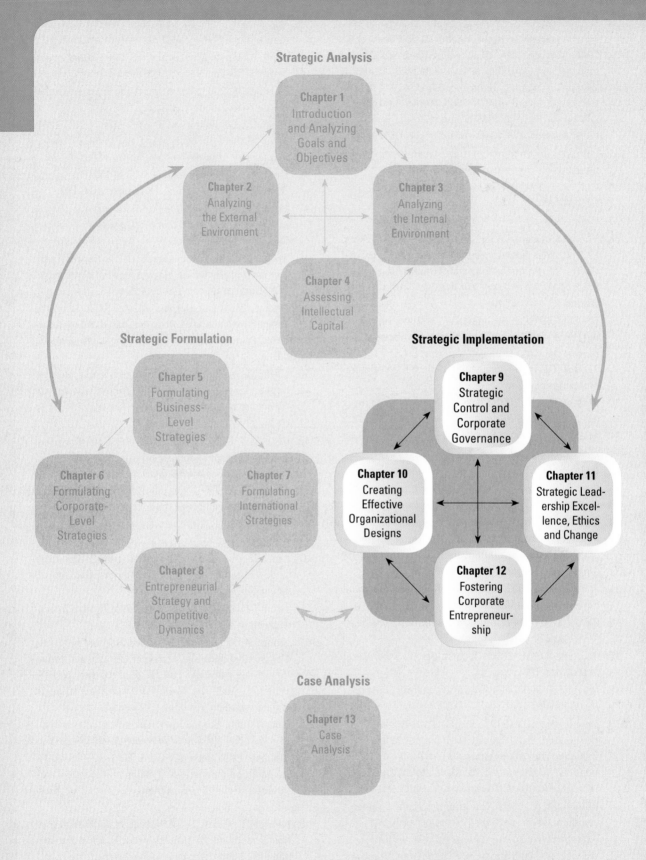

Strategic Analysis

Chapter 1
Introduction
and Analyzing
Goals and
Objectives

Chapter 2
Analyzing
the External
Environment

Chapter 3
Analyzing
the Internal
Environment

Chapter 4
Assessing
Intellectual
Capital

Strategic Formulation

Chapter 5
Formulating
Business-
Level
Strategies

Chapter 6
Formulating
Corporate-
Level
Strategies

Chapter 7
Formulating
International
Strategies

Chapter 8
Entrepreneurial
Strategy and
Competitive
Dynamics

Strategic Implementation

Chapter 9
Strategic
Control and
Corporate
Governance

Chapter 10
Creating
Effective
Organizational
Designs

Chapter 11
Strategic Lead-
ership Excel-
lence, Ethics
and Change

Chapter 12
Fostering
Corporate
Entrepreneur-
ship

Case Analysis

Chapter 13
Case
Analysis

Strategic Implementation

Strategic Control and Corporate Governance

>learning objectives

After reading this chapter, you should have a good understanding of:

LO1 The value of effective strategic control systems in strategy implementation.

LO2 The key difference between "traditional" and "contemporary" control systems.

LO3 The imperative for "contemporary" control systems in today's complex and rapidly changing competitive and general environments.

LO4 The benefits of having the proper balance among the three levers of behavioral control: culture; rewards and incentives; and, boundaries.

LO5 The three key participants in corporate governance: shareholders, management (led by the CEO), and the board of directors.

LO6 The role of corporate governance mechanisms in ensuring that the interests of managers are aligned with those of shareholders from both the United States and international perspectives.

Organizations must have effective strategic controls if they are to successfully implement their strategies. This includes systems that exercise both informational control and behavioral control. In addition, a firm must promote sound corporate governance as well as have controls that are consistent with the strategy that the firm is following.

In the first section, we address the need to have effective informational control, contrasting two approaches to informational control. The first approach, which we call "traditional," is highly sequential. Goals and objectives are set, then implemented, and after a set period of time, performance is compared to the desired standards. In contrast, the second approach, termed "contemporary," is much more interactive. Here, the internal and external environments are continually monitored, and managers determine whether the strategy itself needs to be modified. Today the contemporary approach is required, given the rapidly changing conditions in virtually all industries.

Next, we discuss behavioral control. Here the firm must strive to maintain a proper balance between culture, rewards, and boundaries. We also argue that organizations that have strong, positive cultures and reward systems can rely less on boundaries, such as rules, regulations, and procedures. When individuals in the firm internalize goals and strategies, there is less need for monitoring behavior, and efforts are focused more on important organizational goals and objectives.

The third section addresses the role of corporate governance in ensuring that managerial and shareholder interests are aligned. We provide examples of both effective and ineffective corporate governance practices. We discuss three governance mechanisms for aligning managerial and shareholder interests: a committed and involved board of directors, shareholder activism, and effective managerial rewards and incentives. Public companies are also subject to external control. We discuss several external control mechanisms, such as the market for corporate control, auditors, banks and analysts, the media, and public activists. We close with a discussion of corporate governance from an international perspective.

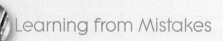

Learning from Mistakes

Recently, the backdating of option grants has prompted the biggest corporate probe since the mid 1970s.[1] By March 2007, about 140 companies were under investigation by the U.S. government for backdating, including Cablevision, Barnes & Noble, and Broadcom. Over 75 of these firms plan to restate earnings to account for charges totaling more than $5 billion. Some 66 executives have lost their jobs, and several have been indicted.

What is backdating all about? Option grants give the recipient a right to buy a stock at a fixed "strike price." This price is generally set at the stock's market price the day of the grant. Typically, a company's board of directors or compensation committee must approve its options grants to executives.

Holders of these grants benefit if the stock rises above the strike price because it enables them to buy stock at the lower price. In the backdating scandal, companies have dated option grants to days when the stock was at a low, thus enhancing the potential payouts. Let's take a look at a particularly egregious case of backdating—Los Angeles–based KB Home:

> KB Home may be only the fifth largest home builder in the United States. However, it easily ranks number one when it comes to paying its chief executive. *[continued]*

Over the last three years, CEO Bruce Karatz made an astonishing $232.6 million in total compensation. That's nearly three times what the chief executives earned at Pulte Homes and Centex Corp.—two rivals that are much larger and more profitable.

Unfortunately, greed got the best of Mr. Karatz and he finds himself homeless (figuratively speaking!). On, November 12, 2006, he fell prey to the backdating scandal and retired under pressure. An internal investigation found that he and another executive handed out options backdated to days when the stock was cheap in order to make them more valuable. The moves cost the company $50 million in additional compensation over a seven-year period ending in 2005. Karatz agreed to pay back $13 million. However, Karatz won't go away empty handed. According to his employment contract, he could walk away with $175 million in severance pay, pension benefits, and stock options. Such a package has prompted fresh criticism from larger shareholder groups that claim that Karatz had been overpaid for years. And there's other bad news: On January 19, 2007, the Securities and Exchange Commission began a formal probe at KB Home because it believed that there was a violation of its rules, and it may subpoena documents and compel testimony.

What factors might explain Karatz's generous windfall at stockholders' expense? One factor sticks out: a very generous and friendly board of directors and compensation committee. The five-man compensation committee was headed by Occidental Chair and Chief Executive Ray Irani, who is no stranger to high pay. Occidental paid him an astonishing $461 million in 2006—much of it in the exercise of stock options! Two other chief executives were also on the committee: Leslie Mooves, of CBS Corporation, who earned $22.8 million in 2005, and J. Terrence Lanni, chairman and CEO of casino company MGM Mirage, who made $9.6 million and was granted options with a potential value of $35.5 million that year.

In response to such largess, Ed Durkin, director of corporate affairs at the United Brotherhood of Carpenters, which has a $40 billion pension fund asserts: "We are always leery when you have another company's CEO on a compensation committee. They don't want people to say no to them, so they are particularly generous."

A fourth member of the compensation committee is James A. Johnson. He has been dubbed a "problem director" by the AFL-CIO. Why? He served on the board of United Health Group Inc. (UHG) whose CEO, William W. McGuire, retired in 2006 in the wake of a stock-option scandal. (McGuire's options were worth an astounding $1.78 billion at some point; he'll get to keep around $1 billion after repricing them.) Johnson's experience with UHG was hardly what KB Home needed!

We now focus on how organizations can develop and use effective strategic control.[2] We first explore two central aspects of strategic control: (1) *informational control,* which is the ability to respond effectively to environmental change, and (2) *behavioral control,* which is the appropriate balance and alignment among a firm's culture, rewards, and boundaries. In the final section of this chapter, we focus on strategic control from a much broader perspective—what is referred to as *corporate governance.* Here, we direct our attention to the need for a firm's shareholders (the owners) and their elected representatives (the board of directors) to ensure that the firm's executives (the management team) strive to fulfill their fiduciary duty of maximizing long-term shareholder value. Clearly, corporate governance was not one of KB Home's noteworthy strengths.

Ensuring Informational Control: Responding Effectively to Environmental Change

>LO1

The value of effective strategic control systems in strategy implementation.

We discuss two broad types of control systems. The first one, labeled "traditional," is based on a feedback approach; that is, there is little or no action taken to revise strategies, goals, and objectives until the end of the time period in question, usually a quarter or a month.

Exhibit 9.1 Traditional Approach to Strategic Control

The second one, which we call "contemporary," emphasizes the importance of continually monitoring the environment (both internal and external) for trends and events that signal the need to make modifications to a firm's strategies, goals, and objectives. As both general and competitive environments become more unpredictable and complex, the need for contemporary systems increases.

A Traditional Approach to Strategic Control

The **traditional approach to strategic control** is sequential: (1) strategies are formulated and top management sets goals, (2) strategies are implemented, and (3) performance is measured against the predetermined goal set, as illustrated in Exhibit 9.1.

Control is based on a feedback loop from performance measurement to strategy formulation. This process typically involves lengthy time lags, often tied to a firm's annual planning cycle. Such traditional control systems, termed "single-loop" learning by Harvard's Chris Argyris simply compare actual performance to a predetermined goal.[3] They are most appropriate when the environment is stable and relatively simple, goals and objectives can be measured with a high level of certainty, and there is little need for complex measures of performance. Sales quotas, operating budgets, production schedules, and similar quantitative control mechanisms are typical. The appropriateness of the business strategy or standards of performance is seldom questioned.[4]

The idea that well-managed companies should move forward in accordance with detailed and precise plans has come under attack.[5] James Brian Quinn of Dartmouth College has argued that grand designs with precise and carefully integrated plans seldom work. Rather, most strategic change proceeds incrementally—one step at a time. Leaders should introduce some sense of direction, some logic in incremental steps.[6]

Similarly, McGill University's Henry Mintzberg has written about leaders "crafting" a strategy.[7] Drawing on the parallel between the potter at her wheel and the strategist, Mintzberg pointed out that the potter begins work with some general idea of the artifact she wishes to create, but the details of design—even possibilities for a different design— emerge as the work progresses. For businesses facing complex and turbulent business environments, the craftsperson's method seems more appropriate than that provided by the traditional, more rational, planner. The former helps us deal with the uncertainty about how a design will work out in practice and allows for a creative element.

Mintzberg's argument, like Quinn's, questions the value of rigid planning and goal-setting processes. Fixed strategic goals also become dysfunctional for firms competing in highly unpredictable competitive environments. Here, strategies need to change frequently and opportunistically. An inflexible commitment to predetermined goals and milestones can prevent the very adaptability that is required of a good strategy.

Even organizations that have been extremely successful in the past can become complacent or fail to adapt their goals and strategies to the new conditions. An example of such a firm is Cisco Systems, whose market value at one time approached an astonishing $600 billion, but as of mid 2007 was about $180 billion. Cisco has minimized the potential for such problems in the future by improving its informational control systems. Other firms such as Siebel Systems (now part of Oracle) have been more successful in anticipating

traditional approach to strategic control a sequential method of organizational control in which (1) strategies are formulated and top management sets goals, (2) strategies are implemented, and (3) performance is measured against the predetermined goal set.

>LO2
The key difference between "traditional" and "contemporary" control systems.

When the Tech Bubble Burst

We can learn some lessons from fallen stars. Cisco Systems, Inc., once the invincible momentum stock adored by Wall Street, came crashing down just as we were beginning the 21st century. What went wrong?

Problems started when Cisco announced a $2.2 billion inventory write-off; Wall Street severely punished the stock as a result. With all of its experience, why didn't Cisco see the problems coming? Cisco made a common mistake: It projected the past into the future.

Past demand had been vigorous, but customers were requiring less and less of the firm's products. And financing was cheap—it was no problem for a company like Cisco to find capital to finance ongoing operations even when things didn't look so bright on the horizon. Overtaken

Sources: Weber, J. 2001. Management lessons from the bust. *BusinessWeek*, August 27: 104–112; Morrison, S. 2001. Positive sales news takes the sting out of Cisco revamp. *Financial Times Online*, August 26; Reuters. 2001. Siebel sees economic rebound late 2002: August 20.

by its own success, Cisco failed to see the slowdown in customer demand. John Sterman at MIT sums up the situation: "If you were in the pasta business, you want to know how much pasta people are cooking and eating, not how much they're buying, and certainly not how much supermarkets and distributors are ordering from the factory." Consumers ultimately determine demand; Cisco missed this important point and inaccurately forecast new sales orders. When the orders didn't materialize, a stockpile of inventory sat on the shelves while Wall Street annulled the short-lived marriage between investors and their beloved Cisco.

In contrast, Siebel Systems, Inc., kept its eye on the future. The company rewarded its sales force for providing accurate information concerning future demand. Salespeople receive commissions not only for sales, but also for forecast information. Haim Mendelson at Stanford University remarked that this provides the company "with a deep understanding of what customers are going to do."

change and have made proper corrections to their strategies. We discuss these firms in Strategy Spotlight 9.1.

Without doubt, the traditional "feedback" approach to strategic control has some important limitations. Is there another, better, way?

A Contemporary Approach to Strategic Control

>LO3

The imperative for "contemporary" control systems in today's complex and rapidly changing competitive and general environments.

Adapting to and anticipating both internal and external environmental change is an integral part of strategic control. The relationships between strategy formulation, implementation, and control are highly interactive, as suggested by Exhibit 9.2. It also illustrates two different types of strategic control: informational control and behavioral control. **Informational control** is primarily concerned with whether or not the organization is "doing the right things." **Behavioral control,** on the other hand, asks if the organization is "doing things right" in the implementation of its strategy. Both the informational and

informational control a method of organizational control in which a firm gathers and analyzes information from the internal and external environment in order to obtain the best fit between the organization's goals and strategies and the strategic environment.

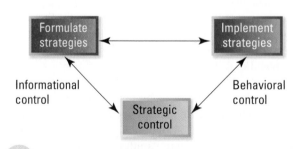

Exhibit 9.2 Contemporary Approach to Strategic Control

behavioral components of strategic control are necessary, but not sufficient, conditions for success. That is, what good is a well-conceived strategy that cannot be implemented? Or, alternatively, what use is an energetic and committed workforce if it is focused on the wrong strategic target?

behavioral control
a method of organizational control in which a firm influences the actions of employees through culture, rewards, and boundaries.

John Weston is the former CEO of ADP Corporation, the largest payroll and taxfiling processor in the world. He captures the essence of contemporary control systems.

> At ADP, 39 plus 1 adds up to more than 40 plus 0. The 40-plus-0 employee is the harried worker who at 40 hours a week just tries to keep up with what's in the "in" basket. He tries to do whatever he thinks he's supposed to do. Because he works with his head down, he takes zero hours to think about what he's doing, why he's doing it, and how he's doing it. Does he need to do it in the first place? On the other hand, the 39-plus-1 employee takes at least 1 of those 40 hours to think about what he's doing and why he's doing it. That's why the other 39 hours are far more productive.[8]

Informational control deals with the internal environment as well as the external strategic context. It addresses the assumptions and premises that provide the foundation for an organization's strategy. The key question becomes: Do the organization's goals and strategies still "fit" within the context of the current strategic environment? Depending on the type of business, such assumptions may relate to changes in technology, customer tastes, government regulation, and industry competition.

This involves two key issues. First, managers must scan and monitor the external environment, as we discussed in Chapter 2. Recall, for example, the failure of Coors to anticipate and act on the trend toward low-carb beer. Also, conditions can change in the internal environment of the firm, as we discussed in Chapter 3, requiring changes in the strategic direction of the firm. These may include, for example, the resignation of key executives or delays in the completion of major production facilities.

In the contemporary approach, information control is part of an ongoing process of organizational learning that continuously updates and challenges the assumptions that underlie the organization's strategy. In such "double-loop" learning, the organization's assumptions, premises, goals, and strategies are continuously monitored, tested, and reviewed. The benefits of continuous monitoring are evident—time lags are dramatically shortened, changes in the competitive environment are detected earlier, and the organization's ability to respond with speed and flexibility is enhanced.

A key question becomes: OK, but how is this done? Contemporary control systems must have four characteristics to be effective.[9]

1. They must focus on constantly changing information that top managers identify as having potential strategic importance.
2. The information is important enough to demand frequent and regular attention from operating managers at all levels of the organization.
3. The data and information generated by the control system are best interpreted and discussed in face-to-face meetings of superiors, subordinates, and peers.
4. The contemporary control system is a key catalyst for an ongoing debate about underlying data, assumptions, and action plans.

An executive's decision to use the control system interactively—in other words, to invest the time and attention to review and evaluate new information—sends a clear signal to the organization about what is important. The dialogue and debate that emerge from such an interactive process can often lead to new strategies and innovations. Strategy Spotlight 9.2 discusses how executives at *USA Today*, Gannett Co.'s daily newspaper, review information delivered each Friday.

Let's now turn our attention to behavioral control.

USA Today's Interactive Control System

Top managers at Gannett-owned *USA Today* meet each Friday to discuss ongoing strategy. Every week, they review information ranging from day-to-day operations to year-to-date data. This information enables top management to check the pulse of the industry on a frequent basis and minimizes the surprises that frequently beset other companies that don't keep close tabs on available information. Senior managers frequently meet with operations-level managers for intensive discussion to analyze the weekly information. The results of these high-level meetings on information control allow managers from the operating core of the newspaper to respond to industry trends and events on nearly a real-time basis.

By controlling information, *USA Today* managers:

- Compare projected advertising volume with actual volume.

Sources: Simons, R. 1995. Control in an age of empowerment. *Harvard Business Review,* 73(2): 80–88; Caney, D. 2001. Gannett, Knight Ridder walloped by ad slump. Reuters, July 17.

- Assess new advertising revenues by client type to better target client markets.

- Quickly discover revenue shortfalls before major problems arise.

- Become aware of unexpected successes that have often led to innovations.

These weekly meetings have returned significant rewards for *USA Today.* Innovations that have been implemented as a result of high information control include:

- A new market survey service targeted at the automobile industry (a potential source of high-volume advertising).

- The addition of fractional page color advertising (increasing the number of advertisers that use color, thereby increasing advertising revenue).

- Expanding the job function of circulation employees to include regional sales of advertising space.

- Developing a program of advertising inserts targeted toward specific customers and products.

Attaining Behavioral Control: Balancing Culture, Rewards, and Boundaries

>LO4

The benefits of having the proper balance among the three levers of behavioral control: culture, rewards and incentives, and boundaries.

Behavioral control is focused on implementation—doing things right. Effectively implementing strategy requires manipulating three key control "levers": culture, rewards, and boundaries. These three levers are illustrated in Exhibit 9.3. Furthermore, there are two compelling reasons for an increased emphasis on culture and rewards in implementing a system of behavioral controls.

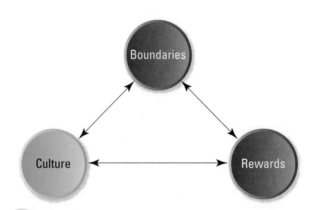

Exhibit 9.3 **Essential Elements of Behavioral Control**

First, the competitive environment is increasingly complex and unpredictable, demanding both flexibility and quick response to its challenges. As firms simultaneously downsize and face the need for increased coordination across organizational boundaries, a control system based primarily on rigid strategies and rules and regulations is dysfunctional. Thus, the use of rewards and culture to align individual and organizational goals becomes increasingly important.

Second, the implicit long-term contract between the organization and its key employees has been eroded.[10] Today's younger managers have been conditioned to see themselves as "free agents" and view a career as a series of opportunistic challenges. As managers are advised to "specialize, market yourself, and have work, if not a job," the importance of culture and rewards in building organizational loyalty claims greater importance. (We addressed this issue at length in Chapter 4.)

Each of the three levers—culture, rewards, and boundaries—must work in a balanced and consistent manner. Let's consider the role of each.

Building a Strong and Effective Culture

What is culture? Consistent with our discussion in Chapter 4, **organizational culture** is a system of shared values (what is important) and beliefs (how things work) that shape a company's people, organizational structures, and control systems to produce behavioral norms (the way we do things around here). How important is culture? Very. Over the years, numerous best sellers, such as *Theory Z, Corporate Cultures, In Search of Excellence,* and *Good to Great,*[11] have emphasized the powerful influence of culture on what goes on within organizations and how they perform.

organizational culture a system of shared values and beliefs that shape a company's people, organizational structures, and control systems to produce behavioral norms.

Collins and Porras argued in *Built to Last* that the key factor in sustained exceptional performance is a cultlike culture.[12] You can't touch it, you can't write it down, but it's there, in every organization, and its influence is pervasive. It can work for you or against you.[13] Effective leaders understand its importance and strive to shape and use it as one of their important levers of strategic control.[14]

The Role of Culture Culture wears many different hats, each woven from the fabric of those values that sustain the organization's primary source of competitive advantage. Some examples are:

- Federal Express and Southwest Airlines focus on customer service.
- Lexus (a division of Toyota) and Hewlett-Packard emphasize product quality.
- Newell Rubbermaid and 3M place a high value on innovation.
- Nucor (steel) and Emerson Electric are concerned, above all, with operational efficiency.

Culture sets implicit boundaries—that is, unwritten standards of acceptable behavior—in dress, ethical matters, and the way an organization conducts its business.[15] By creating a framework of shared values, culture encourages individual identification with the organization and its objectives. Thus, culture acts as a means of reducing monitoring costs.[16]

Sustaining an Effective Culture Powerful organizational cultures just don't happen overnight, and they don't remain in place without a strong commitment—both in terms of words and deeds—by leaders throughout the organization. A viable and productive organizational culture can be strengthened and sustained. However, it cannot be "built" or "assembled"; instead, it must be cultivated, encouraged, and "fertilized."

Storytelling is one way effective cultures are maintained. Many are familiar with the story of how Art Fry's failure to develop a strong adhesive led to 3M's enormously successful Post-it Notes. Perhaps less familiar is the story of Francis G. Okie.[17] In 1922 Okie came up with the idea of selling sandpaper to men as a replacement for razor blades. The idea obviously didn't pan out, but Okie was allowed to remain at 3M. Interestingly, the technology developed by Okie led 3M to develop its first blockbuster product: a waterproof

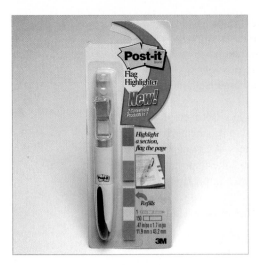

● 3M is well known for its innovative culture. Above is a Yellow 3M Post-It Highlighter Package.

sandpaper that became a staple of the automobile industry. Such stories foster the importance of risk taking, experimentation, freedom to fail, and of course innovation—all vital elements of 3M's culture.

Rallies or "pep talks" by top executives also serve to reinforce a firm's culture. The late Sam Walton was well known for his pep rallies at local Wal-Mart stores. Four times a year, the founders of Home Depot—CEO Bernard Marcus and Arthur Blank—used to don orange aprons and stage Breakfast with Bernie and Arthur, a 6:30 a.m. pep rally, broadcast live over the firm's closed-circuit TV network to most of its 45,000 employees.[18]

Southwest Airlines' "Culture Committee" is a unique vehicle designed to perpetuate the company's highly successful culture. The following excerpt from an internal company publication describes its objectives:

> The goal of the Committee is simple—to ensure that our unique Corporate Culture stays alive. . . . Culture Committee members represent all regions and departments across our system and they are selected based upon their exemplary display of the "Positively Outrageous Service" that won us the first-ever Triple Crown; their continual exhibition of the "Southwest Spirit" to our Customers and to their fellow workers; and their high energy level, boundless enthusiasm, unique creativity, and constant demonstration of teamwork and love for their fellow workers.[19]

Motivating with Rewards and Incentives

Reward and incentive systems represent a powerful means of influencing an organization's culture, focusing efforts on high-priority tasks, and motivating individual and collective task performance.[20] Just as culture deals with influencing beliefs, behaviors, and attitudes of people within an organization, the reward system—by specifying who gets rewarded and why—is an effective motivator and control mechanism.[21] Consider how John Thompson, CEO of $1 billion software security firm Symantec, distributes financial rewards based on contribution:[22]

> When Thompson arrived at Symantec, any executive who was promoted to vice president automatically received a BMW. Senior management's bonuses were paid quarterly and were heavily skewed toward cash, not stock. Thompson says:
>
> > So if the stock didn't do well, they didn't care. We now have a stock option plan that is broad based but not universal. One of the things we recognized early on was that if we were going to grow at the rate that we were growing, we have to be more selective in who we gave options to so as not to dilute the value of our stock. And, the first thing we did was identify a range of employees who were valuable to the company but didn't need equity to come to work, and we focused their compensation around cash bonuses. Then we increased the equity we gave to the engineers and other people that were critical to our long term success.
>
> By paying the two groups of people in a different manner, the new compensation scheme recognizes their distinctive importance.

The Potential Downside   Generally speaking, people in organizations act rationally, each motivated by their personal best interest.[23] However, the collective sum of individual behaviors of an organization's employees does not always result in what is best for the organization; that is, individual rationality is no guarantee of organizational rationality.

As corporations grow and evolve, they often develop different business units with multiple reward systems. They may differ based on industry contexts, business situations, stage of product life cycles, and so on. Thus, subcultures within organizations may reflect differences among an organization's functional areas, products, services, and divisions. To the extent that reward systems reinforce such behavioral norms, attitudes, and belief systems, cohesiveness is reduced; important information is hoarded rather than shared, individuals begin working at cross-purposes, and they lose sight of overall goals.

Such conflicts are commonplace in many organizations. For example, sales and marketing personnel promise unrealistically quick delivery times to bring in business, much to the dismay of operations and logistics; overengineering by R&D creates headaches for manufacturing; and so on. Conflicts also arise across divisions when divisional profits become a key compensation criterion. As ill will and anger escalate, personal relationships and performance may suffer.

Creating Effective Reward and Incentive Programs   To be effective, incentive and reward systems need to reinforce basic core values and enhance cohesion and commitment to goals and objectives. They also must not be at odds with the organization's overall mission and purpose.[24]

At General Mills, a manager's interest in the overall performance of his or her unit, half of a manager's annual bonus is linked to business-unit results and half to individual performance.[25] For example, if a manager simply matches a rival manufacturer's performance, his or her salary is roughly 5 percent lower. However, if a manager's product ranks in the industry's top 10 percent in earnings growth and return on capital, the manager's total pay can rise to nearly 30 percent beyond the industry norm.

Effective reward and incentive systems share a number of common characteristics. For example, the perception that a plan is "fair and equitable" is critically important. Similarly, the firm must have the flexibility to respond to changing requirements as its direction and objectives change. In recent years many companies have begun to place more emphasis on growth. Emerson Electric is one company that has shifted its emphasis from cost cutting to growth. To ensure that changes take hold, the management compensation formula has been changed from a largely bottom-line focus to one that emphasizes growth, new products, acquisitions, and international expansion. Discussions about profits are handled separately, and a culture of risk taking is encouraged.[26]

Exhibit 9.4 summarizes some of the attributes of effective reward and evaluation systems.

Setting Boundaries and Constraints

In an ideal world, a strong culture and effective rewards should be sufficient to ensure that all individuals and subunits work toward the common goals and objectives of the whole organization.[27] In practice, however, this is not usually the case. Counterproductive behavior can arise because of motivated self-interest, lack of a clear understanding of goals and

---

• Objectives are clear, well understood, and broadly accepted.
• Rewards are clearly linked to performance and desired behaviors.
• Performance measures are clear and highly visible.
• Feedback is prompt, clear, and unambiguous.
• The compensation "system" is perceived as fair and equitable.
• The structure is flexible; it can adapt to changing circumstances.

Exhibit 9.4

Characteristics of Effective Reward and Evaluation Systems

objectives, or outright malfeasance. Boundaries and constraints, when used properly, can serve many useful purposes for organizations, including:

- Focusing individual efforts on strategic priorities.
- Providing short-term objectives and action plans to channel efforts.
- Improving efficiency and effectiveness.
- Minimizing improper and unethical conduct.

Focusing Efforts on Strategic Priorities   Boundaries and constraints play a valuable role in focusing a company's strategic priorities. A well-known example of a strategic boundary is Jack Welch's (former CEO of General Electric) demand that any business in the corporate portfolio be ranked first or second in its industry. Similarly, Eli Lilly has reduced its research efforts to five broad areas of disease, down from eight or nine a decade ago.[28] This concentration of effort and resources provides the firm with greater strategic focus and the potential for stronger competitive advantages in the remaining areas.

Norman Augustine, Lockheed Martin's former chairman, provided four criteria for selecting candidates for diversification into "closely related" businesses.[29] They must (1) be high tech, (2) be systems-oriented, (3) deal with large customers (either corporations or government) as opposed to consumers, and (4) be in growth businesses. Augustine said, "We have found that if we can meet most of those standards, then we can move into adjacent markets and grow."

Boundaries also have a place in the nonprofit sector. For example, a British relief organization uses a system to monitor strategic boundaries by maintaining a list of companies whose contributions it will neither solicit nor accept. Such boundaries clearly go beyond simply taking the moral high road. Rather, they are essential for maintaining legitimacy with existing and potential benefactors.

Providing Short-Term Objectives and Action Plans   In Chapter 1 we discussed the importance of a firm having a vision, mission, and strategic objectives that are internally consistent and that provide strategic direction. In addition, short-term objectives and action plans provide similar benefits. That is, they represent boundaries that help to allocate resources in an optimal manner and to channel the efforts of employees at all levels throughout the organization.[30] To be effective, short-term objectives must have several attributes. They should:

- Be specific and measurable.
- Include a specific time horizon for their attainment.
- Be achievable, yet challenging enough to motivate managers who must strive to accomplish them.

Research has found that performance is enhanced when individuals are encouraged to attain specific, difficult, yet achievable, goals (as opposed to vague "do your best" goals).[31]

Short-term objectives must provide proper direction and at the same time provide enough flexibility for the firm to keep pace with and anticipate changes in the external environment. Such changes might include new government regulations, a competitor introducing a substitute product, or changes in consumer taste. Additionally, unexpected events within a firm may require a firm to make important adjustments in both strategic and short-term objectives. For example, the emergence of new industries can have a drastic effect on the demand for products and services in more traditional industries.

Along with short-term objectives, action plans are critical to the implementation of chosen strategies. Unless action plans are specific, there may be little assurance that managers have thought through all of the resource requirements for implementing their strategies. In addition, unless plans are specific, managers may not understand what needs to be implemented or have a clear time frame for completion. This is essential for the scheduling of key activities that must be implemented. Finally, individual managers must be held accountable for the implementation of action plans. This helps to provide the necessary motivation and "sense of ownership" to implement action plans on a timely basis. Strategy Spotlight 9.3 illustrates how action plans fit into the mission statement and objectives of a small manufacturer of aircraft interior components. Here, Exhibit 9.5 provides details of an action plan to fulfill one of the firm's objectives.

Improving Operational Efficiency and Effectiveness Rule-based controls are most appropriate in organizations with the following characteristics:

- Environments are stable and predictable.
- Employees are largely unskilled and interchangeable.
- Consistency in product and service is critical.
- The risk of malfeasance is extremely high (e.g., in banking or casino operations), and controls must be implemented to guard against improper conduct.[32]

For example, McDonald's Corp. has extensive rules and regulations that regulate the operation of its franchises.[33] Its policy manual states, "Cooks must turn, never flip, hamburgers. If they haven't been purchased, Big Macs must be discarded in 10 minutes after being cooked and French fries in 7 minutes. Cashiers must make eye contact with and smile at every customer."

Guidelines can also be effective in setting spending limits and the range of discretion for employees and managers, such as the $2,500 limit that hotelier Ritz-Carlton uses to empower employees to placate dissatisfied customers. Regulations also can be initiated to improve the use of an employee's time at work.[34] Computer Associates restricts the use of e-mail during the hours of 10 a.m. to noon and 2 p.m. to 4 p.m. each day.[35]

Minimizing Improper and Unethical Conduct Guidelines can be useful in specifying proper relationships with a company's customers and suppliers.[36] For example, many companies have explicit rules regarding commercial practices, including the prohibition of any form of payment, bribe, or kickback. Cadbury Schweppes has followed a rather simple but effective step in controlling the use of bribes by specifying that all payments, no matter how unusual, are recorded on the company's books. Its chairman, Sir Adrian Cadbury, contended that such a practice causes managers to pause and consider whether a payment is simply a bribe or a necessary and standard cost of doing business.[37] Consulting companies, too, typically have strong rules and regulations directed at protecting client confidentiality and conflicts of interest.

Regulations backed up with strong sanctions can also help an organization avoid conducting business in an unethical manner. In the wake of the corporate scandals of the early 21st century and the passing of the Sarbanes-Oxley Act (which, among other things, provides for stiffer penalties for financial reporting misdeeds), many chief financial officers (CFOs) have taken steps to ensure ethical behavior in the preparation of financial statements. For example, Home Depot's CFO, Carol B. Tome, strengthened the firm's code of ethics and developed stricter guidelines. Now all 25 of her subordinates must sign personal statements that all of their financial statements are correct—just as she and her CEO, have to do now according to the congressional legislation.[38]

Behavioral Control in Organizations: Situational Factors

We have discussed the behavioral dimension of control. Here, the focus is on ensuring that the behavior of individuals at all levels of an organization is directed toward achieving organizational goals and objectives. The three fundamental types of control are culture, rewards and incentives, and boundaries and constraints. An organization may pursue one or a combination of them on the basis of a variety of internal and external factors.

Developing Meaningful Action Plans: Aircraft Interior Products, Inc.

MSA Aircraft Interior Products, Inc., is a manufacturing firm based in San Antonio, Texas, that was founded in 1983 by Mike Spraggins and Robert Plenge. The firm fulfills a small but highly profitable niche in the aviation industry with two key products. The Accordia line consists of patented, light-weight, self-contained window-shade assemblies. MSA's interior cabin shells are state-of-the-art assemblies that include window panels, side panels, headliners, and suspension system structures. MSA's products have been installed on a variety of aircraft, such as the Gulfstream series; the Cessna Citation; and Boeing's 727, 737, 757, and 707.

Much of MSA's success can be attributed to carefully articulated action plans consistent with the firm's mission and objectives. During the past five years, MSA has increased its sales at an annual rate of 15 to 18 percent. It has also succeeded in adding many prestigious companies to its customer base. Below are excerpts from MSA's mission statement and objectives as well as the action plans to achieve a 20 percent annual increase in sales.

Mission Statement

- Be recognized as an innovative and reliable supplier of quality interior products for the high-end, personalized transportation segments of the aviation, marine, and automotive industries.

- Design, develop, and manufacture interior fixtures and components that provide exceptional value to

the customer through the development of innovative designs in a manner that permits decorative design flexibility while retaining the superior functionality, reliability, and maintainability of well-engineered, factory-produced products.

- Grow, be profitable, and provide a fair return, commensurate with the degree of risk, for owners and stockholders.

Objectives

1. Achieve sustained and profitable growth over the next three years:
   - 20 percent annual growth in revenues
   - 12 percent pretax profit margins
   - 18 percent return on shareholder's equity

2. Expand the company's revenues through the development and introduction of two or more new products capable of generating revenues in excess of $8 million a year by 2010.

3. Continue to aggressively expand market opportunities and applications for the Accordia line of window-shade assemblies, with the objective of sustaining or exceeding a 20 percent annual growth rate for at least the next three years.

Exhibit 9.5 details an "Action Plan" for Objective 3.

MSA's action plans are supported by detailed month-by-month budgets and strong financial incentives for its executives. Budgets are prepared by each individual department and include all revenue and cost items. Managers are motivated by their participation in a profit-sharing program, and the firm's two founders each receive a bonus equal to three percent of total sales.

Description	Primary Responsibility	Target Date
1. Develop and implement 2008 marketing plan, including specific plans for addressing Falcon 20 retrofit programs and expanded sales of cabin shells.	R. H. Plenge (V.P. Marketing)	December 15, 2007
2. Negotiate new supplier agreement with Gulfstream Aerospace.	M. Spraggins (President)	March 1, 2008
3. Continue and complete the development of the UltraSlim window and have a fully tested and documented design ready for production at a manufacturing cost of less than $900 per unit.	D. R. Pearson (V.P. Operations)	June 15, 2008
4. Develop a window design suitable for L-1011 and similar wide-body aircraft and have a fully tested and documented design ready for production at a manufacturing cost comparable to the current Boeing window.	D. R. Pearson (V.P. Operations)	September 15, 2008

Exhibit 9.5 Action Plan for Objective Number 3

Not all organizations place the same emphasis on each type of control.[39] For example, in high-technology firms engaged in basic research, members may work under high levels of autonomy. Here, an individual's performance is generally quite difficult to measure accurately because of the long lead times involved in research and development activities. Thus, internalized norms and values become very important.

When the measurement of an individual's output or performance is quite straightforward, control depends primarily on granting or withholding rewards. Frequently, a sales manager's compensation is in the form of a commission and bonus tied directly to his or her sales volume, which is relatively easy to determine. Here, behavior is influenced more strongly by the attractiveness of the compensation than by the norms and values implicit in the organization's culture. Furthermore, the measurability of output precludes the need for an elaborate system of rules to control behavior.

Control in bureaucratic organizations is dependent on members following a highly formalized set of rules and regulations. In such situations, most activities are routine and the desired behavior can be specified in a detailed manner because there is generally little need for innovative or creative activity. For example, managing an assembly plant requires strict adherence to many rules as well as exacting sequences of assembly operations. In the public sector, the Department of Motor Vehicles in most states must follow clearly prescribed procedures when issuing or renewing driver licenses.

Exhibit 9.6 provides alternate approaches to behavioral control and some of the situational factors associated with them.

Evolving from Boundaries to Rewards and Culture

In most environments, organizations should strive to provide a system of rewards and incentives, coupled with a culture strong enough that boundaries become internalized. This reduces the need for external controls such as rules and regulations. We suggest several ways to move in this direction.

First, hire the right people—individuals who already identify with the organization's dominant values and have attributes consistent with them. We addressed this issue in detail in Chapter 4; recall the "Bozo Filter" developed by Cooper Software. Microsoft's David Pritchard is well aware of the consequences of failing to hire properly.

> If I hire a bunch of bozos, it will hurt us, because it takes time to get rid of them. They start infiltrating the organization and then they themselves start hiring people of lower quality. At Microsoft, we are always looking for people who are better than we are.

Exhibit 9.6

Organizational Control: Alternative Approaches

Approach	Some Situational Factors
Culture: A system of unwritten rules that forms an internalized influence over behavior.	• Often found in professional organizations. • Associated with high autonomy. • Norms are the basis for behavior.
Rules: Written and explicit guidelines that provide external constraints on behavior.	• Associated with standardized output. • Tasks are generally repetitive and routine. • Little need for innovation or creative activity.
Rewards: The use of performance-based incentive systems to motivate.	• Measurement of output and performance is rather straightforward. • Most appropriate in organizations pursuing unrelated diversification strategies. • Rewards may be used to reinforce other means of control.

Second, training plays a key role. For example, in elite military units such as the Green Berets and Navy SEALs, the training regimen so thoroughly internalizes the culture that individuals, in effect, lose their identity. The group becomes the overriding concern and focal point of their energies. At firms such as FedEx, training not only builds skills, but also plays a significant role in building a strong culture on the foundation of each organization's dominant values.

Third, managerial role models are vital. Andy Grove at Intel doesn't need (or want) a large number of bureaucratic rules to determine who is responsible for what, who is supposed to talk to whom, and who gets to fly first class (no one does). He encourages openness by not having many of the trappings of success—he works in a cubicle like all the other professionals. Can you imagine any new manager asking whether or not he can fly first class? Grove's personal example eliminates such a need.

Fourth, reward systems must be clearly aligned with the organizational goals and objectives. Where do you think rules and regulations are more important in controlling behavior—Home Depot, with its generous bonus and stock option plan, or Wal-Mart, which does not provide the same level of rewards and incentives?

The Role of Corporate Governance

>LO5

The three key participants in corporate governance: shareholders, management (led by the CEO), and the board of directors.

We have addressed how management can exercise strategic control over the firm's overall operations through the use of informational and behavioral controls. Now we address the issue of strategic control in a broader perspective, typically referred to as "corporate governance." Here we focus on the need for both shareholders (the owners of the corporation) and their elected representatives, the board of directors, to actively ensure that management fulfills its overriding purpose of increasing long-term shareholder value.

Robert Monks and Nell Minow, two leading scholars in **corporate governance,** define it as "the relationship among various participants in determining the direction and performance of corporations. The primary participants are (1) the shareholders, (2) the management (led by the chief executive officer), and (3) the board of directors."* Consistent with Monks and Minow's definition, our discussion will center on how corporations can succeed (or fail) in aligning managerial motives with the interests of the shareholders and their elected representatives, the board of directors. As you will recall from Chapter 1, we discussed the important role of boards of directors and provided some examples of effective and ineffective boards.[40]

corporate governance the relationship among various participants in determining the direction and performance of corporations. The primary participants are (1) the shareholders, (2) the management, and (3) the board of directors.

There is little doubt that effective corporate governance can affect a firm's bottom line. Good corporate governance plays an important role in the investment decisions of major institutions, and a premium is often reflected in the price of securities of companies that practice it. The corporate governance premium is larger for firms in countries with sound corporate governance practices compared to countries with weaker corporate governance standards.[41] In addition, there is a strong correlation between strong corporate governance and superior financial performance. Strategy Spotlight 9.4 briefly summarizes two studies that provide support for this contention.

As indicated in our discussion above and in Strategy Spotlight 9.4, there is solid evidence linking good corporate governance with higher performance. At the same time, few topics in the business press are generating as much interest (and disdain!) as corporate governance.

---

* Management, of course, cannot ignore the demands of other important firm stakeholders such as creditors, suppliers, customers, employees, and government regulators. At times of financial duress, powerful creditors can exert strong and legitimate pressures on managerial decisions. In general, however, the attention to stakeholders other than the owners of the corporation must be addressed in a manner that is still consistent with maximizing long-term shareholder returns. For a seminal discussion on stakeholder management, refer to Freeman, R. E. 1984. *Strategic management: A stakeholder approach.* Boston: Pitman.

Good Corporate Governance and Performance: Research Evidence

Two studies found a positive relationship between the extent to which a firm practices good corporate governance and its performance outcomes. The results of these studies are summarized below.

1. *A strong correlation between corporate governance and price performance of large companies.* Over a recent three-year period, the average return of large capitalized firms with the best governance practices was more than five times higher than the performance of firms in the bottom corporate governance quartile.

2. *Across emerging markets.* In 10 of the 11 Asian and Latin American markets, companies in the top corporate governance quartile for their respective regions had a significantly higher (averaging 10 percentage points) return on capital employed (ROCE) than their market sample. In 12 of the emerging markets analyzed, companies in the lowest corporate governance quartile had a lower ROCE than the market average.

Sources: Gill, A. 2001. Credit Lyonnais Securities (Asia). *Corporate governance in emerging markets: Saints and sinners,* April; and Low, C. K. 2002. *Corporate governance: An Asia-Pacific critique.* Hong Kong: Sweet & Maxwell Asia.

Some recent notable examples of flawed corporate governance include:[42]

- Hewlett-Packard admitted that outside investigators, led by Chairman Patricia Dunn, used a potentially illegal tactic in which they impersonated directors, journalists, and two employees to obtain personal phone records. Dunn resigned as Chairman (September 12, 2006).

- Walter Forbes, former Chairman of Cendant Corp., a travel and real estate company (now known as Avis Budget Group, Inc.), was sentenced to 12 years in prison and ordered to pay $3.3 billion in one of America's biggest accounting scandals. Prosecutors said he oversaw a decade-long accounting scheme that overstated income. He was convicted on one count of conspiracy and two counts of false reporting (January 17, 2006).

- Board members of Nortel Networks meet with governance-minded investors to discuss possible changes to the board. This is after 10 executives and accounting officials are fired for artificially boosting the company's 2003 financial results (September 30, 2004).

- The Chairman of Boeing Company, Philip M. Condit, presides over a series of manipulations in accounting, acquisitions, and strategy. He conceals a $2.6 billion cost overrun from shareholders for months while his merger with McDonnell Douglas Corporation is completed, and as a result, he is forced to resign by the board (December 15, 2003).

- Royal Ahoud NV (owner of Stop and Shop), the world's third largest supermarket operator, fires its CEO and CFO for inappropriate accounting for discounts from suppliers. The company also reduces earnings for the prior two years by $500 million (February 25, 2003).

Clearly, because of the many lapses in corporate governance, we can see the benefits associated with effective practices. However, corporate managers may behave in their own self-interest, often to the detriment of shareholders. Next we address the implications of the separation of ownership and management in the modern corporation, and some mechanisms that can be used to ensure consistency (or alignment) between the interests of shareholders and those of the managers to minimize potential conflicts.

The Modern Corporation: The Separation of Owners (Shareholders) and Management

Some of the proposed definitions for a *corporation* include:

- "The business corporation is an instrument through which capital is assembled for the activities of producing and distributing goods and services and making investments. Accordingly, a basic premise of corporation law is that a business corporation should have as its objective the conduct of such activities with a view to enhancing the corporation's profit and the gains of the corporation's owners, that is, the shareholders." (Melvin Aron Eisenberg, *The Structure of Corporation Law*)

- "A body of persons granted a charter legally recognizing them as a separate entity having its own rights, privileges, and liabilities distinct from those of its members." (*American Heritage Dictionary*)

- "An ingenious device for obtaining individual profit without individual responsibility." (Ambrose Bierce, *The Devil's Dictionary*)[43]

All of these definitions have some validity and each one (including that from *The Devil's Dictionary!*) reflects a key feature of the corporate form of business organization—its ability to draw resources from a variety of groups and establish and maintain its own persona that is separate from all of them. As Henry Ford once said, "A great business is really too big to be human."

corporation a mechanism created to allow different parties to contribute capital, expertise, and labor for the maximum benefit of each party.

Simply put, a **corporation** is a mechanism created to allow different parties to contribute capital, expertise, and labor for the maximum benefit of each party. The shareholders (investors) are able to participate in the profits of the enterprise without taking direct responsibility for the operations. The management can run the company without the responsibility of personally providing the funds. And, in order to make both of these possible, the shareholders have limited liability as well as rather limited involvement in the company's affairs. However, they reserve the right to elect directors who have the fiduciary obligation to protect their interests.

Over 70 years ago, Columbia University professors Adolf Berle and Gardiner C. Means addressed the divergence of the interests of the owners of the corporation from the professional managers who are hired to run it. They warned that widely dispersed ownership "released management from the overriding requirement that it serve stockholders." The separation of ownership from management has given rise to a set of ideas called "agency theory." Central to agency theory is the relationship between two primary players—the *principals* who are the owners of the firm (stockholders) and the *agents,* who are the people paid by principals to perform a job on their behalf (management). The stockholders elect and are represented by a board of directors that has a fiduciary responsibility to ensure that management acts in the best interests of stockholders to ensure long-term financial returns for the firm.

agency theory a theory of the relationship between principals and their agents, with emphasis on two problems: (1) the conflicting goals of principals and agents, along with the difficulty of principals to monitor the agents, and (2) the different attitudes and preferences towards risk of principals and agents.

Agency theory is concerned with resolving two problems that can occur in agency relationships.[44] *The first is the agency problem that arises (1) when the goals of the principals and agents conflict, and (2) when it is difficult or expensive for the principal to verify what the agent is actually doing.* In a corporation, this means that the board of directors would be unable to confirm that the managers were actually acting in the shareholders' interests because, in most cases, managers are "insiders" with regard to the businesses they operate and thus are better informed than the principals. Thus, managers may act "opportunistically" in pursuing their own interests—to the detriment of the corporation.[45] Managers may, for example, spend corporate funds on expensive perquisites (e.g., company jets and expensive art), devote time and resources to pet projects (initiatives in which they have a personal interest but that have limited market potential), engage in power struggles (where they may fight over resources for their own betterment and to the detriment of the firm), and negate (or sabotage) attractive merger offers because they may result in increased employment risk.[46]

Crony Capitalism: Several Examples

When President George W. Bush signed the Sarbanes-Oxley Act into law on July 30, 2002, one of its goals was to prevent the kind of self-dealing and other conflicts of interest that had brought down Enron, WorldCom, Adelphia, and other corporate giants. Among other things, the Sarbanes-Oxley Act bans company loans to executives and prohibits extending the terms of existing loans.

Many companies, however, acted quickly *before* the bill was signed. For example, *one day* before the bill was signed, Crescent Real Estate Equities of Fort Worth, Texas, extended the payback deadline by 10 years on a loan of $26 million to its chief executive, John Goff. And Electronic Arts gave a $4 million loan to Warren Johnson, its chief financial officer, admitting in a filing that it was doing so a month prior to the "prohibition on loans to executive officers."

Despite legislation such as Sarbanes-Oxley and pressures from shareholders, related-party deals are quite common. According to the Corporate Library, a research group in Portland, Maine, 75 percent of 2,000 companies that were studied still engage in them. In essence, that means that companies must make embarrassing disclosures in their proxy statements about nepotism, property leased from top managers, corporate-owned apartments, and other forms of "insiderism."

Consider some examples:

- Two hundred companies have leased or bought airplanes from insiders. For example, Pilgrim's Pride of Pittsburgh, Texas, a chicken processor with $2.6 billion in annual sales has leased an airplane from its chief executive and founder Lonnie Pilgrim since 1985. Mr. Pilgrim made $656,000 in fiscal 2003 from this deal to go along with his $1.7 million in compensation. The company defends the pact as cost-efficient since its headquarters is located in a small town. Pilgrim also provides some bookkeeping services for his personal businesses, but he won't provide details.

- Micky M. Arison is chief executive of Carnival, the big cruise line. He is also chief executive and owner of the Miami Heat of the National Basketball Association. Carnival paid the Heat $675,000 in fiscal 2002 and 2003 for sponsorship and advertising as well as season tickets. Although that may be a rather small sum, given Carnival's $2.2 billion in net income for the period, we could still ask if the money would have been spent on something else if Arison didn't own the team.

- Alliance Semiconductor CEO N. Damodar Reddy has committed $20 million to Solar Ventures, a venture capital company run by his brother C. N. Reddy. Other unnamed insiders purchased undisclosed stakes in Solar. However, Alliance won't disclose whether its CEO is one of them. To date it has invested $12.5 million in Solar. Beth Young, senior research associate of the Corporate Library poses an interesting question: "Is Reddy using shareholder capital just to keep afloat his brother's fund and the insiders' investment?"

Source: MacDonald, E. 2004. Crony capitalism. *Forbes*, June 21: 140–146.

The second issue is the problem of risk sharing. This arises when the principal and the agent have different attitudes and preferences toward risk. For example, the executives in a firm may favor additional diversification initiatives because, by their very nature, they increase the size of the firm and thus the level of executive compensation. At the same time, such diversification initiatives may erode shareholder value because they fail to achieve some of the synergies that we discussed in Chapter 6 (e.g., building on core competencies, sharing activities, or enhancing market power). In effect, agents (executives) may have a stronger preference toward diversification than shareholders because it reduces their personal level of risk from potential loss of employment. In contrast, research has shown that executives who have large holdings of stock in their firms were more likely to have diversification strategies that were more consistent with shareholder interests—that is, increasing long-term returns.[47]

At times, top-level managers engage in actions that reflect their self-interest rather than the interests of shareholders. Some examples of such conflicts of interest are addressed in Strategy Spotlight 9.5.

Governance Mechanisms: Aligning the Interests of Owners and Managers

>LO6

The role of corporate governance mechanisms in ensuring that the interests of managers are aligned with those of shareholders from both the United States and international perspectives.

As noted above, a key characteristic of the modern corporation is the separation of ownership from control. To minimize the potential for managers to act in their own self-interest, or "opportunistically," the owners can implement some governance mechanisms.[48] We address three of these in the next sections. First, there are two primary means of monitoring the behavior of managers. These include (1) a committed and involved *board of directors* that acts in the best interests of the shareholders to create long-term value and (2) *shareholder activism,* wherein the owners view themselves as share*owners* instead of share*holders* and become actively engaged in the governance of the corporation. As we will see later in this section, shareholder activism has increased dramatically in recent years. Finally, there are managerial incentives, sometimes called "contract-based outcomes," which consist of *reward and compensation agreements.* Here the goal is to carefully craft managerial incentive packages to align the interests of management with those of the stockholders.

board of directors a group that has a fiduciary duty to ensure that the company is run consistently with the long-term interests of the owners, or shareholders, of a corporation and that acts as an intermediary between the shareholders and management.

A Committed and Involved Board of Directors   The **board of directors** acts as a fulcrum between the owners and controllers of a corporation. In effect, they are the intermediaries who provide a balance between a small group of key managers in the firm based at the corporate headquarters and a sometimes vast group of shareholders. In the United States, the law imposes on the board a strict and absolute fiduciary duty to ensure that a company is run consistent with the long-term interests of the owners—the shareholders. The reality, as we have seen, is somewhat more ambiguous.[49]

The Business Roundtable, representing the largest U.S. corporations, describes the duties of the board as follows:

1. Select, regularly evaluate, and, if necessary, replace the chief executive officer. Determine management compensation. Review succession planning.
2. Review and, where appropriate, approve the financial objectives, major strategies, and plans of the corporation.
3. Provide advice and counsel to top management.
4. Select and recommend to shareholders for election an appropriate slate of candidates for the board of directors; evaluate board processes and performance.
5. Review the adequacy of the systems to comply with all applicable laws/regulations.[50]

Given these principles, what makes for a good board of directors? According to the Business Roundtable, the most important quality is a board of directors who are active, critical participants in determining a company's strategies.[51] That does not mean board members should micromanage or circumvent the CEO. Rather, they should provide strong oversight going beyond simply approving the CEO's plans. A board's primary responsibilities are to ensure that strategic plans undergo rigorous scrutiny, evaluate managers against high performance standards, and take control of the succession process.

Although boards in the past were often dismissed as CEO's rubber stamps, increasingly they are playing a more active role by forcing out CEOs who cannot deliver on performance. According to a recent study by the consulting firm Booz Allen Hamilton, the rate of CEO departures for performance reasons has more than tripled, from 1.3 percent to 4.2 percent, between 1995 and 2002.[52] And the trend has continued. In 2006, turnover among CEOs increased 30 percent over the previous year.[53] Well-known CEOs like Gerald M. Levin of AOL Time Warner and Jack M. Greenberg of McDonald's paid the price for poor financial performance by being forced to leave. Others, such as Bernard Ebbers of WorldCom, Inc., and Dennis Kozlowski of Tyco International, lost their jobs due to scandals. "Deliver or depart" is clearly the new message from the boards.

Another key component of top-ranked boards is director independence.[54] Governance experts believe that a majority of directors should be free of all ties to either the CEO or the company. That means a minimum of "insiders" (past or present members of the management team) should serve on the board, and that directors and their firms should be barred from doing consulting, legal, or other work for the company.[55] Interlocking directorships—in which CEOs and other top managers serve on each other's boards—are not desirable. But perhaps the best guarantee that directors act in the best interests of shareholders is the simplest: Most good companies now insist that directors own significant stock in the company they oversee.[56]

Such guidelines are not always followed. At times, the practices of the boards of directors are the antithesis of such guidelines. Consider the Walt Disney Co. Over a recent five-year period, Michael Eisner pocketed an astonishing $531 million. He likely had very little resistance from his board of directors:

> Many investors view the Disney board as an anachronism. Among Disney's 16 directors is Eisner's personal attorney—who for several years was chairman of the company's compensation committee! There was also the architect who designed Eisner's Aspen home and his parents' apartment. Joining them are the principal of an elementary school once attended by his children and the president of a university to which Eisner donated $1 million. The board also includes the actor Sidney Poitier, seven current and former Disney executives, and an attorney who does business with Disney. Moreover, most of the outside directors own little or no Disney stock. "It is an egregiously bad board—a train wreck waiting to happen," warns Michael L. Useem, a management professor at the University of Pennsylvania's Wharton School.[57]

This example also shows that "outside directors" are only beneficial to strong corporate governance if they are vigilant in carrying out their responsibilities.[58] As humorously suggested by Warren Buffett, founder and chairman of Berkshire Hathaway: "The ratcheting up of compensation has been obscene. . . . There is a tendency to put cocker spaniels on compensation committees, not Doberman pinschers."[59]

Many firms do have exemplary board practices. Below, for example, we list some of the excellent practices at Intel Corp., the world's largest semiconductor chip manufacturer, with $35 billion in revenues:[60]

- *Mix of inside and outside directors.* The board believes that there should be a majority of independent directors on the board. However, the board is willing to have members of management, in addition to the CEO, as directors.
- *Board presentations and access to employees.* The board encourages management to schedule managers to be present at meetings who: (1) can provide additional insight into the items being discussed because of personal involvement in these areas, or (2) have future potential that management believes should be given exposure to the board.
- *Formal evaluation of officers.* The Compensation Committee conducts, and reviews with the outside directors, an annual evaluation to help determine the salary and executive bonus of all officers, including the chief executive officer.

Exhibit 9.7 provides some suggestions for how boards of directors can improve their practices.

Shareholder Activism   As a practical matter, there are so many owners of the largest American corporations that it makes little sense to refer to them as "owners" in the sense of individuals becoming informed and involved in corporate affairs. However, even an individual shareholder has several rights, including (1) the right to sell the stock, (2) the right to vote the proxy (which includes the election of board members), (3) the right to bring suit for damages if the corporation's directors or managers fail to meet their obligations, (4) the right to certain information from the company, and (5) certain residual rights following the company's liquidation (or its filing for reorganization under bankruptcy laws), once creditors and other claimants are paid off.[61]

Exhibit 9.7

Best Practice Ideas: The New Rules for Directors

Issue	Suggestion
Pay	**Know the Math**
Companies will disclose full details of CEO payouts for the first time in their 2007 SEC filings. Activist investors are already drawing up hit lists of companies where CEO paychecks are out of line with performance.	Before okaying any financial package, directors must make sure they can explain the numbers. They need to adopt the mindset of an activist investor and ask: What's the harshest criticism someone could make about this package?
Strategy	**Make It a Priority**
Boards have been so focused on compliance that duties like strategy and leadership oversight too often get ignored. Only 59 percent of directors in a recent study rated their board favorably on setting strategy	To avoid spending too much time on compliance issues, move strategy up to the beginning of the meeting. Annual one-, two- or three-day offsite meetings on strategy alone are becoming standard for good boards.
Financials	**Put in the Time**
Although 95 percent of directors in the recent study said they were doing a good job of monitoring financials, the number of earnings restatements hit a new high in 2006, after breaking records in 2004 and 2005.	Even nonfinancial board members need to monitor the numbers and keep a close eye on cash flows. Audit committee members should prepare to spend 300 hours a year on committee responsibilities.
Crisis Management	**Dig in**
Some 120 companies are under scrutiny for options backdating, and the 100 largest companies have replaced 56 CEOs in the past five years—nearly double the terminations in the prior five years.	The increased scrutiny on boards means that a perfunctory review will not suffice if a scandal strikes. Directors can no longer afford to defer to management in a crisis. They must roll up their sleeves and move into watchdog mode.

Source: Byrnes, N., & Sassen, J. 2007. Board of hard knocks. *BusinessWeek*. January 22: 36–39.

Collectively, shareholders have the power to direct the course of corporations.[62] This may involve acts such as being party to shareholder action suits and demanding that key issues be brought up for proxy votes at annual board meetings.[63] In addition, the power of shareholders has intensified in recent years because of the increasing influence of large institutional investors such as mutual funds (e.g., T. Rowe Price and Fidelity Investments) and retirement systems such as TIAA-CREF (for university faculty members and school administrative staff).[64] Institutional investors hold approximately 50 percent of all listed corporate stock in the United States.

shareholder activism actions by large shareholders to protect their interests when they feel that managerial actions of a corporation diverge from shareholder value maximization.

Shareholder activism refers to actions by large shareholders, both institutions and individuals, to protect their interests when they feel that managerial actions diverge from shareholder value maximization.

Many institutional investors are aggressive in protecting and enhancing their investments. In effect, they are shifting from traders to owners. They are assuming the role of permanent shareholders and rigorously analyzing issues of corporate governance. In the process they are reinventing systems of corporate monitoring and accountability.[65]

Consider the proactive behavior of CalPERS, the California Public Employees' Retirement System, which manages over $200 billion in assets and is the third largest pension fund in the world. Every year CalPERS reviews the performance of U.S. companies in its stock portfolio and identifies those that are among the lowest long-term relative performers and have governance structures that do not ensure full accountability to company owners. This generates a long list of companies, each of which may potentially be publicly identified as a CalPERS "Focus Company"—corporations to which CalPERS directs specific suggested governance reforms. CalPERS meets with the directors of each of these companies to discuss performance and governance issues. The CalPERS Focus List contains those companies that continue to merit public and market attention at the end of the process.

On April 19, 2006, CalPERS released its annual Focus List, which singled out six U.S. companies for poor financial and corporate governance.[66]

Firms on the list were: *Brocade Communications* of San Jose California; *Cardinal Health* of Dublin, Ohio; *Clear Channel Communications* of San Antonio Texas; *Mellon Financial* of Pittsburgh, Pennsylvania; *OfficeMax* of Itasca, Illinois; and *Sovereign Bancorp* of Philadelphia.

A few of CalPERS's concerns:

- Clear Channel Communications, a diversified media company that owns hundreds of radio stations, has excessive executive compensation and severance agreements, and lost 42 percent in stock value over the past five years compared with a 26 percent decline for industry peers.
- OfficeMax, a U.S. provider of office supplies, technology products and solutions, and furniture, has takeover defenses that are excessive, including an 80 percent supermajority requirement to amend bylaws. It performed well below its peer group for the past five years.

While appearing punitive to company management, such aggressive activism has paid significant returns for CalPERS (and other stockholders of the "Focused" companies). For example, a Wilshire Associates study of the "CalPERS Effect" of corporate governance examined the performance of 62 targets over a five-year period. The results indicated that, while the stock of these companies trailed the Standard & Poors Index by 89 percent in the five-year period before CalPERS acted, the same stocks outperformed the index by 23 percent in the following five years, adding approximately $150 million annually in additional returns to the fund.

Perhaps no discussion of shareholder activism would be complete without mention of Carl Icahn, a famed activist with a personal net worth of about $13 billion. As he forcefully points out:

> The bogeyman I am now chasing is the structure of American corporations, which permit managements and boards to rule arbitrarily and too often receive egregious compensation even after doing a subpar job. Yet they remain accountable to no one.[67]

Managerial Rewards and Incentives   As we discussed earlier in the chapter, incentive systems must be designed to help a company achieve its goals.[68] Similarly, from the perspective of governance, one of the most critical roles of the board of directors is to create incentives that align the interests of the CEO and top executives with the interests of owners of the corporation—long-term shareholder returns.[69] After all, shareholders rely on CEOs to adopt policies and strategies that maximize the value of their shares.[70] A combination of three basic policies may create the right monetary incentives for CEOs to maximize the value of their companies:

1. Boards can require that the CEOs become substantial owners of company stock.
2. Salaries, bonuses, and stock options can be structured so as to provide rewards for superior performance and penalties for poor performance.
3. Threat of dismissal for poor performance can be a realistic outcome.

In recent years the granting of stock options has enabled top executives of publicly held corporations to earn enormous levels of compensation. In 2005, the average CEO in the Standard & Poor's 500 stock index took home 369 times the pay of the average worker—up from 28 times the average in 1970. Needless to say, the counterargument, that the ratio is down from the 514 multiple in 2000, doesn't get much traction![71] And it has been estimated that there could be as many as 50 or more companies with CEO pay packages over $150 million.[72]

Many boards have awarded huge option grants despite poor executive performance, and others have made performance goals easier to reach. In 2002 nearly 200 companies swapped or repriced options—all to enrich wealthy executives who are already among the country's richest people. However, stock options can be a valuable governance mechanism to align the CEO's interests with those of the shareholders. The extraordinarily high level of compensation can, at times, be grounded in sound governance principles.[73] For example, Howard Solomon, CEO of Forest Laboratories, received a total compensation of $148.5 million in 2001.[74] This represented $823,000 in salary, $400,000 in bonus, and $147.3 million in stock options that were exercised. However, shareholders also did well, receiving gains of 40 percent. The firm has enjoyed spectacular growth over the past five years and Solomon has been CEO since 1977. Thus, huge income is attributed largely to gains that have built up over many years. As stated by compensation committee member Dan Goldwasser, "If a CEO is delivering substantial increases in shareholder value . . . it's only appropriate that he be rewarded for it."

However, the "pay for performance" principle doesn't always hold. In addition to the granting of stock options, boards of directors are often failing to fulfill their fiduciary responsibilities to shareholders when they lower the performance targets that executives need to meet in order to receive millions of dollars. At General Motors, for example, CEO G. Richard Wagoner, Jr., and other top executives were entitled to a special performance bonus if the company's net profit margin reached five percent by the end of 2003. However, the five percent target was later lowered.

TIAA-CREF has provided several principles of corporate governance with regard to executive compensation.[75] These include the importance of aligning the rewards of all employees—rank and file as well as executives—to the long-term performance of the corporation; general guidelines on the role of cash compensation, stock, and "fringe benefits"; and the mission of a corporation's compensation committee. Exhibit 9.8 addresses TIAA-CREF's principles on the role of stock in managerial compensation.

external governance control mechanisms methods that ensure that managerial actions lead to shareholder value maximization and do not harm other stakeholder groups and that are outside the control of the corporate governance system.

External Governance Control Mechanisms

Thus far, we've discussed internal governance mechanisms. Internal controls, however, are not always enough to ensure good governance. The separation of ownership and control that we discussed earlier requires multiple control mechanisms, some internal and some external, to ensure that managerial actions lead to shareholder value maximization. Further, society-at-large wants some assurance that this goal is met without harming other stakeholder groups. Now we discuss several **external governance control mechanisms** that have developed in most modern economies. These include the market for corporate

Exhibit 9.8
TIAA-CREF's Principles
on the Role of
Stock in Executive
Compensation

Stock-based compensation plans are a critical element of most compensation programs and can provide opportunities for managers whose efforts contribute to the creation of shareholder wealth. In evaluating the suitability of these plans, considerations of reasonableness, scale, linkage to performance, and fairness to shareholders and all employees also apply. TIAA-CREF, the largest pension system in the world, has set forth the following guidelines for stock-based compensation. Proper stock-based plans should:

- Allow for creation of executive wealth that is reasonable in view of the creation of shareholder wealth. Management should not prosper through stock while shareholders suffer.

- Have measurable and predictable outcomes that are directly linked to the company's performance.

- Be market oriented, within levels of comparability for similar positions in companies of similar size and business focus.

- Be straightforward and clearly described so that investors and employees can understand them.

- Be fully disclosed to the investing public and be approved by shareholders.

Source: www.tiaa-cref.org/pubs.

control, auditors, governmental regulatory bodies, banks and analysts, media, and public activists.

The Market for Corporate Control   Let us assume for a moment that internal control mechanisms in a company are failing. This means that the board is ineffective in monitoring managers and is not exercising the oversight required of them and that shareholders are passive and are not taking any actions to monitor or discipline managers. Under these circumstances managers may behave opportunistically.[76] Opportunistic behavior can take many forms. First, they can *shirk* their responsibilities. Shirking means that managers fail to exert themselves fully, as is required of them. Second, they can engage in *on the job consumption.* Examples of on the job consumption include private jets, club memberships, expensive artwork in the offices, and so on. Each of these represents consumption by managers that does not in any way increase shareholder value. Instead, they actually diminish shareholder value. Third, managers may engage in *excessive product-market diversification.*[77] As we discussed in Chapter 6, such diversification serves to reduce only the employment risk of the managers rather than the financial risk of the shareholders, who can more cheaply diversify their risk by owning a portfolio of investments. Is there any external mechanism to stop managers from shirking, consumption on the job, and excessive diversification?

The **market for corporate control** is one such external mechanism that provides at least some partial solution to the problems described. If internal control mechanisms fail and the management is behaving opportunistically, the likely response of most shareholders will be to sell their stock rather than engage in activism.[78] As more and more stockholders vote with their feet, the value of the stock begins to decline. As the decline continues, at some point the market value of the firm becomes less than the book value. That is, a corporate raider can take over the company for a price less than the book value of the assets of the company. The first thing that the raider may do on assuming control over the company will be to fire the underperforming management. The risk of being acquired by a hostile raider

market for corporate control
an external control mechanism in which shareholders dissatisfied with a firm's management sell their shares.

takeover constraint
the risk to
management of the
firm being acquired
by a hostile raider.

is often referred to as the **takeover constraint.** The takeover constraint deters management from engaging in opportunistic behavior.[79]

Although in theory the takeover constraint is supposed to limit managerial opportunism, in recent years its effectiveness has become diluted as a result of a number of defense tactics adopted by incumbent management (see Chapter 6). Foremost among them are poison pills, greenmail, and golden parachutes. Poison pills are provisions adopted by the company to reduce its worth to the acquirer. An example would be payment of a huge one-time dividend, typically financed by debt. Greenmail involves buying back the stock from the acquirer, usually at an attractive premium. Golden parachutes are employment contracts that cause the company to pay lucrative severance packages to top managers fired as a result of a takeover, often running to several million dollars.

Auditors   Even when there are stringent disclosure requirements, there is no guarantee that the information disclosed will be accurate. Managers may deliberately disclose false information or withhold negative financial information as well as use accounting methods that distort results based on highly subjective interpretations. Therefore, all accounting statements are required to be audited and certified to be accurate by external auditors. These auditing firms are independent organizations staffed by certified professionals who verify the firm's books of accounts. Audits can unearth financial irregularities and ensure that financial reporting by the firm conforms to standard accounting practices.

Recent developments leading to the bankruptcy of firms such as Enron and WorldCom and a spate of earnings restatements raise questions about the failure of the auditing firms to act as effective external control mechanisms. Why did an auditing firm like Arthur Andersen, with decades of good reputation in the auditing profession at stake, fail to raise red flags about accounting irregularities? First, auditors are appointed by the firm being audited. The desire to continue that business relationship sometimes makes them overlook financial irregularities. Second, most auditing firms also do consulting work and often have lucrative consulting contracts with the firms that they audit. Understandably, some of them tend not to ask too many difficult questions, because they fear jeopardizing the consulting business, which is often more profitable than the auditing work.

The recent restatement of earnings by Xerox is an example of the lack of independence of auditing firms. The SEC filed a lawsuit against KPMG, the world's third largest accounting firm, in January 2003 for allowing Xerox to inflate its revenues by $3 billion between 1997 and 2000. Of the $82 million that Xerox paid KPMG during those four years, only $26 million was for auditing. The rest was for consulting services. When one of the auditors objected to Xerox's practice of booking revenues for equipment leases earlier than it should have, Xerox asked KPMG to replace him. It did.[80]

Banks and Analysts   Commercial and investment banks have lent money to corporations and therefore have to ensure that the borrowing firm's finances are in order and that the loan covenants are being followed. Stock analysts conduct ongoing in-depth studies of the firms that they follow and make recommendations to their clients to buy, hold, or sell. Their rewards and reputation depend on the quality of these recommendations. Their access to information, knowledge of the industry and the firm, and the insights they gain from interactions with the management of the company enable them to alert the investing community of both positive and negative developments relating to a company.

It is generally observed that analyst recommendations are often more optimistic than warranted by facts. "Sell" recommendations tend to be exceptions rather than the norm. Many analysts seem to have failed to grasp the gravity of the problems surrounding failed companies such as Enron and Global Crossing till the very end. Part of the explanation may lie in the fact that most analysts work for firms that also have investment banking relationships with the companies they follow. Negative recommendations by analysts can displease the management, who may decide to take their investment banking business to a rival firm. Thus, otherwise independent and competent analysts may be pressured to overlook negative information or tone down their criticism. A recent settlement between the Securities and Exchange Commission and the New York State Attorney General with 10 banks requires them to pay $1.4 billion in penalties and to fund independent research for investors.[81]

Regulatory Bodies   All corporations are subject to some regulation by the government. The extent of regulation is often a function of the type of industry. Banks, utilities, and pharmaceuticals, for example, are subject to more regulatory oversight because of their importance to society. Public corporations are subject to more regulatory requirements than private corporations.

All public corporations are required to disclose a substantial amount of financial information by bodies such as the Securities and Exchange Commission. These include quarterly and annual filings of financial performance, stock trading by insiders, and details of executive compensation packages. There are two primary reasons behind such requirements. First, markets can operate efficiently only when the investing public has faith in the market system. In the absence of disclosure requirements, the average investor suffers from a lack of reliable information and therefore may completely stay away from the capital market. This will negatively impact an economy's ability to grow. Second, disclosure of information such as insider trading protects the small investor to some extent from the negative consequences of information asymmetry. That is, the insiders and large investors typically have more information than the small investor and can therefore use that information to buy or sell before the information becomes public knowledge.

The failure of a variety of external control mechanisms led the U.S. Congress to pass the Sarbanes-Oxley Act in 2002. This act calls for many stringent measures that would ensure better governance of U.S. corporations. Some of these measures include:[82]

- *Auditors* are barred from certain types of nonaudit work. They are not allowed to destroy records for five years. Lead partners auditing a client should be changed at least every five years.
- *CEOs* and *CFOs* must fully reveal off-balance-sheet finances and vouch for the accuracy of the information revealed.
- *Executives* must promptly reveal the sale of shares in firms they manage and are not allowed to sell when other employees cannot.
- *Corporate lawyers* must report to senior managers any violations of securities law lower down.

Strategy Spotlight 9.6 discusses some of the expenses that companies have incurred in complying with the Sarbanes-Oxley Act. There has been much debate as to whether the costs outweigh some of the benefits.

Media and Public Activists   The press is not usually recognized as an external control mechanism in the literature on corporate governance. There is, however, no denying that in all developed capitalist economies, the financial press and media play an important indirect role in monitoring the management of public corporations. In the United States, business magazines such as *BusinessWeek* and *Fortune,* financial newspapers such as *The Wall Street Journal* and *Investors Business Daily,* as well as television networks like Financial News Network and CNBC are constantly reporting on companies. Public perceptions about a company's financial prospects and the quality of its management are greatly influenced by the media. For example, Food Lion's reputation was sullied when ABC's *Prime Time Live*

Governance Reform: The Costs Add Up

In the aftermath of Enron and Worldcom and a spate of corporate scandals early in the decade, the U.S. Congress passed the Sarbanes-Oxley Act in 2002. It was an effort to restore investor confidence in the governance of corporations in general and financial reporting in particular. Three years later, a backlash seems to be developing among executives about the high compliance costs and some of the more draconian requirements.

The major source of resentment is the issue of cost. It is estimated that large corporations with revenues over $4 billion have to spend an average of $35 million a year to implement Sarbanes-Oxley. Medium-sized companies spend $3.1 million a year on average. Smaller companies find the cost of compliance particularly burdensome because they have a smaller revenue base. Some critics go to the extent of arguing that this amounts to a form of regressive taxation against small businesses. Many are even considering delisting to avoid compliance costs.

Costs are not the only problem that companies face. Meeting the requirements of Sarbanes-Oxley is very time consuming as well. For example, the law requires that financial numbers such as value of inventory and receivables are cross-checked. But it requires an army of addi-

tional people and significant additional costs to ensure this. Yellow Roadway Corporation, the nation's largest trucking firm, had to use 200 employees and $9 million to accomplish this in 2004. This was three percent of their total profits. And just think of the lost productivity!

Nasdaq officials say the Sarbanes-Oxley burden is heaviest on the smallest companies, and firms with less than $100 million in revenues make up half of Nasdaq's 3,000 listings. The regulatory costs average two percent of revenue at firms with revenue under $100 million, while they are only 0.1 percent for the biggest companies. Theodore Stebbins, chairman of investment banking at Canaccord Adams says, "Clearly, the low end of the Nasdaq is broken. We can no longer in good conscience recommend to our small clients that they go public on Nasdaq."

How much has Sarbanes-Oxley succeeded in improving governance and ensuring the accuracy and reliability of financial reporting? While it is too early to assess the impact, there is at least some anecdotal evidence that it is having some impact. Visteon Corp., an auto-parts supplier, reported that they uncovered problems with their accounts receivable while complying with the requirements of the act. Similarly, SunTrust Banks Inc. fired three officers after discovering errors in the calculation of loan allowances in their portfolios. Tough but fair regulations can improve governance, but the costs of compliance cannot be ignored.

Source: Brown, E. 2006. London calling. *Forbes*, May 8: 51–52; and Henry, D. 2005. Death, taxes & Sarbanes-Oxley? *BusinessWeek*, January 17: 28–31.

in 1992 charged the company with employee exploitation, false package dating, and unsanitary meat handling practices. Bethany McLean of *Fortune* magazine is often credited as the first to raise questions about Enron's long-term financial viability.[83]

Similarly, consumer groups and activist individuals often take a crusading role in exposing corporate malfeasance. Well-known examples include Ralph Nader and Erin Brockovich, who played important roles in bringing to light the safety issues related to GM's Corvair and environmental pollution issues concerning Pacific Gas and Electric Company, respectively. Ralph Nader has created over 30 watchdog groups including:[84]

- *Aviation Consumer Action Project.* Works to propose new rules to prevent flight delays, impose penalties for deceiving passengers about problems, and push for higher compensation for lost luggage.
- *Center for Auto Safety.* Helps consumers find plaintiff lawyers and agitate for vehicle recalls, increased highway safety standards, and lemon laws.
- *Center for Study of Responsive Law.* This is Nader's headquarters. Home of a consumer project on technology, this group sponsored seminars on Microsoft remedies and pushed for tougher Internet privacy rules. It also took on the drug industry over costs.

- ***Pension Rights Center.*** This center helped employees of IBM, General Electric, and other companies to organize themselves against cash-balance pension plans.

Corporate Governance: An International Perspective

As we have noted in this chapter (and in Chapter 1), the topic of corporate governance has long been dominated by agency theory and based on the explicit assumption of the separation of ownership and control.[85] The central conflicts are principal–agent conflicts between shareholders and management. However, such an underlying assumption seldom applies outside of the United States and the United Kingdom. This is particularly true in emerging economies and continental Europe. Here, there is often concentrated ownership, along with extensive family ownership and control, business group structures, and weak legal protection for minority shareholders. Thus, serious conflicts tend to exist between two classes of principals: controlling shareholders and minority shareholders. Such conflicts can be called **principal–principal (PP) conflicts** as opposed to *principal–agent* conflicts. Exhibits 9.9 and 9.10 address how principal–principal conflicts and principal–agent conflicts differ.

> **principal–principal conflicts** conflicts between two classes of principals—controlling shareholders and minority shareholders—within the context of a corporate governance system.

Strong family control is one of the leading indicators of concentrated ownership. For example, in East Asia (excluding China), approximately 57 percent of the corporations have board chairmen and CEOs from the controlling families. In continental Europe, this number is 68 percent. A very common practice is the appointment of family members as board chairman, CEOs, and other top executives. This happens because the families are controlling (not necessarily majority) shareholders. For example, in 2003, 30-year-old James Murdoch was appointed CEO of British Sky Broadcasting (BSkyB), Europe's largest satellite broadcaster. There was very vocal resistance by minority shareholders. Why was he appointed in the first place? James's father just happened to be Rupert Murdoch, who controlled 35 percent of BSkyB and chaired the board. Clearly, this is a case of a principal–principal conflict.

In general, three conditions must be met for PP conflicts to occur. There must be:

● In Hong Kong, strong family control is characteristic of many corporations. At times, this has led to principal–principal (PP) conflicts. Above is Hong Kong's spectacular skyline, as seen from Victoria Point.

- A dominant owner or group of owners who have interests that are distinct from minority shareholders.
- Motivation for the controlling shareholders to exercise their dominant positions to their advantage.
- Few formal (such as legislation or regulatory bodies) or informal constraints that would discourage or prevent the controlling shareholders from exploiting their advantageous positions.

The result is often that family managers, who represent (or actually are) the controlling shareholders, engage in *expropriation* of minority shareholders, which is defined as activities that enrich the controlling shareholders at the expense of minority shareholders. What is their motive? After all, controlling shareholders have incentives to maintain firm value. But controlling shareholders may take actions that decrease aggregate firm performance if their personal gains from expropriation exceed their personal losses from their firm's lowered performance.

	Principal–Agent Conflicts	Principal–Principal Conflicts
Goal Incongruence	Between shareholders and professional managers who own a relatively small portion of the firm's equity.	Between controlling shareholders and minority shareholders.
Ownership Pattern	Dispersed—5%–20% is considered "concentrated ownership."	Concentrated—Often greater than 50% of equity is controlled by controlling shareholders.
Manifestations	Strategies that benefit entrenched managers at the expense of shareholders in general (e.g., shirking, pet projects, excessive compensation, and empire building).	Strategies that benefit controlling shareholders at the expense of minority shareholders (e.g., minority shareholder expropriation, nepotism, and cronyism).
Institutional Protection of Minority Shareholders	Formal constraints (e.g., judicial reviews and courts) set an upper boundary on potential expropriation by majority shareholders. Informal norms generally adhere to shareholder wealth maximization.	Formal institutional protection is often lacking, corrupted, or un-enforced. Informal norms are typically in favor of the interests of controlling shareholders ahead of those of minority investors.

Source: Adapted from Young, M., Peng, M. W., Ahlstrom, D., & Bruton, G. 2002. Governing the corporation in emerging economies: A principal–principal perspective. *Academy of Management Best Papers Proceedings,* Denver.

Exhibit 9.9 Traditional Principal–Agent Conflicts versus Principal–Principal Conflicts: How they Differ Along Dimensions

Exhibit 9.10 Principal–Agent Conflicts and Principal–Principal Conflicts: A Diagram

Source: Young, M. N., Peng, M. W., Ahlstrom, D., Bruton, G. D., Jiang, Y. forthcoming. Principal–principal conflicts in corporate governance (*Journal of Management Studies*); and Peng, M. V. 2006. *Global strategy*. Cincinnati: Thomson South-Western. We are very appreciative of the helpful comments of Mike Young of Hong Kong Baptist University and Mike Peng of the University of Texas at Dallas.

Effective and Ineffective Corporate Governance in Hong Kong

Finding examples of exemplary corporate governance in Hong Kong isn't easy due to the high incidence of family-controlled corporations and the lack of laws to protect minority shareholders. An exception is CLP, one of the largest electric utilities in Asia, which is 35 percent controlled by Chairman Michael Kadoorie and his family. Admirers say it is an example of how even a family-controlled company can move toward more transparency. The company's board has several independent directors, and its Web site gives comprehensive information on its corporate governance policy. Kadoorie says family shareholders are treated the same as others.

At the other end of the continuum is Henderson Land Development. The company is controlled by Lee Shau Kee, one of Hong Kong's wealthiest tycoons. In its latest corporate-governance snafu, Henderson attempted to buy 73 percent of its publicly listed subsidiary, Henderson

Investment, for 30 percent below its reported net asset value. However, the related transaction was thwarted by minority shareholders, including the powerful Templeton Asset Management. At the time, Henderson Land Vice-Chairman Colin Lam insisted the dissenting investors had placed "a very, very high valuation on Henderson Investment," implying that this placed too high a value on its shares. Needless to say, the minority shareholders would hardly agree. However, it was perfectly legal in Hong Kong, and had it gone through, the minority shareholders would have been left holding the bag.

Had the Henderson Investment deal occurred in the United States, a shareholder lawsuit would have been launched. In Hong Kong, however, class-action lawsuits are not allowed. Consider the sentiment of Andrew Sheng, head of the Hong Kong Securities & Futures Commission, in the face of an action by another company taking advantage of minority shareholders: if the investors didn't like what was happening, they could simply sell their shares. Such a "buyer beware" attitude, even by regulatory bodies in one of the most developed emerging economies, causes firms to trade at a discount compared to firms in more mature economies.

Sources: Balfour, F., & Tashiro, H. 2004. A change in attitude. *BusinessWeek,* May 17: 48–50; Clifford, M. 2002. China Journal: Hong Kong's cautionary Christmas carol. *BusinessWeek* Online, August; and Young, M. N., Peng, M. W., Ahlstrom, D., Bruton, G. D., & Jiang, Y. forthcoming. Principal–principal conflicts in corporate governance. *Journal of Management Studies.*

Another ubiquitous feature of corporate life outside of the United States and Great Britain are *business groups* such as the keiretsus of Japan and the chaebols of South Korea. This is particularly dominant in emerging economies. A **business group** is "a set of firms that, though legally independent, are bound together by a constellation of formal and informal ties and are accustomed to taking coordinated action."[86] Business groups are especially common in emerging economies, and they are different from other organizational forms in that the groups are communities of firms without clear boundaries.

Business groups have many advantages that can enhance the value of a firm. For example, they often facilitate technology transfer or intergroup capital allocation that otherwise might be impossible because of inadequate institutional infrastructure such as excellent financial services firms. On the other hand, informal ties—such as cross-holdings, board interlocks, and coordinated actions—can often result in intragroup activities and transactions, often at very favorable terms to member firms. For example, expropriation can be legally done through *related transactions,* which can occur when controlling owners sell firm assets to another firm they own at below market prices or spin off the most profitable part of a public firm and merge it with another of their private firms.

Strategy Spotlight 9.7 provides examples from Hong Kong of effective corporate governance. It also shows how a firm attempted a related transaction that would have benefited controlling shareholders at the expense of minority shareholders.

> **business groups** a set of firms that, though legally independent, are bound together by a constellation of formal and informal ties and are accustomed to taking coordinated action.

Reflecting on Career Implications . . .

- **Behavioral Control:** What sources of behavioral control does your organization employ? In general, too much emphasis on rules and regulations may stifle initiative and be detrimental to your career opportunities.
- **Rewards and Incentives:** Are your organization's reward structure fair and equitable? Does it effectively reward outstanding performance? If not, there may be a long-term erosion of morale which may have long-term adverse career implications for you.
- **Culture:** Consider the type of organization culture that would provide the best work environment for your career goals. How does your organization's culture deviate from this concept? Does your organization have a strong and effective culture? If so, professionals are more likely to develop strong "firm specific" ties, which further enhances collaboration.
- **Corporate Governance:** Does your organization practice effective corporate governance? Such practices will enhance a firm's culture and it will be easier to attract top talent. Operating within governance guidelines is usually a strong indicator of organizational citizenship which, in turn, should be good for your career prospects.

Summary

For firms to be successful, they must practice effective strategic control and corporate governance. Without such controls, the firm will not be able to achieve competitive advantages and outperform rivals in the marketplace.

We began the chapter with the key role of informational control. We contrasted two types of control systems: what we termed "traditional" and "contemporary" information control systems. Whereas traditional control systems may have their place in placid, simple competitive environments, there are fewer of those in today's economy. Instead, we advocated the contemporary approach wherein the internal and external environment are constantly monitored so that when surprises emerge, the firm can modify its strategies, goals, and objectives.

Behavioral controls are also a vital part of effective control systems. We argued that firms must develop the proper balance between culture, rewards and incentives, and boundaries and constraints. Where there are strong and positive cultures and rewards, employees tend to internalize the organization's strategies and objectives. This permits a firm to spend fewer resources on monitoring behavior, and assures the firm that the efforts and initiatives of employees are more consistent with the overall objectives of the organization.

In the final section of this chapter, we addressed corporate governance, which can be defined as the relationship between various participants in determining the direction and performance of the corporation. The primary participants include shareholders, management (led by the chief executive officer), and the board of directors. We reviewed studies that indicated a consistent relationship between effective corporate governance and financial performance. There are also several internal and external control mechanisms that can serve to align managerial interests and shareholder interests. The internal mechanisms include a committed and involved board of directors, shareholder activism, and effective managerial incentives and rewards. The external mechanisms include the market for corporate control, banks and analysts, regulators, the media, and public activists. We also addressed corporate governance from both a United States and an international perspective.

Summary Review Questions

1. Why are effective strategic control systems so important in today's economy?
2. What are the main advantages of "contemporary" control systems over "traditional" control systems? What are the main differences between these two systems?
3. Why is it important to have a balance between the three elements of behavioral control—culture; rewards and incentives; and, boundaries?

4. Discuss the relationship between types of organizations and their primary means of behavioral control.

5. Boundaries become less important as a firm develops a strong culture and reward system. Explain.

6. Why is it important to avoid a "one best way" mentality concerning control systems? What are the consequences of applying the same type of control system to all types of environments?

7. What is the role of effective corporate governance in improving a firm's performance? What are some of the key governance mechanisms that are used to ensure that managerial and shareholder interests are aligned?

8. Define principal–principal (PP) conflicts. What are the implications for corporate governance?

Key Terms

Experiential Exercise

McDonald's Corporation, the world's largest fast-food restaurant chain, with 2006 revenues of $22 billion, has recently been on a "roll." Its shareholder value has more than tripled between March 2003 and March 2007. Using the Internet or library sources, evaluate the quality of the corporation in terms of management, the board of directors, and shareholder activism. Are the issues you list favorable or unfavorable for sound corporate governance?

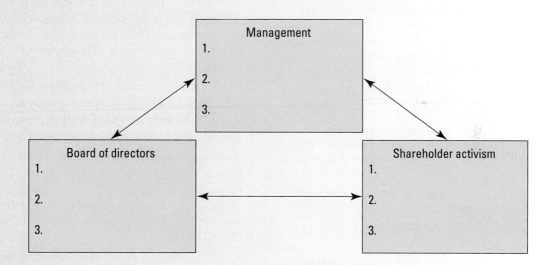

Application Questions Exercises

1. The problems of many firms may be attributed to a "traditional" control system that failed to continuously monitor the environment and make necessary changes in their strategy and objectives. What companies are you familiar with that responded appropriately (or inappropriately) to environmental change?

2. How can a strong, positive culture enhance a firm's competitive advantage? How can a weak, negative culture erode competitive advantages? Explain and provide examples.

3. Use the Internet to research a firm that has an excellent culture and/or reward and incentive system. What are this firm's main financial and nonfinancial benefits?

4. Using the Internet, go to the Web site of a large, publicly held corporation in which you are interested. What evidence do you see of effective (or ineffective) corporate governance?

Ethics Questions

1. Strong cultures can have powerful effects on employee behavior. How does this create inadvertent control mechanisms? That is, are strong cultures an ethical way to control behavior?

2. Rules and regulations can help reduce unethical behavior in organizations. To be effective, however, what other systems, mechanisms, and processes are necessary?

References

1. Burrows, P. 2007. A smaller options scandal? *Business-Week*, March 5: 28–31; Maurer, H. (Ed.). 2006. Options watch. *BusinessWeek*, October 30: 32; Anonymous. 2006. Exit of the week. *BusinessWeek*, November 27: 31; Anonymous. 2006. How KB Home CEO's pay went through the roof. www.hobb.org. December 17, np.; and Anonymous. 2006. Backdating. *Business-Week*. December 18: 108.

2. This chapter draws upon Picken, J. C., & Dess, G. G. 1997. *Mission critical*. Burr Ridge, IL: Irwin Professional Publishing.

3. Argyris, C. 1977. Double-loop learning in organizations. *Harvard Business Review,* 55: 115–125.

4. Simons, R. 1995. Control in an age of empowerment. *Harvard Business Review,* 73: 80–88. This chapter draws on this source in the discussion of informational control.

5. Goold, M., & Quinn, J. B. 1990. The paradox of strategic controls. *Strategic Management Journal,* 11: 43–57.

6. Quinn, J. B. 1980. *Strategies for change*. Homewood, IL: Richard D. Irwin.

7. Mintzberg, H. 1987. Crafting strategy. *Harvard Business Review,* 65: 66–75.

8. Weston, J. S. 1992. Soft stuff matters. *Financial Executive,* July–August: 52–53.

9. This discussion of control systems draws upon Simons, op. cit.

10. For an interesting perspective on this issue and how a downturn in the economy can reduce the tendency toward "free agency" by managers and professionals, refer to Morris, B. 2001. White collar blues. *Fortune,* July 23: 98–110.

11. Ouchi, W. 1981. *Theory Z*. Reading, MA: Addison-Wesley; Deal, T. E., & Kennedy, A. A. 1982. *Corporate cultures*. Reading, MA: Addison-Wesley; Peters, T. J., & Waterman, R. H. 1982. *In search of excellence*. New York: Random House; Collins, J. 2001. *Good to great*. New York: HarperCollins.

12. Collins, J. C., & Porras, J. I. 1994. *Built to last: Successful habits of visionary companies*. New York: Harper Business.

13. Lee, J., & Miller, D. 1999. People matter: Commitment to employees, strategy, and performance in Korean firms. *Strategic Management Journal,* 6: 579–594.

14. For an insightful discussion of IKEA's unique culture, see Kling, K., & Goteman, I. 2003. IKEA CEO Anders Dahlvig on international growth and IKEA's unique corporate culture and brand identity. *Academy of Management Executive,* 17(1): 31–37.

15. For a discussion of how professionals inculcate values, refer to Uhl-Bien, M., & Graen, G. B. 1998. Individual self-management: Analysis of professionals' self-managing activities in functional and cross-functional work teams. *Academy of Management Journal,* 41(3): 340–350.

16. A perspective on how antisocial behavior can erode a firm's culture can be found in Robinson, S. L., & O'Leary-Kelly, A. M. 1998. Monkey see, monkey do: The influence of work groups on the antisocial behavior of employees. *Academy of Management Journal,* 41(6): 658–672.

17. Mitchell, R. 1989. Masters of innovation. *Business-Week,* April 10: 58–63.

18. Sellers, P. 1993. Companies that serve you best. *Fortune,* May 31: 88.

19. Southwest Airlines Culture Committee. 1993. *Luv Lines* (company publication), March–April: 17–18; for an interesting perspective on the "downside" of strong "cultlike" organizational cultures, refer to Arnott, D. A. 2000. *Corporate cults*. New York: AMACOM.

20. Kerr, J., & Slocum, J. W., Jr. 1987. Managing corporate culture through reward systems. *Academy of Management Executive,* 1(2): 99–107.

21. For a unique perspective on leader challenges in managing wealthy professionals, refer to Wetlaufer, S. 2000. Who wants to manage a millionaire? *Harvard Business Review,* 78(4): 53–60.

22. Neilson, G. L., Pasternack, B. A., & Van Nuys, K. E. 2005. The passive-aggressive organization. *Harvard Business Review,* 83(10): 82–95.

23. These next two subsections draw upon Dess, G. G., & Picken, J. C. 1997. *Beyond Productivity*. New York: AMACOM.

24. For a discussion of the benefits of stock options as executive compensation, refer to Hall, B. J. 2000. What you need to know about stock options. *Harvard Business Review,* 78(2): 121–129.

25. Tully, S. 1993. Your paycheck gets exciting. *Fortune,* November 13: 89.

26. Zellner, W., Hof, R. D., Brandt, R., Baker, S., & Greising, D. 1995. Go-go goliaths. *BusinessWeek,* February 13: 64–70.

27. This section draws on Dess & Picken, op. cit.: chap. 5.

28. Simons, op. cit.

29. Davis, E. 1997. Interview: Norman Augustine. *Management Review,* November: 11.

30. This section draws upon Dess, G. G., & Miller, A. 1993. *Strategic management.* New York: McGraw-Hill.

31. For a good review of the goal-setting literature, refer to Locke, E. A., & Latham, G. P. 1990. *A theory of goal setting and task performance.* Englewood Cliffs, NJ: Prentice Hall.

32. For an interesting perspective on the use of rules and regulations that is counter to this industry's (software) norms, refer to Fryer, B. 2001. Tom Siebel of Siebel Systems: High tech the old fashioned way. *Harvard Business Review,* 79(3): 118–130.

33. Thompson, A. A., Jr., & Strickland, A. J., III. 1998. *Strategic management: Concepts and cases* (10th ed.): 313. New York: McGraw-Hill.

34. Ibid.

35. Teitelbaum, R. 1997. Tough guys finish first. *Fortune,* July 21: 82–84.

36. Weaver, G. R., Trevino, L. K., & Cochran, P. L. 1999. Corporate ethics programs as control systems: Influences of executive commitment and environmental factors. *Academy of Management Journal,* 42(1): 41–57.

37. Cadbury, S. A. 1987. Ethical managers make their own rules. *Harvard Business Review,* 65: 3, 69–73.

38. Weber, J. 2003. CFOs on the hot seat. *BusinessWeek,* March 17: 66–70.

39. William Ouchi has written extensively about the use of clan control (which is viewed as an alternate to bureaucratic or market control). Here, a powerful culture results in people aligning their individual interests with those of the firm. Refer to Ouchi, op. cit. This section also draws on Hall, R. H. 2002. *Organizations: Structures, processes, and outcomes* (8th ed.). Upper Saddle River, NJ: Prentice Hall.

40. Monks, R., & Minow, N. 2001. *Corporate governance* (2nd ed.). Malden, MA: Blackwell.

41. Pound, J. 1995. The promise of the governed corporation. *Harvard Business Review,* 73(2): 89–98.

42. Heinzl, M. 2004. Nortel's directors and investors discuss changes to the board. *The Wall Street Journal,* September 30: B4; Editorial. 2003. Pulling Boeing out of a tailspin. *BusinessWeek,* December 15: 136; and Zimmerman, A., Ball, D., & Veen, M. 2003. A global journal report: Supermarket giant Ahoud ousts CEO in big accounting scandal. *The Wall Street Journal,* February 25: A1; Ibid; and Maurer, H. 2006. Is this 'the HP way'? *BusinessWeek,* September 25: 34.

43. This discussion draws upon Monks & Minow, op. cit.

44. Eisenhardt, K. M. 1989. Agency theory: An assessment and review. *Academy of Management Review,* 14(1): 57–74. Some of the seminal contributions to agency theory include Jensen, M., & Meckling, W. 1976. Theory of the firm: Managerial behavior, agency costs, and ownership structure. *Journal of Financial Economics,* 3: 305–360; Fama, E., & Jensen, M. 1983. Separation of ownership and control. *Journal of Law and Economics,* 26: 301, 325; and Fama, E. 1980. Agency problems and the theory of the firm. *Journal of Political Economy,* 88: 288–307.

45. Managers may also engage in "shirking"—that is, reducing or withholding their efforts. See, for example, Kidwell, R. E., Jr., & Bennett, N. 1993. Employee propensity to withhold effort: A conceptual model to intersect three avenues of research. *Academy of Management Review,* 18(3): 429–456.

46. For an interesting perspective on agency and clarification of many related concepts and terms, visit the following Web site: www.encycogov.com.

47. Argawal, A., & Mandelker, G. 1987. Managerial incentives and corporate investment and financing decisions. *Journal of Finance,* 42: 823–837.

48. For an insightful, recent discussion of the academic research on corporate governance, and in particular the role of boards of directors, refer to Chatterjee, S., & Harrison, J. S. 2001. Corporate governance. In Hitt, M. A., Freeman, R. E., & Harrison, J. S. (Eds.). *Handbook of strategic management:* 543–563. Malden, MA: Blackwell.

49. This opening discussion draws on Monks & Minow, op. cit. 164, 169; see also Pound, op. cit.

50. Business Roundtable. 1990. *Corporate governance and American competitiveness,* March: 7.

51. Byrne, J. A., Grover, R., & Melcher, R. A. 1997. The best and worst boards. *BusinessWeek,* November 26: 35–47. The three key roles of boards of directors are monitoring the actions of executives, providing advice, and providing links to the external environment to provide resources. See Johnson, J. L., Daily, C. M., & Ellstrand, A. E. 1996. Boards of directors: A review and research agenda. *Academy of Management Review,* 37: 409–438.

52. McGeehan, P. 2003. More chief executives shown the door, study says. *New York Times,* May 12: C2.

53. Gerdes, L. 2007. Hello, goodbye. *BusinessWeek,* January 22: 16.

54. For an analysis of the effects of outside director's compensation on acquisition decisions, refer to Deutsch, T., Keil, T., & Laamanen, T. 2007. Decision making in acquisitions: The effect of outside directors' compensation on acquisition patterns. *Journal of Management,* 33(1): 30–56.

55. There are benefits, of course, to having some insiders on the board of directors. Inside directors would be more aware of the firm's strategies. Additionally, outsiders may rely too often on financial performance indicators because of information asymmetries. For an interesting discussion, see Baysinger, B. D., & Hoskisson, R. E. 1990. The composition of boards of directors and strategic control: Effects on corporate strategy. *Academy of Management Review,* 15: 72–87.

56. Hambrick, D. C., & Jackson, E. M. 2000. Outside directors with a stake: The linchpin in improving governance. *California Management Review,* 42(4): 108–127.

57. Ibid.

58. Disney has begun to make many changes to improve its corporate governance, such as assigning only independent directors to important board committees, restricting directors from serving on more than three boards, and appointing a lead director who can convene the board without approval by the CEO. In recent years, the Disney Co. has shown up on some "best" board lists. In addition Eisner has recently relinquished the chairman position.

59. Talk show. 2002. *BusinessWeek,* September 30: 14.

60. Ward, R. D. 2000. *Improving corporate boards.* New York: Wiley.

61. Monks and Minow, op. cit.: 93.

62. A discussion of the factors that lead to shareholder activism is found in Ryan, L. V., & Schneider, M. 2002. The antecedents of institutional investor activism. *Academy of Management Review,* 27(4): 554–573.

63. For an insightful discussion of investor activism, refer to David, P., Bloom, M., & Hillman, A. 2007. Investor activism, managerial responsiveness, and corporate social performance. *Strategic Management Journal,* 28(1): 91–100.

64. There is strong research support for the idea that the presence of large block shareholders is associated with value-maximizing decisions. For example, refer to Johnson, R. A., Hoskisson, R. E., & Hitt, M. A. 1993. Board of director involvement in restructuring: The effects of board versus managerial controls and characteristics. *Strategic Management Journal,* 14: 33–50.

65. For an interesting perspective on the impact of institutional ownership on a firm's innovation strategies, see Hoskisson, R. E., Hitt, M. A., Johnson, R. A., & Grossman, W. 2002. *Academy of Management Journal,* 45(4): 697–716.

66. www.calpers.ca.gov/index.jsp

67. Icahn, C. 2007. Icahn: On activist investors and private equity run wild. *BusinessWeek,* March 12: 21–22. For an interesting perspective on Carl Icahn's transition (?) from corporate raider to shareholder activist, read Grover, R. 2007. Just don't call him a raider. *BusinessWeek,* March 5: 68–69. The quote in the text is part of Icahn's response to the article by R. Grover.

68. For a study of the relationship between ownership and diversification, refer to Goranova, M., Alessandri, T. M., Brandes, P., & Dharwadkar, R. 2007. Managerial ownership and corporate diversification: A longitudinal view, *Strategic Management Journal,* 28(3): 211–226.

69. Jensen, M. C., & Murphy, K. J. 1990. CEO incentives—It's not how much you pay, but how. *Harvard Business Review,* 68(3): 138–149.

70. For a perspective on the relative advantages and disadvantages of "duality"—that is, one individual serving as both Chief Executive Office and Chairman of the Board, see Lorsch, J. W., & Zelleke, A. 2005. Should the CEO be the chairman? *MIT Sloan Management Review,* 46(2): 71–74.

71. Sasseen, J. 2007. A better look at the boss's pay. *BusinessWeek,* February 26: 44–45.

72. Byrnes, N., & Sasseen, J. 2007. Board of hard knocks. *BusinessWeek,* January 22: 36–39.

73. Research has found that executive compensation is more closely aligned with firm performance in companies with compensation committees and boards dominated by outside directors. See, for example, Conyon, M. J., & Peck, S. I. 1998. Board control, remuneration committees, and top management compensation. *Academy of Management Journal,* 41: 146–157.

74. Lavelle, L., Jespersen, F. F., & Arndt, M. 2002. Executive pay. *BusinessWeek,* April 15: 66–72.

75. www.tiaa-cref.org/pubs.

76. Such opportunistic behavior is common in all principal-agent relationships. For a description of agency problems, especially in the context of the relationship between shareholders and managers, see Jensen, M. C., & Meckling, W. H. 1976. Theory of the firm: Managerial behavior, agency costs, and ownership structure. *Journal of Financial Economics,* 3: 305–360.

77. Hoskisson, R. E., & Turk, T. A. 1990. Corporate restructuring: Governance and control limits of the internal market. *Academy of Management Review,* 15: 459–477.

78. For an insightful perspective on the market for corporate control and how it is influenced by knowledge intensity, see Coff, R. 2003. Bidding wars over R&D-intensive firms: Knowledge, opportunism, and the market for corporate control. *Academy of Management Journal,* 46(1): 74–85.

79. Walsh, J. P., & Kosnik, R. D. 1993. Corporate raiders and their disciplinary role in the market for corporate control. *Academy of Management Journal,* 36: 671–700.

80. Gunning for KPMG. 2003. *Economist,* February 1: 63.

81. Timmons, H. 2003. Investment banks: Who will foot their bill? *BusinessWeek,* March 3: 116.

82. Wishy-washy: The SEC pulls its punches on corporate-governance rules. 2003. *Economist,* February 1: 60.

83. McLean, B. 2001. Is Enron overpriced? *Fortune,* March 5: 122–125.

84. Bernstein, A. 2000. Too much corporate power. *BusinessWeek,* September 11: 35–37.

85. This section draws upon Young, M. N., Peng, M. W., Ahlstrom, D., Bruton, G. D., Jiang, Y. 2005. Principal–principal conflicts in corporate governance (unpublished manuscript); and, Peng, M. W. 2006. *Globalstrategy*. Cincinnati: Thomson South-Western. We are very appreciative of the helpful comments of Mike Young of Hong Kong Baptist University and Mike Peng of the University of Texas at Dallas.

86. Khanna, T., & Rivkin, J. 2001. Estimating the performance effects of business groups in emerging markets. *Strategic Management Journal*, 22: 45–74.

chapter 10

Creating Effective Organizational Designs

>learning objectives

After reading this chapter, you should have a good understanding of:

LO1 The importance of organizational structure and the concept of the "boundaryless" organization in implementing strategies.

LO2 The growth patterns of major corporations and the relationship between a firm's strategy and its structure.

LO3 Each of the traditional types of organizational structure: simple, functional, divisional, and matrix.

LO4 The relative advantages and disadvantages of traditional organizational structures.

LO5 The implications of a firm's international operations for organizational structure.

LO6 Why there is no "one best way" to design strategic reward and evaluation systems, and the important contingent roles of business- and corporate-level strategies.

LO7 The different types of boundaryless organizations—barrier-free, modular, and virtual—and their relative advantages and disadvantages.

LO8 The need for creating ambidextrous organizational designs that enable firms to explore new opportunities and effectively integrate existing operations.

*t*o implement strategies successfully, firms must have appropriate organizational structures. These include the processes and integrating mechanisms necessary to ensure that boundaries among internal activities and external parties, such as suppliers, customers, and alliance partners, are flexible and permeable. A firm's performance will suffer if its managers don't carefully consider both of these organizational design attributes.

In the first section, we begin by discussing the growth patterns of large corporations to address the important relationships between the strategy that a firm follows and its corresponding structure. For example, as firms diversify into related product-market areas, they change their structure from functional to divisional. We then address the different types of traditional structures—simple, functional, divisional, and matrix—and their relative advantages and disadvantages. We close with a discussion of the implications of a firm's international operations for the structure of its organization.

The second section takes the perspective that there is no "one best way" to design an organization's strategic reward and evaluation system. Here we address two important contingencies: business- and corporate-level strategy. For example, when strategies require a great deal of collaboration, as well as resource and information sharing, there must be incentives and cultures that encourage and reward such initiatives.

The third section discusses the concept of the "boundaryless" organization. We do *not* argue that organizations should have no internal and external boundaries. Instead, we suggest that in rapidly changing and unpredictable environments, organizations must strive to make their internal and external boundaries both flexible and permeable. We suggest three different types of boundaryless organizations: barrier-free, modular, and virtual.

The fourth section focuses on the need for managers to recognize that they typically face two opposing challenges: (1) being proactive in taking advantage of new opportunities and (2) ensuring the effective coordination and integration of existing operations. This suggests the need for ambidextrous organizations; that is, firms that can both be efficient in how they manage existing assets and competencies and take advantage of opportunities in rapidly changing and unpredictable environments—conditions that are becoming more pronounced in today's global markets.

Learning from Mistakes

As 2007 began, Airbus' A380 double-decker jet was two years behind schedule, sending about $6 billion in potential profits down the drain.[1] However, the root of the problem may appear to be too simple to be true. Let's take a look.

Airbus factories in Germany and France were using incompatible design software. Engineers in Hamburg were drawing on a two-dimensional computer program, while their counterparts in Toulouse were working in 3-D. Thus, wiring produced in Hamburg didn't fit properly into the plane on the assembly line in Toulouse. As noted by Hans Weber, CEO of San Diego–based consultant Tecop International, "The various Airbus locations had their own legacy software, methods, procedures, and Airbus never succeeded in unifying all those efforts." (There are 348 *miles* of bundled wiring in each A380.)

The A380 fiasco has become one of the costliest blunders in the history of commercial aviation and plunged Airbus into crisis. Chief Executive Christian Streiff quit in October, 2006 after only three months on the job. He clashed with Airbus' parent, European Aeronautic Defense & Space (EADS) Company, over how to sort out the mess. EADS will probably wind up taking a $6 billion hit to its *[continued]* profit—measured by the expected loss in earnings from production delays over the next four years. Further, the resulting cash crunch could slow Airbus' plans to develop a new midsize wide-body plane to challenge Boeing's highly successful 787 Dreamliner. Through September 2006, Airbus fell far behind Boeing on total aircraft orders, logging only 226 versus 723 for its U.S. rival.

What Went Wrong?

The software debacle exposes a salient flaw in Airbus. Although it likes to project a seamless, pan-European image, Airbus is terribly balkanized. Its factories in Germany, France, Britain, and Spain cling to traditional operating methods and harbor cross-border jealousies. As Strieff told the French newspaper *Le Figaro* in an interview, "It is still, in part, a juxtaposition of four companies."

Each of those four companies comes, as one would expect, with a government attached. In essence, constant political meddling is the price Airbus must pay for the billions of dollars in low-interest government loans that have helped it launch new designs. Politicians have a powerful weapon with which to exert influence to spread work across Airbus's 16 European factories. As noted by *Washington Post* writer Steven Peaerlstein: ". . . it's about the pigheadedness of . . . partners who care less about how many planes Airbus sells than how the work is divided between the countries." Such attitudes sap efficiency and increase the risk of production glitches. Eric Chaney, Morgan Stanley's chief European economist asserts: "The fairy tale has turned into a nightmare that even the fiercest Euro-skeptics wouldn't have imagined possible."

There is, however, good news in all of this—for Boeing. The delays on the Airbus A380 have created a sort of virtuous cycle. First, they force air transport companies to switch freighter orders, as both International Lease Finance and FedEx did. Second, the delays in the passenger version of the A380 mean potential customers have to keep older planes, such as Boeing 747-400s, in passenger service longer, instead of converting them into cargo haulers—a much cheaper option than buying new. So fewer used jets lying around means more demand for the new cargo jets, which Boeing is happy to sell.

>LO1

The importance of organizational structure and the concept of the "boundaryless" organization in implementing strategies.

One of the central concepts in this chapter is the importance of boundaryless organizations. That is, successful organizations create permeable boundaries among the internal activities as well as between the organization and its external customers, suppliers, and alliance partners. We introduced this idea in Chapter 3 in our discussion of the value-chain concept, which consisted of several primary (e.g., inbound logistics, marketing and sales) and support activities (e.g., procurement, human resource management). Clearly, the underlying cause of Airbus' problem was its inability to establish close and effective working relationships between its various factories operating in four countries. Frequently, managers (and politicians) were seemingly more focused on national interests instead of what was best for Airbus' shareholders.

The most important implication of this chapter is that today's managers are faced with two ongoing and vital activities in structuring and designing their organizations. First, they must decide on the most appropriate type of organizational structure. Second, they need to assess what mechanisms, processes, and techniques are most helpful in enhancing the permeability of both internal and external boundaries.

Traditional Forms of Organizational Structure

Organizational structure refers to the formalized patterns of interactions that link a firm's tasks, technologies, and people.[2] Structures help to ensure that resources are used effectively in accomplishing an organization's mission. Structure provides a means of balancing two conflicting forces: a need for the division of tasks into meaningful groupings and the need to integrate such groupings in order to ensure efficiency and effectiveness. Structure identifies the executive, managerial, and administrative organization of a firm and indicates responsibilities and hierarchical relationships. It also influences the flow of information as well as the context and nature of human interactions.

Most organizations begin very small and either die or remain small. Those few that survive and prosper embark on strategies designed to increase the overall scope of operations and enable them to enter new product-market domains. Such growth places additional pressure on executives to control and coordinate the firm's increasing size and diversity. The most appropriate type of structure depends on the nature and magnitude of growth in a firm. Next, we address various types of structural forms, their advantages and disadvantages, and their relationships to the strategies that organizations undertake.

Patterns of Growth of Large Corporations: Strategy-Structure Relationships

A firm's strategy and structure change as it increases in size, diversifies into new product markets, and expands its geographic scope.[3] Exhibit 10.1 illustrates some of the common growth patterns that firms may follow.

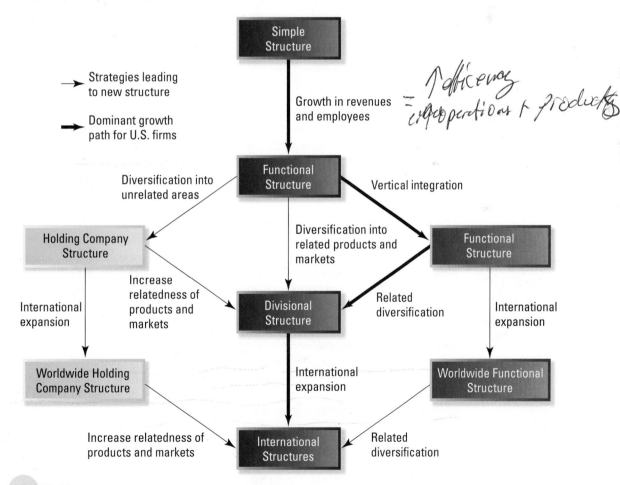

Exhibit 10.1 **Dominant Growth Patterns of Large Corporations**

Source: From *Strategy Implementation: Structure, Systems and Process,* 2nd edition by J. R. Galbraith and R. K. Kazanjian. Copyright © 1986. Reprinted with permission of South-Western, a division of Thomson Learning: www.thomsonrights.com. Fax: 800-730-2215.

A new firm with a *simple structure* typically increases its sales revenue and volume of outputs over time. It may also engage in some vertical integration to secure sources of supply (backward integration) as well as channels of distribution (forward integration). After a time, the simple-structure firm implements a *functional structure* to concentrate efforts on both increasing efficiency and enhancing its operations and products. This structure enables the firm to group its operations into either functions, departments, or geographic areas. As its initial markets mature, a firm looks beyond its present products and markets for possible expansion.

A strategy of related diversification requires a need to reorganize around product lines or geographic markets. This leads to a *divisional structure.* As the business expands in terms of sales revenues, and domestic growth opportunities become somewhat limited, a firm may seek opportunities in international markets. At this time, a firm has a wide variety of structures to choose from. These include *international division, geographic area, worldwide product division, worldwide functional,* and *worldwide matrix.* As we will see later in this section, deciding upon the most appropriate structure when a firm has international operations depends on three primary factors: the extent of international expansion, type of strategy (global, multidomestic, or transnational), and the degree of product diversity.[4]

There are some other common growth patterns. For example, some firms may find it advantageous to diversify into several product lines rather than focus their efforts on strengthening distributor and supplier relationships through vertical integration. Thus, they would organize themselves according to product lines by implementing a divisional structure. Also, some firms may choose to move into unrelated product areas, typically by acquiring existing businesses. Frequently, their rationale is that acquiring assets and competencies is more economical or expedient than developing them internally. Such an unrelated, or conglomerate, strategy requires relatively little integration across businesses and sharing of resources. Thus, a *holding company structure* becomes appropriate. As we would expect, there are many other growth patterns, but these are the most common.*

Now we will discuss some of the most common types of organizational structures—simple, functional, divisional (including two variants: *strategic business unit* and *holding company*), and matrix and their advantages and disadvantages. We will close the section with a discussion of the structural implications when a firm expands its operations into international markets.

Simple Structure

>LO3

Each of the traditional types of organizational structure: simple, functional, divisional, and matrix.

The **simple organizational structure** is the oldest, and most common, organizational form. After all, most organizations are very small and have a single or very narrow product line in which the owner-manager (or top executive) makes most of the decisions. In effect, the owner-manager controls all activities, and the staff serves as an extension of the top executive.

Advantages   The simple structure is highly informal and the coordination of tasks is accomplished by direct supervision. Decision making is highly centralized, there is little specialization of tasks, few rules and regulations, and an informal evaluation and reward system. Although the owner-manager is intimately involved in almost all phases of the business, a manager is often employed to oversee day-to-day operations.

simple organizational structure an organizational form in which the owner-manager makes most of the decisions and controls activities, and the staff serves as an extension of the top executive.

* The lowering of transaction costs and globalization have led to some changes in the common historical patterns that we have discussed. Some firms are, in effect, bypassing the vertical integration stage. Instead, they focus on core competencies and outsource other value-creation activities. Also, even relatively young firms are going global early in their history because of lower communication and transportation costs. For an interesting perspective on global start-ups, see McDougall, P. P., & Oviatt, B. M. 1996. New venture internationalization, strategic change and performance: A follow-up study. *Journal of Business Venturing,* 11: 23–40; and McDougall, P. P., & Oviatt, B. M. (Eds.). 2000. The special research forum on international entrepreneurship. *Academy of Management Journal,* October: 902–1003.

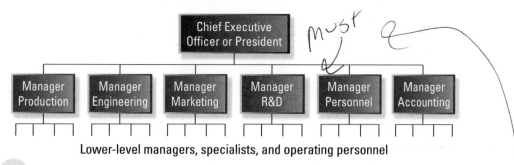

Exhibit 10.2 **Functional Organizational Structure**

Disadvantages   A simple structure may often foster creativity and individualism since there are generally few rules and regulations. However, such "informality" may lead to problems. Employees may not clearly understand their responsibilities, which can lead to conflict and confusion. Employees also may take advantage of the lack of regulations and act in their own self-interest. Such actions can erode motivation and satisfaction as well as lead to the possible misuse of organizational resources. Further, small organizations have flat structures that limit opportunities for upward mobility. Without the potential for future advancement, recruiting and retaining talent may become very difficult.

Functional Structure

When an organization is small (15 employees or less), it is not necessary to have a variety of formal arrangements and groupings of activities. However, as firms grow, excessive demands may be placed on the owner-manager in order to obtain and process all of the information necessary to run the business. Chances are the owner will not be skilled in all specialties (e.g., accounting, engineering, production, marketing). Thus, he or she will need to hire specialists in the various functional areas. Such growth in the overall scope and complexity of the business necessitates a **functional organizational structure** wherein the major functions of the firm are grouped internally. The coordination and integration of the functional areas becomes one of the most important responsibilities of the chief executive of the firm. Exhibit 10.2 presents a diagram of a functional organizational structure.

Functional structures are generally found in organizations in which there is a single or closely related product or service, high production volume, and some vertical integration. Initially, firms tend to expand the overall scope of their operations by penetrating existing markets, introducing similar products in additional markets, or increasing the level of vertical integration. Such expansion activities clearly increase the scope and complexity of the operations. Fortunately, the functional structure provides for a high level of centralization that helps to ensure integration and control over the related product-market activities or multiple primary activities (from inbound logistics to operations to marketing, sales, and service) in the value chain (addressed in Chapters 3 and 4).

Strategy Spotlight 10.1 provides an example of an effective functional organization structure—Parkdale Mills.

Advantages   As with any type of organizational structure, there are some relative advantages and disadvantages associated with the functional structure. By bringing together specialists into functional departments, a firm is able to enhance its coordination and control within each of the functional areas. The structure also ensures that decision making in the firm will be centralized at the top of the organization. This enhances the organizational-level (as opposed to functional area) perspective across the various functions in the organization. In addition, the functional structure provides for a more efficient use of managerial and

functional organizational structure an organizational form in which the major functions of the firm, such as production, marketing, R&D, and accounting, are grouped internally.

>LO4
The relative advantages and disadvantages of traditional organizational structures.

Parkdale Mills: A Successful Functional Organizational Structure

For more than 80 years, Parkdale Mills, with approximately $1 billion in revenues, has been the industry leader in the production of cotton and cotton blend yarns. Their expertise comes by concentrating on a single product line, perfecting processes, and welcoming innovation. According to CEO Andy Warlick, "I think we've probably spent more than any two competitors combined on new

Sources: Stewart, C. 2003. The perfect yarn. *The Manufacturer.com*, July 31; www.parkdalemills.com; Berman, P. 1987. The fast track isn't always the best track. *Forbes*, November 2: 60–64; and personal communication with Duke Kimbrell, March 11, 2005.

equipment and robotics. We do this because we have to compete in a global market where a lot of the competition has a lower wage structure and gets subsidies that we don't receive, so we really have to focus on consistency and cost control." Yarn making is generally considered to be a commodity business, and Parkdale is the industry's low-cost producer.

Tasks are highly standardized and authority is centralized with Duke Kimbrell, founder and chairman, and CEO Andy Warlick. The firm operates a bare-bones staff with a small staff of top executives. Kimbrell and Warlick are considered shrewd about the cotton market, technology, customer loyalty, and incentive pay.

---

technical talent since functional area expertise is pooled in a single department (e.g., marketing) instead of being spread across a variety of product-market areas. Finally, career paths and professional development in specialized areas are facilitated.

Disadvantages   There also are some significant disadvantages associated with the functional structure. First, the differences in values and orientations among functional areas may impede communication and coordination. Edgar Schein of MIT has argued that shared assumptions, often based on similar backgrounds and experiences of members, form around functional units in an organization. This leads to what are often called "stove pipes" or "silos," in which departments view themselves as isolated, self-contained units with little need for interaction and coordination with other departments. This erodes communication because functional groups may have not only different goals but also differing meanings of words and concepts. According to Schein:

> The word "marketing" will mean product development to the engineer, studying customers through market research to the product manager, merchandising to the salesperson, and constant change in design to the manufacturing manager. When they try to work together, they will often attribute disagreements to personalities and fail to notice the deeper, shared assumptions that color how each function thinks.[5]

Such narrow functional orientations also may lead to short-term thinking based largely upon what is best for the functional area, not the entire organization. For example, in a manufacturing firm, sales may want to offer a wide range of customized products to appeal to the firm's customers; research and development may overdesign products and components to achieve technical elegance; and manufacturing may favor no-frills products that can be produced at low cost by means of long production runs. In addition, functional structures may overburden the top executives in the firm because conflicts have a tendency to be "pushed up" to the top of the organization since there are no managers who are responsible for the specific product lines. Finally, functional structures make it difficult to establish uniform performance standards across the entire organization. Whereas it may be relatively easy to evaluate production managers on the basis of production volume and cost control, establishing performance measures for engineering, research and development, and accounting become more problematic.

Divisional Structure

The **divisional organizational structure** (sometimes called the multidivisional structure or M-Form) is organized around products, projects, or markets. Each of the divisions, in turn, includes its own functional specialists who are typically organized into departments. A divisional structure encompasses a set of relatively autonomous units governed by a central corporate office. The operating divisions are relatively independent and consist of products and services that are different from those of the other divisions. Operational decision making in a large business places excessive demands on the firm's top management. In order to attend to broader, longer-term organizational issues, top-level managers must delegate decision making to lower-level managers. Thus, divisional executives play a key role. In conjunction with corporate-level executives, they help to determine the product-market and financial objectives for the division as well as their division's contribution to overall corporate performance.[6] The rewards are based largely on measures of financial performance such as net income and revenue. Exhibit 10.3 illustrates a divisional structure.

General Motors was among the earliest firms to adopt the divisional organizational structure.[7] In the 1920s the company formed five major product divisions (Cadillac, Buick, Oldsmobile, Pontiac, and Chevrolet) as well as several industrial divisions. Since then, many firms have discovered that as they diversified into new product-market activities, functional structures—with their emphasis on single functional departments—were unable to manage the increased complexity of the entire business.

Advantages   There are many advantages associated with the divisional structure. By creating separate divisions to manage individual product markets, there is a separation of strategic and operating control. That is, divisional managers can focus their efforts on improving operations in the product markets for which they are responsible, and corporate officers can devote their time to overall strategic issues for the entire corporation. The focus on a division's products and markets—by the divisional executives—provides the corporation with an enhanced ability to respond quickly to important changes in the external environment. Since there are functional departments within each division of the corporation, the problems associated with sharing resources across functional departments are minimized.

> **divisional organizational structure** an organizational form in which products, projects, or product markets are grouped internally.

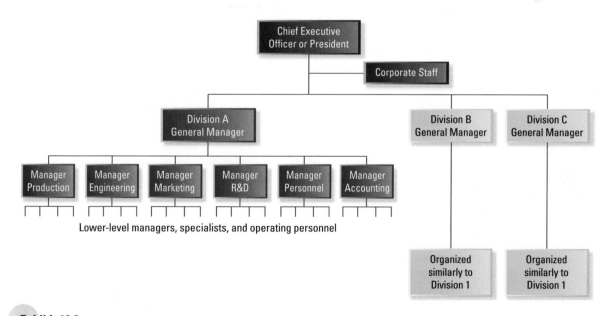

Exhibit 10.3 **Divisional Organizational Structure**

Brinker International Changes to a Divisional Organizational Structure

Although Brinker International had a traditional functional structure, changes in its competitive outlook forced management to take a closer look at the organizational design of the firm. The firm controls a variety of restaurant chains and bakeries, including Wildfire, Big Bowl, and Chili's.

With all these interests under one corporate roof, management of these disparate entities became difficult. The fragmented $330 billion restaurant and bakery industry caters to highly focused market niches. The original

Source: CEO interview: Ronald A. McDougall, Brinker International. 1999. *Wall Street Transcript*, January 20: 1–4.

functional design of the Brinker chain had some disadvantages as the company grew. With areas separated by function, it became hard to focus efforts on a single restaurant chain. The diverse markets served by the bakeries and restaurants began to lose their focus.

As a result, Brinker International changed to a divisional structure. This allowed the company to consolidate individuals who worked with a single restaurant or bakery chain into a separate division. Brinker referred to these as concept teams, with each concept team responsible for the operation of a single line of business. This focused effort streamlined the company's ability to concentrate on the market niche served by each of its restaurants and bakeries.

Finally, because there are multiple levels of general managers (that is, executives responsible for integrating and coordinating all functional areas), the development of general management talent is enhanced. Strategy Spotlight 10.2 discusses the rationale behind Brinker Corporation's change in structure from functional to divisional.

Disadvantages   A divisional structure also has potential disadvantages. First, it can be very expensive; that is, there can be increased costs due to the duplication of personnel, operations, and investment since each division must staff multiple functional departments. There also can be dysfunctional competition among divisions since each division tends to become concerned solely about its own operations. Further, divisional managers are often evaluated on common measures such as return on assets and sales growth. Thus, if goals are conflicting, there can be a sense of a "zero-sum" game that would discourage sharing ideas and resources among the divisions for the common good of the corporation. Ghoshal and Bartlett, two leading strategy scholars, note:

> As their label clearly warns, divisions divide. The divisional model fragmented companies' resources; it created vertical communication channels that insulated business units and prevented them from sharing their strengths with one another. Consequently, the whole of the corporation was often less than the sum of its parts.[8]

Another potential disadvantage is that with many divisions providing different products and services, there is the chance that differences in image and quality may occur across divisions. For example, one division may offer no-frills products of lower quality that may erode the brand reputation of another division that has top quality, highly differentiated offerings. Finally, since each division is evaluated in terms of financial measures such as return on investment and revenue growth, there is often an urge to focus on short-term performance. For example, if corporate management uses quarterly profits as the key performance indicator, divisional management may tend to put significant emphasis on "making the numbers" and minimizing activities, such as advertising, maintenance, and capital investments, which would detract from short-term performance measures.

Before moving on, we'll discuss two variations of the divisional form of organizational structure: the strategic business unit (SBU) and holding company structures.

Strategic Business Unit (SBU) Structure Highly diversified corporations such as ConAgra, a $12 billion food producer, may consist of dozens of different divisions.[9] If ConAgra were to use a purely divisional structure, it would be nearly impossible for the corporate office to plan and coordinate activities because the span of control would be too large. Instead, to attain synergies, ConAgra has put its diverse businesses into three primary SBUs: food service (restaurants), retail (grocery stores), and agricultural products.

With a **strategic business unit (SBU) structure,** divisions with similar products, markets, and/or technologies are grouped into homogenous units to achieve some synergies. These include those discussed in Chapter 6 for related diversification, such as leveraging core competencies, sharing infrastructures, and market power. Generally speaking, the more related businesses are within a corporation, the fewer SBUs will be required. Each of the SBUs in the corporation operates as a profit center.

> **strategic business unit (SBU) structure** an organizational form in which products, projects, or product market divisions are grouped into homogeneous units.

Advantages The major advantage of the SBU structure is that it makes the task of planning and control by the corporate office more manageable. Also, with greater decentralization of authority, individual businesses can react more quickly to important changes in the environment than if all divisions had to report directly to the corporate office.

Disadvantages There are also some disadvantages to the SBU structure. Since the divisions are grouped into SBUs, it may become difficult to achieve synergies across SBUs. That is, if divisions that are included in different SBUs have potential sources of synergy, it may become difficult for them to be realized. The additional level of management increases the number of personnel and overhead expenses, while the additional hierarchical level removes the corporate office further from the individual divisions. Thus, the corporate office may become unaware of key developments that could have a major impact on the corporation.

Holding Company Structure The **holding company structure** (sometimes referred to as a *conglomerate*) is also a variation of the divisional structure. Whereas the SBU structure is often used when similarities exist between the individual businesses (or divisions), the holding company structure is appropriate when the businesses in a corporation's portfolio do not have much in common. Thus, the potential for synergies is limited.

> **holding company structure** an organizational form that is a variation of the divisional organizational structure in which the divisions have a high degree of autonomy both from other divisions and from corporate headquarters.

Holding company structures are most appropriate for firms with a strategy of unrelated diversification. Companies such as Hanson Trust, ITT, and the CP group of Thailand have used holding company structure to implement their unrelated diversification strategies. Since there are few similarities across the businesses, the corporate offices in these companies provide a great deal of autonomy to operating divisions and rely on financial controls and incentive programs to obtain high levels of performance from the individual businesses. Corporate staffs at these firms tend to be small because of their limited involvement in the overall operation of their various businesses.[10]

Advantages An important advantage of the holding company structure is the cost savings associated with fewer personnel and the lower overhead resulting from a small corporate office and fewer hierarchical levels. In addition, the autonomy of the holding company structure increases the motivational level of divisional executives and enables them to respond quickly to market opportunities and threats.

Disadvantages The primary disadvantage of the holding company structure is the inherent lack of control and dependence that corporate-level executives have on divisional executives. Major problems could arise if key divisional executives leave the firm, because the corporate office has very little "bench strength"—that is, additional managerial talent ready to quickly fill key positions. And, if problems arise in a division, it

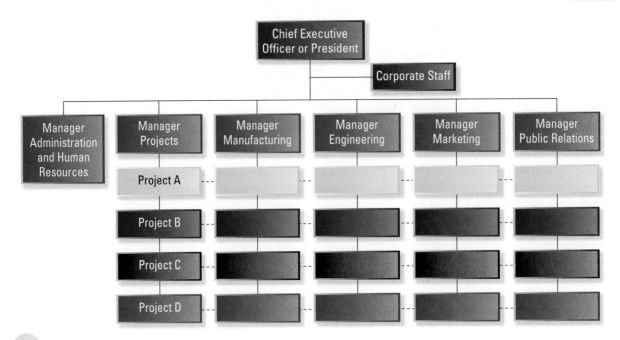

Exhibit 10.4 **Matrix Organizational Structure**

may become very difficult to turn around individual businesses because of limited staff support in the corporate office.

Matrix Structure

At times, managers may find that none of the structures that we have described above fully meet their needs. One approach that tries to overcome the inadequacies inherent in the other structures is the **matrix organizational structure.** It is, in effect, a combination of the functional and divisional structures. Most commonly, functional departments are combined with product groups on a project basis. For example, a product group may want to develop a new addition to its line; for this project, it obtains personnel from functional departments such as marketing, production, and engineering. These personnel work under the manager of the product group for the duration of the project, which can vary from a few weeks to an open-ended period of time. The individuals who work in a matrix organization become responsible to two managers: the project manager and the manager of their functional area. Exhibit 10.4 illustrates a matrix structure.

In addition to the product-function matrix, other bases may be related in a matrix. Some large multinational corporations rely on a matrix structure to combine product groups and geographical units. Product managers have global responsibility for the development, manufacturing, and distribution of their own line, while managers of geographical regions have responsibility for the profitability of the businesses in their regions. In the mid-1990s, Caterpillar, Inc., implemented this type of structure.

Dell Computer relies on the matrix concept, with its dual reporting responsibility, to enhance accountability as well as develop general managers. According to former CEO Kevin Rollins:[11]

> . . . we're organized in a matrix of sales regions and product groups. Then we break each of those groups down to a pretty fine level of sub-products and sales sub-segments. Dell has more P&L managers, and smaller business units, than most companies its size. This not only increases accountability to the customer, it helps train general managers by moving them from smaller to larger businesses as their skills develop.

Our matrix organization has a third level—our business councils. For example, we have a small-business sales group in each country, along with product development people who become very familiar with what small-business customers buy. In addition, we have our worldwide small-business council made up of all our small-business GMs and product managers. Everyone in these councils sees everyone else's P&L, so it provides another set of checks and balances.

Advantages A primary advantage of the matrix structure is that it facilitates the use of specialized personnel, equipment, and facilities. Instead of duplicating functions, as would be the case in a divisional structure based on products, the resources are shared. Individuals with high expertise can divide their time among multiple projects. Such resource sharing and collaboration enable a firm to use resources more efficiently and to respond more quickly and effectively to changes in the competitive environment. In addition, the flexibility inherent in a matrix structure provides professionals with a broader range of responsibility. Such experience enables them to develop their skills and competencies.

Disadvantages Matrix structures have many potential disadvantages. The dual-reporting structures can result in uncertainty and lead to intense power struggles and conflict over the allocation of personnel and other resources. Additionally, working relationships become more complicated. This may result in excessive reliance on group processes and teamwork, along with a diffusion of responsibility, which in turn may erode timely decision making. Exhibit 10.5 briefly summarizes the advantages and disadvantages of the functional, divisional, and matrix organizational structures.

International Operations: Implications for Organizational Structure

Today's managers must maintain an international outlook on their firm's businesses and competitive strategies. To be successful in the global marketplace, managers must ensure consistency between their strategies (at the business, corporate, and international levels) and the structure of their organization. As firms expand into foreign markets, they generally follow a pattern of change in structure that parallels the changes in their strategies. Three major contingencies that influence the chosen structure are (1) the type of strategy that is driving a firm's foreign operations, (2) product diversity, and (3) the extent to which a firm is dependent on foreign sales.[12]

>LO5
The implications of a firm's international operations for organizational structure.

As international operations become an important part of a firm's overall operations, managers must make changes that are consistent with their firm's structure. The primary types of structures used to manage a firm's international operations are:[13]

- International division
- Geographic-area division
- Worldwide functional
- Worldwide product division
- Worldwide matrix

As we discussed in Chapter 7, multidomestic strategies are driven by political and cultural imperatives requiring managers within each country to respond to local conditions. The structures consistent with such a strategic orientation are the *international division* and *geographic-area division* structures. Here local managers are provided with a high level of autonomy to manage their operations within the constraints and demands of their geographic market. As a firm's foreign sales increase as a percentage of its total sales, it will likely change from an international division to a geographic-area division structure. And,

Functional Structure	
Advantages	**Disadvantages**
• Pooling of specialists enhances coordination and control. • Centralized decision making enhances an organizational perspective across functions. • Efficient use of managerial and technical talent. • Facilitates career paths and professional development in specialized areas.	• Differences in functional area orientation impede communication and coordination. • Tendency for specialists to develop short-term perspective and narrow functional orientation. • Functional area conflicts may overburden top-level decision makers. • Difficult to establish uniform performance standards.

Divisional Structure	
Advantages	**Disadvantages**
• Increases strategic and operational control, permitting corporate-level executives to address strategic issues. • Quick response to environmental changes. • Increases focus on products and markets. • Minimizes problems associated with sharing resources across functional areas. • Facilitates development of general managers.	• Increased costs incurred through duplication of personnel, operations, and investment. • Dysfunctional competition among divisions may detract from overall corporate performance. • Difficult to maintain uniform corporate image. • Overemphasis on short-term performance.

Matrix Structure	
Advantages	**Disadvantages**
• Increases market responsiveness through collaboration and synergies among professional colleagues. • Allows more efficient utilization of resources. • Improves flexibility, coordination, and communication. • Increases professional development through a broader range of responsibility.	• Dual-reporting relationships can result in uncertainty regarding accountability. • Intense power struggles may lead to increased levels of conflict. • Working relationships may be more complicated and human resources duplicated. • Excessive reliance on group processes and teamwork may impede timely decision making.

Exhibit 10.5 Functional, Divisional, and Matrix Organizational Structures: Advantages and Disadvantages

as a firm's product and/or market diversity becomes large, it is likely to benefit from a *worldwide matrix structure.*

Global strategies, on the other hand, are driven by economic pressures that require managers to view operations in different geographic areas to be managed for overall efficiency. The structures consistent with the efficiency perspective are the *worldwide functional* and *worldwide product division* structures. Here, division managers view the marketplace as homogeneous and devote relatively little attention to local market, political, and economic factors. The choice between these two types of structures is guided largely by the extent of product diversity. Firms with relatively low levels of product diversity may opt for a worldwide product division structure. However, if significant product–market diversity results from highly unrelated international acquisitions, a worldwide holding company structure should be implemented. Such firms have very little commonality among products, markets, or technologies, and have little need for integration.

Global Start-Ups: A New Phenomenon

Earlier, we suggested that international expansion occurs rather late for most corporations, typically after possibilities of domestic growth are exhausted. Increasingly, we are seeing two interrelated phenomena. First, many firms now expand internationally relatively early in their history. Second, some firms are "born global"—that is, from the very beginning, many start-ups are global in their activities. For example, Logitech Inc., the leading producer of the "mouse" that helps you use the personal computer, was global from day one. Founded in 1982 by a Swiss national and two Italians, the company was headquartered both in California and Switzerland. R&D and manufacturing were also conducted in both locations and, subsequently, in Taiwan and Ireland as well.[14]

The success of companies such as Logitech challenges the conventional wisdom that a company must first build up assets, internal processes, and experience before venturing into faraway lands. It also raises a number of questions: What exactly is a global start-up? Under what conditions should a company start out as a global start-up? What does it take to succeed as a global start-up?

A **global start-up** has been defined as a business organization that, from inception, seeks to derive significant competitive advantage from the use of resources and the sale of outputs in multiple countries. That is, right from the beginning, it uses inputs from around the world and sells its products and services to customers around the world. Geographical boundaries of nation-states are, by and large, irrelevant for a global start-up.

global start-up a business organization that, from inception, seeks to derive significant advantage from the use of resources and the sale of outputs in multiple countries.

There is no reason for every start-up to be global. Being global necessarily involves higher communication, coordination, and transportation costs. Therefore, it is important to identify the circumstances under which going global from the beginning is advantageous.[15] First, if the required human resources are globally dispersed, going global may be the best way to access those resources. For example, Italians are masters in fine leather and Europeans in ergonomics. Second, in many cases foreign financing may be easier to obtain and more suitable. Traditionally, U.S. venture capitalists have shown greater willingness to bear risk, but they have shorter time horizons in their expectations for return. If a U.S. start-up is looking for patient capital, it may be better off looking overseas. Third, the target customers in many specialized industries are located in other parts of the world. Fourth, in many industries a gradual move from domestic markets to foreign markets is no longer possible because, if a product is successful, foreign competitors may immediately imitate it. Therefore, preemptive entry into foreign markets may be the only option. Finally, because of high up-front development costs, a global market is often necessary to recover the costs. This is particularly true for start-ups from smaller nations that do not have access to large domestic markets.

Successful management of a global start-up presents many challenges. Communication and coordination across time zones and cultures are always problematic. Since most global start-ups have far less resources than well-established corporations, one key for success is to internalize few activities and outsource the rest. It is absolutely important that managers of such firms have considerable prior international experience so that they can

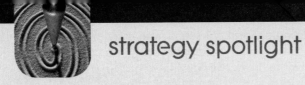
Israel: Home of Global Start-Ups

Israel may be a minor player in the world of international commerce, but surprisingly, the country has been the home base for a disproportionately large number of global start-ups. Blue chip venture capital firms and private equity firms from the United States funded as many as 111 start-ups in Israel in the fourth quarter of 2003.

Why is Israel home to so many global start-ups? First, being a small country of 6 million people, the home market is too small to support the growth of domestic companies. Second, the political uncertainties of the region encourage entrepreneurs to diversify their risk by establishing an international presence. Third, many younger generation Israelis have international networks of contacts either due to education or travel. More importantly, the country has an educated workforce with a work ethic second to none. No wonder, many international start-ups are blooming in this desert country! Here are three examples:

- Cash-U, founded by Gal Nachum and Amir Peleg, initially thought of developing games for cell phones but soon realized that it was difficult to come up with games that have universal appeal. Instead, they now supply a software platform that helps others develop games for cell phones. Once they created the product in their labs outside Tel Aviv,

they opened sales offices in London and Singapore. Today, their customers include firms such as Vodafone and Telefonica and their revenue growth is around 75 percent annually.

- Baradok Pridor, 38, and Yonatan Aumann, 42, founders of ClearForest, developed an innovative software product—a program that can analyze unstructured electronic data, such as a Web page or a video clip, as if it were already in a spreadsheet or database. Instead of waiting for customers to show up, right from the beginning, they started sending their engineers to make presentations to potential clients around the world. Today the company's customers include Dow Chemical, Thomson Financial, and the FBI itself! They have raised $33 million so far in three rounds of venture financing. Interestingly, the headquarters of the 83-person company is in Boston!

- HyperRoll, a company that makes software for analyzing massive databases, has raised $28 million in venture funding. Referring to their hiring practices, Yossi Matias, founder of HyperRoll, says, "We build the strongest team possible, unconstrained by locality, affinity, or culture. It requires every employee to accept and support a multicultural environment." Although essentially an Israeli start-up, he even banned the use of Hebrew in the office to facilitate greater integration between the American and Israeli employees!

Sources: Copeland, M. V. 2004. The start-up oasis. *Business 2.0*, August 46–48; and Brown, E. 2004. Global start-up. *Forbes*, November 29: 150–161.

successfully handle the inevitable communication problems and cultural conflicts. Another key for success is to keep the communication and coordination costs low. The only way to achieve this is by creating less costly administrative mechanisms. The boundaryless organizational designs that we discuss in the next section are particularly suitable for global start-ups because of their flexibility and low cost.

Strategy Spotlight 10.3 discusses two global start-ups that are based in Israel.

How an Organization's Structure Can Influence Strategy Formulation

Discussions of the relationship between strategy and structure usually strongly imply that structure follows strategy. That is, the strategy that a firm chooses (e.g., related diversification) dictates such structural elements as the division of tasks, the need for integration of activities, and authority relationships within the organization. However, an existing structure can influence strategy formulation. For example, once a firm's structure

How the Role of the Chief Diversity Officer (CDO) at Russell Athletic has Paid Off

Corporations have been adding "lighter" titles over the years such as Chief Yahoo, Chief Fun Office, and the like. In 1995, Denny's added a new "chief" title—Chief Diversity Officer. But this new title certainly wasn't done in an effort to inspire humor and lightheartedness. Rather, it was a direct result of their infamous class action discrimination lawsuit. In fact, Denny's Ray Hood-Phillips became the first Chief Diversify Officer in America. She claims, "I'm responsible for driving the cultural and structural change throughout the whole organization. And I take diversity and leverage it into a business advantage of the company."

In the corporate world, CDO's have been in vogue since Denny's initiative over 10 years ago. The more progressive companies are releasing CDOs from the confines of human resources and positioning them to work closely with the heads of product development, business development, marketing, and sales. *This change in reporting rela-*

tionships (a key component of organization structure) allows the CDO to more easily detect innovation opportunities throughout the organization. "Increasingly, CDOs report to the CEO, outside of HR," asserts Edie Fraser, founder and president of Diversity Best Practices, an organization that tracks diversity initiatives by corporations.

One company that has taken this approach is Russell Corporation, with $1.5 billion in revenues. The company (recently acquired by Berkshire Hathaway), founded in 1902, now has three business segments: apparel, sports equipment, and athletic shoes. At Russell, the human resources function handles the traditional diversity matters such as affirmative action, recruiting, and legal issues. However, CDO Kevin Clayton is busy turning a separate diversity department into a profit center. For example, Clayton's group discovered that a large number of Russell's employees had graduated from historically black colleges and universities. The group then used those graduates' ideas to create products for the black university market, resulting in an $8 million- to $10-million contract. Since then, Clayton has created several additional development groups that combine employees of different ethnicities and religions. Clayton is expecting to significantly increase revenues in the future.

Sources: Johansson, F. 2006. Masters of the multicultural. *Harvard Business Review,* 83(10): 18–19; Wells, J. 2003. Grandiose titles are proliferating in corporate boardrooms. www.msnbc.msn.com. August 12: np; and Young, N. 2006. Berkshire Hathaway to acquire Russell Corporation. *Press Release.* April 17.

is in place, it is very difficult and expensive to change.[16] Executives may not be able to modify their duties and responsibilities greatly, or may not welcome the disruption associated with a transfer to a new location. Further, there are costs associated with hiring, training, and replacing executive, managerial, and operating personnel. Thus, strategy cannot be formulated without considering structural elements.

The type of organizational structure can also strongly influence a firm's strategy, day-to-day operations, and performance.[17] We discussed Brinker International's move to a divisional structure in order to organize its restaurant groups into different units to focus on market niches. This new structure should enable the firm to adapt to change more rapidly and innovate more effectively with the various restaurant brands. Brinker's management did not feel that they were as effective with their previous functional organizational structure.

An organization's structure can also have an important influence on how it competes in the marketplace. Strategy Spotlight 10.4 discusses how a new role in many corporations, a Chief Diversity Officer (CDO), can promote diversity and spur innovation.

● Today's organizations need to be designed to draw on the strengths of a diversified workforce.

Linking Strategic Reward and Evaluation Systems to Business-Level and Corporate-Level Strategies

>LO6

Why there is no "one best way" to design strategic reward and evaluation systems, and the important contingent roles of business- and corporate-level strategies.

The effective use of reward and evaluation systems can play a critical role in motivating managers to conform to organizational strategies, achieve performance targets, and reduce the gap between organizational and individual goals. In contrast, reward systems, if improperly designed, can lead to behaviors that either are detrimental to organizational performance or can lower morale and cause employee dissatisfaction.

As we will see in this section, there is no "one best way" to design reward and evaluation systems. Instead, it is contingent on many factors. Two of the most important factors are a firm's business-level strategy (see Chapter 5) and its corporate-level strategy (see Chapter 6).

Business-Level Strategy: Reward and Evaluation Systems

In Chapter 5 we discussed two approaches that firms may take to secure competitive advantages: overall cost leadership and differentiation.[18] As we might expect, implementing these strategies requires fundamentally different organizational arrangements, approaches to control, and reward and incentive systems.

Overall Cost Leadership This strategy requires that product lines remain rather stable and that innovations deal mostly with production processes. Given the emphasis on efficiency, costly changes even in production processes tend to be rare. Since products are quite standardized and change rather infrequently, procedures can be developed to divide work into its basic components—those that are routine, standardized, and ideal for semi-skilled and unskilled employees. As such, firms competing on the basis of cost must implement tight cost controls, frequent and comprehensive reports to monitor the costs associated with outputs, and highly structured tasks and responsibilities. Incentives tend to be based on explicit financial targets since innovation and creativity are expensive and might tend to erode competitive advantages. Let's look at Nucor, a highly successful steel producer with $15 billion in revenues.

Nucor competes primarily on the basis of cost and, has a reward and incentive system that is largely based on financial outputs and financial measures.[19] Nucor uses four incentive compensation systems that correspond to the levels of management.

1. *Production incentive program.* Groups of 20 to 40 people are paid a weekly bonus based on either anticipated product time or tonnage produced. Each shift and production line is in a separate bonus group.
2. *Department managers.* Bonuses are based on divisional performance, primarily measured by return on assets.
3. *Employees not directly involved in production.* These include engineers, accountants, secretaries, receptionists, and others. Bonuses are based on two factors: divisional and corporate return on assets.
4. *Senior incentive programs.* Salaries are lower than comparable companies, but a significant portion of total compensation is based on return on stockholder equity. A portion of pretax earnings is placed in a pool and divided among officers as bonuses that are part cash and part stock.

The culture at Nucor reflects its reward and incentive system. Since incentive compensation can account for more than half of their paychecks, employees become nearly obsessed with productivity and apply a lot of pressure on each other. Ken Iverson, a former CEO, recalled an instance in which one employee arrived at work in sunglasses instead of safety glasses, preventing the team from doing any work. Furious, the other workers chased him around the plant with a piece of angle iron!

Differentiation This strategy typically involves the development of innovative products and services that require using experts who can identify the crucial elements of intricate, creative designs and marketing decisions. Highly trained professionals such as scientists and engineers are essential for devising, assessing, implementing and continually changing complex product designs. New product design also requires extensive collaboration and cooperation among specialists and functional managers from different areas within a firm. Such individuals must, for example, evaluate and implement a new design, constantly bearing in mind marketing, financial, production, and engineering considerations.

Given the need for cooperation and coordination among professionals in many functional areas, it becomes quite difficult to evaluate individuals using set quantitative criteria. It also is difficult to measure specific outcomes of such efforts and attribute outcomes to specific individuals. Thus, more behavioral measures (such as how effectively employees collaborate and share information) and intangible incentives and rewards become necessary to support a strong culture and to motivate employees. Consider 3M, a highly innovative company whose core value is innovation.

> At 3M, rewards are tied closely to risk-taking and innovation-oriented behavior. Managers are not penalized for product failures. Instead, those same people are encouraged to work on another project that borrows from their shared experience and insight. A culture of creativity and "thinking out of the box" is reinforced by their well-known "15 percent rule," which permits employees to set aside 15 percent of their work time to pursue personal research interests. And a familiar 3M homily, "Thou shall not kill new ideas for products," is known as the 11th commandment. It is the source of countless stories, including one that tells how L. D. DeSimone (3M's former CEO) tried five times (and failed) to kill the project that yielded the 3M blockbuster product, Thinsulate.[20]

Corporate-Level Strategy: Strategic Reward and Evaluation Systems

In Chapter 6 we discussed two broad types of diversification strategies: related and unrelated. The type of diversification strategy that a firm follows has important implications for the type of reward and evaluation systems that it should use.

Sharp Corporation, a $25 billion Japanese consumer electronics giant follows a strategy of *related* diversification.[21] Its most successful technology has been liquid crystal displays (LCDs) that are critical components in nearly all of the firm's products. With their expertise in this area, they are moving into high-end displays for cellular telephones, hand-held computers, and digital computers.[22]

Given the need to leverage such technologies across multiple product lines, Sharp needs reward and evaluation systems that foster coordination and sharing. It must focus more on individuals' behavior rather than on short-term financial outcomes. For example, promotion is a powerful incentive, and it is generally based on seniority and subtle skills exhibited over time, such as teamwork and communication. It helps to ensure that the company's reward system will not reward short-term self-interested orientations.

Like many Japanese companies, Sharp's culture reinforces the view that the firm is a family or community whose members should cooperate for the greater good. In accordance with the policy of lifetime employment, turnover is low. This encourages employees to pursue what is best for the entire company. Such an outlook lessens the inevitable conflict over sharing important resources such as R&D knowledge.

In contrast to Sharp, firms such as Hanson PLC (a British conglomerate) followed a strategy of unrelated diversification for most of its history. At one time it owned as many as 150 operating companies in areas such as tobacco, footwear, building products, brewing, and food. There were limited product similarities across businesses and therefore little need for sharing of resources and knowledge across divisional boundaries. James Hanson and Gordon White, founders of the company, actually did not permit any sharing of resources between operating companies even if it was feasible!

Their reward and evaluation system placed such heavy emphasis on individual accountability that they viewed resource sharing, with its potential for mutual blaming, unacceptable. The operating managers had more than 60 percent of their compensation tied to annual financial performance of their subsidiaries. All decision making was decentralized so that subsidiary managers could be held responsible for the return on capital they employed. However, there was one area in which they had to obtain approval from the corporate office. No subsidiary manager was allowed to incur a capital expenditure greater than $3,000 without permission from the corporate office. Hanson managed to be successful with a very small corporate office because of its decentralized structure, tight financial controls, and an incentive system that motivated managers to meet financial goals. Gordon White was proud of claiming that he had never visited any of the operating companies that were part of the Hanson empire.[23]

To summarize, the key issue becomes the need for *in*dependence versus *inter*dependence. With cost leadership strategies and unrelated diversification, there tends to be less need for interdependence. Thus, the reward and evaluation systems focus more on the use of financial indicators because unit costs, profits, and revenues can be rather easily attributed to a given business unit or division.

In contrast, firms that follow differentiation or related diversification strategies have intense needs for tight interdependencies among the functional areas and business units. Here, sharing of resources, including raw materials, R&D knowledge, marketing information, and so on, is critical to organizational success. That is, it is more important to achieve synergies with value-creating activities and business units than with cost leadership or unrelated strategies. To facilitate sharing and collaboration, reward and evaluation systems tend to incorporate more behavioral indicators. Exhibit 10.6 summarizes our discussion of the relationship between strategies and control systems.

We must apply an important caveat. Although Exhibit 10.6 suggests guidelines on how an organization should match its strategies to its evaluation and reward systems, all organizations must have combinations of both financial and behavioral rewards. Both overall cost leadership and unrelated diversification strategies require a need for collaboration and the sharing of best practices across both value-creating activities and business units. General Electric, for example, has developed many integrating mechanisms to enhance sharing "best practices" across what would appear to be rather unrelated businesses such as jet engines, appliances, and network television. And, for both differentiation and related diversification strategies, financial indicators such as revenue growth and profitability should not be overlooked at both the business-unit and corporate levels.

Exhibit 10.6

Summary of Relationships between Reward and Evaluation Systems and Business-Level and Corporate-Level Strategies

Level of Strategy	Types of Strategy	Need for Interdependence	Primary Type of Reward and Evaluation System
Business-level	Overall cost leadership	Low	Financial
Business-level	Differentiation	High	Behavioral
Corporate-level	Related diversification	High	Behavioral
Corporate-level	Unrelated diversification	Low	Financial

strategy spotlight

10.5

Boundary Types

There are primarily four types of boundaries that place limits on organizations. In today's dynamic business environment, different types of boundaries are needed to foster high degrees of interaction with outside influences and varying levels of permeability.

1. *Vertical boundaries between levels in the organization's hierarchy.* SmithKline Beecham asks employees at different hierarchical levels to brainstorm ideas for managing clinical trial data. The ideas are incorporated into action plans that significantly cut the new product approval time of its breakthrough pharmaceuticals. This would not have been possible if the barriers between levels of individuals in the organization had been too high.

2. *Horizontal boundaries between functional areas.* Fidelity Investments makes the functional barriers more porous and flexible among divisions, such as marketing, operations, and customer service, in order to offer customers a more integrated experience when conducting business with the company. Customers can take their questions to one person, reducing the chance that customers will "get the runaround" from employees who feel customer service is not their responsibility. At Fidelity, customer service is everyone's business, regardless of functional area.

3. *External boundaries between the firm and its customers, suppliers, and regulators.* GE Lighting, by working closely with retailers, functions throughout the value chain as a single operation. This allows GE to track point-of-sale purchases, giving it better control over inventory management.

4. *Geographic boundaries between locations, cultures, and markets.* The global nature of today's business environment spurred PricewaterhouseCoopers to use a global groupware system. This allows the company to instantly connect to its 26 worldwide offices.

Source: Ashkenas, R. 1997. The organization's new clothes. In Hesselbein, F., Goldsmith, M., and Beckhard, R. (Eds.). *The organization of the future:* 104–106. San Francisco: Jossey Bass.

Boundaryless Organizational Designs

The term *boundaryless* may bring to mind a chaotic organizational reality in which "anything goes." This is not the case. As Jack Welch, GE's former CEO, has suggested, boundaryless does not imply that all internal and external boundaries vanish completely. Although boundaries may continue to exist in some form, they become more open and permeable.[24] Strategy Spotlight 10.5 discusses four types of boundaries and provides examples of how organizations have made them more permeable.

We are not suggesting that **boundaryless organizational designs** replace the traditional forms of organizational structure, but rather that they should complement them. For example, Sharp Corp. has implemented a functional structure to attain economies of scale with its applied research and manufacturing skills. However, to bring about this key objective, Sharp has relied on several integrating mechanisms and processes:

> To prevent functional groups from becoming vertical chimneys that obstruct product development, Sharp's product managers have responsibility—but not authority—for coordinating the entire set of value-chain activities. And the company convenes enormous numbers of cross-unit and corporate committees to ensure that shared activities, including the corporate R&D unit and sales forces, are optimally configured and allocated among the different product lines. Sharp invests in such time-intensive coordination to minimize the inevitable conflicts that arise when units share important activities.[25]

We will discuss three approaches to making boundaries more permeable. These approaches help to facilitate the widespread sharing of knowledge and information across both the internal and external boundaries of the organization. We'll begin with the *barrier-free*

>LO7
The different types of boundaryless organizations— barrier-free, modular, and virtual—and their relative advantages and disadvantages.

boundaryless organizational designs organizations in which the boundaries, including vertical, horizontal, external, and geographic boundaries, are permeable.

type, which involves making all organizational boundaries—internal and external—more permeable. We'll place particular emphasis on team concepts, because teams as a central building block for implementing the boundaryless organization. In the next two sections, we will address the *modular* and *virtual* types of organizations. These forms focus on the need to create seamless relationships with external organizations such as customers or suppliers. While the modular type emphasizes the outsourcing of noncore activities, the virtual (or network) organization focuses on alliances among independent entities formed to exploit specific market opportunities.

The Barrier-Free Organization

The "boundary" mind-set is ingrained deeply into bureaucracies. It is evidenced by such clichés as "That's not my job," "I'm here from corporate to help," or endless battles over transfer pricing. In the traditional company, boundaries are clearly delineated in the design of an organization's structure. Their basic advantage is that the roles of managers and employees are simple, clear, well-defined, and long-lived. A major shortcoming was pointed out to the authors during an interview with a high-tech executive: "Structure tends to be divisive; it leads to territorial fights."

Today such structures are being replaced by fluid, ambiguous, and deliberately ill-defined tasks and roles. Just because work roles are no longer clearly defined, however, does not mean that differences in skills, authority, and talent disappear.

A **barrier-free organization** enables a firm to bridge real differences in culture, function, and goals to find common ground that facilitates information sharing and other forms of cooperative behavior. Eliminating the multiple boundaries that stifle productivity and innovation can enhance the potential of the entire organization.

Strategy Spotlight 10.6 describes how United Technologies Corporation used the boundaryless concept to develop a revolutionary product, PureCycle.

Creating Permeable Internal Boundaries For barrier-free organizations to work effectively, the level of trust and shared interests among all parts of the organization must be raised. Similarly, the organization needs to develop among its employees the skill level needed to work in a more democratic organization. Barrier-free organizations also require a shift in the organization's philosophy from executive development to organizational development, and from investments in high-potential individuals to investments in leveraging the talents of all individuals.

Teams can be an important aspect of barrier-free structures.[26] Jeffrey Pfeffer, author of several insightful books, including *The Human Equation,* suggests that teams have three primary advantages.[27] First, teams substitute peer-based control for hierarchical control of work activities. In essence, employees control themselves, reducing the time and energy management needs to devote to control.

Second, teams frequently develop more creative solutions to problems because they encourage the sharing of the tacit knowledge held by individuals.[28] Brainstorming, or group problem solving, involves the pooling of ideas and expertise to enhance the chances that at least one group member will think of a way to solve the problems at hand.

Third, by substituting peer control for hierarchical control, teams permit the removal of layers of hierarchy and absorption of administrative tasks previously performed by specialists. This avoids the costs of having people whose sole job is to watch the people who watch other people do the work. As Norman Augustine humorously pointed out in *Augustine's Laws,* "If a sufficient number of management layers are superimposed on top of each other, it can be assured that disaster is not left to chance!"[29]

Effective barrier-free organizations must go beyond achieving close integration and coordination within divisions in a corporation. Research on multidivisional organizations

barrier-free organization an organizational design in which firms bridge real differences in culture, function, and goals to find common ground that facilitates information sharing and other forms of cooperative behavior.

strategy spotlight

United Technologies Corporation's PureCycle: An Effective Use of the Boundaryless Concept

United Technologies Corporation is a giant manufacturing conglomerate that has been on a roll. Revenues and profits for 2006 were $48 billion and $3.7 billion, respectively, which represents an annual increase of over 15 percent over the most recent four-year period.

Like many diversified firms, UTC faced a challenge in developing synergies across business units. UTC's wide variety of products include Carrier heating and air conditioning, Hamilton Sundstrand aerospace systems and industrial products, Otis elevators and escalators, Pratt & Whitney aircraft engines, Sikorsky helicopters, UTC Fire & Security systems, and UTC Power fuel cells. Overall, UTC spends a huge amount of money on research—about 3.5 percent of total revenues.

Historically, UTC's culture placed a high value on decentralized decision making, with each unit operating almost entirely independently of the others. Such an approach may have motivational benefits and helps each unit focus their efforts. However, it leads to "silo business units" and prevents the corporation from generating innovations in the white spaces between business units.

This approach to business troubled UTC senior vice president John Cassidy and Carl Nett, director of the firm's corporate research center, UTRC. The center is staffed with nearly 500 scientists, engineers, and staff who are charged with "bringing future technologies to the point of product insertion." They both believed that

Sources: www.utc.com; 2005 *UTC Annual Report;* Davidson, A. 2007. Conglomerates: United Technologies. *Forbes,* January 8: 96; and Cross, R., Liedtka, J., & Weiss, L. 2005. A practical guide to social networks. *Harvard Business Review,* 83(3): 92–101.

tremendous potential for growth existed in the junctures between the business units. However, such collaboration was not consistent with the history, work practices, and cultural norms at UTC. In fact, Cassidy felt that integrating expertise and talent across business units was an "unnatural act."

What did they do? In 2002, the two executives invited top technical talent from each unit to several brainstorming sessions. The goal was to bring together a diverse set of talented professionals to create and service new markets.

Early on, a potential winner emerged from the intersection of cooling, heating, and power. Engineers from Carrier, Pratt & Whitney, and UTRC recognized that using cooling and heating equipment could transform an innovative power generation concept into a revolutionary product. Called PureCycle, the product contained virtually no new components. However, it offered a breakthrough value proposition: Customers could convert waste heat to electricity at rates substantially below those of utilities. The product held great promise because U.S. industrial plants emit roughly as much waste heat as a 50-gigawatt power plant generates (enough to run most major U.S. cities).

In retrospect, engineers involved in the PureCycle project find it hard to believe that nobody had previously thought of the idea. Thierry Jomard, a former Carrier engineer who transferred to UTRC to head the effort explains, "Carrier people are trained to think in terms of using heat exchange to produce cold air—that's the output that counts: the compressor is just there to move the fluid. Pratt & Whitney engineers, on the other hand, are power people. The outcome they are about is power, and they use turbines to get it." It wasn't until they began their collaboration that anyone recognized the opportunities before them.

has stressed the importance of interdivisional coordination and resource sharing.[30] This requires interdivisional task forces and committees, reward and incentive systems that emphasize interdivisional cooperation, and common training programs.

Given the importance of collaboration and collective efforts, effective teams become critical. Frank Carruba (former head of Hewlett-Packard's labs) provides some interesting insights.[31] He found that the difference between mediocre teams and good teams was generally varying levels of motivation and talent. But what explained the difference between good teams and truly superior teams? Carruba found that the key difference—and this explained a 40 percent overall difference in performance—was the way members treated each other; that is, the degree to which they believed in one another and created an atmosphere of encouragement rather than competition. In other words, vision, talent, and motivation could carry a team only so far. What clearly stood out in the "super" teams were higher levels of authenticity and caring, which allowed the full synergy of their individual talents, motivation, and vision.

Developing Effective Relationships with External Constituencies

In barrier-free organizations, managers must also create flexible, porous organizational boundaries and establish communication flows and mutually beneficial relationships with internal (e.g., employees) and external (e.g., customers) constituencies. Michael Dell, founder and CEO of Dell Computer, is a strong believer in fostering close relationships with his customers. In an interview, he explained:

> We're not going to be just your PC vendor anymore. We're going to be your IT department for PCs. Boeing, for example, has 100,000 Dell PCs, and we have 30 people that live at Boeing, and if you look at the things we're doing for them or for other customers, we don't look like a supplier, we look more like Boeing's PC department. We become intimately involved in planning their PC needs and the configuration of their network.
>
> It's not that we make these decisions by ourselves. They're certainly using their own people to get the best answer for the company. But the people working on PCs together, from both Dell and Boeing, understand the needs in a very intimate way. They're right there living it and breathing it, as opposed to the typical vendor who says, "Here are your computers. See you later."[32]

Thus far, we have argued that barrier-free organizations create successful relationships between both internal and external constituencies. However, there is one additional constituency—competitors—with whom some organizations have benefited as they developed cooperative relationships.

For example, after years of seeing its empty trucks return from warehouses back to production facilities after deliveries, General Mills teamed up with 16 of its competitors. They formed an e-commerce business to help the firms to find carriers with empty cargo trailers to piggyback freight loads to distributors near the production facilities.[33] This increases revenue for all network members and reduces fuel costs.

Risks, Challenges, and Potential Downsides

Despite its potential benefits, many firms find that creating and managing a barrier-free organization can be frustrating.[34] For example, Puritan-Bennett Corporation, a Lenexa, Kansas, manufacturer of respiratory equipment, found that its product development time more than doubled after it adopted team management. Roger J. Dolida, director of R&D, attributed this failure to a lack of top management commitment, high turnover among team members, and infrequent meetings. Often, managers trained in rigid hierarchies find it difficult to make the transition to the more democratic, participative style that teamwork requires.

Christopher Barnes, now a consultant with PricewaterhouseCoopers in Atlanta, previously worked as an industrial engineer for Challenger Electrical Distribution (a subsidiary of Westinghouse, now part of CBS) at a plant in Jackson, Mississippi, which produced circuit-breaker boxes. His assignment was to lead a team of workers from the plant's troubled final-assembly operation with the mission: "Make things better." Not surprisingly, that vague notion set the team up for failure.

After a year of futility, the team was disbanded. In retrospect, Barnes identified several reasons for the debacle: (1) limited personal credibility—he was viewed as an "outsider"; (2) a lack of commitment to the team—everyone involved was forced to be on the team; (3) poor communications—nobody was told why the team was important; (4) limited autonomy—line managers refused to give up control over team members; and (5) misaligned incentives—the culture rewarded individual performance over team performance. Barnes's experience has implications for all types of teams, whether they are composed of

Exhibit 10.7

Pros and Cons of
Barrier-Free Structures

Pros	Cons
• Leverages the talents of all employees. • Enhances cooperation, coordination, and information sharing among functions, divisions, SBUs, and external constituencies. • Enables a quicker response to market changes through a single-goal focus. • Can lead to coordinated win–win initiatives with key suppliers, customers, and alliance partners.	• Difficult to overcome political and authority boundaries inside and outside the organization. • Lacks strong leadership and common vision, which can lead to coordination problems. • Time-consuming and difficult-to-manage democratic processes. • Lacks high levels of trust, which can impede performance.

managerial, professional, clerical, or production personnel.[35] The pros and cons of barrier-free structures are summarized in Exhibit 10.7.

The Modular Organization

As Charles Handy, author of *The Age of Unreason,* has noted:

> Organizations have realized that, while it may be convenient to have everyone around all the time, having all of your workforce's time at your command is an extravagant way of marshaling the necessary resources. It is cheaper to keep them outside the organization, employed by themselves or by specialist contractors, and to buy their services when you need them.[36]

Consistent with Handy's vision, the **modular organization** outsources nonvital functions, tapping into the knowledge and expertise of "best in class" suppliers, but retains strategic control. Outsiders may be used to manufacture parts, handle logistics, or perform accounting activities. As we discussed in Chapters 3 and 5, the value chain can be used to identify the key primary and support activities performed by a firm to create value. The key question becomes: Which activities do we keep "in-house" and which activities do we outsource to suppliers?[37] The organization becomes a central hub surrounded by networks of outside suppliers and specialists and, much like Lego blocks, parts can be added or taken away. Both manufacturing and service units may be modular.[38]

modular organization an organization in which nonvital functions are outsourced, which uses the knowledge and expertise of outside suppliers while retaining strategic control.

Apparel is an industry in which the modular type has been widely adopted. Nike and Reebok, for example, concentrate on their strengths: designing and marketing high-tech, fashionable footwear. Nike has few production facilities and Reebok owns no plants. These two companies contract virtually all their footwear production to suppliers in China, Vietnam, and other countries with low-cost labor. Avoiding large investments in fixed assets helps them derive large profits on minor sales increases. Thus, Nike and Reebok can keep pace with changing tastes in the marketplace because their suppliers have become expert at rapidly retooling to produce new products.

● Adidas is one of many athletic shoe companies that has outsourced most of its production to low-cost labor countries such as China and Vietnam.

In a modular company, outsourcing the noncore functions offers three advantages.

1. A firm can decrease overall costs, stimulate new product development by hiring suppliers whose talent may be superior to that of in-house personnel, avoid idle capacity, reduce inventories, and avoid being locked into a particular technology.
2. Outsourcing enables a company to focus scarce resources on the areas where it holds a competitive advantage. These benefits can translate into more funding for research and development, hiring the best engineers, and providing continuous training for sales and service staff.
3. By enabling an organization to tap into the knowledge and expertise of its specialized supply-chain partners, it adds critical skills and accelerates organizational learning.[39]

The modular type enables a company to leverage relatively small amounts of capital and a small management team to achieve seemingly unattainable strategic objectives.[40] Freed from the need to make big investments in fixed assets, the modular company can grow rapidly. Certain preconditions are necessary before the modular approach can be successful. First, the company must work closely with suppliers to ensure that the interests of each party are being fulfilled. Companies need to find loyal, reliable vendors who can be trusted with trade secrets. They also need assurances that suppliers will dedicate their financial, physical, and human resources to satisfy strategic objectives such as lowering costs or being first to market.

Second, the modular company must be sure that it selects the proper competencies to keep in-house. For Nike and Reebok, the core competencies are design and marketing, not shoe manufacturing; for Honda, the core competence is engine technology. These firms are unlikely to outsource any activity that involves their core competence. An organization must avoid outsourcing components that may compromise its long-term competitive advantages.

Strategic Risks of Outsourcing   While adopting the modular form clearly has some advantages, managers must also weigh associated risks. The main strategic concerns are (1) loss of critical skills or developing the wrong skills, (2) loss of cross-functional skills, and (3) loss of control over a supplier.[41]

Too much outsourcing can result in a firm "giving away" too much skill and control. Outsourcing relieves companies of the requirement to maintain skill levels needed to manufacture essential components. Over time, these skills that were once part of the knowledge base of the company disappear. At one time, semiconductor chips seemed like a simple technology to outsource. But now, they have become a critical component of a wide variety of products. Companies that have outsourced the manufacture of these chips run the risk of losing the ability to manufacture them as the technology escalates. Thus, they become more dependent upon their suppliers.

Cross-functional skills refer to the skills acquired through the interaction of individuals in various departments within a company. Often, such interaction assists a department in solving problems as employees interface with others across functional units. However, if a firm outsources key functional responsibilities, such as manufacturing, communication across departments can become more difficult. This is because a firm and its employees must now integrate their activities with a new, outside supplier. This typically brings about new challenges in the coordination of joint efforts.

Another drawback occurs when the outsourced products give suppliers too much power over the manufacturer. This happens when the manufacturer is dependent on a single supplier, or just a few suppliers, for critical components. Suppliers that are key to a manufacturer's success can, in essence, hold the manufacturer "hostage." Nike manages this potential problem by sending full-time "product expatriates" to work at the plants of its suppliers. Also, Nike often brings top members of supplier management and technical teams to its headquarters. This way, Nike keeps close tabs on the pulse of new developments, builds rapport and trust with suppliers, and develops long-term relationships with suppliers to prevent hostage situations.

Outsourcing for Talent: How Sony Develops Video Games

The convergence of Hollywood and Silicon Valley has led to the explosive growth of the worldwide video game industry, with revenues of $24.5 billion in 2004. Recently, it has overtaken the movie industry's box office receipts. The industry's sales are expected to soar to $55 billion by 2008, according to PricewaterhouseCoopers.

While broadcast TV audiences dwindle and moviegoing stagnates, gaming is emerging as the newest and perhaps strongest pillar in the media world. So it's no surprise that film studios, media giants, gamemakers, and Japanese electronics companies are all battling to win the "Games Wars." "This is a huge shift we're seeing, and nobody wants to be left behind," says Sony Entertainment Chairman, Michael Lynton.

In this sprawling market where controlling a broad portfolio of businesses is crucial, nobody is better positioned than Sony. Unlike other rivals, it has already assembled all of the pieces of a true video game empire. It sells hardware with its PlayStation consoles, and it has developed its handheld PlayStation Portable product. It also develops games such as the popular *Gran Turismo* racing and *EverQuest* online. And it owns Sony Pictures and MGM movie studios, whose Spider-Man and James Bond franchises have been mega hit games for Activision

and EA. This combination has enabled Sony to sell 80 million Play Station 2 (PS2) consoles worldwide.

The real payoff for Sony comes in game software sales. While Sony and other console makers sell their hardware for a loss, they typically make $5 to $10 in royalties for every game sold on their platform. PS2 has more than 2,000 software titles, with more than 775 million total game copies sold.

Central to Sony's strategy is how it has used outside developers to produce most of its games. It has even reached out to gamers themselves. "We didn't want outside developers to be peripheral to our business model," says Andrew House, an early PlayStation team member and executive vice president of Sony Computer Entertainment America. "We knew that the widest variety of content possible was the best way to build the largest consumer base possible."

Sony has searched high and low for talent. In 1997, it launched a developer kit aimed at hobbyists. "We sent it to budding college developers who wanted to try their hands," House says. Ideas from those amateurs made their way into commercial games in Japan. Meanwhile, externally developed titles like *Final Fantasy* and *Madden NFL Football* helped put Sony's second generation console, the PS2, at the top of the heap in 2001. Sony also launched a Linux developer kit for just $199 in 2002. "It's our way of feeding the market for the future. Some of the first great games were developed by people at home in their garages," say House. "If we're not getting people involved and looking for opportunities very early on, we really are missing out."

Sources: House, A. 2004. Sony. *Fast Company*, April: 65; and Grover, R. Edwards, C., Rowley, I., & Moon, I. 2005. Game wars. *BusinessWeek*, February 28: 35–40.

Strategy Spotlight 10.7 discusses how Sony outsources for talent to develop games for its highly successful video game business. Exhibit 10.8 summarizes the pros and cons of modular structures.[42]

The Virtual Organization

In contrast to the "self-reliant" thinking that guided traditional organizational designs, the strategic challenge today has become doing more with less and looking outside the firm for opportunities and solutions to problems. The virtual organization provides a new means of leveraging resources and exploiting opportunities.[43]

The **virtual organization** can be viewed as a continually evolving network of independent companies—suppliers, customers, even competitors—linked together to share skills, costs, and access to one another's markets.[44] The members of a virtual organization, by pooling and sharing the knowledge and expertise of each of the component organizations, simultaneously "know" more and can "do" more than any one member of the group could do alone. By working closely together, each gains in the long run from individual and organizational learning.[45] The term *virtual*, meaning "being in effect but not actually so," is commonly used in the computer industry. A computer's ability to appear to have

virtual organization
a continually evolving network of independent companies that are linked together to share skills, costs, and access to one another's markets.

Exhibit 10.8

Pros and Cons of Modular Structures

Pros	Cons
• Directs a firm's managerial and technical talent to the most critical activities.	• Inhibits common vision through reliance on outsiders.
• Maintains full strategic control over most critical activities—core competencies.	• Diminishes future competitive advantages if critical technologies or other competences are outsourced.
• Achieves "best in class" performance at each link in the value chain.	• Increases the difficulty of bringing back into the firm activities that now add value due to market shifts.
• Leverages core competencies by outsourcing with smaller capital commitment.	• Leads to an erosion of cross-functional skills.
• Encourages information sharing and accelerates organizational learning.	• Decreases operational control and potential loss of control over a supplier.

more storage capacity than it really possesses is called virtual memory. Similarly, by assembling resources from a variety of entities, a virtual organization may seem to have more capabilities than it really possesses.[46]

The virtual organization is a grouping of units from different organizations that have joined in an alliance to exploit complementary skills in pursuing common strategic objectives. A case in point is Lockheed Martin's use of specialized coalitions between and among three entities—the company, academia, and government—to enhance competitiveness. According to former CEO Norman Augustine:

> The underlying beauty of this approach is that it forces us to reach outward. No matter what your size, you have to look broadly for new ideas, new approaches, new products. Lockheed Martin used this approach in a surprising manner when it set out during the height of the Cold War to make stealth aircraft and missiles. The technical idea came from research done at the Institute of Radio Engineering in Moscow in the 1960s that was published, and publicized, quite openly in the academic media.
>
> Despite the great contrasts among government, academia and private business, we have found ways to work together that have produced very positive results, not the least of which is our ability to compete on a global scale.[47]

Virtual organizations need not be permanent and participating firms may be involved in multiple alliances. Virtual organizations may involve different firms performing complementary value activities, or different firms involved jointly in the same value activities, such as production, R&D, and distribution. The percentage of activities that are jointly performed with partners may vary significantly from alliance to alliance.[48]

How does the virtual type of structure differ from the modular type? Unlike the modular type, in which the focal firm maintains full strategic control, the virtual organization is characterized by participating firms that give up part of their control and accept interdependent destinies. Participating firms pursue a collective strategy that enables them to cope with uncertainty through cooperative efforts. The benefit is that, just as virtual memory increases storage capacity, the virtual organizations enhance the capacity or competitive advantage of participating firms. Strategy Spotlight 10.8 addresses the variety of collaborative relationships in the biotechnology industry.

Each company (as Strategy Spotlight 10.8 illustrates) that links up with others to create a virtual organization contributes only what it considers its core competencies. It will mix and match what it does best with the best of other firms by identifying its critical capabilities and the necessary links to other capabilities.[49]

Collaborative Relationships in Biotechnology

Collaboration in biotechnology has benefited a variety of firms. Amgen collaborates with a number of smaller firms including ARRIS, Environgen, Glycomex, and Interneuron, among others. The companies work on joint marketing projects and bring R&D scientists together to explore opportunities for new pharmaceutical product development. In exchange for the expertise of the scientists and marketers at the smaller companies, Amgen provides financial

Source: Powell, W. W. 1998. Learning from collaboration: Knowledge and networks in the biotechnology and pharmaceutical industries. *California Management Review*, 40 (3): 228–240; Williams, E., & Langreth, R. 2001. "A biotech wonder grows up. *Forbes*, September 3: 118.

clout and technical assistance when new-product opportunities are identified.

Another biotech company that utilizes collaborative relationships with competitors is Biogen. This large pharmaceutical firm once outsourced clinical testing of its new drugs. But now, the company brings experts from other firms to Biogen laboratories to work with their scientists.

Chiron, one of the largest pharmaceutical firms, with over 7,500 employees, makes extensive use of collaborative efforts with its competitors. The company currently collaborates with over 1,400 companies, tapping into the knowledge base of R&D experts with a wide variety of skill and expertise in the field. Chiron considers this network one of its core competencies.

Challenges and Risks   Despite their many advantages, such alliances often fail to meet expectations. For example, the alliance between IBM and Microsoft soured in early 1991 when Microsoft began shipping Windows in direct competition to OS/2, which they jointly developed. The runaway success of Windows frustrated IBM's ability to set an industry standard. In retaliation, IBM entered into an alliance with Microsoft's archrival, Novell, to develop network software to compete with Microsoft's LAN Manager.

The virtual organization demands a unique set of managerial skills. Managers must build relationships with other companies, negotiate win–win deals for all parties involved, find the right partners with compatible goals and values, and provide the right balance of freedom and control. In addition, information systems must be designed and integrated to facilitate communication with current and potential partners.

Managers must be clear about the strategic objectives while forming alliances. Some objectives are time bound, and those alliances need to be dissolved once the objective is fulfilled. Some alliances may have relatively long-term objectives and will need to be clearly monitored and nurtured to produce mutual commitment and avoid bitter fights for control. The highly dynamic personal computer industry, for example, is characterized by multiple temporary alliances among hardware, operating systems, and software producers.[50] But alliances in the more stable automobile industry, such as those involving Nissan and Volkswagen as well as Mazda and Ford, have long-term objectives and tend to be relatively stable.

The virtual organization is a logical culmination of joint-venture strategies of the past. Shared risks, shared costs, and shared rewards are the facts of life in a virtual organization.[51] When virtual organizations are formed, they involve tremendous challenges for strategic planning. As with the modular corporation, it is essential to identify core competencies. However, for virtual structures to be successful, a strategic plan is also needed to determine the effectiveness of combining core competencies.

The strategic plan must address the diminished operational control and overwhelming need for trust and common vision among the partners. This new structure may be appropriate for firms whose strategies require merging technologies (e.g., computing and communication) or for firms exploiting shrinking product life cycles that require simultaneous entry into multiple geographical markets. Further, it may be effective for firms that desire to be quick to the

Exhibit 10.9

**Pros and Cons of
Virtual Structures**

Pros	Cons
• Enables the sharing of costs and skills.	• Harder to determine where one company ends and another begins, due to close interdependencies among players.
• Enhances access to global markets.	
• Increases market responsiveness.	• Leads to potential loss of operational control among partners.
• Creates a "best of everything" organization since each partner brings core competencies to the alliance.	• Results in loss of strategic control over emerging technology.
• Encourages both individual and organizational knowledge sharing and accelerates organizational learning.	• Requires new and difficult-to-acquire managerial skills.

Source: Miles, R. E., & Snow, C. C. 1986. Organizations: New concepts for new forms. *California Management Review,* Spring: 62–73; Miles & Snow. 1999. Causes of failure in network organizations. *California Management Review,* Summer: 53–72; and Bahrami, H. 1991. The emerging flexible organization: Perspectives from Silicon Valley. *California Management Review,* Summer: 33–52.

market with a new product or service. For example, the recent profusion of alliances among airlines was primarily motivated by the need to provide seamless travel demanded by the full-fare paying business traveler. Exhibit 10.9 summarizes the advantages and disadvantages of the virtual form.

Boundaryless Organizations: Making Them Work

Designing an organization that simultaneously supports the requirements of an organization's strategy, is consistent with the demands of the environment, and can be effectively implemented by the people around the manager is a tall order for any manager.[52] The most effective solution is usually a combination of organizational types. That is, a firm may outsource many parts of its value chain to reduce costs and increase quality, engage simultaneously in multiple alliances to take advantage of technological developments or penetrate new markets, and break down barriers within the organization to enhance flexibility. In Strategy Spotlight 10.9, we see how an innovative firm, Technical Computer Graphics, combines both barrier-free and virtual organizational forms.

When an organization faces external pressures, resource scarcity, and declining performance, it tends to become more internally focused, rather than directing its efforts toward managing and enhancing relationships with existing and potential external stakeholders. We believe that this may be the most opportune time for managers to carefully analyze their value-chain activities and evaluate the potential for adopting elements of modular, virtual, and barrier-free organizational types.

Regardless of the form of organization ultimately chosen, achieving the coordination and integration necessary to maximize the potential of an organization's human capital involves much more than just creating a new structure. Techniques and processes to ensure the coordination and integration of an organization's key value-chain activities are critical. Teams are key building blocks of the new organizational forms, and teamwork requires new and flexible approaches to coordination and integration.

Managers trained in rigid hierarchies may find it difficult to make the transition to the more democratic, participative style that teamwork requires. As Douglas K. Smith, co-author of *The Wisdom of Teams,* pointed out, "A completely diverse group must agree on a goal, put the notion of individual accountability aside and figure out how to work with each other. Most of all, they must learn that if the team fails, it's everyone's fault."[53] Within the framework of an appropriate organizational design, managers must select a mix and

Technical Computer Graphics' Boundaryless Organization

The Technical Computer Graphics (TCG) group manufactures items such as handheld bar code readers and scanning software. The company uses 13 "alliances," or small project teams, employing a total of 200 employees. Each team is responsible for either specific customers or specific products. Alliance teams share a common infrastructure, but they can develop new business opportunities without approval from upper management. Projects often emerge from listening to what customers need.

TCG uses a "triangulation approach"—alliances that include customers, suppliers, and other alliances. Suppliers and customers who provide funding are involved at the outset of the project. The alliances recognize that attaining the initial customer funding is crucial; it stimulates them to focus on what customers have to say. With an emphasis on speed, new products come to market quickly, providing the firm and its partners with tangible benefits. Sometimes another alliance acts as either the customer or the supplier and provides funding.

While each alliance is independent, it shares financial concern for other alliance teams. When a new business opportunity is discovered, an alliance draws on technical expertise from the other alliances. The purpose is not only to acquire additional knowledge, but also to share accumulated learning. There's no benefit to hoarding information: Learning gained from one software project might prove especially valuable to one under way in another alliance. This technological diffusion of information produces products that quickly reach the market.

TCG's formal structure is designed to ensure that such knowledge diffusion occurs. The company's culture is structured to encourage this as well. The TCG culture attracts both the entrepreneur and the team-oriented person at the same time. Working with multiple stakeholders through TCG's triangulation model forces employees to listen to the customers and respond quickly. Because the customer matters more than the functional title, teams lend expertise to each other in return for sharing the gains realized from supplying value to the customer.

Source: Snow, C. 1997. Twenty-first century organizations: Implications for a new marketing paradigm. *Journal of the Academy of Marketing Science,* Winter: 72–74; Allred, B. Snow, C. & Miles, R. 1996. Characteristics of managerial careers of the 21st century. *Academy of Management Executive,* November: 17–27; Herzog, V. L. 2001. Trust building on corporate collaborative teams. *Project Management Journal,* March: 28–41.

balance of tools and techniques to facilitate the effective coordination and integration of key activities. Some of the factors that must be considered include:

- Common culture and shared values.
- Horizontal organizational structures.
- Horizontal systems and processes.
- Communications and information technologies.
- Human resource practices.

Common Culture and Shared Values   Shared goals, mutual objectives, and a high degree of trust are essential to the success of boundaryless organizations. It is neither feasible nor desirable to attempt to "control" suppliers, customers, or alliance partners in the traditional sense. In the fluid and flexible environments of the new organizational architectures, common cultures, shared values, and carefully aligned incentives are often less expensive to implement and are often a more effective means of strategic control than rules, boundaries, and formal procedures.

Horizontal Organizational Structures   Horizontal organizational structures, which group similar or related business units under common management control, facilitate sharing resources and infrastructures to exploit synergies among operating units and help to create a sense of common purpose. Consistency in training and the development of similar structures across business units facilitates job rotation and cross training and enhances understanding of common problems and opportunities. Cross-functional teams and interdivisional committees and task groups represent important opportunities to improve understanding and foster cooperation among operating units.

Horizontal Systems and Processes Organizational systems, policies, and procedures are the traditional mechanisms for achieving integration among functional units. Too often, however, existing policies and procedures do little more than institutionalize the barriers that exist from years of managing within the framework of the traditional model. The concept of business reengineering focuses primarily on these internal processes and procedures. Beginning with an understanding of basic business processes in the context of "a collection of activities that takes one or more kinds of input and creates an output that is of value to the customer," Michael Hammer and James Champy's 1993 best-selling *Reengineering the Corporation* outlined a methodology for redesigning internal systems and procedures that has been embraced, in its various forms, by many organizations.[54] Proponents claim that successful reengineering lowers costs, reduces inventories and cycle times, improves quality, speeds response times, and enhances organizational flexibility. Others advocate similar benefits through the reduction of cycle times, total quality management, and the like.

Communications and Information Technologies Improved communications through the effective use of information technologies can play an important role in bridging gaps and breaking down barriers between organizations. Electronic mail and videoconferencing can improve lateral communications across long distances and multiple time zones and circumvent many of the barriers of the traditional model. Information technology can be a powerful ally in the redesign and streamlining of internal business processes and in improving coordination and integration between suppliers and customers. Internet technologies have eliminated the paperwork of purchase order and invoice documentation in many buyer–supplier relationships, enabling cooperating organizations to reduce inventories, shorten delivery cycles, and reduce operating costs. Today, information technology must be viewed more as a prime component of an organization's overall strategy than simply in terms of its more traditional role as administrative support. The close relationships that must exist between technology and other value-creating activities were addressed in Chapters 3, 4, and 5.

Human Resource Practices Change, whether in structure, process, or procedure, always involves and impacts the human dimension of organizations. As we noted in Chapter 4, the attraction, development, and retention of human capital are vital to value creation. As boundaryless structures are implemented, processes are reengineered, and organizations become increasingly dependent on sophisticated information technologies, the skills of workers and managers alike must be upgraded to realize the full benefits.

Creating Ambidextrous Organizational Designs

>LO8

The need for creating ambidextrous organizational designs that enable firms to explore new opportunities and effectively integrate existing operations.

In Chapter 1, we introduced the concept of "ambidexterity," which incorporates two contradictory challenges faced by today's managers.[55] First, managers must explore new opportunities and adjust to volatile markets in order to avoid complacency. They must ensure that they maintain *adaptability* and remain proactive in expanding and/or modifying their product–market scope to anticipate and satisfy market conditions. Such competences are especially challenging when change is rapid and unpredictable—conditions that are becoming more pronounced in global markets.

Second, managers must also effectively exploit the value of their existing assets and competencies. They need to have *alignment,* which is a clear sense of how value is being created in the short term and how activities are integrated and properly coordinated. Firms that achieve both adaptability and alignment are considered *ambidextrous organizations*—aligned and efficient in how they manage today's business but flexible enough to changes in the environment so that they will prosper tomorrow.

As we would expect, handling such opposing demands is difficult because there will always be some degree of conflict. Such trade-offs can never really be entirely eliminated, and firms often suffer when they place too strong a priority on either adaptability or alignment. If it places too much focus on adaptability, the firm will suffer low profitability in the short term. On the other hand, if managers direct their efforts primarily at alignment, they will likely miss out on promising business opportunities.

Ambidextrous Organizations: Key Design Attributes

A recent study by Charles O'Reilly and Michael Tushman[56] provides some insights into how some firms were able to create successful **ambidextrous organizational designs.** They investigated companies that attempted to simultaneously pursue modest, incremental innovations as well as more dramatic, breakthrough innovations. In all, the team investigated 35 attempts to launch breakthrough innovations undertaken by 15 business units in nine different industries. They studied the organizational designs and the processes, systems, and cultures associated with the breakthrough projects as well as their impact on the operations and performance of the traditional businesses.

> **ambidextrous organizational designs** organization designs that attempt to simultaneously pursue modest, incremental innovations as well as more dramatic, breakthrough innovations.

Companies structured their breakthrough projects in one of four primary ways:

- Seven were carried out within existing *functional organizational structures*. The projects were completely integrated into the regular organizational and management structure.
- Nine were organized as *cross-functional teams*. The groups operated within the established organization but outside of the existing management structure.
- Four were organized as *unsupported teams*. Here, they became independent units set up outside the established organization and management hierarchy.
- Fifteen were conducted within *ambidextrous organizations*. Here, the breakthrough efforts were organized within structurally independent units, each having its own processes, structures, and cultures. However, they were integrated into the existing senior management structure.

The performance results of the 35 initiatives were tracked along two dimensions:

- Their success in creating desired innovations was measured by either the actual commercial results of the new product or the application of practical market or technical learning.
- The performance of the existing business was evaluated.

The study found that the organizational structure and management practices employed had a direct and significant impact on the performance of both the breakthrough initiative and the traditional business. The ambidextrous organizational designs were more effective than the other three designs on both dimensions: launching breakthrough products or services (i.e., adaptation) and improving the performance of the existing business (i.e., alignment).

Why Was the Ambidextrous Organization the Most Effective Structure?

The study found that there were many factors. A clear and compelling vision, consistently communicated by the company's senior management team was critical in building the ambidextrous designs. The structure enabled cross-fertilization among business units while avoiding cross-contamination. The tight coordination and integration at the managerial levels enabled the newer units to share important resources from the traditional units such as cash, talent, expertise, and so on. Such sharing was encouraged and facilitated by effective reward systems that emphasized overall company goals. At the same time, the organizational separation ensured that the new units' distinctive processes, structures, and cultures were not overwhelmed by the forces of "business as usual." Furthermore, the established units were shielded from the distractions of launching new businesses, and they continued to focus all of their attention and energy on refining their operations, enhancing their products, and serving their customers.

Reflecting on Career Implications . . .

- **Strategy–Structure:** Is there an effective "fit" between your organization's strategy and its structure? If not, there may be inconsistencies in how you are evaluated which often leads to role ambiguity and confusion. A poor fit could also affect communication among departments as well as across the organization's hierarchy.
- **Matrix Structure:** If your organization employs elements of a matrix structure (e.g., dual reporting relationships), are there effective structural supporting elements (e.g., culture and rewards)? If not, there could be a high level of dysfunctional conflict among managers.
- **The "Fit" Between Rewards and Incentives and "Levels of Strategy" (Business- and Corporate-Level):** What metrics are used to evaluate the performance of your work unit? Are there strictly financial measures of success or are you also rewarded for achieving competitive advantages (through effective innovation, organizational learning, or other activities that increase knowledge but may be costly in the short run)?
- **Boundaryless Organizational Designs:** Does your firm have structural mechanisms (e.g., culture, human resource practices) that facilitate sharing of information across boundaries? If so, you should be better able to enhance your human capital by leveraging your talents and competencies.

Summary

Successful organizations must ensure that they have the proper type of organizational structure. Furthermore, they must ensure that their firms incorporate the necessary integration and processes so that the internal and external boundaries of their firms are flexible and permeable. Such a need is increasingly important as the environments of firms become more complex, rapidly changing, and unpredictable.

In the first section of the chapter, we discussed the growth patterns of large corporations. Although most organizations remain small or die, some firms continue to grow in terms of revenues, vertical integration, and diversity of products and services. In addition, their geographical scope may increase to include international operations. We traced the dominant pattern of growth, which evolves from a simple structure to a functional structure as a firm grows in terms of size and increases its level of vertical integration. After a firm expands into related products and services, its structure changes from a functional to a divisional form of organization. Finally, when the firm enters international markets, its structure again changes to accommodate the change in strategy.

We also addressed the different types of organizational structure—simple, functional, divisional (including two variations—strategic business unit and holding company), and matrix—as well as their relative advantages and disadvantages. We closed the section with a discussion of the implications for structure when a firm enters international markets. The three primary factors to take into account when determining the appropriate structure are type of international strategy, product diversity, and the extent to which a firm is dependent on foreign sales.

In the second section, we took a contingency approach to the design of reward and evaluation systems. That is, we argued that there is no one best way to design such systems; rather, it is dependent on a variety of factors. The two that we discussed are business- and corporate-level strategies. With an overall cost leadership strategy and unrelated diversification, it is appropriate to rely primarily on cultures and reward systems that emphasize the production outcomes of the organization, because it is rather easy to quantify such indicators. In contrast, differentiation strategies and related diversification require cultures and incentive systems that encourage and reward creativity initiatives as well as the cooperation among professionals in many different functional areas. Here it becomes more difficult to measure accurately each individual's contribution, and more subjective indicators become essential.

The third section of the chapter introduced the concept of the boundaryless organization. We did not suggest that the concept of the boundaryless organization replaces the traditional forms of organizational structure. Rather, it should complement them. This is necessary to cope with the increasing complexity and change in the competitive environment. We addressed three types of boundaryless organizations. The barrier-free type focuses on the need for the internal and external boundaries of a firm to be more flexible and permeable. The modular type emphasizes the strategic outsourcing of noncore activities. The virtual type centers on the strategic benefits of alliances and the forming of network organizations. We discussed both the advantages and disadvantages of each type of boundaryless organization as well as suggested some techniques and processes that are necessary to successfully implement them. These are common culture and values, horizontal organizational structures, horizontal systems and processes, communications and information technologies, and human resource practices.

The final section addresses the need for managers to develop ambidextrous organizations. In today's rapidly changing global environment, managers must be responsive and proactive in order to take advantage of new opportunities. At the same time, they must effectively integrate and coordinate existing operations. Such requirements call for organizational designs that establish project teams that are structurally independent units, with each having its own processes, structures, and cultures. But, at the same time, each unit needs to be effectively integrated into the existing management hierarchy.

Summary Review Questions

1. Why is it important for managers to carefully consider the type of organizational structure that they use to implement their strategies?

2. Briefly trace the dominant growth pattern of major corporations from simple structure to functional structure to divisional structure. Discuss the relationship between a firm's strategy and its structure.

3. What are the relative advantages and disadvantages of the types of organizational structure—simple, functional, divisional, matrix—discussed in the chapter?

4. When a firm expands its operations into foreign markets, what are the three most important factors to take into account in deciding what type of structure is most appropriate? What are the types of international structures discussed in the text and what are the relationships between strategy and structure?

5. Briefly describe the three different types of boundaryless organizations: barrier-free, modular, and virtual.

6. What are some of the key attributes of effective groups? Ineffective groups?

7. What are the advantages and disadvantages of the three types of boundaryless organizations: barrier-free, modular, and virtual?

8. When are ambidextrous organizational designs necessary? What are some of their key attributes?

Key Terms

simple organizational structure, 342
functional organizational structure, 343
divisional organizational structure, 345
strategic business unit (SBU) structure, 347
holding company structure, 347
matrix organizational structure, 348
global start-up, 351
boundaryless organizational designs, 357
barrier-free organization, 358
modular organization, 361
virtual organization, 368
ambidextrous organizational designs, 369

Experiential Exercise

Many firms have recently moved toward a modular structure. For example, they have increasingly outsourced many of their information technology (IT) activities. Identify three such organizations. Using secondary sources, evaluate (1) the firm's rationale for IT outsourcing and (2) the implications for performance.

Firm	Rationale	Implication(s) for Performance
1.		
2.		
3.		

Application Questions Exercises

1. Select an organization that competes in an industry in which you are particularly interested. Go on the Internet and determine what type of organizational structure this organization has. In your view, is it consistent with the strategy that it has chosen to implement? Why? Why not?

2. Choose an article from *BusinessWeek, Fortune, Forbes, Fast Company,* or any other well-known publication that deals with a corporation that has undergone a significant change in its strategic direction. What are the implications for the structure of this organization?

3. Go on the Internet and look up some of the public statements or speeches of an executive in a major corporation about a significant initiative such as entering into a joint venture or launching a new product line. What do you feel are the implications for making the internal and external barriers of the firm more flexible and permeable? Does the executive discuss processes, procedures, integrating mechanisms, or cultural issues that should serve this purpose? Or are other issues discussed that enable a firm to become more boundaryless?

4. Look up a recent article in the publications listed in question 2 above that addresses a firm's involvement in outsourcing (modular organization) or in strategic alliance or network organizations (virtual organization). Was the firm successful or unsuccessful in this endeavor? Why? Why not?

Ethics Questions

1. If a firm has a divisional structure and places extreme pressures on its divisional executives to meet short-term profitability goals (e.g., quarterly income), could this raise some ethical considerations? Why? Why not?

2. If a firm enters into a strategic alliance but does not exercise appropriate behavioral control of its employees (in terms of culture, rewards and incentives, and boundaries—as discussed in Chapter 9) that are involved in the alliance, what ethical issues could arise? What could be the potential long-term and short-term downside for the firm?

References

1. Tomanio, J., Burke, D. & Morser, B. 2007. Missed connections. *Fortune,* March 5: 103–108; Schwartz, N. D. 2007. Big plane, big problems. *Fortune,* March 5: 95–98; Anonymous. 2007. Hard landing. *The Economist.* February 17: 68; Pearlstein, S. 2006. Political winds are pushing Airbus. www.washingtonpost.com. October 11: D01; Holmes, S. 2007. The secret weapon of Boeing. *BusinessWeek,* January 8: 34; Matlack, C. 2006. Wayward Airbus. *BusinessWeek,* October 23: 46–48; and Matlack, C. 2006. Airbus: First, blame the software. *BusinessWeek,* October 5, np.

2. This introductory discussion draws upon Hall, R. H. 2002. *Organizations: Structures, processes, and outcomes* (8th ed.). Upper Saddle River, NJ: Prentice Hall; and Duncan, R. E. 1979. What is the right organization structure? Decision-tree analysis provides the right answer. *Organizational Dynamics,* 7(3): 59–80. For an insightful discussion of strategy-structure relationships in the organization theory and strategic management literatures, refer to Keats, B., & O'Neill, H. M. 2001. Organization structure: Looking through a strategy lens. In Hitt, M. A., Freeman, R. E., & Harrison, J. S. 2001. *The Blackwell handbook of strategic management:* 520–542. Malden, MA: Blackwell.

3. This discussion draws upon Chandler, A. D. 1962. *Strategy and structure.* Cambridge, MA: MIT Press; Galbraith J. R., & Kazanjian, R. K. 1986. *Strategy implementation: The role of structure and process.* St. Paul, MN: West Publishing; and Scott, B. R. 1971. Stages of corporate development. Intercollegiate Case Clearing house, 9-371-294, BP 998. Harvard Business School.

4. Our discussion of the different types of organizational structures draws on a variety of sources, including Galbraith & Kazanjian, op. cit.; Hrebiniak, L. G., & Joyce, W. F. 1984. *Implementing strategy.* New York: Macmillan; Distelzweig, H. 2000. Organizational structure. In Helms, M. M. (Ed.). *Encyclopedia of management:* 692–699. Farmington Hills, MI: Gale; and Dess, G. G., & Miller, A. 1993. *Strategic management.* New York: McGraw-Hill.

5. Schein, E. H. 1996. Three cultures of management: The key to organizational learning. *Sloan Management Review,* 38(1): 9–20.

6. For a discussion of performance implications, refer to Hoskisson, R. E. 1987. Multidivisional structure and performance: The contingency of diversification strategy. *Academy of Management Journal,* 29: 625–644.

7. For a thorough and seminal discussion of the evolution toward the divisional form of organizational structure in the United States, refer to Chandler, op. cit. A rigorous empirical study of the strategy and structure relationship is found in Rumelt, R. P. 1974. *Strategy, structure, and economic performance.* Cambridge, MA: Harvard Business School Press.

8. Ghoshal, S., & Bartlett, C. A. 1995. Changing the role of management: Beyond structure to processes. *Harvard Business Review,* 73(1): 88.

9. Koppel, B. 2000. Synergy in ketchup? *Forbes,* February 7: 68–69; and Hitt, M. A., Ireland, R. D., & Hoskisson, R. E. 2001. *Strategic management: Competitiveness and globalization* (4th ed.). Cincinnati, OH: Southwestern Publishing.

10. Pitts, R. A. 1977. Strategies and structures for diversification. *Academy of Management Journal,* 20(2): 197–208.

11. Dell, M., & Rollins, K. 2005. Execution without excuses. *Harvard Business Review,* 83(3): 102–111.

12. Daniels, J. D., Pitts, R. A., & Tretter, M. J. 1984. Strategy and structure of U.S. multinationals: An exploratory study. *Academy of Management Journal,* 27(2): 292–307.

13. Habib, M. M., & Victor, B. 1991. Strategy, structure, and performance of U.S. manufacturing and service MNCs: A comparative analysis. *Strategic Management Journal,* 12(8): 589–606.

14. Our discussion of global start-ups draws from Oviatt, B. M., & McDougall, P. P. 2005. The internationalization of entrepreneurship. *Journal of International Business Studies,* 36(1): 2–8; Oviatt, B. M., & McDougall, P. P. 1994. Toward a theory of international new ventures. *Journal of International Business Studies,* 25(1): 45–64; and Oviatt, B. M., & McDougall, P. P. 1995. Global start-ups: Entrepreneurs on a worldwide stage. *Academy of Management Executive,* 9(2): 30–43.

15. Some useful guidelines for global start-ups are provided in Kuemmerle, W. 2005. The entrepreneur's path for global expansion. *MIT Sloan Management Review,* 46(2): 42–50.

16. See, for example, Miller, D., & Friesen, P. H. 1980. Momentum and revolution in organizational structure. *Administrative Science Quarterly,* 13: 65–91.

17. Many authors have argued that a firm's structure can influence a firm's strategy and performance. These include Amburgey, T. L., & Dacin, T. 1995. As the left foot follows the right? The dynamics of strategic and structural change. *Academy of Management Journal,* 37: 1427–1452; Dawn, K., & Amburgey, T. L. 1991. Organizational inertia and momentum: A dynamic model of strategic change. *Academy of Management Journal,* 34: 591–612; Fredrickson, J. W. 1986. The strategic decision process and organization structure. *Academy of Management Review,* 11: 280–297; Hall, D. J., & Saias, M. A. 1980. Strategy follows structure! *Strategic Management Journal,* 1: 149–164; and Burgelman, R. A. 1983. A model of the interaction of strategic behavior, corporate context, and the concept of strategy. *Academy of Management Review,* 8: 61–70.

18. This discussion of generic strategies and their relationship to organizational control draws upon Porter, M. E. 1980. *Competitive strategy.* New York: Free Press; and Miller, D. 1988. Relating Porter's business strategies to environment and structure: Analysis and performance implications. *Academy of Management Journal,* 31(2): 280–308.

19. Rodengen, J. L. 1997. *The legend of Nucor Corporation.* Fort Lauderdale, FL: Write Stuff Enterprises.

20. The 3M example draws upon *Blueprints for service quality.* 1994. New York: American Management Association; personal communication with Katerine Hagmeier, program manager, external communications, 3M Corporation, March 26, 1998; Lei, D., Slocum, J. W., & Pitts, R. A. 1999. Designing organizations for competitive advantage: The power of unlearning and learning. *Organizational Dynamics,* 27(3): 24–38; and Graham, A. B., & Pizzo, V. G. 1996. A question of balance: Case studies in strategic knowledge management. *European Management Journal,* 14(4): 338–346.

21. The Sharp Corporation and Hanson plc examples are based on Collis, D. J., & Montgomery, C. A. 1998. Creating corporate advantage. *Harvard Business Review,* 76(3): 70–83.

22. Kunii, I. 2002. Japanese companies' survival skills. *BusinessWeek,* November 18: 18.

23. White, G. 1988. How I turned $3,000 into $10 billion. *Fortune,* November 7: 80–89. After the death of the founders, the Hanson plc conglomerate was found to be too unwieldy and was broken up into several separate, publicly traded corporations. For more on its more limited current scope of operations, see www.hansonplc.com.

24. An interesting discussion on how the Internet has affected the boundaries of firms can be found in Afuah, A. 2003. Redefining firm boundaries in the face of the Internet: Are firms really shrinking? *Academy of Management Review,* 28(1): 34–53.

25. Collis & Montgomery, op. cit.

26. For a discussion of the role of coaching on developing high performance teams, refer to Kets de Vries, M. F. R. 2005. Leadership group coaching in action: The zen of creating high performance teams. *Academy of Management Executive,* 19(1): 77–89.

27. Pfeffer, J. 1998. *The human equation: Building profits by putting people first.* Cambridge, MA: Harvard Business School Press.

28. For a discussion on how functional area diversity affects performance, see Bunderson, J. S., & Sutcliffe, K. M. 2002. *Academy of Management Journal,* 45(5): 875–893.

29. Augustine, N. R. 1983. *Augustine's laws.* New York: Viking Press.

30. See, for example, Hoskisson, R. E., Hill, C. W. L., & Kim, H. 1993. The multidivisional structure: Organizational fossil or source of value? *Journal of Management,* 19(2): 269–298.

31. Pottruck, D. A. 1997. Speech delivered by the co-CEO of Charles Schwab Co., Inc., to the Retail Leadership Meeting, San Francisco, CA, January 30; and Miller, W. 1999. Building the ultimate resource. *Management Review,* January: 42–45.

32. Magretta, J. 1998. The power of virtual integration: An interview with Dell Computer's Michael Dell. *Harvard Business Review,* 76(2): 75.

33. Forster, J. 2001. Networking for cash. *BusinessWeek,* January 8: 129.

34. Dess, G. G., Rasheed, A. M. A., McLaughlin, K. J., & Priem, R. 1995. The new corporate architecture. *Academy of Management Executive,* 9(3): 7–20.

35. Barnes, C. 1998. A fatal case. *Fast Company,* February–March: 173.

36. Handy, C. 1989. *The age of unreason.* Boston: Harvard Business School Press; Ramstead, E. 1997. APC maker's low-tech formula: Start with the box. *The Wall Street Journal,* December 29: B1; Mussberg, W. 1997. Thin screen PCs are looking good but still fall flat. *The Wall Street Journal,* January 2: 9; Brown, E. 1997. Monorail: Low cost PCs. *Fortune,* July 7: 106–108; and Young, M. 1996. Ex-Compaq executives start new company. *Computer Reseller News,* November 11: 181.

37. For a discussion of some of the downsides of outsourcing, refer to Rossetti, C., & Choi, T. Y. 2005. On the dark side of strategic sourcing: Experiences from the aerospace industry. *Academy of Management Executive,* 19(1): 46–60.

38. Tully, S. 1993. The modular corporation. *Fortune,* February 8: 196.

39. Quinn, J. B. 1992. *Intelligent enterprise: A knowledge and service based paradigm for industry.* New York: Free Press.

40. For an insightful perspective on outsourcing and its role in developing capabilities, read Gottfredson, M.,

Puryear, R., & Phillips, C. 2005. Strategic sourcing: From periphery to the core. *Harvard Business Review,* 83(4): 132–139.

41. This discussion draws upon Quinn, J. B., & Hilmer, F. C. 1994. Strategic outsourcing. *Sloan Management Review,* 35(4): 43–55.

42. See also Stuckey, J., & White, D. 1993. When and when not to vertically integrate. *Sloan Management Review,* Spring: 71–81; Harrar, G. 1993. Outsource tales. *Forbes ASAP,* June 7: 37–39, 42; and Davis, E. W. 1992. Global outsourcing: Have U.S. managers thrown the baby out with the bath water? *Business Horizons,* July–August: 58–64.

43. For a discussion of knowledge creation through alliances, refer to Inkpen, A. C. 1996. Creating knowledge through collaboration. *California Management Review,* 39(1): 123–140; and Mowery, D. C., Oxley, J. E., & Silverman, B. S. 1996. Strategic alliances and interfirm knowledge transfer. *Strategic Management Journal,* 17 (Special Issue, Winter): 77–92.

44. Doz, Y., & Hamel, G. 1998. *Alliance advantage: The art of creating value through partnering.* Boston: Harvard Business School Press.

45. DeSanctis, G., Glass, J. T., & Ensing, I. M. 2002. Organizational designs for R&D. *Academy of Management Executive,* 16(3): 55–66.

46. Barringer, B. R., & Harrison, J. S. 2000. Walking a tightrope: Creating value through interorganizational alliances. *Journal of Management,* 26: 367–403.

47. Davis, E. 1997. Interview: Norman Augustine. *Management Review,* November: 14.

48. One contemporary example of virtual organizations is R&D consortia. For an insightful discussion, refer to Sakaibara, M. 2002. Formation of R&D consortia: Industry and company effects. *Strategic Management Journal,* 23(11): 1033–1050.

49. Bartness, A., & Cerny, K. 1993. Building competitive advantage through a global network of capabilities. *California Management Review,* Winter: 78–103. For an insightful historical discussion of the usefulness of alliances in the computer industry, see Moore, J. F. 1993. Predators and prey: A new ecology of competition. *Harvard Business Review,* 71(3): 75–86.

50. See Lorange, P., & Roos, J. 1991. Why some strategic alliances succeed and others fail. *Journal of Business Strategy,* January–February: 25–30; and Slowinski, G. 1992. The human touch in strategic alliances. *Mergers and Acquisitions,* July–August: 44–47. A compelling argument for strategic alliances is provided by Ohmae, K. 1989. The global logic of

strategic alliances. *Harvard Business Review,* 67(2): 143–154.

51. Some of the downsides of alliances are discussed in Das, T. K., & Teng, B. S. 2000. Instabilities of strategic alliances: An internal tensions perspective. *Organization Science,* 11: 77–106.

52. This section draws upon Dess, G. G., & Picken, J. C. 1997. *Mission critical.* Burr Ridge, IL: Irwin Professional Publishing.

53. Katzenbach, J. R., & Smith, D. K. 1994. *The wisdom of teams: Creating the high performance organization.* New York: HarperBusiness.

54. Hammer, M., & Champy, J. 1993. *Reengineering the corporation: A manifesto for business revolution.* New York: HarperCollins.

55. This section draws on Birkinshaw, J., & Gibson, C. 2004. Building ambidexterity into an organization. *MIT Sloan Management Review,* 45(4): 47–55; and Gibson, C. B., & Birkinshaw, J. 2004. The antecedents, consequences, and mediating role of organizational ambidexterity. *Academy of Management Journal,* 47(2): 209–226. Robert Duncan is generally credited with being the first to coin the term "ambidextrous organizations" in his article entitled: Designing dual structures for innovation. In Kilmann, R. H., Pondy, L. R., & Slevin, D. (Eds.). 1976. *The management of organizations,* vol. 1: 167–188. For a seminal academic discussion of the concept of exploration and exploitation, which parallels adaptation and alignment, refer to: March, J. G. 1991. Exploration and exploitation in organizational learning. *Organization Science,* 2: 71–86.

56. This section is based on O'Reilly, C. A., & Tushman, M. L. 2004. The ambidextrous organization. *Harvard Business Review,* 82(4): 74–81.

chapter 11

Strategic Leadership:

Creating a Learning Organization and an Ethical Organization

>learning objectives

After reading this chapter, you should have a good understanding of:

LO1 The three key interdependent activities in which all successful leaders must be continually engaged.

LO2 The salience of power in overcoming resistance to change.

LO3 The crucial role of emotional intelligence (EI) in successful leadership as well as its potential drawbacks.

LO4 The value of creating and maintaining a "learning organization" in today's global marketplace.

LO5 The leader's role in establishing an ethical organization.

LO6 The difference between integrity-based and compliance-based approaches to organizational ethics.

LO7 Several key elements that organizations must have to become an ethical organization.

*t*o compete in the global marketplace, organizations need to have strong and effective leadership. This involves the active process of both creating and implementing proper strategies. In this chapter we address key activities in which leaders throughout the organization must be involved to be successful in creating and sustaining competitive advantages.

In the first section we provide a brief overview of the three key leadership activities. These are (1) setting a direction, (2) designing the organization, and (3) nurturing a culture committed to excellence and ethical behavior. Each of these activities is "necessary but not sufficient"; that is, to be effective, leaders must give proper attention to each of them. We also address the importance of a leader's effective use of power to overcome resistance to change.

The second section discusses the vital role of emotional intelligence (EI) in effective strategic leadership. EI refers to an individual's capacity for recognizing his or her emotions and those of others. It consists of five components: self-awareness, self-regulation, motivation, empathy, and social skills. We also address potential downsides or drawbacks that may result from the ineffective use of EI.

Next we address the important role of a leader in creating a "learning organization." Here, leaders must strive to harness the individual and collective talents of individuals throughout the entire organization. Creating a learning organization becomes particularly important in today's competitive environment, which is increasingly unpredictable, dynamic, and interdependent. Clearly, everyone must be involved in learning. It can't be only a few people at the top of the organization. The key elements of a learning organization are inspiring and motivating people with a mission or purpose, empowering employees at all levels, accumulating and sharing internal and external information, and challenging the status quo to enable creativity.

The final section discusses a leader's challenge in creating and maintaining an ethical organization. There are many benefits of having an ethical organization. In addition to financial benefits, it can enhance human capital and help to ensure positive relationships with suppliers, customers, society at large, and governmental agencies. On the other hand, the costs of ethical crises can be very expensive for many reasons. We address four key elements of an ethical organization: role models, corporate credos and codes of conduct, reward and evaluation systems, and policies and procedures.

 Learning from Mistakes

Scott A. Livengood was fired as Chief Executive Officer (CEO) of Krispy Kreme on January 19, 2005.[1] He hasn't received very much good news lately. The firm's stock went up 10 percent the day of that announcement. And he received some rather dubious honors: he was recognized as one of *BusinessWeek*'s seven "Worst Managers" of 2004 and he was named 2004's "Worst CEO of the Year by Herb Greenberg of CBS MarketWatch.

What brought about the demise of Livengood, a 28-year veteran of the doughnut maker who had been CEO since 1998? Let's look at two of the central issues.

First, under his direction Krispy Kreme expanded far too rapidly. After its initial public offering in 2001, it continued to open stores at breakneck speed. Hoping to cash in on the nation's sweet tooth, the chain created media events in places like New York, San Francisco, and Boston. At times, cars would line up for blocks just to bring a box of the tasty confections to work. Unfortunately, while the craze faded, the costs of operating the franchises did not. By 2003, same-store sales had declined 16 percent, *[continued]* while the company's overhead continued to rise. In short, the brand quickly lost its novelty. Soon Krispy Kreme realized that many of its franchises would fail.

Recent financial results reflect the poor strategy. The once high-flying company posted a $3 million third-quarter loss in November 2004—its second losing quarter of the year. And in February 2005, the firm stated that it would restate earnings for the previous year, lowering previously reported income by as much as 8.6 percent.

Second, there are what *Fortune* has called "shady deals" surrounding how the firm conducted buybacks of some franchises owned by corporate insiders. For example, Krispy Kreme didn't disclose that a California franchise it repurchased in 2004 was partly owned by Livengood's ex-wife, whose stake was valued at $1.5 million. While executives aren't required to disclose transactions with former spouses, Livengood could be in trouble if the deal was made as part of a settlement or in lieu of alimony.

An even more troubling transaction is the 2003 deal in which the chain repurchased six stores in Dallas and Shreveport, Louisiana, that were partly owned by Krispy Kreme's former chairman and current director, Joseph McAleer. McAleer got a pretty good deal—$67 million (or $11 million per store). This comes to more than three times what the firm paid for many other shops! According to David Gourevitch, a former Securities and Exchange Commission (SEC) enforcement attorney, "At some point a transaction is not remotely reasonable, and it approximates a gift or payoff." Worst case scenario: The SEC could impose fines and require some officials to step down.

The SEC continues to investigate the firm and it upgraded its informal inquiry to a formal probe. Although customers may continue to enjoy Krispy Kreme's products, the investors have hardly had a pleasant experience. Krispy Kreme's stock price has continued to sink. By early 2007, it was at $12—less than one-fourth of the $50 peak that it reached in August 2003. This fall reflects a loss of market capitalization of $2 billion.

Clearly, many of the decisions and actions of Scott A. Livengood were not in the best interests of the firm and its shareholders. In contrast, effective leaders play an important and often pivotal role in creating and implementing strategies.

This chapter provides insights into how organizations can more effectively manage, change, and cope with increased environmental complexity and uncertainty. Below we will define leadership and introduce what are considered to be the three most important leadership activities as well as the important role of power. The second section focuses on a key trait—emotional intelligence—that has become increasingly recognized as critical to successful leadership. Then, the third major section, "Developing a Learning Organization," provides a useful framework for how leaders can help their firms learn and proactively adapt in the face of accelerating change. Central to this contemporary idea is the concept of empowerment, wherein employees and managers throughout the organization truly come to have a sense of self-determination, meaning, competence, and impact. The fourth section addresses the leader's role in building an ethical organization. Here, we address both the value of an ethical culture for a firm as well as the key elements that it encompasses.

Leadership: Three Interdependent Activities

In today's chaotic world, few would argue against the need for leadership, but how do we go about encouraging it? Let's focus on business organizations. Is it enough to merely keep the organization afloat, or is it essential to make steady progress toward some well-defined objective? We believe custodial management is not leadership. Rather, leadership is proactive, goal-oriented, and focused on the creation and implementation of a creative vision.

Leadership is the process of transforming organizations from what they are to what the leader would have them become. This definition implies a lot: *dissatisfaction* with the status quo, a *vision* of what should be, and a *process* for bringing about change. An insurance company executive recently shared the following insight on leadership, "I lead by the Noah Principle: It's all right to know when it's going to rain, but, by God, you had better build the ark."

leadership the process of transforming organizations from what they are to what the leader would have them become.

Doing the right thing is becoming increasingly important. Many industries are declining; the global village is becoming increasingly complex, interconnected, and unpredictable; and product and market life cycles are becoming increasingly compressed. Recently, when asked to describe the life cycle of his company's products, the CEO of a supplier of computer components replied, "Seven months from cradle to grave—and that includes three months to design the product and get it into production!" Richard D'Aveni, author of *Hypercompetition,* went even further. He argued that in a world where all dimensions of competition appear to be compressed in time and heightened in complexity, *sustainable* competitive advantages are no longer possible.

Despite the importance of doing the "right thing," leaders must also be concerned about doing "things right." Charan and Colvin argued strongly that implementation (or execution) is also essential to success.

> Any way that you look at it, mastering execution turns out to be the odds-on best way for a CEO to keep his job. So what's the right way to think about that sexier obsession, strategy? It's vitally important—obviously. The problem is that our age's fascination feeds the mistaken belief that developing exactly the right strategy will enable a company to rocket past competitors. In reality, that's less than half the battle.[2]

Thus, leaders are change agents whose success is measured by how effectively they implement a strategic vision and mission.

Accordingly, many authors contend that successful leaders must recognize three interdependent activities that must be continually reassessed for organizations to succeed. As shown in Exhibit 11.1, these are: (1) determining a direction, (2) designing the organization, and (3) nurturing a culture dedicated to excellence and ethical behavior.[3]

>LO1

The three key interdependent activities in which all successful leaders must be continually engaged.

The interdependent nature of these three activities is self-evident. Consider an organization with a great mission and a superb organizational structure and design, but a culture that implicitly encourages shirking and unethical behavior. Or a strong culture and organizational design but little direction and vision—in caricature, a highly ethical and efficient buggy whip manufacturer. Or one with a sound direction and strong culture, but counterproductive teams

Exhibit 11.1 Three Interdependent Activities of Leadership

and a "zero-sum" reward system that leads to the dysfunctional situation in which one party's gain is viewed as another party's loss, and collaboration and sharing are severely hampered.

Often, failure of today's organizations can be attributed to a lack of equal consideration of these three activities. The imagery of a three-legged stool is instructive: It will collapse if one leg is missing or broken. Let's briefly look at each of these activities.

Setting a Direction

A holistic understanding of an organization's stakeholders requires an ability to scan the environment to develop a knowledge of all of the company's stakeholders (e.g., customers, suppliers, shareholders) and other salient environmental trends and events. Managers must integrate this knowledge into a vision of what the organization could become. It necessitates the capacity to solve increasingly complex problems, become proactive in approach, and develop viable strategic options. As noted in Chapter 1, a strategic vision provides many benefits: a clear future direction; a framework for the organization's mission and goals; and enhanced employee communication, participation, and commitment.

At times the creative process involves what the CEO of Yokogawa, GE's Japanese partner in the Medical Systems business, called "bullet train" thinking.[4] That is, if you want to increase the speed by 10 miles per hour, you look for incremental advances. However, if you want to double the speed, you've got to think "out of the box" (e.g., widen the track, change the overall suspension system). In today's challenging times, leaders typically need more than just keeping the same train with a few minor tweaks. Instead, they must come up with more revolutionary visions.

Consider how Robert Tillman, CEO of Lowe's, dramatically revitalized his firm by setting a clear and compelling direction:

> He made Lowe's into a formidable competitor to Home Depot, Inc., the Goliath of the home-improvement and hardware retailing industry.[5] In his six years as CEO, Tillman has transformed the $43 billion chain, based in Wilkesboro, North Carolina. Its shares have more than doubled over the past four years, while Home Depot's have fallen about 20 percent.
>
> Tillman has redirected Lowe's strategy by responding effectively to research showing that women initiate 80 percent of home projects. While Home Depot has focused on the professionals and male customers, Tillman has redesigned Lowe's stores to give them a brighter appearance, stocked them with more appliances, and focused on higher-margin goods (including everything from Laura Ashley paints to high-end bathroom fixtures). And, like Wal-Mart, Lowe's has one of the best inventory systems in retailing. As a result, Lowe's profits are expected to continue to rise faster than Home Depot's.

Let's now turn to another key leadership activity: the design of the organization's structure, processes, and evaluation and control systems.

Designing the Organization

At times, almost all leaders have difficulty implementing their vision and strategies. Such problems—discussed in Chapter 10—may stem from a variety of sources, including:

- Lack of understanding of responsibility and accountability among managers.
- Reward systems that do not motivate individuals (or collectives such as groups and divisions) toward desired organizational goals.
- Inadequate or inappropriate budgeting and control systems.
- Insufficient mechanisms to integrate activities across the organization.

Successful leaders are actively involved in building structures, teams, systems, and organizational processes that facilitate the implementation of their vision and strategies. For example, we discussed the necessity for consistency between business-level and corporate-level strategies and organizational control in Chapter 9. For example, a firm would generally be unable to attain an overall low-cost advantage without closely monitoring its costs through detailed and formalized cost and financial control procedures. With regard to corporate-level strategy, in Chapter 9 we addressed how a related diversification strategy would necessitate reward systems that emphasize behavioral measures to promote sharing across divisions within a firm, whereas an unrelated strategy should rely more on financial (or objective) indicators of performance, such as revenue gains and profitability, since there is less need for collaboration across business units because they would have little in common.

Nurturing a Culture Dedicated to Excellence and Ethical Behavior

In Chapter 9 we discussed how organizational culture can be an effective means of organizational control. Leaders play a key role in developing and sustaining—as well as changing, when necessary—an organization's culture. Hector Ruiz is a good role model. After he became CEO of AMD, a $6 billion microprocessor producer, he dramatically improved his firm's competitive position vis-à-vis Intel—a firm six times as large. He says:[6]

> We have gotten larger and more complex. By definition that means we're going to make some mistakes. I'm much more comfortable in an environment when I know that's going to happen. That means we're learning. An aura of confidence begins to develop around people who can make mistakes and learn and go forward. At employee meetings I say, "Please, go get speeding tickets. I don't want you to get parking tickets."

In sharp contrast, leaders can also have a very detrimental effect on a firm's culture and ethics. Imagine the negative impact that Todd Berman's illegal activities have had on a firm that he cofounded—New York's private equity firm Chartwell Investments.[7] He recently began serving a five-year sentence in a Pennsylvania prison for stealing more than $3.6 million from the firm and its investors. Berman pleaded guilty to fraud charges brought by the Justice Department. For 18 months he misled Chartwell's investors concerning the financial condition of one of the firm's portfolio companies by falsely claiming it needed to borrow funds to meet operating expenses. Instead, Berman transferred the money to his personal bank account, along with fees paid by portfolio companies. Clearly, a leader's ethical behavior can make a strong impact on an organization—for good or for bad. Given the importance of this topic, we address it in detail in the last major section of this chapter.

Managers and top executives must also accept personal responsibility for developing and strengthening ethical behavior throughout the organization. They must consistently demonstrate that such behavior is central to the vision and mission of the organization. Several elements must be present and reinforced for a firm to become a highly ethical organization: role models, corporate credos and codes of conduct, reward and evaluation systems, and policies and procedures.

Strategy Spotlight 11.1 discusses how Nancy Snyder epitomizes the aforementioned three leadership activities. She was very effective in instilling a culture of innovation at Whirlpool Corporation.

Overcoming Barriers to Change and the Effective Use of Power

After discussing the three interdependent activities that leaders perform, we must address a key question: What are the **barriers to change** that leaders often encounter, and how can they use power to bring about organizational change? After all, people generally have some level of choice about how strongly they support or resist a leader's change initiatives. Why

barriers to change
characteristics of individuals and organizations that prevent a leader from transforming an organization.

>LO2
The salience of power in overcoming resistance to change.

Whirlpool: Becoming a Leader in Innovation

David R. Whitwam realized he had a major problem. The Chairman and CEO had helped build Whirlpool into the world's number one maker of big-ticket appliances, attaining unmatched economies of scale. He had also repeatedly cut costs by hundreds of millions of dollars. However, in 1999, everything—the stock price, profit margins, market share—had been about where it was a decade earlier. At the time, housing and sales of Whirlpool appliances were booming. Despite the strong demand, prices were falling by an average of 3.4 percent a year. The underlying problem was that its machines had been reduced to commodities. The solution was straightforward: Whirlpool had to come up with exciting new products that could command premium prices.

Whitman's goal of "innovation from everyone, everywhere" required major changes in the firm's management processes and culture, which had been designed to drive operational efficiency. He appointed Nancy Snyder, a corporate vice president to be Whirlpool's first "innovation czar." She rallied her colleagues around what was to become a five-year quest to reinvent the company's management processes. Key changes included:

- Making innovation a central topic in Whirlpool's leadership development programs.

- Setting aside $45 million from the capital budget for innovation in 2000 and doubling it in 2001 for projects that met a stringent standard of innovativeness.

- Requiring every product development plan to contain a sizable component of new-to-market innovation.

Sources: Arndt, M. 2006. Creativity overflowing. www.businessweek.com. May 8: np; Hamel, G. 2006. The why, what, and how of management innovation. *Harvard Business Review,* 84(2): 72–87; and, Salter, C. 2005. Whirlpool finds its cool. *Fast Company,* June: 73.

- Training more than 600 innovation mentors charged with encouraging a culture of innovation throughout the company.

- Setting up an intranet site that offered a do-it-yourself course on innovation and listing every project in the pipeline.

- Establishing innovation as a significant component of senior management's compensation program. If they failed to meet annual revenue and pipeline targets, they could lose 30 percent of their annual bonus.

- Setting aside time in quarterly business review meetings for an in-depth discussion of each unit's innovation performance.

Whirlpool's innovation efforts are paying off. The Duet, a matching washer and dryer introduced in 2001, has become a must-have appliance that seems to be selling like iPods. At $2,000, it is the company's most expensive washer-dryer set. With its stylish lines, portholelike door, and eye-catching colors, the Duet, says Chuck Jones, Whirlpool's Design Chief, "is like a Ferrari in your laundry room." That same year, Paris's Louvre Museum displayed Whirlpool's next generation concept products. And, in 2002, the Smithsonian Institution named Whirlpool the winner of its annual National Design Award in corporate achievement.

The bottom line results of Snyder's initiatives have been impressive. Since 2001, revenues from products that fit the company's definition of innovation have soared from $10 million to $760 million by 2005, or over five percent of the firm's record $14.3 billion revenue. Whirlpool's shares as of early 2007 were around $90—nearly double what they were five years ago. And prices are no longer eroding. Over the past three years, the average price of Whirlpool's appliances has risen five percent annually.

is there often so much resistance? There are many reasons why organizations at all levels are prone to inertia and are slow to learn, adapt, and change:

1. Many people have **vested interests in the status quo.** People, in general, tend to be risk averse and resistant to change. Further, there is a broad stream of research on the subject of "escalation," wherein certain individuals continue to throw "good money at bad decisions" despite negative performance feedback.[8]

2. There are **systemic barriers.** Here, the design of the organization's structure, information processing, reporting relationships, and so forth impede the proper flow and evaluation of information. A bureaucratic structure with multiple layers, onerous requirements for documentation, and rigid rules and procedures will often "inoculate" the organization against change.

systemic barriers
barriers to change that stem from an organizational design that impedes the proper flow and evaluation of information.

3. **Behavioral barriers** cause managers to look at issues from a biased or limited perspective. This can be attributed to their education, training, work experiences, and so forth. For example, consider an incident shared by David Lieberman, marketing director at GVO, an innovation consulting firm:

> A company's creative type had come up with a great idea for a new product. Nearly everybody loved it. However, it was shot down by a high-ranking manufacturing representative who exploded: "A new color? Do you have any idea of the spare-parts problem that it will create?" This was not a dimwit exasperated at having to build a few storage racks at the warehouse. He'd been hearing for years about cost cutting, lean inventories, and "focus." Lieberman's comment: "Good concepts, but not always good for innovation."

4. **Political barriers** refer to conflicts arising from power relationships. This can be the outcome of a myriad of symptoms such as vested interests (e.g., the aforementioned escalation problems), refusal to share information, conflicts over resources, conflicts between departments and divisions, and petty interpersonal differences.

5. **Personal time constraints** bring to mind the old saying about "not having enough time to drain the swamp when you are up to your neck in alligators." In effect, Gresham's law of planning states that operational decisions will drive out the time necessary for strategic thinking and reflection. This tendency is accentuated in organizations experiencing severe price competition or retrenchment wherein managers and employees are spread rather thin.

Successful leadership requires effective use of power in overcoming barriers to change.[9] As humorously noted by Mark Twain, "I'm all for progress. It's change I object to."

Power refers to a leader's ability to get things done in a way he or she wants them to be done. It is the ability to influence other people's behavior, to persuade them to do things that they otherwise would not do, and to overcome resistance and opposition to changing direction. Effective exercise of power is essential for successful leadership.[10]

A leader derives his or her power from several sources or bases. Numerous classifications of such sources or bases abound in the literature on power. However, the simplest way to understand the bases of power is by classifying them as organizational and personal, as shown in Exhibit 11.2.

behavioral barriers barriers to change associated with the tendency for managers to look at issues from a biased or limited perspective based on their prior education and experience.

political barriers barriers to change related to conflicts arising from power relationships.

power a leader's ability to get things done in a way he or she wants them to be done.

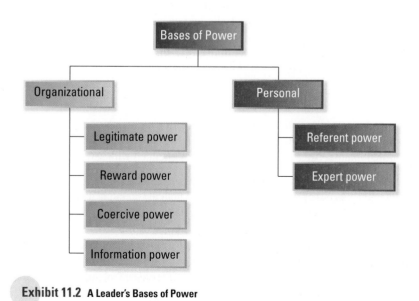

Exhibit 11.2 A Leader's Bases of Power

Organizational bases of power refer to the power that a person wields because of holding a formal management position. These include legitimate power, reward power, coercive power, and information power. *Legitimate power* is derived from organizationally conferred decision-making authority and is exercised by virtue of a manager's position in the organization. *Reward power* depends on the ability of the leader or manager to confer rewards for positive behaviors or outcomes. *Coercive power* is the power a manager exercises over employees using fear of punishment for errors of omission or commission. *Information power* arises from a manager's access, control, and distribution of information that is not freely available to everyone in an organization.

Apart from the organizationally derived power, a leader might be able to influence subordinates because of his or her personality characteristics and behavior. These would be considered the **personal bases of power.** The personal bases of power are referent power and expert power. The source of *referent power* is a subordinate's identification with the leader. A leader's personal attributes or charisma might influence subordinates and make them devoted to that leader. On the other hand, the source of *expert power* is the leader's expertise and knowledge in a particular field. The leader is the expert on whom subordinates depend for information that they need to do their jobs successfully.

personal bases of power power that stems from a leader's personality characteristics and behavior.

Successful leaders use the different bases of power, and often a combination of them, as appropriate to meet the demands of a situation, such as the nature of the task, the personality characteristics of the subordinates, the urgency of the issue, and other factors. Leaders must recognize that persuasion and developing consensus are often essential, but so is pressing for action. Clearly, at some point stragglers must be prodded into line.[11] Peter Georgescu, who recently retired as CEO of Young & Rubicam (an advertising and media giant acquired by the UK-based WPP Group in 2000), summarized a leader's dilemma brilliantly (and humorously), "I have knee pads and a .45. I get down and beg a lot, but I shoot people too."[12]

Strategy Spotlight 11.2 addresses some of the subtleties of power. It focuses on William Bratton, Chief of the Los Angeles Police Department, who has enjoyed a very successful career in law enforcement.

Emotional Intelligence: A Key Leadership Trait

>LO3

The crucial role of emotional intelligence (EI) in successful leadership as well as its potential drawbacks.

In the previous section, we discussed three activities of strategic leadership. The focus was on "what leaders *do*." Now, the issue becomes "who leaders *are*," that is, what are the most important traits (or capabilities) of leaders. Clearly, these two issues are related, because successful leaders possess the valuable traits that enable them to perform effectively in order to create value for their organization.

There has been a vast amount of literature on the successful traits of leaders, including business leaders at the highest level.[13] These traits include integrity, maturity, energy, judgment, motivation, intelligence, expertise, and so on. However, for simplicity, these traits may be grouped into three broad sets of capabilities:

- Purely technical skills (like accounting or operations research).
- Cognitive abilities (like analytical reasoning or quantitative analysis).
- Emotional intelligence (which includes skills associated with self-management and managing relationships).

emotional intelligence (EI) an individual's capacity for recognizing his or her own emotions and those of others, including the five components of self awareness, self regulation, motivation, empathy, and social skills.

"Emotional intelligence (EI)" has become popular in both the literature and management practice in recent years.[14] Some evidence of this popularity is that *Harvard Business Review* articles published in 1998 and 2000 by psychologist/journalist Daniel Goleman, who is most closely associated with the concept, have become *HBR*'s most highly requested reprint articles. And two of Goleman's recent books, *Emotional Intelligence* and *Working with Emotional Intelligence,* were both on the *New York Times*'s best-seller lists. Goleman defines **emotional intelligence** as the capacity for recognizing one's own emotions and those of others.[15]

William Bratton: Using Multiple Bases of Power

William Bratton, Chief of the Los Angeles Police Department has an enviable track record in turning around police departments in crime-ridden cities. First, while running the police division of Massachusetts Bay Transit Authority (MBTA) in Boston, then as police commissioner of New York in the mid-1990s, and now in Los Angeles since 2002, Chief Bratton is credited with reducing crime and improving police morale in record time. An analysis of his success at each of these organizations reveals very similar patterns both in terms of the problems he faced and the many ways in which he used the different bases of power to engineer a rapid turnaround.

In Boston, New York, and Los Angeles, Chief Bratton faced similar hurdles: organizations wedded to the status quo, limited resources, demotivated staffs, and opposition from powerful vested interests. But he does not give up in the face of these seemingly insurmountable problems. He is persuasive in calls for change, capable of mobilizing the commitment of key players, silencing vocal naysayers, and building rapport with superiors and subordinates while building bridges with external constituencies.

Chief Bratton's persuasion tactics are unconventional, yet effective. When he was running the MBTA police, the Transit Authority decided to buy small squad cars, which are cheaper to buy and to run, but very inadequate for the police officer's task. Instead of arguing, Bratton invited the general manager for a tour of the city. He rode with the general manager in exactly the same type of car that was ordered for ordinary officers, and drove over every pothole on the road. He moved the seats forward so that the general manager could feel how little leg room was there. And he put on his belt, cuffs, and gun so that the general manager could understand how limited the space was. After two hours in the cramped car, the general manager was ready to change the order and get more suitable cars for the officers!

Another tactic Bratton used effectively was insisting on community meetings between police officers and citizens. This went against the long-standing practice of detachment between police and community to decrease the chances of corruption. The result was that his department had a better understanding of public concerns and rearranged their priorities, which in turn led to better community relations. For internal communications, he relied mainly on professionally produced videos instead of long, boring memos.

Chief Bratton also shows a remarkable talent for building political bridges and silencing naysayers. As he was introducing his zero-tolerance policing approach that aggressively targets "quality of life" crimes such as panhandling, drunkenness, and prostitution, opposition came from the city's courts which feared being inundated by a large number of small-crimes cases. Bratton enlisted the support of Rudolph Giuliani, the mayor of New York, who had considerable influence over the district attorneys, the courts, and the city jail. He also took the case to the *New York Times,* and managed to get the issue of zero-tolerance on the front pages of the newspaper. The courts were left with no alternative but to cooperate.

To a great extent, Bratton's success can be attributed to his understanding of the subtleties of power, including persuasion, motivation, coalition building, empathy for subordinates, and a focus on goals.

Sources: Chan Kim, W., & Renee Mauborgne, R. 2003. Tipping point leadership. *Harvard Business Review,* 81(4): 60–69; and McCarthy, T. 2004. The gang buster. *Time,* January 19: 56–58.

Recent studies of successful managers have found that effective leaders consistently have a high level of emotional intelligence.[16] Findings indicate that EI is a better predictor of life success (economic well-being, satisfaction with life, friendship, family life), including occupational attainments, than IQ. Such evidence has been extrapolated to the catchy phrase: "IQ gets you hired, but EQ (Emotional Quotient) gets you promoted." And surveys show that human resource managers believe this statement to be true, even for highly technical jobs such as those of scientists and engineers.

This is not to say that IQ and technical skills are irrelevant. Obviously, they do matter, but they become "threshold capabilities." That is, they are the necessary requirements for attaining higher-level managerial positions. EI, on the other hand, is essential for leadership success. Without it, Goleman claims, a manager can have excellent training, an incisive analytical mind, and many smart ideas but will still not be a great leader.

	Definition	Hallmarks
Self-management skills:		
Self-awareness	• The ability to recognize and understand your moods, emotions, and drives, as well as their effect on others.	• Self-confidence • Realistic self-assessment • Self-deprecating sense of humor
Self-regulation	• The ability to control or redirect disruptive impulses and moods. • The propensity to suspend judgment—to think before acting.	• Trustworthiness and integrity • Comfort with ambiguity • Openness to change
Motivation	• A passion to work for reasons that go beyond money or status. • A propensity to pursue goals with energy and persistence.	• Strong drive to achieve • Optimism, even in the face of failure • Organizational commitment
Managing relationships:		
Empathy	• The ability to understand the emotional makeup of other people. • Skill in treating people according to their emotional reactions.	• Expertise in building and retaining talent • Cross-cultural sensitivity • Service to clients and customers
Social skill	• Proficiency in managing relationships and building networks. • An ability to find common ground and build rapport.	• Effectiveness in leading change • Persuasiveness • Expertise in building and leading teams

Source: Adapted and reprinted by permission of *Harvard Business Review.* Exhibit from "What Makes a Leader," by D. Goleman, January 2004. Copyright © 2004 by the Harvard Business School Publishing Corporation; all rights reserved.

Exhibit 11.3 The Five Components of Emotional Intelligence at Work

There are five components of EI: self-awareness, self-regulation, motivation, empathy, and social skill. They are included in Exhibit 11.3. We now discuss each of them.

Self-Awareness

Self-awareness is the first component of EI and brings to mind that Delphic oracle who gave the advice "know thyself" thousands of years ago. Self-awareness involves a person having a deep understanding of his or her emotions, strengths, weaknesses, and drives. People with strong self-awareness are neither overly critical nor unrealistically optimistic. Instead, they are honest with themselves and others.

People generally admire and respect candor. Further, leaders are constantly required to make judgment calls that require a candid assessment of capabilities—their own and those of others. People who assess themselves honestly (i.e., self-aware people) are well suited to do the same for the organizations they run.

Self-Regulation

Biological impulses drive our emotions. Although we cannot do away with them, we can strive to manage them. Self-regulation, which is akin to an ongoing inner conversation, frees us from being prisoners of our feelings. People engaged in such conversation feel bad moods and emotional impulses just as everyone else does. However, they find ways to control them and even channel them in useful ways.

People who are in control of their feelings and impulses are able to create an environment of trust and fairness. In such an environment, political behavior and infighting are sharply reduced and productivity tends to be high. Further, people who have mastered their emotions are better able to bring about and implement change in an organization. When a new initiative is announced, they are less likely to panic; rather, they are able to suspend judgment, seek out information, and listen to executives explain the new program.

Motivation

Successful executives are driven to achieve beyond expectations—their own and everyone else's. They are driven to achieve. Although many people are driven by external factors, such as money and prestige, those with leadership potential are driven by a deeply embedded desire to achieve for the sake of achievement.

How can a person tell if he or she is motivated by a drive for achievement instead of external rewards? Look for a sign of passion for the work itself, such as seeking out creative challenges, a love of learning, and taking pride in a job well done. Also, motivated people have a high level of energy to do things better as well as a restlessness with the status quo. They are eager to explore new approaches to their work.

Empathy

Empathy is probably the most easily recognized component of EI. In a business setting, empathy means thoughtfully considering an employee's feelings, along with other factors, in the process of making intelligent decisions. Empathy is particularly important in today's business environment for at least three reasons: the increasing use of teams, the rapid pace of globalization, and the growing need to retain talent.[17]

When leading a team, a manager is often charged with arriving at a consensus—often in the face of a high level of emotions. Empathy enables a manager to sense and understand the viewpoints of everyone around the table.

Globalization typically involves cross-cultural dialogue that can easily lead to miscues. Empathetic people are attuned to the subtleties of body language; they can hear the message beneath the words being spoken. In a more general sense, they have a deep understanding of the existence and importance of cultural and ethnic differences.

Empathy also plays a key role in retaining talent. As we discussed in Chapter 4, human capital is particularly important to a firm in the knowledge economy when it comes to creating advantages that are sustainable. Leaders need empathy to develop and keep top talent. Today, that's even more important, because when high performers leave, they take their tacit knowledge with them.

At times, leaders in organizations can make blunders that exacerbate unfavorable situations—a time when effective leadership is essential. Astonishingly, Northwest Airlines sent a booklet entitled *101 Ways to Save Money* to a number of employees who were undergoing steep pay cuts or layoffs. "Helpful" suggestions included:

- (Tip #15) Get hand-me-down clothes and toys for your kids from family and friends.
- (Tip #18) Take shorter showers.
- (Tip #21) Make your own baby food.
- (Tip #39) Shop in thrift stores.
- (Tip #46) Don't be shy about pulling something you like out of the trash.

Would any of us want the manager(s) who came up with these ideas to be the one to comfort or counsel us during a personal misfortune or tragedy? We'd probably all agree that handing out this booklet would be the antithesis of empathy!

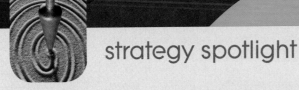

strategy spotlight

11.3

Emotional Intelligence: Cisco Systems' CEO John Chambers

John Chambers recently shared his insights on how he goes about performing his responsibilities as CEO of Cisco Systems. He exemplifies many of the concepts of emotional intelligence and, in his 15 years at Cisco Systems, has become one of the most respected high-tech executives in the world. Chambers' brief essay is one of a series in *Fortune* magazine on the topic of "How I Work."

I started with the classic communications methods when I got here 15 years ago. I'd walk around and talk to small groups and larger groups. I'd see whose car is out in the parking lot. Then e-mail became very effective, because it gave me the ability to send a message to the whole group. But I'm a voice person. I communicate with emotion that way. I like to listen to emotion too. It's a lot easier to listen to a key customer if I hear how they're describing a problem to me. I'll leave 40 or 50 voicemails a day. I do them on the way to work and coming back from work. The newest thing for me is video on demand, which is my primary communication vehicle

today. We have a small studio downstairs. We probably tape ten to fifteen videos a quarter. That way employees, and customers, can watch them when they want.

As far as how I hear from employees, I host a monthly birthday breakfast. Anybody who has a birthday in that month gets to come and quiz me for an hour and 15 minutes. No directors or VPs in the room. It's how I keep my finger on the pulse of what's working and what's not. It's brutal, but it's my most enjoyable session.

To be informed, I like summaries. Because of my dyslexia, I do very little novel reading or that type of activity. I love quick articles. Before every meeting and every panel I study briefing binders with all the information I need: What we're doing in a presentation, who we're meeting with, backgrounds on them, etc. It's two or three pages on each topic, and that is how I like to learn.

I usually wrap up my day just before my wife, Elaine, and I go to bed. I review my critical accounts around the world and summarize a little bit. And then Elaine and I go to sleep talking. My wife has been my partner for 33 years, and we dated for seven years before that, so she understands my strengths and my limitations remarkably well. We make decisions together. My family is the most important thing in the world to me.

Source: Chambers, J. 2006. Lights! Camera! Cue From CEO! *Fortune*, August 21: 27. (Interviewed by Adam Lashinsky.) Copyright © 2006 Time, Inc. All rights reserved.

● The booklet *101 Ways to Save Money* sent out by Northwest Airlines' management was *not* well received by its employees.

Social Skill

While the first three components of emotional intelligence are all self-management skills, the last two—empathy and social skill—concern a person's ability to manage relationships with others. Social skill may be viewed as friendliness with a purpose: moving people in the direction you desire, whether that's agreement on a new marketing strategy or enthusiasm about a new product.

Socially skilled people tend to have a wide circle of acquaintances as well as a knack for finding common ground and building rapport. They recognize that nothing gets done alone, and they have a network in place when the time for action comes.

Social skill can be viewed as the culmination of the other dimensions of EI. People will be effective at managing relationships when they can understand and control their own emotions and empathize with others' feelings. Motivation also contributes to social skill. People who are driven to achieve tend to be optimistic, even when confronted with setbacks. And when people are upbeat, their "glow" is cast upon conversations and other social encounters. They are popular, and for good reason.

Strategy Spotlight 11.3 provides John Chambers' personal reflection on how he goes about his job as Chief Executive Officer of Cisco Systems, the $28 billion networking giant. This empathetic leader has become one of America's most respected high-tech executives.

Emotional Intelligence: Some Potential Drawbacks and Cautionary Notes

Many great leaders have been found to have great reserves of empathy, interpersonal astuteness, awareness of their own feelings, and an awareness of their impact on others.[18] And, more importantly, they apply these capabilities judiciously as best benefits the situation. In essence, the key to this is self-regulation; having some minimum level of these emotional intelligences will help a person be effective as a leader as long as they are channeled appropriately. However, if a person has a high level of these capabilities it may become "too much of a good thing" if they are allowed to drive inappropriate behaviors. Some additional potential drawbacks of EI can be gleaned from the flip side of the benefits from some of its essential components.

Effective Leaders Have Empathy for Others   However, they also must be able to make the "tough decisions." Leaders must be able to appeal to logic and reason and acknowledge others' feelings so that people feel the decisions are correct. However, it is easy to overidentify with others or confuse empathy with sympathy. This will make it more difficult to make the tough decisions.

Effective Leaders Are Astute Judges of People   A danger is that leaders may become judgmental and overly critical about the shortcomings they perceive in others. They are likely to dismiss other people's insights, making them feel undervalued.

Effective Leaders Are Passionate about What They Do, and They Show It   This doesn't mean that they are always cheerleaders. Rather, they may express their passion as persistence in pursuing an objective or a relentless focus on a valued principle. However, there is a fine line between being excited about something and letting your passion close your mind to other possibilities or cause you to ignore realities that others may see.

Effective Leaders Create Personal Connections with Their People   Most effective leaders take time to engage employees individually and in groups, listening to their ideas, suggestions and concerns, and responding in ways that make people feel that their ideas are respected and appreciated. However, the downside of such visibility is that if the leader makes too many unannounced visits, it may create a culture of fear and micromanagement. Clearly, striking a correct balance is essential.

Finally, from a moral standpoint, emotional leadership is neither good nor bad. Emotional leaders can be altruistic, focused on the general welfare of the company and its employees, and highly principled. On the other hand, they can be manipulative, selfish, and dishonest. For example, if a person is using leadership solely to gain formal or informal power, that is not leadership at all.[19] Rather, they are using their EI to grasp what people want and pander to those desires in order to gain authority and influence. After all, easy answers sell.

In the next section, we will discuss some guidelines for developing a "learning organization." In today's competitive environment, the old saying about "a chain is only as strong as the weakest link" applies more than ever before. People throughout organizations must become involved in leadership processes and play greater roles in the formulation and implementation of an organization's strategies and tactics. Put another way, to learn and adapt proactively, firms need "eyes, ears, and brains" throughout all parts of the organization. One person, or a small group of individuals, can no longer think and learn for the entire entity.

Developing a Learning Organization

>LO4
The value of creating and maintaining a "learning organization" in today's global marketplace.

Charles Handy, author of *The Age of Unreason* and *The Age of Paradox* and one of today's most respected business visionaries, shared an amusing story:

> The other day, a courier could not find my family's remote cottage. He called his base on his radio, and the base called us to ask directions. He was just around the corner, but his base managed to omit a vital part of the directions. So he called them again, and they called us again. Then the courier repeated the cycle a third time to ask whether we had a dangerous dog. When he eventually arrived, we asked whether it would not have been simpler and less aggravating to everyone if he had called us directly from the roadside telephone booth where he had been parked. "I can't do that," he said, "because they won't refund any money I spend." "But it's only pennies!" I exclaimed. "I know," he said, "but that only shows how little they trust us!"[20]

At first glance, it would appear that the story simply epitomizes the lack of empowerment and trust granted to the hapless courier: Don't ask questions, Do as you're told![21] However, implicit in this scenario is also the message that learning, information sharing, adaptation, decision making, and so on are *not* shared throughout the organization. In contrast to this admittedly rather extreme case, leading-edge organizations recognize the importance of having everyone involved in the process of actively learning and adapting. As noted by today's leading expert on learning organizations, MIT's Peter Senge, the days when Henry Ford, Alfred Sloan, and Tom Watson *learned **for** the organization* are gone.

> In an increasingly dynamic, interdependent, and unpredictable world, it is simply no longer possible for anyone to "figure it all out at the top." The old model, "the top thinks and the local acts," must now give way to integrating thinking and acting at all levels. While the challenge is great, so is the potential payoff. "The person who figures out how to harness the collective genius of the people in his or her organization," according to former Citibank CEO Walter Wriston, "is going to blow the competition away."[22]

Learning and change typically involve the ongoing questioning of an organization's status quo or method of procedure. This means that all individuals throughout the organization—not just those at the top—must reflect. Although this seems simple enough, it is easy to ignore. After all, many organizations get so caught up in carrying out their day-to-day work that they rarely, if ever, stop to think objectively about themselves and their businesses. They often fail to ask the probing questions that might lead them to call into question their basic assumptions, to refresh their strategies, or to reengineer their work processes. According to Michael Hammer and Steven Stanton, the pioneer consultants who touched off the reengineering movement:

> Reflection entails awareness of self, of competitors, of customers. It means thinking without preconception. It means questioning cherished assumptions and replacing them with new approaches. It is the only way in which a winning company can maintain its leadership position, by which a company with great assets can ensure that they continue to be well deployed.[23]

learning organizations organizations that create a proactive, creative approach to the unknown, characterized by (1) inspiring and motivating people with a mission and purpose, (2) empowering employees at all levels, (3) accumulating and sharing internal knowledge, (4) gathering and integrating external information, and (5) challenging the status quo and enabling creativity.

Successful **learning organizations** create a proactive, creative approach to the unknown, actively solicit the involvement of employees at all levels, and enable all employees to use their intelligence and apply their imagination. Higher-level skills are required of everyone, not just those at the top. A learning environment involves organizationwide commitment to change, an action orientation, and applicable tools and methods.[24] It must be viewed by everyone as a guiding philosophy and not simply as another change program that is often derisively labeled the new "flavor of the month."

A critical requirement of all learning organizations is that everyone feels and supports a compelling purpose. In the words of William O'Brien, CEO of Hanover Insurance, "Before there can be meaningful participation, people must share certain values and pictures about where we are trying to go. We discovered that people have a real need to feel that they're part of an enabling mission."[25]

These are the five key elements of a learning organization. Each of these items should be viewed *as necessary, but not sufficient.* That is, successful learning organizations need all five elements.

1. Inspiring and motivating people with a mission or purpose.
2. Empowering employees at all levels.
3. Accumulating and sharing internal knowledge.
4. Gathering and integrating external information.
5. Challenging the status quo and enabling creativity.

Inspiring and motivating people with a mission or purpose is a necessary but not sufficient condition for developing an organization that can learn and adapt to a rapidly changing, complex, and interconnected environment.

We briefly addressed the importance of articulating a mission or purpose. Exhibit 11.4 lists all five elements of a learning organization.

Empowering Employees at All Levels

"The great leader is a great servant," asserted Ken Melrose, CEO of Toro Company and author of *Making the Grass Greener on Your Side.*[26] A manager's role becomes one of creating an environment where employees can achieve their potential as they help move the organization toward its goals. Instead of viewing themselves as resource controllers and power brokers, leaders must envision themselves as flexible resources willing to assume numerous roles as coaches, information providers, teachers, decision makers, facilitators, supporters, or listeners, depending on the needs of their employees.

The central key to empowerment is effective leadership. Empowerment can't occur in a leadership vacuum. According to Melrose, "I came to understand that you best lead by serving the needs of your people. You don't do their jobs for them; you enable them to learn and progress on the job." Robert Quinn and Gretchen Spreitzer made an interesting point about two diametrically opposite perspectives on empowerment.[27] In the top-down perspective, empowerment is about delegation and accountability—senior management has developed a clear vision and has communicated specific plans to the rest of the organization. This strategy for empowerment encompasses the following:

- Start at the top.
- Clarify the organization's mission, vision, and values.
- Clearly specify the tasks, roles, and rewards for employees.
- Delegate responsibility.
- Hold people accountable for results.

By contrast, the bottom-up view looks at empowerment as concerned with risk taking, growth, and change. It involves trusting people to "do the right thing" and having a tolerance for failure. It encourages employees to act with a sense of ownership and typically "ask for forgiveness rather than permission." Here the salient elements of empowerment are:

- Start at the bottom by understanding the needs of employees.
- Teach employees self-management skills and model desired behavior.
- Build teams to encourage cooperative behavior.
- Encourage intelligent risk taking.
- Trust people to perform.

Clearly, these two perspectives draw a sharp contrast in assumptions that people make about trust and control. Interestingly, Quinn and Spreitzer recently shared these contrasting

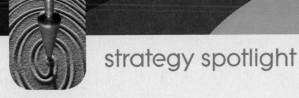

Employee Empowerment at Chaparral Steel

Managers at Chaparral Steel, a steel minimill in Midlothian, Texas, are convinced that employee ownership empowers workers to act in the best interests of the company. They believe that ownership is not composed solely of the firm's equity but also of its knowledge. By sharing financial and knowledge resources with employees, Chaparral Steel is a model of employee empowerment—90 percent of its employees own company stock and everyone is salaried, wears the same white hard hats, drinks the same free coffee, and has access to the knowledge that goes into the innovative processes at the firm's manufacturing plants.

Sources: Johnson, D. 1998. Catching the third wave: How to succeed in business when it's changing at the speed of light. *Futurist*, March: 32–38; Petry, C. 1997. Chaparral poised on the brink of breakthrough: Chaparral Steel developing integrated automobile shredder-separation facility. *American Metal Market*, September 10: 18; Leonard-Barton, D. 1992. The factory as a learning laboratory. *Sloan Management Review*, 34: 23–38; and TXI Chaparral Steel Midlothian registered to ISO 2002. Chaparral Steel press release, July 8, 2001.

Rather than using managers as buffers between customers and line workers, Chaparral directly involves employees with customers. Customer concerns are routed directly to the line workers responsible for manufacturing a customer's specific products. "Everyone here is part of the sales department," president and CEO Gordon Forward said. "They carry their own business cards. If they visit a customer, we want them to come back and look at their own process differently. This helps employees from all levels to view operations from the customer's perspective." Forward believes that "if a melt shop crew understands why a customer needs a particular grade of steel, it will make sure the customer gets that exact grade."

This encourages employees to think beyond traditional functional boundaries and find ways to improve the organization's processes. By integrating the customer's perspective into their efforts, employees at Chaparral Steel become more than just salaried workers; they feel responsible to the firm as if each production process was their own creation and responsibility.

views of empowerment with a senior management team. After an initial heavy silence, someone from the first group voiced a concern about the second group's perspective, "We can't afford loose cannons around here." A person in the second group retorted, "When was the last time you saw a cannon of any kind around here?"

Many leading-edge organizations are moving in the direction of the second perspective—recognizing the need for trust, cultural control, and expertise (at all levels) instead of the extensive and cumbersome rules and regulations inherent in hierarchical control.[28] Some have argued that too often organizations fall prey to the "heroes-and-drones syndrome," wherein the value of those in powerful positions is exalted and the value of those who fail to achieve top rank is diminished. Such an attitude is implicit in phrases such as "Lead, follow, or get out of the way" or, even less appealing, "Unless you're the lead horse, the view never changes." Of course, few will ever reach the top hierarchical positions in organizations, but in the information economy, the strongest organizations are those that effectively use the talents of all the players on the team. Strategy Spotlight 11.4 illustrates how one company, Chaparral Steel, empowers its employees.

Accumulating and Sharing Internal Knowledge

Effective organizations must also *redistribute information, knowledge* (i.e., skills to act on the information), and *rewards*.[29] For example, a company might give frontline employees the power to act as "customer advocates," doing whatever is necessary to satisfy customers. Employees, however, also need to have the appropriate training. The company needs to disseminate information by sharing customer expectations and feedback as well as financial information. The employees must know about the goals of the business as well as how key value-creating activities in the organization are related to each other. Finally, organizations should allocate rewards on how effectively employees use information, knowledge, and power to improve customer service quality and the company's overall performance.

Jack Stack is the president and CEO of Springfield ReManufacturing Corporation (SRC) in Springfield, Missouri, and author of *The Great Game of Business.* He is generally considered the pioneer of "open book" management—an innovative way to gather and disseminate internal information. Implementing this system involves three core activities.[30] First, numbers are generated daily for each of the company's employees, reflecting his or her work performance and production costs. Second, this information is aggregated once a week and shared with all of the company's people from secretaries to top management. Third, employees receive extensive training in how to use and interpret the numbers—how to understand balance sheets as well as cash flows and income statements.

In explaining why SRC embraces open book management, Stack provided an insightful counterperspective to the old adage "Information is power."

> We are building a company in which everyone tells the truth every day—not because everyone is honest but because everyone has access to the same information: operating metrics, financial data, valuation estimates. The more people understand what's really going on in their company, the more eager they are to help solve its problems. Information isn't power. It's a burden. Share information, and you share the burdens of leadership as well.

Let's take a look at Whole Foods Market, Inc., the largest natural foods grocer in the United States.[31] An important benefit of the sharing of internal information at Whole Foods becomes the active process of *internal benchmarking*. Competition is intense at Whole Foods. Teams compete against their own goals for sales, growth, and productivity; they compete against different teams in their stores; and they compete against similar teams at different stores and regions. Similarly, there is an elaborate system of peer reviews through which teams benchmark each other. The "Store Tour" is the most intense. On a periodic schedule, each Whole Foods store is toured by a group of as many as 40 visitors from another region. Lateral learning—discovering what your colleagues are doing right and carrying those practices into your organization—has become a driving force at Whole Foods.

In addition to enhancing the sharing of company information both up and down as well as across the organization, leaders also have to develop means to tap into some of the more informal sources of internal information. In a recent survey of presidents, CEOs, board members, and top executives in a variety of nonprofit organizations, respondents were asked what differentiated the successful candidates for promotion. The consensus: The executive was seen as a person who listens. According to Peter Meyer, the author of the study, "The value of listening is clear: You cannot succeed in running a company if you do not hear what your people, customers, and suppliers are telling you. Poor listeners do not survive. Listening and understanding well are key to making good decisions."[32]

Strategy Spotlight 11.5 addresses a critical aspect of obtaining information from internal sources—listening skills. General Peter Pace, Chairman of the Joint Chiefs of Staff, shares his perspective on this topic. He is the highest-ranking military officer in the United States.

Gathering and Integrating External Information

Recognizing opportunities, as well as threats, in the external environment is vital to a firm's success. Focusing exclusively on the efficiency of internal operations may result in a firm becoming, in effect, the world's most efficient producer of manual typewriters or leisure suits—hardly an enviable position! As organizations *and* environments become more complex and evolve rapidly, it is far more critical for employees and managers to become more aware of environmental trends and events—both general and industry-specific—and more knowledgeable about their firm's competitors and customers. Next, we will discuss some ideas on how to do it.

First, the Internet has dramatically accelerated the speed with which anyone can track down useful information or locate people who might have useful information. Prior to the Net, locating someone who used to work at a company—always a good source of

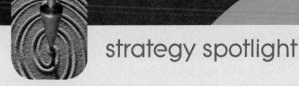

Listening Skills: A Key to Obtaining Valuable Internal Information

"I don't want any yes-men around me," movie mogul Samuel Goldwyn once said. "I want them to tell me the truth, even if it costs them their jobs." We may laugh because it is often true. Organizations are usually not in the habit of rewarding people who speak uncomfortable truths—or, in the vernacular, "going against the company line." However, we need to hear from them.

According to General Peter Pace, "If you walk into a room as a senior person and innocently say, 'Here's what I'm thinking about this,' you have already skewed people's

thinking. His approach: "Start out with a question and don't voice an opinion."

Why? People can't support your position if they do not know where you stand on the issue. After all, supporting the boss is usually the politically expedient thing to do! Further, if you present subordinates with an intellectual challenge, they feel freer to offer their opinions without fear of offending somebody ranking higher in the organization. "If you are looking for answers, ask the question," suggests Pace, and "if you are looking for an honest critique, you ought to be the first person to self-critique." This is different from generals' metaphorically taking off their stars to ask for honest feedback. People know the stars will be back!

Source: Useem, M., & Useem, J. 2005. Great escapes. *Fortune*, June 27: 98, 100.

information—was quite a challenge. However, today people post their résumés on the Web; they participate in discussion groups and talk openly about where they work.

Marc Friedman, manager of market research at $1 billion Andrew Corporation, a fast-growing manufacturer of wireless communications products provides an example of effective Internet use.[33] One of Friedman's preferred sites to visit is Corptech's Web site, which provides information on 45,000 high-tech companies and more than 170,000 executives. One of his firm's product lines consisted of antennae for air-traffic control systems. He got a request to provide a country-by-country breakdown of upgrade plans for various airports. He knew nothing about air-traffic control at the time. However, he found a site on the Internet for the International Civil Aviation Organization. Fortunately, it had a great deal of useful data, including several research companies working in his area of interest.

Second, in addition to the Internet, company employees at all levels can use "garden variety" traditional sources to acquire external information. Much can be gleaned by reading trade and professional journals, books, and popular business magazines such as *BusinessWeek, Forbes, Fortune,* and *Fast Company.* Other venues for gathering external information include membership in professional or trade organizations and attendance at meetings and conventions. Networking among colleagues inside and outside of your industry is also very useful. Intel's Andy Grove, for example, gathers information from people like DreamWorks SKG's Steven Spielberg and Tele-Communications Inc.'s John Malone.[34] He believes that such interaction provides insights into how to make personal computers more entertaining and better at communicating. Internally, Grove spends time with the young "propeller-heads" who run Intel Architecture labs, an Oregon-based facility that Grove hopes will become the de facto R&D lab for the entire PC industry.

Third, benchmarking can be a useful means of employing external information. Here managers seek out the best examples of a particular practice as part of an ongoing effort to improve the corresponding practice in their own organization.[35] There are two primary types of benchmarking. *Competitive benchmarking* restricts the search for best practices to competitors, while *functional benchmarking* endeavors to determine best practices regardless of industry. Industry-specific standards (e.g., response times required to repair power outages in the electric utility industry) are typically best handled through competitive benchmarking, whereas more generic processes (e.g., answering 1-800 calls) lend themselves to functional benchmarking because the function is essentially the same in any industry.

Ford Motor Company used benchmarking to study Mazda's accounts payable operations.[36] Its initial goal of a 20 percent cut in its 500-employee accounts payable staff was ratcheted up to 75 percent—and met. Ford found that staff spent most of their time trying to match often conflicting data in a mass of paper, including purchase orders, invoices, and receipts. Following Mazda's example, Ford created an "invoiceless system" in which invoices no longer trigger payments to suppliers. The receipt does the job.

Fourth, focus directly on customers for information. For example, William McKnight, head of 3M's Chicago sales office, required that salesmen of abrasives products talk directly to the workers in the shop to find out what they needed, instead of calling on only front-office executives.[37] This was very innovative at the time—1909! But it illustrates the need to get to the end user of a product or service. (McKnight went on to become 3M's president from 1929 to 1949 and chairman from 1949 to 1969.) More recently, James Taylor, senior vice president for global marketing at Gateway 2000, discussed the value of customer input in reducing response time, a critical success factor in the PC industry.

> We talk to 100,000 people a day—people calling to order a computer, shopping around, looking for tech support. Our Web site gets 1.1 million hits per day. The time it takes for an idea to enter this organization, get processed, and then go to customers for feedback is down to minutes. We've designed the company around speed and feedback.[38]

Challenging the Status Quo and Enabling Creativity

Earlier in this chapter we discussed some of the barriers that leaders face when trying to bring about change in an organization. These included vested interests in the status quo, systemic barriers, behavioral barriers, political barriers, and personal time constraints. For a firm to become a "learning organization," it must overcome such barriers in order to foster creativity and enable it to permeate the firm. This becomes quite a challenge, of course, if the firm is entrenched in a status quo mentality.

Perhaps the best way to challenge the status quo is for the leader to forcefully create a sense of urgency. For example, Tom Kasten, vice president of Levi Strauss, has a direct approach to initiating change. He is charged with leading the campaign to transform the company for the 21st century.

> You create a compelling picture of the risks of *not* changing. We let our people hear directly from customers. We videotaped interviews with customers and played excerpts. One big customer said, "We trust many of your competitors implicitly. We sample their deliveries. We open *all* Levi's deliveries." Another said, "Your lead times are the worst. If you weren't Levi's, you'd be gone." It was powerful. I wish we had done more of it.[39]

Such initiative—if sincere and credible—establishes a shared mission and the need for major transformations. If effective, it can channel energies to bring about both change and creative endeavors.

Establishing a "culture of dissent" can be another effective means of questioning the status quo and serving as a spur toward creativity. Here norms are established whereby dissenters can openly question a superior's perspective without fear of retaliation or retribution. Consider the perspective of Steven Balmer, Microsoft's CEO.

> Bill [Gates] brings to the company the idea that conflict can be a good thing. . . . Bill knows it's important to avoid that gentle civility that keeps you from getting to the heart of an issue quickly. He likes it when anyone, even a junior employee, challenges him, and you know he respects you when he starts shouting back.[40]

Motorola has, in effect, gone a step further and institutionalized its culture of dissent.[41] By filing a "minority report," an employee can go above his or her immediate supervisor's head and officially lodge a different point of view on a business decision. According to former CEO George Fisher, "I'd call it a healthy spirit of discontent and a freedom by and large to express your discontent around here or to disagree with whoever it is in the company, me or anybody else."

It's innovation's great paradox: Success—that is, true breakthroughs—usually comes through failure. Here are some ideas on how to help your team get comfortable with taking risks and learning from mistakes:

- **Formalize Forums for Failure**
  To keep failures and the valuable lessons they offer from getting swept under the rug, *carve out time for reflection.* GE recently began sharing lessons from failures by bringing together managers whose "Imagination Breakthrough" efforts are put on the shelf.

- **Move the Goalposts**
  Innovation requires flexibility in meeting goals, since early predictions are often little more than educated guesses. Intuit's Scott Cook even suggests that teams developing new products ignore forecasts in the early days. "For every one of our failures, we had spreadsheets that looked awesome," he says.

- **Share Personal Stories**
  If employees hear leaders discussing their own failures, *they'll feel more comfortable talking about their own.* But it's not just the CEO's job. Front-line leaders are even more important, says Harvard Business School professor Amy Edmondson. "That person needs to be inviting, curious, and the first to say: 'I made a mistake'."

- **Bring in Outsiders**
  Outsiders can *help neutralize the emotions and biases that prop up a flop.* Customers can be the most valuable. After its DNA chip failed, Corning brought pharmaceutical companies in early to test its new drug-discovery technology, Epic.

- **Prove Yourself Wrong, Not Right**
  Development teams tend to look for supporting, rather than countervailing, evidence. "You have to reframe what you're seeking in the early days," says Innosight's Scott Anthony. *"You're not really seeking proof that you have the right answer.* It's more about testing to prove yourself wrong."

- **Celebrate Smart Failures**
  Managers should design performance-management systems that reward risk taking and foster a long-term view. But they should also *celebrate failures that teach something new,* energizing people to try again and offering them closure.

Source: McGregor, J. 2006. How failure breeds success. *BusinessWeek.* July10: 42–52.

Exhibit 11.5 Best Practices: Learning from Failures

Closely related to the culture of dissent is the fostering of a culture that encourages risk taking. "If you're not making mistakes, you're not taking risks, and that means you're not going anywhere," claimed John Holt, coauthor of *Celebrate Your Mistakes.*[42] "The key is to make errors faster than the competition, so you have more chances to learn and win."

Companies that cultivate cultures of experimentation and curiosity make sure that *failure* is not, in essence, an obscene word. People who stretch the envelope and ruffle feathers are protected. More importantly, they encourage mistakes as a key part of their competitive advantage. This philosophy was shared by Stan Shih, CEO of Acer, a Taiwan-based computer company. If a manager at Acer took an intelligent risk and made a mistake—even a costly one—Shih wrote off the loss as tuition payment for the manager's education. Such a culture must permeate the entire organization. As a high-tech executive told us during an interview: "Every person has a freedom to fail."

Exhibit 11.5 has insights on how organizations can both embrace risk and learn from failure.

ethics a system of right and wrong that assists individuals in deciding when an act is moral or immoral and/or socially desirable or not.

>LO5

The leader's role in establishing an ethical organization.

Creating an Ethical Organization

Ethics may be defined as a system of right and wrong.[43] Ethics assists individuals in deciding when an act is moral or immoral, socially desirable or not. The sources for an individual's ethics include religious beliefs, national and ethnic heritage, family practices, community standards, educational experiences, and friends and neighbors. Business ethics is the application of ethical standards to commercial enterprise.

Individual Ethics versus Organizational Ethics

Many leaders may think of ethics as a question of personal scruples, a confidential matter between employees and their consciences. Such leaders are quick to describe any wrongdoing as an isolated incident, the work of a rogue employee. They assume the company should not bear any responsibility for an individual's misdeeds. After all, in their view, ethics has nothing to do with leadership.

In fact, ethics has everything to do with leadership. Seldom does the character flaw of a lone actor completely explain corporate misconduct. Instead, unethical business practices typically involve the tacit, if not explicit, cooperation of others and reflect the values, attitudes, and behavior patterns that define an organization's operating culture. Ethics is as much an organizational as a personal issue. Leaders who fail to provide proper leadership to institute proper systems and controls that facilitate ethical conduct share responsibility with those who conceive, execute, and knowingly benefit from corporate misdeeds.

The ethical orientation of a leader is a key factor in promoting ethical behavior. Ethical leaders must take personal, ethical responsibility for their actions and decision making. Leaders who exhibit high ethical standards become role models for others and raise an organization's overall level of ethical behavior. In essence, ethical behavior must start with the leader before the employees can be expected to perform accordingly.

Over the last few decades, there has been a growing interest in corporate ethical performance. Perhaps some reasons for this trend may be the increasing lack of confidence regarding corporate activities, the growing emphasis on quality of life issues, and a spate of recent corporate scandals at such firms as Enron, Tyco, and others. Merely adhering to the minimum regulatory standards may not be enough to remain competitive in a world that is becoming more socially conscious.

Without a strong ethical culture, the chance of ethical crises occurring is enhanced. Ethical crises can be very expensive—both in terms of financial costs and in the erosion of human capital and overall firm reputation. Consider, for example, Texaco's class-action discrimination lawsuit.

> In 1994 a senior financial analyst, Bari-Ellen Roberts, and one of her co-workers, Sil Chambers, filed a class-action discrimination suit against Texaco after enduring racial slurs and being passed over for promotion on several occasions. The discrimination suit charged Texaco with using an "old boys network" to systematically discriminate against African Americans.
>
> Roberts remembers, "The hardest part of the suit was deciding to do it. I'd worked so hard to get where I was, and I had to risk all of that. Then I had to deal with loneliness and isolation. Even some of the other African Americans viewed me as a troublemaker. When you're standing up and calling for change, it makes people fear for their own security."
>
> Two years later, in 1996, Texaco settled the suit, paying $141 million to its African-American workers. This was followed with an additional $35 million to remove discriminatory practices.[44]

Please note that the financial cost alone of $176 million was certainly not the proverbial "drop in the bucket." This amount represented nearly 10 percent of Texaco Inc.'s entire net income for 1996.

As we are all aware, the past several years have been characterized by numerous examples of unethical and illegal behavior by many top-level corporate executives. These include executives of firms such as Enron, Tyco, Worldcom, Inc., Adelphia, and Healthsouth Corp., who were all forced to resign and are facing (or have been convicted of) criminal charges. And, recall the example of greed in the opening case of Chapter 9. Here KB Home's CEO Bruce Karatz made millions on options backdating. The resulting scandal eventually forced him to retire. And that's

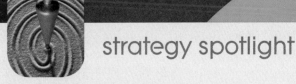

strategy spotlight

11.6

Procter & Gamble: Using Ethics to "Build the Spirit of the Place"

John Pepper, former CEO and chairman of Procter & Gamble Company, shares his perspective on ethics.

Let me start by saying that while ethics may seem like a soft concept—not as hard, say, as strategy or budgeting or operations—it is, in fact, a very hard concept. It is tangible. It is crucial . . . it is good for business.

There are several reasons for this. First, a company's values have a tremendous impact on who is attracted to your company and who will stay with it. We only have one life to live. All of us want to live it as part of an institution committed to high goals and high-sighted means of reaching these goals. This is true everywhere I've been. In our most mature countries and our newest.

Strong corporate values greatly simplify decision making. It is important to know the things you won't even

think about doing. Diluting a product. Paying a bribe. Not being fair to a customer or an employee.

Strong values earn the respect of customers and suppliers and governments and other companies, too. This is absolutely crucial over the long term.

A company which pays bribes in a foreign market becomes an open target for more bribes when the word gets out. It never stops.

A company which is seen to be offering different trade terms to different customers based on how big they are or how hard they push will forever be beset by requests for special terms.

A company which is seen by a government as having weak or varying standards will not be respected by that government.

And more positively, governments and other companies really do want to deal with companies they feel are pursuing sound values because in many, if not most, cases, they believe it will be good for them.

One final but very fundamental reason for operating ethically is that strong values create trust and pride among employees. Simply put, they build the spirit of the place.

Source: Pepper, J. E. 1997. The boa principle: Operating ethically in today's business environment. Speech presented at Florida A&M University, Tallahassee, January 30.

---

just one example of what has taken place in more than 200 companies that have faced questions about backdating—in many cases leading to indictments and criminal penalties.

The ethical organization is characterized by a conception of ethical values and integrity as a driving force of the enterprise.[45] Ethical values shape the search for opportunities, the design of organizational systems, and the decision-making process used by individuals and groups. They provide a common frame of reference that serves as a unifying force across different functions, lines of business, and employee groups. Organizational ethics helps to define what a company is and what it stands for.

There are many potential benefits of an ethical organization, but they are often indirect. Research has found somewhat inconsistent results concerning the overall relationship between ethical performance and measures of financial performance.[46] However, positive relationships have generally been found between ethical performance and strong organizational culture, increased employee efforts, lower turnover, higher organizational commitment, and enhanced social responsibility.

Clearly, the advantages of a strong ethical orientation can have a positive effect on employee commitment and motivation to excel. This is particularly important in today's knowledge-intensive organizations, where human capital is critical in creating value and competitive advantages. As we discussed in Chapter 4, positive, constructive relationships among individuals (i.e., social capital) are vital in leveraging human capital and other resources in an organization. However, there are many other potential benefits as well. Drawing on the concept of stakeholder management that we discussed in Chapter 1, an ethically sound organization can also strengthen its bonds among its suppliers, customers, and governmental agencies. John E. Pepper, former chairman of Procter & Gamble, addresses such a perspective in Strategy Spotlight 11.6.

Integrity-Based versus Compliance-Based Approaches to Organizational Ethics

>LO6
The difference between integrity-based and compliance-based approaches to organizational ethics.

Before discussing the key elements of an ethical organization, one must understand the links between organizational integrity and the personal integrity of an organization's members.[47] There cannot be high-integrity organizations without high-integrity individuals. However, individual integrity is rarely self-sustaining. Even good people can lose their bearings when faced with pressures, temptations, and heightened performance expectations in the absence of organizational support systems and ethical boundaries. Organizational integrity, goes beyond personal integrity. It rests on a concept of purpose, responsibility, and ideals for an organization as a whole. An important responsibility of leadership in building organizational integrity is to create this ethical framework and develop the organizational capabilities to make it operational.

Lynn Paine, an ethics scholar at Harvard, identifies two approaches: the compliance-based approach and the integrity-based approach. (See Exhibit 11.6 for a comparison of compliance-based and integrity-based strategies.) Faced with the prospect of litigation, several organizations reactively implement **compliance-based ethics programs.** Such programs are typically designed by a corporate counsel with the goal of preventing, detecting, and punishing legal violations. But being ethical is much more than being legal, and an integrity-based approach addresses the issue of ethics in a more comprehensive manner.

Integrity-based ethics programs combine a concern for law with an emphasis on managerial responsibility for ethical behavior. It is broader, deeper, and more demanding than a legal compliance initiative. It is broader in that it seeks to enable responsible conduct. It is deeper in that it cuts to the ethos and operating systems of an organization and its members, their core guiding values, thoughts, and actions. And it is more demanding because it requires an active effort to define the responsibilities and aspirations that constitute an organization's ethical compass. Most importantly, in this approach, organizational ethics is seen as the work of management.

A corporate counsel may play a role in designing and implementing integrity strategies, but it is managers at all levels and across all functions that are involved in the process. Once integrated into the day-to-day operations, such strategies can prevent damaging ethical lapses, while tapping into powerful human impulses for moral thought and action. Ethics becomes the governing ethos of an organization and not burdensome

compliance-based ethics programs programs for building ethical organizations that have the goal of preventing, detecting, and punishing legal violations.

integrity-based ethics programs programs for building ethical organizations that combine a concern for law with an emphasis on managerial responsibility for ethical behavior, including (1) enabling ethical conduct; (2) examining the organization's and members' core guiding values, thoughts, and actions; and (3) defining the responsibilities and aspirations that constitute an organization's ethical compass.

Characteristics	Compliance-Based Approach	Integrity-Based Approach
Ethos	Conformity with externally imposed standards	Self-governance according to chosen standards
Objective	Prevent criminal misconduct	Enable responsible conduct
Leadership	Lawyer-driven	Management-driven with aid of lawyers, HR, and others
Methods	Education, reduced discretion, auditing and controls, penalties	Education, leadership, accountability, organizational systems and decision processes, auditing and controls, penalties
Behavioral Assumptions	Autonomous beings guided by material self-interest	Social beings guided by material self-interest, values, ideals, peers

Source: Reprinted by permission of *Harvard Business Review*. Exhibit from "Managing Organizational Integrity," by L. S. Paine. Copyright 1994 by the Harvard Business School Publishing Corporation; all rights reserved.

Exhibit 11.6 Approaches to Ethics Management

constraints. Here is an example of an organization that goes beyond mere compliance to laws in building an ethical organization:

> In teaching ethics to its employees, Texas Instruments, the $14 billion chip and electronics manufacturer, asks them to run an issue through the following steps: Is it legal? Is it consistent with the company's stated values? Will the employee feel bad doing it? What will the public think if the action is reported in the press? Does the employee think it is wrong? Further, if the employees are not sure of the ethicality of the issue, they are encouraged to ask someone until they are clear about it. In the process, employees can approach high-level personnel and even the company's lawyers. As can be clearly noted, at Texas Instruments, the question of ethics goes much beyond merely being legal. It is no surprise, therefore, that this company is a benchmark for corporate ethics and has been a recipient of three ethics awards: the David C. Lincoln Award for Ethics and Excellence in Business, American Business Ethics Award, and Bentley College Center for Business Ethics Award.[48]

>LO7

Several key elements that organizations must have to become an ethical organization.

To sum up, compliance-based approaches are externally motivated—that is, based on the fear of punishment for doing something unlawful. On the other hand, integrity-based approaches are driven by a personal and organizational commitment to ethical behavior.

A firm must have several key elements before it can become a highly ethical organization. The following elements must be both present and constantly reinforced:

- Role models.
- Corporate credos and codes of conduct.
- Reward and evaluation systems.
- Policies and procedures.

These elements are highly interrelated. For example, reward structures and policies will be useless if leaders are not sound role models. That is, leaders who implicitly say, "Do as I say, not as I do," will quickly have their credibility eroded and such actions will, in effect, sabotage other elements that are essential to building an ethical organization.

Role Models

For good or for bad, leaders are role models in their organizations. As we noted in Chapter 9, leaders must "walk the talk"; that is, they must be consistent in their words and deeds. The values as well as the character of leaders become transparent to an organization's employees through their behaviors. In addition, when leaders do not believe in the ethical standards that they are trying to inspire, they will not be effective as good role models. Being an effective leader often includes taking responsibility for ethical lapses within the organization—even though the executives themselves are not directly involved. Consider, for example, the perspective of Dennis Bakke, CEO of AES, the $12 billion global electricity company based in Arlington, Virginia.

> There was a major breach (in 1992) of the AES values. Nine members of the water treatment team in Oklahoma lied to the EPA about water quality at the plant. There was no environmental damage, but they lied about the test results. A new, young chemist at the plant discovered it, told a team leader, and we then were notified. Now, you could argue that the people who lied were responsible and were accountable, but the senior management team also took responsibility by taking pay cuts. My reduction was about 30 percent.[49]

Such action enhances the loyalty and commitment of employees throughout the organization. Many would believe that it would have been much easier (and personally less expensive!) for Bakke and his management team to merely take strong punitive action against the nine individuals who were acting contrary to the behavior expected in AES's ethical culture. However, by taking responsibility for the misdeeds, the top executives—through their highly visible action—made it very clear that responsibility and penalties for ethical lapses go well beyond the "guilty" parties. Such courageous behavior by leaders helps to strengthen an organization's ethical environment.

Corporate Credos and Codes of Conduct

Corporate credos or codes of conduct are mechanisms that provide a statement and guidelines for norms and beliefs as well as guidelines for decision making. They provide employees with a clear understanding of the organization's position regarding employee behavior. Such guidelines also provide the basis for employees to refuse to commit unethical acts and help to make them aware of issues before they are faced with the situation. For such codes to be truly effective, organization members must be aware of them and what behavioral guidelines they contain.[50]

Large corporations are not the only ones to develop and use codes of conduct. Consider the example of Wetherill Associates (WAI), a small, privately held supplier of electrical parts to the automotive market.

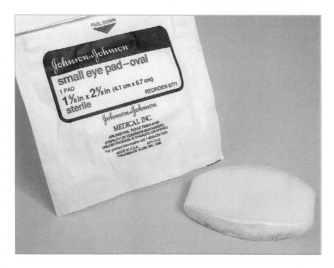

● Johnson & Johnson is well known for its credo, which stresses honesty, integrity, superior products, and putting people before profits. Above is one of its many products.

> Rather than a conventional code of conduct, WAI has a Quality Assurance Manual—a combination of philosophy text, conduct guide, technical manual, and company profile—that describes the company's commitment to honesty, ethical action, and integrity.
>
> Interestingly, WAI doesn't have a corporate ethics officer, because the company's corporate ethics officer is Marie Bothe, WAI's chief executive officer. She sees her main function as keeping the 350-employee company on the path of ethical behavior and looking for opportunities to help the community. She delegates the "technical" aspects of the business—marketing, finance, personnel, and operations—to other members of the organization.[51]

Perhaps the best-known credo, a statement describing a firm's commitment to certain standards, is that of Johnson & Johnson (J&J). It is reprinted in Exhibit 11.7. The credo stresses honesty, integrity, superior products, and putting people before profits. What distinguishes the J&J credo from those of other firms is the amount of energy the company's top managers devote to ensuring that employees live by its precepts:

> Over a three-year period, Johnson & Johnson undertook a massive effort to assure that its original credo, already decades old, was still valid. More than 1,200 managers attended two-day seminars in groups of 25, with explicit instructions to challenge the credo. The president or CEO of the firm presided over each session. In the end, the company came out of the process believing that its original document was still valid. However, the questioning process continues. Such "challenge meetings" are still replicated every other year for all new managers. These efforts force J&J to question, internalize, and then implement its credo. Such investments have paid off handsomely many times—most notably in 1982, when eight people died from swallowing capsules of Tylenol, one of its flagship products, that someone had laced with cyanide. Leaders such as James Burke, who without hesitation made an across-the-board recall of the product even though it affected only a limited number of untraceable units, send a strong message throughout the firm.

Reward and Evaluation Systems

It is entirely possible for a highly ethical leader to preside over an organization that commits several unethical acts. How? It may reflect a flaw in the organization's reward structure. A reward and evaluation system may inadvertently cause individuals to act in an inappropriate manner if rewards are seen as being distributed on the basis of outcomes instead of the means by which goals and objectives are achieved.[52]

Consider the example of Sears, Roebuck & Co.'s automotive operations. Here, unethical behavior, rooted in a faulty reward system, took place primarily at the operations level: its automobile repair facilities.[53]

Exhibit 11.7

Johnson & Johnson's Credo

We believe our first responsibility is to the doctors, nurses and patients, to mothers and fathers and all others who use our products and services. In meeting their needs everything we do must be of high quality. We must constantly strive to reduce our costs in order to maintain reasonable prices. Customers' orders must be serviced promptly and accurately. Our suppliers and distributors must have an opportunity to make a fair profit.

We are responsible to our employees, the men and women who work with us throughout the world. Everyone must be considered as an individual. We must respect their dignity and recognize their merit. They must have a sense of security in their jobs. Compensation must be fair and adequate, and working conditions clean, orderly, and safe. We must be mindful of ways to help our employees fulfill their family responsibilities. Employees must feel free to make suggestions and complaints. There must be equal opportunity for employment, development, and advancement for those qualified. We must provide competent management, and their actions must be just and ethical.

We are responsible to the communities in which we live and work and to the world community as well. We must be good citizens—support good works and charities and bear our fair share of taxes. We must encourage civic improvements and better health and education. We must maintain in good order the property we are privileged to use, protecting the environment and natural resources.

Our final responsibility is to our stockholders. Business must make a sound profit. We must experiment with new ideas. Research must be carried on, innovative programs developed, and mistakes paid for. New equipment must be purchased, new facilities provided, and new products launched. Reserves must be created to provide for adverse times. When we operate according to these principles, the stockholders should realize a fair return.

Source: Reprinted with permission of Johnson & Johnson Co.

In 1992 Sears was flooded with complaints about its automotive service business. Consumers and attorneys general in more than 40 states accused the firm of misleading customers and selling them unnecessary parts and services, from brake jobs to front-end alignments. What were the causes?

In the face of declining revenues and eroding market share, Sears's management attempted to spur the performance of its auto centers by introducing new goals and incentives for mechanics. Automotive service advisers were given product-specific quotas for a variety of parts and repairs. Failure to meet the quotas could lead to transfers and reduced hours. Many employees spoke of "pressure, pressure, pressure" to bring in sales.

Not too surprisingly, the judgment of many employees suffered. In essence, employees were left to chart their own course, given the lack of management guidance and customer ignorance. The bottom line: In settling the spate of lawsuits, Sears offered coupons to customers who had purchased certain auto services over the most recent two-year period. The total cost of the settlement, including potential customer refunds, was estimated to be $60 million. The cost in terms of damaged reputation? Difficult to assess, but certainly not trivial.

This example makes two points. First, inappropriate reward systems may cause individuals at all levels throughout an organization to commit unethical acts that they might not otherwise commit. Second, the penalties in terms of damage to reputations, human capital erosion, and financial loss—in the short run and long run—are typically much higher than any gains that could be obtained through such unethical behavior.

Many companies have developed reward and evaluation systems that evaluate whether a manager is acting in an ethical manner. For example, Raytheon, a $20 billion defense contractor, incorporates the following items in its "Leadership Assessment Instrument":[54]

- Maintains unequivocal commitment to honesty, truth, and ethics in every facet of behavior.
- Conforms with the letter and intent of company policies while working to affect any necessary policy changes.

No More Whistleblowing Woes!

The landmark Sarbanes-Oxley Act of 2002 gives those who expose corporate misconduct strong legal protection. Henceforth, an executive who retaliates against the corporate whistleblower can be held criminally liable and imprisoned for up to 10 years. That's the same sentence a mafia don gets for threatening a witness. The Labor Department can order a company to rehire an employee without going to court. If the fired workers feel their case is moving too slowly, they can request a federal jury after six months.

Companies need to revisit their current policies, including nondisclosure pacts. They may no longer be able to enforce rules requiring employees to get permission to speak to the media or lawyers. Even layoffs should be planned in advance, lest they seem retaliatory.

Sources: www.sarbanes-oxley.com/pcaob.php/level=2&pub_id=Sarbanes-Oxley&chap_id=PCAOB11; Dwyer, P., Carney, D., Borrus, A., Woellert,L., & Palmeri, C. 2002. Year of the Whistle Blower. *BusinessWeek*, December 16: 107–109; and www.buchalter.com/FSL5CS/articles/articles204.asp.

Employees of publicly traded companies are now the most protected whistleblowers. Provisions coauthored by Senator Grassley in the Sarbanes-Oxley corporate-reform law:

- Make it unlawful to "discharge, demote, suspend or threaten, harass, or in any manner discriminate against" a whistleblower.
- Establish criminal penalties of up to 10 years in jail for executives who retaliate against whistleblowers.
- Require board audit committees to establish procedures for hearing whistleblower complaints.
- Allow the secretary of labor to order a company to rehire a terminated whistleblower with no court hearings whatsoever.
- Give a whistleblower a right to jury trial, bypassing months or years of cumbersome administrative hearings.

- Actions are consistent with words; follows through on commitments; readily admits mistakes.
- Is trusted and inspires others to be trusted.

As noted by Dan Burnham, Raytheon's former CEO: "What do we look for in a leadership candidate with respect to integrity? What we're really looking for are people who have developed an inner gyroscope of ethical principles. We look for people for whom ethical thinking is part of what they do—no different from 'strategic thinking' or 'tactical thinking.'"

Policies and Procedures

Many situations that a firm faces have regular, identifiable patterns. Typically, leaders tend to handle such routine by establishing a policy or procedure to be followed that can be applied uniformly to each occurrence. As noted in Chapter 9, such guidelines can be useful in specifying the proper relationships with a firm's customers and suppliers. For example, Levi Strauss has developed stringent global sourcing guidelines and Chemical Bank (part of J. P. Morgan Chase Bank) has a policy of forbidding any review that would determine if suppliers are Chemical customers when the bank awards contracts.

Carefully developed policies and procedures guide behavior so that all employees will be encouraged to behave in an ethical manner. However, it is not enough merely to have policies and procedures "on the books." Rather, they must be reinforced with effective communication, enforcement, and monitoring, as well as sound corporate governance practices. Strategy Spotlight 11.7 describes how the recently enacted Sarbanes-Oxley Act provides considerable legal protection to employees of publicly traded companies who report unethical or illegal practices.

We close our chapter on strategic leadership with a brief discussion of the Goolsby Leadership Model. It is addressed in Strategy Spotlight 11.8 and includes three dimensions: integrity, courage, and impact. The Goolsby Model synthesizes many of the ideas that we have addressed in this chapter and has important implications for career success.

The Goolsby Leadership Model: Integrity, Courage, and Impact

For many years there has been a focus in leadership research on inspirational styles that emphasize such traits as vision, charisma, and transformation. Some have criticized such approaches and have suggested that they may lead to unethical behavior. Why? They appeal to emotion rather than reason, lack checks and balances, and exploit followers to their detriment and to the benefit of the leader(s). Thus, some writers have begun to distinguish between authentic and inauthentic leaders. The Goolsby Leadership Model grows from the transformational leadership tradition and is anchored in the more recent emphasis on authentic leadership.

Clearly, most would agree that a healthy leader is at the heart of a healthy organization. Consider the alternative: The unhealthy leader has drawn attention to the damaging and debilitating effects—on both individuals and organizations—that result from such behaviors as excessive narcissism and toxic micromanagement. Also, recall the unethical and illegal activities in which some leaders participate that we addressed earlier in this chapter and in our discussion on corporate governance in Chapter 9. The Goolsby Leadership Model, in contrast, sets forth a healthy, positive model based on three core concepts: integrity, courage, and impact. It suggests that healthy leaders have integrity; act with courage and passion; and achieve high impact results for themselves, other individuals, and the organization. This model is shown in Exhibit 11.8. Next, we address each of the model's three dimensions.

Integrity

Integrity, a concept at the heart of good business practice, can be defined as consistency between word and deed as well as sound moral character. The four core questions of the Rotary Four-Way Test aim to test personal integrity. These questions evolved from a 100-word statement developed by Herbert J. Taylor during the economic challenges of the 1930s in the United States. Taylor was engineering a major business turnaround of Club Aluminum Corporation of America and the following questions were aimed at lifting his company above the competition and to giving them a competitive advantage:

1. Is it the truth?
2. Is it fair to all concerned?
3. Will it build goodwill and better friendships?
4. Will it be beneficial to all concerned?

In building on these questions, we suggest two key attributes of integrity in the healthy leader: authenticity and emotional competence. These two attributes, in part, draw on the concept of emotional intelligence (EI) that we addressed earlier in the chapter. As indicated in Exhibit 11.8, authenticity includes self-awareness, transparency, positive psychological states, and personal integrity. An authentic leader possesses good self-awareness, is transparent to others while being consistent, engenders positive psychological states within himself and his followers, and is widely known for having personal integrity. Essentially, authentic leaders are who they say they are; that is, there is a consistency between their values and intentions, their beliefs, their spoken words, and their actions and behaviors. In effect, the opposite of an authenticity is duplicity, which is a type of Jekyll-and-Hyde personality.

The second dimension of integrity is emotional competence, which involves the integration of thought and emotion, goes to the authentic characteristic of self-awareness, and is defined by its four dimensions shown in Exhibit 11.8: awareness of self, management of self, awareness of others, and management of others. Emotionally *(continued)*

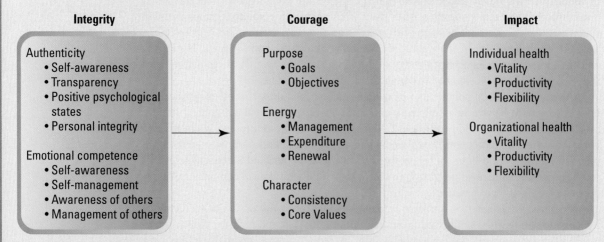

Exhibit 11.8 The Goolsby Leadership Model

Source: Quick, J. C., Macik-Frey, M., & Cooper, C. L. 2007. *Journal of Management Studies,* 44(2):195. Reprinted with permission of Wiley-Blackwell Publishing Ltd.

(continued) competent leaders are aware of their own feelings and emotions and aware of the feelings and emotions in other people. In addition, the emotionally competent leader is able to act in ways that appropriately manage his own emotions while accommodating the emotions of others. Emotional competence helps the healthy leader to be hopeful, positive, and compassionate in his actions and behaviors.

Courage

Courage, the second element in the Goolsby Leadership Model as indicated in Exhibit 11.8, is defined as the capacity to act, even in the presence of adversity, fear, and danger. Courage involves purpose, energy, and character. Courage matters; it makes a difference in the course of human events. After conducting in-depth interviews with 28 senior executives, researchers recently found a wide variety of attributes and characteristics of great leaders. However, there was no variance along the dimension of purpose. Purpose is the heart of great leadership and the heart of character.

Energy and energy management are essential for healthy productivity and achievement. While many leaders may focus on time management, energy management becomes more important. Consider, for example, the personal leadership track at PepsiCo's, corporate leadership program in Purchase, New York. Here, consultants found that energy expenditure through full engagement is what leads to productive achievement and meaningful work accomplishment. The executive team at PepsiCo, agrees, and PepsiCo, as a corporation, has enjoyed an impressive

Source: This Strategy Spotlight draws upon Quick, J. C., Macik-Frey, M., & Cooper, C. L. 2007. Managerial dimensions of organizational health: The healthy leader at work. *Journal of Management Studies,* 44(2): 189–295.

12 percent annual growth in market valuation over the most recent four-year period. This is over twice the growth of its long-time rival, Coca Cola, whose corresponding figure is only 5 percent. Interestingly, to be most effective, the power of full engagement must be balanced with strategic disengagement through which leaders are able to achieve renewal based on the process of energy recovery. Rather than a marathon, good leadership may be viewed as a series of short runs punctuated by periods of rest and recovery.

A third dimension of courage is character, and it can be defined as who you are when no one is looking. Character has an important role because it leads to consistency in actions and behaviors based on core values and principles. It's been suggested that character can be measured and that strength and character is a powerful force that enables leaders to act with courage in the midst of business crises or disasters. Therefore, courageous leaders are purposeful, energetic, and possess strong character.

Impact

Strategic leadership is neither a philosophical nor contemplative activity. Great leaders have a strong impact on their followers and on the businesses they lead. Consider, for example, the impacts of such well-known leaders as Andy Grove at Intel, Richard Branson at Virgin, Inc., and Lou Gerstner at IBM. The Goolsby Leadership Model suggests that the important impacts of integrity and courage are individual and that organizational health and the characteristics of vitality, productivity, and flexibility are essential to effective organizations. When individuals and organizations function in a healthy manner, they get results and make a positive impact for a wide range of organizational stakeholders.

Reflecting on Career Implications . . .

- *Strategic Leadership:* Do managers in your firm effectively set the direction; design the organization; and, instill a culture committed to excellence and ethical behavior? If you are in a position of leadership, do you practice all of these three elements effectively?
- *Power:* What sources of power do managers in your organization use? For example, if there is an overemphasis on organizational sources of power (e.g., position power); there could be negative implications for creativity, morale and turnover among professionals. How much power do you have? What is the basis of it? How might it be used to both advance your career goals and benefit the firm?
- *Emotional Intelligence:* Do leaders of your firm have sufficient levels of EI? Alternatively, are there excessive levels of EI present that have negative implications for your organization? Is your level of EI sufficient to allow you to have effective interpersonal and judgment skills in order to enhance your career success?
- *Learning Organization:* Does your firm effectively practice all five elements of the learning organization? If one or more elements are absent, adaptability and change will be compromised. What can you do to enhance any of the elements that might be lacking?
- *Ethics:* Does your organization practice a compliance-based or integrity-based ethical culture? Integrity-based cultures can enhance your personal growth. In addition, such cultures foster greater loyalty and commitment among all employees.

Summary

Strategic leadership is vital in ensuring that strategies are formulated and implemented in an effective manner. Leaders must play a central role in performing three critical and interdependent activities: setting the direction, designing the organization, and nurturing a culture committed to excellence and ethical behavior. In the chapter we provided the imagery of these three activities as a "three-legged stool." If leaders ignore or are ineffective at performing any one of the three, the organization will not be very successful. Leaders must also use power effectively to overcome barriers to change.

For leaders to effectively fulfill their activities, emotional intelligence (EI) is very important. Five elements that contribute to EI are self-awareness, self-regulation, motivation, empathy, and social skill. The first three elements pertain to self-management skills, whereas the last two are associated with a person's ability to manage relationships with others. We also addressed some of the potential drawbacks from the ineffective use of EI. These include the dysfunctional use of power as well as a tendency to become overly empathetic, which may result in unreasonably lowered performance expectations.

Leaders must also play a central role in creating a learning organization. Gone are the days when the top-level managers "think" and everyone else in the organization "does." With the rapidly changing, unpredictable, and complex competitive environments that characterize most industries, leaders must engage everyone in the ideas and energies of people throughout the organization. Great ideas can come from anywhere in the organization—from the executive suite to the factory floor. The five elements that we discussed as central to a learning organization are inspiring and motivating people with a mission or purpose, empowering people at all levels throughout the organization, accumulating and sharing internal knowledge, gathering external information, and challenging the status quo to stimulate creativity.

In the final section of the chapter, we addressed a leader's central role in instilling ethical behavior in the organization. We discussed the enormous costs that firms face when ethical crises arise—costs in terms of financial and reputational loss as well as the erosion of human capital and relationships with suppliers, customers, society at large, and governmental agencies. And, as we would expect, the benefits of having a strong ethical organization are also numerous. We contrasted compliance-based and integrity-based approaches to organizational ethics. Compliance-based approaches are largely externally motivated; that is, they are motivated by the fear of punishment for doing something that is unlawful. Integrity-based approaches, on the other hand, are driven by a personal and organizational commitment to ethical behavior. We also addressed the four key elements of an ethical organization: role models, corporate credos and codes of conduct, reward and evaluation systems, and policies and procedures.

Key Terms

leadership, 379
barriers to change, 381
systemic barriers, 382
behavioral barriers, 383
political barriers, 383
power, 383
organizational bases of power, 384

personal bases of power, 384
emotional intelligence, 384
learning organizations, 390
ethics, 396
compliance-based ethics programs, 399
integrity-based ethics programs, 399

Summary Review Questions

1. Three key activities—setting a direction, designing the organization, and nurturing a culture and ethics—are all part of what effective leaders do on a regular basis. Explain how these three activities are interrelated.

2. Define emotional intelligence (EI). What are the key elements of EI? Why is EI so important to successful strategic leadership? Address potential "downsides."

3. The knowledge a firm possesses can be a source of competitive advantage. Describe ways that a firm can continuously learn to maintain its competitive position.

4. How can the five central elements of "learning organizations" be incorporated into global companies?

5. What are the benefits to firms and their shareholders of conducting business in an ethical manner?

6. Firms that fail to behave in an ethical manner can incur high costs. What are these costs and what is their source?

7. What are the most important differences between an "integrity organization" and a "compliance organization" in a firm's approach to organizational ethics?

8. What are some of the important mechanisms for promoting ethics in a firm?

Experiential Exercise

Select two well-known business leaders—one you admire and one you do not. Evaluate each of them on the five characteristics of emotional intelligence.

Emotional Intelligence Characteristics	Admired Leader	Leader Not Admired
Self-awareness		
Self-regulation		
Motivation		
Empathy		
Social skills		

Application Questions Exercises

1. Identify two CEOs whose leadership you admire. What is it about their skills, attributes, and effective use of power that causes you to admire them?

2. Founders have an important role in developing their organization's culture and values. At times, their influence persists for many years. Identify and describe two organizations in which the cultures and values established by the founder(s) continue to flourish. You may find research on the Internet helpful in answering these questions.

3. Some leaders place a great emphasis on developing superior human capital. In what ways does this help a firm to develop and sustain competitive advantages?

4. In this chapter we discussed the five elements of a "learning organization." Select a firm with which you are familiar and discuss whether or not it epitomizes some (or all) of these elements.

Ethics Questions

1. Sometimes organizations must go outside the firm to hire talent, thus bypassing employees already working for the firm. Are there conditions under which this might raise ethical considerations?

2. Ethical crises can occur in virtually any organization. Describe some of the systems, procedures, and processes that can help to prevent such crises.

References

1. Gagnier, M. 2005. Kremed again. *BusinessWeek,* January 17:40; Anonymous. 2005. Worst managers. *BusinessWeek,* January 10: 74–77; Stires, D. 2004. Krispy Kreme is in the hole—again. *Fortune,* November 11: 42–43; and, McGowan, W. P. 2005. Krispy Kreme: A recipe for business failure. *Canyon News,* 19: 23.

2. Charan, R., & Colvin, G. 1999. Why CEOs fail. *Fortune,* June 21: 68–78.

3. These three activities and our discussion draw from Kotter, J. P. 1990. What leaders really do. *Harvard Business Review,* 68(3): 103–111; Pearson, A. E. 1990. Six basics for general managers. *Harvard Business Review,* 67(4): 94–101; and Covey, S. R. 1996. Three roles of the leader in the new paradigm. In *The leader of the future:* 149–160. Hesselbein, F., Goldsmith, M., & Beckhard, R. (Eds.). San Francisco: Jossey-Bass. Some of the discussion of each of the three leadership activity concepts draws on Dess, G. G., & Miller, A. 1993. *Strategic management:* 320–325. New York: McGraw-Hill.

4. Day, C., Jr., & LaBarre, P. 1994. GE: Just your average everyday $60 billion family grocery store. *Industry Week,* May 2: 13–18.

5. The best (& worst) managers of the year. 2003. *BusinessWeek,* January 13: 63.

6. Kirkpatrick, D. 2006. Use humility as a weapon. *Fortune.* October 30: 118.

7. Anonymous. 2006. Looking out for number one. *BusinessWeek,* October 30: 66.

8. For insightful perspectives on escalation, refer to Brockner, J. 1992. The escalation of commitment to a failing course of action. *Academy of Management Review,* 17(1): 39–61; and Staw, B. M. 1976. Knee-deep in the big muddy: A study of commitment to a chosen course of action. *Organizational Behavior and Human Decision Processes,* 16: 27–44. The discussion of systemic, behavioral, and political barriers draws on Lorange, P., & Murphy, D. 1984. Considerations in implementing strategic control. *Journal of Business Strategy,* 5: 27–35. In a similar vein, Noel M. Tichy has addressed three types of resistance to change in the context of General Electric: technical resistance, political resistance, and cultural resistance. See Tichy, N. M. 1993. Revolutionalize your company. *Fortune,* December 13: 114–118. Examples draw from O'Reilly, B. 1997. The secrets of America's most admired corporations: New ideas and new products. *Fortune,* March 3: 60–64.

9. This section draws on Champoux, J. E. 2000. *Organizational behavior: Essential tenets for a new millennium.* London: South-Western; and The mature use of power in organizations. 2003. *RHR International-Executive Insights,* May 29, 12.19.168.197/execinsights/8-3.htm.

10. An insightful perspective on the role of power and politics in organizations is provided in Ciampa, K. 2005. Almost ready: How leaders move up. *Harvard Business Review,* 83(1): 46–53.

11. A discussion of the importance of persuasion in bringing about change can be found in Garvin, D. A., & Roberto, M. A. 2005. Change through persuasion. *Harvard Business Review,* 83(4): 104–113.

12. Lorsch, J. W., & Tierney, T. J. 2002. *Aligning the stars: How to succeed when professionals drive results.* Boston: Harvard Business School Press.

13. For a review of this literature, see Daft, R. 1999. *Leadership: Theory and practice.* Fort Worth, TX: Dryden Press.

14. This section draws on Luthans, F. 2002. Positive organizational behavior: Developing and managing psychological strengths. *Academy of Management Executive,* 16(1): 57–72; and Goleman, D. 1998. What makes a leader? *Harvard Business Review,* 76(6): 92–105.

15. EI has its roots in the concept of "social intelligence" that was first identified by E. L. Thorndike in 1920 (Intelligence and its uses. *Harper's Magazine,* 140: 227–235). Psychologists have been uncovering other intelligences for some time now and have grouped them into such clusters as abstract intelligence (the ability to understand and manipulate verbal and mathematical symbols), concrete intelligence (the ability to understand and manipulate objects), and social intelligence (the ability to understand and relate to people). See Ruisel, I. 1992. Social intelligence: Conception and methodological problems. *Studia Psychologica,* 34(4–5): 281–296. Refer to trochim.human. cornell.edu/gallery.

16. See, for example, Luthans, op. cit.; Mayer, J. D., Salvoney, P., & Caruso, D. 2000. Models of emotional intelligence. In Sternberg, R. J. (Ed.). *Handbook of intelligence.* Cambridge, UK: Cambridge University Press; and Cameron, K. 1999. Developing emotional intelligence at the Weatherhead School of Management. *Strategy: The Magazine of the Weatherhead School of Management,* Winter: 2–3.

17. An insightful perspective on leadership, which involves discovering, developing and celebrating what is unique about each individual, is found in Buckingham, M. 2005. What great managers do. *Harvard Business Review,* 83(3): 70–79.

18. This section draws upon Klemp. G. 2005. *Emotional intelligence and leadership: What really matters.* Cambria Consulting, Inc., www.cambriaconsulting.com.

19. Heifetz, R. 2004. Question authority. *Harvard Business Review,* 82(1): 37.

20. Handy, C. 1995. Trust and the virtual organization. *Harvard Business Review,* 73(3): 40–50.

21. This section draws upon Dess, G. G., & Picken, J. C. 1999. *Beyond productivity.* New York: AMACOM. The elements of the learning organization in this section are consistent with the work of Dorothy Leonard-Barton. See, for example, Leonard-Barton, D. 1992. The factory as a learning laboratory. *Sloan Management Review,* 11: 23–38.

22. Senge, P. M. 1990. The leader's new work: Building learning organizations. *Sloan Management Review,* 32(1): 7–23.

23. Hammer, M., & Stanton, S. A. 1997. The power of reflection. *Fortune,* November 24: 291–296.

24. For some guidance on how to effectively bring about change in organizations, refer to Wall, S. J. 2005. The protean organization: Learning to love change. *Organizational Dynamics,* 34(1): 37–46.

25. Covey, S. R. 1989. *The seven habits of highly effective people: Powerful lessons in personal change.* New York: Simon & Schuster.

26. Melrose, K. 1995. *Making the grass greener on your side: A CEO's journey to leading by servicing.* San Francisco: Barrett-Koehler.

27. Quinn, R. C., & Spreitzer, G. M. 1997. The road to empowerment: Seven questions every leader should consider. *Organizational Dynamics,* 25: 37–49.

28. Helgesen, S. 1996. Leading from the grass roots. In *Leader of the future:* 19–24 Hesselbein et al.

29. Bowen, D. E., & Lawler, E. E., III. 1995. Empowering service employees. *Sloan Management Review,* 37: 73–84.

30. Stack, J. 1992. *The great game of business.* New York: Doubleday/Currency.

31. Schafer, S. 1997. Battling a labor shortage? It's all in your imagination. *Inc.,* August: 24.

32. Meyer, P. 1998. So you want the president's job . . . *Business Horizons,* January–February: 2–8.

33. Imperato, G. 1998. Competitive intelligence: Get smart! *Fast Company,* May: 268–279.

34. Novicki, C. 1998. The best brains in business. *Fast Company,* April: 125.

35. The introductory discussion of benchmarking draws on Miller, A. 1998. *Strategic management:* 142–143. New York: McGraw-Hill.

36. Port, O., & Smith, G. 1992. Beg, borrow—and benchmark. *BusinessWeek,* November 30: 74–75.

37. Main, J. 1992. How to steal the best ideas around. *Fortune,* October 19: 102–106.

38. Taylor, J. T. 1997. What happens after what comes next? *Fast Company,* December–January: 84–85.

39. Sheff, D. 1996. Levi's changes everything. *Fast Company,* June–July: 65–74.

40. Isaacson, W. 1997. In search of the real Bill Gates. *Time,* January 13: 44–57.

41. Baatz, E. B. 1993. Motorola's secret weapon. *Electronic Business,* April: 51–53.

42. Holt, J. W. 1996. *Celebrate your mistakes.* New York: McGraw-Hill.

43. This opening discussion draws upon Conley, J. H. 2000. Ethics in business. In Helms, M. M. (Ed.). *Encyclopedia of management* (4th ed.): 281–285; Farmington Hills, MI: Gale Group; Paine, L. S. 1994. Managing for organizational integrity. *Harvard Business Review,* 72(2): 106–117; and Carlson, D. S., & Perrewe, P. L. 1995. Institutionalization of organizational ethics through transformational leadership. *Journal of Business Ethics,* 14: 829–838.

44. Kiger, P. J. 2001. Truth and consequences. *Working Woman,* May: 57–61.

45. Soule, E. 2002. Managerial moral strategies—in search of a few good principles. *Academy of Management Review,* 27(1): 114–124.

46. Carlson & Perrewe, op. cit.

47. This discussion is based upon Paine. Managing for organizational integrity; Paine, L. S. 1997. *Cases in leadership, ethics, and organizational integrity: A Strategic approach.* Burr Ridge, IL: Irwin; and Fontrodona, J. 2002. Business ethics across the Atlantic. Business Ethics Direct, www.ethicsa.org/BED_art_fontrodone.html.

48. www.ti.com/corp/docs/company/citizen/ethics/benchmark. shtml; and www.ti.com/corp/docs/company/citizen/ethics/quicktest.shtml.

49. Wetlaufer, S. 1999. Organizing for empowerment: An interview with AES's Roger Sant and Dennis Bakke. *Harvard Business Review,* 77(1): 110–126.

50. For an insightful, academic perspective on the impact of ethics codes on executive decision making, refer to Stevens, J. M., Steensma, H. K., Harrison, D. A., & Cochran, P. S. 2005. Symbolic or substantive document? The influence of ethics code on financial executives' decisions. *Strategic Management Journal,* 26(2): 181–195.

51. Paine. Managing for organizational integrity.

52. For a recent study on the effects of goal setting on unethical behavior, read Schweitzer, M. E., Ordonez, L., & Douma, B. 2004. Goal setting as a motivator of unethical behavior. *Academy of Management Journal,* 47(3): 422–432.

53. Paine. Managing for organizational integrity.

54. Fulmer, R. M. 2004. The challenge of ethical leadership. *Organizational Dynamics,* 33 (3): 307–317.

chapter 12

Managing Innovation and Fostering Corporate Entrepreneurship

>learning objectives

After reading this chapter, you should have a good understanding of:

LO1 The importance of implementing strategies and practices that foster innovation.

LO2 The challenges and pitfalls of managing corporate innovation processes.

LO3 How independent venture teams and business incubators are used to develop corporate ventures.

LO4 How corporations create an internal environment and culture that promote entrepreneurial development.

LO5 The role of product champions in internal corporate venturing.

LO6 How corporate entrepreneurship achieves both financial goals and strategic goals.

LO7 The benefits and potential drawbacks of real options analysis in making resource deployment decisions in corporate entrepreneurship contexts.

LO8 How an entrepreneurial orientation can enhance a firm's efforts to develop promising corporate venture initiatives.

*t*o remain competitive, established firms must continually seek out opportunities for growth and new methods for strategically renewing their performance. Changes in customer needs, new technologies, and shifts in the competitive landscape require that companies continually innovate and initiate corporate ventures in order to compete effectively. This chapter addresses how entrepreneurial activities can be an avenue for achieving competitive advantages.

In the first section, we address the importance of innovation in identifying venture opportunities and strategic renewal. Innovations can take many forms, including radical breakthrough innovations as well as incremental innovative improvements, and be used either to update products or renew organizational processes. We discuss how firms can successfully manage the innovation process. Impediments and challenges to effective innovation are discussed, and examples of good innovation practices are presented.

We discuss the unique role of corporate entrepreneurship in the strategic management process in the second section. Here we highlight two types of activities corporations use to remain competitive—focused and dispersed. New venture groups and business incubators are often used to focus a firm's entrepreneurial activities. In other corporations, the entrepreneurial spirit is dispersed throughout the organization and gives rise to product champions and other autonomous strategic behaviors that organizational members engage in to foster internal corporate venturing. We also discuss the benefits and potential drawbacks of real options analysis in making decisions about which venture activities merit additional investment and which should be abandoned.

In the final section we describe how a firm's entrepreneurial orientation can contribute to its growth and renewal as well as enhance the methods and processes strategic managers use to recognize opportunities and develop initiatives for internal growth and development. The chapter also evaluates the pitfalls that firms may encounter when implementing entrepreneurial strategies.

Learning from Mistakes

Companies often grow by commercializing new technologies. This is one of the most important paths to corporate entrepreneurship. But technologies change and yesterday's exciting innovation eventually becomes today's old news. Consider the case of Polaroid, a company that captivated the marketplace with its instant photography technology and grew to become a multibillion dollar enterprise on the strength of that innovation.[1]

Polaroid Corporation's founder, Edward Land, was a Harvard dropout. He was also a genius in optics, chemistry, and engineering who started his Cambridge, Massachusetts, company in 1937 to focus on sunglasses and other technologies that polarize light. During World War II, the company built infrared filters for gunsights and dark-adaptation goggles. It was after the war, however, that one of Land's innovations struck gold. In 1947 he introduced a single-step photographic process that would develop film in 60 seconds and launched the Land Camera. Over the next 30 years, the camera and its film evolved into the Polaroid One-Step, and sales surged to $1.4 billion by 1978.

In the process, Polaroid became one of the most admired companies and a best bet among stock pickers. It was a member of the "Nifty Fifty," a group of companies known for their innovative ideas whose stocks regularly traded at 40 or more times earnings. In 1991 it won a huge patent infringement lawsuit against rival Eastman Kodak, which had to pay Polaroid $925 million. The company also continued to launch new products using its instant film technology in a variety of different cameras with updated features. *[continued]*

● Polaroid's cameras were a stunning success when they were first introduced. However, the firm began to stumble in the 1990s after its founder, Edward Land, died.

On the surface, Polaroid seemed to be the picture of success. Land had been hailed as a new breed of corporate leader—both technically savvy and entrepreneurial. But by 1991, the year Land died, the company he built was unraveling. Instead of using the cash from the Kodak lawsuit to pay down its heavy debt, Polaroid spent the money to develop a new camera—the Captiva—which flopped in the marketplace. A few years later the I-Zone Pocket Camera, a product targeted at adolescents, had weak sales because the image quality was inconsistent and replacement film was considered too expensive for teens. Meanwhile, internally, Polaroid was spending 37 percent of its sales on administrative costs, compared to Kodak's 21 percent. Even though the company continued to sell millions of cameras each year—a record 13.1 million in 2000—its strength was deteriorating.

Polaroid's most serious problems began when it failed to get on the digital photography bandwagon. Rather than make the move into digital, Polaroid decided to stick with its proprietary technology. Once Polaroid realized the extent of the digital photography trend, it was too late. It eventually introduced digital cameras but they were often ranked low in consumer ratings. Polaroid even developed digital printing technologies, called Opal and Onyx, designed to deliver high resolution digital images. But because of its weakened financial state, it could not get the funding from investors to advertise and develop them. By 2001, it was in real trouble. Its debt was $950 million, it laid off 2,950 employees—35 percent of its workforce—and began missing interest payments to bondholders. In October 2001, it filed for Chapter 11 bankruptcy protection. Sale of its stock, which had traded as high as $60 in July 1997, was halted at 28 cents per share on the New York Stock Exchange.

The final blow to its reputation came in 2005 when it was announced, as part of a deal to sell Polaroid to a Minnesota-based conglomerate, that thousands of former Polaroid employees would have their pensions wiped out. Retirees and ex-employees, who also lost their health coverage and life insurance, received a total of just $47 for their years of service, while four former Polaroid executives split a $30 million dollar settlement among them![2]

What went wrong at Polaroid? Considered by many to be one of the first great research-based companies, Polaroid failed largely because it lost its ability to effectively innovate and launch new products. Many factors contributed to its downfall. Clearly, its failure to respond quickly to the digital photography phenomenon caused a serious setback. But the roots of the problem were deeper. As one writer put it, "They overestimated the value of their core business." That is, Polaroid's overconfidence in its early success prevented it from envisioning a purpose beyond its instant imaging capability. This phenomenon is sometimes referred to as "the innovator's dilemma"—firms become so preoccupied with meeting current needs that they fail to take steps to meet future needs.[3] This dilemma inhibited Polaroid's ability to change and affected every aspect of its business:

- Even though sales of its core products were strong, it lost touch with its customers. As a result, several of its innovations failed in the marketplace.
- It did not have a long-term strategy for financing growth. Because it relied heavily on investors to finance new product initiatives, when one failed, it created cash flow problems. To regain profitability, Polaroid would offer more shares and bonds to investors, which, in turn, devalued the stock and created even more indebtedness. Eventually, investors turned away. *[continued]*

- Buoyed by revenues that grew annually for over 30 years, it failed to control personnel costs and was weighed down by too many employees. Eventually these expenses overtook its sales.

In short, Polaroid stopped thinking and acting like an entrepreneurial firm. As a result of its lack of vision and failure to change, what had once been a leading innovator and top financial performer slowly fizzled out.[4]

Managing change, as we suggested in Chapter 11, is one of the most important functions performed by strategic leaders. What options are available to organizations that want to change and grow? This chapter addresses two major avenues through which companies can expand or improve their business—innovation and corporate entrepreneurship. These two activities go hand-in-hand because they both have similar aims. The first is strategic renewal. Innovations help an organization stay fresh and reinvent itself as conditions in the business environment change. This is why managing innovation is such an important strategic implementation issue. The second is the pursuit of venture opportunities. Innovative breakthroughs, as well as new product concepts, evolving technologies, and shifting demand, create opportunities for corporate venturing. In this chapter we will explore these topics—how change and innovation can stimulate strategic renewal and foster corporate entrepreneurship. First we turn to the challenge of managing innovation.

>LO1
The importance of implementing strategies and practices that foster innovation.

Managing Innovation

One of the most important sources of growth opportunities is innovation. **Innovation** involves using new knowledge to transform organizational processes or create commercially viable products and services. The sources of new knowledge may include the latest technology, the results of experiments, creative insights, or competitive information. However it comes about, innovation occurs when new combinations of ideas and information bring about positive change.

The emphasis on newness is a key point. For example, for a patent application to have any chance of success, one of the most important attributes it must possess is novelty. You can't patent an idea that has been copied. This is a central idea. In fact, the root of the word *innovation* is the Latin *novus,* which means new. Innovation involves introducing or changing to something new.[5]

Among the most important sources of new ideas is new technology. Technology creates new possibilities. Technology provides the raw material that firms use to make innovative new products and services. But technology is not the only source of innovations. There can be innovations in human resources, firm infrastructure, marketing, service, or in many other value-adding areas that have little to do with anything "high-tech." Strategy Spotlight 12.1 highlights a simple but effective innovation implemented by Target stores.

As the Target example suggests, innovation can take many forms. Next we will consider two frameworks that are often used to distinguish types of innovation.

innovation the use of new knowledge to transform organizational processes or create commercially viable products and services.

Types of Innovation

Although innovations are not always high-tech, changes in technology can be an important source of change and growth. When an innovation is based on a sweeping new technology, it often has a more far-reaching impact. However, sometimes even a small innovation can add value and create competitive advantages. Innovation can and should occur throughout an organization—in every department and all aspects of the value chain.

One way to view the impact of an innovation is in terms of its degree of innovativeness, which falls somewhere on a continuum that extends from incremental to radical.[6]

- *Radical innovations* produce fundamental changes by evoking major departures from existing practices. These breakthrough innovations usually occur because of

radical innovation an innovation that fundamentally changes existing practices.

Target's Low-Tech, High-Value Design Innovation

Sometimes a simple change can make a vast improvement. That's what Target discovered when it adopted a new design for the traditional amber-colored prescription pill bottle. The new design literally flips the old bottle on its head. The base of the bottle is a large cap that uses color-coded rings to help family members distinguish between different containers. The upper part includes a flat surface that holds wider and easier-to-read labels. "They're much easier to use, and it's a lot easier to read," says to Target customer Pat Howell.

Design student Deborah Adler came up with the new bottle after her grandmother Helen accidentally took her grandfather Herman's prescription. She noticed that the small lettering on the curved label of a traditional pill bottle was hard to read. Target, which commissioned a study that found that nearly 60 percent of prescription drugs are taken improperly, welcomed the design innovation. The new bottle, called the ClearRX, has won several design awards and improved Target's prescription drug sales by 14 percent—from $1.4 billion to $1.6 billion in a recent year.

Sources: Anonymous. 2005. Target turns old pill bottle design on its head. *MSNBC.com*, www.msnbc.com, April 26; Finn, B. 2006. Target ClearRX bottle. *Business 2.0*, April: 120; and www.target.com.

technological change. They tend to be highly disruptive and can transform a company or even revolutionize a whole industry. They may lead to products or processes that can be patented, giving a firm a strong competitive advantage. Examples include electricity, the telephone, the transistor, desktop computers, fiber optics, artificial intelligence, and genetically engineered drugs.

- ***Incremental innovations*** enhance existing practices or make small improvements in products and processes. They may represent evolutionary applications within existing paradigms of earlier, more radical innovations. Because they often sustain a company by extending or expanding its product line or manufacturing skills, incremental innovations can be a source of competitive advantage by providing new capabilities that minimize expenses or speed productivity. Examples include frozen food, sports drinks, steel-belted radial tires, electronic bookkeeping, shatterproof glass, and digital telephones.

incremental innovation an innovation that enhances existing practices or makes small improvements in products and processes.

Some innovations are highly radical; others are only slightly incremental. But most innovations fall somewhere between these two extremes. Exhibit 12.1 shows where several innovations fall along the radical–incremental continuum.

Another distinction that is often used when discussing innovation is between process innovation and product innovation.[7] *Product innovation* refers to efforts to create product designs and applications of technology to develop new products for end users. Recall from Chapter 5 how generic strategies were typically different depending on the stage of the industry life cycle. Product innovations tend to be more radical and are more common during the earlier stages of an industry's life cycle. As an industry matures, there are fewer opportunities for newness, so the innovations tend to be more incremental. Product innovations are also commonly associated with a differentiation strategy. Firms that differentiate by providing customers with new products or services that offer unique features or quality enhancements often engage in product innovation.

Process innovation, by contrast, is typically associated with improving the efficiency of an organizational process, especially manufacturing systems and operations. By drawing on new technologies and an organization's accumulated experience (Chapter 5), firms can often improve materials utilization, shorten cycle time, and increase quality. Process innovations are more likely to occur in the later stages of an industry's life cycle as companies seek ways to remain viable in markets where demand has flattened out and competition is more intense. As a result, process innovations are often associated with overall

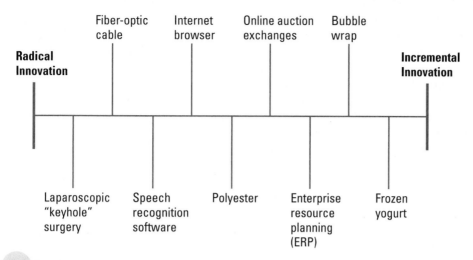

Exhibit 12.1 Continuum of Radical and Incremental Innovations

cost leader strategies, because the aim of many process improvements is to lower the costs of operations.

Innovation is a force in both the external environment (technology, competition) and also a factor affecting a firm's internal choices (generic strategy, value-adding activities). Nevertheless, innovation can be quite difficult for some firms to manage, especially those that have become comfortable with the status quo. Next, we turn to the challenges associated with successful innovation.

Challenges of Innovation

>LO2

The challenges and pitfalls of managing corporate innovation processes.

Innovation is essential to sustaining competitive advantages. Recall from Chapter 3 that one of the four elements of the Balanced Scorecard is the innovation and learning perspective. The extent and success of a company's innovation efforts are indicators of its overall performance. As management guru Peter Drucker warned, "An established company which, in an age demanding innovation, is not capable of innovation is doomed to decline and extinction."[8] To put it simply, in today's competitive environment, most firms have only one choice: "Innovate or die."

As with change, however, firms are often resistant to innovation. Only those companies that actively pursue innovation, even though it is often difficult and uncertain, will get a payoff from their innovation efforts. But managing innovation is challenging. As former Pfizer chairman and CEO William Steere puts it: "In some ways, managing innovation is analogous to breaking in a spirited horse. You are never sure of success until you achieve your goal. In the meantime, everyone takes a few lumps."[9]

What is it that makes innovation so difficult? Clearly the uncertainty about outcomes is one factor. Companies are often reluctant to invest time and resources into activities with an unknown future. Another factor is that the innovation process involves so many choices. These choices present five dilemmas that companies must wrestle with when pursuing innovation.[10]

- **Seeds versus Weeds.** Most companies have an abundance of innovative ideas. They must decide which of these is most likely to bear fruit—the "Seeds"—and which should be cast aside—the "Weeds." This is an ongoing dilemma that is often complicated by the fact that some innovation projects require a considerable level of investment before a firm can fully evaluate whether they are worth pursuing. As a result, firms need a mechanism with which they can choose among various innovation projects.
- **Experience versus Initiative.** Companies must decide who will lead an innovation project. Senior managers may have experience and credibility but tend to be more

risk averse. Midlevel employees, who may be the innovators themselves, may have more enthusiasm because they can see firsthand how an innovation would address specific problems. As a result, firms need to support and reward organizational members who bring new ideas to light.

- **Internal versus External Staffing.** Innovation projects need competent staffs to succeed. People drawn from inside the company may have greater social capital and know the organization's culture and routines. But this knowledge may actually inhibit them from thinking outside the box. Staffing innovation projects with external personnel requires that project managers justify the hiring and spend time recruiting, training, and relationship building. As a result, firms need to streamline and support the process of staffing innovation efforts.

- **Building Capabilities versus Collaborating.** Innovation projects often require new sets of skills. Firms can seek help from other departments and/or partner with other companies that bring resources and experience as well as share costs of development. However, such arrangements can create dependencies and inhibit internal skills development. Further, struggles over who contributed the most or how the benefits of the project are to be allocated may arise. As a result, firms need a mechanism for forging links with outside parties to the innovation process.

- **Incremental versus Preemptive Launch.** Companies must manage the timing and scale of new innovation projects. An incremental launch is less risky because it requires fewer resources and serves as a market test. But a launch that is too tentative can undermine the project's credibility. It also opens the door for a competitive response. A large-scale launch requires more resources, but it can effectively preempt a competitive response. As a result, firms need to make funding and management arrangements that allow for projects to hit the ground running and be responsive to market feedback.

These dilemmas highlight why the innovation process can be daunting even for highly successful firms. Strategy Spotlight 12.2 addresses the challenges and pitfalls that Microsoft faces in its efforts to be a strong innovator. How can companies successfully address these innovation challenges? Next, we consider four steps that firms can take to manage the innovation process.[11]

Defining the Scope of Innovation

Firms must have a means to focus their innovation efforts. By defining the "strategic envelope"—that is, the scope of a firm's innovation efforts—firms ensure that their innovation efforts are not wasted on projects that are outside the firm's domain of interest. Strategic enveloping defines the range of acceptable projects. As Alistair Corbett, an innovation expert who directs the Toronto office of the global consulting firm Bain & Company, recently said, "One man's radical innovation is another man's incremental innovation."[12] Thus, a strategic envelope creates a firm-specific view of innovation that defines how a firm can create new knowledge and learn from an innovation initiative even if the project fails. It also gives direction to a firm's innovation efforts, which helps separate seeds from weeds and builds internal capabilities.

One way to determine which projects to work on is to focus on a common technology. Then, innovation efforts across the firm can aim at developing skills and expertise in a given technical area. Another potential focus is on a market theme. Consider how DuPont responded to a growing concern for environmentally sensitive products:

> In the early 1990s, DuPont sought to use its knowledge of plastics to identify products to meet a growing market demand for biodegradable products. Over the next decade, it conducted numerous experiments with a biodegradable polyester resin it named Biomax. By trying different applications and formulations demanded by potential customers, the company was finally able to create a product that could be produced economically and had market appeal. Recently, Biomax was certified biodegradable and compostable by the Biodegradable Products Institute, an endorsement that should further boost sales.[13]

Microsoft's Innovation Challenges

You would think that Microsoft, the dominant software seller in the world with a $6.8 billion annual research and development budget, would be a major innovator. Instead, innovation seems to be Microsoft's Achilles' heel. From its earliest days, Microsoft has had far more success as an imitator than an innovator. Despite having well-funded research labs at its Redmond, Washington, headquarters, Microsoft has little to show for years of efforts to come up with the next big breakthrough innovation. Why is Microsoft is so innovation-challenged?

- **Innovation is hard.** There is no doubt that Microsoft is working hard at it. From 2000 to 2005, Microsoft acquired 2,188 patents to protect its researchers' work. But creating a commercially viable breakthrough innovation such as the Web browser (created by Netscape), the streaming media player (by Real-Networks) or interactive television (TiVo) is not easy. In many cases, it is more about luck and timing than money, dedication, and brilliance.

- **Bigger isn't better.** Large companies simply find it more difficult than smaller ones to sustain rapid growth through innovation. Good ideas are scarce everywhere and most new innovations take a few years to get off the ground. Because of Microsoft's sheer size, the contribution that a new product can make is relatively small. For example, if Microsoft had matched Google's recent growth record, that business activity would have added only 4 percent to Microsoft's top line.

- **Defense is easier.** Most of Microsoft's research efforts go to helping it sustain its strong leadership in software products such as MS Office. Of every dollar it spends on research and development (R&D), "probably something on the order of 90 percent is directly in line, or in service of, the existing business groups," according to Craig Mundie, Microsoft's co-chief technology officer. In this respect, Microsoft is a victim of "the innovator's dilemma"—spending so much more time protecting its established lines of business and satisfying existing customers that it misses opportunities to make breakthroughs.

Microsoft continues to support innovation and its breakthrough product may come any day. But even its new project, the second generation videogame console known as XBox 360, lags far behind Sony's PlayStation2 in sales and market penetration. Microsoft may not be producing the next big thing, but as a fast follower of technology breakthroughs, it has been highly successful.

Sources: Grossman, L. 2005. Out of the Xbox. *Time,* May 23: 44–53; and Hawn, C. 2004. What money can't buy. *Fast Company,* 89: 68–73.

In defining a strategic envelope, companies must be clear not only about the kinds of innovation they are looking for but also the expected results. Therefore, each company needs to develop a set of questions to ask itself about its innovation efforts:

- How much will the innovation initiative cost?
- How likely is it to actually become commercially viable?
- How much value will it add; that is, what will it be worth if it works?
- What will be learned if it does not pan out?

In other words, however a firm envisions its innovation goals, it needs to develop a systematic approach to evaluating its results and learning from its innovation initiatives. Viewing innovation from this perspective helps firms manage the process.[14]

Managing the Pace of Innovation

Along with clarifying the scope of an innovation by defining a strategic envelope, firms also need to regulate the pace of innovation. An advantage of assessing the extent to which an innovation is radical or incremental is that it helps determine how long it will take for an innovation initiative to realistically come to fruition. The project time line of an incremental innovation may be 6 months to 2 years, whereas a more radical innovation is typically long term—10 years or more.[15] Thus, radical innovations often begin with a long period of exploration in which experimentation makes strict timelines unrealistic. In contrast, firms that are innovating incrementally in order to exploit a window of opportunity may use a milestone approach that is more stringently driven by goals and deadlines. This kind of sensitivity to realistic time frames helps companies separate dilemmas temporally so they are easier to manage.

The idea of time pacing can also be a source of competitive advantage, because it helps a company manage transitions and develop an internal rhythm.[16] Time pacing does not mean the company ignores the demands of market timing. Instead, it means that companies have a sense of their own internal clock in a way that allows them to thwart competitors by controlling the innovation process.

Not all innovation lends itself to speedy development, however. Radical innovation often involves open-ended experimentation and time-consuming mistakes. Further, the creative aspects of innovation are often difficult to time. When software maker Intuit's new CEO, Steve Bennett, began to turn around that troubled business, he required every department to implement Six Sigma, a quality control management technique that focuses on being responsive to customer needs. Everybody, that is, but the techies.

> "We're not GE, we're not a company where Jack says 'Do it,' and everyone salutes," says Bill Hensler, Intuit's vice president for process excellence. That's because software development, according to many, is more of an art than a science. At the Six Sigma Academy, president of operations Phil Samuel says even companies that have embraced Six Sigma across every other aspect of their organization usually maintain a hands-off policy when it comes to software developers. Techies, it turns out, like to go at their own pace.[17]

The example of software developers makes an important point about strategic pacing: some projects can't be rushed. Companies that hurry up their research efforts or go to market before they are ready can damage their ability to innovate—and their reputation. Thus, managing the pace of innovation can be an important factor in long-term success.

Staffing to Capture Value from Innovation

People are central to the processes of identifying, developing, and commercializing innovations effectively. Not only do they need broad sets of skills, but they also need experience—experience working with teams and experience working on successful innovation projects. To capture value from innovation activities, therefore, companies must provide strategic decision makers with staff members who make it possible to reap the benefits of innovative behavior.

This insight led strategy experts Rita Gunther McGrath and Thomas Keil to research the types of human resource management practices that effective firms use to capture value from their innovation efforts.[18] Four practices are especially important when creating staffs to engage in business venturing:

- Create innovation teams with experienced players who know what it is like to deal with uncertainty and can help new staff members learn venture management skills.
- Require that employees seeking to advance their career with the organization serve in the new venture group as part of their career climb.
- Once people have experience with the new venture group, transfer them to mainstream management positions where they can use their skills and knowledge to revitalize the company's core business.
- Separate the performance of individuals from the performance of the innovation. Otherwise, strong players may feel stigmatized if the innovation effort they worked on fails.

There are other staffing practices that may sound as if they would benefit a firm's innovation activities but may, in fact, be counterproductive. These include:

- Creating a staff that consists only of strong players whose primary experience is related to the company's core business. This provides too few people to deal with the uncertainty of innovation projects and may cause good ideas to be dismissed because they do not appear to fit with the core business.

Staffing for Innovation Success at Air Products

When it comes to implementing its innovation efforts, Air Products and Chemicals, Inc. (APCI) recognizes the importance of staffing for achieving success. Air Products is a global manufacturer of industrial gases, chemicals, and related equipment. Headquartered in Allentown, Pennsylvania, Air Products has annual sales of $5 billion, manufacturing facilities in over 30 countries, and 17,000 employees worldwide. The company has a strong reputation for effectively embedding innovation into its culture through its unique employee engagement processes.

Ron Pierantozzi, a 30-year veteran of the company and its director of innovation and new product development, says "Innovation is about discipline.... It requires a different

Sources: Chesbrough, H. 2007. Why bad things happen to good technology. *The Wall Street Journal:* April 28–29, R11; Leavitt, P. 2005. Delivering the difference: Business process management at APCI. *APQC,* www.apqc.com; McGrath, R. G., & Keil, T. 2007. The value captor's process: Getting the most out of your new business ventures. *Harvard Business Review,* May: 128–136; and www.apci.com.

type of training, different tools and new approaches to experimentation." To enact this philosophy, Pierantozzi begins with his people. He recruits people with diverse backgrounds and a wide range of expertise including engineers, entrepreneurs, and government officials. It is made clear to those on his innovation teams that they will return to mainstream operations after four years—a fact that most consider a plus since working in the innovation unit usually provides a career boost. He also assures players that there is no stigma associated with a failed venture because experimentation is highly valued.

Innovation teams are created to manage the company's intellectual assets and determine which technologies have the most potential value. A key benefit of this approach has been to more effectively leverage its human resources to achieve innovative outcomes without increasing its R&D expenses. These efforts resulted in an innovation award from APQC (formerly known as the American Productivity and Quality Center) which recognizes companies for exemplary practices that increase productivity.

- Creating a staff that consists only of volunteers who want to work on projects they find interesting. Such players are often overzealous about new technologies or overly attached to product concepts, which can lead to poor decisions about which projects to pursue or drop.
- Creating a climate where innovation team members are considered second-class citizens. In companies where achievements are rewarded, the brightest and most ambitious players may avoid innovation projects with uncertain outcomes.

Unless an organization can align its key players into effective new venture teams, it is unlikely to create any differentiating advantages from its innovation efforts.[19] An enlightened approach to staffing a company's innovation efforts provides one of the best ways to ensure that the challenges of innovation will be effectively met. Strategy Spotlight 12.3 describes the approach Air Products and Chemicals, Inc. is using to enhance its innovation efforts.

Collaborating with Innovation Partners

It is rare for any one organization to have all the information it needs to carry an innovation from concept to commercialization. Even a company that is highly competent with its current operations usually needs new capabilities to achieve new results. Innovation partners can provide the skills and insights that are often needed to make innovation projects succeed.

Innovation partners may come from many sources, including research universities and the federal government. Each year the federal government issues requests for proposals (RFPs) asking private companies for assistance in improving services or finding solutions to public problems. Universities are another type of innovation partner. Chip-maker Intel, for example, has benefited from underwriting substantial amounts of university research. Rather than hand universities a blank check, Intel bargains for rights to patents that emerge

strategy spotlight

InnoCentive's Collaborative Approach to Innovation

Eli Lilly's patent expired recently on its blockbuster drug Prozac, which accounted for 34 percent of Lilly's annual sales. Rather than launch a new drug, however, Lilly launched a new business: InnoCentive, LLC. InnoCentive, as the name implies, provides incentives for innovation. It does so by providing a platform for scientists from around the world to work in virtual communities to solve complex problems. The effort does not just benefit Lilly but provides a virtual, open source R&D organization that any member company can use.

Here's how it works: Drug companies, called "Seekers," put up "Wanted" posters describing problems that need addressing. Bounty-hunting scientists, labeled "Solvers," sign confidentiality agreements that gain them admission to a secure project room where they can access data and product specifications related to the problem. If they solve the problem, they get a reward of as much as $100,000 depending on

the problem. Clients such as Procter & Gamble and Boeing have already benefited from this network approach to innovation. Procter & Gamble reports that a third of its new product concepts now originate outside the company.

Not only is InnoCentive a savvy application of digital technology, it is also an example of what Harvard Business Professor Henry Chesbrough calls "open innovation." The concept of open innovation builds on two other concepts seen in previous chapters—the importance of intellectual assets in today's economy (Chapter 4) and the use of boundaryless organizational arrangements to achieve strategic objectives (Chapter 10). Successful innovation, according to Chesbrough, involves collaborating and drawing on the knowledge and resources of competitors and other strategic partners. In other words, disclose your intellectual property (IP), cross organizational boundaries to achieve innovation goals, and let others share in the wealth. InnoCentive's collaborative model is on the cutting edge of this new approach to innovation. It remains to be seen whether other companies will adopt open innovation, but Chesbrough is convinced that the ones that are willing to seize this new approach will be the long-term winners.

Sources: Breen, B. 2002. Lilly's R&D prescription. *Fast Company*, 57: 44; Chesbrough, H. *Open innovation: The new imperative for creating and profiting from technology.* 2003. Boston; Harvard Business School Press; Vencat, E. F. 2006. The power of we. *MSNBC/Newsweek International*, www.msnbc.msn.com, November 20; and www.innocentive.com.

---

from Intel-sponsored research. The university retains ownership of the patent, but Intel gets royalty-free use of it.[20]

Strategic partnering requires firms to identify their strengths and weaknesses and make choices about which capabilities to leverage, which need further development, and which are outside the firm's current or projected scope of operations. Consider Nextel in its decision to partner with RadioFrame Networks, a Seattle-based start-up.

> RadioFrame had developed an innovative radio transmitter that could be used inside buildings to make cell-phone signals clearer. Nextel, which did not have as much network capacity as some of its larger competitors, saw this as a way to increase bandwidth and add value to its existing set of services. Not only did the two firms form a partnership, but Nextel also became involved in the development process by providing senior engineers and funding to help build the system. "We really worked hand-in-hand with Nextel," says RadioFrame CEO Jeff Brown, "from user requirements to how to physically get the finished product into their distribution systems."[21]

To choose partners, firms need to ask what competencies they are looking for and what the innovation partner will contribute.[22] These contributions might include knowledge of markets, technology expertise, or contacts with key players in an industry. Innovation partnerships also typically need to specify how the rewards of the innovation will be shared and who will own the intellectual property that is developed.[23]

Innovation efforts that involve multiple partners and the speed and ease with which partners can network and collaborate are changing the way innovation is conducted. Strategy Spotlight 12.4 highlights the role of InnoCentive, which emphasizes collaboration and partnerships in a new approach to innovation labeled "open innovation."

Successful innovation involves a companywide commitment because the results of innovation affect every part of the organization. Innovation also requires an entrepreneurial spirit and skill set to be effective. Few companies have a more exemplary reputation than W. L. Gore Exhibit 12.2 highlights the policies that help make Gore an innovation leader. One of the most important ways that companies improve and grow is when innovation is put to the task of creating new corporate ventures. We will look at that topic next.

Exhibit 12.2

W. L. Gore's New Rules for Fostering Innovation

Rule	Implications
The power of small teams	Gore believes that small teams promote familiarity and autonomy. Even its manufacturing plants are capped at just 200 people. That way everyone can get to know one another on a first-name basis and work together with minimal rules. This also helps to cultivate "an environment where creativity can flourish," according to CEO Chuck Carroll.
No ranks, no titles, no bosses	Because Gore believes in maximizing individual potential, employees, dubbed "associates," decide for themselves what new commitments to take on. Associates have "sponsors," rather than bosses, and there are no standardized job descriptions or categories. Everyone is supposed to take on a unique role. Committees of co-workers evaluate each team member's contribution and decide on compensation.
Take the long view	Although impatient about the status quo, Gore exhibits great patience with the time—often years, sometimes decades—it takes to nurture and develop breakthrough products and bring them to market.
Make time for face time	Gore avoids the traditional hierarchical chain of command, opting instead for a team-based environment that fosters personal initiative. Gore also discourages memos and e-mail and promotes direct, person-to-person communication among all associates—anyone in the company can talk to anyone else.
Lead by leading	Associates are encouraged to spend about 10 percent of their time pursuing speculative new ideas. Anyone is free to champion products, as long as they have the passion and ideas to attract followers. Many of Gore's breakthroughs started with one person acting on his or her own initiative and developed as colleagues helped in their spare time.
Celebrate failure	When a project doesn't work out and the team decides to kill it, they celebrate just as they would if it had been a success—with some beer and maybe a glass of champagne. Rather than condemning failure, Gore figures that celebrating it encourages experimentation and risk taking.

Source: Deutschman, A. 2004. The fabric of creativity. *Fast Company,* 89: 54–62; Levering, R., & Moskowitz, M. 2006. The 100 best companies to work for. *Fortune,* www.fortune.com, January, and www.gore.com.

Corporate Entrepreneurship

corporate entrepreneurship
the creation of new value for a corporation, through investments that create either new sources of competitive advantage or renewal of the value proposition.

Corporate entrepreneurship (CE) has two primary aims: the pursuit of new venture opportunities and strategic renewal.[24] The innovation process keeps firms alert by exposing them to new technologies, making them aware of marketplace trends, and helping them evaluate new possibilities. Corporate entrepreneurship uses the fruits of the innovation process to help firms build new sources of competitive advantage and renew their value propositions. Just as the innovation process helps firms to make positive improvements, corporate entrepreneurship helps firms identify opportunities and launch new ventures.

Corporate new venture creation was labeled "intrapreneuring" by Gifford Pinchot because it refers to building entrepreneurial businesses within existing corporations.[25] However, to engage in corporate entrepreneurship that yields above-average returns and contributes to sustainable advantages, it must be done effectively. In this section we will examine the sources of entrepreneurial activity within established firms and the methods large corporations use to stimulate entrepreneurial behavior.

In a typical corporation, what determines how entrepreneurial projects will be pursued? That depends on many factors, including:

- Corporate culture.
- Leadership.
- Structural features that guide and constrain action.
- Organizational systems that foster learning and manage rewards.

In other words, all of the factors that influence the strategy implementation process will also shape how corporations engage in internal venturing.

Other factors will also affect how entrepreneurial ventures will be pursued.

- The use of teams in strategic decision making.
- Whether the company is product or service oriented.
- Whether its innovation efforts are aimed at product or process improvements.
- The extent to which it is high-tech or low-tech.

Because these factors are different in every organization, some companies may be more involved than others in identifying and developing new venture opportunities. These factors will also influence the nature of the CE process. In this section, we will address several avenues by which companies pursue growth and profit opportunities through entrepreneurial activities.

Successful corporate entrepreneurship typically requires firms to reach beyond their current operations and markets in the pursuit of new opportunities. In fact, it is often the breakthrough opportunities that provide the greatest returns. Such strategies are not without risks, however. In the sections that follow, we will address some of the strategic choice and implementation issues that influence the success or failure of CE activities. How various companies approach corporate venturing is a key factor.

Two distinct approaches to corporate venturing are found among firms that pursue entrepreneurial aims. The first is *focused* corporate venturing, in which CE activities are isolated from a firm's existing operations and worked on by independent work units. The second approach to CE is *dispersed,* in which all parts of the organization and every organization member are engaged in intrapreneurial activities. In the next two sections, we will address these approaches and provide examples of each.

Focused Approaches to Corporate Entrepreneurship

Firms using a focused approach typically separate the corporate venturing activity from the other ongoing operations of the firm. That is, corporate entrepreneurship is usually the domain of autonomous work groups that pursue entrepreneurial aims independent of the rest of the firm. The advantage of this approach is that it frees entrepreneurial team members to think and act without the constraints imposed by existing organizational norms and routines. This independence is often necessary for the kind of open-minded creativity that leads to strategic breakthroughs. The disadvantage is that, because of their isolation from the corporate mainstream, the work groups that concentrate on internal ventures may fail to obtain the resources or support needed to carry an entrepreneurial project through to completion. Two forms—new venture groups (NVGs) and business incubators—are among the most common types of focused approaches.

>LO3

How independent venture teams and business incubators are used to develop corporate ventures.

New Venture Groups (NVGs)   Corporations often form new venture groups whose goal is to identify, evaluate, and cultivate venture opportunities. These groups typically function as semi-autonomous units with little formal structure. The **new venture group** may simply be a committee that reports to the president on potential new ventures. Or it may be organized as a corporate division with its own staff and budget. The aims of the new venture group may be open-ended in terms of what ventures it may consider. Alternatively, some corporations use them to promote concentrated effort on a specific problem. In both cases, they usually have a substantial amount of freedom to take risks and a supply of resources to do it with.[26]

new venture group
a group of individuals, or a division within a corporation, that identifies, evaluates, and cultivates venture opportunities.

New venture groups usually have a larger mandate than a typical R&D department. That is, their involvement extends beyond innovation and experimentation to coordinating with other corporate divisions, identifying potential venture partners, gathering resources, and, in some cases, actually launching the venture.

Firms that want to expand by way of new venture start-ups usually acquire existing ventures, as discussed in Chapter 6, or develop ventures internally. Strategy Spotlight 12.5 describes a third alternative for firms that want to be entrepreneurial but still maintain their autonomy: corporate venture funding.[27]

Business Incubators   The term *incubator* was originally used to describe a device in which eggs are hatched. **Business incubators** are designed to "hatch" new businesses. They are a type of corporate new venture group with a somewhat more specialized purpose—to support and nurture fledgling entrepreneurial ventures until they can thrive on their own as stand-alone businesses. Corporations use incubators as a way to grow businesses identified by the new venture group. Although they often receive support from many parts of the corporation, they still operate independently until they are strong enough to go it alone. Then, depending on the type of business, they are either integrated into an existing corporate division or continue to operate as a subsidiary of the parent firm. Additionally, the type of corporate venturing support reported in Strategy Spotlight 12.5 that external new ventures receive may also include allowing a young venture into the corporation's incubator.

business incubator
a corporate new venture group that supports and nurtures fledgling entrepreneurial ventures until they can thrive on their own as stand-alone businesses.

Incubators typically provide some or all of the following five functions.[28]

- *Funding.* Usually includes capital investments but may also include in-kind investments and loans.
- *Physical space.* A common problem for new ventures; incubators in which several start-ups share space often provide fertile ground for new ideas and collaboration.
- *Business services.* Along with office space, young ventures need basic services and infrastructure; may include anything from phone systems and computer networks to public relations and personnel management.
- *Mentoring.* Senior executives and skilled technical personnel often provide coaching and experience-based advice.
- *Networking.* Contact with other parts of the firm and external resources such as suppliers, industry experts, and potential customers facilitates problem solving and knowledge sharing.

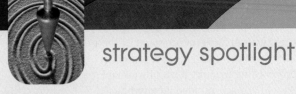
Corporate Venture Capital

What does a company do when it wants to enjoy the benefits of an entrepreneurial start-up but does not want to acquire a venture or take time to develop one internally? It finances one by providing venture capital.

Since the 1970s, major U.S. corporations such as Exxon Mobil have invested in externally generated business ideas in order to strengthen their innovation profile. Some firms invest in technologies that are similar to their core business or provide potential future synergies. Intel, for example, has invested in several e-business start-ups that are in a position to increase demand for Intel processors. With the high growth potential of industries such as information technology and biotechnology, the level of corporate venture capital is increasing. During the booming dot-com era, corporate venture unit investments jumped by a factor of five, from $1.4 billion to $7.8 billion. In 2000 alone, corporations worldwide invested nearly $17 billion in venture capital.

Several major corporations have launched venture financing efforts. In Germany alone there are over 20 corporate venture funds, including global players Siemens, Bertelsmann, and Deutsche Telekom. Even utilities are investing in emerging companies. AEP, a major U.S. electric power company, recently invested in PHPK, a cryogenics firm based in Columbus, Ohio. PHPK is poised to provide support of superconductivity applications, a rapidly growing energy niche that is seeking innovations. AEP prefers expansion-stage firms that need capital and guidance rather than earlier-stage firms. And AEP invests only in energy-related companies. PHPK has nearly doubled its business since AEP made its investment, which served as an immediate endorsement of PHPK's technology and capabilities.

The result? Intel, for one, has enjoyed tremendous returns. It has a portfolio of businesses worth $8 billion. But Intel's goal is not just to make money—it is looking for ways to cement ties early with promising start-ups. "Companies have discovered that it's a good way to do market development," according to Les Vadasz, head of Intel's venture program. "I do see it as a competitive weapon."

Louis Rajczi, managing partner at Siemens Venture Capital, agrees. Unlike traditional VCs which invest in businesses strictly for the financial returns, corporations invest in new ventures to advance their strategic vision and beat the competition. "If we get in on more good deals at an earlier stage than our competitors, we'll end up getting ahead," says Rajczi. "That will increase the value of the company and increase our returns."

Even so, corporate funding for external ventures dried up rapidly after the technology bubble burst in the early 2000s. In the first half of 2002, only $1.1 billion was invested, compared to $17 billion in 2000. Not only have new investments by corporations dropped dramatically, but also corporations such as Hewlett-Packard and Accenture have sold off large portions of their portfolios. Nevertheless, as a long-term strategy, corporate venture funding can benefit both new ventures and corporations and remains a viable alternative to internal corporate venturing.

Sources: Stein, T. 2002. Rip cord. *Red Herring,* November 28, www.redherring .com; Franzke, E. 2001. Four keys to corporate venturing success. *European Venture Capital Journal,* June 1: 36–37; Letzelter, J. 2000. The new venture capitalists: Utilities go shopping for deals. *Public Utilities Fortnightly,* December: 34–38; Rabinovitz, J. 2000. Venture capital, Inc. *Industry Standard,* April 17: 88–90; and, Worrell, D. 2003. The big guns. *Entrepreneur,* November, www.entrepreneur.com.

The risks associated with incubating ventures should not be overlooked. Companies have at times spent millions on new ideas with very little to show for it. Major corporations such as Lucent, British Airways, and Hewlett-Packard inactivated their incubators and scaled back new venture portfolios after experiencing major declines in value since the early 2000s.[29]

Thus, to encourage entrepreneurship, corporations sometimes need to do more than create independent work groups or venture incubators to generate new enterprises. In some firms, the entrepreneurial spirit is spread throughout the organization. It is this dispersed approach to corporate entrepreneurship that we turn to next.

Dispersed Approaches to Corporate Entrepreneurship

The second type of corporate entrepreneurship is dispersed. For some companies, a dedication to the principles and practices of entrepreneurship is spread throughout the organization. One advantage of this approach is that organizational members don't have to be reminded to think entrepreneurially or be willing to change. The ability to change is considered to be a core capability. This leads to a second advantage: Because of the firm's entrepreneurial reputation, stakeholders such as vendors, customers, or alliance partners can bring new ideas or venture opportunities to anyone in the organization and expect them to be well-received. Such opportunities make it possible for the firm to stay ahead of the competition. However, there are disadvantages as well. Firms that are overzealous about corporate entrepreneurship sometimes feel they must change for the sake of change, causing them to lose vital competencies or spend heavily on R&D and innovation to the detriment of the bottom line. Two related aspects of dispersed entrepreneurship include entrepreneurial cultures that have an overarching commitment to CE activities and the use of product champions in promoting entrepreneurial behaviors.

>LO4
How corporations create an internal environment and culture that promote entrepreneurial development.

Entrepreneurial Culture   In some large corporations, the corporate culture embodies the spirit of entrepreneurship. A culture of entrepreneurship is one in which the search for venture opportunities permeates every part of the organization. Recall from Chapter 3 that the key to creating value successfully is viewing every value-chain activity as a source of competitive advantage. In a similar way, the effect of corporate entrepreneurship on a firm's strategic success is strongest when it animates all parts of an organization. It is found in companies where the strategic leaders and the culture together generate a strong impetus to innovate, take risks, and seek out new venture opportunities.

In companies with an entrepreneurial culture, everyone in the organization is attuned to opportunities to help create new businesses. Many such firms use a top-down approach to stimulate entrepreneurial activity. That is, the top leaders of the organization support programs and incentives that foster a climate of entrepreneurship. Many of the best ideas for new corporate ventures, however, come from the bottom up. Here's what Martin Sorrell, CEO of the WPP Group, a London-based global communication services group, says about drawing on the talents of lower-level employees:

> The people at the so-called bottom of an organization know more about what's going on than the people at the top. The people in the trenches are the ones in the best position to make critical decisions. It's up to the leaders to give those people the freedom and the resources they need.[30]

Thus, an entrepreneurial culture is one in which change and renewal are on everybody's mind. Sony, 3M, Intel, and Cisco are among the corporations best known for their corporate venturing activities. Many fast-growing young corporations also attribute much of their success to an entrepreneurial culture. Best Buy's CEO Brad Anderson considers an entrepreneurial spirit to be essential for success in retailing. Strategy Spotlight 12.6 describes the kinds of activities that promote an entrepreneurial culture at Best Buy.

>LO5
The role of product champions in internal corporate venturing.

Product Champions   CE does not always involve making large investments in start-ups or establishing incubators to spawn new divisions. Often, innovative ideas emerge in the normal course of business and are brought forth and become part of the way of doing business. Entrepreneurial champions are often needed to take charge of internally generated ventures. **Product** (or project) **champions** are those individuals working within a corporation who bring entrepreneurial ideas forward, identify what kind of market exists for the product or service, find resources to support the venture, and promote the venture concept to upper management.[31]

When lower-level employees identify a product idea or novel solution, they will take it to their supervisor or someone in authority. Similarly, a new idea that is generated in a technology lab may be introduced to others by its inventor. If the idea has merit, it gains support and builds momentum across the organization.[32] Thus, even though the corporation may not be looking for new ideas or have a program for cultivating internal ventures, the independent behaviors of a few organizational members can have important strategic consequences.

product champion an individual working within a corporation who brings entrepreneurial ideas forward, identifies what kind of market exists for the product or service, finds resources to support the venture, and promotes the venture concept to upper management.

strategy spotlight

Best Buy's Spirit of Innovation

Best Buy remains the number one electronics retailer despite intense competition from competitors such as Circuit City and Wal-Mart (see Strategy Spotlight 8.9). A major key to its success is the climate of innovation that permeates the company. According to Shari Ballard, Best Buy's vice president for human resources, "If you're going to turn on an innovation engine, a lot depends on whether managers listen for the brilliance in their employees' ideas." Here are a couple of Best Buy's recent innovation successes:

- Project manager Nate Omann noticed that a high number of flat-panel TVs were being damaged during home delivery. It was making customers angry and running up replacement costs. So Nate came up with the "TV taco"—a reusable device that fits around TVs to better protect them during transit. It is expected to save the company millions of dollars.

- *Sound and Vision Magazine* awarded Best Buy the Retail Innovation Award in 2005 for its Magnolia Home Theatre store-within-a-store concept. This innovation offers the kind of services usually found only at small specialty stores—quiet demo rooms, comfortable seating, a highly knowledgeable staff, and top quality brands.

More radical than its store innovations, Best Buy is also winning kudos for innovative human resources management. It implemented a program, called ROWE for "results-only work environment," designed to dramatically increase employee autonomy by focusing on output instead of hours worked. The program has been so successful, in fact, that Best Buy formed a subsidiary named CultureRx to implement similar programs at other companies. What it implements, however, is not the usual flextime, telecommuting program. ROWE co-founders Jody Thompson and Cali Ressler consider those programs, which still focus on hours worked, to be overly bureaucratic. ROWE employees, by contrast, are required to put in only as much time as it actually takes to do their work.

Is it working? In 2006, Best Buy's procurement department increased savings by 50 percent over the previous year after it entered the ROWE program. In the online ordering division, orders processed by people not working in the office were as much as 18 percent higher than those working in the office. Across the company, voluntary turnover has decreased significantly and ROWE participants report that they feel 35 percent more productive. As a result, Workforce Management gave Best Buy and CultureRx its 2007 Optimas Award for innovation.

Sources: Anonymous. 2006. 2005 Editor's Choice Awards: Best Buy. *Sound and Vision Magazine*, www.soundandvision.mag, February; Ballard, S. 2006. Fast talk: Best brains, *Fast Company*, November: 66; Conlin, M. 2006. Smashing the clock. *BusinessWeek*, www.businessweek.com, December 11; and Frauenheim, E. 2007. Best Buy & CultureRx: Optimas Award Winner for Innovation, *Workforce Management*, www.workforce.com, March 26.

No matter how an entrepreneurial idea comes to light, however, a new venture concept must pass through two critical stages or it may never get off the ground: project definition and project impetus:

1. *Project definition.* A promising opportunity has to be justified in terms of its attractiveness in the marketplace and how well it fits with the corporation's other strategic objectives.
2. *Project impetus.* For a project to gain impetus, its strategic and economic impact must be supported by senior managers who have experience with similar projects. The project then becomes an embryonic business with its own organization and budget.

For a project to advance through these stages of definition and impetus, a product champion is often needed to generate support and encouragement. Champions are especially important during the time after a new project has been defined but before it gains momentum. They form a link between the definition and impetus stages of internal development, which they do by procuring resources and stimulating interest for the product among potential customers.[33] Often, they must work quietly and alone. Consider the example of Ken Kutaragi, the Sony engineer who championed the PlayStation.

Even though Sony had made the processor that powered the first Nintendo video games, no one at Sony in the mid-1980s saw any future in such products. "It was a kind of snobbery," Kutaragi recalled. "For Sony people, the Nintendo product would have been very embarrassing to make because it was only a toy." But Kutaragi was convinced he could make a better product. He began working secretly on a video game. Kutaragi said, "I realized that if it was visible, it would be killed." He quietly began enlisting the support of senior executives, such as the head of R&D. He made a case that Sony could use his project to develop capabilities in digital technologies that would be important in the future. It was not until 1994, after years of "underground" development and quiet building of support, that Sony introduced the PlayStation. By the year 2000, Sony had sold 55 million of them, and Kutaragi became CEO of Sony Computer Entertainment. By 2005, Kutagari was Sony's Chief Operating Officer, and plans to launch the third generation version of the market-leading PlayStation (PS3) were well under way.[34]

● Sony's PlayStation is an exemplary example of successful product championing.

Thus, product champions play an important entrepreneurial role in a corporate setting by encouraging others to take a chance on promising new ideas.[35]

Measuring the Success of Corporate Entrepreneurship Activities

At this point in the discussion, it is reasonable to ask whether corporate entrepreneurship is successful. Corporate venturing, like the innovation process, usually requires a tremendous effort. Is it worth it? In this section we consider factors that corporations need to take into consideration when evaluating the success of CE programs. We also examine techniques that companies can use to limit the expense of venturing or to cut their losses when CE initiatives appear doomed.

Comparing Strategic and Financial CE Goals   Not all corporate venturing efforts are financially rewarding. In terms of financial performance, slightly more than 50 percent of corporate venturing efforts reach profitability (measured by ROI) within six years of their launch.[36] If this were the only criterion for measuring success, it would seem to be a rather poor return. On the one hand, these results should be expected, because CE is riskier than other investments such as expanding ongoing operations. On the other hand, corporations expect a higher return from corporate venturing projects than from normal operations. Thus, in terms of the risk–return trade-off, it seems that CE often falls short of expectations.[37]

>LO6
How corporate entrepreneurship achieves both financial goals and strategic goals.

There are several other important criteria, however, for judging the success of a corporate venture initiative. In addition to financial goals, most CE programs have strategic goals. The strategic reasons for undertaking a corporate venture include strengthening competitive position, entering into new markets, expanding capabilities by learning and acquiring new knowledge, and building the corporation's base of resources and experience. Three questions should be used to assess the effectiveness of a corporation's venturing initiatives:[38]

1.   *Are the products or services offered by the venture accepted in the marketplace?* That is, is the venture considered to be a market success? If so, the financial returns are likely to be satisfactory. In addition, the venture may open doors into other markets and suggest avenues for other venture projects.

2. *Are the contributions of the venture to the corporation's internal competencies and experience valuable?* That is, does the venture add to the worth of the firm internally? If so, strategic goals such as leveraging existing assets, building new knowledge, and enhancing firm capabilities are likely to be met.

3. *Is the venture able to sustain its basis of competitive advantage?* That is, does the value proposition offered by the venture insulate it from competitive attack? If so, it is likely to place the corporation in a stronger position relative to competitors and provide a base from which to build other advantages.

As you can see, these criteria include both strategic and financial goals of CE. Another way to evaluate a corporate venture is in terms of the four criteria from the Balanced Scorecard (Chapter 3). In a successful venture, not only are financial and market acceptance (customer) goals met but so are the internal business and innovation and learning goals. Thus, when assessing the success of corporate venturing, it is important to look beyond simple financial returns and consider a well-rounded set of criteria.[39]

Next, we consider the role of "exit champions" in helping corporations limit their exposure to venture projects that are unlikely to succeed.

Exit Champions   Although a culture of championing venture projects is advantageous for stimulating an ongoing stream of entrepreneurial initiatives, many—in fact, most—of the ideas will not work out. At some point in the process, a majority of initiatives will be abandoned. Sometimes, however, companies wait too long to terminate a new venture and do so only after large sums of resources are used up or, worse, result in a marketplace failure. Motorola's costly global satellite telecom project known as Iridium provides a useful illustration. Even though problems with the project existed during the lengthy development process, Motorola refused to pull the plug. Only after investing $5 billion and years of effort was the project abandoned.[40]

How can companies avoid these costly and discouraging defeats? One way is to support a key role in the CE process: **exit champions.** In contrast to product champions and other entrepreneurial enthusiasts within the corporation, exit champions are willing to question the viability of a venture project.[41] By demanding hard evidence and challenging the belief system that is carrying an idea forward, exit champions hold the line on ventures that appear shaky.

Both product champions and exit champions must be willing to energetically stand up for what they believe. Both put their reputations on the line. But they also differ in important ways. Product champions deal in uncertainty and ambiguity. Exit champions reduce ambiguity by gathering hard data and developing a strong case for why a project should be killed. Product champions are often thought to be willing to violate procedures and operate outside normal channels. Exit champions, by contrast, often have to reinstate procedures and reassert the decision-making criteria that are supposed to guide venture decisions. Whereas product champions often emerge as heroes, exit champions run the risk of losing status by opposing popular projects.

Thus, the role of exit champion may seem unappealing. But it is one that could save a corporation both financially and in terms of its reputation in the marketplace. It is especially important because one measure of the success of a firm's CE efforts is the extent to which it knows when to cut its losses and move on. To address this, we turn to real options analysis, a useful tool in analyzing strategic decisions.

Real Options Analysis: A Useful Tool

One way firms can minimize failure and avoid losses from pursuing faulty ideas is to apply the logic of real options. **Real options analysis** (ROA) is an investment analysis tool from the field of finance. It has been slowly, but increasingly, adopted by consultants and executives to support strategic decision making in firms. What does real options analysis consist of and how can

exit champion an individual working within a corporation who is willing to question the viability of a venture project by demanding hard evidence of venture success and challenging the belief system that carries a venture forward.

real options analysis an investment analysis tool that looks at an investment or activity as a series of sequential steps, and for each step the investor has the option of (a) investing additional funds to grow or accelerate, (b) delaying, (c) shrinking the scale of, or (d) abandoning the activity.

it be appropriately applied to the investments required to initiate strategic decisions? To understand *real* options it is first necessary to have a basic understanding of what *options* are.

>LO7
The benefits and potential drawbacks of real options analysis in making resource deployment decisions in corporate entrepreneurship contexts.

Options exist when the owner of the option has the right but not the obligation to engage in certain types of transactions. The most common are stock options. A stock option grants the holder the right to buy (call option) or sell (put option) shares of the stock at a fixed price (strike price) at some time in the future.[42] Another aspect of stock options important to note is that the investment to be made immediately is small, whereas the investment to be made in the future is generally larger. For example, an option to buy a rapidly rising stock currently priced at $50 might cost as little as $.50.[43] An important point to note is that owners of such a stock option have limited their losses to $.50 per share, while the upside potential is unlimited. This aspect of options is attractive because options offer the prospect of high gains with relatively small up-front investments that represent limited losses.

The phrase "real options" applies to situations where options theory and valuation techniques are applied to real assets or physical things as opposed to financial assets. Applied to entrepreneurship, real options suggest a path that companies can use to manage the uncertainty associated with launching new ventures. Some of the most common applications of real options are with property and insurance. A real estate option grants the holder the right to buy or sell a piece of property at an established price some time in the future. The actual market price of the property may rise above the established (or strike) price—or the market value may sink below the strike price. If the price of the property goes up, the owner of the option is likely to buy it. If the market value of the property drops below the strike price, the option holder is unlikely to execute the purchase. In the latter circumstance, the option holder has limited his or her loss to the cost of the option, but during the life of the option retains the right to participate in whatever the upside potential might be.

Applications of Real Options Analysis to Strategic Decisions

The concept of options can also be applied to strategic decisions where management has flexibility; that is, the situation will permit management to decide whether to invest additional funds to grow or accelerate the activity, perhaps delay in order to learn more, shrink the scale of the activity, or even abandon it. Decisions to invest in new ventures or other business activities such as R&D, motion pictures, exploration and production of oil wells, and the opening and closing of copper mines often have this flexibility.[44] Important issues to note are the following:

- Real options analysis is appropriate to use when investments can be staged; in other words, a smaller investment up front can be followed by subsequent investments. In short, real options can be applied to an investment decision that gives the company the right, but not the obligation, to make follow-on investments.
- The strategic decision makers have "tollgates" or key points at which they can decide whether to continue, delay, or abandon the project. In short, the executives have the flexibility. There are opportunities to make other go or no-go decisions associated with each phase.
- It is expected that there will be increased knowledge about outcomes at the time of the next investment and that additional knowledge will help inform the decision makers about whether to make additional investments (i.e., whether the option is in the money or out of the money).

Many strategic decisions have the characteristic of containing a series of options. The phenomenon is called "embedded options," a series of investments in which at each stage of the investment there is a go/no–go decision. Consider the real options logic that Johnson Controls, a maker of car seats, instrument panels, and interior control systems uses to advance or eliminate entrepreneurial ideas.[45] Johnson options each new innovative idea by making a small investment in it. To decide whether to exercise an option, the idea must

strategy spotlight

Using Real Options Analysis to Evaluate a Pharmaceutical Venture

Pharmaceutical companies often use real options analysis in evaluating decisions about whether to invest in new R&D ventures. Developing new pharmaceutical products requires at least four stages of investments: basic research to yield new compounds and three FDA-mandated phases of clinical trials. Generally, each phase is more expensive to undertake than the previous phase. However, as each phase unfolds, management knows more about the underlying drug and its many sources of uncertainty, including the technical difficulties it faces and external market conditions that could affect sales. With this information, management can make the decision to invest more, speed up the process, delay the start of the next phase, or even abandon the R&D project.

Consider, for example, a privately held biotechnology firm that used real options analysis to evaluate whether to invest in a veterinary pharmaceutical product. The firm had developed a unique technology for introducing the coat protein of a particular virus into animal feedstocks. Ingesting the coat protein generated an immune response, thus protecting

Sources: Janney, J. J. &, Dess, G. G. 2004. Can real-options analysis improve decision making? Promises and pitfalls. *Academy of Management Executive,* 18(4): 60–75; Stockley, R. L., Jr., Curtis, S., Jafari, J., & Tibbs, K. 2003. The options value of an early-stage biotechnology investment. *Journal of Applied Finance,* 15(2): 44–55; and Triantis, A., et al. 2003. University of Maryland roundtable on real options and corporate practice. *Journal of Applied Corporate Finance,* 15(2): 8–23.

the animal from the virus. The firm was at the beginning of the preclinical trials stage, the first of a series of tests required by FDA regulation and conducted through the FDA subagency called the Center for Veterinary Medicine.

The company expected the stage to take 18 months and cost $2 million. Long-standing experience indicated that 95 percent of new drug investigations are abandoned during this phase. Abandonment rates in subsequent stages would decrease somewhat, but costs would rise, with a total outflow from 2002 through its anticipated launch in 2007 of at least $18.5 million. The company's best estimate of the market from 2007 through 2017 was about $85 million per year. Still, there was a possibility the product would gain as much as a 50 percent market share. In short, there was huge potential, but in the interim there was a tremendous chance of failure (i.e., high risk), significant early outflows, and delayed inflows of revenue.

A traditional net present value (NPV) analysis (which sums revenues and costs for the life of the project and then discounts them using current interest rates) yielded a negative $2 million with an 11 percent risk-adjusted discount rate. However, viewing the investment as a multi-stage option and incorporating management's flexibility to alter its decision at least four times between 2002 and 2007 changes the valuation markedly. That is, a real options analysis demonstrated a present value of about $22 million. The question, then, was not whether to risk $18.5 million, but whether to invest $2 million today for the opportunity to earn $22 million at a future date.

---

continue to prove itself at each stage of development. Here's how Jim Geschke, vice president and general manager of electronics integration at Johnson, describes the process:

> Think of Johnson as an innovation machine. The front end has a robust series of gates that each idea must pass through. Early on, we'll have many ideas and spend a little money on each of them. As they get more fleshed out, the ideas go through a gate where a go or no-go decision is made. A lot if ideas get filtered out, so there are far fewer items, and the spending on each goes up. . . . Several months later each idea will face another gate. If it passes, that means it's a serious idea that we are going to develop. Then the spending goes way up, and the number of ideas goes way down. By the time you reach the final gate, you need to have a credible business case in order to be accepted. At a certain point in the development process, we take our idea to customers and ask them what they think. Sometimes they say, "That's a terrible idea. Forget it." Other times they say, "That's fabulous. I want a million of them."

This process of evaluating ideas by separating winning ideas from losing ones in a way that keeps investments low has helped Johnson Controls grow its revenues to over $33 billion a year. Thus, using real options logic to advance the development process is a key way that firms reduce uncertainty and minimize innovation-related failures.[46]

Strategy Spotlight 12.7 provides an example of a pharmaceutical company that used ROA to guide its decision-making process.

Potential Pitfalls of Real Options Analysis

Despite the many benefits that can be gained from using real options analysis, managers must be aware of its potential limitations or pitfalls. Below we will address three major issues.[47]

Agency Theory and the Back-Solver Dilemma   Let's assume that companies adopting a real-options perspective invest heavily in training and that their people understand how to effectively estimate variance—that is, the amount of dispersion or range that is estimated for potential outcomes. Such training can help them use ROA. However, it does not solve another inherent problem: managers may have an incentive and the know-how to "game the system." Most electronic spreadsheets permit users to simply back-solve any formula; that is, you can type in the answer you want and ask what values are needed in a formula to get that answer. If managers know that a certain option value must be met in order for the proposal to get approved, they can back-solve the model to find a variance estimate needed to arrive at the answer that upper management desires. What would be the manager's motive to do this?

Agency problems are typically inherent in investment decisions. They may occur when the managers of a firm are separated from its owners—that is, when managers act as "agents" rather than "principals" (owners). Such problems could occur because a manager may have something to gain by not acting in the owner's best interests, or the interests of managers and owners are not co-aligned. Agency theory suggests that as managerial and owner interests diverge, managers will follow the path of their own self-interests. Sometimes this is to secure better compensation: Managers who propose projects may believe that if their projects are approved, they stand a much better chance of getting promoted. So while managers have an incentive to propose projects that *should* be successful, they also have an incentive to propose projects that *might* be successful. And because of the subjectivity involved in formally modeling a real option, managers may have an incentive to choose variance values that increase the likelihood of approval.

Managerial Conceit: Overconfidence and the Illusion of Control   Often, poor decisions are the result of such traps as biases, blind spots, and other human frailties. Much of this literature falls under the concept of *managerial conceit*.[48] Understanding how these traps affect decision makers can help to improve decision making.

First, managerial conceit occurs when decision makers who have made successful choices in the past come to believe that they possess superior expertise for managing uncertainty. They believe that their abilities can, therefore, reduce the risks inherent in decision making to a much greater extent than they actually can. Such managers are more likely to shift away from analysis to trusting their own judgment. In the case of real options, they can simply declare that any given decision is a real option and proceed as before. If asked to formally model their decision, they are more likely to employ variance estimates that support their viewpoint.

Second, employing the real-options perspective can encourage decision makers toward a bias for action. Such a bias may lead to carelessness. Managerial conceit is as much a problem (if not more so) for small decisions as for big ones. Why? The cost to write the first stage of an option is much smaller than the cost of full commitment, and managers pay less attention to small decisions than to large ones. Because real options are designed to minimize potential losses while preserving potential gains, any problems that arise are likely to be smaller at first, causing less concern for the manager. Managerial conceit could suggest that managers will assume that those problems are the easiest to solve and control—a concern referred to as the illusion of control. Managers may fail to respond appropriately because they overlook the problem or believe that since it is small, they can easily resolve it. Thus, managers may approach each real-option decision with less care and diligence than if they had made a full commitment to a larger investment.

Managerial Conceit: Irrational Escalation of Commitment   A strength of a real options perspective is also one of its Achilles heels. Both real options and decisions involving escalation of commitment require specific environments with sequential decisions.[49] As the escalation-of-commitment literature indicates, simply separating a decision into multiple parts does not guarantee that decisions made will turn out well. This condition is potentially present whenever the exercise decision retains some uncertainty, which most still do. The decision to abandon also has strong psychological factors associated with it that affect the ability of managers to make correct exercise decisions.[50]

An option to exit requires reversing an initial decision made by someone in the organization (such as an exit champion). Organizations typically encourage managers to "own their decisions" in order to motivate them. One result is that as managers invest themselves in their decision, it proves harder for them to lose face by reversing course. In effect, for managers making the decision, it feels as if they made the wrong decision in the first place, even if it was initially a good decision. The more specific the manager's human capital becomes, the harder it is to transfer it to other organizations. Hence, there is a greater likelihood that managers will stick around and try to make an existing decision work. They are more likely to continue an existing project even if it should perhaps be ended.[51]

Despite the potential pitfalls of a real options approach, many of the strategic decisions that product champions and top managers must make are enhanced when decision makers have an entrepreneurial mind-set. In the next section, we look at the practices and characteristics associated with an entrepreneurial orientation.

Entrepreneurial Orientation

>LO8
How an entrepreneurial orientation can enhance a firm's efforts to develop promising corporate venture initiatives.

Firms that want to engage in successful corporate entrepreneurship need to have an entrepreneurial orientation (EO). EO refers to the strategy-making practices that businesses use in identifying and launching corporate ventures. It represents a frame of mind and a perspective toward entrepreneurship that is reflected in a firm's ongoing processes and corporate culture.[52]

An entrepreneurial orientation has five dimensions that permeate the decision-making styles and practices of the firm's members. These are autonomy, innovativeness, proactiveness, competitive aggressiveness, and risk taking. These factors can work together to enhance a firm's entrepreneurial performance. But even those firms that are strong in only a few aspects of EO can be very successful.[53] Exhibit 12.3 summarizes the dimensions of an **entrepreneurial orientation.** Below we discuss the five dimensions of entrepreneurial orientation and how they have been used to enhance internal venture development.

entrepreneurial orientation the strategy-making practices that businesses use in identifying and launching new ventures, consisting of autonomy, innovativeness, proactiveness, competitive aggressiveness, and risk taking.

Autonomy

Autonomy refers to a willingness to act independently in order to carry forward an entrepreneurial vision or opportunity. It applies to both individuals and teams that operate outside an organization's existing norms and strategies. In the context of corporate entrepreneurship, autonomous work units are often used to leverage existing strengths in new arenas, identify opportunities that are beyond the organization's current capabilities, and encourage development of new ventures or improved business practices.[54]

The need for autonomy may apply to either dispersed or focused entrepreneurial efforts. Clearly, because of the emphasis on venture projects that are being developed outside of the normal flow of business, a focused approach suggests a working environment that is relatively autonomous. But autonomy may also be important in an organization where entrepreneurship is part of the corporate culture. Everything from the methods of group interaction to the firm's reward system must make organizational members feel as if they can think freely about venture opportunities, take time to investigate them, and act without fear of condemnation. This implies a respect for the autonomy of each individual

autonomy independent action by an individual or team aimed at bringing forth a business concept or vision and carrying it through to completion.

Exhibit 12.3
Dimensions of
Entrepreneurial
Orientation

Dimension	Definition
Autonomy	Independent action by an individual or team aimed at bringing forth a business concept or vision and carrying it through to completion.
Innovativeness	A willingness to introduce novelty through experimentation and creative processes aimed at developing new products and services as well as new processes.
Proactiveness	A forward-looking perspective characteristic of a marketplace leader that has the foresight to seize opportunities in anticipation of future demand.
Competitive aggressiveness	An intense effort to outperform industry rivals characterized by a combative posture or an aggressive response aimed at improving position or overcoming a threat in a competitive marketplace.
Risk taking	Making decisions and taking action without certain knowledge of probable outcomes; some undertakings may also involve making substantial resource commitments in the process of venturing forward.

Sources: Dess, G. G., & Lumpkin, G. T. 2005. The role of entrepreneurial orientation in stimulating effective corporate entrepreneurship. *Academy of Management Executive,* 19(1): 147–156; Covin, J. G., & Slevin, D. P. 1991. A conceptual model of entrepreneurship as firm behavior. *Entrepreneurship Theory & Practice,* Fall: 7–25; Lumpkin, G. T., and Dess, G. G. 1996. Clarifying the entrepreneurial orientation construct and linking it to performance. *Academy of Management Review,* 21: 135–172; Miller, D. 1983. The correlates of entrepreneurship in three types of firms. *Management Science,* 29: 770–791.

and an openness to the independent thinking that goes into championing a corporate venture idea. Thus, autonomy represents a type of empowerment (see Chapter 11) that is directed at identifying and leveraging entrepreneurial opportunities.

Exhibit 12.4 identifies two techniques that organizations often use to promote autonomy.

Creating autonomous work units and encouraging independent action may have pitfalls that can jeopardize their effectiveness. Autonomous teams, for example, often lack coordination. Excessive decentralization has a strong potential to create inefficiencies, such as duplication of effort and wasting resources on projects with questionable feasibility. For example, Chris Galvin, former CEO of Motorola, scrapped the skunkworks approach the company had been using to develop new wireless phones. Fifteen teams had created 128 different phones, which led to spiraling costs and overly complex operations.[55]

Thus, for autonomous work units and independent projects to be effective, such efforts have to be measured and monitored. This requires a delicate balance: companies must have the patience and budget to tolerate the explorations of autonomous groups and the strength to cut back efforts that are not bearing fruit. It must be undertaken with a clear sense of purpose—namely, to generate new sources of competitive advantage.

Innovativeness

Innovativeness refers to a firm's efforts to find new opportunities and novel solutions. In the beginning of this chapter we discussed innovation; here the focus is on innovativeness—that is, a firm's attitude toward innovation and willingness to innovate. It involves creativity and experimentation that result in new products, new services, or improved technological processes. Innovativeness is one of the major components of an entrepreneurial

innovativeness a willingness to introduce novelty through experimentation and creative processes aimed at developing new products and services as well as new processes.

Autonomy		
Technique	**Description/Purpose**	**Example**
Use skunkworks to foster entrepreneurial thinking	Skunkworks are independent work units, often physically separate from corporate headquarters. They allow employees to get out from under the pressures of their daily routines to engage in creative problem solving.	Overstock.com created a skunkworks to address the problem of returned merchandise. The solution was a business within-a-business: Overstock auctions. The unit has grown by selling products returned to Overstock and offers fees 30 percent lower than eBay's auction service.
Design organizational structures that support independent action	Established companies with traditional structures often need to break out of such old forms to compete more effectively.	Deloitte Consulting, a division of Deloitte Touche Tohmatsu, found it difficult to compete against young agile firms. So it broke the firm into small autonomous units called "chip-aways" that operate with the flexibility of a start-up. In its first year, revenues were $40 million—10 percent higher than its projections.

Sources: Conlin, M. 2006. Square feet. Oh how square! *BusinessWeek,* www.businessweek.com, July 3; Cross, K. 2001. Bang the drum quickly. *Business 2.0,* May: 28–30; Sweeney, J. 2004. A firm for all reasons. *Consulting Magazine,* www.consultingmag.com; and Wagner, M. 2005. Out of the skunkworks. *Internet Retailer,* January, www.internetretailer.com.

Exhibit 12.4
Autonomy Techniques

strategy. As indicated at the beginning of the chapter, however, the job of managing innovativeness can be very challenging.

Innovativeness requires that firms depart from existing technologies and practices and venture beyond the current state of the art. Inventions and new ideas need to be nurtured even when their benefits are unclear. However, in today's climate of rapid change, effectively producing, assimilating, and exploiting innovations can be an important avenue for achieving competitive advantages.

As our earlier discussion of CE indicated, many corporations owe their success to an active program of innovation-based corporate venturing.[56] Exhibit 12.5 highlights two of the methods companies can use to enhance their competitive position through innovativeness.

Innovativeness can be a source of great progress and strong corporate growth, but there are also major pitfalls for firms that invest in innovation. Expenditures on R&D aimed at identifying new products or processes can be a waste of resources if the effort does not yield results. Another danger is related to the competitive climate. Even if a company innovates a new capability or successfully applies a technological breakthrough, another company may develop a similar innovation or find a use for it that is more profitable. Finally, in many firms, R&D and other innovation efforts are among the first to be cut back during an economic downturn.

Therefore, even though innovativeness is an important means of internal corporate venturing, it also involves major risks because investments in innovations may not pay off. For strategic managers of entrepreneurial firms, however, successfully developing and adopting innovations can generate competitive advantages and provide a major source of growth for the firm.

Proactiveness

proactiveness a forward-looking perspective characteristic of a marketplace leader that has the foresight to seize opportunities in anticipation of future demand.

Proactiveness refers to a firm's efforts to seize new opportunities. Proactive organizations monitor trends, identify the future needs of existing customers, and anticipate changes in demand or emerging problems that can lead to new venture opportunities. Proactiveness involves not only

Innovativeness		
Technique	**Description/Purpose**	**Example**
Foster creativity and experimentation	Companies that support idea exploration and allow employees to express themselves creatively enhance innovation outcomes.	To tap into its reserves of innovative talent, Royal Dutch/Shell created "GameChanger" to help employees develop promising ideas. The process provides funding up to $600,000 for would-be entrepreneurs to pursue innovative projects and conduct experiments.
Invest in new technology, R&D, and continuous improvement	The latest technologies often provide sources of new competitive advantages. To extract value from a new technology, companies must invest in it.	Dell Computer Corporation's new OptiPlex manufacturing system revolutionized the traditional assembly line. Hundreds of custom-built computers can be made in an eight-hour shift using state of the art automation techniques that have increased productivity per person by 160 percent.

Sources: Breen, B. 2004. Living in Dell time. *Fast Company,* November: 88–92: Hammonds, K. H. 2002. Size is not a strategy. *Fast Company,* August: 78–83; Perman, S. 2001. Automate or die. eCompanyNow.com, July; Dell, M. 1999. *Direct from Dell.* New York: HarperBusiness; and Watson, R. 2006. Expand your innovation horizons. *Fast Company,* www.fastcompany.com, May.

Exhibit 12.5

Innovativeness Techniques

recognizing changes but also being willing to act on those insights ahead of the competition. Strategic managers who practice proactiveness have their eye on the future in a search for new possibilities for growth and development. Such a forward-looking perspective is important for companies that seek to be industry leaders. Many proactive firms seek out ways not only to be future oriented but also to change the very nature of competition in their industry.

Proactiveness is especially effective at creating competitive advantages, because it puts competitors in the position of having to respond to successful initiatives. The benefit gained by firms that are the first to enter new markets, establish brand identity, implement administrative techniques, or adopt new operating technologies in an industry is called first mover advantage.[57]

First movers usually have several advantages. First, industry pioneers, especially in new industries, often capture unusually high profits because there are no competitors to drive prices down. Second, first movers that establish brand recognition are usually able to retain their image and hold on to the market share gains they earned by being first. Sometimes these benefits also accrue to other early movers in an industry, but, generally speaking, first movers have an advantage that can be sustained until firms enter the maturity phase of an industry's life cycle.[58]

First movers are not always successful. The customers of companies that introduce novel products or embrace breakthrough technologies may be reluctant to commit to a new way of doing things. In his book *Crossing the Chasm,* Geoffrey A. Moore noted that most firms seek evolution, not revolution, in their operations. This makes it difficult for a first mover to sell promising new technologies.[59]

Even with these caveats, however, companies that are first movers can enhance their competitive position. Exhibit 12.6 illustrates two methods firms can use to act proactively.

Proactiveness		
Technique	**Description/Purpose**	**Example**
Introduce new products or technological capabilities ahead of the competition.	Being a first mover provides companies with an ability to shape the playing field and shift competitive advantages in their favor.	Sony's mission states, "We should always be the pioneers with our products—out front leading the market." This philosophy has made Sony technologically strong with industry-leading products such as the PlayStation and Vaio laptop computers.
Continuously seek out new product or service offerings.	Firms that provide new resources or sources of supply can benefit from a proactive stance.	Costco seized a chance to leverage its success as a warehouse club that sells premium brands when it introduced Costco Home Stores. The home stores are usually located near its warehouse stores and its rapid inventory turnover gives it a cost advantage of 15 to 25 percent over close competitors such as Bassett Furniture and the Bombay Company.

Sources: Bryce, D. J., & Dyer, J. H. 2007. Strategies to crack well-guarded markets. *Harvard Business Review,* May: 84–92; Collins, J. C., & Porras, J. I. 1997. *Built to last.* New York: HarperBusiness; Robinson, D. 2005. Sony pushes reliability in Vaio laptops. *IT Week,* www.itweek.co.uk, October 12; and www.sony.com

Exhibit 12.6

Proactiveness Techniques

Being an industry leader does not always lead to competitive advantages. Some firms that have launched pioneering new products or staked their reputation on new brands have failed to get the hoped-for payoff. Two major beverage companies—Coca-Cola and PepsiCo—invested $75 million to launch sodas that would capitalize on the low-carb diet trend. But with half the carbohydrates taken out, neither *C2,* Coke's entry, nor *Pepsi Edge* tasted very good. The two new brands combined never achieved more than one percent market share. PepsiCo announced in would halt production in 2006 and Coca-Cola was expected to follow suit.[60] Such missteps are indicative of the dangers of trying to proactively anticipate demand. Strategy Spotlight 12.8, in contrast, describes another type of proactiveness—how some organizations are using entrepreneurial thinking and practices to effectively promote corporate social responsibility.

Thus, careful monitoring and scanning of the environment, as well as extensive feasibility research, are needed for a proactive strategy to lead to competitive advantages. Firms that do it well usually have substantial growth and internal development to show for it. Many of them have been able to sustain the advantages of proactiveness for years.

Competitive Aggressiveness

competitive aggressiveness an intense effort to outperform industry rivals characterized by a combative posture or an aggressive response aimed at improving position or overcoming a threat in a competitive marketplace.

Competitive aggressiveness refers to a firm's efforts to outperform its industry rivals. Companies with an aggressive orientation are willing to "do battle" with competitors. They might slash prices and sacrifice profitability to gain market share or spend aggressively to obtain manufacturing capacity. As an avenue of firm development and growth, competitive aggressiveness may involve being very assertive in leveraging the results of other entrepreneurial activities such as innovativeness or proactiveness.

Unlike innovativeness and proactiveness, however, which tend to focus on market opportunities, competitive aggressiveness is directed toward competitors. The SWOT

Socially Responsible Corporate Entrepreneurship

One of the most important trends in U.S. business today is corporate social responsibility (CSR). Proactively oriented firms are seizing opportunities to take a leading role in issues such as the environment, product safety, and fair trade. Among the most interesting examples of this, as suggested in the Chapter 1 section on social innovation, are those firms that are taking an entrepreneurial approach to CSR. That is, they are using new technologies, environmentally friendly ventures, and entrepreneurial practices to advance their social responsibility goals. Following is a sample of three corporations that are taking a very entrepreneurial approach to corporate social responsibility.

Whirlpool Corporation—From efficiency to advocacy

Whirlpool is perhaps best known for its "white boxes"— the refrigerators, freezers, and laundry appliances that account for over 60 percent of its $13 billion in annual sales. To explore what creates customer loyalty, Whirlpool conducted a global survey of its customers. "We discovered there is a strong correlation between a company's performance in appliance markets and their social response to issues such as energy efficiency and pollution," said Steve Willis, director of Whirlpool's global environment, health, and safety programs. One result has been its innovative Duet Series of washers and dryers that significantly reduces energy consumption. Recently, Whirlpool decided to take its environmental efforts a step farther: It joined The Natural Step, an entrepreneurial organization that is advancing the movement toward environmental sustainability by advocating the development of innovative products that meet high standards of ecological sustainability.

Interface, Inc.—Doing more with less

In Chapter 1, we saw how some companies have changed their corporate missions to include socially responsible goals like protecting the environment. Carpet maker Interface Inc. has found a way not only to become more environmentally friendly but also to achieve a universal entrepreneurial objective: Do more with less. By leasing rather than selling carpets, Georgia-based Interface is able to take back worn carpets and "remanufacture" them. As a result, it has cut its raw materials input costs by nearly 100 percent and its business customers get to deduct the cost of leasing. "Our costs are down, not up," according to chairman Ray Anderson. "Sustainability doesn't cost more, it saves." Recently, Interface instituted a program known as EcoSense to educate its employees about sustainability and reward them for making environmental improvements. These savings helped Interface survive the 40 percent decline in sales of office furnishings that followed the dot-com collapse and the September 11th terrorist attack. "We might not have made it if it were not for our EcoSense programs," says Anderson.

Green Mountain Coffee Roasters—Empowering local entrepreneurs

As the name suggests, this NASDAQ-listed corporation (GMCR) is located in the Green Mountains of Vermont. But its reach is global. As a roaster and distributor of specialty coffees, GMCR has become a leading advocate for fair trade practices and providing financial support for local coffee growers. "Our president and CEO Robert Stiller visited places where coffee is grown and was struck by the levels of poverty. He wanted to do something about it," said Rick Peyser, director of public relations. As a result, GMCR now purchases coffee beans from small farm cooperatives in Peru, Mexico, and Sumatra. It also provides micro-loans to underwrite family businesses that are trying to create more diverse agricultural economies. Back home in its Waterbury, Vermont, roasting facility, GMCR uses a 95-kilowatt cogeneration system that captures waste heat from its propane-fired generator and recycles it for both coffee roasting and space heating.

Each of these companies has recently been named one of the 100 Best Corporate Citizens by *Business Ethics* magazine. However, major corporations still have their critics. In fact, companies that claim to be making progress in advancing CSR are often the most loudly criticized. For example, British Petroleum, which has endeavored to be an oil industry leader in supporting environmentally sensitive energy development, is often attacked by environmental groups despite initiatives such as investing $48 million to develop the world's largest solar energy project. Despite such criticism, it is encouraging to note that entrepreneurial activities can help companies achieve their social responsibility goals as well as their innovation and growth goals.

Sources: Asmus, P. 2005. 100 best corporate citizens for 2005. *Business Ethics*, www.business-ethics.com; Asmus, P. 2003. 100 best corporate citizens for 2003. *Business Ethics*, www.business-ethics.com; Baker, M. 2001. BP anounces world's largest solar project. *Business Respect*, 1: April 6; Hawken, P., Lovins, A., & Lovins, H. 2000. *Natural capitalism*. Boston: Back Bay Books; see also www.bp.com; www.domini.com; www.hoovers.com; and www.ifsia.com.

Competitive Aggressiveness		
Technique	**Description/Purpose**	**Example**
Enter markets with drastically lower prices.	Narrow operating margins make companies vulnerable to extended price competition.	Using open source software, California-based Zimbra, Inc. has become a leader in messaging and collaboration software. Its product costs about one-third less than its direct competitor Microsoft Exchange. Zimbra now has over 4 million users including 12,000 H&R Block tax preparers.
Find successful business models and copy them.	As long as a practice is not protected by intellectual property laws, it's probably okay to imitate it. Finding solutions to existing problems is generally quicker and cheaper than inventing them.	Best Practices, LLC is a North Carolina consulting group that seeks out best practices and then repackages and resells them. With annual revenues in excess of $8 million, Best Practices has become a leader in continuous improvement and benchmarking strategies.

Sources: Guth, R. A. 2006. Trolling the web for free labor, software upstarts are new force. *The Wall Street Journal,* November 12: 1; Mochari, I. 2001. Steal this strategy. *Inc.,* July: 62–67; www.best-in-class.com; and www.zimbra.com.

Exhibit 12.7
Competitive Aggressiveness Techniques

(strengths, weaknesses, opportunities, threats) analysis discussed in Chapters 2 and 3 provides a useful way to distinguish between these different approaches to corporate entrepreneurship. Proactiveness, as we saw in the last section, is a response to opportunities—the O in SWOT. Competitive aggressiveness, by contrast, is a response to threats—the T in SWOT. A competitively aggressive posture is important for firms that seek to enter new markets in the face of intense rivalry.

Strategic managers can use competitive aggressiveness to combat industry trends that threaten their survival or market position. Sometimes firms need to be forceful in defending the competitive position that has made them an industry leader. Firms often need to be aggressive to ensure their advantage by capitalizing on new technologies or serving new market needs. Exhibit 12.7 suggests two of the ways competitively aggressive firms enhance their entrepreneurial position.

Another practice companies use to overcome the competition is to make preannouncements of new products or technologies. This type of signaling is aimed not only at potential customers but also at competitors to see how they will react or to discourage them from launching similar initiatives. Sometimes the preannouncements are made just to scare off competitors, an action that has potential ethical implications.

Competitive aggressiveness may not always lead to competitive advantages. Some companies (or their CEOs) have severely damaged their reputations by being overly aggressive. Microsoft is a good example. Although it continues to be a dominant player, its highly aggressive profile makes it the subject of scorn by some businesses and individuals. Efforts to find viable replacements for the Microsoft products have helped fuel the open source software movement that threatens to erode Microsoft's leading role as a software provider.[61]

Therefore, competitive aggressiveness is a strategy that is best used in moderation. Companies that aggressively establish their competitive position and vigorously exploit opportunities to achieve profitability may, over the long run, be better able to sustain their competitive advantages if their goal is to defeat, rather than decimate, their competitors.

Risk Taking

Risk taking refers to a firm's willingness to seize a venture opportunity even though it does not know whether the venture will be successful—to act boldly without knowing the consequences. To be successful through corporate entrepreneurship, firms usually have to take on riskier alternatives, even if it means forgoing the methods or products that have worked in the past. To obtain high financial returns, firms take such risks as assuming high levels of debt, committing large amounts of firm resources, introducing new products into new markets, and investing in unexplored technologies.

risk taking making decisions and taking action without certain knowledge of probable outcomes. Some undertakings may also involve making substantial resource commitments in the process of venturing forward.

In some ways, all of the approaches to internal development that we have discussed are potentially risky. Whether they are being aggressive, proactive, or innovative, firms on the path of corporate entrepreneurship must act without knowing how their actions will turn out. Before launching their strategies, corporate entrepreneurs must know their firm's appetite for risk. How far is it willing to go without knowing what the outcome will be?

Three types of risk that organizations and their executives face are business risk, financial risk, and personal risk:

- *Business risk taking* involves venturing into the unknown without knowing the probability of success. This is the risk associated with entering untested markets or committing to unproven technologies.
- *Financial risk taking* requires that a company borrow heavily or commit a large portion of its resources in order to grow. In this context, risk is used to refer to the risk/return trade-off that is familiar in financial analysis.
- *Personal risk taking* refers to the risks that an executive assumes in taking a stand in favor of a strategic course of action. Executives who take such risks stand to influence the course of their whole company, and their decisions also can have significant implications for their careers.

In many business situations, all three types of risk taking are present. Taking bold new actions rarely affects just one part of the organization. Consider the example of David D'Alessandro of John Hancock Financial Services, Inc.

> David D'Alessandro joined insurance giant John Hancock in 1984 as its vice president of corporate communications. At the time, Hancock's image was weak due in part to a series of forgettable TV ads that failed to distinguish it from other insurance carriers. D'Alessandro championed a new advertising campaign that featured "real life" images, such as a husband and wife arguing, and a lesbian couple adopting a Vietnamese baby. Although it was costly to produce and risky for the image of the traditional insurance carrier, sales surged 17 percent in the first year of the ad campaign. The risk also paid off for D'Alessandro personally: In May 2000 he was named the youngest chairman and CEO in John Hancock's history. (In 2004, John Hancock was acquired by Toronto-based Manulife Financial Corporation.)[62]

Even though risk taking involves taking chances, it is not gambling. The best-run companies investigate the consequences of various opportunities and create scenarios of likely outcomes. As we saw in the section on product champions, a key to managing entrepreneurial risks is to evaluate new venture opportunities thoroughly enough to reduce the uncertainty surrounding them. Exhibit 12.8 indicates two methods companies can use to strengthen their competitive position through risk taking.

Risk taking, by its nature, involves potential dangers and pitfalls. Only carefully managed risk is likely to lead to competitive advantages. Actions that are taken without sufficient forethought, research, and planning may prove to be very costly. Therefore, strategic managers must always remain mindful of potential risks. In his book *Innovation and Entrepreneurship,* Peter Drucker argued that successful entrepreneurs are typically not risk

Risk Taking		
Technique	**Description/Purpose**	**Example**
Research and assess risk factors to minimize uncertainty	Companies that "do their homework"—that is, carefully evaluate the implications of bold actions—reduce the likelihood of failure.	Graybar Electric Co. took a risk when it invested $144 million to revamp its distribution system. It consolidated 231 small centers into 16 supply warehouses and installed the latest communications network. Graybar is now considered a leader in facility redesign and its sales have increased steadily since the consolidation, topping $4 billion in sales in a recent year.
Use techniques that have worked in other domains	Risky methods that other companies have tried may provide an avenue for advancing company goals.	Autobytel.com, one of the first companies to sell cars online, decided on an approach that worked well for others—advertising during the Super Bowl. It was the first dot–com ever to do so and its $1.2 million 30-second ad paid off well by generating weeks of free publicity and favorable business press.

Sources: Anonymous. 2006. Graybar offers data center redesign seminars. *Cabling Installation and Maintenance,* www.cim.pennnet.com, September 1; Keenan, F., & Mullaney, T. J. 2001. Clicking at Graybar. *BusinessWeek,* June 18: 132–34; Weintraub, A. 2001. Make or break for Autobytel. *BusinessWeek e.biz,* July 9: EB30-EB32; www.autobytel.com; and www.graybar.com.

Exhibit 12.8

Risk Taking Techniques

takers. Instead, they take steps to minimize risks by carefully understanding them. That is how they avoid focusing on risk and remain focused on opportunity.[63] Thus, risk taking is a good place to close this chapter on corporate entrepreneurship. Companies that choose to grow through internal corporate venturing must remember that entrepreneurship always involves embracing what is new and uncertain.

Reflecting on Career Implications . . .

- *Innovation:* Look around at the types of innovations being pursued by your company. Do they tend to be incremental or radical? Product-related or process-related? What new types of innovations might benefit your organization? How can you add value to such innovations?
- *Managing Innovation:* How might your organization's chances of a successful innovation increase through collaboration with innovation partners? Your ability to collaborate with individuals from other departments and firms will make you more receptive to and capable of innovation initiatives and enhance your career opportunities.
- *Corporate Entrepreneurship:* Do you consider the company you work for to be entrepreneurial? If not, what actions might you take to enhance its entrepreneurial spirit? If so, what have been the keys to its entrepreneurial success? Can these practices be repeated to achieve future successes?
- *Entrepreneurial Orientation:* Consider the five dimensions of entrepreneurial orientation. Is your organization especially strong at any of these? Especially weak? What are the career implications of your company's entrepreneurial strengths or weaknesses?

Summary

To remain competitive in today's economy, established firms must find new avenues for development and growth. This chapter has addressed how innovation and corporate entrepreneurship can be a means of internal venture creation and strategic renewal, and how an entrepreneurial orientation can help corporations enhance their competitive position.

Innovation is one of the primary means by which corporations grow and strengthen their strategic position. Innovations can take several forms, ranging from radical breakthrough innovations to incremental improvement innovations. Innovations are often used to update products and services or for improving organizational processes. Managing the innovation process is often challenging, because it involves a great deal of uncertainty and there are many choices to be made about the extent and type of innovations to pursue. By defining the scope of innovation, managing the pace of innovation, staffing to capture value from innovation, and collaborating with innovation partners, firms can more effectively manage the innovation process.

We also discussed the role of corporate entrepreneurship in venture development and strategic renewal. Corporations usually take either a focused or dispersed approach to corporate venturing. Firms with a focused approach usually separate the corporate venturing activity from the ongoing operations of the firm in order to foster independent thinking and encourage entrepreneurial team members to think and act without the constraints imposed by the corporation. In corporations where venturing activities are dispersed, a culture of entrepreneurship permeates all parts of the company in order to induce strategic behaviors by all organizational members. In measuring the success of corporate venturing activities, both financial and strategic objectives should be considered. Real options analysis is often used to make better quality decisions in uncertain entrepreneurial situations. However, a real options approach has potential drawbacks.

Most entrepreneurial firms need to have an entrepreneurial orientation: the methods, practices, and decision-making styles that strategic managers use to act entrepreneurially. Five dimensions of entrepreneurial orientation are found in firms that pursue corporate venture strategies. Autonomy, innovativeness, proactiveness, competitive aggressiveness, and risk taking each make a unique contribution to the pursuit of new opportunities. When deployed effectively, the methods and practices of an entrepreneurial orientation can be used to engage successfully in corporate entrepreneurship and new venture creation. However, strategic managers must remain mindful of the pitfalls associated with each of these approaches.

Summary Review Questions

1. What is meant by the concept of a continuum of radical and incremental innovations?
2. What are the dilemmas that organizations face when deciding what innovation projects to pursue? What steps can organizations take to effectively manage the innovation process?
3. What is the difference between focused and dispersed approaches to corporate entrepreneurship?
4. How are business incubators used to foster internal corporate venturing?
5. What is the role of the product champion in bringing a new product or service into existence in a corporation? How can companies use product champions to enhance their venture development efforts?
6. Explain the difference between proactiveness and competitive aggressiveness in terms of achieving and sustaining competitive advantage.
7. Describe how the entrepreneurial orientation (EO) dimensions of innovativeness, proactiveness, and risk taking can be combined to create competitive advantages for entrepreneurial firms.

Key Terms

innovation 413	real options analysis 428
radical innovation 413	entrepreneurial
incremental innovation 414	orientation 432
corporate	autonomy 432
entrepreneurship 422	innovativeness 433
new venture group 423	proactiveness 434
business incubator 423	competitive
product champion 425	aggressiveness 436
exit champion 428	risk taking 439

Experiential Exercise

Select two different major corporations from two different industries (you might use Fortune 500 companies to make your selection). Compare and contrast these organizations in terms of their entrepreneurial orientation.

Entrepreneurial Orientation	Company A _____	Company B _____
Autonomy		
Innovativeness		
Proactiveness		
Competitive Aggressiveness		
Risk Taking		

Based on Your Comparison:

1. How is the corporation's entrepreneurial orientation reflected in its strategy?
2. Which corporation would you say has the stronger entrepreneurial orientation?
3. Is the corporation with the stronger entrepreneurial orientation also stronger in terms of financial performance?

Application Questions Exercises

1. Select a firm known for its corporate entrepreneurship activities. Research the company and discuss how it has positioned itself relative to its close competitors. Does it have a unique strategic advantage? Disadvantage? Explain.
2. Explain the difference between product innovations and process innovations. Provide examples of firms that have recently introduced each type of innovation. What are the types of innovations related to the strategies of each firm?
3. Using the Internet, select a company that is listed on the NASDAQ or New York Stock Exchange. Research the extent to which the company has an entrepreneurial culture. Does the company use product champions? Does it have a corporate venture capital fund? Do you believe its entrepreneurial efforts are sufficient to generate sustainable advantages?
4. How can an established firm use an entrepreneurial orientation to enhance its overall strategic position? Provide examples.

Ethics Questions

1. Innovation activities are often aimed at making a discovery or commercializing a technology ahead of the competition. What are some of the unethical practices that companies could engage in during the innovation process? What are the potential long-term consequences of such actions?
2. Discuss the ethical implications of using entrepreneurial policies and practices to pursue corporate social responsibility goals. Are these efforts authentic and genuine or just an attempt to attract more customers?

References

1. Sources for the Polaroid example include Charan, R., & Useem, J. 2002. Why companies fail. *Fortune,* May 15; Knox, N. 2001. Rivals push Polaroid toward Chapter 11. *USA Today,* October 11; McLaughlin, T. 2001. Harvard dropout made Polaroid an icon. *Toronto Star,* October 15; Pope, J. 2001. Polaroid's fortunes rose with Land, but fell under the burden of debt. *Daily Kent Stater* (OH), October 15; and www.polaroid.com.
2. Eagan, M. 2005. How did Polaroid's faithful ever land in this predicament? *Boston Herald,* April 28: 20; and St. Anthony, N. 2005. Petters wraps up Polaroid. *Star Tribune,* April 28: 1D.
3. Christensen, C. M. 1997. *The innovator's dilemma: When new technologies cause great firms to fail.* Cambridge, MA: Harvard Business School Press.

4. For a discussion about Polaroid, see Gavetti, G., & Levinthal, D. 2000. Looking forward and looking backward: Cognitive and experiential search. *Administrative Science Quarterly,* 45: 113–137.

5. For an interesting discussion, see Johannessen, J. A., Olsen, B., & Lumpkin, G. T. 2001. Innovation as newness: What is new, how new, and new to whom? *European Journal of Innovation Management,* 4(1): 20–31.

6. The discussion of radical and incremental innovations draws from Leifer, R., McDermott, C. M., Colarelli, G., O'Connor, G. C., Peters, L. S., Rice, M. P., & Veryzer, R. W. 2000. *Radical innovation: How mature companies can outsmart upstarts.* Boston: Harvard Business School Press; Damanpour, F. 1996. Organizational complexity and innovation: Developing and testing multiple contingency models. *Management Science,* 42(5): 693–716; and Hage, J. 1980. *Theories of organizations.* New York: Wiley.

7. The discussion of product and process innovation is based on Roberts, E. B. (Ed.). 2002. *Innovation: Driving product, process, and market change.* San Francisco: Jossey-Bass; Hayes, R., & Wheelwright, S. 1985. Competing through manufacturing. *Harvard Business Review,* 63(1): 99–109; and Hayes, R., & Wheelwright, S. 1979. Dynamics of product–process life cycles. *Harvard Business Review,* 57(2): 127–136.

8. Drucker, P. F. 1985. *Innovation and entrepreneurship:* 2000 New York: Harper & Row.

9. Steere, W. C., Jr., & Niblack, J. 1997. Pfizer, Inc. In Kanter, R. M., Kao, J., & Wiersema, F. (Eds.), *Innovation: Breakthrough thinking at 3M, DuPont, GE, Pfizer, and Rubbermaid:* 123–145. New York: HarperCollins.

10. Morrissey, C. A. 2000. Managing innovation through corporate venturing. *Graziadio Business Report,* Spring, gbr.pepperdine.edu; and Sharma, A. 1999. Central dilemmas of managing innovation in large firms. *California Management Review,* 41(3): 147–164.

11. Sharma, op. cit.

12. Canabou, C. 2003. Fast ideas for slow times. *Fast Company,* May: 52.

13. Biodegradable Products Institute. 2003. "Compostable Logo" of the Biodegradable Products Institute gains momentum with approval of DuPont™ Biomax® resin, www.bpiworld.org, June 12; Leifer et al., op. cit.

14. For more on defining the scope of innovation, see Valikangas, L., & Gibbert, M. 2005. Boundary-setting strategies for escaping innovation traps. *MIT Sloan Management Review,* 46(3): 58–65.

15. Leifer et al., op. cit.

16. Bhide, A. V. 2000. *The origin and evolution of new businesses.* New York: Oxford University Press; Brown, S. L., & Eisenhardt, K. M. 1998. *Competing on the edge: Strategy as structured chaos.* Cambridge, MA: Harvard Business School Press.

17. Caulfield, B. 2003. Why techies don't get Six Sigma. *Business 2.0,* June: 90.

18. McGrath, R. G., & Keil, T. 2007. The value captor's process: Getting the most out of your new business ventures. *Harvard Business Review,* May: 128–136.

19. For an interesting discussion of how sharing technology knowledge with different divisions in an organization can contribute to innovation processes, see Miller, D. J., Fern, M. J., & Cardinal, L. B. 2007. The use of knowledge for technological innovation within diversified firms. *Academy of Management Journal,* 50(2): 308–326.

20. Chesbrough, H. 2003. *Open innovation: The new imperative for creating and profiting from technology.* Boston: Harvard Business School Press.

21. Bick, J. 2003. Gold bond. *Entrepreneur,* March: 54–57.

22. For a recent study of what makes alliance partnerships successful, see Sampson, R. C. 2007. R&D alliances and firm performance: The impact of technological diversity and alliance organization on innovation. *Academy of Management Journal,* 50(2): 364–386.

23. For an interesting perspective on the role of collaboration among multinational corporations see Hansen, M. T., & Nohria, N. 2004. How to build collaborative advantage. *MIT Sloan Management Review,* 46(1): 22–30.

24. Guth, W. D., & Ginsberg, A. 1990. Guest editor's introduction: Corporate entrepreneurship. *Strategic Management Journal,* 11: 5–15.

25. Pinchot, G. 1985. *Intrapreneuring.* New York: Harper & Row.

26. Birkinshaw, J. 1997. Entrepreneurship in multinational corporations: The characteristics of subsidiary initiatives. *Strategic Management Journal,* 18(3): 207–229; and Kanter, R. M. 1985. *The change masters.* New York: Simon & Schuster.

27. For a closer look at how established firms can create value by investing in new ventures, see Dushnitsky, G., & Lenox, M. J. 2006. When does corporate venture capital investment create firm value? *Journal of Business Venturing,* 21: 753–772.

28. Hansen, M. T., Chesbrough, H. W., Nohria, N., & Sull, D. 2000. Networked incubators: Hothouses of the new economy. *Harvard Business Review,* 78(5): 74–84.

29. Stein, T. 2002. Corporate venture investors are bailing out. *Red Herring,* December: 74–75.

30. Is your company up to speed? 2003. *Fast Company,* June: 86.

31. For an interesting discussion, see Davenport, T. H., Prusak, L., & Wilson, H. J. 2003. Who's bringing you hot ideas and how are you responding? *Harvard Business Review,* 80(1): 58–64.

32. Howell, J. M. 2005. The right stuff. Identifying and developing effective champions of innovation. *Academy of Management Executive,* 19(2): 108–119. See also Greene, P., Brush, C., & Hart, M. 1999. The corporate venture champion: A resource-based approach to role and process. *Entrepreneurship Theory & Practice,* 23(3): 103–122; and Markham, S. K., & Aiman-Smith, L. 2001. Product champions: Truths, myths and management. *Research Technology Management,* May–June: 44–50.

33. Burgelman, R. A. 1983. A process model of internal corporate venturing in the diversified major firm. *Administrative Science Quarterly,* 28: 223–244.

34. Hamel, G. 2000. *Leading the revolution.* Boston: Harvard Business School Press.

35. Greene, Brush, & Hart, op. cit.; and Shane, S. 1994. Are champions different from non-champions? *Journal of Business Venturing,* 9(5): 397–421.

36. Block, Z., & MacMillan, I. C. 1993. *Corporate venturing—Creating new businesses with the firm.* Cambridge, MA: Harvard Business School Press.

37. For an interesting discussion of these trade-offs, see Stringer, R. 2000. How to manage radical innovation. *California Management Review,* 42(4): 70–88; and Gompers, P. A., & Lerner, J. 1999. *The venture capital cycle.* Cambridge, MA: MIT Press.

38. Albrinck, J., Hornery, J., Kletter, D., & Neilson, G. 2001. Adventures in corporate venturing. *Strategy + Business,* 22: 119–129; and McGrath, R. G., & MacMillan, I. C. 2000. *The entrepreneurial mind-set.* Cambridge, MA: Harvard Business School Press.

39. For an interesting discussion of how different outcome goals affect organizational learning and employee motivation, see Seijts, G. H., & Latham, G. P. 2005. Learning versus performance goals: When should each be used? *Academy of Management Executive,* 19(1): 124–131.

40. Crockett, R. O. 2001. Motorola. *BusinessWeek,* July 15: 72–78.

41. The ideas in this section are drawn from Royer, I. 2003. Why bad projects are so hard to kill. *Harvard Business Review,* 80(1): 48–56.

42. Hoskin, R. E. 1994. *Financial Accounting.* New York: Wiley.

43. We know stock options as derivative assets—that is, "an asset whose value depends on or is derived from the value of another, the underlying asset": Amram, M., & Kulatilaka, N. 1999. *Real options: Managing strategic investment in an uncertain world:* 34. Boston: Harvard Business School Press.

44. For an interesting discussion on why it is difficult to "kill options," refer to Royer, I. 2003. Why bad projects are so hard to kill. *Harvard Business Review,* 81(2): 48–57.

45. Slywotzky, A., & Wise, R. 2003. Double-digit growth in no-growth times. *Fast Company,* April: 66–72; www.hoovers.com; and www.johnsoncontrols.com.

46. For more on the role of real options in entrepreneurial decision making, see Folta, T. B., & O'Brien, J. P. 2004. Entry in the presence of dueling options. *Strategic Management Journal,* 25: 121–138.

47. This section draws on Janney, J. J., & Dess, G. G. 2004. Can real options analysis improve decision-making? Promises and pitfalls. *Academy of Management Executive,* 18(4): 60–75. For additional insights on pitfalls of real options, consider McGrath, R. G. 1997. A real options logic for initiating technology positioning investment. *Academy of Management Review,* 22(4): 974–994; Coff, R. W., & Laverty, K. J. 2001. Real options on knowledge assets: Panacea or Pandora's box. *Business Horizons,* 73: 79, McGrath, R. G. 1999. Falling forward: Real options reasoning and entrepreneurial failure. *Academy of Management Review,* 24(1): 13–30; and, Zardkoohi, A. 2004.

48. For an understanding of the differences between how managers say they approach decisions and how they actually do, March and Shapira's discussion is perhaps the best. March, J. G., & Shapira, Z. 1987. Managerial perspectives on risk and risk-taking. *Management Science,* 33(11): 1404–1418.

49. A discussion of some factors that may lead to escalation in decision making is included in Choo, C. W. 2005. Information failures and organizational disasters. *MIT Sloan Management Review,* 46(3): 8–10.

50. For an interesting discussion of the use of real options analysis in the application of wireless communications, which helped to lower the potential for escalation, refer to McGrath, R. G., Ferrier, W. J., &

Mendelow, A. L. 2004. Real options as engines of choice and heterogeneity. *Academy of Management Review,* 29(1): 86–101.

51. One very useful solution for reducing the effects of managerial conceit is to incorporate an "exit champion" into the decision process. Exit champions provide arguments for killing off the firm's commitment to a decision. For a very insightful discussion on exit champions, refer to Royer, I. 2003. Why bad projects are so hard to kill. *Harvard Business Review,* 81(2): 49–56.

52. Covin, J. G., & Slevin, D. P. 1991. A conceptual model of entrepreneurship as firm behavior. *Entrepreneurship Theory and Practice,* 16(1): 7–24; Lumpkin, G. T., & Dess, G. G. 1996. Clarifying the entrepreneurial orientation construct and linking it to performance. *Academy of Management Review,* 21(1): 135–172; and McGrath, R. G., & MacMillan, I. C. 2000. *The entrepreneurial mind-set.* Cambridge, MA: Harvard Business School Press.

53. Lumpkin, G. T., & Dess, G. G. 2001. Linking two dimensions of entrepreneurial orientation to firm performance: The moderating role of environment and life cycle. *Journal of Business Venturing,* 16: 429–451.

54. For an interesting discussion, see Day, J. D., Mang, P. Y., Richter, A., & Roberts, J. 2001. The innovative organization: Why new ventures need more than a room of their own, *McKinsey Quarterly,* 2: 21–31.

55. Crockett, R. O. 2001. Chris Galvin shakes things up—again. *BusinessWeek,* May 28: 38–39.

56. For an interesting discussion of the impact of innovativeness on organizational outcomes see Cho, H. J., & Pucik, V. 2005. Relationship between innovativeness, quality, growth, profitability, and market value. *Strategic Management Journal,* 26(6): 555–575.

57. Lieberman, M. B., & Montgomery, D. B. 1988. First mover advantages. *Strategic Management Journal,* 9 (Special Issue): 41–58.

58. The discussion of first mover advantages is based on several articles, including Lambkin, M. 1988. Order of entry and performance in new markets. Strategic Management Journal, 9: 127–140; Lieberman & Montgomery, op. cit.: 41–58; and Miller, A., & Camp, B. 1985. Exploring determinants of success in corporate ventures. Journal of Business Venturing, 1(2): 87–105.

59. Moore, G. A. 1999. Crossing the chasm (2nd ed.). New York: HarperBusiness.

60. Mallas, S. 2005. PepsiCo loses its Edge. The Motley *Fool,* June 1, www.fool.com.

61. Lyons, D. 2006. The cheap revolution. *Forbes,* September 18: 102–111.

62. Helman, C. 2001. Stand-up brand. *Forbes,* July 9: 27; and www.hoovers.com.

63. Drucker, op. cit., pp. 109–110.

Strategic Analysis

Chapter 1
Introduction and Analyzing Goals and Objectives

Chapter 2
Analyzing the External Environment

Chapter 3
Analyzing the Internal Environment

Chapter 4
Assessing Intellectual Capital

Strategic Formulation

Chapter 5
Formulating Business-Level Strategies

Chapter 6
Formulating Corporate-Level Strategies

Chapter 7
Formulating International Strategies

Chapter 8
Entrepreneurial Strategy and Competitive Dynamics

Strategic Implementation

Chapter 9
Strategic Control and Corporate Governance

Chapter 10
Creating Effective Organizational Designs

Chapter 11
Strategic Leadership Excellence, Ethics and Change

Chapter 12
Fostering Corporate Entrepreneurship

Case Analysis

Chapter 13
Case Analysis

part four 4

Case Analysis

13 Analyzing Strategic Management Cases

Cases

Analyzing Strategic Management Cases

>learning objectives

After reading this chapter, you should have a good understanding of:

LO1 How strategic case analysis is used to simulate real-world experiences.

LO2 How analyzing strategic management cases can help develop the ability to differentiate, speculate, and integrate when evaluating complex business problems.

LO3 The steps involved in conducting a strategic management case analysis.

LO4 How to get the most out of case analysis.

LO5 How conflict-inducing discussion techniques can lead to better decisions.

LO6 How to use the strategic insights and material from each of the 12 previous chapters in the text to analyze issues posed by strategic management cases.

Case analysis is one of the most effective ways to learn strategic management. It provides a complement to other methods of instruction by asking you to use the tools and techniques of strategic management to deal with an actual business situation. Strategy cases include detailed descriptions of management challenges faced by executives and business owners. By studying the background and analyzing the strategic predicaments posed by a case, you first see that the circumstances businesses confront are often difficult and complex. Then you are asked what decisions you would make to address the situation in the case and how the actions you recommend will affect the company. Thus, the processes of analysis, formulation, and implementation that have been addressed by this textbook can be applied in a real-life situation.

In this chapter we will discuss the role of case analysis as a learning tool in both the classroom and the real world. One of the benefits of strategic case analysis is to develop the ability to differentiate, speculate, and integrate. We will also describe how to conduct a case analysis and address techniques for deriving the greatest benefit from the process, including the effective use of conflict-inducing decision techniques. Finally, we will discuss how case analysis in a classroom setting can enhance the process of analyzing, making decisions, and taking action in real-world strategic situations.

Why Analyze Strategic Management Cases?

It is often said that the key to finding good answers is to ask good questions. Strategic managers and business leaders are required to evaluate options, make choices, and find solutions to the challenges they face every day. To do so, they must learn to ask the right questions. The study of strategic management poses the same challenge. The process of analyzing, decision making, and implementing strategic actions raises many good questions.

>LO1
How strategic case analysis is used to simulate real-world experiences.

- Why do some firms succeed and others fail?
- Why are some companies higher performers than others?
- What information is needed in the strategic planning process?
- How do competing values and beliefs affect strategic decision making?
- What skills and capabilities are needed to implement a strategy effectively?

How does a student of strategic management answer these questions? By strategic case analysis. **Case analysis** simulates the real-world experience that strategic managers and company leaders face as they try to determine how best to run their companies. It places students in the middle of an actual situation and challenges them to figure out what to do.[1]

Asking the right questions is just the beginning of case analysis. In the previous chapters we have discussed issues and challenges that managers face and provided analytical frameworks for understanding the situation. But once the analysis is complete, decisions have to be made. Case analysis forces you to choose among different options and set forth a plan of action based on your choices. But even then the job is not done. Strategic case analysis also requires that you address how you will implement the plan and the implications of choosing one course of action over another.

A strategic management case is a detailed description of a challenging situation faced by an organization.[2] It usually includes a chronology of events and extensive support materials, such as financial statements, product lists, and transcripts of interviews with employees. Although names or locations are sometimes changed to provide anonymity, cases usually report the facts of a situation as authentically as possible.

case analysis a method of learning complex strategic management concepts such as environmental analysis, the process of decision making, and implementing strategic actions through placing students in the middle of an actual situation and challenging them to figure out what to do.

One of the main reasons to analyze strategic management cases is to develop an ability to evaluate business situations critically. In case analysis, memorizing key terms and conceptual frameworks is not enough. To analyze a case, it is important that you go beyond textbook prescriptions and quick answers. It requires you to look deeply into the information that is provided and root out the essential issues and causes of a company's problems.

The types of skills that are required to prepare an effective strategic case analysis can benefit you in actual business situations. Case analysis adds to the overall learning experience by helping you acquire or improve skills that may not be taught in a typical lecture course. Three capabilities that can be learned by conducting case analysis are especially useful to strategic managers—the ability to differentiate, speculate, and integrate.[3] Here's how case analysis can enhance those skills.

>LO2
How analyzing strategic management cases can help develop the ability to differentiate, speculate, and integrate when evaluating complex business problems.

1. **Differentiate.** Effective strategic management requires that many different elements of a situation be evaluated at once. This is also true in case analysis. When analyzing cases, it is important to isolate critical facts, evaluate whether assumptions are useful or faulty, and distinguish between good and bad information. Differentiating between the factors that are influencing the situation presented by a case is necessary for making a good analysis. Strategic management also involves understanding that problems are often complex and multilayered. This applies to case analysis as well. Ask whether the case deals with operational, business-level, or corporate issues. Do the problems stem from weaknesses in the internal value chain or threats in the external environment? Dig deep. Being too quick to accept the easiest or least controversial answer will usually fail to get to the heart of the problem.

2. **Speculate.** Strategic managers need to be able to use their imagination to envision an explanation or solution that might not readily be apparent. The same is true with case analysis. Being able to imagine different scenarios or contemplate the outcome of a decision can aid the analysis. Managers also have to deal with uncertainty since most decisions are made without complete knowledge of the circumstances. This is also true in case analysis. Case materials often seem to be missing data or the information provided is contradictory. The ability to speculate about details that are unknown or the consequences of an action can be helpful.

3. **Integrate.** Strategy involves looking at the big picture and having an organization-wide perspective. Strategic case analysis is no different. Even though the chapters in this textbook divide the material into various topics that may apply to different parts of an organization, all of this information must be integrated into one set of recommendations that will affect the whole company. A strategic manager needs to comprehend how all the factors that influence the organization will interact. This also applies to case analysis. Changes made in one part of the organization affect other parts. Thus, a holistic perspective that integrates the impact of various decisions and environmental influences on all parts of the organization is needed.

In business, these three activities sometimes "compete" with each other for your attention. For example, some decision makers may have a natural ability to differentiate among elements of a problem but are not able to integrate them very well. Others have enough innate creativity to imagine solutions or fill in the blanks when information is missing. But they may have a difficult time when faced with hard numbers or cold facts. Even so, each of these skills is important. The mark of a good strategic manager is the ability to simultaneously make distinctions and envision the whole, and to imagine a future scenario while staying focused on the present. Thus, another reason to conduct case analysis is to help you develop and exercise your ability to differentiate, speculate, and integrate.

Case analysis takes the student through the whole cycle of activity that a manager would face. Beyond the textbook descriptions of concepts and examples, case analysis asks

Analysis, Decision Making, and Change at Sapient Health Network

Sapient Health Network (SHN) had gotten off to a good start. CEO Jim Kean and his two cofounders had raised $5 million in investor capital to launch their vision: an Internet-based health care information subscription service. The idea was to create an Internet community for people suffering from chronic diseases. It would provide members with expert information, resources, a message board, and chat rooms so that people suffering from the same ailments could provide each other with information and support. "Who would be more voracious consumers of information than people who are faced with life-changing, life-threatening illnesses?" thought Bill Kelly, one of SHN's cofounders. Initial market research and beta tests had supported that view.

During the beta tests, however, the service had been offered for free. The troubles began when SHN tried to convert its trial subscribers into paying ones. Fewer than 5 percent signed on, far less than the 15 percent the company had projected. Sapient hired a vice president of marketing who launched an aggressive promotion, but after three months of campaigning SHN still had only 500 members. SHN was now burning through $400,000 per month, with little revenue to show for it.

At that point, according to SHN board member Susan Clymer, "there was a lot of scrambling around trying to figure out how we could wring value out of what we'd already accomplished." One thing SHN had created was an expert software system which had two components: an "intelligent profile engine" (IPE) and an "intelligent query engine" (IQE). SHN used this system to collect detailed information from its subscribers.

SHN was sure that the expert system was its biggest selling point. But how could they use it? Then the founders remembered that the original business plan had suggested there might be a market for aggregate data about patient populations gathered from the Web site. Could they turn the business around by selling patient data? To analyze the possibility, Kean tried out the idea on the market research arm of a huge East Coast health care conglomerate. The officials were intrigued. SHN realized that its expert system could become a market research tool.

Once the analysis was completed, the founders made the decision: They would still create Internet communities for chronically ill patients, but the service would be free. And they would transform SHN from a company that processed subscriptions to one that sold market research.

Finally, they enacted the changes. Some of it was painful, including laying off 18 employees. Instead, SHN needed more health care industry expertise. It even hired an interim CEO, Craig Davenport, a 25-year veteran of the industry, to steer the company in its new direction. Finally, SHN had to communicate a new message to its members. It began by reimbursing the $10,000 of subscription fees they had paid.

All of this paid off dramatically in a matter of just two years. Revenues jumped to $1.9 million in 1998. Early in 1999 SHN was purchased by WebMD and less than a year later, WebMD merged with Healtheon. The combined company still operates a thriving office out of SHN's original location in Portland, Oregon.

Sources: Ferguson, S. 2007. Health care gets a better IT prescription. *Baseline*, www.baselinemag.com, May 24. Brenneman, K. 2000. Healtheon/WebMD's local office is thriving. *Business Journal of Portland*, June 2; Raths, D. 1998. Reversal of fortune. *Inc. Technology*, 2: 52–62.

you to "walk a mile in the shoes" of the strategic decision maker and learn to evaluate situations critically. Executives and owners must make decisions every day with limited information and a swirl of business activity going on around them. Consider the example of Sapient Health Networks, an Internet start-up that had to undergo some analysis and problem solving just to survive. Strategy Spotlight 13.1 describes how this company transformed itself after a serious self-examination during a time of crisis.

As you can see from the experience of Sapient Health Networks, businesses are often faced with immediate challenges that threaten their lives. The Sapient case illustrates how the strategic management process helped it survive. First, the company realistically assessed the environment, evaluated the marketplace, and analyzed its resources. Then it made tough decisions, which included shifting its market focus, hiring and firing, and redeploying its assets. Finally, it took action. The result was not only firm survival, but also a quick turnaround leading to rapid success.

How to Conduct a Case Analysis

The process of analyzing strategic management cases involves several steps. In this section we will review the mechanics of preparing a case analysis. Before beginning, there are two things to keep in mind that will clarify your understanding of the process and make the results of the process more meaningful.

First, unless you prepare for a case discussion, there is little you can gain from the discussion and even less that you can offer. Effective strategic managers don't enter into problem-solving situations without doing some homework—investigating the situation, analyzing and researching possible solutions, and sometimes gathering the advice of others. Good problem solving often requires that decision makers be immersed in the facts, options, and implications surrounding the problem. In case analysis, this means reading and thoroughly comprehending the case materials before trying to make an analysis.

The second point is related to the first. To get the most out of a case analysis you must place yourself "inside" the case—that is, think like an actual participant in the case situation. However, there are several positions you can take. These are discussed in the following paragraphs:

- *Strategic decision maker.* This is the position of the senior executive responsible for resolving the situation described in the case. It may be the CEO, the business owner, or a strategic manager in a key executive position.
- *Board of directors.* Since the board of directors represents the owners of a corporation, it has a responsibility to step in when a management crisis threatens the company. As a board member, you may be in a unique position to solve problems.
- *Outside consultant.* Either the board or top management may decide to bring in outsiders. Consultants often have an advantage because they can look at a situation objectively. But they also may be at a disadvantage since they have no power to enforce changes.

Before beginning the analysis, it may be helpful to envision yourself assuming one of these roles. Then, as you study and analyze the case materials, you can make a diagnosis and recommend solutions in a way that is consistent with your position. Try different perspectives. You may find that your view of the situation changes depending on the role you play. As an outside consultant, for example, it may be easy for you to conclude that certain individuals should be replaced in order to solve a problem presented in the case. However, if you take the role of the CEO who knows the individuals and the challenges they have been facing, you may be reluctant to fire them and will seek another solution instead.

The idea of assuming a particular role is similar to the real world in various ways. In your career, you may work in an organization where outside accountants, bankers, lawyers, or other professionals are advising you about how to resolve business situations or improve your practices. Their perspective will be different from yours but it is useful to understand things from their point of view. Conversely, you may work as a member of the audit team of an accounting firm or the loan committee of a bank. In those situations, it would be helpful if you understood the situation from the perspective of the business leader who must weigh your views against all the other advice that he or she receives. Case analysis can help develop an ability to appreciate such multiple perspectives.

One of the most challenging roles to play in business is as a business founder or owner. For small businesses or entrepreneurial start-ups, the founder may wear all hats at once—key decision maker, primary stockholder, and CEO. Hiring an outside consultant may not be an option. However, the issues faced by young firms and established firms are often not that different, especially when it comes to formulating a plan of action. Business plans that entrepreneurial firms use to raise money or propose a business expansion typically revolve around a

Using a Business Plan Framework to Analyze Strategic Cases

Established businesses often have to change what they are doing in order to improve their competitive position or sometimes simply to survive. To make the changes effectively, businesses usually need a plan. Business plans are no longer just for entrepreneurs. The kind of market analysis, decision making, and action planning that is considered standard practice among new ventures can also benefit going concerns that want to make changes, seize an opportunity, or head in a new direction.

The best business plans, however, are not those loaded with decades of month-by-month financial projections or that depend on rigid adherence to a schedule of events that is impossible to predict. The good ones are focused on four factors that are critical to new-venture success. These same factors are important in case analysis as well because they get to the heart of many of the problems found in strategic cases.

1. *The People.* "When I receive a business plan, I always read the résumé section first," says Harvard Professor William Sahlman. The people questions that are critically important to investors include: What are their skills? How much experience do they have? What is their reputation? Have they worked together as a team? These same questions also may be used in case analysis to evaluate the role of individuals in the strategic case.

2. *The Opportunity.* Business opportunities come in many forms. They are not limited to new ventures.

Sources: Wasserman, E. 2003. A simple plan. *MBA Jungle,* February: 50–55; DeKluyver, C. A. 2000. *Strategic thinking: An executive perspective.* Upper Saddle River, NJ: Prentice Hall; and Sahlman, W. A. 1997. How to write a great business plan. *Harvard Business Review,* 75(4): 98–108.

The chance to enter new markets, introduce new products, or merge with a competitor provide many of the challenges that are found in strategic management cases. What are the consequences of such actions? Will the proposed changes affect the firm's business concept? What factors might stand in the way of success? The same issues are also present in most strategic cases.

3. *The Context.* Things happen in contexts that cannot be controlled by a firm's managers. This is particularly true of the general environment where social trends, economic changes, or events such as the September 11, 2001, terrorist attacks can change business overnight. When evaluating strategic cases, ask: Is the company aware of the impact of context on the business? What will it do if the context changes? Can it influence the context in a way that favors the company?

4. *Risk and Reward.* With a new venture, the entrepreneurs and investors take the risks and get the rewards. In strategic cases, the risks and rewards often extend to many other stakeholders, such as employees, customers, and suppliers. When analyzing a case, ask: Are the managers making choices that will pay off in the future? Are the rewards evenly distributed? Will some stakeholders be put at risk if the situation in the case changes? What if the situation remains the same? Could that be even riskier?

Whether a business is growing or shrinking, large or small, industrial or service oriented, the issues of people, opportunities, context, and risks and rewards will have a large impact on its performance. Therefore, you should always consider these four factors when evaluating strategic management cases.

---

few key issues that must be addressed no matter what the size or age of the business. Strategy Spotlight 13.2 reviews business planning issues that are most important to consider when evaluating any case, especially from the perspective of the business founder or owner.

Next we will review five steps to follow when conducting a strategic management case analysis: becoming familiar with the material, identifying the problems, analyzing the strategic issues using the tools and insights of strategic management, proposing alternative solutions, and making recommendations.[4]

>LO3

The steps involved in conducting a strategic management case analysis.

Become Familiar with the Material

Written cases often include a lot of material. They may be complex and include detailed financials or long passages. Even so, to understand a case and its implications, you must become familiar with its content. Sometimes key information is not immediately apparent.

It may be contained in the footnotes to an exhibit or an interview with a lower-level employee. In other cases the important points may be difficult to grasp because the subject matter is so unfamiliar. When you approach a strategic case try the following technique to enhance comprehension:

- Read quickly through the case one time to get an overall sense of the material.
- Use the initial read-through to assess possible links to strategic concepts.
- Read through the case again, in depth. Make written notes as you read.
- Evaluate how strategic concepts might inform key decisions or suggest alternative solutions.
- After formulating an initial recommendation, thumb through the case again quickly to help assess the consequences of the actions you propose.

Identify Problems

When conducting case analysis, one of your most important tasks is to identify the problem. Earlier we noted that one of the main reasons to conduct case analysis was to find solutions. But you cannot find a solution unless you know the problem. Another saying you may have heard is, "A good diagnosis is half the cure." In other words, once you have determined what the problem is, you are well on your way to identifying a reasonable solution.

Some cases have more than one problem. But the problems are usually related. For a hypothetical example, consider the following: Company A was losing customers to a new competitor. Upon analysis, it was determined that the competitor had a 50 percent faster delivery time even though its product was of lower quality. The managers of company A could not understand why customers would settle for an inferior product. It turns out that no one was marketing to company A's customers that its product was superior. A second problem was that falling sales resulted in cuts in company A's sales force. Thus, there were two related problems: inferior delivery technology and insufficient sales effort.

When trying to determine the problem, avoid getting hung up on symptoms. Zero in on the problem. For example, in the company A example above, the symptom was losing customers. But the problems were an underfunded, understaffed sales force combined with an outdated delivery technology. Try to see beyond the immediate symptoms to the more fundamental problems.

Another tip when preparing a case analysis is to articulate the problem.[5] Writing down a problem statement gives you a reference point to turn to as you proceed through the case analysis. This is important because the process of formulating strategies or evaluating implementation methods may lead you away from the initial problem. Make sure your recommendation actually addresses the problems you have identified.

One more thing about identifying problems: Sometimes problems are not apparent until *after* you do the analysis. In some cases the problem will be presented plainly, perhaps in the opening paragraph or on the last page of the case. But in other cases the problem does not emerge until after the issues in the case have been analyzed. We turn next to the subject of strategic case analysis.

Conduct Strategic Analyses

This textbook has presented numerous analytical tools (e.g., five-forces analysis and value-chain analysis), contingency frameworks (e.g., when to use related rather than unrelated diversification strategies), and other techniques that can be used to evaluate strategic situations. The previous 12 chapters have addressed practices that are common in strategic management, but only so much can be learned by studying the practices and concepts. The best way to understand these methods is to apply them by conducting analyses of specific cases.

The first step is to determine which strategic issues are involved. Is there a problem in the company's competitive environment? Or is it an internal problem? If it is internal, does it have to do with organizational structure? Strategic controls? Uses of technology? Or perhaps the company has overworked its employees or underutilized its intellectual capital. Has the company mishandled a merger? Chosen the wrong diversification strategy? Botched a new product introduction? Each of these issues is linked to one or more of the concepts discussed earlier in the text. Determine what strategic issues are associated with the problems you have identified. Remember also that most real-life case situations involve issues that are highly interrelated. Even in cases where there is only one major problem, the strategic processes required to solve it may involve several parts of the organization.

Once you have identified the issues that apply to the case, conduct the analysis. For example, you may need to conduct a five-forces analysis or dissect the company's competitive strategy. Perhaps you need to evaluate whether its resources are rare, valuable, difficult to imitate, or difficult to substitute. Financial analysis may be needed to assess the company's economic prospects. Perhaps the international entry mode needs to be reevaluated because of changing conditions in the host country. Employee empowerment techniques may need to be improved to enhance organizational learning. Whatever the case, all the strategic concepts introduced in the text include insights for assessing their effectiveness. Determining how well a company is doing these things is central to the case analysis process.

Financial ratio analysis is one of the primary tools used to conduct case analysis. Appendix 1 to Chapter 13 includes a discussion and examples of the financial ratios that are often used to evaluate a company's performance and financial well-being. Exhibit 13.1 provides a summary of the financial ratios presented in Appendix 1 to this chapter.

In this part of the overall strategic analysis process, it is also important to test your own assumptions about the case.[6] First, what assumptions are you making about the case materials? It may be that you have interpreted the case content differently than your team members or classmates. Being clear about these assumptions will be important in determining how to analyze the case. Second, what assumptions have you made about the best way to resolve the problems? Ask yourself why you have chosen one type of analysis over another. This process of assumption checking can also help determine if you have gotten to the heart of the problem or are still just dealing with symptoms.

As mentioned earlier, sometimes the critical diagnosis in a case can only be made after the analysis is conducted. However, by the end of this stage in the process, you should know the problems and have completed a thorough analysis of them. You can now move to the next step: finding solutions.

financial ratio analysis a method of evaluating a company's performance and financial well-being through ratios of accounting values, including short-term solvency, long-term solvency, asset utilization, profitability, and market value ratios.

Propose Alternative Solutions

It is important to remember that in strategic management case analysis, there is rarely one right answer or one best way. Even when members of a class or a team agree on what the problem is, they may not agree upon how to solve the problem. Therefore, it is helpful to consider several different solutions.

After conducting strategic analysis and identifying the problem, develop a list of options. What are the possible solutions? What are the alternatives? First, generate a list of all the options you can think of without prejudging any one of them. Remember that not all cases call for dramatic decisions or sweeping changes. Some companies just need to make small adjustments. In fact, "Do nothing" may be a reasonable alternative in some cases. Although that is rare, it might be useful to consider what will happen if the company does nothing. This point illustrates the purpose of developing alternatives: to evaluate what will happen if a company chooses one solution over another.

Thus, during this step of a case analysis, you will evaluate choices and the implications of those choices. One aspect of any business that is likely to be highlighted in this part of the analysis is strategy implementation. Ask how the choices made will be implemented. It may be that what seems like an obvious choice for solving a problem creates

Ratio	What It Measures
Short-term solvency, or liquidity, ratios:	
Current ratio	Ability to use assets to pay off liabilities.
Quick ratio	Ability to use liquid assets to pay off liabilities quickly.
Cash ratio	Ability to pay off liabilities with cash on hand.
Long-term solvency, or financial leverage, ratios:	
Total debt ratio	How much of a company's total assets are financed by debt.
Debt-equity ratio	Compares how much a company is financed by debt with how much it is financed by equity.
Equity multiplier	How much debt is being used to finance assets.
Times interest earned ratio	How well a company has its interest obligations covered.
Cash coverage ratio	A company's ability to generate cash from operations.
Asset utilization, or turnover, ratios:	
Inventory turnover	How many times each year a company sells its entire inventory.
Days' sales in inventory	How many days on average inventory is on hand before it is sold.
Receivables turnover	How frequently each year a company collects on its credit sales.
Days' sales in receivables	How many days on average it takes to collect on credit sales (average collection period).
Total asset turnover	How much of sales is generated for every dollar in assets.
Capital intensity	The dollar investment in assets needed to generate $1 in sales.
Profitability ratios:	
Profit margin	How much profit is generated by every dollar of sales.
Return on assets (ROA)	How effectively assets are being used to generate a return.
Return on equity (ROE)	How effectively amounts invested in the business by its owners are being used to generate a return.
Market value ratios:	
Price–earnings ratio	How much investors are willing to pay per dollar of current earnings.
Market-to-book ratio	Compares market value of the company's investments to the cost of those investments.

Exhibit 13.1 Summary of Financial Ratio Analysis Techniques

an even bigger problem when implemented. But remember also that no strategy or strategic "fix" is going to work if it cannot be implemented. Once a list of alternatives is generated, ask:

- Can the company afford it? How will it affect the bottom line?
- Is the solution likely to evoke a competitive response?
- Will employees throughout the company accept the changes? What impact will the solution have on morale?
- How will the decision affect other stakeholders? Will customers, suppliers, and others buy into it?

- How does this solution fit with the company's vison, mission, and objectives?
- Will the culture or values of the company be changed by the solution? Is it a positive change?

The point of this step in the case analysis process is to find a solution that both solves the problem and is realistic. A consideration of the implications of various alternative solutions will generally lead you to a final recommendation that is more thoughtful and complete.

Make Recommendations

The basic aim of case analysis is to find solutions. Your analysis is not complete until you have recommended a course of action. In this step the task is to make a set of recommendations that your analysis supports. Describe exactly what needs to be done. Explain why this course of action will solve the problem. The recommendation should also include suggestions for how best to implement the proposed solution because the recommended actions and their implications for the performance and future of the firm are interrelated.

Recall that the solution you propose must solve the problem you identified. This point cannot be overemphasized; too often students make recommendations that treat only symptoms or fail to tackle the central problems in the case. Make a logical argument that shows how the problem led to the analysis and the analysis led to the recommendations you are proposing. Remember, an analysis is not an end in itself; it is useful only if it leads to a solution.

The actions you propose should describe the very next steps that the company needs to take. Don't say, for example, "If the company does more market research, then I would recommend the following course of action. . . ." Instead, make conducting the research part of your recommendation. Taking the example a step further, if you also want to suggest subsequent actions that may be different *depending* on the outcome of the market research, that's OK. But don't make your initial recommendation conditional on actions the company may or may not take.

In summary, case analysis can be a very rewarding process but, as you might imagine, it can also be frustrating and challenging. If you will follow the steps described above, you will address the different elements of a thorough analysis. This approach can give your analysis a solid footing. Then, even if there are differences of opinion about how to interpret the facts, analyze the situation, or solve the problems, you can feel confident that you have not missed any important steps in finding the best course of action.

Students are often asked to prepare oral presentations of the information in a case and their analysis of the best remedies. This is frequently assigned as a group project. Or you may be called upon in class to present your ideas about the circumstances or solutions for a case the class is discussing. Exhibit 13.2 provides some tips for preparing an oral case presentation.

How to Get the Most from Case Analysis

One of the reasons case analysis is so enriching as a learning tool is that it draws on many resources and skills besides just what is in the textbook. This is especially true in the study of strategy. Why? Because strategic management itself is a highly integrative task that draws on many areas of specialization at several levels, from the individual to the whole of society. Therefore, to get the most out of case analysis, expand your horizons beyond the concepts in this text and seek insights from your own reservoir of knowledge. Here are some tips for how to do that.[7]

>LO4
How to get the most out of case analysis.

- ***Keep an open mind.*** Like any good discussion, a case analysis discussion often evokes strong opinions and high emotions. But it's the variety of perspectives that makes case analysis so valuable: Many viewpoints usually lead to a more complete analysis. Therefore, avoid letting an emotional response to another person's style or opinion keep you from hearing what he or she has to say. Once you evaluate what is said, you may

Rule	Description
Organize your thoughts.	Begin by becoming familiar with the material. If you are working with a team, compare notes about the key points of the case and share insights that other team members may have gleaned from tables and exhibits. Then make an outline. This is one of the best ways to organize the flow and content of the presentation.
Emphasize strategic analysis.	The purpose of case analysis is to diagnose problems and find solutions. In the process, you may need to unravel the case material as presented and reconfigure it in a fashion that can be more effectively analyzed. Present the material in a way that lends itself to analysis—don't simply restate what is in the case. This involves three major categories with the following emphasis:

Background/Problem Statement 10–20%
Strategic Analysis/Options 60–75%
Recommendations/Action Plan 10–20%

	As you can see, the emphasis of your presentation should be on analysis. This will probably require you to reorganize the material so that the tools of strategic analysis can be applied.
Be logical and consistent.	A presentation that is rambling and hard to follow may confuse the listener and fail to evoke a good discussion. Present your arguments and explanations in a logical sequence. Support your claims with facts. Include financial analysis where appropriate. Be sure that the solutions you recommend address the problems you have identified.
Defend your position.	Usually an oral presentation is followed by a class discussion. Anticipate what others might disagree with and be prepared to defend your views. This means being aware of the choices you made and the implications of your recommendations. Be clear about your assumptions. Be able to expand on your analysis.
Share presentation responsibilities.	Strategic management case analyses are often conducted by teams. Each member of the team should have a clear role in the oral presentation, preferably a speaking role. It's also important to coordinate the different parts of the presentation into a logical, smooth-flowing whole. How well a team works together is usually very apparent during an oral presentation.

Exhibit 13.2 Preparing an Oral Case Presentation

disagree with it or dismiss it as faulty. But unless you keep an open mind in the first place, you may miss the importance of the other person's contribution. Also, people often place a higher value on the opinions of those they consider to be good listeners.

- *Take a stand for what you believe.* Although it is vital to keep an open mind, it is also important to state your views proactively. Don't try to figure out what your friends or the instructor wants to hear. Analyze the case from the perspective of your own background and belief system. For example, perhaps you feel that a decision is unethical or that the managers in a case have misinterpreted the facts. Don't be afraid to assert that in the discussion. For one thing, when a person takes a strong stand, it often encourages others to evaluate the issues more closely. This can lead to a more thorough investigation and a more meaningful class discussion.
- *Draw on your personal experience.* You may have experiences from work or as a customer that shed light on some of the issues in a case. Even though one of the purposes of

case analysis is to apply the analytical tools from this text, you may be able to add to the discussion by drawing on your outside experiences and background. Of course, you need to guard against carrying that to extremes. In other words, don't think that your perspective is the only viewpoint that matters! Simply recognize that firsthand experience usually represents a welcome contribution to the overall quality of case discussions.

- *Participate and persuade.* Have you heard the phrase, "Vote early . . . and often"? Among loyal members of certain political parties, it has become rather a joke. Why? Because a democratic system is built on the concept of one person, one vote. Even though some voters may want to vote often enough to get their candidate elected, it is against the law. Not so in a case discussion. People who are persuasive and speak their mind can often influence the views of others. But to do so, you have to be prepared and convincing. Being persuasive is more than being loud or long-winded. It involves understanding all sides of an argument and being able to overcome objections to your own point of view. These efforts can make a case discussion more lively. And they parallel what happens in the real world; in business, people frequently share their opinions and attempt to persuade others to see things their way.

- *Be concise and to the point.* In the previous point, we encouraged you to speak up and "sell" your ideas to others in a case discussion. But you must be clear about what you are selling. Make your arguments in a way that is explicit and direct. Zero in on the most important points. Be brief. Don't try to make a lot of points at once by jumping around between topics. Avoid trying to explain the whole case situation at once. Remember, other students usually resent classmates who go on and on, take up a lot of "airtime," or repeat themselves unnecessarily. The best way to avoid this is to stay focused and be specific.

- *Think out of the box.* It's OK to be a little provocative; sometimes that is the consequence of taking a stand on issues. But it may be equally important to be imaginative and creative when making a recommendation or determining how to implement a solution. Albert Einstein once stated, "Imagination is more important than knowledge." The reason is that managing strategically requires more than memorizing concepts. Strategic management insights must be applied to each case differently—just knowing the principles is not enough. Imagination and out-of-the-box thinking help to apply strategic knowledge in novel and unique ways.

- *Learn from the insights of others.* Before you make up your mind about a case, hear what other students have to say. Get a second opinion, and a third, and so forth. Of course, in a situation where you have to put your analysis in writing, you may not be able to learn from others ahead of time. But in a case discussion, observe how various students attack the issues and engage in problem solving. Such observation skills also may be a key to finding answers within the case. For example, people tend to believe authority figures, so they would place a higher value on what a company president says. In some cases, however, the statements of middle managers may represent a point of view that is even more helpful for finding a solution to the problems presented by the case.

- *Apply insights from other case analyses.* Throughout the text, we have used examples of actual businesses to illustrate strategy concepts. The aim has been to show you how firms think about and deal with business problems. During the course, you may be asked to conduct several case analyses as part of the learning experience. Once you have performed a few case analyses, you will see how the concepts from the text apply in real-life business situations. Incorporate the insights learned from the text examples and your own previous case discussions into each new case that you analyze.

- *Critically analyze your own performance.* Performance appraisals are a standard part of many workplace situations. They are used to determine promotions, raises, and work assignments. In some organizations, everyone from the top executive down is subject to such reviews. Even in situations where the owner or CEO is not evaluated by others, they often find it useful to ask themselves regularly, Am I being effective? The same can be applied to your performance in a case analysis situation. Ask yourself, Were my comments insightful? Did I make a good contribution? How might I improve next time? Use the same criteria on yourself that you use to evaluate others. What grade would you give yourself? This technique will not only make you more fair in your assessment of others but also will indicate how your own performance can improve.

- *Conduct outside research.* Many times, you can enhance your understanding of a case situation by investigating sources outside the case materials. For example, you may want to study an industry more closely or research a company's close competitors. Recent moves such as mergers and acquisitions or product introductions may be reported in the business press. The company itself may provide useful information on its Web site or in its annual reports. Such information can usually spur additional discussion and enrich the case analysis. (*Caution:* It is best to check with your instructor in advance to be sure this kind of additional research is encouraged. Bringing in outside research may conflict with the instructor's learning objectives.)

Several of the points suggested above for how to get the most out of case analysis apply only to an open discussion of a case, like that in a classroom setting. Exhibit 13.3 provides some additional guidelines for preparing a written case analysis.

Rule	Description
Be thorough.	Many of the ideas presented in Exhibit 13.2 about oral presentations also apply to written case analysis. However, a written analysis typically has to be more complete. This means writing out the problem statement and articulating assumptions. It is also important to provide support for your arguments and reference case materials or other facts more specifically.
Coordinate team efforts.	Written cases are often prepared by small groups. Within a group, just as in a class discussion, you may disagree about the diagnosis or the recommended plan of action. This can be healthy if it leads to a richer understanding of the case material. But before committing your ideas to writing, make sure you have coordinated your responses. Don't prepare a written analysis that appears contradictory or looks like a patchwork of disconnected thoughts.
Avoid restating the obvious.	There is no reason to restate material that everyone is familiar with already, namely, the case content. It is too easy for students to use up space in a written analysis with a recapitulation of the details of the case—this accomplishes very little. Stay focused on the key points. Only restate the information that is most central to your analysis.
Present information graphically.	Tables, graphs, and other exhibits are usually one of the best ways to present factual material that supports your arguments. For example, financial calculations such as break-even analysis, sensitivity analysis, or return on investment are best presented graphically. Even qualitative information such as product lists or rosters of employees can be summarized effectively and viewed quickly by using a table or graph.
Exercise quality control.	When presenting a case analysis in writing, it is especially important to use good grammar, avoid misspelling words, and eliminate typos and other visual distractions. Mistakes that can be glossed over in an oral presentation or class discussion are often highlighted when they appear in writing. Make your written presentation appear as professional as possible. Don't let the appearance of your written case keep the reader from recognizing the importance and quality of your analysis.

Exhibit 13.3 Preparing a Written Case Analysis

Using Conflict-Inducing Decision-Making Techniques in Case Analysis

Next we address some techniques often used to improve case analyses that involve the constructive use of conflict. In the classroom—as well as in the business world—you will frequently be analyzing cases or solving problems in groups. While the word *conflict* often has a negative connotation (e.g., rude behavior, personal affronts), it can be very helpful in arriving at better solutions to cases. It can provide an effective means for new insights as well as for rigorously questioning and analyzing assumptions and strategic alternatives. In fact, if you don't have constructive conflict, you may only get consensus. When this happens, decisions tend to be based on compromise rather than collaboration.

In your organizational behavior classes, you probably learned the concept of "groupthink."[8] Groupthink, a term coined by Irving Janis after he conducted numerous studies on executive decision making, is a condition in which group members strive to reach agreement or consensus without realistically considering other viable alternatives. In effect, group norms bolster morale at the expense of critical thinking and decision making is impaired.[9]

Many of us have probably been "victims" of groupthink at one time or another in our life. We may be confronted with situations when social pressure, politics, or "not wanting to stand out" may prevent us from voicing our concerns about a chosen course of action. Nevertheless, decision making in groups is a common practice in the management of many businesses. Most companies, especially large ones, rely on input from various top managers to provide valuable information and experience from their specialty area as well as their unique perspectives. Chapter 11 emphasized the importance of empowering individuals at all levels to participate in decision-making processes. In terms of this course, case analysis involves a type of decision making that is often conducted in groups. Strategy Spotlight 13.3 provides guidelines for making team-based approaches to case analysis more effective.

Clearly, understanding how to work in groups and the potential problems associated with group decision processes can benefit the case analysis process. Therefore, let's first look at some of the symptoms of groupthink and suggest ways of preventing it. Then, we will suggest some conflict-inducing decision-making techniques—devil's advocacy and dialectical inquiry—that can help to prevent groupthink and lead to better decisions.

Symptoms of Groupthink and How to Prevent It

Irving Janis identified several symptoms of groupthink, including:

- ***An illusion of invulnerability.*** This reassures people about possible dangers and leads to overoptimism and failure to heed warnings of danger.
- ***A belief in the inherent morality of the group.*** Because individuals think that what they are doing is right, they tend to ignore ethical or moral consequences of their decisions.

● Effectively working in teams is a critical skill—both in the classroom and in business organizations.

Making Case Analysis Teams More Effective

Working in teams can be very challenging. Not all team members have the same skills, interests, or motivations. Some team members just want to get the work done. Others see teams as an opportunity to socialize. Occasionally, there are team members who think they should be in charge and make all the decisions; other teams have free-loaders—team members who don't want to do anything except get credit for the team's work.

One consequence of these various styles is that team meetings can become time wasters. Disagreements about how to proceed, how to share the work, or what to do at the next meeting tend to slow down teams and impede progress toward the goal. While the dynamics of case analysis teams are likely to always be challenging depending on the personalities involved, one thing nearly all members realize is that, ultimately, the team's work must be completed. Most team members also aim to do the highest quality work possible. The following guidelines provide some useful insights about how to get the work of a team done more effectively.

Spend More Time Together

One of the factors that prevents teams from doing a good job with case analysis is their failure to put in the necessary time. Unless teams really tackle the issues surrounding case analysis—both the issues in the case itself and organizing how the work is to be conducted—the end result will probably be lacking because decisions that are made too quickly are unlikely to get to the heart of the problem(s) in the case. "Meetings should be a precious resource, but they're treated like a necessary evil," says Kenneth Sole, a consultant who specializes in organizational behavior. As a result, teams that care more about finishing the analysis than getting the analysis right often make poor decisions.

Therefore, expect to have a few meetings that run long, especially at the beginning of the project when the work is being organized and the issues in the case are being sorted out, and again at the end when the team must coordinate the components of the case analysis that will be presented. Without spending this kind of time together, it is doubtful that the analysis will be comprehensive and the presentation is likely to be choppy and incomplete.

Make a Focused and Disciplined Agenda

To complete tasks and avoid wasting time, meetings need to have a clear purpose. To accomplish this at Roche, the Swiss drug and diagnostic product maker, CEO Franz Humer implemented a "decision agenda." The agenda

focuses only on Roche's highest value issues and discussions are limited to these major topics. In terms of case analysis, the major topics include sorting out the issues of the case, linking elements of the case to the strategic issues presented in class or the text, and assigning roles to various team members. Such objectives help keep team members on track.

Agendas also can be used to address issues such as the time line for accomplishing work. Otherwise the purpose of meetings may only be to manage the "crisis" of getting the case analysis finished on time. One solution is to assign a team member to manage the agenda. That person could make sure the team stays focused on the tasks at hand and remains mindful of time constraints. Another role could be to link the team's efforts to the steps presented in Exhibits 13.2 and 13.3 on how to prepare a case analysis.

Pay More Attention to Strategy

Teams often waste time by focusing on unimportant aspects of a case. These may include details that are interesting but irrelevant or operational issues rather than strategic issues. It is true that useful clues to the issues in the case are sometimes embedded in the conversations of key managers or the trends evident in a financial statement. But once such insights are discovered, teams need to focus on the underlying strategic problems in the case. To solve such problems, major corporations such as Cadbury Schweppes and Boeing hold meetings just to generate strategic alternatives for solving their problems. This gives managers time to consider the implications of various courses of action. Separate meetings are held to evaluate alternatives, make strategic decisions, and approve an action plan.

Once the strategic solutions or "course corrections" are identified—as is common in most cases assigned—the operational implications and details of implementation will flow from the strategic decisions that companies make. Therefore, focusing primarily on strategic issues will provide teams with insights for making recommendations that are based on a deeper understanding of the issues in the case.

Produce Real Decisions

Too often, meetings are about discussing rather than deciding. Teams often spend a lot of time talking without reaching any conclusions. As Raymond Sanchez, CEO of Florida-based Security Mortgage Group, says, meetings are often used to "rehash the hash that's already been hashed." To be efficient and productive, team meetings need to be about more than just information sharing and group input. For example, an initial meeting may result in the team realizing that it needs to study the case in greater depth and examine links to strategic issues *(continued)*

- *Stereotyped views of members of opposing groups.* Members of other groups are viewed as weak or not intelligent.
- *The application of pressure to members who express doubts about the group's shared illusions or question the validity of arguments proposed.*
- *The practice of self-censorship.* Members keep silent about their opposing views and downplay to themselves the value of their perspectives.
- *An illusion of unanimity.* People assume that judgments expressed by members are shared by all.
- *The appointment of mindguards.* People sometimes appoint themselves as mindguards to protect the group from adverse information that might break the climate of consensus (or agreement).

Clearly, groupthink is an undesirable and negative phenomenon that can lead to poor decisions. Irving Janis considers it to be a key contributor to such faulty decisions as the failure to prepare for the attack on Pearl Harbor, the escalation of the Vietnam conflict, and the failure to prepare for the consequences of the Iraqi invasion. Many of the same sorts of flawed decision making occur in business organizations—as we discussed above with the EDS example. Janis has provided several suggestions for preventing groupthink that can be used as valuable guides in decision making and problem solving:

- Leaders must encourage group members to address their concerns and objectives.
- When higher-level managers assign a problem for a group to solve, they should adopt an impartial stance and not mention their preferences.
- Before a group reaches its final decision, the leader should encourage members to discuss their deliberations with trusted associates and then report the perspectives back to the group.
- The group should invite outside experts and encourage them to challenge the group's viewpoints and positions.
- The group should divide into subgroups, meet at various times under different chairpersons, and then get together to resolve differences.
- After reaching a preliminary agreement, the group should hold a "second chance" meeting which provides members a forum to express any remaining concerns and rethink the issue prior to making a final decision.

Using Conflict to Improve Decision Making

In addition to the above suggestions, the effective use of conflict can be a means of improving decision making. Although conflict can have negative outcomes, such as ill will, anger, tension, and lowered motivation, both leaders and group members must strive to assure that it is managed properly and used in a constructive manner.

Two conflict-inducing decision-making approaches that have become quite popular are *devil's advocacy* and *dialectical inquiry.* Both approaches incorporate conflict into the decision-making process through formalized debate. A group charged with making a decision or solving a problem is divided into two subgroups and each will be involved in the analysis and solution.

Devil's Advocacy   With the devil's advocate approach, one of the groups (or individuals) acts as a critic to the plan. The devil's advocate tries to come up with problems with the proposed alternative and suggest reasons why it should not be adopted. The role of the devil's advocate is to create dissonance. This ensures that the group will take a hard look at its original proposal or alternative. By having a group (or individual) assigned the role of devil's advocate, it becomes clear that such an adversarial stance is legitimized. It brings out criticisms that might otherwise not be made.

Some authors have suggested that the use of a devil's advocate can be very helpful in helping boards of directors to ensure that decisions are addressed comprehensively and to avoid groupthink.[10] And Charles Elson, a director of Sunbeam Corporation, has argued that:

> Devil's advocates are terrific in any situation because they help you to figure a decision's numerous implications. . . . The better you think out the implications prior to making the decision, the better the decision ultimately turns out to be. That's why a devil's advocate is always a great person, irritating sometimes, but a great person.

As one might expect, there can be some potential problems with using the devil's advocate approach. If one's views are constantly criticized, one may become demoralized. Thus, that person may come up with "safe solutions" in order to minimize embarrassment or personal risk and become less subject to criticism. Additionally, even if the devil's advocate is successful with finding problems with the proposed course of action, there may be no new ideas or counterproposals to take its place. Thus, the approach sometimes may simply focus on what is wrong without suggesting other ideas.

Dialectical Inquiry   Dialectical inquiry attempts to accomplish the goals of the devil's advocate in a more constructive manner. It is a technique whereby a problem is approached from two alternative points of view. The idea is that out of a critique of the opposing perspectives—a thesis and an antithesis—a creative synthesis will occur. Dialectical inquiry involves the following steps:

1. Identify a proposal and the information that was used to derive it.
2. State the underlying assumptions of the proposal.
3. Identify a counterplan (antithesis) that is believed to be feasible, politically viable, and generally credible. However, it rests on assumptions that are opposite to the original proposal.
4. Engage in a debate in which individuals favoring each plan provide their arguments and support.
5. Identify a synthesis which, hopefully, includes the best components of each alternative.

There are some potential downsides associated with dialectical inquiry. It can be quite time consuming and involve a good deal of training. Further, it may result in a series of compromises between the initial proposal and the counterplan. In cases where the original proposal was the best approach, this would be unfortunate.

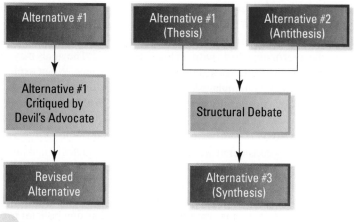

Exhibit 13.4 Two Conflict-Inducing Decision-Making Processes

Despite some possible limitations associated with these conflict-inducing decision-making techniques, they have many benefits. Both techniques force debate about underlying assumptions, data, and recommendations between subgroups. Such debate tends to prevent the uncritical acceptance of a plan that may seem to be satisfactory after a cursory analysis. The approach serves to tap the knowledge and perspectives of group members and continues until group members agree on both assumptions and recommended actions. Given that both approaches serve to use, rather than minimize or suppress, conflict, higher quality decisions should result. Exhibit 13.4 briefly summarizes these techniques.

Following the Analysis-Decision-Action Cycle in Case Analysis

In Chapter 1 we defined strategic management as the analysis, decisions, and actions that organizations undertake to create and sustain competitive advantages. It is no accident that we chose that sequence of words because it corresponds to the sequence of events that typically occurs in the strategic management process. In case analysis, as in the real world, this cycle of events can provide a useful framework. First, an analysis of the case in terms of the business environment and current events is needed. To make such an analysis, the case background must be considered. Next, based on that analysis, decisions must be made. This may involve formulating a strategy, choosing between difficult options, moving forward aggressively, or retreating from a bad situation. There are many possible decisions, depending on the case situation. Finally, action is required. Once decisions are made and plans are set, the action begins. The recommended action steps and the consequences of implementing these actions are the final stage.

Each of the previous 12 chapters of this book includes techniques and information that may be useful in a case analysis. However, not all of the issues presented will be important in every case. As noted earlier, one of the challenges of case analysis is to identify the most critical points and sort through material that may be ambiguous or unimportant.

In this section we draw on the material presented in each of the 12 chapters to show how it informs the case analysis process. The ideas are linked sequentially and in terms of an overarching strategic perspective. One of your jobs when conducting case analysis is to see how the parts of a case fit together and how the insights from the study of strategy can help you understand the case situation.

>LO6

How to use the strategic insights and material from each of the 12 previous chapters in the text to analyze issues posed by strategic management cases.

1. *Analyzing organizational goals and objectives.* A company's vision, mission, and objectives keep organization members focused on a common purpose. They also influence how an organization deploys its resources, relates to its stakeholders, and matches its short-term objectives with its long-term goals. The goals may even impact how a company formulates and implements strategies. When exploring issues of goals and objectives, you might ask:
   - Has the company developed short-term objectives that are inconsistent with its long-term mission? If so, how can management realign its vision, mission, and objectives?
   - Has the company considered all of its stakeholders equally in making critical decisions? If not, should the views of all stakeholders be treated the same or are some stakeholders more important than others?
   - Is the company being faced with an issue that conflicts with one of its long-standing policies? If so, how should it compare its existing policies to the potential new situation?

2. *Analyzing the external environment.* The business environment has two components. The general environment consists of demographic, sociocultural, political/legal, technological, economic, and global conditions. The competitive environment includes rivals, suppliers, customers, and other factors that may directly affect a company's success. Strategic managers must monitor the environment to identify opportunities and threats that may have an impact on performance. When investigating a firm's external environment, you might ask:
   - Does the company follow trends and events in the general environment? If not, how can these influences be made part of the company's strategic analysis process?
   - Is the company effectively scanning and monitoring the competitive environment? If so, how is it using the competitive intelligence it is gathering to enhance its competitive advantage?
   - Has the company correctly analyzed the impact of the competitive forces in its industry on profitability? If so, how can it improve its competitive position relative to these forces?

3. *Analyzing the internal environment.* A firm's internal environment consists of its resources and other value-adding capabilities. Value-chain analysis and a resource-based approach to analysis can be used to identify a company's strengths and weaknesses and determine how they are contributing to its competitive advantages. Evaluating firm performance can also help make meaningful comparisons with competitors. When researching a company's internal analysis, you might ask:
   - Does the company know how the various components of its value chain are adding value to the firm? If not, what internal analysis is needed to determine its strengths and weakness?
   - Has the company accurately analyzed the source and vitality of its resources? If so, is it deploying its resources in a way that contributes to competitive advantages?
   - Is the company's financial performance as good as or better than that of its close competitors? If so, has it balanced its financial success with the performance criteria of other stakeholders such as customers and employees?

4. *Assessing a firm's intellectual assets.* Human capital is a major resource in today's knowledge economy. As a result, attracting, developing, and retaining talented workers is a key strategic challenge. Other assets such as patents and trademarks are also critical. How companies leverage their intellectual assets through social networks and strategic alliances, and how technology is used to manage knowledge may be a major

influence on a firm's competitive advantage. When analyzing a firm's intellectual assets, you might ask:

- Does the company have underutilized human capital? If so, what steps are needed to develop and leverage its intellectual assets?
- Is the company missing opportunities to forge strategic alliances? If so, how can it use its social capital to network more effectively?
- Has the company developed knowledge-management systems that capture what it learns? If not, what technologies can it employ to retain new knowledge?

5. *Formulating business-level strategies.* Firms use the competitive strategies of differentiation, focus, and overall cost leadership as a basis for overcoming the five competitive forces and developing sustainable competitive advantages. Combinations of these strategies may work best in some competitive environments. Additionally, an industry's life cycle is an important contingency that may affect a company's choice of business-level strategies. When assessing business-level strategies, you might ask:

- Has the company chosen the correct competitive strategy given its industry environment and competitive situation? If not, how should it use its strengths and resources to improve its performance?
- Does the company use combination strategies effectively? If so, what capabilities can it cultivate to further enhance profitability?
- Is the company using a strategy that is appropriate for the industry life cycle in which it is competing? If not, how can it realign itself to match its efforts to the current stage of industry growth?

6. *Formulating corporate-level strategies.* Large firms often own and manage portfolios of businesses. Corporate strategies address methods for achieving synergies among these businesses. Related and unrelated diversification techniques are alternative approaches to deciding which business should be added to or removed from a portfolio. Companies can diversify by means of mergers, acquisitions, joint ventures, strategic alliances, and internal development. When analyzing corporate-level strategies, you might ask:

- Is the company competing in the right businesses given the opportunities and threats that are present in the environment? If not, how can it realign its diversification strategy to achieve competitive advantages?
- Is the corporation managing its portfolio of businesses in a way that creates synergies among the businesses? If so, what additional business should it consider adding to its portfolio?
- Are the motives of the top corporate executives who are pushing diversification strategies appropriate? If not, what action can be taken to curb their activities or align them with the best interests of all stakeholders?

7. *Formulating international-level strategies.* Foreign markets provide both opportunities and potential dangers for companies that want to expand globally. To decide which entry strategy is most appropriate, companies have to evaluate the trade-offs between two factors that firms face when entering foreign markets: cost reduction and local adaptation. To achieve competitive advantages, firms will typically choose one of three strategies: global, multidomestic, or transnational. When evaluating international-level strategies, you might ask:

- Is the company's entry into an international marketplace threatened by the actions of local competitors? If so, how can cultural differences be minimized to give the firm a better chance of succeeding?
- Has the company made the appropriate choices between cost reduction and local adaptation to foreign markets? If not, how can it adjust its strategy to achieve competitive advantages?

- Can the company improve its effectiveness by embracing one international strategy over another? If so, how should it choose between a global, multidomestic, or transnational strategy?

8. *Formulating entrepreneurial strategies.* New ventures add jobs and create new wealth. To do so, they must identify opportunities that will be viable in the marketplace as well as gather resources and assemble an entrepreneurial team to enact the opportunity. New entrants often evoke a strong competitive response from incumbent firms in a given marketplace. When examining the role of strategic thinking on the success of entrepreneurial ventures and the role of competitive dynamics, you might ask:
   - Is the company engaged in an ongoing process of opportunity recognition? If not, how can it enhance its ability to recognize opportunities?
   - Do the entrepreneurs who are launching new ventures have vision, dedication and drive, and a commitment to excellence? If so, how have these affected the performance and dedication of other employees involved in the venture?
   - Have strategic principles been used in the process of developing strategies to pursue the entrepreneurial opportunity? If not, how can the venture apply tools such as five-forces analysis and value-chain analysis to improve its competitive position and performance?

9. *Achieving effective strategic control.* Strategic controls enable a firm to implement strategies effectively. Informational controls involve comparing performance to stated goals and scanning, monitoring, and being responsive to the environment. Behavioral controls emerge from a company's culture, reward systems, and organizational boundaries. When assessing the impact of strategic controls on implementation, you might ask:
   - Is the company employing the appropriate informational control systems? If not, how can it implement a more interactive approach to enhance learning and minimize response times?
   - Does the company have a strong and effective culture? If not, what steps can it take to align its values and rewards system with its goals and objectives?
   - Has the company implemented control systems that match its strategies? If so, what additional steps can be taken to improve performance?

10. *Creating effective organizational designs.* Organizational designs that align with competitive strategies can enhance performance. As companies grow and change, their structures must also evolve to meet new demands. In today's economy, firm boundaries must be flexible and permeable to facilitate smoother interactions with external parties such as customers, suppliers, and alliance partners. New forms of organizing are becoming more common. When evaluating the role of organizational structure on strategy implementation, you might ask:
    - Has the company implemented organizational structures that are suited to the type of business it is in? If not, how can it alter the design in ways that enhance its competitiveness?
    - Is the company employing boundaryless organizational designs where appropriate? If so, how are senior managers maintaining control of lower-level employees?
    - Does the company use outsourcing to achieve the best possible results? If not, what criteria should it use to decide which functions can be outsourced?

11. *Creating a learning organization and an ethical organization.* Strong leadership is essential for achieving competitive advantages. Two leadership roles are especially important. The first is creating a learning organization by harnessing talent and encouraging the development of new knowledge. Second, leaders play a vital role in

motivating employees to excellence and inspiring ethical behavior. When exploring the impact of effective strategic leadership, you might ask:

- Do company leaders promote excellence as part of the overall culture? If so, how has this influenced the performance of the firm and the individuals in it?
- Is the company committed to being a learning organization? If not, what can it do to capitalize on the individual and collective talents of organizational members?
- Have company leaders exhibited an ethical attitude in their own behavior? If not, how has their behavior influenced the actions of other employees?

12. ***Fostering corporate entrepreneurship.*** Many firms continually seek new growth opportunities and avenues for strategic renewal. In some corporations, autonomous work units such as business incubators and new-venture groups are used to focus corporate venturing activities. In other corporate settings, product champions and other firm members provide companies with the impetus to expand into new areas. When investigating the impact of entrepreneurship on strategic effectiveness, you might ask:

- Has the company resolved the dilemmas associated with managing innovation? If so, is it effectively defining and pacing its innovation efforts?
- Has the company developed autonomous work units that have the freedom to bring forth new product ideas? If so, has it used product champions to implement new venture initiatives?
- Does the company have an entrepreneurial orientation? If not, what can it do to encourage entrepreneurial attitudes in the strategic behavior of its organizational members?

Summary

Strategic management case analysis provides an effective method of learning how companies analyze problems, make decisions, and resolve challenges. Strategic cases include detailed accounts of actual business situations. The purpose of analyzing such cases is to gain exposure to a wide variety of organizational and managerial situations. By putting yourself in the place of a strategic decision maker, you can gain an appreciation of the difficulty and complexity of many strategic situations. In the process you can learn how to ask good strategic questions and enhance your analytical skills. Presenting case analyses can also help develop oral and written communication skills.

In this chapter we have discussed the importance of strategic case analysis and described the five steps involved in conducting a case analysis: becoming familiar with the material, identifying problems, analyzing strategic issues, proposing alternative solutions, and making recommendations. We have also discussed how to get the most from case analysis. Finally, we have described how the case analysis process follows the analysis-decision-action cycle of strategic management and outlined issues and questions that are associated with each of the previous 12 chapters of the text.

Key Terms

case analysis 449

financial ratio analysis 455

References

1. The material in this chapter is based on several sources, including Barnes, L. A., Nelson, A. J., & Christensen, C. R. 1994. *Teaching and the case method: Text, cases and readings.* Boston: Harvard Business School Press: Guth, W. D. 1985. Central concepts of business unit and corporate strategy. In W. D. Guth (Ed.). *Handbook of business strategy:* 1–9. Boston: Warren, Gorham & Lamont; Lundberg,

C. C., & Enz, C. 1993. A framework for student case preparation. *Case Research Journal,* 13 (Summer): 129–140; and Ronstadt, R. 1980. *The art of case analysis: A guide to the diagnosis of business situations.* Dover, MA: Lord Publishing.

2. Edge, A. G., & Coleman, D. R. 1986. *The guide to case analysis and reporting* (3rd ed.). Honolulu, HI: System Logistics.

3. Morris, E. 1987. Vision and strategy: A focus for the future. *Journal of Business Strategy* 8: 51–58.

4. This section is based on Lundberg & Enz, op. cit., and Ronstadt, op. cit.

5. The importance of problem definition was emphasized in Mintzberg, H., Raisinghani, D., & Theoret, A. 1976. The structure of "unstructured" decision processes. *Administrative Science Quarterly,* 21(2): 246–275.

6. Drucker, P. F. 1994. The theory of the business. *Harvard Business Review,* 72(5): 95–104.

7. This section draws on Edge & Coleman, op. cit.

8. Irving Janis is credited with coining the term *groupthink,* and he applied it primarily to fiascos in government (such as the Bay of Pigs incident in 1961). Refer to Janis, I. L. 1982. *Victims of groupthink* (2nd ed.). Boston: Houghton Mifflin.

9. Much of our discussion is based upon Finkelstein, S., & Mooney, A. C. 2003. Not the usual suspects: How to use board process to make boards better. *Academy of Management Executive,* 17(2): 101–113; Schweiger, D. M., Sandberg, W. R., & Rechner, P. L. 1989. Experiential effects of dialectical inquiry, devil's advocacy, and consensus approaches to strategic decision making. *Academy of Management Journal,* 32(4): 745–772; and Aldag, R. J., & Stearns, T. M. 1987. *Management.* Cincinnati: South-Western Publishing.

10. Finkelstein and Mooney, op. cit.

APPENDIX 1 TO CHAPTER 13

Financial Ratio Analysis

Standard Financial Statements

One obvious thing we might want to do with a company's financial statements is to compare them to those of other, similar companies. We would immediately have a problem, however. It's almost impossible to directly compare the financial statements for two companies because of differences in size.

For example, Oracle and IBM are obviously serious rivals in the computer software market, but IBM is much larger (in terms of assets), so it is difficult to compare them directly. For that matter, it's difficult to even compare financial statements from different points in time for the same company if the company's size has changed. The size problem is compounded if we try to compare IBM and, say, SAP (of Germany). If SAP's financial statements are denominated in German marks, then we have a size *and* a currency difference.

To start making comparisons, one obvious thing we might try to do is to somehow standardize the financial statements. One very common and useful way of doing this is to work with percentages instead of total dollars. The resulting financial statements are called *common-size statements.* We consider these next.

Common-Size Balance Sheets

For easy reference, Prufrock Corporation's 2006 and 2007 balance sheets are provided in Exhibit 13A.1. Using these, we construct common-size balance sheets by expressing each item as a percentage of total assets. Prufrock's 2006 and 2007 common-size balance sheets are shown in Exhibit 13A.2.

Notice that some of the totals don't check exactly because of rounding errors. Also notice that the total change has to be zero since the beginning and ending numbers must add up to 100 percent.

In this form, financial statements are relatively easy to read and compare. For example, just looking at the two balance sheets for Prufrock, we see that current assets were 19.7 percent of total assets

Source: Adapted from Rows, S. A., Westerfield, R. W., & Jordan, B. D. 1999. *Essentials of Corporate Finance* (2nd ed.). chap. 3. New York: McGraw-Hill, 1999.

Exhibit 13A.1
Prufrock Corporation
Balance Sheets as
of December 31,
2006 and 2007
($ in millions)

	2006	2007
Assets		
Current assets		
Cash	$ 84	$ 98
Accounts receivable	165	188
Inventory	393	422
Total	$ 642	$ 708
Fixed assets		
Net plant and equipment	$2,731	$2,880
Total assets	$3,373	$3,588
Liabilities and Owners' Equity		
Current liabilities		
Accounts payable	$ 312	$ 344
Notes payable	231	196
Total	$ 543	$ 540
Long-term debt	$ 531	$ 457
Owners' equity		
Common stock and paid-in surplus	$ 500	$ 550
Retained earnings	1,799	2,041
Total	$2,299	$2,591
Total liabilities and owners' equity	$3,373	$3,588

in 2006, up from 19.1 percent in 2007. Current liabilities declined from 16.0 percent to 15.1 percent of total liabilities and equity over that same time. Similarly, total equity rose from 68.1 percent of total liabilities and equity to 72.2 percent.

Overall, Prufrock's liquidity, as measured by current assets compared to current liabilities, increased over the year. Simultaneously, Prufrock's indebtedness diminished as a percentage of total assets. We might be tempted to conclude that the balance sheet has grown "stronger."

Common-Size Income Statements

A useful way of standardizing the income statement, shown in Exhibit 13A.3, is to express each item as a percentage of total sales, as illustrated for Prufrock in Exhibit 13A.4.

This income statement tells us what happens to each dollar in sales. For Prufrock, interest expense eats up $.061 out of every sales dollar and taxes take another $.081. When all is said and done, $.157 of each dollar flows through to the bottom line (net income), and that amount is split into $.105 retained in the business and $.052 paid out in dividends.

These percentages are very useful in comparisons. For example, a relevant figure is the cost percentage. For Prufrock, $.582 of each $1.00 in sales goes to pay for goods sold. It would be interesting to compute the same percentage for Prufrock's main competitors to see how Prufrock stacks up in terms of cost control.

Ratio Analysis

Another way of avoiding the problems involved in comparing companies of different sizes is to calculate and compare *financial ratios*. Such ratios are ways of comparing and investigating the relationships

Exhibit 13A.2

Prufrock Corporation

Common-Size Balance Sheets as of December 31, 2006 and 2007 (%)

	2006	2007	Change
Assets			
Current assets			
Cash	2.5%	2.7%	+ .2%
Accounts receivable	4.9	5.2	+ .3
Inventory	11.7	11.8	+ .1
Total	19.1	19.7	+ .6
Fixed assets			
Net plant and equipment	80.9	80.3	− .6
Total assets	100.0%	100.0%	.0%
Liabilities and Owners' Equity			
Current liabilities			
Accounts payable	9.2%	9.6%	+ .4%
Notes payable	6.8	5.5	−1.3
Total	16.0	15.1	− .9
Long-term debt	15.7	12.7	−3.0
Owners' equity			
Common stock and paid-in surplus	14.8	15.3	+ .5
Retained earnings	53.3	56.9	+3.6
Total	68.1	72.2	+4.1
Total liabilities and owners' equities	100.0%	100.0%	.0%

Note: Numbers may not add up to 100.0% due to rounding.

Exhibit 13A.3

Prufrock Corporation

2007 Income Statement ($ in millions)

Sales		$2,311
Cost of goods sold		1,344
Depreciation		276
Earnings before interest and taxes		$ 691
Interest paid		141
Taxable income		$ 550
Taxes (34%)		187
Net income		$ 363
Dividends	$121	
Addition to retained earnings	242	

between different pieces of financial information. We cover some of the more common ratios next, but there are many others that we don't touch on.

One problem with ratios is that different people and different sources frequently don't compute them in exactly the same way, and this leads to much confusion. The specific definitions we use here

Sales		100.0%
Cost of goods sold		58.2
Depreciation		11.9
Earnings before interest and taxes		29.9
Interest paid		6.1
Taxable income		23.8
Taxes (34%)		8.1
Net income		15.7%
Dividends	5.2%	
Addition to retained earnings	10.5	

may or may not be the same as others you have seen or will see elsewhere. If you ever use ratios as a tool for analysis, you should be careful to document how you calculate each one, and, if you are comparing your numbers to those of another source, be sure you know how its numbers are computed.

For each of the ratios we discuss, several questions come to mind:

1. How is it computed?
2. What is it intended to measure, and why might we be interested?
3. What is the unit of measurement?
4. What might a high or low value be telling us? How might such values be misleading?
5. How could this measure be improved?

Financial ratios are traditionally grouped into the following categories:

1. Short-term solvency, or liquidity, ratios.
2. Long-term solvency, or financial leverage, ratios.
3. Asset management, or turnover, ratios.
4. Profitability ratios.
5. Market value ratios.

We will consider each of these in turn. In calculating these numbers for Prufrock, we will use the ending balance sheet (2007) figures unless we explicitly say otherwise. The numbers for the various ratios come from the income statement and the balance sheet.

Short-Term Solvency, or Liquidity, Measures

As the name suggests, short-term solvency ratios as a group are intended to provide information about a firm's liquidity, and these ratios are sometimes called *liquidity measures*. The primary concern is the firm's ability to pay its bills over the short run without undue stress. Consequently, these ratios focus on current assets and current liabilities.

For obvious reasons, liquidity ratios are particularly interesting to short-term creditors. Since financial managers are constantly working with banks and other short-term lenders, an understanding of these ratios is essential.

One advantage of looking at current assets and liabilities is that their book values and market values are likely to be similar. Often (though not always), these assets and liabilities just don't live long enough for the two to get seriously out of step. On the other hand, like any type of near cash, current assets and liabilities can and do change fairly rapidly, so today's amounts may not be a reliable guide to the future.

Current Ratio   One of the best-known and most widely used ratios is the *current ratio*. As you might guess, the current ratio is defined as:

$$\text{Current ratio} = \frac{\text{Current assets}}{\text{Current liabilities}}$$

For Prufrock, the 2007 current ratio is:

$$\text{Current ratio} = \frac{\$708}{\$540} = 1.31 \text{ times}$$

Because current assets and liabilities are, in principle, converted to cash over the following 12 months, the current ratio is a measure of short-term liquidity. The unit of measurement is either dollars or times. So, we could say Prufrock has $1.31 in current assets for every $1 in current liabilities, or we could say Prufrock has its current liabilities covered 1.31 times over.

To a creditor, particularly a short-term creditor such as a supplier, the higher the current ratio, the better. To the firm, a high current ratio indicates liquidity, but it also may indicate an inefficient use of cash and other short-term assets. Absent some extraordinary circumstances, we would expect to see a current ratio of at least 1, because a current ratio of less than 1 would mean that net working capital (current assets less current liabilities) is negative. This would be unusual in a healthy firm, at least for most types of businesses.

The current ratio, like any ratio, is affected by various types of transactions. For example, suppose the firm borrows over the long term to raise money. The short-run effect would be an increase in cash from the issue proceeds and an increase in long-term debt. Current liabilities would not be affected, so the current ratio would rise.

Finally, note that an apparently low current ratio may not be a bad sign for a company with a large reserve of untapped borrowing power.

Quick (or Acid-Test) Ratio Inventory is often the least liquid current asset. It's also the one for which the book values are least reliable as measures of market value, since the quality of the inventory isn't considered. Some of the inventory may later turn out to be damaged, obsolete, or lost.

More to the point, relatively large inventories are often a sign of short-term trouble. The firm may have overestimated sales and overbought or overproduced as a result. In this case, the firm may have a substantial portion of its liquidity tied up in slow-moving inventory.

To further evaluate liquidity, the *quick,* or *acid-test, ratio* is computed just like the current ratio, except inventory is omitted:

$$\text{Quick ratio} = \frac{\text{Current assets} - \text{Inventory}}{\text{Current liabilities}}$$

Notice that using cash to buy inventory does not affect the current ratio, but it reduces the quick ratio. Again, the idea is that inventory is relatively illiquid compared to cash.

For Prufrock, this ratio in 2007 was:

$$\text{Quick ratio} = \frac{\$708 - 422}{\$540} = .53 \text{ times}$$

The quick ratio here tells a somewhat different story than the current ratio, because inventory accounts for more than half of Prufrock's current assets. To exaggerate the point, if this inventory consisted of, say, unsold nuclear power plants, then this would be a cause for concern.

Cash Ratio A very short-term creditor might be interested in the *cash ratio:*

$$\text{Cash ratio} = \frac{\text{Cash}}{\text{Current liabilities}}$$

You can verify that this works out to be .18 times for Prufrock.

Long-Term Solvency Measures

Long-term solvency ratios are intended to address the firm's long-run ability to meet its obligations, or, more generally, its financial leverage. These ratios are sometimes called *financial leverage ratios* or just *leverage ratios.* We consider three commonly used measures and some variations.

Total Debt Ratio   The *total debt ratio* takes into account all debts of all maturities to all creditors. It can be defined in several ways, the easiest of which is:

$$\text{Total debt ratio} = \frac{\text{Total assets} - \text{Total equity}}{\text{Total assets}}$$

$$= \frac{\$3,588 - 2,591}{\$3,588} = .28 \text{ times}$$

In this case, an analyst might say that Prufrock uses 28 percent debt.[1] Whether this is high or low or whether it even makes any difference depends on whether or not capital structure matters.

Prufrock has $.28 in debt for every $1 in assets. Therefore, there is $.72 in equity ($1 − .28) for every $.28 in debt. With this in mind, we can define two useful variations on the total debt ratio, the *debt-equity ratio* and the *equity multiplier:*

$$\text{Debt-equity ratio} = \text{Total debt/Total equity}$$

$$= \$.28/\$.72 = .39 \text{ times}$$

$$\text{Equity multiplier} = \text{Total assets/Total equity}$$

$$= \$1/\$.72 = 1.39 \text{ times}$$

The fact that the equity multiplier is 1 plus the debt-equity ratio is not a coincidence:

$$\text{Equity multiplier} = \text{Total assets/Total equity} = \$1/\$.72 = 1.39$$

$$= (\text{Total equity} + \text{Total debt})/\text{Total equity}$$

$$= 1 + \text{Debt-equity ratio} = 1.39 \text{ times}$$

The thing to notice here is that given any one of these three ratios, you can immediately calculate the other two, so they all say exactly the same thing.

Times Interest Earned   Another common measure of long-term solvency is the *times interest earned* (TIE) *ratio*. Once again, there are several possible (and common) definitions, but we'll stick with the most traditional:

$$\text{Times interest earned ratio} = \frac{\text{EBIT}}{\text{Interest}}$$

$$= \frac{\$691}{\$141} = 4.9 \text{ times}$$

As the name suggests, this ratio measures how well a company has its interest obligations covered, and it is often called the interest coverage ratio. For Prufrock, the interest bill is covered 4.9 times over.

Cash Coverage   A problem with the TIE ratio is that it is based on earnings before interest and taxes (EBIT), which is not really a measure of cash available to pay interest. The reason is that depreciation, a noncash expense, has been deducted. Since interest is most definitely a cash outflow (to creditors), one way to define the *cash coverage ratio* is:

$$\text{Cash coverage ratio} = \frac{\text{EBIT} + \text{Depreciation}}{\text{Interest}}$$

$$= \frac{\$691 + 276}{\$141} = \frac{\$967}{\$141} = 6.9 \text{ times}$$

The numerator here, EBIT plus depreciation, is often abbreviated EBDIT (earnings before depreciation, interest, and taxes). It is a basic measure of the firm's ability to generate cash from operations, and it is frequently used as a measure of cash flow available to meet financial obligations.

---

[1]Total equity here includes preferred stock, if there is any. An equivalent numerator in this ratio would be (Current liabilities + Long-term debt).

Asset Management, or Turnover, Measures

We next turn our attention to the efficiency with which Prufrock uses its assets. The measures in this section are sometimes called *asset utilization ratios.* The specific ratios we discuss can all be interpreted as measures of turnover. What they are intended to describe is how efficiently, or intensively, a firm uses its assets to generate sales. We first look at two important current assets: inventory and receivables.

Inventory Turnover and Days' Sales in Inventory   During the year, Prufrock had a cost of goods sold of $1,344. Inventory at the end of the year was $422. With these numbers, *inventory turnover* can be calculated as:

$$\text{Inventory turnover} = \frac{\text{Cost of goods sold}}{\text{Inventory}}$$

$$= \frac{\$1,344}{\$422} = 3.2 \text{ times}$$

In a sense, we sold off, or turned over, the entire inventory 3.2 times. As long as we are not running out of stock and thereby forgoing sales, the higher this ratio is, the more efficiently we are managing inventory.

If we know that we turned our inventory over 3.2 times during the year, then we can immediately figure out how long it took us to turn it over on average. The result is the average *days' sales in inventory:*

$$\text{Days's sales in inventory} = \frac{365 \text{ days}}{\text{Inventory turnover}}$$

$$= \frac{365}{3.2} = 114 \text{ days}$$

This tells us that, on average, inventory sits 114 days before it is sold. Alternatively, assuming we used the most recent inventory and cost figures, it will take about 114 days to work off our current inventory.

For example, we frequently hear things like "Majestic Motors has a 60 days' supply of cars." This means that, at current daily sales, it would take 60 days to deplete the available inventory. We could also say that Majestic has 60 days of sales in inventory.

Receivables Turnover and Days' Sales in Receivables   Our inventory measures give some indication of how fast we can sell products. We now look at how fast we collect on those sales. The *receivables turnover* is defined in the same way as inventory turnover:

$$\text{Receivables turnover} = \frac{\text{Sales}}{\text{Accounts receivable}}$$

$$= \frac{\$2,311}{\$188} = 12.3 \text{ times}$$

Loosely speaking, we collected our outstanding credit accounts and reloaned the money 12.3 times during the year.[2]

This ratio makes more sense if we convert it to days, so the *days' sales in receivables* is:

$$\text{Days' sales in receivables} = \frac{365 \text{ days}}{\text{Receivables turnover}}$$

$$= \frac{365}{12.3} = 30 \text{ days}$$

Therefore, on average, we collect on our credit sales in 30 days. For obvious reasons, this ratio is very frequently called the *average collection period* (ACP).

Also note that if we are using the most recent figures, we can also say that we have 30 days' worth of sales currently uncollected.

---

[2]Here we have implicitly assumed that all sales are credit sales. If they were not, then we would simply use total credit sales in these calculations, not total sales.

Total Asset Turnover   Moving away from specific accounts like inventory or receivables, we can consider an important "big picture" ratio, the *total asset turnover ratio*. As the name suggests, total asset turnover is:

$$\text{Total asset turnover} = \frac{\text{Sales}}{\text{Total assets}}$$

$$= \frac{\$2,311}{\$3,588} = .64 \text{ times}$$

In other words, for every dollar in assets, we generated $.64 in sales.

A closely related ratio, the *capital intensity ratio,* is simply the reciprocal of (i.e., 1 divided by) total asset turnover. It can be interpreted as the dollar investment in assets needed to generate $1 in sales. High values correspond to capital intensive industries (e.g., public utilities). For Prufrock, total asset turnover is .64, so, if we flip this over, we get that capital intensity is $1/.64 = $1.56. That is, it takes Prufrock $1.56 in assets to create $1 in sales.

Profitability Measures

The three measures we discuss in this section are probably the best known and most widely used of all financial ratios. In one form or another, they are intended to measure how efficiently the firm uses its assets and how efficiently the firm manages its operations. The focus in this group is on the bottom line, net income.

Profit Margin   Companies pay a great deal of attention to their *profit margin:*

$$\text{Profit margin} = \frac{\text{Net income}}{\text{Sales}}$$

$$= \frac{\$363}{\$2,311} = 15.7\%$$

This tells us that Prufrock, in an accounting sense, generates a little less than 16 cents in profit for every dollar in sales.

All other things being equal, a relatively high profit margin is obviously desirable. This situation corresponds to low expense ratios relative to sales. However, we hasten to add that other things are often not equal.

For example, lowering our sales price will usually increase unit volume, but will normally cause profit margins to shrink. Total profit (or, more importantly, operating cash flow) may go up or down; so the fact that margins are smaller isn't necessarily bad. After all, isn't it possible that, as the saying goes, "Our prices are so low that we lose money on everything we sell, but we make it up in volume!"[3]

Return on Assets   *Return on assets* (ROA) is a measure of profit per dollar of assets. It can be defined several ways, but the most common is:

$$\text{Return on assets} = \frac{\text{Net income}}{\text{Total assets}}$$

$$= \frac{\$363}{\$3,588} = 10.12\%$$

Return on Equity   *Return on equity* (ROE) is a measure of how the stockholders fared during the year. Since benefiting shareholders is our goal, ROE is, in an accounting sense, the true bottom-line measure of performance. ROE is usually measured as:

$$\text{Return on equity} = \frac{\text{Net income}}{\text{Total equity}}$$

$$= \frac{\$363}{\$2,591} = 14\%$$

---

[3]No, it's not; margins can be small, but they do need to be positive!

For every dollar in equity, therefore, Prufrock generated 14 cents in profit, but, again, this is only correct in accounting terms.

Because ROA and ROE are such commonly cited numbers, we stress that it is important to remember they are accounting rates of return. For this reason, these measures should properly be called *return on book assets* and *return on book equity.* In addition, ROE is sometimes called *return on net worth.* Whatever it's called, it would be inappropriate to compare the results to, for example, an interest rate observed in the financial markets.

The fact that ROE exceeds ROA reflects Prufrock's use of financial leverage. We will examine the relationship between these two measures in more detail below.

Market Value Measures

Our final group of measures is based, in part, on information not necessarily contained in financial statements—the market price per share of the stock. Obviously, these measures can only be calculated directly for publicly traded companies.

We assume that Prufrock has 33 million shares outstanding and the stock sold for $88 per share at the end of the year. If we recall that Prufrock's net income was $363 million, then we can calculate that its earnings per share were:

$$\text{EPS} = \frac{\text{Net income}}{\text{Shares outstanding}} = \frac{\$363}{33} = \$11$$

Price-Earnings Ratio The first of our market value measures, the *price-earnings,* or PE, *ratio* (or multiple), is defined as:

$$\text{PE ratio} = \frac{\text{Price per share}}{\text{Earnings per share}}$$

$$= \frac{\$85}{\$11} = 8 \text{ times}$$

In the vernacular, we would say that Prufrock shares sell for eight times earnings, or we might say that Prufrock shares have, or "carry," a PE multiple of 8.

Since the PE ratio measures how much investors are willing to pay per dollar of current earnings, higher PEs are often taken to mean that the firm has significant prospects for future growth. Of course, if a firm had no or almost no earnings, its PE would probably be quite large; so, as always, be careful when interpreting this ratio.

Market-to-Book Ratio A second commonly quoted measure is the *market-to-book ratio:*

$$\text{Market-to-book ratio} = \frac{\text{Market value per share}}{\text{Book value per share}}$$

$$= \frac{\$88}{(\$2,591/33)} = \frac{\$88}{\$78.5} = 1.12 \text{ times}$$

Notice that book value per share is total equity (not just common stock) divided by the number of shares outstanding.

Since book value per share is an accounting number, it reflects historical costs. In a loose sense, the market-to-book ratio therefore compares the market value of the firm's investments to their cost. A value less than 1 could mean that the firm has not been successful overall in creating value for its stockholders.

Conclusion

This completes our definition of some common ratios. Exhibit 13A.5 summarizes the ratios we've discussed.

I. Short-term solvency, or liquidity, ratios

$$\text{Current ratio} = \frac{\text{Current assets}}{\text{Current liabilities}}$$

$$\text{Quick ratio} = \frac{\text{Current assets} - \text{Inventory}}{\text{Current liabilities}}$$

$$\text{Cash ratio} = \frac{\text{Cash}}{\text{Current liabilities}}$$

II. Long-term solvency, or financial leverage, ratios

$$\text{Total debt ratio} = \frac{\text{Total assets} - \text{Total equity}}{\text{Total assets}}$$

$$\text{Debt-equity ratio} = \text{Total debt/Total equity}$$

$$\text{Equity multiplier} = \text{Total assets/Total equity}$$

$$\text{Times interest earned ratio} = \frac{\text{EBIT}}{\text{Interest}}$$

$$\text{Cash coverage ratio} = \frac{\text{EBIT} + \text{Depreciation}}{\text{Interest}}$$

III. Asset utilization, or turnover, ratios

$$\text{Inventory turnover} = \frac{\text{Cost of goods sold}}{\text{Inventory}}$$

$$\text{Days' sales in inventory} = \frac{365 \text{ days}}{\text{Inventory turnover}}$$

$$\text{Receivables turnover} = \frac{\text{Sales}}{\text{Accounts receivable}}$$

$$\text{Days' sales in receivables} = \frac{365 \text{ days}}{\text{Receivables turnover}}$$

$$\text{Total asset turnover} = \frac{\text{Sales}}{\text{Total assets}}$$

$$\text{Capital intensity} = \frac{\text{Total assets}}{\text{Sales}}$$

IV. Profitability ratios

$$\text{Profit margin} = \frac{\text{Net income}}{\text{Sales}}$$

$$\text{Return on assets (ROA)} = \frac{\text{Net income}}{\text{Total assets}}$$

$$\text{Return on equity (ROE)} = \frac{\text{Net income}}{\text{Total equity}}$$

$$\text{ROE} = \frac{\text{Net income}}{\text{Sales}} \times \frac{\text{Sales}}{\text{Assets}} \times \frac{\text{Assets}}{\text{Equity}}$$

V. Market value ratios

$$\text{Price-earnings ratio} = \frac{\text{Price per share}}{\text{Earnings per share}}$$

$$\text{Market-to-book ratio} = \frac{\text{Market value per share}}{\text{Book value per share}}$$

Exhibit 13A.5 A Summary of Five Types of Financial Ratios

APPENDIX 2 TO CHAPTER 13

Sources of Company and Industry Information*

For business executives to make the best decisions when developing corporate and/or business strategies, it is critical for them to be knowledgeable about their competitors and about the industries in which they compete. The process used by corporations to learn as much as possible about competitors is called "competitive intelligence." This appendix provides an overview of important and widely available sources of information that may be useful in conducting basic competitive intelligence. Much information of this nature is available in libraries, article databases, business reference books, and on Web sites. This list provides a variety of recommendations. Ask a librarian for assistance because library collections and resources vary.

The information sources are organized into 10 categories: Competitive Intelligence; Public or Private, Subsidiary or Division, U.S. or Foreign?; Annual Report Collections—Public Companies; Guides and Tutorials; SEC Filings/EDGAR—Company Disclosure Reports; Company Rankings; Business Metasites and Portals; Strategic and Competitive Analysis—Information Sources; Sources for Industry Research and Analysis; and Search Engines.

Competitive Intelligence

Students and other researchers who want to learn more about the value and process of competitive intelligence should see four recent books on this subject.

*This information was compiled by Ruthie Brock and Carol Byrne, Business Librarians at The University of Texas at Arlington. We greatly appreciate their valuable contribution.

Craig Fleisher and Babette Bensoussan. *Business and Competitive Analysis: Effective Application of New and Classic Methods.* Philadelphia, PA: Wharton School, 2007.

Leonard M. Fuld. *The Secret Language of Competitive Intelligence.* New York: Crown Business, 2006.

David L. Blenkhorn and Craig S. Fleisher, eds. *Competitive Intelligence and Global Business.* Westport, CT: Praeger Publishers, 2005.

Benjamin Gilad. *Early Warning: Using Competitive Intelligence to Anticipate Market Shifts, Control Risk, and Create Powerful Strategies.* New York: American Management Association, 2004.

Public or Private, Subsidiary or Division, U.S. or Foreign?

Companies traded on stock exchanges in the United States are required to file a variety of reports that disclose information about the company. This begins the process that produces a wealth of data on public companies and at the same time distinguishes them from private companies, which often lack available data. Similarly, financial data of subsidiaries and divisions are typically filed in a consolidated financial statement by the parent company instead of being treated independently, thus limiting the kind of data available on them. On the other hand, foreign companies that trade on U.S. stock exchanges are required to file 20F reports, similar to the 10-K for U.S. companies—the most comprehensive of the required reports—although the number of foreign companies doing so is relatively small.

Corporate Directory of U.S. Public Companies. San Mateo, CA: Walker's Research, LLC, 2007.
The Corporate Directory provides company profiles of more than 9,000 publicly traded companies in the United States, including foreign companies trading on the U.S. exchanges (American depository receipts or ADRs). Some libraries may subscribe to an alternative online version at http://www.walkersresearch.com.

Corporate Affiliations. New Providence, NJ: A LexisNexis Group, 2006.
This directory features brief profiles of major U.S. and foreign corporations, both public and private, as well as their subsidiaries, divisions, and affiliates. The directory also indicates hierarchy of corporate relationships. An online version of the directory allows retrieval of a list of companies that meet specific criteria. Results can be downloaded to a spreadsheet. The online version requires a subscription.

ReferenceUSA. Omaha, NE: infoUSA, 2007
ReferenceUSA is an online directory of more than 14 million businesses located in the United States. One of its unique features is that it includes public and private companies, both large and small. Also, results can be analyzed using the data summary feature, which allows for a snapshot of how the industry breaks down by size, geographic location, etc. Library subscriptions may vary.

Ward's Business Directory of U.S. Private and Public Companies. Detroit, MI: Thomson Gale, 2007. 8 volumes.
Ward's Business Directory lists brief profiles on more than 110,000 public and private companies and indicates whether they are public or private and a subsidiary or division. Two volumes of the set are arranged using the Standard Industrial Classifications (SIC) and the North American Industry Classification System (NAICS) and feature company rankings within industries.

Annual Report Collections—Public Companies

Most companies have their Annual Report to Shareholders and other financial reports available on their corporate Web site. A few "aggregators" also conveniently provide an accumulation of links to many reports of U.S. and international corporations or include a PDF document as part of their database.

AnnualReports.com. IR Solutions. Weston, FL.
This Web site contains annual reports in HTML or PDF format. Reports can be retrieved by company name, ticker symbol, exchange, industry, or sector.
http://www.annualreports.com

Company Annual Reports Online (CAROL). Carol Ltd. London, UK.
This Web site is based in the United Kingdom, so many reports are European. Links are also provided for companies in Asia and the United States. A pull-down menu allows selection of companies within an industry. Access is free, but registration is required.
http://www.carol.co.uk/

Public Register's Online Annual Report Service. Baytact Corp. Woodstock Valley, CT.
Visitors to this Web site may choose from more than 4,500 company annual reports and 10-K filings to view online or order a paper copy. Access is free, but registration is required.
www.annualreportservice.com/

Mergent Online. Mergent, Inc. New York, NY.
Mergent Online provides company financial data for public companies headquartered in the United States, as well as those headquartered in other countries, including a large collection of corporate annual reports in PDF format. For industry ratios, Mergent Online offers an advanced search option. Industry reports are available as a subscription add-on. Library subscriptions to Mergent Online may vary.

Guides and Tutorials

Researching Companies Online. Debbie Flanagan. Fort Lauderdale, FL.
This site provides a step-by-step process for finding free company & industry information on the Web.
www.learnwebskills.com/company/

Annual Reports and Financial Statements: An Introduction. IBM. Armonk, NY.
These educational guides, located on IBM's Web site, provide basic information on how to read financial statements and other information in annual reports.
http://www.ibm.com/investor/tools/annualreportsAnatomy.phtml
http://www.ibm.com/investor/tools/financials.phtml

EDGAR Full-Text Search Frequently Asked Questions (FAQ). U.S. Securities and Exchange Commission. Washington D.C.
The capability to search full-text SEC filings (popularly known as EDGAR filings) was vastly improved when the SEC launched its new search form in late 2006. Features are explained at the FAQ page.
http://www.sec.gov/edgar/searchedgar/edgarfulltextfaq.htm

Locating Company Information. Tutorial. William and Joan Schreyer Business Library. Penn State University. University Park, PA.
Created by librarians at Penn State, this outstanding tutorial provides suggestions for online and print resources for company information. Click on "how to" links for each item to view a brief instruction vignette.
http://www.libraries.psu.edu/instruction/business/information/companyi.htm Lo

Locating Industry Information. Tutorial. William and Joan Schreyer Business Library. Penn State University. University Park, PA.
Created by librarians at Penn State, this outstanding tutorial provides suggestions for online and print resources for industry information. Click on "how to" links for each item to view a brief instruction vignette.
http://www.libraries.psu.edu/instruction/business/information/industryi.htm

Ten Steps to Industry Intelligence. Industry Tutorial. George A. Smathers Libraries. University of Florida. Gainesville, FL
A step by step approach is provided for finding information about industries, with embedded links to recommended sources.
http://web.uflib.ufl.edu/cm/business/tutors/indtutor.htm

SEC Filings/EDGAR—Company Disclosure Reports

SEC Filings are the various reports that publicly traded companies must file with the Securities Exchange Commission to disclose information about their corporation. These are often referred to as "EDGAR" filings, an acronym for the Electronic Data Gathering, Analysis and Retrieval System. Some Web sites and commercial databases improve access to these reports by offering additional retrieval features not available on the official (www.sec.gov) Web site.

EDGAR Database Full-Text Search. U.S. Securities and Exchange Commission (SEC). Washington D.C.
The 10-K reports, and other corporate documents, are made available in the EDGAR database within 24 hours after being filed. Annual reports, on the other hand, are typically sent directly to

shareholders and are not required as part of EDGAR by the SEC, although some companies voluntarily include them. Both 10-Ks and shareholder's annual reports are considered basic sources of company research. In late 2006, the SEC launched their new and improved search interface for full-text searching of the content and exhibits of EDGAR SEC filings. The advanced search can be used to locate "hard to find" information within documents filed by corporations and their competitors. Searches for specific types of reports or certain industries can also be performed. http://searchwww.sec.gov/EDGARFSClient/jsp/EDGAR_MainAccess.jsp

EdgarScan—An Interface to the SEC EDGAR Database. PricewaterhouseCoopers. New York, NY. Using filings from the SEC's servers, EdgarScan's intelligent interface parses the data automatically into a common format that is comparable across companies. A small Java applet called the "Benchmarking Assistant" performs graphical financial benchmarking interactively. Extracted financial data from the 10-K includes ratios with links to indicate where the data were derived and how it was computed. Tables showing company comparisons can be downloaded as Excel charts. http://edgarscan.pwcglobal.com/servlets/edgarscan

LexisNexis Academic—SEC Filings & Reports. LexisNexis. Bethesda, MD. EDGAR filings and reports are available through the "Business" option of LexisNexis Academic. These reports and filings can be retrieved by company name, industry code (SIC), or ticker symbol for a particular time period or by a specific report. Proxy, prospectus and registration filings are also available.

Mergent Online—EDGAR. Mergent, Inc. New York, NY. From the "EDGAR Search" tab within Mergent Online, EDGAR SEC filings and reports can be searched by company name or ticker symbol, filing date range and file type (10-K, 8-K, ARS). The reports are available in HTML or Word format. Using the "Find in Page" option from the browser provides the capability of jumping to specific sections of an SEC report.

Company Rankings

Fortune 500. Time Inc. New York, NY. The Fortune 500 list and other company rankings are published in the printed edition of *Fortune* magazine, and are also available online. http://money.cnn.com/magazines/fortune/fortune500/index.html

Hoover's Handbook of American Business. Austin, TX: Hoovers, Inc., 2007. This two-volume set gives a company overview, a list of competitors, and basic financial information for large U.S. companies. A special feature is a section called "The List Lovers' Companion," which includes a variety of lists with company rankings, some that include companies listed in Hoover's Handbooks; others reprinted from *Fortune, Forbes,* and other publications. In addition to the American edition, Hoover's handbooks are available for private companies, emerging companies, and companies headquartered outside of the United States.

Ward's Business Directory of U.S. Private and Public Companies. Detroit, MI: Thomson Gale, 2006. 8 volumes. *Ward's Business Directory* is one of the few directories to rank both public and private companies together by sales within an industry, using both the Standard Industrial Classification system (in Volume 5 only) and the North American Industry Classification System (in Volume 8 only). With this information, it is easy to spot who the big players are in a particular product or industry category. Market share within an industry group can be calculated by determining what percentage a company's sales figure is of the total given by Ward's for that industry group.

Business Metasites and Portals

Yahoo Finance. Sunnyvale, CA: Yahoo! Inc. This metasite links to information on U.S. markets, world markets, data sources, finance references, investment editorials, financial news, and other helpful websites. http://finance.yahoo.com

Hoover's Online. Hoover's, Inc., Dun & Bradstreet Corporation. Short Hills, NJ. Hoover's Online includes a limited amount of free information on companies, industries, and executives. The subscribers' edition provides more in-depth information, especially for competitors and industries. http://www.hoovers.com/free

VIBES—Virtual International Business & Economic Sources
VIBES provides over 3,000 links to Internet sources of international business and economic information in English and available free of charge. Links include full-text articles, research reports, statistical tables, and portals linking to other sources.
http://library.uncc.edu/vibes/

Strategic and Competitive Analysis—Information Sources

Analyzing a company can take the form of examining its internal and external environment. In the process, it is useful to identify the company's strengths, weaknesses, opportunities, and threats (SWOT). Sources for this kind of analysis are varied, but perhaps the best would be to locate articles from *The Wall Street Journal,* business magazines, and industry trade publications. Publications such as these can be found in the following databases available at many public and academic libraries. When using a database that is structured to allow it, try searching the company name combined with one or more key words, such as "IBM and competition" or "Microsoft and lawsuits" or "AMR and fuel costs," to retrieve articles relating to the external environment.

ABI/Inform Complete. Ann Arbor, MI: ProQuest–CSA LLC, 2007.
ABI/Inform Complete provides abstracts and full text articles covering management, law, taxation, human resources, and company and industry information from more than 4,000 business and management journals. It also includes market condition reports, corporate strategies, case studies, executive profiles, and global industry conditions.

Business & Company Resource Center. Detroit, MI: Thomson Gale.
Business & Company Resource Center provides company and industry intelligence for a selection of public and private companies. Company profiles include parent–subsidiary relationships, industry rankings, products and brands, investment reports, industry statistics, and financial ratios. A selection of full-text investment reports from Investext Plus is also available.

Business Source Complete. Ipswich, MA: EBSCO Publishing.
Business Source Complete is a full text database with over 3,800 scholarly business journals covering management, economics, finance, accounting, international business, and more. The database also includes detailed company profiles of the world's 10,000 largest companies as well as selected country economic reports provided by the Economist Intelligence Unit (EIU). The database includes case studies, investment and market research reports, SWOT analyses, and more. Business Source Complete contains over 1,100 peer-reviewed business journals.

Investext Plus. Detroit, MI: Thomson Gale.
Investext Plus offers full-text analytical reports on more than 47,000 public companies and 54 industries. The reports are excellent sources for strategic and financial profiles of a company, its competitors, and industry trends. Developed by a global roster of brokerage, investment banking, and research firms, these full-text investment reports include a wealth of current and historical information useful for evaluating a company or industry over time.

International Directory of Company Histories. Detroit, MI: St. James Press, 1988 to present. 84 volumes to date.
This directory covers more than 4,500 multinational companies and the series is still adding volumes. Each company history is approximately three to five pages in length and provides a summary of the company's mission, goals, and ideals, followed by company milestones, principal subsidiaries, and competitors. Strategic decisions made by the company are usually noted. This series covers public and private companies and nonprofit entities. Entry information includes a company's legal name, headquarters information, URL, incorporation date, ticker symbol, stock exchange, sales figures, and the primary North American Industry Classification System (NAICS) code. Further reading selections complete the entry information.

LexisNexis Academic. Bethesda, MD: LexisNexis.
The "Business" category in *LexisNexis Academic* provides access to timely business articles from newspapers, magazines, journals, wires, and broadcast transcripts. Other information available in this section includes detailed company financials, company comparisons, and industry and market information for over 25 industries.

LexisNexis Statistical. Bethesda, MD: LexisNexis.

LexisNexis Statistical provides access to a variety of statistical publications indexed in the American Statistics Index (ASI), Statistical Reference Index (SRI) and the Index to International Statistics (IIS). Use the PowerTables search to locate historical trends, future projections, and industry or demographic information. LexisNexis Statistical provides links to originating government Web sites when available.

The Wall Street Journal. New York: Dow Jones & Company.

This respected business newspaper is available in searchable full text from 1984 to present in the Factiva database. The "News Pages" link provides access to current articles and issues of *The Wall Street Journal.* Dow Jones, publisher of the print version of *The Wall Street Journal,* also has an online subscription available at wsj.com.

Sources for Industry Research and Analysis

Factiva. New York: Dow Jones & Company.

The Factiva database has several options for researching an industry. One is to search the database for articles in the business magazines and industry trade publications. The second option is to search in the Companies/Markets category for company/industry comparison reports.

Mergent Online. New York, Mergent Inc.

Mergent Online is a searchable database of over 10,000 U.S. public companies and more than 18,000 international public companies. The database offer worldwide industry reports, U.S. and global competitors, and executive biographical information. Mergent's enhanced Basic Search option features searching by primary industry codes (either SIC or NAICS). Once the search is executed, companies in that industry should be listed. A comparison or standard peer group analysis can be created to analyze companies in the same industry on various criteria. The improved Advanced Search allows the user to search a wider range of financial and textual information. Results, including ratios for a company and its competitors, can be downloaded to a spreadsheet.

North American Industry Classification (NAICS)

The North American Industry Classification System has officially replaced the Standard Industrial Classification (SIC) as a numerical structure used to define and analyze industries, although some publications and databases offer both classification systems. The NAICS codes are used in Canada, the United States, and Mexico. In the United States, the NAICS codes are used to conduct an Economic Census every five years, providing a snapshot of the U.S. economy at a given moment in time.

NAICS—http://www.census.gov/epcd/www/naics.html
Economic Census—http://www.census.gov/econ/census02/

NetAdvantage. New York: Standard & Poor's.

The database includes company, financial and investment information as well as the well-known publication *Industry Surveys.* Each industry report includes information on the current environment, industry trends, key industry ratios and statistics, and comparative company financial analysis. It is available in HTML, PDF, or Excel formats.

Search Engines

Google. Mountain View, CA: Google, Inc. Recognized for its advanced technology, quality of results and simplicity, the search engine Google is highly recommended by librarians and other expert Web "surfers."
http://www.google.com

Clusty. Pittsburgh, PA: Vivisimo, Inc. This search engine not only finds relevant results, but organizes it in logical subcategories.
http://www.clusty.com

photo credits

Chapter 1: page 8, Photo by Jocelyn Augustino/FEMA; page 21, Royalty-Free/CORBIS

Chapter 2: page 42, Getty Images; page 65, The McGraw-Hill Companies, Inc./John Flournoy, photographer

Chapter 3: page 81, The McGraw-Hill Companies, Inc./Lars A. Niki, photographer; page 94, Royalty-Free/CORBIS

Chapter 4: page 128, © Digital Vision/Punchstock; page 143, Royalty-Free/CORBIS

Chapter 5: page 164, The McGraw-Hill Companies, Inc./John Flournoy, photographer; page 182, The McGraw-Hill Companies, Inc./Andrew Resek, photographer

Chapter 6: page 197, The McGraw-Hill Companies, Inc./Christopher Kerrigan, photographer; page 209, B. Drake/PhotoLink/Getty Images

Chapter 7: page 234, © David Zurick; page 253, Cartesia/PhotoDisc Imaging/Getty Images

Chapter 8: page 266, Royalty-Free/CORBIS; page 279, JupiterImages

Chapter 9: page 310, The McGraw-Hill Companies/Jill Braaten, photographer; page 329, Royalty-Free/CORBIS

Chapter 10: page 353, © Flying Colours Ltd / Getty Images; page 361, The McGraw-Hill Companies, Inc./Jill Braaten, photographer

Chapter 11: page 388, © imageshop - zefa visual media uk ltd / Alamy; page 401, The McGraw-Hill Companies, Inc./Rick Brady, photographer

Chapter 12: page 412, Royalty-Free/CORBIS; page 427, © image100/PunchStock

Chapter 13: page 461, Digital Vision/Getty Images

company index

U

Under Armour, 279–280
Unilever, 251
    competition with Procter & Gamble,
        179–180
Unilever Bestfoods, 238
Union Pacific Railroad, market-book value
        ratio, 118
United Airlines, 93
United Health Group, 304
United Parcel Service, 28
United States Trust Corporation, 213
United Technologies Corporation, 358
    boundaryless concept, 359
    competitive intelligence, 41
Unocal, 203
US Airways, 288
USA Today, 307
    interactive control system, 308
UTC Fire & Security, 359
UTC Power, 359
UTStarcom, 282–283

V

Values Technology, 126
Vanguard, as workplace, 126
Veritas Software Corporation, 212
Verizon Wireless, as workplace, 126
VF Corporation, 198
Viacom International, 129
ViAir, 131
Viewpoint DataLabs International, profit
        generation, 95–96
Viore TV, 291
Virgin Group, 24
Virgin Inc., 405

Visteon Corporation, 328
Visto, 143
Vivendi International, 219
Vodafone, 352
Volkswagen, 49, 365
Volvo, 67

W

W. L. Gore Company, rules for innovation, 421
Walgreen Company, 29, 85
Walker's Research LLC, 480
Wal-Mart Stores, 10, 66, 75, 76, 170, 171,
        178, 212, 247, 288, 290, 294, 310,
        316, 380, 426
    cutthroat pricing schemes, 291
    problems in South Korea, 227–228
    success in combination strategies, 171
Walnut Venture Associates, 273
Walt Disney Company, 198, 265, 321
Wang Laboratories, 38
Warner Brothers, 25
Warner Brothers Publications, 199
Warner-Lambert Company, 212
Waste Management, 218
Waterman pens, 197
WD-40 Company, 283
WebMD, 451
Wegman's Food Markets, 80
WellPoint Health Network, 27, 63, 161
    and Food and Drug Administration,
        159–160
Wells Fargo, 26, 29, 122
Wendy's International, 256
Westinghouse, 360
Wetherill Associates, 401
Whirlpool Corporation, 24, 381
    advocacy programs, 437
    innovation at, 382

Whole Foods Market, Inc., internal
        benchmarking, 393
Wildfire Restaurants, 346
Wildflower Group, employee problems,
        115–116
Wilshire Associates, 323
Winnebago, 201–202
Wipro, 234
WorldCom, 18, 47, 218, 219, 319, 320, 326,
        328, 397
WPP Group PLC, 137, 384, 425
Wrangler tires, 75

X

Xerox Corporation, 26, 326
XM Satellite Radio, and Sirius, 295

Y

Yahoo! Inc., 274, 287, 294, 482
    market-book value ratio, 118
Yellow Roadway Corporation, 328
Yokogawa, 380
Yoplait, 253
Young & Rubicam, 384
YouTube, 287
Yugo, 158
Yum! Brands, 200

Z

Zimbra, Inc., 438
Zurich Financial Services, 245

name index

subject index

d

Database research, 40
Days' sales in inventory, 98, 456, 476
Days' sales in receivables, 98, 456, 476
Debt–equity mix, 206
Debt–equity ratio, 98, 456, 475
Debt financing, 272
Decentralization, excessive, 433
Decentralized network organization, 131–132
Decision making
 in entry strategy, 277–278
 and managerial conceit, 431–432
 stakeholders included in, 11
 for strategic management, 449
Decisions, 8–9
Decline stage strategies, 180–183
 consolidation, 182
 definition, 180
 examples, 182
 exiting the market, 182
 harvesting, 182
 maintaining, 182
Dedication, 276
Defense industry, 182
Defensive actions, 293
Deliberate strategy, 13
Demand
 aggregate, 179
 and blue ocean strategy, 281
 knowledge of future, 306
 selective, 179
Demand conditions
 in India, 234
 for national competitiveness, 231
Demand volatility, 203
Demographic environment, 45
 industries affected, 50
 key trends and events, 46
Demographic trends, 127
Denmark, demand conditions, 231
Department of Defense, 182
Department of Education, 45
Department of Energy, 182
Department of Justice, 381
Department of Labor, 403
Developing countries, potential purchasing
 power, 230
Developing human capital, 119, 122–124
Devil's advocacy, 464
Devils' Dictionary (Bierce), 318
Dialectical inquiry, 464–465
Diet trends, 37
Differentiating skills, 450
Differentiation
 blue ocean strategy, 281
 competitive parity based on, 158–159
 easily imitated, 166
 excessive, 166
 lacking uniqueness, 165–166
 lack of parity in, 162

Differentiation strategies, 135; *see also*
 Combination strategies
 cost parity, 164
 definition, 156
 effects of Internet, 173
 enhanced by sharing activities,
  197–198
 examples, 163–164
 and five-forces model, 164–165
 forms of, 163
 integration of value chain, 164
 for multidomestic strategy, 246–248
 for new ventures, 283
 potential Internet-related
  pitfalls, 174
 potential pitfalls
  consumer perceptions, 166–167
  diluting brand identity, 166
  easy imitation, 166
  too high price premiums, 166
  too much differentiation, 166
  uniqueness not valuable, 165–166
 price premiums, 164
 and product innovation, 414
 reward and evaluation systems, 355
 Starbucks model, 165
Digital technologies, 51
 benefits to industry, 63
 customer feedback, 111
 disadvantages to industry, 63
 effect on competitive strategies
  combination strategies, 175–176
  differentiation strategies, 173–174
  focus strategy, 174–175
  overall cost leadership, 172–173
 effect on five-forces model
  bargaining power of buyers, 60
  bargaining power of suppliers, 61
  competitive rivalry, 62
  threat of new entrants, 58
  threat of substitutes, 61–62
 entertainment programming, 111
 evaluation activities, 110
 expertise, 111
 to identify substitutes, 55–56, 61–62
 impact on doing business, 172
 problem-solving activities, 110–111
 search activities, 109–110
 transaction activities, 111
Direction, setting, 379
Direct sales, 91
Disclosure requirements, 326
Disintermediation, 61
 lowering transaction costs, 172
Dispersed approaches to CE
 advantages, 424–425
 definition, 422
 disadvantages, 425
 entrepreneurial culture, 425
 product champions, 425–427
Dissatisfaction with status quo, 379
Dissolution, 214n

Distribution channels
 access to, 53
 Internet, 58
 new, 292
Diversification; *see also* Related
  diversification; Unrelated
  diversification
 achieving
  by internal development, 216–217
  joint ventures, 214–216
  mergers and acquisitions,
   210–214
  strategic alliances, 214–216
 disappointing, 192
 expensive blunders, 193
 hierarchical relationships, 194
 horizontal relationships, 194
 learning from mistakes, 191–192
 by PepsiCo, 200
 related, 342, 355
 successful, 193–194
 for synergies, 194
 unrelated, 347
 value creation by, 193–194
Diversity, 127–128
 benefits of, 129
Diversity management
 examples, 353
 guidelines, 127–129
Divestment
 examples, 214
 means of, 214n
 objectives, 214
 by Philips Electronics, 215
Divisional organizational structure
 advantages, 345–346, 350
 at Brinker International, 346
 characteristics, 345
 competition between divisions, 346
 definition, 345
 disadvantages, 346, 350
 at General Motors, 345
 from related diversification, 342
Dogs, 207
Dollar weakness, 211
Domestic rivalry, 232
Double-loop learning, 307
Dow Jones Industrial Average, 49
Dr. Atkins New Diet Revolution
 (Atkins), 37
Drive, 276
Durable opportunities, 271

e

*Early Warning: Using Competitive
 Intelligence to Anticipate Market
 Shifts* (Gilad), 480
Earnings restatements, 326
Eastern Europe, Internet users, 51

Mexico
  Ford operations in, 249
  maquiladoras, 236
  United States expansion problems, 250
Microchip industry, 289
Micro credit, 230
Middle class, in China, 235
Middle East, 238
  Internet users, 51
Millennials, 122
Mindguards, 463
Mind-sets, 136
Mission, 5
  employee identification with, 125–126
Mission statement
  change of, 28
  compared to vision, 27
  definition, 27
  effective, 27–28
  of MSA Aircraft Interior Products, 314
  strategic priorities, 27
Mobile workplace, 56
Mobility, barriers to, 66
Modular organizational structure
  compared to virtual organization, 364
  definition, 361
  outsourcing by, 361–362
  pros and cons, 364
  strategic risks in outsourcing, 362
Monitoring costs, 204
Monopoly power of 3M Corporation, 201
Motivation, 386, 387
Multidomestic strategy
  adaptation vs. cost structure, 247–248
  cultural differences, 247
  differentiation strategies, 246–248
  evolution of adaptation, 248
  local adaptation, 246–248
  rejection of adaptation, 248
  risks and challenges, 247–248
  strengths, 248
  weaknesses, 248
Multinational corporations
  beachhead strategy, 252
  centralized R&D/dispersed
    production, 244
  and child labor, 237
  dealing with bribery, 247
  exporting for market entry, 252–253
  franchising problems, 254
  sales distribution of firms, 251
Multitaskers, 12
My True Diary (Messier), 219

n

Nanotechnology, 48
NASCAR, 160
National Aeronautics and Space
    Administration, 145, 182, 278

National Association of Manufacturers, 45
National competitive advantage
  factors affecting, 230–232
    demand conditions, 230, 231
    factor conditions, 230, 231
    firm strategy, structure, and rivalry,
      231, 232
    related and supporting industries,
      231–232
  in India, 233–234
National Design Award, 382
National Economic Research Institute,
    China, 235
National Federation of Independent
    Business, 275
Negotiating costs, 204
NetAdvantage, 484
Net disposable income, 39
Net present value analysis, 430
Networking, 121–122, 394
  function of business incubators, 423
New competitive actions
  and market commonality, 287–289
  reasons for, 286
  and resource similarity, 287–289
  sources of competitive attacks, 286–287
  threat analysis, 287–289
New Economy, 130, 229
New entrants, 168
New markets, entering, 292
New product design, 355
New product introduction, 292
New venture groups, 423
New venture opportunities, 422
New ventures, 265; *see also* Corporate
    entrepreneurship
  bootstrapping, 273
  business incubators, 423–424
  close competitors, 285
  combination strategies, 284–285
  competitive dynamics
    choosing not to react, 294–295
    likelihood of competitive reaction,
      293–294
    motivation & capability to respond,
      290–291
    new competitive actions, 286–289
    types of competitive actions, 291–293
  corporate venture capital, 424
  critical success factors, 453
  differentiation strategies, 283
  factors necessary for, 267
  failures, 436
  feasibility analysis, 271
  financial resources, 271–273
  and five-forces model, 267
  focus strategies, 283–284
  formulating strategy, 468
  government resources, 274–276
  human capital, 273
  idea sources, 425
  market potential evaluation, 271

New ventures—*Cont.*
  opportunity discovery, 270
  overall cost leadership, 281–283
  preannouncements, 438
  product champions, 425–427
  social capital, 274
New York State Attorney General, 327
Niche marketing, 167
  airports as opportunity for, 280
  effect of Internet, 164
Noncompete employment contracts, 149n
Nonfinancial rewards, 127
Nonfinancial strategic objectives, 29
North America, Internet users, 51
North American Free Trade Agreement,
    49, 251
North American Industry Classification, 484

O

Objectives
  of MSA Aircraft Interior Products, 314
  short-term, 312–313
One-Click purchasing technology, 61
101 Ways to Save Money, 387, 388
Online procurement systems, 61
On the job consumption, 325
Open book management, 393
Open innovation, 420
Open source software movement, 293
Operating cost reductions, 235
Operational effectiveness, 10
Operational efficiency and
    effectiveness, 313
Operations, 79–80
  of service organizations, 86
  summary of, 79
Opportunistic managers, 325
Opportunities, 77; *see also*
    SWOT analysis
  achievable, 271
  attractive, 271
  durable, 271
  evaluation of, 270–271
  recognizing, 38
  value-creating, 271
Opportunity analysis framework,
    269–270
Opportunity recognition, 269–270
  examples, 270
Optimas Award, 426
Options, 429
Option to exit, 432
Oral case presentation guidelines, 458
Organizational bases of power, 384
Organizational capabilities
  causal ambiguity, 93
  characteristics, 90–91
  kinds of, 89
Organizational conflicts, 311

The Reviewer Hall of Fame

We would like to thank the dedicated instructors who have graciously provided their insights since the inception of *Strategic Management: Creating Competitive Advantages* and *Strategic Management: Text and Cases.*

Acquaah, Moses — University of North Carolina-Greensboro

Alessandri, Todd — Syracuse University

Alexander, Larry — Virginia Polytechnic Institute

Amason, Allen C. — University of Georgia

Anders, Kathy — Arizona State University

Antoniou, Peter H. — California State University, San Marcos

Arnott, Dave — Dallas Baptist University

Azriel, Jay — Seton Hall University

Bailey, Jeffrey J. — University of Idaho

Barringer, Bruce — University of Central Florida

Beal, Brent D. — Louisiana State University

Beggs, Joyce — University of North Carolina-Charlotte

Bell DeTienne, Kristen — Brigham Young University

Bernstein, Eldon — Lynn University

Bodie, Dusty — Boise State University

Bogner, William — Georgia State University

Calhoun, Mikelle A. — Valparaiso University

Cappel, Samuel D. — Southeastern Louisiana State University

Carini, Gary — Baylor University

Carraher, Shawn M. — Texas A&M University, Commerce

Caruth, Don — Amberton University

Castrogiovanni, Gary J. — University of Tulsa

Chaganti, Radha — Rider University

Cho, Theresa — Rutgers University

Coffey, Betty S. — Appalachian State University

Coggins, Wade — Webster University, Fort Smith Metro Campus

Coombs, Joseph — University of Richmond

Cordeiro, James J. — SUNY Brockport

Covin, Jeffrey — Indiana University

Datta, Deepak — University of Texas at Arlington

Davis, James — University of Notre Dame

Deresky, Helen — State University of New York, Plattsburgh

DeWitt, Rocki-Lee — University of Vermont

Dial, Jay — Ohio State University

Dobbs, Michael E. — Arkansas State University

Doh, Jonathan — Villanova University

Douglas, Tom — Clemson University

Down, Jon — Oregon State University

Engle, Clare — Concordia University

Evans, William A. — Troy State University, Dothan

Fabian, Frances H. — University of North Carolina, Charlotte

Fanelli, Angelo — Warrington College of Business

Fathi, Michael — Georgia Southwestern University

Fausnaugh, Carolyn J. — Florida Institute of Technology

Ferguson, Tamela D. — University of Louisiana at Lafayette

Flanagan, David — Western Michigan University

Fox, Isaac — University of Minnesota

Frankforter, Steven A. — Winthrop University

Fried, Vance — Oklahoma State University

Gardberg, Naomi A. — Bernard M. Baruch College

Geringer, J. Michael — California Polytechnic State University

Gilbertson, Diana L. — California State University, Fresno

Gilley, Matt — Oklahoma State University

Gilliard, Debora — Metropolitan State College of Denver

Godiwalla, Yezdi H. — University of Wisconsin-Whitewater

Goel, Sanjay — University of Minnesota, Duluth

Gough, Sandy — Boise State University

Hatfield, Donald — Virginia Polytechnic Institute

Harrison, Niran — University of Oregon

Harveston, Paula — Berry College

Hester, Kim — Arkansas State University

Hironaka, John — California State University, Sacramento

Hoffman, Alan — Bentley College

Holbein, Gordon — Northern Kentucky University

Hough, Jill — University of Tulsa

Humphreys, John — Eastern New Mexico University

Ibe, James G. — Morris College

Janney, Jay J. — University of Dayton

Jauch, Lawrence — University of Louisiana - Monroe

Johnson, Dana M. — Michigan Technical University

Katzenstein, James — California State University, Dominguez Hills

Kellermanns, Franz — Mississippi State University

Kelley, Donna — Babson College

Kelley, Craig — California State University, Sacramento

Ketchen, Dave — Florida State University

Kilpatrick, John A. — Idaho State University

Korn, Helaine — Bernard M. Baruch College

Kowalczyk, Stan — San Francisco State University

Kraska, Daniel — North Central State College

Kreps, Donald E. — Kutztown University

Kroeger, Jim — Cleveland State University

Kulkarni, Subdoh P. — Howard University

Lant, Theresa — New York University

Legatski, Ted — Texas Christian University

Lengnick-Hall, Cynthia — University of Texas at San Antonio

Lester, Donald L. — Arkansas State University

Lester, Wanda — North Carolina A&T State University

Lemak, David J. — Washington State University-Tri-Cities

Lichtenstein, Benyamin — University of Massachusetts at Boston

Lockhart, Dan — University of Kentucky

Logan, John — University of South Carolina

Lowe, Kevin — University of North Carolina-